Baby
DAY BY DAY

In-depth, daily advice on your baby's growth,
care, and development in the first year

Baby
DAY BY DAY

CANADIAN EDITION

Editor-in-chief **Dr. Ilona Bendefy**

Senior Editors Victoria Heyworth-Dunne, Amanda Lebentz
Senior Designers Nicola Rodway, Pamela Shiels
Editorial Assistant Kathryn Meeker
Canadian Editor Barbara Campbell
Consultant Editor Lisa Fields
Senior Production Editor Clare McLean
Production Controller Seyhan Esen
Creative Technical Support Sonia Charbonnier
New Photography Vanessa Davies
Art Direction for Photography Emma Forge
Managing Editor Penny Smith
Managing Art Editor Marianne Markham
Publishing Manager Anna Davidson
Publisher Peggy Vance

DK INDIA
Senior Editor Alicia Ingty
Editors Janashree Singha and Himanshi Sharma
Art Editor Ira Sharma
Assistant Art Editor Ridhi Khanna
Managing Editor Glenda Fernandes
Managing Art Editor Navidita Thapa
DTP Manager Sunil Sharma
DTP Designers Anurag Trivedi and Satish Chandra Gaur

First Canadian edition, 2012

DK Publishing is represented in Canada by Tourmaline Editions Inc.,
662 King Street West, Suite 304, Toronto, Ontario M5V 1M7

12 13 14 15 10 9 8 7 6 5 4 3 2 1
001–183083–September 2012
Copyright © 2012 Dorling Kindersley Limited
All rights reserved.

Every effort has been made to ensure that the information in this book is complete and accurate. However, neither the publisher nor the authors are engaged in rendering professional advice or services to the individual reader. The contents of this book are not intended as a substitute for consulting with your healthcare provider. All matters regarding the health of you and your baby require medical supervision. Neither the publisher nor the authors shall be liable or responsible for any loss or damage allegedly arising from any information or suggestions in this book.

Published in Great Britain by Dorling Kindersley Ltd.

Library and Archives Canada Cataloguing in Publication
Baby day by day : in-depth, daily advice on your baby's growth,
care, and development in the first year / editor-in-chief Ilona Bendefy.
Includes index.
ISBN 978-1-55363-184-2
1. Infants--Care. 2. Infants--Growth.
3. Infants--Development. I. Bendefy, Ilona
RJ61.B226 2012   649'.122   C2012-900595-9

DK books are available at special discounts when purchased in bulk for corporate sales, sales promotions, premiums, fund-raising, or educational use. For details, please contact specialmarkets@tourmaline.ca.

Printed and bound by Hung Hing, China

Discover more at **www.dk.com**

Editor-in-chief

Dr. Ilona Bendefy MB, BS, MRCP (Paeds) is a GP, community pediatrician, and mother of four. After getting a medical degree at St. Thomas' Hospital in London, Dr. Bendefy worked as a hospital pediatrician for seven years. She went on to train as a GP in a London practice where she became a partner. In 1997, she moved from London to Derbyshire, where she worked for a time as a pediatrician at Sheffield Children's Hospital. She now practices as a GP in Derbyshire.

Contributors

Bella Dale RM is a midwife and infant feeding specialist with extensive experience supporting new mothers breast-feeding their babies. She was nominated for Midwife of the Year in 2007 and 2008. She has three children.

Dr. Carol Cooper MA, MB, BChir, MRCP is a GP in London, as well as a prolific medical writer and broadcaster. She also teaches at Imperial College Medical School. After graduating with a degree in medicine from Cambridge University, she spent nine years as a hospital physician before entering general practice. She has three sons.

Dr. Claire Halsey AFBPsS, ClinPsyD, MSc is a consultant clinical psychologist of 30 years' standing, working mainly with children. She is a journalist and author in the field of child psychology, parenting, and child development, and is a mother of three.

Fiona Wilcock MSc, PGCE, RPHNut is a registered Public Health Nutritionist and food writer, who has written widely on diet in pregnancy and the early years, as well as providing nutrition consultancy to several manufacturers and retailers. She runs a baby and toddler group and has two children.

Jenny Hall BSc, RGN, RN (Child) worked as a children's nurse before becoming a health visitor 12 years ago. She has two daughters.

Judy Barratt is a highly experienced child-care author specializing in children's nutrition and development. She is a mother of two.

Karen Sullivan is an author and child-care expert with degrees in developmental and educational psychology. She has three sons.

Dr. Mary Steen RGN, RM, BHSc, PGCRM, PGDipHE, MCGI, PhD has practiced as a midwife in the UK for 24 years and is a mother of three. She has received awards for original research, clinical innovation, and outstanding services to Midwifery. In 2010, she was made Professor of Midwifery at the University of Chester.

Dr. Su Laurent MRCP, FRCPCH is is a consultant pediatrician at Barnet Hospital, London, where she supervises the care of children of all ages, from extremely premature babies to teenagers. She is a trustee of The Child Bereavement Charity and a mother of three.

Contents

Introduction

In these days of advanced technology when so much can be achieved at the touch of a screen, there is still nothing to compare with the miracle of a new baby. For new parents, the reality of having created this little being is stunning; a whole life is theirs to care for; their baby's future is in their hands. The sense of achievement and responsibility will change them as people.

By adulthood, most of us have learned what we need to get a job, run a home, and have a social life. The one area most first-time parents have not learned about is how to bring up a baby. Once, families would hand down child-rearing skills, for better or worse. These days, families may be scattered across countries or continents; grandparents may be working. Parents cannot always take family support for granted. At the same time, research and medical care have improved child health dramatically and advanced our knowledge of how best to raise babies. Parents want to have real input into how their child develops, because they have a vision of the kind of person they hope their child will grow up to be.

The first year of a baby's life is the time of most rapid growth and development. Parents see their baby changing almost day by day. They will be filled with wonder and pride but may be overwhelmed by how much they need to learn. At this time, more than at any other age, they need reliable, balanced, and reassuring information about what to expect and what to do for their baby.

In *Baby Day by Day*, parents will find a comprehensive guide to each step of their baby's first year of life. There is specialized advice on each stage of their baby's growth and development, with current evidence-based guidelines on breast- and bottle-feeding, starting solid food, sleeping, health screening, and immunizations. Common problems and worries are discussed, with friendly, reassuring help. A detailed medical section provides an accessible reference to common illnesses and first aid. Supportive information is given for parents, from breast-feeding and postpartum care for mothers, to work options, child care, family networks, and maintaining parents' identities and relationships.

The book is written for mothers, fathers, and anyone involved in raising children. The aim is to make this first year a happy, rewarding, and confident start to the rest of baby's and parents' lives together.

Dr. Ilona Bendefy

Once your baby is born, you'll find that life takes on a new momentum as you grapple with all the first-time experiences that caring for a growing baby involves. The first days—and weeks—can pass in a bit of a blur, so this chapter gives you the kind of background information that's so useful to know from the beginning. From bonding and parenting approaches to your rights and benefits, to feeding your baby, choosing diapers, and buying equipment, it's essential preparation for parenthood.

 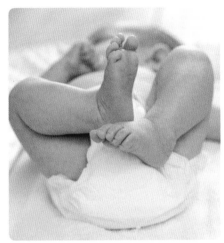 

Your new baby

Being a parent

IT'S A LIFELONG AND, AT TIMES, DEMANDING JOB—BUT THE REWARDS ARE AMAZING

You have anticipated this moment for the past nine months, if not longer. Now that your baby has arrived, you have someone else to love and care for, someone for whom you must create a safe, nurturing environment, and whose needs come before your own.

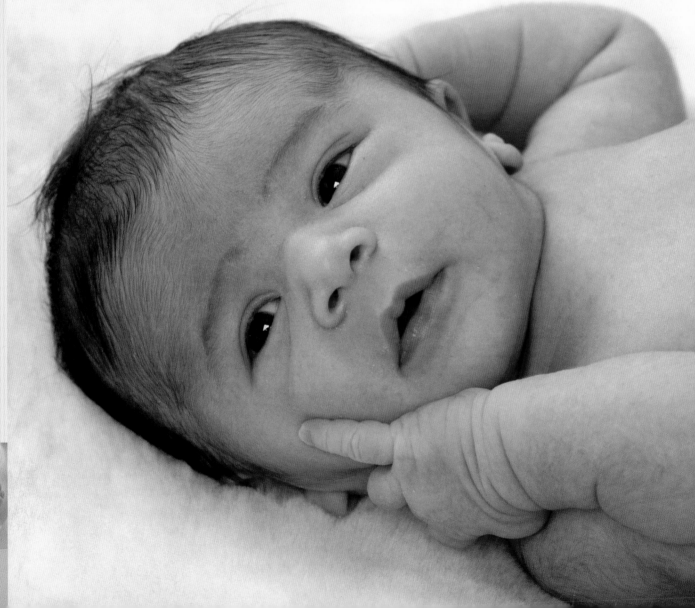

Adjusting to parenthood

Your baby is roughly as long as your elbow to your fingertips, yet he is able to turn your whole world on its head. Welcome to parenthood!

No one can prepare you for the whirlwind that is your baby. Although you may have already made practical adjustments to your life—put a crib in your bedroom, dedicated a drawer to diapers and another to sleep sacks and so on—the reality of living with and having complete responsibility for your baby can come as a bit of a shock.

Time difference The most dramatic change you will notice at first is how, by and large, your time is no longer your own—both day and night. Particularly in the early weeks, your baby will need almost constant care. He will wake for feedings when you would rather sleep, and chances are he will need a diaper change just as you sit down with a cup of coffee. This is physically exhausting and a time of both emotional highs and lows as you adjust to your new role. However, even at your most tired, be assured that this is just a phase, and it also involves the pleasure of learning all about your baby and how to take care of him.

As you get to know your baby and start to feel more confident as a parent, you should find that life settles down into a more predictable pattern. That's not to say that you'll be back to eight hours' sleep a night any time soon, but after about three months, your baby will probably be sleeping longer at night and less during the day. By 12 months, most babies sleep for around 10–12 hours at night and have a couple of naps during the day, so rest assured that "normal" life will resume—eventually.

Trusting your instincts Becoming a parent is the most exciting and fulfilling experience imaginable—but along with the highs comes an entirely new realm of fears and worries. Is my baby feeding too much or too little? Am I playing with him enough? Is my baby ill? Is he developing normally? Is he under- or

Duty of care You might be surprised at how fiercely protective of your baby you feel—that's your maternal instinct kicking in.

overstimulated? There's no antidote to the anxiety of new parenthood, but two main lessons you can learn are to trust your instincts and never be afraid to share your concerns and ask for help. It's worthwhile to remember that no matter how much well-meaning advice you receive, you are the best authority on your baby. Nature has an amazing knack of tuning you in to your baby's needs—and if you don't know the answer right away, you'll soon figure it out. If you can't, then seek advice.

Talk to your partner, too. In addition to being an extra pair of hands, your partner shares the responsibility of caring for your baby, and talking about your hopes, fears, and concerns divides the burden. Even if you don't find the answers, reaffirming that you are in this together is an essential part of dealing with the demands of being a parent.

TWINS

Learning to juggle

The responsibility of a new life in duplicate (or multiple) can be overwhelming. Both you and your partner will need lots of support from family and friends. Try to concentrate solely on your babies, and forget about housework or doing much else for at least the first three months. Delegate making meals and running the home to your partner and family, and spend this precious time getting to know your twins and focusing on the best ways to juggle their needs.

Two's company Every mom could use two pairs of hands, but with twins, sharing the care is even more of a necessity.

Becoming a family

As soon as you have a baby, you become a family. This changes the dynamics of your relationship with your partner and your relatives.

Family unit Having a baby creates a unique bond between you and your partner as you strive to provide for and care for your child.

You and your partner Before your baby came along, your spare time could be dedicated to one another. If you have individual hobbies, each of you could pursue them without feeling tied to home. However, as soon as you have a baby, your time for each other, and for individual pursuits, is much less of a priority. None of this matters, of course, because your baby is the center of your world, but inevitably there will come a moment when the full realization dawns of how life has changed for you, particularly as a couple.

Remind each other every so often that you are in this together. You will be tired and fretful, you may even be snappy or tearful, making it more important than ever that you actively lean on one another for support. Keep talking and try to make time for each other—even if it is just 20 minutes to sit down and eat a meal together—every day. Reassure yourselves that the fatigue of the early days passes soon enough, and that this is the beginning of a journey in which every step you take together in the common goal of doing the best for your baby (even when he's old enough to make decisions for himself) is a step that brings you closer together and reaffirms the strength of your relationship.

One common point of tension in the early months is when a new work–life balance begins as one of you goes back to work. The stay-at-home parent may feel that their independence has been dramatically reduced, while little has changed in the life of the parent who has gone back to work. They may feel that the burden of responsibility for the family's day-to-day welfare falls too heavily on their shoulders. On the other hand, the parent who is working may feel left out or alienated, and that their contribution as the breadwinner separates them from the fun part of being a parent.

In fact, you both have crucial roles for the family's well-being and it is important that you love, support, and respect one another for the choices you have made. When the weekend comes, try to give the primary care giver even just a few hours' time out, while the working parent immerses him- or herself in family life.

Both of you juggling work and child care puts its own strain on your relationship. In this case, you both need to share as many of the household tasks as you can, and be ready to ask each other for help when you need it. Try not to make assumptions about what the other is going to take on and which tasks fall to you, since this often leads to misunderstandings. Make lists or notes every morning if it helps, keep talking, and be prepared to be flexible.

Brothers and sisters If you already have other children, the arrival of a new baby will cause a shift in their lives, too. It is extremely rare that any family completely escapes some form of sibling rivalry along the way (be prepared that it may not happen immediately). If you can show each other and all your children love and respect, siblings are much more likely to show love and

Sibling rivalry Giving your toddler time and attention will help her accept the new arrival more readily and lessen feelings of jealousy.

respect toward one another, even if they squabble at some point about having to share you. Involving all your children with the baby care is important, and so is making time for each child individually—and that goes for step-children or children from a previous relationship, too.

In time, siblings become a support network for you and your baby, providing help for you, and unconditional love for your baby, well into adulthood.

Step-children A new baby provides step-children with an unmistakable reminder that one of their parents has moved on beyond their original family. Some step-children see the new sibling as the glue that bonds the whole family—old and new—together, and welcome the new life gladly, but others feel resentful. Give step-siblings as much opportunity as possible to play and help with the new baby. Try to avoid terms such as "half brother" or "half sister," which create a distance. Instead, talk about how much the baby is going to love having a big brother or sister.

If your step-child doesn't live with you, keep to the same visiting schedule, and plan activities that you all can enjoy together on those days. Reassure your step-child that your love for him or her won't ever change.

Extended family You have become parents, but your parents, your in-laws, and your siblings have become grandparents and aunts and uncles, too. Welcoming your wider family into your baby's life, and ensuring they have regular contact, gives him the opportunity to have a distinct sense of family identity and to know his place in the world. Today, we are often scattered from our own parents or siblings, and it may not always be easy to spend time together. If this is true for you, consider inviting your parents or in-laws to stay every so often, or going

Family ties Involving your family in your baby's life will not only gain you much-needed practical help, but will also allow your child to build close and lasting relationships.

to stay with them. It may be a little daunting taking your baby to stay with relatives, but there are positive gains to be made. Grandparents who see a lot of their grandchildren and are actively involved in their care share a much closer bond than those who become acquainted on the occasional fleeting visit. And the love you all have for your child gives you a common link that can bring you closer.

For week-to-week contact, join a social networking site through which you can contact relatives and share photos; or download a social chat program, and invest in a webcam—even if you are at opposite ends of the country, or the world, your baby can still grow up with a sense of his family connections. Finally, babies love to look at faces so, as he matures, do show him photographs of relatives, pointing at them and naming them one by one. This is a great way of providing your baby with a sense of his wider family.

SINGLE PARENTING

It takes only two—you and your baby—to make a family and you can provide your baby with everything he needs, from food to clothing and especially love. You are also the person who best knows your baby, so your instincts will ensure that you make no more mistakes than anyone else who ventures into the world of parenthood for the first time. Being a single parent does not mean that you are alone. If you feel isolated, pick up the phone and talk to someone—a friend, a midwife, a family member—to share how you feel. During the first few weeks, in particular, be prepared to ask for help from willing friends and family; you may even want to consider staying with someone, such as your own parents, while you adjust to being a mom.

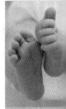

Parenting approaches

There are no hard-and-fast rules when it comes to good parenting practice. Your own approach to parenting will emerge in time.

Perfect parent Of course, there's no such thing, but with plenty of love, kindness, and consistency you'll be the best parent there is.

Before you had your baby you may have had some fixed ideas about the right and wrong ways to bring up a baby. The reality is that as you settle into your new role, some of the ideas about parenting you thought were non-negotiable suddenly become less important, while others move up the agenda. Beyond the fundamental requirements to love, nurture, respond to, feed, and clothe your baby, there is so much to learn as you go along. It is essential to talk to your partner about how you will raise your baby and how, in the years to come, you will set expectations for behavior.

One thing is certain—as your baby becomes a toddler, he will soon learn if one of you is a soft touch and one the disciplinarian, and whether or not he can play one of you off against the other. Presenting a united front and giving a clear, consistent message is the key to success, whatever approach to parenting you decide to take.

Reflecting you Your approach to parenting will inevitably, in part, reflect the ways in which your parents brought you up. In addition, it will demonstrate your own culture and values, and your faith if you have one. It will also reflect your personality: if you tend to be laid back, it's more likely that your parenting style will be laid back; if you are a list-maker and organizer, the chances are that your approach will be more routine based. No approach is definitive, but you need to be comfortable with the one you choose, so that you can stick by it and provide a secure environment in which your baby can develop.

Setting boundaries A newborn baby does not yet have the mental acuity to understand right from wrong, yes from no, good from bad. But in only a matter of months, he will begin to explore the world by such actions as reaching and grabbing, at which point, gently setting him boundaries gives him the opportunity to discover what's around him, but also keeps him safe.

Furthermore, as he becomes more aware, your boundaries will make him feel secure in what is otherwise a baffling melee of sight, sound, taste, touch, and scent. He needs you to guide him on appropriate behavior and actions. Setting boundaries isn't about becoming a disciplinarian with a strict rule book. Rather, boundaries provide an important structure for your baby's life, and when it comes to right and wrong, a moral code for his behavior. Ultimately, they make him feel secure.

Out of harm's way Once she's mobile, you'll need to remove her repeatedly from danger. Explain why some things are out of bounds, and distract her by moving her to a safer place or activity.

Introducing discipline During your baby's first year, there are very few reasons for saying "No." You cannot teach a baby to control his behavior at this age because he is unable to do so—the part of his brain that controls social understanding and behavior won't be fully developed for another year or two. So "discipline" at this stage should be about gentle correction or distraction, and saying "No" only when your baby is doing something that is unsafe for him, or for others.

Whatever boundaries you set, it is important to follow the same pattern of correction each time. One useful approach is "repeat, remove, distract." So, you repeat the boundary (for example, "Don't touch the vase, it may break"), then remove the temptation (put the vase away) or remove your baby from the danger, if relevant, and then distract him quickly. The next time he does the same thing, respond with the same sequence: repeat, remove, distract. Through the consistency of your words and actions, from about nine months, your baby should begin to associate certain commands with certain consequences. This is a vital lesson for the toddler years when all children learn to push boundaries, as he will trust that you mean what you say.

Tell her why Explaining why some things shouldn't be done will help her understand—but don't expect too much too early.

Giving reasons When you ask your baby not to do something, let him know why in very simple terms: "Don't touch the oven—it's hot, ouch," and mime touching something hot. He won't fully understand, but he'll begin to get the idea during his first year. Getting upset with your baby won't achieve anything. As he matures, he will listen and respond more readily when you are calm. Get his attention, speak clearly, and show him by acting it out yourself.

Positive parenting

Whatever your values and the specifics of the way in which you want to raise your baby, there are certain fundamentals of parenting that will make your approach more effective and loving, and some methods that are best avoided. Positive parenting is about championing the good in your child. Children thrive on praise, and they also love attention. If they get lots of praise and attention for good behavior, but find that bad behavior is reprimanded or ignored, they soon learn to focus on the good.

Key positive parenting traits

- Give lots of extra praise and attention when your baby does as he is asked.
- Show how proud you are of your baby. Even minor achievements can be celebrated with clapping and cheering. Your baby will love this and soon want to elicit those reactions again.
- Show respect to your baby.
- Be consistent in your rules or expectations and follow through with rewards for positive behavior.
- Show your baby you love him by giving him your undivided attention and lots of physical affection.

Parenting traits to avoid

- Even if you feel frustrated, try not to react angrily toward your baby. If you stay calm, your baby will stay calm and be far more likely to respond positively to you.
- It is never appropriate to criticize your baby. As he gets older, focus on behavior ("You did not share your toy"), not him ("You are selfish").
- Stick to your rules and routines: your baby will feel more secure when he knows what's expected.

ASK A... CHILD PSYCHOLOGIST

When does parenting become "pushy" as opposed to "encouraging"? We live in a competitive world and there is a growing trend for parents to fill their children's—even their babies'—time with activities to race them through developmental milestones. However, children will rarely be hurried. Encouraging your child to learn means giving him time to explore the world himself, and giving him a degree of autonomy to discover what is around him and to discover the principles of cause and effect (whether that's in actions, language, or sounds). It also means giving him lots of praise when he makes a new discovery, behaves well, or learns to do something for himself. Above all, children learn best through play, when they are happy, relaxed, and able to work at their own pace. If you allow lots of playtime, and read stories and sing songs together, your baby will have all the encouragement he needs to develop his mental acuity at a perfect pace, without being pushed to go too fast.

Maternity rights and benefits

Once your child is born, you will have paperwork to fill out, and if you're employed, you may be eligible for paid or unpaid leave.

In the blur of a new baby's arrival, filling out forms can feel like the last thing you want to do. However, there are certain forms that should be submitted before you leave the hospital, and other notifications that should be made within 30 days of the baby's birth. Even though you have other things on your mind right now, it's important to sift through the paperwork and make the necessary phone calls to make everything fall into place.

Registering the birth Registering your baby's birth with your province or territory allows you to apply for a birth certificate, and this should be done as soon as possible after your baby is born. The registration process differs depending on where you live; your provincial or territorial government will have information on your particular situation, including how soon you are required to fill out the registration forms after birth.

In some provinces, you can use the online Newborn Registration Service to complete your baby's birth registration, and you may be able to apply for your child's birth certificate and Social Insurance Number (SIN) at the same time. You may also be able to apply online for Canada Child Benefits, which include the Canada Child Tax Benefit and the Universal Child Care Benefit, and the GST/HST credit. Be sure to review the requirements for registering so you can ensure that you have all of the information that you need to complete the process. If both parents are going to be named on the birth registration, both must be available to sign the form.

It's a good idea to apply for your baby's SIN as soon as possible as well.

You will need it if you plan to start saving for your child's education through a Registered Education Savings Plan (RESP) or a Canada Learning Bond. Your baby will also need a SIN to work legally in Canada, although this is far down the road at this point!

Applying for a health card Your province or territory will provide your baby with his or her own health card, which will allow access to insured health care services. In many cases, you can get health card application forms online; go to your provincial or territorial government website for more details.

Your right to time off work
In Canada, you are entitled to take a certain amount of time off work (called

"leave") after your baby is born, and you retain your right to return to the same or an equivalent position. Each province and territory has its own legislation regarding job protection during pregnancy, as well as maternity and parental leave, so check with your local government for the specifics of your situation.

Maternity leave is available for birth mothers, and ranges from 15–18 weeks. Parental leave can be taken by either parent or sometimes shared between them, and ranges from 35–52 weeks. In most provinces and territories, you must have completed a specific period of continuous employment with a company to qualify for leave. Your employer is not required to pay you during your leave, although some of

Seeing what help is available You have certain rights and benefits depending on your circumstances so make sure you find out what you're entitled to so that you don't miss out.

Parental leave

In 2001, federal EI parental benefits were increased from 10 to 35 weeks, and since then, the number of Canadian fathers that are choosing to stay home for a time to care for their newborns has been steadily rising.

Canadian dads are entitled to any part of the 35-week parental benefits offered by Employment Insurance, provided they have worked a minimum of 600 hours of insured work in the last 52 weeks. While most dads aren't taking the full 35 weeks, recent statistics show an average of 17 weeks' leave is the norm outside of Quebec, and 7 weeks' leave within Quebec. Quebec is the only province that offers 5 weeks of paid paternity leave that cannot be transferred to the mother.

More dads who are not eligible for paid leave are also taking some time off after the birth of their babies, either by accumulating vacation days or taking unpaid time off.

Regardless of how much time they have off, most dads agree that the time they spend bonding with and caring for a new baby is precious. Recent studies have shown that the role dads play in the early lives of their infants has important and long-lasting effects. Children of loving and involved dads are more likely to have good self-esteem, succeed in school, and to integrate well in social situations as compared to those with uninvolved fathers.

Hands-on dad Parental leave gives dads a chance to get to learn the practicalities of babycare when their help is needed most.

them do—speak to your human resources department.

During your leave, you may be entitled to receive maternity and/or parental benefits through the federal Employment Insurance Act (EI), which will pay you a certain percentage of your wage provided you have worked a certain minimum of hours and have been contributing to the EI program. Eligible birth mothers are entitled to a maximum of 15 weeks of paid maternity benefits. Parental benefits of up to 35 weeks are available to either eligible parent, and can be shared between them. If the birth mother decides to take both the maternity and complete parental benefits, she could receive a total of 50 weeks' benefits. EI benefits are considered taxable income, which means that both federal and provincial taxes will be deducted from your payment. You will need to apply for EI benefits as soon as you stop working, either in person at a Service Canada Center or online at www.servicecanada.gc.ca.

Your employer may also top up the amount that you receive from EI, and allow you to add on accumulated vacation or sick days to your leave. Speak to your human resources department about what additional benefits may be available to you.

If you are a resident of Quebec, you are covered by the Quebec Parental Insurance Plan instead of the federal Employment Insurance Act. Go to www.rqap.gouv.qc.ca for more details.

Breast-feeding at work Provincial Human Rights Codes in Canada protect a woman's right to breast-feed in public, as does the Canadian Charter of Rights and Freedoms. Some provinces specifically address the right to breast-feed in the workplace. These laws generally outline ways that employers should accommodate a woman who needs to pump breast milk during business hours—for example, supplying a secluded place near an electrical outlet where a woman can plug in her pump and express milk undisturbed.

Is there any support system available for single parents? You may find it difficult to juggle your parenting responsibilities along with everything else, particularly when you've got a newborn who is completely dependent upon you. Accept any and all offers of help when you're just starting out; let someone else cook or clean while you nurse the baby, or let someone else babysit while you nap or pay the bills. Check for government programs that may help you financially, such as the Canada Child Tax Benefit, the Universal Child Care Benefit, and the Employment Insurance Family Supplement. And take advantage of eager babysitters in the form of parents or siblings, who may be thrilled to spend time with your baby. Single parenthood has become more prevalent in recent decades, so there's no need to feel alone.

Maternity rights and benefits

Understanding your child

YOU'LL DISCOVER MORE AND MORE ABOUT WHAT MAKES YOUR BABY TICK AS EACH MONTH GOES BY

Your baby has her own unique genetic makeup, of course, but at least some of her characteristics are inherited from you. In the first year, as she negotiates developmental milestones and develops her own personality, you will gather clues as to what kind of child she will eventually become.

Your child's inheritance

Friends and family always look to see which parent a baby resembles. As he grows, you may recognize traits he's inherited from both of you.

Your genes and your partner's genes are the ingredients that make up your baby. He has inherited these from both of you because both your DNA was locked in the chromosomes that created him. Those chromosomes divided and replicated, making new chromosomes that mixed your and your baby's father's DNA to create cells that are individual to your baby. So your baby has inherited traits from both of you, but won't exactly replicate either of you. Furthermore, your own DNA consists of your parents' DNA, which is why some children show striking likenesses to one or other of their grandparents.

Dominant and recessive genes

Certain physical traits are determined by the presence or absence of a dominant or recessive gene, meaning that you will be able to predict certain aspects of your baby's appearance. For example, when he is born, he will have blue or gray eyes, but they may not stay that way. If both you and your partner have blue eyes, your baby will have blue eyes, because he will have inherited recessive blue genes from both of you. However, if you have brown eyes and your partner has blue, you have to look at your parents for the outcome. If there is a chance that you have one brown gene and one blue gene (giving you brown eyes, because brown is dominant), there is a chance that your baby will be blue eyed. However, if you have two brown genes, even if your partner has blue eyes, your baby will have brown eyes, because he will always inherit one dominant brown eye gene from you. Other characteristics that work this way are hair color (dark hair is dominant; fair or red hair recessive) and hair type (curly is dominant; straight is recessive).

Polygenic traits A polygenic trait is a characteristic that is determined by a combination of genes, rather than just one. For example, height is a polygenic trait and this makes it hard to predict

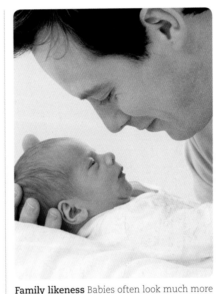

Family likeness Babies often look much more like their fathers at first, but the resemblance tends to fade as they grow older.

how tall your baby will eventually be. As a guideline, experts say that taking the average of the height of both parents and then subtracting 2 in (5 cm) for a girl and adding 2 in (5 cm) for a boy gives a good idea of how tall your baby may grow. However, genes themselves contain dominant and recessive triggers, called alleles. Even if you and your baby's father are both short, you may still have "tall" (dominant) alleles within your genes, it's just that you have more short (recessive) ones, which collectively dominate. If your baby inherited genes made up of most or all of your "tall" alleles, and only a few or none of the "short" alleles, he could end up being taller. Polygenic traits are also often influenced by environmental factors, such as good or poor nutrition. Other polygenic traits include intelligence and skin color.

ASK A... PEDIATRICIAN

Is my baby likely to be musical like me or athletic like his father? In 2001, geneticists at St. Thomas's Hospital in London, working with the Institute for Deafness in Maryland, US, published a study of hundreds of twins that supported the notion that musical ability is inherited. Certainly, Johann Sebastian Bach came from a long line of well-respected musicians. So, generally, yes, it is likely that your baby will be musical like you, especially if you encourage his innate talent by playing a variety of music to him and offering him instruments to play with. Equally, if you are a natural athlete, you are likely to produce children with the physical build and, say, hand–eye coordination to follow in your footsteps. Inevitably, though, nurture also comes into play. If you are musical, you will naturally encourage your child to love music; if you love sports, you'll encourage him to play sports, which in turn hones his talent.

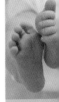

Your developing child

Your baby's growth in the first year is remarkable. At no other time in human life is development so evident and so rapid.

Soft focus At first, your baby must be up close to see your face; by eight months, she'll identify people and objects from across the room.

ASK A... CHILD PSYCHOLOGIST

Can I spoil my baby with love?

Babies need to feel secure and you and your partner are the people best placed to ensure that happens. Showing your baby love by giving him lots of attention, in the form of playing with him, attending to his needs, being close at all times, and giving him plenty of embraces and kisses does not spoil him—it confirms for him that he is the center of your world. With a deep sense of security in you, he will develop confidence to explore his world independently. As your baby matures, you can also show love by setting boundaries and limits: giving in to him every time isn't in his best interests; it's more important to show him what is safe and to teach him right from wrong.

Physical milestones The most striking physical change during your baby's first year is his size. By the time he is one, he will be around 12 in (30 cm) longer than he was at birth, and about three times as heavy. During that time, his muscle tone and physical coordination will develop so that by two months, he will be able to hold up his head for a few seconds, and at three months, he may be able to flip over. By the time he is 6–7 months, he will have developed enough muscle strength to sit unaided, and from sitting he will learn to crawl (usually by 6–9 months), and then, by a year, he will be able to stand up, possibly unaided, and may even be able to walk.

His fine motor skills will progress from swiping at objects at about three months to holding a small object using a pincer grip at 8–10 months. At around 10 months, he can use a sippy cup and drink with help, and by 12 months can make a mark on paper with a big crayon or piece of chalk.

These major physical milestones are among the most visible, but his body is developing in many unseen ways, too. Over the first year, his sight will improve from being able to focus only on objects as little as 8–10 in (20–25 cm) away from his face to being able to distinguish depth and distance at a year. He rapidly learns to recognize sounds, so that by only a few months old, he will know where a sound is coming from and even turn his head toward it.

Early learning milestones Your baby's brain has "plasticity," which means that it is able to create, adapt, and change its neural pathways according to all the new experiences life brings. This plasticity ensures your baby's rapid intellectual development. Within a few days of birth, he will prefer your face to anyone else's and he will recognize your scent. These experiences make him feel secure.

By six months, his language skills will have developed enough that he may recognize his own name when you say it, and by nine months, he'll understand when you say "no" (although he may not

Head control After a couple of months, babies' neck muscles are strong enough to allow them to lift their heads (left). **Sitting comfortably** Around the middle of the first year, they can sit up unaided (middle). **Standing up** By the end of their first year, most can stand with a little support (right).

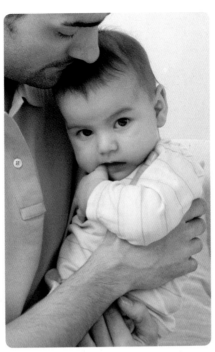

Chit chat Your baby will love to exchange looks, "words," and laughter with those closest to her (left). **Don't go** At around 6–8 months, your baby will experience separation anxiety, preferring mom or dad over other people and being upset at first if he has to go to anyone else (right).

always comply), and he may even be able to look at the correct image of an object in a book if you ask him to find it.

He will begin to make recognizable sounds. At first, at a few months old, he may coo, gurgle, or make strange vowel sounds, but by around 10 months, these may become a discernible "mama" or "dada," although it's unlikely he will use them discriminately. However, by a year, he may have managed his first meaningful word—often "dada" when referring to daddy (because babies find the consonant "d" easier to sound out than the "m" sound required for mama), although "cat" and "spoon" are often cited as first words, too.

Behavioral and personality milestones By the end of your baby's first year, you've gone from having a bundle of mystery to a young toddler, who is already showing clear signs of the person he is going to be.

You might be relieved to hear that his behavior with regard to sleeping will gradually improve month by month, as his stomach grows to hold enough food to prevent him from waking up for feedings. By the time he is one year old, he should be sleeping through the night, going to bed at around seven o'clock, and waking about 12 hours later.

At first, he will show preferences for certain people—you, his father, siblings, and other caregivers—and by six months old, may become wary of strangers. When he is six months old, he will begin to display distinct personality traits, such as the sort of things he finds amusing and the things that make him frustrated. He may throw away toys when he becomes upset with them, or cry in anger.

By eight months old, he will object to you taking away a toy and believes that everything belongs to him. He'll still be anxious if he has to leave you, but will be interested in other babies and "chat" with adults he is close to. He wants to please you and will thrive on your love and affection.

Girls and boys All children develop at different rates, regardless of their gender. However, there are certain aspects of early learning that seem to favor girls over boys, or vice versa. For example, studies show that girls learn to understand language and talk more quickly and they have more honed fine motor skills (girls will write sooner, for example). On the other hand, boys tend to be more physical and their gross motor skills are often ahead of girls, certainly by the time they reach toddler age.

One study at Cambridge University indicated that boys understand the laws of motion more quickly than girls—for example, they understand the speed and direction of a rolling ball sooner than girls tend to. Girls tend to be more wary; boys more fearless. Needless to say, things inevitably even themselves out, and whether nature or nurture results in stereotypical behavior for girls and boys is still the subject of much debate.

Baby basics

GETTING TO KNOW THE BASICS OF BABYCARE WILL HELP PREPARE YOU FOR THE FIRST WEEKS

There's an enormous amount to take in immediately after your baby is born, so the more you can learn beforehand about feeding your baby, putting him down to sleep, changing him, and keeping him clean, the more confident and in control you're likely to feel.

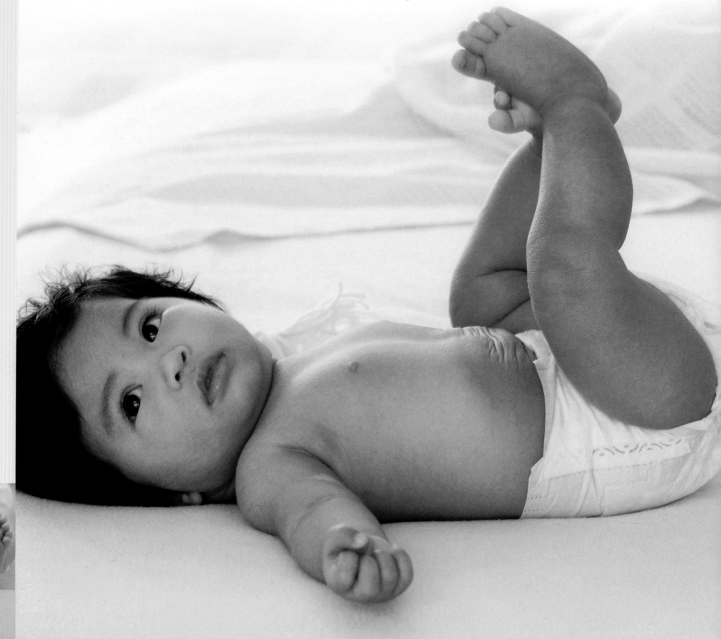

Feeding your baby

For the first year, milk will form your baby's main diet, providing him with the nutrients he needs for optimum growth and development.

Whether you choose to breast-feed or bottle-feed, understanding the basics of early nutrition and feeding practices can help give you a flying start when your baby is born. It's completely normal and understandable to be a little nervous or anxious about feeding. You want what's best for your baby to ensure that he gets the best possible start in life. Knowing what to expect can make the process that much easier, successful, and relaxing.

Why breast-feed? Breast-feeding is the best way to ensure that your baby gets all the nutrients he needs, and there is a host of health benefits (see box, right). The composition of your breast milk will change to meet the needs of your growing baby. It includes healthy fats (including essential fatty acids—EFAs) that are necessary for healthy growth and optimum development (particularly in the brain), and the calcium it contains is better utilized by babies than that in formula.

Breast milk contains certain hormones and growth factors that encourage healthy weight gain and development. It also reduces your baby's risk of acquiring diabetes and both childhood and adult obesity, as well as protecting against allergies, asthma, and eczema. Most importantly, perhaps, breast-feeding reduces your baby's risk of crib death or sudden infant death syndrome, (SIDS, see p.31), improves the process of bonding, and, according to new research, promotes the development of your baby's facial structure, which can enhance speech and vision.

You may be interested to know that breast-feeding is considered to be the "fourth trimester" in terms of your baby's brain growth and development. You'll also be passing on your antibodies to your baby through your breast milk, which can help to keep him well until his immune system matures.

Benefits for you Not only is breast-feeding good for your baby, but it's also the healthiest choice for you. It reduces your risk of breast and ovarian cancer and of osteoporosis. There's also growing evidence to suggest that women who breast-feed may be lowering their risk of having a heart attack, heart disease, or stroke. Breast-feeding uses up around 500 calories per day, so it can promote postpartum weight loss, as well as delay the return of menstruation. Last, but not least, breast-feeding is very convenient—there are no bottles to wash or sterilize, nothing to prepare, and no equipment to transport around.

AS A MATTER OF FACT

Research has found that breast-fed babies have fewer incidences of vomiting and diarrhea, and are protected against gastroenteritis, as well as ear infections, respiratory illnesses, pneumonia, bronchitis, kidney infections, and septicemia (blood poisoning). There is also a reduced risk of chronic constipation, colic, and other tummy disorders.

There are also elements in breast milk that are known to destroy bacteria such as E. coli and salmonella. There are many more health benefits for your baby, including a reduced risk of heart disease, obesity, and iron-deficiency anemia. Unless you really cannot manage it (see p.28), this is by far the best way to feed your baby.

YOUR BABY'S FIRST YEAR

In most cases, your baby will have a milk-only diet until he is around six months old. Whether you choose bottle- or breast-feeding, he will need an increasing amount of milk over the coming months, and milk should remain the mainstay of his diet throughout his first year (see p.199).

Starting solids normally begins at around six months (see pp.234–235), when your baby will start on very liquid purées—usually baby rice mixed with a little of his usual milk—and puréed fruits and vegetables. Once these foods are accepted, a range of others can be introduced—particularly those that are rich in iron and protein, such as meat, fish, and eggs. The texture of foods should change as quickly as your baby finds acceptable, from purées to mashed to lumpy and then chopped foods. By the end of the year, your baby should be enjoying three meals a day.

Throughout this book, we'll guide you through the stages of starting solids, helping you make the right choices for your baby at the right times. You may decide to choose "baby-led" eating, in which your baby is started on whole foods, rather than purées, at his own pace (see p.235).

How breast-feeding works

It's a natural process based on supply and demand—letting your baby nurse will trigger your breasts to make more milk to satisfy him.

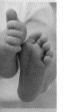

CHECKLIST

Breast-feeding

■ Breast-feeding will be much more successful when you are relaxed, so find a comfortable place to sit down and put your feet up.

■ Breast-feeding moms will need (often instant) access to their breasts, so loose-fitting, comfortable clothing that unzips or unbuttons easily is essential. You'll also need a nursing bra that you can open and close with one hand.

■ Your baby will feed until he has had enough. If he dozes off after a few moments, gently wake him by burping him or stroking his cheek.

■ Check that your entire areola is in his mouth; he will stimulate the release—and resupply—of your milk by pressing on the milk sinuses (see right). If he's only hitting a few, you could end up with blocked ducts (see p.59), sore nipples, and a hungry baby!

■ Don't worry about whether he is getting enough. Your baby's weight gain will be monitored over the first few weeks of his life, and as long as he puts on weight, has plenty of wet diapers (see pp.44–5), and seems alert when he is awake, all will be fine.

■ Try not to give up! Breast-feeding can take a little while to settle into a comfortable experience, but it does become easier over the first few weeks. Try to remember that you are doing what's best for your baby.

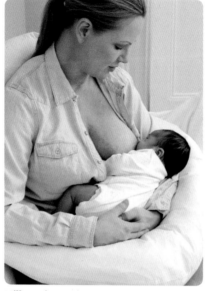

Milk on demand Your baby's sucking triggers the release of the hormone prolactin, which stimulates the production of more milk.

During pregnancy, your body begins to prepare for breast-feeding. Your areola becomes darker (which some people believe helps your baby to see it and encourages feeding), tiny bumps around your areola grow bigger and more noticeable (known as Montgomery's tubercles, these secrete oil that lubricates your nipples to prevent drying, cracking, and infections while feeding), and your placenta stimulates the release of hormones that make milk production possible.

All women are born with milk ducts (a series of channels that transport milk through your breasts) and during pregnancy, these begin to prepare for feeding. Your milk glands expand dramatically so that by the end of pregnancy, each breast may be up to 1 lb 5 oz (600 g) heavier!

Your lactation system, inside your breasts, is somewhat like a small tree, with milk glands forming clusters like grapes high up in your breast. These make milk. This milk travels down from the glands through the milk ducts, which widen beneath the areola to form milk "sinuses." These empty into about 20 little openings in your nipple, which release milk when they are stimulated by your baby's sucking.

This sucking sends a message to the pituitary gland to release oxytocin, a hormone that makes you feel calm and loving, and prompts your milk-producing cells to empty their milk into the ducts. This is known as the "let-down" reflex, and it can also be triggered when you hear your baby cry (and sometimes other babies!), or even simply think about your baby.

Once your milk is let down, your baby's gums compress the sinuses where the milk begins to pool. If he sucks on your nipple rather than the whole areola, only a little milk can be drawn out and you may experience some discomfort. This is why it is essential to get your baby's "latch" correct from the outset (see opposite).

Your baby's sucking also stimulates nerves in your nipple that send messages to the pituitary gland in your brain to secrete the hormone prolactin. This hormone is responsible for ensuring that your milk is continually produced according to your baby's needs. The more milk that is removed from your breasts, the more milk your body makes to replace it, so even expressing milk can help to keep up your supply if you are unable to breast-feed immediately.

Colostrum From about 15–16 weeks of pregnancy, your breasts begin to produce colostrum, which is your baby's first milk. This is a very nutritious, deep-yellow liquid containing high levels of protein, carbohydrates, healthy fat, and antibodies. It is very easy to digest, and just a few teaspoons will provide hugely concentrated nutrition for your baby, and keep him hydrated before your milk "comes in." Colostrum has a laxative effect on your baby, helping him pass his early stools (meconium), which is important for the excretion of excess bilirubin, which may otherwise cause jaundice (see p.404).

Consistency of breast milk When your milk comes in two to three days after your baby's birth (although sometimes a little later, if you've had a cesarean), your breasts will feel engorged and perhaps even a little painful. Each time your baby suckles, he will receive two types of milk. The first milk out of the breast is known as "foremilk," which is thinner in consistency and slightly bluish white in color. This hydrates your baby and satisfies his thirst. Next, he will receive "hindmilk," which is the thicker, more nutrient-dense, and calorific milk that provides everything your baby needs for

ASK A... BREAST-FEEDING EXPERT

Do I need to give my breast-fed baby vitamin supplements? While breast milk is the perfect first food, it only contains small amounts of vitamin D, which is necessary for healthy bone development. Health Canada recommends a vitamin D supplement of 400 IU per day for breast-fed babies during their first year. If you live in a northern community (latitude of 55 degrees or on par with Edmonton), your baby may require a larger supplement.

HOW TO...

Latch your baby on to your breast

Gently stroking your baby's cheek or the corner of his mouth will stimulate his rooting reflex, and he will naturally open his mouth to seek out food. The next step is to ensure he is correctly latched on to your breast. Getting this right can make breast-feeding more comfortable and efficient.

When your baby opens his mouth wide, bring him to your breast—not the other way around! His tongue should be down and forward, and your nipple should be aimed at the roof of his mouth as you draw him on to your breast. When he is properly latched on, all of the nipple and some of the breast tissue should be in his mouth. Your baby is correctly positioned if his tummy is to yours—tummy-to-tummy. His lower lip will be rolled out and his chin will be against your breast. His lower arm may be tucked beneath you, and his upper arm may reach around to hold your breast. His nose should be free of your breast so he can breathe comfortably.

If your baby is correctly latched on, you should hear only a low-pitched swallowing noise—not a clicking or smacking noise—and should see his jaw moving, a sign that he is feeding successfully. Your breasts may be tender at first; trying a few different positions can improve comfort (see p.58).

Rooting reflex Help your baby root for your nipple by stroking the cheek closest to it. He will purse his lips, ready to suck.

Get it right Make sure your baby's tongue is down and forward, and your nipple is aimed at the roof of his mouth before he latches on.

Latch on Make sure your baby takes the nipple and a good proportion of the areola into his mouth for a good latch.

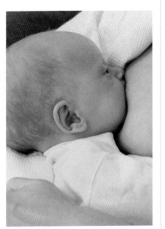

Best position Your baby's head and body must be in a straight line so he can swallow easily, and his chin should touch your breast.

growth, development, and energy. It's important to empty your breast completely at each sitting to ensure that your baby gets both types of milk. If he gets only a little of your foremilk, he may be hungry soon afterward and need another feeding.

Feeding on demand Feeding your baby whenever he is hungry will encourage your breasts to produce the milk he needs. While it can be tempting to put your baby on a schedule, he may be left bewildered and hungry, and your breasts will fail to meet his demands (see p.58). A good feeding normally lasts about 20 to 30 minutes, but a young baby will probably want to nurse every couple of hours, so you might feel as if you're feeding around the clock. If he's falling asleep on the breast, or losing concentration and looking around, it may be that he isn't very hungry, and you'll be better off trying again later.

Getting support Breast-feeding is not always easy in the beginning, and you may require the support of your ob/gyn, your baby's pediatrician, or a lactation consultant to help to get it established, or go to a mothers' group. You'll need support from your partner, too. You'll be spending very long hours feeding your baby, and until you are able to express a little milk that can be fed to your baby via a bottle (see box, below), your partner won't be very involved. He will need to understand that you are breast-feeding to give your baby the best possible start in life. Studies have shown that family and friends play an important role in the decisions that new moms make about feeding. Women who are supported feel more confident and tend to breast-feed longer.

EXPRESSING BREAST MILK

Once your milk supply is established—at around a month or six weeks after the birth—you can begin to express a little milk. This will not only buy you some freedom, allowing dad or someone else to feed him from time to time, but it will also provide you with a store of frozen milk that can be used if and when you go back to work.

Not everyone finds expressing easy, and you may need to experiment with different pumps (for example, manual, battery-operated, or electric) or do it by hand (see p.85) to produce enough milk. If you're nursing eight times a day, 3 oz (90 ml) is usually adequate for a single feeding, so don't worry if you don't manage to extract much at first. Relaxing somewhere near your baby can make the process more successful, and you may find that if your baby regularly feeds from only one breast in a sitting, you can simultaneously express from the other.

If your baby is born prematurely, he may not be able to feed at the breast initially, in which case you will be helped to express and get your milk supply established, ready for when he is physically able to manage feeding.

 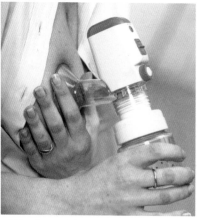

Manual pump Hand or manual pumps are affordable, lightweight, quiet, and easy to use—you simply operate the plunger to express milk (left). **Electric pump** This pump is automatic, so generally quicker and better if you need to express milk quite frequently (right).

ASK A... BREAST-FEEDING EXPERT

Is there any reason why I won't be able to breast-feed? Almost all women can breast-feed, and provide sufficient milk to meet their babies' needs. Even women with small breasts or inverted nipples can successfully nurse, so try not to worry. Women often "decide" in advance that it will be too difficult, but with the support of your partner and midwife, you can succeed if you make the commitment.

There are some cases when breast-feeding may not be possible. These include taking some types of medication, which would be unsafe for your baby, or suffering from a breast infection or disease, such as cancer. Very, very rarely, some women don't generate enough milk for their babies, although current support makes this less likely. Women who have had a breast reduction may find feeding difficult (although not always impossible); similarly, your baby may be unable to breast-feed because she is premature, too small, has a problem sucking, or birth defects in her mouth, such as cleft palate, or digestive problems, in which case you may want to express milk (see box, left).

Bottle-feeding

If you can't or do not want to breast-feed, or plan to do so for a short period of time, you'll need to master the art of bottle-feeding.

Comforting feeding Making eye contact with your baby while you bottle-feed helps promote bonding and makes him feel secure.

Moms who cannot, or choose not to breast-feed should not feel guilty. There is a very good range of formulas on the market that will encourage healthy growth and development, and it's perfectly possible to make bottle-feeding sessions warm, nurturing, and positive (see p.59).

Bottle-feeding equipment You'll need six–eight bottles, nipples, and caps, a bottle-brush for cleaning, a sterilizer (optional), a measuring cup, formula, and a pot to boil water, which is then cooled to make up the feed. There are many bottles and nipples available, and you can buy anything from colic bottles and self-sterilizing, to "natural" and slow- or fast-flow nipples. You may need to experiment when your baby is born, to see what works best for him.

Nipples should be slow-flowing for new babies, and gradually become "faster" as they get a little older. Silicone nipples are more durable; however, latex tends to be closer to the sensation of a nipple. Choose from a traditional bell shape, an "orthodontic" nipple that manufacturers claim most resembles a nipple, or a flatter nipple that is particularly easy for young babies to manage.

Choosing formula Choose an iron-fortified formula that is appropriate for your baby's age. Most formulas contain roughly the same beneficial ingredients, but you may want to look for one that contains probiotics to encourage digestive health, and omega oils, which aid brain development. You can make formula from a powder or a liquid, or buy it ready made. Breast milk contains two types of protein: whey and casein. The balance in breast milk is in favor of whey, with a 60:40 ratio (60 percent whey, and 40 percent casein). It is a good idea, therefore, to look for a formula with this same ratio intact. Formulas that have a greater percentage of casein tend to be harder for your baby to digest. Formula is designed to provide your baby with the right amounts of essential nutrients. It is balanced to ensure that it is easily digestible, and meets your baby's needs for both fluid and food. It is, therefore, extremely important to follow the manufacturer's instructions to the letter.

Your first bottle-feeding Many hospitals supply you with formula for your baby, although if you have a strong preference for a particular brand, you may want to take some ready-made cartons to the hospital with you (there may not be time or opportunity to make liquid or powdered formula while you're there). You'll need some bottles, too.

Hold your baby close, skin-to-skin, to mimic the breast-feeding experience, and look into his eyes when you feed to promote bonding. Your nurse will be able to show you the best positions for bottle-feeding (see p.59). He'll feed little and often at first, so don't force him to finish a bottle. Give him as much as he wants, when he wants.

ASK A... MIDWIFE

Do I need to sterilize all my baby's feeding equipment? Washing bottles carefully is important because every trace of milk needs to be removed. While many experts feel it isn't necessary in places with safe drinking water, you may choose to sterilize your baby's feeding equipment as well. There are several methods to choose from: You can use high heat, such as steam, or a chemical cold-water treatment that is designed to kill any germs. There is a wide variety of sterilizers available, including those that work in the microwave. It's also fine to use your dishwasher, as long as your machine reaches a hot temperature of at least 176°F (80°C) or more, which is necessary to kill any harmful bacteria or viruses. This will help your baby avoid germs that cause illness.

Sleeping arrangements

Your baby will spend a lot of time asleep in the coming months, so you want him to be comfortable and safe while he's sleeping.

ASK A... DOCTOR

I'd like my baby to sleep in our bed, but is it safe? There's a lot of controversy over whether it's safe to co-sleep, so really it's up to you to weigh the arguments and decide what's best for you. Proponents of co-sleeping say it's convenient for breast-feeding because your baby can nurse easily and you both can doze off when finished. It is also thought that babies settle down better when their mothers are close, being reassured by their familiar scent and rhythmic breathing. Some research suggests that babies who co-sleep grow up to be more independent and secure. Other studies point to a lower incidence of SIDS, perhaps because babies learn to mimic adult breathing patterns earlier.

Some experts, however, say that co-sleeping should not be done with babies under any circumstances, because there's a risk of a baby being suffocated by pillows or loose blankets or crushed by a sleeping parent who has rolled onto the baby. A parent who is intoxicated, a deep sleeper, or who takes medication that induces deep sleep, or who smokes, should not co-sleep. To protect your baby, you may want to invest in a baby nest or bed divider, or a bassinet or Moses basket that you can place beside your bed within easy reach. Some moms warn that babies who get used to sleeping with their parents find it difficult to sleep alone later on. There are also consequences for your relationship with your partner.

There is a wealth of options when it comes to choosing your baby's first bed, and you can spend a lot of money on features that may not be necessary. For example, although a rocking cradle might look like a good way to settle him down at night, he may get used to being rocked to sleep, and find the transition to a crib or bed more difficult. Whatever your budget, the most important considerations are safety and comfort.

Little beds After having been tightly confined in your uterus for months, your baby is likely to settle down better and feel more secure in a snug environment. For this reason, his "first" bed should be small enough to make him feel cozy and comfortable. Experts now recommend that your baby sleeps in the same room as you for the first six months of his life, so a "portable" bed, such as a Moses basket, is a practical choice. (Just be aware that you should avoid putting your baby's Moses basket directly on a heated floor since this puts your baby at risk of overheating.)

Cradles and cribs are less mobile, which can be a disadvantage in the early days, but many parents like something sturdier. This first bed will probably only last a few months, so it isn't usually worthwhile spending a lot! If you buy used, it's recommended that you buy a new mattress, to help lower the risk of Sudden Infant Death Syndrome (SIDS) (see box, right), and be sure that any used crib meets the current consumer product

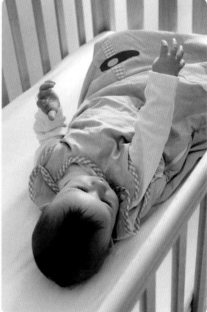

Portable Moses basket A lightweight Moses basket is ideal for a young baby because you can move it around to keep her close when she sleeps (left) **Sleeping bag** For older wiggly babies who are always losing their blankets, sleeping bags are a good way to ensure they stay snug.

safety standards of Health Canada (www.hc-sc.gc.ca).

If you go for a full-sized crib, there are certain features that will help ensure your baby's safety and help you get the most for your money (see p.113). Mattresses can be made of foam, natural, or hollow fibers, and must fit the crib snugly so that there are no gaps in which a baby could get trapped. The mattress cover should be easy to clean. You can put a carry crib or Moses basket inside a crib when your baby is small, which helps ease the transition to a big crib later.

Your baby's bedding You will need two or three mattress protectors, three fitted sheets, a mattress pad, and a waterproof mattress protector, but nothing more. Newborns and infants shouldn't be put into cribs with loose top sheets or blankets, quilts, or comforters, pillows, or even bumper pads, since they all pose a risk of suffocation. If they go over your sleeping baby's nose or mouth, he won't have the coordination or inclination to push them off. To keep your baby warm, consider purchasing a baby sleeping bag, or wrap him in a tight swaddle. If you insist upon putting your baby under a blanket on cold nights, for his own safety, place your baby's feet at the bottom of the crib, then securely tuck the blanket under the mattress on three sides and place the top of the blanket no higher than his chest.

What temperature? It is important to keep the temperature of your baby's bedroom on the cool side. Not only will he sleep better, but also he will have far less risk of overheating—something that has been linked to SIDS. A room temperature of 60.8–68°F (16–20°C) is ideal. As a general rule, if the room temperature is 60.8°F (16°C), your baby will need a 2.5 tog (medium weight) sleeping bag plus a blanket, or a sheet and three layers of blanket. The warmer the room is, the fewer layers he'll need.

Sudden Infant Death Syndrome (SIDS or "crib death") is the unexplained death of a baby. It occurs most often in babies under four months, but can occur up to the age of one. The cause is still largely unknown, but a lot of research has gone into identifying risk factors and the measures that can be taken to prevent it.

Remember that crib death is rare, so don't let yourself worry about it so much that you stop enjoying your baby's first few months of life. However, follow the advice below to reduce the risk as much as possible:

■ Use baby sleeping bags, swaddles, or place his feet at the bottom of the crib, then securely tuck a blanket under three sides of the mattress, placing the top edge no higher than the chest.

■ Keep your baby in a crib in a room with you for the first six months.

■ Keep your baby's head uncovered to prevent the baby from getting too hot.

■ Don't smoke in pregnancy and don't let anyone smoke in the same room—or house—as your baby.

■ Never fall asleep with your baby on a sofa or armchair.

■ Avoid overheating by keeping the room temperature at about 65°F (18°C).

■ Never allow your baby to sleep with a hot-water bottle, electric blanket, next to a radiator, heater, or fire, or in direct sunshine.

■ Avoid sleeping with your baby if he was premature (born before 37

Safe sleeping To reduce the risk of SIDS, your baby should sleep on her back with her feet at the foot of the bed.

weeks) or if he weighed less than 5½lb (2.5kg) at birth, or if you or your partner are smokers (even if you never smoke in the house), feel very tired, or have recently drunk alcohol or taken medication or drugs that make you sleep heavily. Official guidelines advise that you do not co-sleep with a baby under any circumstances.

■ Breast-feeding your baby reduces the risk of crib death.

■ A pacifier can cut the risk of SIDS in half. However don't use one for a breast-fed baby under four weeks, and only use it when your baby is going to sleep.

Early routines Many babies feel more secure when they are in the same place every day (for naps) and at night. Creating a familiar environment, which your baby associates with sleep, will help him settle down more easily—and sleep longer. Create a sleep corner in your bedroom, or move his bed around so that you can keep an eye on him when he sleeps during the day.

Some moms prefer to stick to a regular "bed" at night, and use a carry crib or even a carriage for their baby's naps. This has the advantage of helping your baby differentiate between daytime sleeps (shorter) and nighttime sleeps (longer).

This also allows for a bit more flexibility, because it means that your baby can enjoy his nap in the carriage wherever you happen to be.

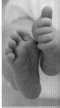

All about diapers

Your baby will be in diapers for at least a couple of years, so choosing the type of diaper that bests suits your lifestyle is important.

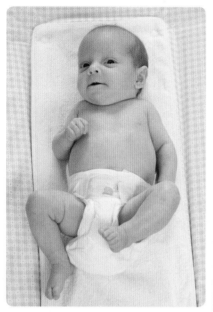

Disposable diapers Disposables are very convenient and absorbent, but can be costly.

There are two main types of diapers: disposables and reusables, both of which have their advantages and disadvantages. Many parents choose to use a combination of the two—disposables when they are out and about and on vacation, and sometimes even at night, because they tend to be more absorbent, and reusables the rest of the time. Figure out a system that's best for you. There's not much point in feeling virtuous about doing your part for the environment if your stress load hits the ceiling and you end up using an environmentally unfriendly tumble dryer to try to get through a pile of laundry.

If your baby is prone to diaper rashes, his skin may respond better to disposables. If your budget is tight and your organizational skills are immaculate, reusables may be right for you. There is no right way. It's a question of balance and practicality.

Disposable diapers These are undoubtedly more convenient and there appear to be fewer cases of diaper rash, fewer leaks, and fewer changes necessary with disposables. They are, however, much more expensive, produce a high level of waste, and must be disposed of properly. The majority contain man-made chemicals, too.

Your baby will go through approximately 5,000 disposable diapers from birth to potty training, and this can have a pretty dramatic effect on the environment. Go for disposables that do not contain any bleaching agents, which are a major source of pollution during manufacture and decomposition.

Diapers that are better for your baby's bottom and to the environment are those that don't contain gels, perfumes, dyes, and/or latex. Those that are at least 50 percent biodegradable can help reduce the growing problem with landfills, and diapers that use sustainable resources (that is "fluff" from wood that has been cultivated sustainably) will also make an impact.

If you go with disposables, keep in mind that you'll need an average of 8–12 diapers per day, so make sure you stock up! Ask your doctor to assess the probable size and weight of your baby, so that you don't end up buying a lot of diapers that will instantly be too small. It's best to buy one or two packages of newborn disposables, and then see if he's ready to move up. "Bikini diapers," which fold down, will help keep his umbilical cord free from irritation.

CHANGING PLACES

Although you may have created a lovely set-up on the changing table in your baby's bedroom, this may not always be practical. Babies often need fairly "instant" changes, particularly in the middle of a feed, or in the event of a sudden explosion at the bottom end! You may find it useful to keep a diaper bag handy or to set up mini changing stations in rooms where you plan to feed your baby, near his bed, and where you'll spend time playing. Fill a basket with diapers, wipes, barrier cream, diaper sacks, and/or a plastic bag or tub to contain reusables, and a fold-up changing mat. Check the stations every evening, so that you can keep them fresh, tidy, and fully stocked!

Changing unit A purpose-made station is ideal for the bedroom where pre- and post-sleep diaper changes normally happen.

Change a reusable diaper

Gone are the days when we had to rely on terry or cotton diaper squares that had to be folded and pinned—no easy task with a small, fractious baby to change. Today's reusables come in a variety of styles and colors, and often use easy-to-manage clips or Velcro tabs to make fastening them quick and efficient. Set up a clean, dry area in a warm room to change your baby—on a changing table is ideal—and gather all the supplies you need: a clean diaper; cotton pads and water, or baby wipes; a diaper bucket or bag to store the dirty diaper; and some emollient cream if your baby is prone to diaper rash.

If you are using flushable liners, you can flush the dirty one after you remove the diaper; if you are using reusable liners, you will need to shake or rinse off any excess feces before putting the liner in the diaper bucket to be washed.

When you put the clean diaper on, make sure that it fits snugly, but it should not be too tight or it might pinch the skin.

Get the diaper ready Lay the diaper out on the changing mat and place the lining on top so that you're all prepared. Move it to one side while removing your baby's dirty diaper.

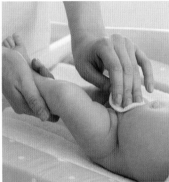

Wash your baby Clean the diaper area thoroughly with cotton pads and water or a baby wipe.

Comfortable fit Slide the diaper under the baby's bottom, fold the outer edge over, and fasten the tabs or snaps.

Most parents purchase diaper sacks (biodegradable), to efficiently dispose of diapers at home and out of the house. (See also "How to change a disposable diaper, p.44).

Reusable diapers Reusables produce less waste and use fewer raw materials in their manufacture. Your baby will also be wearing soft, natural fibers next to his skin. However, washing reusables can waste a lot of water, and requires cleansing agents. It can also be very time consuming, unless you can afford a laundry service. Your baby will also need to be changed more often, since reusables tend to be less absorbent.

There are two main types of reusables. Two-part diapers consist of a diaper and a wrap. Diapers can be traditional terry cloth, which will require pins or clips, a folded diaper (known as a pre-fold, and which also requires a fastener), or a shaped diaper. On top, you will place a wrap designed to keep the moisture in and prevent leaking. Wraps can take the form of a pull-up pant, or wrap around with fastenings (often Velcro). All-in-one diapers combine the inner diaper and the "wrap" in a single waterproof garment. These diapers look a little more like disposables, and are normally self-fastening. Some moms find them harder to wash and thoroughly dry; they also tend to leak. You'll also need disposable diaper liners, which provide a barrier between the fabric and your baby's skin, and make it easier to lift out and dispose of bowel movements. Booster pads can be useful at night to provide greater absorbency. If you choose pre-folds or terry cloth, you'll need diaper pins or clips. Plastic diaper clips are a great alternative to pins, not only because they are easier to fasten, but because they'll prevent accidental pricking. Finally, you'll need a large bucket with a lid to store dirty diapers, and a plastic carrier to transport dirty diapers when you are out and about.

Reusables also come in "sizes" according to the weight of your baby, and you'll need to purchase about 20 diapers and three or four wraps to begin with. Don't buy too many; your baby will grow and move on to the next size more quickly than you think. Equally, however, you don't want to be left with only one clean diaper and a pile of unwashed, dirty ones! Although they can require a hefty investment every few months, reusables should prove to be cheaper in the long run.

Essential equipment

Although a visit to the store may suggest otherwise, you don't need a huge pile of new gadgets and equipment—just some key items.

Feeding equipment

Breast-feeding doesn't require any equipment to start with; however, there are a few items that will aid your comfort and are necessary for expressing milk (see p.28). Bottle-feeding does require a few essentials.

Breast-feeding

■ 3–4 good-quality nursing bras that you can open with one hand.
■ Breast pads for leaks.
■ Breast shells to catch those leaks.
■ Nipple cream for sore or chapped nipples; choose a lanolin-based one that can stay on your breast while you are nursing.
■ A pump, if you want to express, and 2–3 feeding bottles (with caps and nipples) to store your expressed milk. Some people use special freezer bags designed for breast milk.
■ A U-shaped feeding pillow to stay comfortable during long feedings.

Bottle-feeding

■ 6–8 bottles; smaller bottles are more appropriate for newborns and babies who do not consume much milk at one sitting. You'll need caps and nipples, too.
■ Cleaning equipment and a bottle brush.
■ A teapot—you might want a quick and regular source of fresh, boiled water for making up bottles.
■ A designated measuring cup, spoon, and knife.

In the bedroom

■ A Moses basket, crib, or cradle, which will keep your baby secure in the early days. They are soon outgrown, so if your budget is tight, go for a full-sized crib.
■ A full-sized crib that meets Health Canada's crib safety standards (cribs made before 1986 do not).
■ Bedding (see p.31).
■ A changing table. Any hard surface at hip height will work, including the top of his chest of drawers. If you are purchasing one, look for one with a lip to prevent him from rolling off.
■ A changing mat—go for one that is easily washed and comfortable; you may want a few fold-up spares for your mini changing stations.
■ A baby monitor; a two-way monitor is ideal, so you can hear your baby and he can hear you!
■ Diapers and the other elements of a changing station (see p.32).
■ A bouncy chair that can be moved from room to room.
■ A night-light, to help those late-night feedings, or a light that will keep the room dim enough to see your baby, but discourages him from fully waking.
■ Chest of drawers or baskets for storage.
■ A diaper bucket for reusables, or a container for disposables.
■ If you are planning to co-sleep, you may want to invest in a baby nest or bed divider (see p.30).

Burp cloths It's definitely worth stocking up on burp cloths since they're invaluable for protecting clothing and mopping up mess.

Crib Your baby's crib is an important purchase, so do your research beforehand to help you make the right choice.

Changing mat Keep a couple of mats in strategic locations around the home, and at least one foldable mat to fit in your diaper bag.

Flat out A carriage can provide a convenient place for your baby to sleep when planning an outing, instead of her Moses basket.

Out and about

■ A rear-facing car seat is required for all infants, with an easy-to-manage five-point harness. Second-hand car seats are not recommended for safety reasons. Your car seat may come as part of a travel system, which can include various fittings, including a stroller and carry crib that fit onto one base.

■ A baby carrier for transporting your baby or keeping him calm when you need your hands free. Choose one with wide shoulder straps to protect your back. Be careful with babies under four months old in front carriers; these can be a suffocation hazard for infants with weak neck muscles.

■ A carriage or stroller. Newborn babies need to lie flat, and a traditional carriage with a flat base provides a perfect secure environment. Most strollers can be adjusted to lie flat, so are suitable from birth, and the seat can be raised so your baby can sit up when he is older. There are many different types, but make sure the one you choose has a five-point harness and a double-locking folding mechanism; is easy to fold and erect; comfortable for your height; and suits your lifestyle. If you do more shopping than jogging, storage space may be more useful than a reinforced suspension. Your baby's first stroller should be rear-facing, that is, facing you.

■ A diaper bag. Ideal for transporting all your baby's paraphernalia; some come with detachable changing mats. Plenty of pockets means you can keep bottles, diapers, and clean clothes separate.

Staying clean

■ Wipes—choose water-based wipes with no fragrance or other chemicals; biodegradable are best.

■ Small, thin washcloths for reaching those tiny folds and crevices, or cotton pads (cotton balls sometimes leave skin-irritating fluff behind).

■ An all-in-one bath and shampoo product designed for babies. You'll only need a little, so investing in a good,

Bouncy chair These chairs help babies see what's going on around them and their gentle rocking or bouncing motion is soothing.

natural product is probably worthwhile.

■ Burp cloths, which can be used to mop up spit-up, leaks, and drool, and protect your clothes when burping and feeding.

■ Washable bibs that will slip over or fasten behind your baby's neck easily. These are helpful to protect his clothing during feedings.

■ A baby bath—although this is not essential. It's perfectly acceptable to wash your baby in a full-sized bath or even the kitchen sink. Invest in a nonslip mat if you use the tub, and line the sink with an old sheet or dish towel

to keep him comfortable. If you purchase a baby bath, make sure it is sturdy and you can easily fill and drain it.

■ A thermometer, if you aren't confident about assessing the temperature of your baby's bath water.

■ 2–4 towels—preferably hooded, which will keep your baby's head warm and dry while you use the body of the towel to dry him off. You'll probably use two when you bathe him (see p.57), and the others may well be in the wash!

■ A bowl for sponge baths (see p.45).

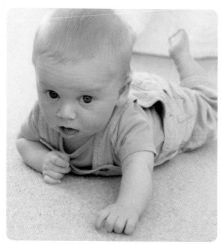

Your baby's first year whizzes by so fast, yet every single day is a new adventure for you and your child, punctuated by triumphs and tears, amazing developments, and the occasional setback. There's also so much to learn, so this chapter acts as your companion, day by precious day, pointing out the highlights and pitfalls you are likely to encounter along the way. From feeding and sleeping to crawling and communicating (and staying sane as a parent, too), it's a unique and illuminating insight into an unforgettable 12 months.

Your baby
day by day

Your baby at 1 to 3 months

WEEK | 1 | 2 | 3 | 4 | 5 | 6 | 7 | 8 | 9 | **10** | **11** | **12** | **13** | 14 | 15 | 16 | 17 | 18 | 19 | 20 | 21 | 22 | 23 | 24 | 25 | 26

Head support A young baby has virtually no muscle control and is unable to hold her head up. You'll need to support your baby's neck and head for the first month or so.

Frequent feedings Young babies feed a lot—breast-feeding on demand helps stimulate your milk supply.

Physical contact Being held and touched makes your baby feel secure and aids her emotional development.

Helpless newborn Your baby is fully dependent, but her senses function well—she'll know your smell and voice.

Did you know? By the end of the first month, most babies are alert for about 2–3 hours of every day.

Blurry vision Your baby's early vision is fuzzy but she can focus on your face if it's within a 12 in (30 cm) range. By six weeks, she can see up to 24 in (60 cm) away.

Built-in reflexes Your baby is born with reflexes that are part of her survival kit. These include the rooting, grasp, and crawling reflexes shown here, but there are many others. Some of these reflexes disappear over the first three months.

Sleepy baby Initially, your baby will sleep up to 18 hours a day, decreasing to about 15 hours by three months. However, it's not likely that she'll sleep through the night.

From a helpless newborn to a smiling baby with a mind of her own, your baby's development is astonishing.

First smile Usually, babies produce their first real smile between six and eight weeks, once their facial muscles have developed.

Head lift By about eight weeks, your baby may be able to lift her head briefly—and possibly turn it from side to side—while lying on her tummy.

Cooing baby Your baby will start to make soft vowel sounds such as "ooh-ooh" and "ah-ah." He may even add consonants, to make sounds like "ah-goo."

Discovering hands At about two months, your baby may discover his hands but he doesn't yet realize they're his.

Reaching out Once she's discovered her hands, your baby will start swiping at objects within reach.

Did you know? Many—although not all—three-month-olds can lift their heads up to a 90-degree angle when lying on their stomachs.

Self-expression Your two- to three-month-old can now make use of a range of facial expressions to tell you how he feels or whether he's tired or hungry.

Getting a grasp By her third month, your baby will have greater hand control. She may be able to grasp a rattle, possibly firmly enough to give it a shake.

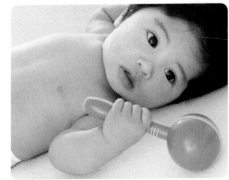

The first seven days

SOME BABIES ARE BORN WITH A FULL HEAD OF HAIR WHILE OTHERS ARE NEARLY BALD

Skin-to-skin contact with your baby immediately after birth as well as in the weeks and months to come helps you form a close bond with her. Such contact also stabilizes your baby's heart and breathing rates and helps her to maintain a normal body temperature.

After your baby's birth

While you gaze in wonder at your new baby, your doctor or midwife will check that all is well. Then you'll be able to say hello properly.

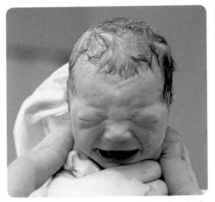

First impressions Newborn babies often look somewhat squashed and wrinkly, but within a day or two their appearance smoothes out.

After nine long months of pregnancy, today you can finally hold your baby in your arms for the first time. You may experience an overwhelming rush of emotions, ranging from tearfulness, pride, and intense love, to exhaustion and elation. You may also feel somewhat daunted by the prospect of caring for such a tiny, fragile human being, and nervous about her health and well-being. Labor takes an enormous physical and emotional toll, and you will need time to rest and recover after the birth.

Your baby's appearance Don't be surprised if your newborn looks nothing like you had imagined. She may be covered in a white, waxy substance known as vernix, which has protected her skin in the amniotic fluid, and she may be streaked with blood from the birth canal. If she had a bowel movement during labor, her skin, hair, and nails may be stained with a blackish, tarlike substance called meconium that forms her first bowel movements. If your baby is premature, she may also have a covering of fine hair, known as "lanugo."

Your baby's genitals may be enlarged and her head may look squashed or elongated, because babies' skulls change shape to negotiate the birth canal. Her nose may be flattened and her eyes might be puffy or even sealed shut. If you do glimpse her eyes, they'll probably be blue or gray. All babies have blue eyes in the uterus, which are lighter or darker depending on their ethnic origin. The irises develop their final color between six months and three years after birth.

Many newborns have birthmarks such as stork marks on the eyelids or nape of the neck that fade over time.

HOW TO...

Breast-feed after birth

Even if you don't plan to breast-feed after this, offering your baby her first feeding within an hour of birth ensures that she receives colostrum, your early milk, which contains high levels of nutrients, antibodies, and other health benefits (see p.27). It also reduces your risk of heavy bleeding after birth and stimulates mild contractions that help your uterus shrink back to normal size.

Your nurse or midwife will help you into position and your baby may root around to find your breast and begin nursing. Encourage her by lying her next to you under your arm to nurse easily. Her mouth should open wide and take in the whole areola. This is known as latching on (see p.27).

Straight to the breast Putting your baby to your breast soon after birth has proven health benefits for both of you.

THE APGAR TEST

After your baby is born, her breathing, pulse, movements, skin color, and responses are assessed. This test, known as the Apgar test, is done at one and five minutes, and sometimes 10 minutes, after the birth. Each of these indicators is given a score of between zero and two, and all the scores are added together to calculate your baby's Apgar score. A total of seven or more at one minute is normal; under seven means that help may be needed. Many babies are groggy after birth or need a little help breathing and responding to the outside world.

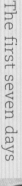

41

You and your new arrival

As your baby begins to acclimatize to her new environment, your doctor will check to see that you are recovering well.

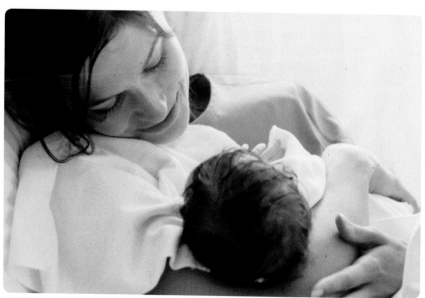

The first hours Now you can spend time getting to know your brand new baby, bonding with her, and admiring every precious little feature as you hold her in your arms.

After the exertion of giving birth, you'll probably feel sticky, sweaty, and in need of a shower. You may also want to use the bathroom. The first time you urinate it can sting, especially if you've had stitches, so it can help to take a cup with you, fill it with warm water, and pour it over the area as you urinate.

Your body after the birth It's a good idea to replenish your depleted energy reserves—a cool drink and a snack should taste delicious right now.

The doctor or labor nurse will check your pulse and blood pressure to ensure they are returning to normal. Your uterus will be gently palpated to observe if it is well-contracted, vaginal blood loss will be checked to ensure it is not excessive, and your perineum will be examined to assess whether or not

any cuts or tears need stitching. Your temperature will also be taken. It is normal to experience a slightly raised temperature after the birth, but if it remains high, or begins to rise, this can be a sign of infection. Your urine may be tested to make sure your kidneys are

working normally and you'll be asked to confirm that you've urinated. It's normal to experience continued vaginal blood loss, known as lochia, after birth. The bleeding is usually heavier than during a normal period and small blood clots are common for the first few days. You'll need maternity pads to deal with the flow—you should not use tampons because they could cause infection.

Your baby after the birth During the first 12 hours, in addition to checking your baby's Apgar score (see p.41), a doctor or nurse will give your baby a quick check. Your baby will probably become increasingly alert during the hours following the birth, opening her eyes frequently and gazing at your face. Her tiny fingers and toes will have nails, and she may have some mild spots or a rash. After months curled up in the confines of your uterus, her arms and legs will be bent, but will straighten out over the coming weeks. Your baby will probably respond to the sound of your voice, and exhibit some reflexes (see p.47). She may cry, sleep, or simply look

AFTER A CESAREAN

A cesarean section is major surgery, so you need to give your body time to recover. It is normal to feel shaky, tired, tearful, drowsy, and nauseous after the surgery, and you will be given medication to help you deal with any pain. If your cesarean was unplanned, you may feel the need to talk through why it was necessary with your doctor. Your body will be somewhat

compromised by the incision, so your nurse and/or doctor will advise you on how to breast-feed comfortably, use the bathroom, roll out of bed, and lift your baby without causing damage to the incision. Medical staff will encourage you to become mobile, which will prevent clots from forming in your legs. But try to rest as much as you can.

around at her new environment, although she won't see much beyond about 12 in (30 cm) at this point (the approximate distance your face is from your breast when you breast-feed her).

The golden hour The hour immediately after your baby's birth is known as the golden hour because it is an important time for the attachment process between mother and baby. New moms experience changes in brain chemistry immediately after birth that increase their desire for nurturing. Holding your baby naked, skin-to-skin, at this stage has been shown to promote bonding, calm your baby, increase her resistance to infection, and get breast-feeding off to a good start.

Try not to worry if you miss out on this first hour of bonding, perhaps because your baby requires medical attention right after birth. Obviously, it's much more important that she receives the care she needs first. You can make up for any lost time later by giving her "Kangaroo care" (see p.54).

On the labor floor If the birth was straightforward, you may be able to go home within a few hours. A long or difficult birth, a cesarean, or concerns about your baby may mean a slightly longer stay. If you do need to stay in the hospital, use the opportunity to rest and to ask for help with feeding, or about any aspect of taking care of your baby, from the experienced staff on hand.

Prime time In the hour after birth, skin-to-skin contact is beneficial for both of you.

NEWBORN CHECKUPS

An examination will be done by a hospital pediatrician before you return home, or within 72 hours by your own pediatrician or midwife if you have had a home birth. Your baby will be weighed and measured from the top of her head to her heel and around the head. The measurements are plotted on a chart to show you her size in relation to that of other babies. Her stomach will be palpated to check the organs. The opening of her anus will be examined and, if your baby is a boy, the doctor will look at his penis and check that his testicles have descended into the scrotum. Your baby's eyes will also be checked for cataracts and she will be given a hearing screening test. If this doesn't take place in hospital, it will be arranged by your own pediatrician.

Once your baby has passed all the checkups on her scheduled discharge day, (most babies do without any problems), she will be allowed to go home. Assuming all is well, her next checkup will take place within one to two weeks.

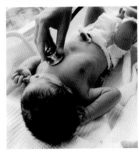

Heart and lungs The doctor uses a stethoscope to listen to your baby's heartbeat and to check that her lungs sound healthy and free of fluid.

Head shape The head is carefully examined and the fontanelles (soft areas between the skull bones) are checked for irregularities.

Feet and hands The palms and soles of the feet are checked, all the toes and fingers are counted, and reflexes are tested.

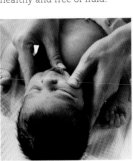

Mouth and palate The mouth is examined to check that the roof (palate) is normal, and that the tongue can move freely.

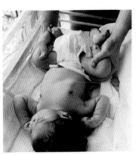

Hips The legs are opened wide and bent upward to check the stability of joints and look for "clicky" hips or other signs of dislocation.

Spine Your baby will be held up so that her spine can be examined to check that it is straight and there is no sign of abnormality.

Early care

Your initial efforts to feed, change, and calm your baby may feel a bit clumsy, but don't worry—you'll soon be up to speed.

Learning to feed your baby If you are breast-feeding, try not to worry if your first sessions haven't gone perfectly well. Over the next day or two, your baby's attempts to nurse may be a little erratic, particularly in the first 24 hours after birth, when she's resting. Just let her nurse when she wants to, and don't expect any kind of pattern to emerge. For the next two to three days, your breasts will be producing mainly colostrum. This is a highly concentrated deep yellow liquid that is rich in antibodies, immunity boosters, and proteins that help nurture and protect your baby from illness. Your breasts probably won't feel very different at this stage because the amount of colostrum your baby needs is very small—she can't fit much more than a few teaspoonfuls at a time into her tiny tummy.

Although your baby doesn't need a lot of milk now, let her nurse whenever she needs to, since this will stimulate the production of mature milk over the next day or two, and help to prevent your breasts from feeling overly full and engorged when this milk does come in.

Keep going with skin-to-skin contact and encouraging your baby to latch-on well—this will make breast-feeding more comfortable for both of you.

If you are bottle-feeding, your baby will also want the bottle little and often, so offer her a bottle every two to three hours. Let her feed for as long as she wants to—if she's had enough of her bottle, don't push her to drink more.

Your baby's diapers Your newborn can have as many as eight to 10 bowel movements in every 24 hours, so you

---

HOW TO...

Change a disposable diaper

It's important to change your baby's diaper regularly because urine, combined with the bacteria in feces, can make his bottom very sore. Diaper changing takes a bit of practice if you've never done it before, but you'll soon be up to speed on the best ways to keep diapers straight and secure (especially after a few leaks). Gather all the equipment you need beforehand to make the change as quick and easy as possible. If your baby doesn't particularly like being changed, and objects to a cold plastic changing mat, try placing a towel over it to make him feel a bit more comfortable.

When cleaning your baby's bottom, remember to wipe from front to back if your baby is a girl, away from the vagina. This minimizes the risk of infection. If you're changing a boy, keep his penis covered with a clean cloth or diaper so that you don't get caught by an unexpected sprinkle!

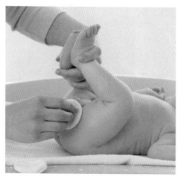

Clean his bottom Holding your baby's ankles, lift his bottom, and gently clean with a damp cotton pad.

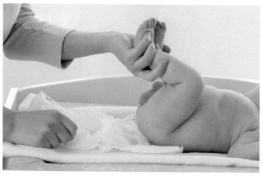

Position the diaper Lift up your baby by the ankles and slide the opened-out diaper beneath his bottom so that the back of the diaper (with the tabs) lines up with his waist.

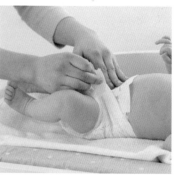

Secure tabs Pull the tabs over the front flap to fasten. Fold down the flap so that the cord stump is open to the air.

Give a sponge bath

Sponge bathing is a good alternative to a full bath for a young baby and to keep an older baby clean between baths. It simply involves gently wiping her from head to toe, paying attention to all those little dimply folds and creases in-between. It's important to do this every day because if dirt, fluff, or milk is allowed to accumulate, it can make your baby's sensitive skin feel irritated and sore. It also prevents skin infections.

Gather all you need before you start: a bowl of lukewarm water; a washcloth or cotton pads; a towel; clean diaper; diaper cream, if used; and fresh clothes if necessary. Keeping your baby's undershirt on to start, gently clean her face, under her chin, neck, hands and feet, and diaper area. Finally, remove her undershirt and clean her tummy, paying attention to the cord stump (see p.51) and under her arms, where dirt is often trapped.

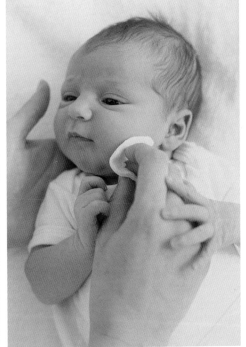

Face and neck Clean your baby's face and neck; use a fresh pad for each eye, and then wipe over and behind (but not inside) each ear (left). **Hands and feet** Wipe her hands and feet, being careful to clean in-between all her fingers and toes (top right). **Diaper area** Clean your baby's bottom and her thigh creases, changing cotton pads frequently (bottom right).

---

will need to change her diaper about eight to 10 times to keep her comfortable and prevent diaper rash. A bowel movement often happens right after feeding, but if it doesn't, don't worry: as long as she has at least one movement per day, she's probably fine. For the first couple of days after birth, your baby will pass meconium, a black, tarry substance that filled her bowels when she was in the uterus. You can't see if your baby's diaper is wet, but you can tell by its weight. If her diaper is heavier than a clean one when you change her, this indicates that she is well-hydrated.

Staying clean You don't even need to think about bathing your baby yet. Some experts recommend not giving her a full bath until the umbilical stump has completely fallen off, and that could take several weeks. For the time being, it's much easier to give her a sponge bath (see box, above). Be sure to check that the warm water in the bowl you're using doesn't become cold before you're done, or your baby won't be happy.

Skin-to-skin contact If you haven't had the opportunity for much skin-to-skin contact so far, you can indulge yourself and your baby now that you've had a little more chance to recover after the birth. This can help to improve the way she latches on during breast-feeding which in turn boosts your milk supply.

The optimum time for this type of contact is when she is feeding. If you are breast-feeding, open your baby's sleep suit or lift up her undershirt, and let her tummy press against yours. If it's not too cool, she can wear just a diaper. Drape a light blanket or sheet over her to protect her from drafts. Many women who experience difficulties with breast-feeding in the early days notice that they have more success when there is skin-to-skin contact.

If you are bottle-feeding, lift up or open your own top to allow skin-to-skin contact. It will promote bonding and help your baby feel secure.

Dads can also remove their tops and go skin-to-skin to establish their own warm relationship.

When your baby is a little older, you or your partner may want to bathe with her to achieve skin-to-skin contact, which is particularly helpful if she is frightened by the bath. When she is difficult to calm, holding her skin close to yours may be all she needs to settle down.

Finding your way

Taking care of your new baby may be confusing at first and you may not know what she needs from you—try to relax and go with the flow.

If you've had a normal birth, or a home birth, you may already be settled in at home and able to introduce your baby to her new environment. You'll probably be most comfortable keeping her next to you most of the time and, in fact, experts recommend that she sleeps in your room for the first six months. Although it's tempting to hold her constantly, it's important to settle her down so that you can get some rest, too. Even the easiest labor is physically and emotionally exhausting, and it will take some time for you to feel like yourself again. Your baby will let you know when she needs you, and you'll soon be able to discern between her cries. In the early days, she'll sleep a great deal, and wake when she's hungry—or simply wants the comfort of being held.

Going home If you are in the hospital, you will be discharged when the doctors are confident that both you and your baby are well, and that you are comfortable taking care of her. Most women are discharged within 24–48 hours of an uncomplicated vaginal birth, but if you've had a cesarean you will need to stay a bit longer, usually three or four days. When you are discharged from the hospital, you'll need to settle your baby in her car seat for the trip home. You may find it easier to sit in the back seat of the car with her, to reassure her of your presence.

A doctor will examine you before you're discharged, and then you won't be seen again for six weeks. Your baby, however, will be seen within one to two weeks by his own pediatrician or family doctor. He was probably examined by a staff pediatrician at the hospital, so this may be their first meeting.

Feeding You will continue to produce colostrum, which is your baby's ideal first food. Exactly how much milk your baby needs depends on her, but, on average, a two-day-old baby will probably take just under 3 teaspoons (14 ml) at each feeding. You can expect feeding to take 40 minutes or longer at the moment. If your nipples are starting to feel sore, or breast-feeding is at all painful, it's likely that your baby isn't latching on correctly. Try to ensure that you get all your areola into her mouth, and adjust her position so that her tummy is against yours (see p.27). If you do experience discomfort, ask for help from your baby's pediatrician, or a lactation (breast-feeding) consultant. Nipple cream can help to ease discomfort. Look for a brand that can be left on while nursing. Pat your

---

HOW TO...

Handle your newborn

You may feel a little daunted at the prospect of handling your tiny baby, but it will soon become instinctive. Your baby is not as fragile as you think, but it is important to handle her gently in order to keep her feeling snug, secure, and safe. Hold her firmly in case she jerks her body backward.

Babies are born with a "startle" reflex (see box, opposite), and will thrust their arms outward if you do not support their neck and head.

A newborn's neck muscles are fairly weak and dangling limbs will make her uncomfortable, so hold her entire body by cradling her close to you.

Pick her up Slide one hand under your baby's neck to support her head, place the other hand beneath her bottom, and lift her gently (left). **Support her head** Rest your baby's head in the palm of your hand, keeping it raised slightly higher than her body (middle). **Face-down hold** Support your baby on one arm with her head near the crook of your elbow and slide your other arm between her legs so that both hands are supporting her stomach (right).

YOUR BABY'S REFLEXES

Your baby is born with over 70 reflexes, which are nature's way of protecting her from harm and promoting her survival. Most of these disappear in six months. The main reflexes are:

- **Moro or startle reflex** If her neck or head are unsupported, your baby will thrust out her arms.
- **Grasp reflex** This reflex is also known as the Palmar grasp. If you place your finger in the palm of your baby's hand, her fingers will instinctively curl around it and grip onto it tightly.
- **Sucking reflex** Your baby sucks when something is placed in her mouth; this ensures she will get nourishment.
- **Rooting reflex** If you stroke your baby's cheek, it will make her turn toward you, looking for food.
- **Stepping reflex** If you hold your baby upright on a flat, hard surface, she will "walk" by placing one foot in front of the other as you support her weight.

Moro reflex Your baby may throw out her arms in response to a sudden noise that startles her (top left). **Stepping reflex** Newborns are able to make stepping movements (far right). **Grasp reflex** This reflex may be an evolutionary legacy from primates, who need to cling to their mothers from birth (right).

nipples dry before rubbing a pea-sized amount on to each nipple.

If you are bottle-feeding, your baby may take more milk but probably not more than a few teaspoons (30 ml) at each feeding. Bottle-feeding tends to be quicker, but this is not always the case. Your formula-fed baby will probably feed for between 20 and 40 minutes.

Weight loss It is normal for newborn babies to lose weight during the first week after birth. Breast-fed babies tend to lose 7–10 percent of their birth weight; bottle-fed babies lose an average of five percent. It is thought that newborns lose weight because they are born with a little extra to begin with to ensure their survival after birth. Most regain this weight by the time they are 10–14 days old. If your baby is feeding well, is urinating, having bowel movements, and appears healthy, there shouldn't be anything to worry about.

Diaper contents Your baby will continue to pass meconium, which can be very sticky and difficult to clean! Warm water and a drop of baby bath can help to clean up the worst of it, but try to use only plain water on your baby's genitals. Your baby's urine should be pale or straw colored; if it becomes dark or smelly, talk to your pediatrician.

ASK A... DOCTOR

My baby sounds very snuffly when she sleeps, and she's constantly snorting and hiccuping. Is this normal? Babies can be very noisy sleepers, and you can expect to hear grunts, groans, little mewling sounds, short cries, and even snorts and hiccups. Your baby may also appear to stop breathing for up to 15 seconds, which is known as "periodic breathing" and can occur until your baby is six months old. She may have a buildup of mucus in her respiratory system, including her nose, after the birth, which may cause her to snuffle, cough, and snort to clear it. This normally passes by the time she's 4–6 weeks old. If her nose seems blocked and she is struggling to feed, talk to your pediatrician; she may have a cold or other infection, and she may need saline nose drops to help clear her nose (see p.408).

How should I care for my baby's genitals? Your baby's genitals may appear swollen for a couple of weeks after the birth, which is caused by pregnancy hormones in her system. Her genitals are very delicate and will need to be carefully cleaned with warm water for a few weeks after the birth; after this, you can use a little of your baby's pH-neutral baby bath to keep the area scrupulously clean. Always clean from front to back in baby girls; lift a baby boy's penis and scrotum to clean around them, and be careful not to pull back the foreskin. If your baby has been circumcised, your pediatrician will advise you on the best way to keep the area clean. It's normal for there to be a little discharge in the early days, but if it is smelly or yellow, you should report it to your doctor.

Adjusting to your new role

You've now been a mom for 72—mostly waking—hours. It's hard to manage when you're tired, so try to rest whenever you can.

Although your baby may seem impossibly tiny and fragile, she is growing stronger every day and will be alert for longer periods of time. Her needs are quite straightforward at this stage, and regular feeding, changing, and time in your reassuring presence will help her feel secure and content.

However, new babies often cry a lot in the early days, partly in response to the shock of a whole new environment, and also because it is the only way they know how to communicate. This can be very upsetting for new parents, especially when you can't pinpoint what might be wrong. The best thing to do is to work your way through the list of reasons she might be crying and try to address them (see pp.68–69). Keep in mind that this is probably a phase and as you get to know your baby better you will be able to understand her cries and anticipate her needs much more easily.

It isn't possible to "spoil" a newborn baby, and every time you respond to your baby's cries, you will develop a strong bond with her, encourage trust, and teach her that her new world is a safe place to be. Some babies undoubtedly cry more than others as they let you know that something isn't quite right. If she doesn't respond to being held, burped, fed, or changed, you can try to reduce stimulation around her, which can help to soothe her.

Find a comfortable place in a dim, quiet room and lay her on her side. Rhythmically pat her back until she settles down to sleep. Then remember to place her on her back. It's easy to feel inadequate when you can't get your baby to stop crying, but try to relax and remind yourself that this is what babies do, and it is no reflection of your abilities as a parent.

Getting support If you feel like you'll never have a shower or a hot cup of coffee again, you are not alone. Babies have a knack of waking and needing attention just when you think you'll get a break. For the first couple of weeks, it's a real help to have another pair of hands available to hold your baby or calm her when she's crying, to allow you a little time to relax, wash, and eat.

If you're exhausted and finding it difficult to deal with your baby's constant crying, ask your partner or a family member to take over for a couple of hours so that you can sleep. You'll feel much more able to take charge again once you've had real rest.

If your baby becomes distressed when you put her down, try carrying her on your chest in a carrier, which will free your hands and soothe her. Time showers, meals, and naps when you have someone around to help; don't feel guilty about not playing "hostess." Your

HOW TO...

Make formula

It is essential to follow manufacturer's instructions to the letter. Too much formula powder or liquid can cause your baby to become constipated or thirsty; too little may mean that she isn't getting what she needs in terms of nutrition. First, you need to boil the water (to kill any germs) and allow it to cool.

Once you've made the formula, gently warm your baby's bottle in a pitcher of hot water: a microwave can cause "hot spots," which could burn her mouth. It's best to make fresh bottles when you need them. If you need to prepare them in advance, store them in the back of fridge, below 4°C (39° F), and don't keep them more than 24 hours.

Right measurement Level off each scoopful as you measure the formula (left). **Adding the powder** Add the formula to the cooled, boiled water in a feeding bottle (middle). **Mixing it up** Shake the bottle so that there are no lumps and the mixture is smooth (right).

Burp your baby

Most babies take in small amounts of air when feeding. This can become trapped in their intestines, causing pain. Gas can also make your baby feel full, which may prevent her from feeding properly. Burping her encourages your baby to release the air trapped in her digestive system, easing any discomfort. You might want to try a little burping session halfway through her feeding and again at the end. If your baby isn't bringing up any gas after 5–10 minutes, don't keep trying. It may be that she doesn't have any to burp up, or it may be released later.

Hold her over your shoulder Gently rub or pat her back until she burps. She may bring up some milk so place a burp cloth over your shoulder (left). **Sit her on your lap** Lean her slightly forward, support her head, and gently rub or pat her back until she burps (right).

ASK A... DOCTOR

I should be over the moon now that my baby is here, so why am I feeling so tearful and emotional?

Tearfulness, temporary feelings of inadequacy, exhaustion, and anxiety are experienced by about 60 to 80 percent of all new moms in the days following the birth. Commonly known as the "baby blues," these emotions are thought to be caused by a drop in pregnancy hormones, combined with a surge in the hormones that are produced for breast-feeding.

You may find yourself constantly in tears, irritable, frustrated, and weary, and you may wonder how you will cope. Baby blues can last for a few hours or up to five days, and you may feel inexplicably under the weather. Don't be embarrassed about crying or feeling anxious. Explain how you are feeling to your partner, and say yes to offers of support during this period. If you don't feel any better in a week, talk to your doctor who will assess whether you are developing postpartum depression, for which you may need extra help.

helpers will love to spend some time with your baby, and help you recover from the birth. Leave a list of "jobs" on the fridge, so visitors know exactly how they can help around the house.

Your baby's milk Chances are that your milk may "come in" today, which means that your breasts will start producing "transitional" milk, a mixture of colostrum and mature milk that looks yellowish and creamy. Your breasts may become harder and possibly slightly engorged, making it difficult for your baby to latch on. Try to get all of your areola into her mouth (see p.27), and massage your breast downward to release some milk and make it easier for her to get your nipple in her mouth.

Over the next 10 days or so, less and less colostrum will be produced, so that by the time your baby is two weeks old, your breast milk is considered to be "mature." Your body will produce just enough for your baby's needs, so feed her as often as she wants to ensure that your supply meets her demand. The more you feed, the more milk you will make. You may find that you are feeding for between 30 and 60 minutes at each session (and sometimes longer), and your baby may drop off to sleep while she's nursing. Gently nudge her awake by stroking her cheek. When she comes off your breast, burp her before getting her down to sleep. Most breast-fed babies will nurse between eight and 12 times in a 24-hour period. If you've had a cesarean, it may take slightly longer for your milk to come in, but keep her nursing at your breast and report any problems to your doctor.

Life for bottle-feeding moms may be more straightforward at this point because you can see exactly how much milk your baby is getting. You'll still be feeding every 2–3 hours, and your baby will probably need a couple of ounces (30–60 ml) at each feeding for the first week or so, or until she weighs 10 lbs (4.5 kg).

Getting checked

In the first two weeks after birth, you'll venture out to the doctor's office for the first time, to make sure your baby is doing well.

Pediatrician Your baby's pediatrician will examine your baby and ask how breast-feeding is going, so she can offer advice if you need it.

You'll have your baby's first appointment at the pediatrician or family doctor's office in the first one to two weeks after she's born, which offers you opportunities to ask any questions you may have. If you're breast-feeding you'll be offered support. The pediatrician will also check your baby to ensure she is healthy and well and is beginning to put on weight. Report anything that concerns you, no matter how minor it may seem. Being responsible for a new life can be daunting at the best of times, and there may be a simple solution to address any problem.

Advice for mom If you're breast-feeding and this is your first child, chances are that you're still trying to get the hang of everything. You might be experiencing pain, your baby might not be latching on properly or your baby might not be gaining enough weight. Don't hesitate to report any problems you may be facing when breast-feeding; it can be very reassuring to get advice and guidance from a professional. Pediatricians often give new moms advice about breast-feeding, and many will offer to watch you breast-feed your baby and critique your technique, with hands-on suggestions for improving the process. Don't feel uncomfortable lifting your shirt in front of the pediatrician; after all, she is a doctor who's seen it all before, and her advice can only benefit you and your baby. If you're still having problems, ask your pediatrician for a referral to a lactation consultant in your area or for the contact information of the local chapter of La Leche League. Both can be invaluable resources for new moms who are trying to figure out the art of breast-feeding while combating sleep deprivation and all of the new responsibilities of motherhood.

Baby checkups You will be asked lots of questions about your baby's feeding and sleeping patterns, bowel movements, wet diapers, and general happiness, which will provide information about her overall health and well-being. Your baby will be weighed during some visits to monitor her weight and see if she is beginning to gain weight.

Weight gain is often slower in breast-fed babies, so don't be alarmed if she doesn't seem to be filling out as quickly as you'd hoped. Your doctor will let you know if she is concerned about your baby's weight, and evaluate your breast-feeding technique. In many cases, improving your baby's latch and allowing her to nurse for long periods in order to build up your milk supply will ensure that she gets what she needs to put on weight and grow at a good rate.

Your baby will probably be undressed for weighing, and your pediatrician will take a look at any rashes or spots, and offer advice. It's normal for babies to look a little mottled in the early days, but if you have concerns, point them out now. Your baby should be given a

TIME TO THINK ABOUT

Newborn screening, or "heel-prick" test

All Canadian babies are offered a blood test, usually between one day and one week old, which checks for three rare but serious disorders: phenylketonuria (PKU), thyroid deficiency, and galactosemia. Several provinces check for up to 25 other hereditary conditions, such as cystic fibrosis and MCADD. It is usually done by a hospital staff doctor or nurse and involves pricking your baby's heel and placing a few drops of blood on an absorbent card that is sent to the lab.

If your baby is on antibiotics, the test should be put off until later, since it can give false results.

full exam, with the pediatrician checking her from head to toe to make sure that everything is all right, since this is probably the first time your pediatrician has met your baby. Your baby's height, weight, and head circumference will be noted in her medical charts and also plotted on percentile graphs to see how she's growing compared to other babies and herself over time. You'll see the pediatrician many times during the first few months, so it's important to feel comfortable with him or her and be able to ask anything that's a concern to you. Be as honest as you can with your pediatrician; there is no shame in admitting that you are struggling to deal with exhaustion or a baby who seems to cry inconsolably. Similarly, don't be afraid to cry or express any anxieties or worries at the doctor's office. Your health practitioners are experienced in all kinds of different scenarios and can offer you invaluable help and advice. If your baby has fallen asleep in the detachable car seat on the drive over to the doctor's office, don't wake her when her name is called; let her sleep while you and the pediatrician discuss other things first; the physical exam can wait until the end of the appointment.

Is my baby suffering from jaundice? About two-thirds of all full-term babies develop jaundice (see p.404) in the first few days after birth. This is caused by a buildup of the pigment bilirubin in your baby's blood. A natural by-product of red blood cells, bilirubin is recycled and cleaned from the blood by the liver. Your baby's liver may take some time to mature in order to deal with the demands placed on it. In most cases, jaundice settles down by about 10 days after the birth. Until then, your baby's eyes may look a little yellow. Make sure she gets plenty of sunlight and feed her often to help encourage her body to excrete the bilirubin.

I have twins. Will my body be able to produce enough milk to feed both of my babies? You are not alone—many new mothers of twins worry that they won't have enough milk to feed two babies. However, breast-feeding works on the principle of supply and demand, so your body will produce milk to the precise requirements of your babies, even during their hungrier periods when they are having a growth spurt.

Should I wake my baby for a feeding? Most parents are reluctant to wake a sleeping baby, since this may be the only opportunity to get some sleep or catch up on chores; however, your baby does need to be fed frequently (at least every two to three hours) to get enough milk for growth and development, so if she is going longer than this, you might need to wake her up to be fed. It's also important to put her to your breast frequently (ideally, about eight to 12 times in every 24-hour period) in order to build up your milk supply.

HOW TO...

Take care of your baby's umbilical cord

It is important to keep your baby's umbilical cord stump clean and dry. It's no longer suggested that alcohol or antiseptic ointments, talc, or liquids be used on it. Instead, plain warm water, with a little baby wash if the area becomes dirty, will do the trick.

Look for "bikini" diapers, which are fastened below the umbilical area to prevent irritation, or you can fold down an ordinary diaper. You can expect the umbilical cord area to look a little mucky in the beginning. However, if it is very red or sore looking, or if there is a smelly discharge, see your doctor, who can rule out infection.

Between five and 15 days after your baby's birth, the umbilical cord stump will dry, blacken, and drop off. Underneath there will be a small wound or sore that will heal over the next few days.

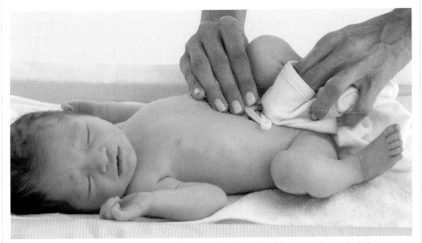

Cleaning the cord To keep infection at bay, gently wipe the skin around your baby's umbilical cord stump with a wet soft washcloth, then dry the area.

51

Bonding with your baby

Bonding begins in pregnancy and continues throughout your lives as you develop a close, powerful connection with each another.

Gentle touch Touching encourages weight gain and reduces fear and anxiety in both of you (left). **Cuddling with dad** Give your partner plenty of opportunities to get involved with your baby's care and spend time with her to establish his own healthy bond with her (right).

Bonding is the development of an intense attachment between parents and their baby. It encourages us to love our babies, feel affection for them, and protect and nourish them. It is what gets us up in the middle of the night to feed them! Bonding also fosters a sense of security and positive self-esteem in your baby. Skin-to-skin contact (see p.45) encourages this process. Your baby's dad can also practice this type of contact to establish his own healthy bond.

Babies are tactile, sensory beings. Caressing your baby will trigger the release of the hormone oxytocin in her. Increased levels of this hormone are associated with feelings of happiness, relaxation, and security. Not all moms find the process of bonding easy, particularly if the birth was difficult. Be patient, look into her eyes, hold her close, and sing and speak to her. She will

respond to your smell and touch, and to your voice, which will be familiar to her from her time in your uterus.

Bonding with dad Your partner may have begun bonding with the baby since the very first ultrasound scan, or when he first felt those magical kicks. It's worth noting that dads often spend less time with their baby directly after the birth, and need to be given the chance to develop confidence in handling and changing their precious newborn. Give your partner plenty of opportunities to be alone with his baby and try to stand back so your partner can find his own style. Help him if need be, and make sure he has all he needs to change her, sponge bathe her, and settle her down to sleep every so often—this way, he'll get to know her as well as you do and develop that all-important bond.

Bonding with twins Parents of twins or multiples can find the bonding process more of a challenge because the huge amount of physical energy needed to take care of twins can sap you of the emotional energy you need to bond. Just like bonding with a single baby, it doesn't always happen instantaneously, and so you need to give yourself time to feel strong attachments to your twins.

Be aware if you are developing more of a bond with one baby than the other. This sometimes happens if one baby needs more time and attention. Try to allocate more relaxed and playful time with the baby you feel less bonded to, as this can help to balance your feelings of closeness more evenly between the two of them.

You may also find that you bond more with one baby, while your partner bonds more easily with the other. This can be a practical measure to ensure both babies develop the security they need for their emotional well-being.

TIME TO THINK ABOUT

Registering the birth

As soon as possible, register your baby's birth with your province or territory, after which you can apply for a birth certificate and a Social Insurance Number (SIN) for your baby. In many cases you can do all this online on the website of your provincial government. You can often apply for Canada Child Benefits at the same time.

Sleeping babies

What a week! Your baby has probably spent most of it sleeping—between feedings—although it certainly may not seem like it!

Sleeping patterns Very few newborns sleep through the night; in fact, the longest stretch they are likely to get will be about five hours.

Most newborns will wake up every two to four hours to be fed. They have tiny tummies and are dependent upon a milk-only diet, which digests very quickly. Your baby will wake when she is hungry and sleep when she is tired, and you cannot force her to do otherwise! It's best to have realistic expectations.

If you are breast-feeding, you can encourage her to sleep well by making sure she fills her tummy. If possible, she should drink from both breasts at each feeding. Now that your milk has come in, she will probably feed on demand for between five and 30 minutes at each breast. She should empty one breast before moving to the other to make sure she gets the fat-rich hindmilk that comes at the end of a feeding.

Bottle-fed babies tend to sleep a little longer because formula is slower to digest than breast milk.

Day and night Many babies wake up for longer periods in the early hours, and sleep all day. In the beginning, it's probably easiest to follow her lead, sleeping when she sleeps. You can start to establish a difference between night and day by keeping things quiet and low key in the run up to bedtime. Try to settle her down while she is still awake. If she falls asleep at the breast she may have discomfort from gas. Allow her to nurse until she is sleepy, but burp her and put her to bed before she is totally asleep.

Avoid the temptation to overdress her. If the weather is warm, just a diaper with a blanket may suffice, and add more layers if she seems cool. When she wakes up at night, feed and change her efficiently, without too much talking.

Most importantly… Lack of sleep can make you anxious and upset. Not only is this transmitted to your baby, making her irritable, it also makes it difficult for you to get a good, restful sleep. Try to be calm when you put her down to sleep. Remember—this is a phase and you'll get your nights back eventually.

HOW TO…

Swaddle your baby

Being wrapped up can help to calm your young baby when she is overstimulated, and prevent her from being disturbed by her own startle reflex (see p.47), which can cause her body to jerk while she is asleep. Choose a soft cotton sheet to swaddle your baby since heavy blankets can cause her to overheat. The idea is to make her feel secure, rather than to keep her warm. Keep her arms free unless she is unsettled, in which case swaddle her loosely with her arms tucked in.

Position your baby Spread out a sheet and fold down a corner to create a long straight edge. Position your baby at top-center (left). **First tuck** Bring across one side of the sheet and tuck it snugly beneath her opposite side. Make sure it's not too tight (middle). **Second tuck** Wrap the other side of the sheet around her. Tuck in the edges beneath her (right).

53

SPOTLIGHT ON...
Your NICU baby

If your baby was born prematurely or wasn't well at birth, she may have been placed in a neonatal intensive care unit (NICU) or a neonatal unit in order to get the best possible medical help and attention from specialist doctors and nurses.

If your baby needs urgent medical care in the NICU, you may not be able to enjoy skin-to-skin contact or encourage the first feeding immediately after birth. You'll probably feel bereft without your baby and extremely anxious about her well-being, especially if she is in an incubator. However, try not to be alarmed by all the tubes and monitors—the incubator protects your baby from infection, provides oxygen if she needs it, and monitors her temperature, oxygen levels, heart rate, and lung capacity.

Feeding your baby If your baby is unable to be fed from your breast or a bottle, tubes may be placed in her mouth or nose, or directly into her stomach. If you want your NICU baby to have your breast milk, you will need to begin expressing (see p.28) as soon as possible after the birth, even if your baby isn't yet ready to take the milk. Breast milk is undoubtedly the best choice for a baby who is small or isn't well as it contains antibodies that can help prevent infection. It also provides all the nutrients she needs for a strong immune system and optimum growth and development.

Hospital staff will show you how to express your milk; most units have a special room with comfortable chairs and an electric breast pump specifically for this purpose. You'll need to keep expressing every couple of hours or so to build up your milk supply. Even if you are able to express only a little in the early days, it should make a big difference to her overall health. Your milk will be fed to your baby through a tube, or possibly via a syringe, bottle, or cup until she is well enough to nurse at your breast.

When you do put your baby to your breast, she may not actually suck, but will enjoy your closeness. If you put a little expressed milk on your nipple,

KANGAROO CARE

Hold her close Research has found that babies benefit greatly from being held closely, skin-to-skin.

One of the best ways of promoting the healthy development of a new baby, whether premature or full term, is to practice Kangaroo care. This simply involves holding her—dressed only in a diaper and probably a hat—against the skin of your chest, between your breasts. Turn her head so her ear is pressed near to your heart, and gather her up against you so she feels your warmth and love. Kangaroo care allows newborns to experience something closer to the containment of the uterus while acclimatizing to the harsher environment of the world.

There is a wealth of benefits associated with Kangaroo care. In fact, research has found that, compared with NICU babies who are not held in this way, those that experience Kangaroo care (even for short periods of time every day) experience:

■ a more stable heart rate
■ more regular breathing (including a 75 percent decreased risk of sleep apnea, which causes babies to stop breathing temporarily during sleep)
■ improved oxygen levels in the blood
■ a regulated body temperature
■ more rapid weight gain and brain development
■ decreased crying
■ longer periods of being alert
■ more successful breast-feeding
■ earlier bonding.

A baby's growth rate increases when held in Kangaroo care mainly because she is able to fall into a deep, restful sleep when snuggled against mom. Sleep allows her to conserve her energy for growth and development. Dads can employ this method of care, too, and aid the process of bonding.

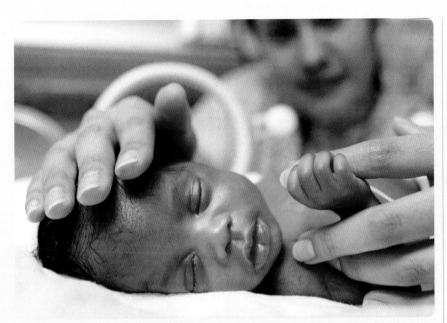

Healing touch It is recommended that you touch and caress your baby, if it is not possible for you to hold her. Spend as much time as possible talking and singing to her to help her relax.

your baby can smell and taste it. A tiny baby will also enjoy catching dribbles of milk in her mouth. Don't expect too much at your first feeding, since premature or sick babies tire easily and need to learn how to suck properly. If your baby is showing definite interest, get some help to make sure she is latching on correctly (see p.27).

Your baby needs you Although she may seem impossibly fragile, and you may be worried about holding her with all of the equipment around her, it is essential that you offer your baby as much close physical contact as you can. She will recognize your voice and smell, and will be comforted by the beating of your heart and your familiar warmth. Holding her as frequently as you can—or, if that is not possible, gently stroking her body in the incubator—can vastly improve her health and well-being. Your regular touch can promote weight gain, encourage healing, and even help her develop more restful sleep patterns. Sing to your baby, talk to her in a calm voice, and reassure her; she will be soothed and positively

stimulated by your voice. Interestingly, research shows that talking to your baby can help to stimulate the developing connections in her brain, yet also makes her feel more relaxed.

Getting involved When it comes to baby care, you may feel out of your depth and want to leave the changing, bathing, and feeding of your baby to the staff, but it can help your baby if you become involved in her regular routine.

Not only will caring for her reassure her and develop the bond between you, but you'll also find the transition to life at home easier. If you are daunted, ask to be shown how to handle her, and be scrupulous about hygiene.

Take care of yourself Rest as often as you can and eat regular, nutritious meals to keep your energy levels up. Get support from family and friends, and try not to feel guilty if you can't be with your baby 24 hours a day.

Keep a journal to record your feelings and celebrate your baby's milestones, no matter how small. Looking back, you'll see her amazing achievements and find comfort in her progress. Also, keep a note of questions you want to ask your baby's doctors and nurses, and write down the answers. We don't always take in all of the information we are given, and you may be in a better position to absorb it when you've had a chance to relax and reflect.

Ask if there is somewhere to stay on the hospital grounds, so that you can have contact with your baby day and night. Above all, recognize that it is normal to experience guilt, distress, anxiety, and a range of other emotions. Talk to your partner and the hospital's health professionals. They are there to support you as well as your baby.

DEVELOPMENT ACTIVITY

Homey atmosphere

Try to interact with your baby as you would if you were taking care of her at home. When you can't be there, decorate her incubator with photos of her family; she'll become familiar with your faces and reassured to see you there. You could play soothing music, or create a recording of your voice to be played during your absences, which will comfort her and help her to develop her connection to you.

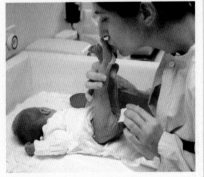

Personal touch Try to forget your clinical surroundings and imagine you're at home.

1 week

DURING THE FIRST FEW WEEKS, BABIES ARE AWAKE ONLY 10 PERCENT OF THE TIME

At this point, your baby's vision will still be blurry, although he has been able to recognize you since shortly after birth. When he's awake, your baby will show great interest in his new world—and you. He'll be fascinated by your eyes and your voice.

Baby knows you

Your voice and smell have been familiar to your baby since birth, but she now recognizes your face and feels secure when she sees you.

Communication Crying is your baby's only way of letting you know he is uncomfortable.

Although your baby is still too young to focus clearly on your face, she can recognize you and likes nothing better than to stare into your eyes. Research has found that babies stare much longer and with greater determination at familiar faces, so you may find her watching you intently. In fact, when she is stimulated and interested, she will stop moving and watch you very carefully. Indulge her passion and look into her eyes. Eye contact is not just essential for the process of bonding, but also acts as an early form of communication between you and your baby. Let her get to know you—position your face around 8–10in (20–25 cm) from hers—this is the optimum focusing distance for her. Your eyes and hairline will offer the most contrast, on which

babies can most easily focus. It won't be very long before she reaches up to touch your face.

Forming an attachment In the early days and weeks after birth, mothers and babies are uniquely primed to want to be close to each other. Continuing with skin-to-skin contact will be reassuring for your baby. She will recognize your heartbeat from the uterus, and your smell comforts her and encourages her to feed. What's more, she is growing familiar with your touch and senses a new confidence in the way you handle her, which help her feel secure.

ASK A... PEDIATRICIAN

Why does my baby cry every time I put her down to sleep? Most babies prefer to be held, particularly in the first week or two when they are adjusting to life outside the uterus. Swaddling (see p.53) can help her feel more secure, or you may want to put her down awake and stroke her until she settles down. Keep in mind that most young babies cry between one and three hours a day—it might be that your baby is tired and needs to unwind with a strong cry.

HOW TO...

Give your baby a bath

If your pediatrician says you don't have to wait for the umbilical cord to fall off, you might want to give your baby her first bath this week. Lots of infants love the sensation of water, and bath time becomes an enjoyable part of your routine. Make sure the room is warm, and gather a clean towel, fresh diaper, and clothes, so everything is ready. Half-fill a baby bath with lukewarm water, testing it with your elbow (98°F/37°C on a thermometer).

Wash hair Wrap her in a towel and support her head and shoulders while you wet her head with your free hand.

Into the tub Lower your baby into the bath tub, carefully supporting her head, shoulders, and bottom.

All clean Support her head; splash water gently all over. Use a washcloth or sponge to wash her if you'd like.

Successful feeding

Feeding your baby will be time consuming, but hugely rewarding as you watch her grow and develop on her milk-only diet.

Breast-feeding

There is no doubt that breast-feeding is an art that takes a little practice—for both you and your baby. Getting latched on correctly can make all the difference when it comes to making sure your baby gets the milk she needs. Once you've both mastered latching on, she will nurse more efficiently, competently stimulating your breasts to supply her with just the right amount of milk, and you'll be less likely to experience discomfort.

Latching on incorrectly can make your nipples sore and cause them to crack. It's common to feel "attachment pain" for the first 10 seconds or so, but pain throughout a feeding needs to be checked. If you find you are experiencing problems, don't hesitate to talk to your pediatrician or breast-feeding consultant. It can take at least a few days for your milk supply to meet your baby's demands, and maybe a bit longer for you to feel entirely comfortable and confident with the process. Some moms who don't enjoy breast-feeding at first are happy they persevered once it's going smoothly two to three weeks later.

How long should a feeding take?

Don't be tempted to time a feeding. Your baby will nurse for as long as it takes for her to get the quantity of milk that is right for her. Sometimes she may empty your breast within 10 minutes. On other occasions she may be sleepy and take 20 minutes on each side, or even longer. Don't rush her. Sometimes she'll simply nurse for comfort, which is nature's way of increasing your milk supply.

Most newborns feed between eight and 12 times a day. For the first few weeks, she may be on your breast every 90 minutes, although she may manage a break as long as three hours if she's had a good breast-feeding.

Emptying each breast It's best to empty each breast fully before moving to the other, since this ensures your baby gets both the hydrating, thirst-quenching foremilk and the nutritious hindmilk.

Emptying each breast fully can also help prevent problems, such as blocked ducts (see box, opposite). If she doesn't manage both breasts in one sitting, start her on the full breast the next time she feeds to make sure that both breasts are eventually emptied. Make a note of the breast on which she last nursed.

HOW TO...

Get into a good position for breast-feeding

For your baby to be able to latch on properly, it's important that you are both positioned well. You should be comfortable, with your back well-supported: cushions or pillows may be helpful. There are a number of different positions to try and you'll probably find one or two that suit you best. Cradling your baby at chest level, with her tummy against yours, can be comfortable. A football hold with your baby under your arm is good if your breasts are sore, as it stops your baby pulling on the breast. For night feedings, or after a cesarean, you might find it helpful to feed your baby lying down on your side. Check that her head is able to tip back slightly as she nurses. Her chin should touch your breast and she should be able to breathe easily.

Cradle hold With your baby on your lap, turn her tummy against yours and cradle her head in the crook of your arm. Extend your forearm to support her and tuck her knees into you with the other arm(left). **Football hold** Tuck your baby's body under your arm, as if holding a football to your chest, and support her neck with your forearm (middle). **Lying down** Lie with your baby facing you and draw her in close to your breast, cradling her with your arm (right).

Breast-feed twins

You may want to begin breast-feeding your babies one at a time until you feel comfortable with it. If you take this route, the milk stimulation in one breast may cause a let-down reflex in your other breast (known as the "double let down"). Place a sterile container nearby to catch any milk that does leak—you can store this in the freezer for later use.

For simultaneous breast-feeding, keep in mind that, in most cases, one twin is a stronger nurser. Put this baby on your breast first, which allows you to spend more time adjusting the position of your second baby. Your second twin will benefit from the simultaneous let-down reflex without having to work too hard for it. If they

Positioning your twins This mother uses a combination of cradle and football holds. In time, you will find what works best for you.

are small you may be able to snuggle both of them in your lap, with their tummies against yours. If this is too awkward, try the football hold (see box, opposite), in which their heads are at your breasts and their bodies are nestled against your sides.

Bottle-feeding

It's equally important to be comfortable when you are bottle-feeding, so make sure you are in a comfy chair with your back well-supported, and position yourself so that you can look into your baby's eyes. Just as with breast-feeding, this is a time for bonding, and this will

Bottle-feeding position Cradle your baby in a semi-upright position and support his head.

happen more naturally if you imitate a breast-feeding position. Hold your baby close against your chest as you feed her so that she can hear your heartbeat, smell your familiar smell, and feel comforted. Switch arms regularly to make sure that both you and your baby are comfortable.

Holding your baby When you are ready to feed your baby, stroke her cheek to stimulate the rooting reflex that encourages her to open her mouth and anticipate feeding. Don't feed your baby when she is lying down—formula can flow into the sinuses or middle ear, causing an infection. Instead, hold her up at a slight angle. To prevent her from swallowing air, tilt the bottle so that the formula fills the nipple and neck of the bottle.

Your newborn will probably take 2–4 oz (60–120 ml) per feeding in her first few weeks, and may be hungry every 3–4 hours. Follow her lead: babies will not overeat, and if she wants more milk than usual, she may be extra hungry.

Common problems

In most cases latching on incorrectly is the cause of discomfort during breast-feeding. Adjusting the feeding position can eradicate annoying problems. Other difficulties include:

Sore or cracked nipples Try rubbing breast milk on your nipples after a feeding, and put a cool washcloth or gel pad in your bra to ease discomfort. Emollient nipple cream may help. "Air" your breasts after feedings, and change breastpads frequently.

Leaking It's normal for breasts to leak in the early days. You may leak from one breast while your baby is nursing from the other, and your baby's cries can also stimulate a "let-down reflex." Wear breastpads and nurse your baby often to prevent overflow. Things usually improve within 6–8 weeks.

Blocked ducts Once breast-feeding is established, an oversupply of milk can build up in the breasts, possibly resulting from poor latching on and/or not completely emptying the breasts during feeding. If you have redness or pain in your breast tissue, feed your baby more often to get the milk flowing. If it doesn't improve, inform your doctor.

Mastitis Inflammation or infection of the breast causes red, inflamed areas and symptoms similar to the flu, such as a high temperature. The affected breast may also feel full and tender. Continue nursing your baby frequently, but if you don't feel better within a few hours, call your doctor.

Thrush This can infect the nipples, causing stabbing pains while nursing. Your doctor may prescribe a gel. Your baby may need to be checked too.

1 week

59

Your baby's weight

At this age, a few ounces matter a lot, especially when you want your tiny baby to start gaining weight steadily.

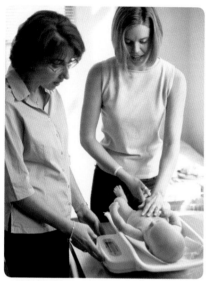

Postpartum weight check Each time your baby is weighed, it will be noted in her medical charts at the pediatrician's office. As long as her weight gain is in a healthy range, all is well.

If you are breast-feeding, your baby's weight is probably a major preoccupation now. When you can't see how much milk your baby is consuming, you're more likely to worry that she's not getting enough to thrive. This is especially the case if your baby lost weight (as is normal) last week and has been slow to regain it. Being told by your doctor that your baby has gained a minimal amount of weight or—worse—none at all, can be enough to send you into a real panic.

There is usually no cause for concern: some babies simply take a little longer than others to start gaining weight. As a rule, once your milk comes in at around three days, your baby should start to gain approximately 1 oz (25 g) a day. Most babies regain their birth weight by two weeks, but some do take a little longer. At this age, weight is less of an issue and your baby's general appearance and well-being are more important indicators of how she's doing. If she is generally alert, waking to be fed, has a good skin color and tone, and is having at least 6–8 wet diapers a day, she should be fine.

If your baby seems lethargic, listless, and pale, passes feces less than once a day, or does small, dark feces after she's five days old, her skin becomes more yellow, rather than less, after the first week, or her skin remains wrinkled after the first week, it's a good idea to get some help to make sure she is feeding efficiently. Just keep breast-feeding on demand and she should soon start to achieve steady weight gain.

If you are bottle-feeding, you can also expect your baby to gain about 1 oz (25 g) in weight per day from now until she is three months old. You will need to give your baby about 2–4 oz (60–120 ml) of formula six to eight times a day: babies have tiny tummies and can't manage too much more in one sitting. There should always be a little milk left in the bottle at the end of each feeding so that you can be sure she's had enough.

HOW TO...

Trim your baby's nails

Babies' fingernails grow fast, so it's a good idea to clip them to prevent them from snagging her skin. Toenails grow more slowly but they can scratch or occasionally become ingrown. It can be daunting to approach her nails with scissors or clippers, but if you use tools made for babies, you're unlikely to hurt her. Cut her nails when she is sleeping or being fed, since she's likely to be calmer. Or you can ask your partner to hold her hands or feet still while you get to work. Don't cut them too short—always leave a little of the white showing. Cut toenails straight across, but fingernails can be slightly rounded.

Scissors Use baby nail scissors that have rounded ends to cut your baby's nails (left).
Clippers The small blades of baby nail clippers are ideal for safely trimming tiny toenails (right).

Going out

If you haven't yet ventured out, you might be going a little stir crazy. Try getting out of the house with your baby now—it will do you good.

Baby carrier A front carrier pack keeps your baby close and snug (left). You can use one from birth, if your baby meets the minimum weight requirements. **Using a carriage** Pushing the carriage can be relaxing for you and the motion is soothing for your baby (right).

Tempting as it is to batten down the hatches and stay indoors with your baby, fresh air and a change of scenery can give you a break from domestic life and lift your mood. Sunshine encourages the production of vitamin D, which you and your baby need for healthy teeth, bones, and restful sleep; vitamin D also helps to prevent depression and ease baby blues.

You may not feel up to walking far (or getting dressed for that matter), but even a short stroll to the nearest store or a walk in the local park will help you feel a bit more connected to the outside world and less isolated if you've been ensconced at home with your baby.

If this is your first trip out, time it after a feeding so your baby is relaxed. Dress her for the weather. In general, put her in the same amount of clothing as you, plus an extra layer to keep out

the wind. If it's cold, a sleep suit, a warm outer suit, a hat, and a blanket should keep her snug. Her head should feel warm, not hot, to the touch; her hands and feet should be a little cooler. Don't forget your keys, cell phone, and purse (fatigue makes you absent-minded), and, above all, enjoy your first outing.

Extra equipment If you're planning to be out longer than half-an-hour or so, you will need to take a few essential items with you. Don't leave home without:
■ **burp cloths** These are perfect for mopping up—and you can drape one over your shoulder whenever you want to breast-feed discreetly.
■ **a diaper bag** with clean diapers, wipes, plastic bags for wet or dirty

clothes or diapers, a change of clothes for your baby, diaper cream if you use it, and a portable changing mat.
■ **formula and bottles** If you're bottle-feeding, take some ready-made cans of formula and sterilized bottles.
■ **water and snacks** Take a bottle of water and something to eat in case you feel in need of an energy boost.

STRAWBERRY MARKS

Also called hemangiomas, strawberry marks are quite common and nothing to worry about. They often form on the head or neck, but can appear anywhere on a baby's body and may be present at birth or develop in the first few weeks. They may start as a small, bright-red flat area, but usually become raised and look like a strawberry. They grow in size for about one to four years, after which they begin to shrink. They can last until 10 years of age, but most are gone by school age with no need for treatment. If they do hamper vision or are in an awkward place, treatment to encourage them to shrink may be advised.

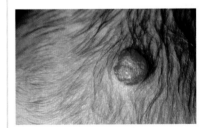

Raised swelling A strawberry mark results from an overgrowth of tiny blood vessels.

1 week

61

Taking care of your health

Your focus is on taking care of your baby, but don't neglect your own health. Being fit and well gives you energy to cope as a new parent.

Eating healthily Quick and easy nutritious meals, such as salads, provide essential vitamins and can help with weight control.

While it can be difficult to find time to put together nutritious meals, it's important to make your diet a priority. Grabbing a sugary snack may keep you going between feeding your baby, but your energy levels and your overall health will eventually suffer.

Fill the fridge with healthy foods that you can eat on the run: seeds, nuts, fresh fruit and vegetables, hummus, yogurt, smoothies, cheese, eggs, whole-grain toast, and lots of water will keep your blood sugar levels stable, and help you feel calm and relaxed.

It is very important to stay well hydrated. Breast-feeding mothers need about 2.8 quarts (2.7 liters) of fluids per day. This can be 70–80 percent from drinks and another 20–30 percent from food. Smoothies and low-fat milk both count. Because caffeine passes into

breast milk, it's best to avoid caffeinated drinks, such as coffee and cola, while you are nursing.

It's perfectly possible to eat well, even when time is tight. A nourishing bowl of soup with a whole-wheat roll can be produced in minutes, as can scrambled eggs on toast or a plate of pasta. Try to eat at least seven or eight servings of fruit and vegetables per day to make sure you get plenty of vitamin C, which your body needs to absorb iron. Iron-rich foods include red meat, dried fruit, fortified breakfast cereals, and legumes.

If friends or family want to cook for you, take advantage of their generosity. There's no shame in accepting help in the kitchen to allow you to concentrate on your new baby and your recovery.

Exercise It's still early, but you should try to get outdoors when you can for some fresh air and a little gentle exercise. Fatigue caused by a lack of sleep is compounded by a lack of activity. It's good for both you and your baby and the exertion will encourage a more restful night's sleep. Try to build a brisk walk in the park into your routine, or walk to the nearby stores instead of getting into the car.

If you've had a cesarean, you might not feel up to going outside for a walk yet, although a gentle daily stroll (even up and down the block or around the backyard) will help your recovery. Go out for a walk only if you're sure you feel able to. If in any doubt, always check with your doctor first.

ASK A... BREAST-FEEDING EXPERT

Is there anything I shouldn't eat while I'm breast-feeding? You can eat normally but you may want to avoid too many "gas-producing" foods, such as onion, garlic, broccoli, and cabbage, or very strong flavors (such as curry), which come through into your milk. It is acceptable to eat peanuts and other allergens, since these may help discourage allergies in later life.

Can I use nipple shields? These are not generally recommended since they can reduce the milk your baby gets, and therefore also milk production.

Is there anything I shouldn't drink? Alcohol should be avoided early on, because it can negatively affect your let-down reflex, but a little is

acceptable later on. Restrict your caffeine intake to one cup of coffee a day since caffeine can make babies more irritable and restless. Be careful not to overdo herbal teas. Mint teas, for example, are thought to help soothe babies' gas and colic when drunk by breast-feeding moms. However, they can also have the effect of decreasing milk supply if consumed in large quantities.

Can I smoke while breast-feeding? You could be putting your baby at risk if you do. Nicotine contains chemicals that can damage her health. Traces of smoke in your baby's environment can increase her risk of SIDS, wheezing, and ear infections.

You know your baby

Parenthood can be quite daunting, and you may worry about getting it right. Trust that you know your baby best.

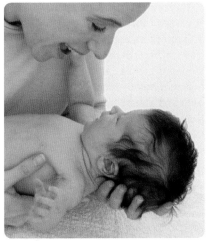

Daily play Eye contact, laughing, talking, and engaging with your baby develop your bond.

If babies came with instruction manuals, the past week and a half might have been easier. But most moms find this steep learning curve difficult, and worry constantly if they are doing the "right thing" for their babies. Your ability to tune in to your baby's needs will guide you in responding to her. Read her signals, and you will be cuddling her, cooing to her, and feeding, changing, and rocking her when she needs it.

There is no "right" way to take care of your baby—and your baby is an individual, so what is right for another baby may not be right for her. Try not to compare your parenting skills with those of other moms either; as you get to know your baby, you will naturally do what is best for her, whether or not your baby manual or friends think differently.

If you are not particularly enjoying taking care of your baby's needs at the moment, try not to worry or think that you are failing as a parent. It's not uncommon for new moms—and dads—to feel that they are just going through the motions rather than actively treasuring every moment with their new baby. For a small number of parents, resentment can start to build about how much time and energy your baby takes up. If this is happening, seek extra support from family and friends and speak to a health professional about how you feel. You may also be exhausted, so arrange for your partner or a friend to take over to give you time to rest.

Don't push yourself too hard, and try not to panic when things don't go as planned. No two days are ever the same in a household with a young baby, and you'll need to be flexible and sometimes lower your expectations of yourself.

ASK A... PEDIATRICIAN

Can I breast-feed when I'm sick?
You may not feel up to it, but do continue breast-feeding to keep up your milk supply. Far from passing infection to your baby, you'll provide her with the antibodies you develop against your illness, making it less likely that she'll catch it. Most over-the-counter analgesics are safe while breast-feeding, but check the label or ask your pharmacist before taking anything. Some antibiotics and decongestants, for example, should be avoided. Talk to your doctor about the safety of any medication you take regularly.

CO-BEDDING TWINS

Putting your twins in the same crib is called co-bedding. Don't worry that your twins will overheat or smother each other. Studies show that the risks to your babies are exactly the same if they are in the same crib as they would be if they were sleeping separately.

It is important that you follow the same rules as you would for one baby. For example, make sure that each baby is feet-to-foot in the crib. This means positioning the babies so that they are on their backs either head to head, with their feet at opposite ends of the crib; or side by side, with their feet at the same end of the crib.

The side-by-side position poses no greater risks, even if one baby flings an arm over the other. In fact, the babies may comfort each other like this. Keeping your twins in the same crib is also more practical, because having them in the same room as you as long as possible—ideally for six months—reduces the risk of SIDS (see p.31).

Sharing a crib It is perfectly safe to have your twins sleep in the same crib, either head to head or side by side.

1 week

Reflecting on the birth

Many new parents want to share and analyze the birth experience. Talking about it is healthy, particularly if it didn't go as planned.

Whether you had an unexpectedly quick and easy birth experience, or found yourself using every medical intervention available even though you had planned to deliver your baby naturally, you'll probably want to talk about the birth—in detail. Having a baby is a life-changing event and a deeply emotive experience. It's normal to be both proud and unsettled after the birth, and it is equally normal to feel as if you need to make sense of the events.

Some women and their partners feel unhappy with their experience of childbirth and a small number feel traumatized. For women, the birth may have been longer or more painful than anticipated, or complications arose. For men, being out of control and distressed

Shared experience Talking about your baby's birth with other moms, who are eager to share their own stories, can be very therapeutic.

about their partner's discomfort may have colored their view. You may wish that things had gone as you had hoped they would, or that you had done things differently, or you might wonder why certain procedures or interventions had been necessary. Equally, you may have had a wonderful, positive birth that has left you bubbling with joy and needing to share your encouraging story. However your experience of childbirth unfolded, part of the process of remembering and understanding does involve talking about it—with your partner, your family, the friends you have met in your childbirth classes, and the doctors or midwives who are responsible for overseeing your care.

Don't hesitate to talk to medical staff and ask questions if you feel uneasy or uncertain about any element of the birth. Health-care professionals are there to support you and will understand that asking questions is part of coming to terms with your experience. The birth of a baby is amazing, and you will find that most people will be fascinated to hear how your baby came into the world.

Focus on the positive Whatever your experience, try to focus on the positive elements, and the fact that you have succeeded in creating a new life. While it is perfectly normal to feel some disappointment or even guilt when things didn't go as planned— particularly if it seems that everyone else had a much better experience, or achieved that "natural" birth—you have a healthy baby in your arms, and there could be no better result. Take pride in the wonderful new life you have created.

ASK A... DOCTOR

My baby's eyes are sticky. Is this normal? It is very common for newborn babies to suffer from a mild eye infection, which is caused by blood or fluid entering her eyes during the birth. Her eyelashes may appear to be crusty or sticky—or even glued together—after sleeping, and there may be a discharge in the inner corner of her eyes. You can keep her eyes clean by gently wiping off any discharge around them. This condition usually clears up on its own, but if symptoms don't improve in three days, see your doctor.

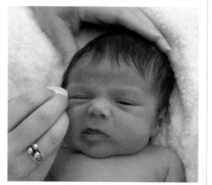

Cleaning a sticky eye Moisten a cotton pad in cooled boiled water or your own breast milk (which contains antibodies). Wipe inside outward. Use a fresh pad for each eye.

Helping your body heal

Even the most straightforward labor can leave you feeling sore and uncomfortable, and if you've had stitches or a cesarean, you may be feeling a bit battered. The good news is that there are ways to encourage healing and get you back on your feet.

Your pelvic floor The weight of your baby, placenta, and amniotic fluid puts a great deal of pressure on your pelvic floor, which supports all the organs in your pelvis. During labor and birth, this area is also stretched to allow your baby's head to pass out of your uterus and through your vagina.

If your baby was big or you had serious tears or an assisted birth, your pelvic floor may have become overstretched and weak, causing you to leak urine when you sneeze, cough, or exercise. This is called stress incontinence and it affects almost half of all new moms—but it usually improves. A weak pelvic floor can also cause discomfort and a feeling of heaviness in the vaginal area.

The good news is that you can do something about it by practicing your pelvic floor exercises (known as Kegels) as soon as you feel comfortable to do so (the sooner the better). Start by doing the exercises while you're lying on your back or side, or in the bath. Here's what to do:

■ Breathe in and as you breathe out gently squeeze your pelvic floor muscles up and in, as though trying to stop yourself from urinating, or passing gas.
■ Hold the squeeze for four or five seconds while you breathe in and out normally, then relax.
■ Repeat five times (stop if you feel at all uncomfortable) five or six times each day. Try to build up to holding a pelvic floor contraction for 10 seconds.

Although it may feel like nothing is happening for the first few days (it can take some time for the muscles to regain enough strength even to move, and for stretched nerves to respond) you will encourage blood supply to the area, promoting healing, and restoring muscle tone. Kegels will also help to deal with hemorrhoids.

If you've had a cesarean, Kegels should be slightly easier because your perineum will be less sore. It's still important to do your exercises though, because pregnancy weakens your pelvic floor muscles.

Your lower abdomen The lower abdomen works with your pelvic floor muscles to help support your back and pelvis. Exercising this may help you regain your pre-pregnancy figure and flatten your tummy. Having strong abdominal muscles can also help relieve back pain. Gentle pelvic tilts (see box, below) are an ideal way to start toning the lower abdomen after childbirth.

Quick relief If your perineum or cesarean incision is tender, apply a cold compress of ice cubes wrapped in a damp kitchen towel, or an icy-cold gel pad to reduce inflammation and ease pain. Take warm baths or showers to help boost circulation and help healing.

HOW TO...

Do a pelvic tilt

Once you've had the all-clear from your doctor after a vaginal birth, you can use pelvic-tilt exercises to strengthen the lower abdominal area. Lie on your back, knees up and your feet flat on the floor. Place your hands on your stomach so you can feel your muscles tightening. Tighten your stomach muscles and push the arch of your back toward the floor. Squeeze your bottom tight. Hold for a count of six, then relax. If you've had a cesarean, wait 6–8 weeks before working your abdomen. To boost blood flow to the area, suck in your tummy and hold it for a minute or two.

Pelvic tilt Tighten your abdominals and push your lower back into the floor—imagine pulling your belly button in toward your backbone. Try to do three sets of 10, but stop if you feel tired.

1 week

2 weeks

MOST BREAST-FED NEWBORN BABIES NURSE BETWEEN EIGHT AND 12 TIMES A DAY

The long, regular feeding sessions your baby has been enjoying make him look plumper, and by now, he should have regained any weight he lost during the first week. Now that he's a little stronger and less vulnerable, you may feel more confident about handling him.

Enjoying family life

Adjusting to a new baby can take time for everyone in the family, but maintaining a strong family unit will benefit you all.

Time for all Giving older siblings attention and time helps them accept the new arrival.

Becoming a family is a wonderful event and your life will never be the same again. You may develop a closer bond with your own parents as they settle into the role of grandparents, and spend more time with your extended family. You may have older children, or children from previous relationships, who will need time to adjust to the idea of a new sibling and a different family unit. Your roles may have changed from being simply "partner" to "partner and parent," and that can alter the way you see and interact with each other. Having a baby offers you an opportunity to build something truly special.

If you have other children, it can be tempting to take turns with your partner to take care of the baby while the other cares for the older children,

however, creating opportunities for family time will reap rewards. Whether you sit down together to watch a movie, head out to the park, play board games, or even just spend some time in the backyard, you will be nourishing the bond that forms the basis of a happy family life.

Spending time together makes every family member feel valued and secure. Even something as simple as cooking or doing the dishes together helps spread the load and makes everyone feel they have a role. Affection, play, communication, and relaxation as a family also improve self-esteem and the family dynamic, and create happy memories, too.

JAUNDICE

This is yellowing of the skin and the whites of the eyes (see p.404). It is common in newborn babies, especially if they are breast-fed, and usually resolves itself within two weeks. Prolonged jaundice, however, requires medical attention. About 10 percent of babies are still jaundiced at two weeks old. It is likely to be "breast milk jaundice," but can also be a sign of an underlying condition such as liver disease, particularly if her stools are chalky white. Speak to your doctor: your baby may need to have a blood test.

THE IMPORTANCE OF GRANDPARENTS

Welcoming grandparents into your baby's life is part of celebrating your growing family. You may or may not appreciate their help, depending on your relationship with them. Let them know what you need, and how they can best help you. For example, if they live nearby, your in-laws could cover the cooking while your parents handle the housework. You may also find that having one set of parents around at a time is enough, since too much "help" can in itself be taxing.

Grandparents are often hugely willing to give advice. Accept it graciously, but believe in your own parenting skills and instincts. There may be gems of wisdom your parents can pass on, so listen, but remember— it's okay to make your own decisions.

In safe hands Grandparents like to shower lots of love and affection on their newborn grandchildren. This helps build strong bonds between them from the beginning.

Crying

All babies cry to communicate and it can be difficult to figure out what they are trying to say at first. You'll soon learn to differentiate between her cries, and find it easier to figure out the very best ways of soothing her.

On average, even the most contented babies cry for between one and three hours a day, and some seem to cry constantly. In the early days, you may be distressed by her cries, and struggle to calm her. The most important thing you can do is to relax and think rationally. Most babies cry for the same reasons, and figuring out what's wrong is the first step to finding a solution. Becoming anxious will only make her more distressed; babies pick up on anxiety and it can compound the situation.

ASK A... PEDIATRICIAN

How can I tell if the crying is caused by colic or reflux? About a quarter of young babies suffer from colic. The cause is unclear, but it is linked to excess gas and is characterized by uncontrollable crying (often around the same time of day or night), and drawing up of their knees in clear discomfort. Most babies outgrow it by three months. (For help with easing colic, see p.77).

Reflux occurs when the acid content of the stomach rises into the esophagus, causing burning and discomfort. This can make a baby very irritable. With reflux, crying often occurs during or just after being fed, unlike colic where crying tends to be worse in the evening. Reflux can also cause babies to regurgitate frequently, sometimes in large amounts. If you suspect that your baby has reflux, talk to your doctor.

Why is my baby crying?

A crying baby is not necessarily unhappy; she's just good at conveying her needs. So when you've walked around the living room for the 50th time in an attempt to soothe her, think positively: you are raising a good communicator! It's time to figure out what makes her cry.

Use a trial-and-error approach to soothing your baby. What works one day may not work the next, or you may find a trick that works every time. If there is one thing at which all parents excel, it's adapting. Over time, you will begin to recognize your baby's cries—you'll know that she is hungry or lonely, or that it's time for a nap. You'll recognize when she needs cuddling or even a little time on her own. She may not enjoy diaper changes or getting dressed, but you'll develop techniques to make these more fun, or become adept at getting them done quickly.

Hunger Babies cry when hungry or thirsty and will not stop until sated. During growth spurts, when your breasts are struggling to keep up with demand, your baby may be hungrier than usual and cry more. Let her nurse at your breast; this action will comfort her and also build up your milk supply.

Feeling too hot or cold Young babies cannot regulate their body temperature. Check that she's not wearing too much clothing, or that she is appropriately dressed. Dressing your baby and putting her to sleep in a swaddle or baby sleeping bag will keep her warmer.

Crying for attention Young babies do not cry without reason; they usually have a genuine need that requires your attention.

If she is small or slim, she may need more clothing to maintain her body temperature. Chubby babies are often happier with fewer layers.

Wet or uncomfortable A wet or dirty diaper can cause discomfort. Some babies are particularly sensitive and need a barrier cream applied to their skin to protect it. If your baby's skin is red, bumpy, or raw in the diaper area, she may have diaper rash (see p.73). Leave her diaper off for short periods of time since this encourages healing.

Loneliness Babies are social creatures and love to be held close. Your baby is stimulated and entertained by your presence and will feel more secure knowing that you are there for her. Don't hesitate to pick her up when she cries. She is communicating a genuine need and it's important to satisfy it.

Understimulation Babies can become bored! If she has been lying in her crib or car seat for hours, she may need some interaction or a change of scenery. Gentle play, talking to her, moving her to a different location in the house, or even putting a mobile over her crib can help entertain her and keep her happy.

Overstimulation A little stimulation encourages development, but babies also need quiet periods, during which skills and information are consolidated. They also need to relax in order to sleep well and adjust to their new world. While play is a wonderful learning experience, a little goes a long way, so avoid long periods of stimulation. If your baby is irritable after periods of activity,

it may be time to help her wind down and sleep. Baby massage (see p.125) or a long feeding can encourage this.

Fatigue Tired babies become irritable and frustrated. Being overstimulated, or not given the opportunity to unwind and relax in order to fall asleep, can make your baby distressed. If she's crying for no apparent reason, rubbing her eyes, and yawning, rock her until she calms, wrap her up tight, and lay her down to sleep. Don't try to put her down when she's angry and upset, or she may resist sleep, compounding the problem.

Wanting comfort Sometimes babies don't know what they want. They just know that they want the comfort of

mom or dad's arms, or some physical contact. Cuddling or a gentle massage can be enough to calm her—or she may want the comfort of nursing at your breast or sucking a pacifier. While you do not want to encourage "snacking," sometimes nothing else will work.

Feeling sick If your baby is sick, she will cry because she is in discomfort, or she may not cry at all, which could be a cause for concern in itself. Check her temperature (see p.395); if she's warm, she may be fighting an infection, and it's worth a trip to the doctor to see what's wrong. It's almost impossible for parents to diagnose illness in a young baby, so if she is crying and clearly uncomfortable, get her checked out.

CHECKLIST

Top tips for soothing your irritable baby

■ Babies respond to being held and rocked. If she is eased off to sleep by rocking, bring her carriage inside and settle yourself in a position where you can comfortably rock it with a free hand or foot.

■ If your baby needs constant comfort, carry her against your chest in a carrier so she can hear your heartbeat.

■ Rhythmical sounds, such as low music, or even the sound of the vacuum cleaner, soothe many babies.

■ Many babies like to feel swaddled (see p.53). Try wrapping her snugly in a crib sheet before settling her down.

■ Some babies need to suck to get to sleep, or to calm down, which is why they feed almost constantly when they are upset. If she's not hungry, she may find comfort from a pacifier.

■ Calm her down by giving her a light massage (see p.125).

■ If crying begins after feeding, after switching from breast milk to formula,

or after switching formula, talk to your pediatrician. The formula she is taking may not be suitable.

■ Take a deep breath, and relax yourself. If necessary, put her down for a few moments and leave the room to give yourself some space to calm down. Crying babies can be exhausting, and you may be at your wits' end. It won't do her harm to be left in a safe place for a few minutes while you take a quick break.

Face-to-face talk Look into your baby's eyes and talk to him to distract him from crying.

Rocking Simply rocking your baby gently back and forth can soothe and comfort him.

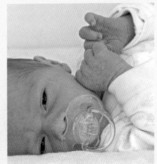

Pacifier Babies like to suck for comfort and a pacifier can help soothe a restless or upset baby.

Baby carrier Your baby may love being held in a carrier, but make sure her neck is well-supported.

Copycat

Your baby mimics your facial expressions, opening her eyes and mouth as you do, and copying the tone of your voice when she coos.

Making faces Using exaggerated facial gestures frequently when you talk with her will make it easier for her to copy expressions.

An amazing study found that when a parent of a newborn sticks out their tongue and moves it from side to side, their baby responds in kind. Researchers concluded that imitation is the most powerful learning tool in your baby's "kit" of instincts. Everything that she will one day do, she will learn from watching and imitating the people around her. You will see her "practice" her new skills until she has honed them.

What's more, if you regularly make the same faces when you play, she'll consider them "familiar" and will respond more and more quickly. Imitation is a sign that your baby is already processing information in a very sophisticated way:

not only does she need to figure out what you are doing, but she also has to control different parts of her body to learn to copy you. This process can start hours after her birth, and continues throughout the first weeks and months of her life. Your baby will also cry with an inflection that matches your accent, something that she has picked up while in the uterus. Researchers have found that babies cry in a way that mimics mom's "native" language (for example, French newborns cry with a rising "accent," while German babies' cries have a falling inflection). This is believed to be an attempt for babies to form an early bond with their mothers.

Baby sounds

Your baby is already learning to talk. Her "oohs" and "aahs" will soon develop into babble that is the basis of early speech. Listen carefully!

TIME TO THINK ABOUT

Your baby's doctor

Your baby can either be taken on as a patient of your family doctor or a pediatrician. Ideally you planned this during your pregnancy, but if not, start looking now—sometimes it's difficult to find a doctor who's accepting new patients. Make sure you apply for your baby's health card as soon as you can.

While crying is undoubtedly your baby's primary, and probably most effective, method of communicating, she'll begin to utter little sounds when she is alert, and you may find that she responds with baby sounds when you speak to her or stimulate her, in response to being startled, or when she recognizes something like your face or Dad's voice.

The first sounds will be vowel sounds, usually "oooooh" and "aaaaah," and little cooing noises. Other than her attempts to talk with you, you can expect to hear plenty of hiccups and sneezes as well!

Encourage your baby to "talk"—move close to her so she can see your face, and talk to her. When she responds with sounds of her own, wait a moment, then "reply" by mimicking her sounds. She's beginning to understand the basics of communication and will respond to this interaction. Talk to her constantly; tell her what you are doing, for example, when you are changing her diaper. She'll listen to your chatter and become familiar with the words you are using, so when it's time for speech, she'll have a good vocabulary to draw from.

"Baby wearing"

All babies love being held. Carrying her against your chest will not only calm and reassure her, it will also encourage bonding.

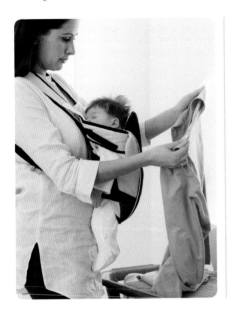

Your baby was tightly confined in your uterus for many long months, and due to this experience became dependent upon touch to feel secure. After the birth, touch is equally important—and reassuring—for babies. Research has found that touch is calming and helps babies adapt to their new surroundings. It encourages bonding and promotes healthy growth, development, and even immunity. In fact, newborns need constant soothing touch to become healthy, happy children. Studies in orphanages have found that babies who are not soothed or nurtured by touch fail to thrive, are slow growers, and develop social problems later in life.

While there can be nothing more rewarding and relaxing than holding your new baby for hours on end, there are things that you will need to get done to keep the household running. Using a carrier to carry your baby is a good way of keeping her in close proximity to you while you do the housework. Your baby is likely to sleep for longer periods when she is held close to you, or is rocked gently to sleep listening to your familiar heartbeat. Your breathing patterns will stimulate hers, and she will be reassured by being able to feel you right there, next to her.

Hands-free baby care Carrying your baby in a carrier (front pack) is the ideal way to keep her close while you do your housework.

SOOTHING YOUR BABY THROUGH TOUCH

Your baby will respond very positively to your touch, and will be soothed and reassured by it, so use touch often, especially when she needs to be comforted and calmed. Hold her close while bottle-feeding or breast-feeding her, ideally with her bare skin against yours (see p.45). Be tactile—stroke her little face, gently rub her back, pat her hands, and feel and explore her body with your hands. Rock or hold her close when she is crying—letting a newborn baby cry sends the message that you are not always there for them, and makes them feel insecure. Infancy is no time for "sleep training." Cuddle with your baby after her bath—she'll be relaxed and ready to settle down when you put her to bed, resulting in a deep, restful sleep.

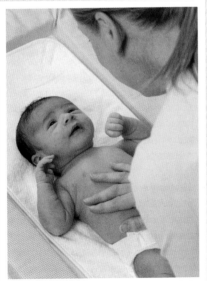

Gentle strokes Softly caressing your baby's body and talking to her as you change her can help her feel less vulnerable.

ASK A... BREAST-FEEDING EXPERT

Can I express yet? While you can express milk as soon as you feel ready after the birth, it's best to wait until your baby is 4–6 weeks old. This is because it takes about this long for your breasts to produce the right amount of milk for your baby, and for your baby to learn to nurse at the breast efficiently. (If you give her a bottle too early, it can cause "nipple confusion," see p.89). Also, at this point, your baby will be feeding eight to 12 times in every 24-hour period, leaving little free time for you to express without disrupting what's available for her next feeding. That said, if you have lots of milk and plan to keep expressing daily to build up a supply of frozen milk for later use, you can give it a try.

2 weeks

Feeling lonely?

If your partner has gone back to work and your mom has headed home, you may find yourself alone with your baby for the first time.

Not only can it be difficult to learn how to take care of your baby on your own—without another pair of arms to hold her or help around the house—but also you may find that long hours of feeding and caring for your baby without adult conversation can be, well, a little boring. You could be missing your social life, too, and the company of friends and colleagues who are busy at work when you'd love the opportunity to talk.

Ask about parent and baby groups in your area, where you can meet other new parents to get support and a little company. If you took childbirth classes, you may be able to arrange get-togethers with your classmates, taking turns hosting. If your baby's grandparents are nearby, you could arrange regular visits, to give you something to look forward to. Talk to your partner about your feelings, too; he may be able to check in by phone more regularly, or arrange to come home earlier sometimes. Ultimately, however, take this time to adjust and put your feet up while you feed your baby. And why not catch up on some good DVDs while you're at it!

ASK A... PEDIATRICIAN

Can I give my baby water to drink?
Breast-fed babies receive a perfect balance of fluid from breast milk and don't require anything else, even if a little dehydrated during illness. Bottle-fed babies should get the fluid they need from formula, but if it's very hot outside, or they have a bug, a little water can be offered. Use previously boiled, cooled water in a sterilized bottle.

Breast-feeding in public

It's one thing to breast-feed in the comfort of your own home, but most women feel a bit reticent at first about doing it in public.

If you're one of the many women who feel embarrassed and self-conscious about breast-feeding in public, chances are you have been avoiding it up until now. But it doesn't have to be a difficult experience and you really don't need to hide to do it.

There are all kinds of ways of breast-feeding discreetly, so give it a try and don't worry about what other people think. It might reassure you to know that, in Canada, you are protected by the Charter of Rights and Freedoms when breast-feeding in a public place. If you are treated unfavorably for doing so, it is considered to be sex discrimination. So if you are breast-feeding in a restaurant and the staff asks you to leave or refuses to serve you, they are breaking the law.

If it makes you feel less awkward, use a shawl to cover your breasts and your baby, and wear feeding-friendly clothes, (see p.111) layering tops so that you can tuck your baby underneath one and still be fully covered. Choose a bra that you can easily open, ideally with one hand.

Above all, try to relax. If you are anxious and uptight, feeding a hungry baby is not likely to be easy.

Discreet feeding A loose top will allow easy access without revealing much flesh. Drape a sarong or shawl around you and your baby for extra coverage if it helps you feel comfortable.

Your baby's thermostat

Babies cannot regulate their own body temperature until they are much older, so it's important to check that they are not too hot or cold.

Dressing your baby Generally, babies need one more layer of clothing than adults.

Babies' bodies are unable to regulate temperature effectively. They lose heat from their heads when very hot but, otherwise, rely upon their caregivers to keep them at the right temperature.

It isn't necessary to take your baby's temperature (see p.395) unless she feels very hot and may have an infection. Instead, examine her regularly by putting your hand against her cheek, which should feel warm to the touch, and checking that her feet and hands are cool, but not hot or cold. Dress her in layers, which can be added or removed as necessary. You'll need to use your instincts to assess the right balance.

Aim for a bedroom temperature of around 60.8–68°F (16–20°C), which is just right for babies. Overheating has been linked with SIDS (see p.31). At night, dress your baby in a onesie and sleep suit, then add a swaddle or baby sleeping bag until she seems cozy.

During the day, your baby should wear roughly the same amount of clothing as you, plus one extra layer. Avoid putting her recliner next to a radiator or fire or in direct sunlight. Keep her away from drafty open windows. Hats are a good idea when it's cool outside, but babies should not wear hats in bed unless very small or premature, so they can cool down when necessary by losing heat from the head. Babies often become very warm in the car, so they don't need a blanket over them unless it is very cold or you have the air conditioning on. Always remember to remove your baby's outdoor clothing when inside.

Most importantly, relax. In most cases, your baby will look and/or feel obviously cold or hot, and you'll soon know at a glance whether she needs a sweater or her socks removed!

TIME TO THINK ABOUT

Contraception

You should decide on the form of contraception you want to use now, and discuss it with your doctor. While the time it takes for fertility to return is very variable, it's important not to take chances. It's possible to find that you are pregnant again within weeks of your baby's birth. Your periods usually return between four and 10 weeks after birth if you are bottle-feeding or combining breast and bottle. Exclusive breast-feeding day and night gives 98 percent protection against pregnancy until your baby is six months, if your period has not returned.

HOW TO...

Deal with diaper rash

Contact with urine or feces irritates your baby's delicate skin and can result in diaper rash. To prevent this, change your baby's diaper frequently. If her bottom does become sore, let her play and kick about without her diaper on at least twice a day, to allow the air to get to the area. If you use reusable diapers, give them an extra rinse. Apply barrier cream to encourage healing, but if her rash does not clear up in a couple of days, see your pediatrician who will check for thrush and may prescribe an antifungal cream.

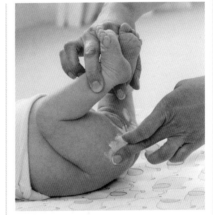

Barrier cream Using a barrier cream, such as zinc oxide, can soothe any inflammation as well as protect your baby's skin when her diaper is dirty.

3 weeks

BABIES CAN CRY, BUT THEY CAN'T MAKE OR SHED TEARS UNTIL THEY ARE ABOUT 3 WEEKS OLD

By now, you might be able to anticipate when your baby is hungry, needs his diaper changed, or is likely to nap. He's probably sleeping 16–18 hours a day, and going for about three or four hours between feedings. He is growing stronger by the day and may turn his head to look at you.

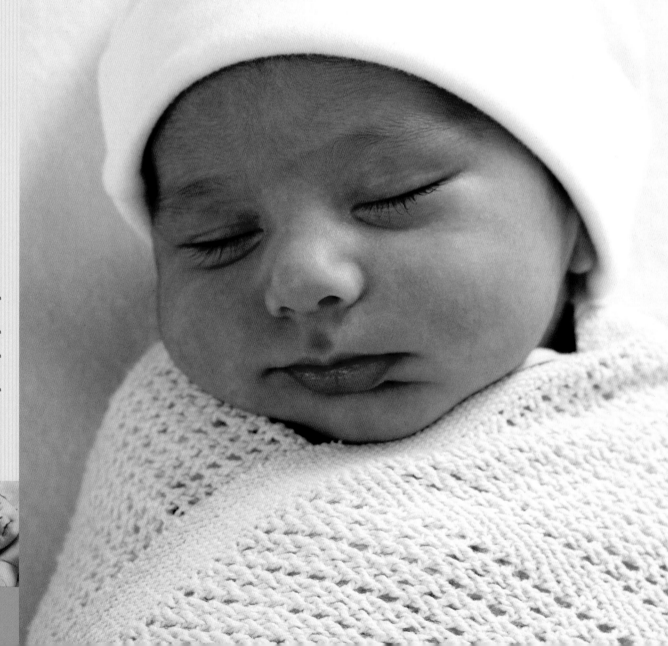

Time to engage

Now that your baby is alert and awake longer, playing with her will help to stimulate her senses and improve her coordination.

Tête-à-tête Making eye contact with your baby, and laughing and talking to her at close quarters stimulates her listening and language skills.

Your three-week-old baby doesn't understand the concept of play yet, of course, but at this age "play" simply means engaging with and spending quality time with your baby. It affords her the opportunity to learn much more than you might think, and it will encourage a healthy bond between you, as well as promote her emotional health and well-being.

While it is important not to overstimulate her, a few 5–10-minute sessions each day, whenever she is calm and alert, will be great fun for both of you, and will help her to develop on all levels. Try to gear your play to her mood—if she is active and alert, try some gentle clapping, tickling games, or carry her outside and show her around the yard; if she's in a quieter mood, talking and singing may be more

appropriate. The point of play is to learn by having fun, so keep it light and cheerful, and forget about what she might be learning. That will become clear before you know it!

Play offers the perfect opportunity to introduce your baby to the wonders of her world in an engaging and happy way. Vary the games you play together to broaden her horizons and develop different parts of her body and brain. She'll be entertained and enjoy the chance to be with you and learn new skills.

Babies instinctively "practice" skills. She may try out her new tricks after the games are done; for example, if you've been encouraging her to stick out her tongue and make faces, she may attempt this each time she sees your face.

Black-and-white patterns

As she begins to interact with the world around her, your very young baby finds boldly contrasting images and distinctive geometric shapes and patterns visually stimulating. To encourage this stimulation, create a black-and-white design for your baby on card stock, using felt-tip pens to make patterns and shapes (stripes and angles are particularly appealing to babies), or purchase a baby book with similar designs. These patterns develop your baby's focusing abilities and encourage her spatial awareness and visual perception. Play this game for a minute or two every day, but don't overdo it. Excessive visual stimulation will distract your baby from the "familiarization process" of getting to know and becoming integrated into her new world.

Visual stimulation Bold, moving patterns will hold your baby's attention and also help develop her ability to focus.

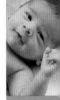

3 weeks

YOUR BABY IS 3 WEEKS AND 1 DAY

Getting your baby to sleep

If you can recognize when your baby needs to sleep, you can catch the wave of her fatigue and send her off into a peaceful slumber.

An overtired baby can be irritable and difficult to calm, so settle her down to sleep as soon as you notice she is tired, when she will be more likely to fall asleep quickly and sleep deeply. In general, following a wakeful period, your baby will need a rest. The length of time that she goes between naps will be individual to her, so it's important that you recognize when she is ready to sleep.

Throughout the day and night, your baby will have drowsy periods when she is more ready to fall asleep. If you miss one window, you may have to wait a good hour or so for the next one, as your baby goes through another active-drowsy-sleeping cycle. Look out for her yawning and rubbing her eyes—these are obvious signs that she is sleepy. She may also cry a little or whine for no obvious reason. She may make grunting noises or growling, beginning quietly and eventually reaching a full-blown cry. Some babies acquire a frown when they are tired, while others become a little jerky, thrashing their limbs—probably in frustration! Don't try to distract her or keep her up when she's tired. She'll become overstimulated and take that much longer to unwind.

ASK A... DOCTOR

My baby brings up a little milk after each feeding. Is she sick? It's normal for babies to "spit up" a little milk after being fed—a result of trapped air surfacing, bringing up a little milk with it. It doesn't cause any pain or discomfort. To prevent spitting up, handle your baby gently after a feeding and when burping her. If she is bringing up large amounts of milk, she may have reflux (see p.401), so take her to see the doctor.

YOUR BABY IS 3 WEEKS AND 2 DAYS

Taking a break

Although it can be tempting to take total charge of your baby, especially if you are breast-feeding, regular breaks will refresh you.

You may be one of the many moms for whom it's difficult to relinquish control—particularly if you've developed tried and tested methods for getting your baby to sleep, or changing and soothing her efficiently. However, it's important to take time off to recharge your batteries and recover fully from the birth. Whether you have a long soak in the tub, meet with a friend, exercise, or get some sleep, a change of scenery and break from routine will make all the difference to your physical and emotional health.

Time with dad Your partner needs to get to know your baby and understand her needs, too.

Dad will welcome the chance to hone his parenting skills and spend time bonding with his baby. He will develop confidence in taking care of her, thereby reducing the pressure on you. Set up a regular time for him to take over—perhaps bath-time, or on Saturday mornings, when he can stroll around town with her in a carrier to pick up a newspaper. Even short periods give them the opportunity to establish their relationship—and give you a rest.

After around 4 weeks, if you are breast-feeding you can start to express milk (see p.28) and Dad can take over feeding from time to time. You can then go farther afield during your breaks.

Feeding on demand

Your baby is learning what hunger feels like, and by satisfying her appetite you reassure her and help her feel more secure.

Food and security Let your baby breast-feed whenever she wants to. Her tummy is still tiny and can only take small amounts, so she needs to nurse on a regular basis.

It is important to continue to feed your baby on demand—whether she is breast- or bottle-fed—because she is learning how to respond to her own hunger cues. She will let you know when she is hungry, and when you satisfy that hunger you are not only encouraging trust and security by meeting her basic needs, but you are also teaching her to eat when she is hungry. Although it may be hard to believe, this can actually help to prevent problems such as obesity in later life.

By now, your baby may be going three or even four hours between feedings, but don't be surprised if this pattern suddenly shifts. Growth spurts and increased physical activity during the day can make her hungrier, and she may seem to nurse endlessly as she works to build up your milk supply.

HOW TO...

Deal with colic

To ease symptoms of colic (see p.68) burp your baby carefully after feeding her (see p.49). Try a warm bath to calm her down, and then rub her abdomen and lower back with a little warm olive or canola oil, using circular motions.

A breast-fed baby may react to Mom's diet. Reducing the amount of dairy products you eat may make a difference, as may avoiding processed foods that contain milk protein, for example some cookies, cakes, and pies. Avoiding garlic, onions, cabbage, beans, and broccoli may also help. If you are bottle-feeding, try a colic bottle, which can reduce the amount of air your baby takes in while feeding. You may also try a different formula, since she may tolerate another type better, but ask your doctor first. Colicky babies are soothed by motion, so try a ride in the car, or carriage, or gentle rocking in a carrier. Try not to take it personally that you can't comfort your colicky baby and make her stop crying. Colic normally subsides at around three months—but if you're at the end of your rope, talk to your pediatrician, who can prescribe a gentle antispasmodic medication.

Colic hold Holding your baby face down along your forearm with your hand firmly between the legs is thought to help soothe colicky babies. Try walking around a little.

YOUR BABY IS 3 WEEKS AND 4 DAYS

Conflicting advice

There is no harm in listening to well-meaning advice given by friends and family, but don't feel under any obligation to act on it.

You may be astonished to find that everyone, from your mother-in-law to the butcher, has very clear ideas about how babies should be treated and cared for, and how children should be raised. It can be very disconcerting to find that, in the eyes of some people, you are doing everything, well, wrong.

One of the most important skills you can learn as a new parent is to sift advice—develop a thick skin, listen politely, and then ignore what doesn't fit in with your parenting philosophy. This skill will be useful not just now but throughout your baby's childhood and

teenage years. When people are offering the advice, no matter how experienced, remember that times change, and that everyone has their own ways of doing things. So what may have been recommended 20 or 30 years ago may not be appropriate now. Also, every baby is different, and requires tailor-made care. Trust your own knowledge, and politely deflect advice and criticism. By all means try anything that sounds potentially useful, and take in well-meaning and practical tips if you want to, but stick to your guns and do things your way.

ASK A... PEDIATRICIAN

My baby's scalp has large patches of loose, dry skin. Is this eczema?
Your baby has cradle cap, a common condition characterized by yellowish, oily, scaly patches on the scalp. To help control it and ease itching and discomfort, massage olive oil into her scalp in the evening and wash it off with a gentle baby shampoo. Brush off loose crusts with a soft brush, but try not to loosen crusts that have not pulled away on their own.

YOUR BABY IS 3 WEEKS AND 5 DAYS

Little explorer

Your baby is starting to show an interest in all the new things around her, and nothing is more fascinating to her than her own little body.

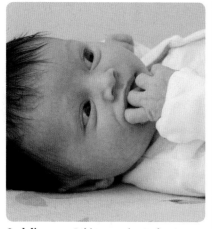

Oral discovery Babies examine and test things out using their tongues and lips.

Around this age, your baby discovers her hands and, possibly, her feet. She'll hold her hands to her face and look at them in wonder, and bring them to her mouth. Sucking on and looking at her hands entertains her and develops early hand–eye coordination (it's not easy to maneuver a little fist into a mouth).

One of the reasons why she finds her hands so interesting is that they fall within her line of vision and she can now focus on them. These wonderful "toys" that appear in and out of her horizon will capture her attention for long periods. She won't, however, know they belong to her for some months yet.

As your baby's neck muscles become stronger, she will turn her head in response to noises and make an effort to maneuver herself into a position where she can see and hear you. Her eyes may open with wonder and interest when a face or a toy is held within her line of vision, and if you move it away, she may make an effort to follow it. This is the beginning of tracking (see p.81), in which her eyes and head follow an object as it moves. Hang a mobile above her bed so that the dangling objects are about 12 in (30 cm) from her. You'll see her eyes move up and down and to the sides to examine it in detail.

Switching diapers

Now that you're feeling a little more settled, you might consider different ways of doing things, such as changing to reusable diapers.

Hands-on help Show family and friends how to change reusables so they can help you out.

Many parents choose disposables in the early days because they are more convenient, and save the presence of an ever-growing pile of dirty diapers threatening your sanity! But as life begins to take on some semblance of a routine, you may find that you can now rearrange your time to wash diapers—or even investigate a diaper service. Babies grow very quickly, so if you have already been using reusables, you may need a new set now.

If you haven't yet used reusables but are thinking about doing so, now could be a good time to make the switch. Once your baby is about 10lbs (4.4kg), you can purchase diapers that can be adjusted to see her through to potty-training days. So at least you won't waste any money on buying the tiny ones. Changing to reusables now should save you money in the long run (disposables are more expensive), and you'll be helping the environment. There's also research to suggest that the shape and design of reusables offer better support for your baby's posture, and can help to keep her legs apart, in a "frog" position, that benefits the development of her hips.

Of course, disposable diapers have their advantages, too, including being super absorbent and easy to put on and take off. So there's no reason to change if you don't want to. Even if you prefer reusables, disposables are handy from time to time—on vacation, out and about, or even when you're just busy and washing diapers is one task too many.

TIME TO THINK ABOUT

Your postpartum checkup

There are just a couple of weeks to go until your postpartum checkup by your doctor to make sure you have fully recovered after the birth of your baby (see pp.94–95). In some cases, an appointment will be made for you by your doctor's office, but you should call and check what the procedure is—you may need to make the appointment yourself. It's a good idea to start jotting down any questions or concerns you have now so that they don't slip your mind during the checkup.

SMILING YOUNG BABIES

It is possible that you've seen your baby smiling in her sleep, and giving a fleeting grin from time to time. This type of smiling is known as "reflex" smiling, and it can occur from birth until she is about eight weeks old. It is believed to make infants more attractive so that they are cared for. Social smiling, which occurs in response to stimuli (such as your smiling face, or a familiar song) is known as "learned" smiling, and can occur as early as four weeks, although usually at 6–8 weeks. But even contented babies might be 12 weeks before they smile. You'll know it's the real thing when your baby smiles with her entire face, including her eyes.

Is she smiling? Until about eight weeks, a baby's smile is the result of a built-in reflex rather than a responsive gesture.

4 weeks

BABIES HAVE OVER 300 BONES; MANY FUSE TOGETHER OVER TIME TO MAKE 206 ADULT BONES

Although she still needs plenty of support, your baby is already trying to hold up her head by herself. She may even lift it briefly when she is resting against your shoulder or on her tummy. Her hands are held in fists for the first few months, but she'll soon start to open and close them.

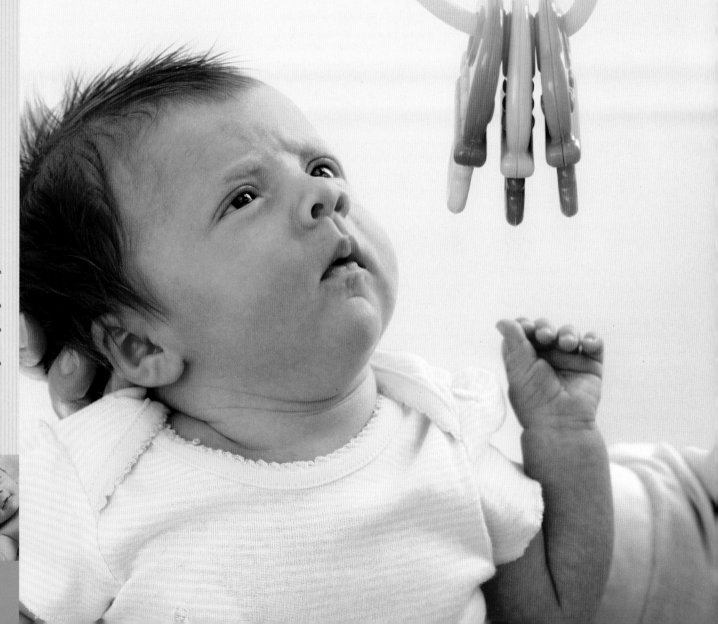

Tracking objects

One of the most exciting developments in your baby's vision is the fact that she can now begin to "track" an object as it moves.

Focusing with both eyes Your baby can focus but she can't see very far, so keep objects of interest within 12 in (30 cm) of her face.

At first, your baby moves her head in order to move her eyes, so a massive movement is required to keep her eyes pinned on a moving object. Initially, she moves her head only horizontally to track objects, largely because it is easier to move her head from side to side than to lift it up and drop it down. If you pass a rattle in front of her eyes, she'll try to move her head to the side to follow it.

In time your baby will start to move her eyes independently of her head and develop "eye-teaming" skills, in which she uses her eyes together. So don't worry if she looks cross-eyed from time to time—in the coming weeks, her eyes will be better coordinated because she will have more control of the nerves and muscles to keep them from crossing.

Your baby will find it easier to track objects that are highly contrasting— your face, for example, or black-and-white geometric shapes and lines, will catch her attention and encourage her to focus. Hold the object of focus in her line of vision and move it slowly from side to side. Her eyes will lock on to it. Gentle movements are easier for her to follow than fast, jerky movements.

Over the coming weeks, you'll notice that she will track things for longer, and show much more interest in the things she tracks. By three months, you can begin to encourage her vertical tracking skills. For now, though, celebrate her wonderful new achievement.

ASK A... DOCTOR

I seem to be leaking urine when I cough or laugh. Shouldn't things have tightened up down there by now? It can take a while for ligaments and muscles to tighten up after pregnancy and childbirth. Like all muscles, your pelvic floor, which supports your bladder, needs to be exercised regularly to become "fit." If you didn't practice these exercises (known as Kegel exercises, see p.65) during pregnancy, it can take longer to tone them after the birth, but it's never too late to start.

TWINS

Telling identical twins apart

Although every parent of identical twins will tell you that there are subtle differences between their babies, the truth is that most parents of identical twins do struggle to tell them apart from time to time, especially in the early weeks, when the different personalities of each baby are not yet established. It can be much easier to know which is which if there is an obvious difference, such as a birthmark, a fuller head of hair, or a different timber of cry.

Many parents choose to color code their children—with red for one and blue for the other, for example. You can choose to keep on your baby's hospital band for a little longer than usual, just to differentiate between

them, and then color-code their clothes so that you'll know who is who. Rest assured that, within a few weeks, their minute differences will become clear, and these will become very big differences with every month that passes.

Color coding Associate one color with each baby to help tell them apart.

4 weeks

YOUR BABY IS 4 WEEKS AND 1 DAY

Taking a time out

Even an hour away from the routine of taking care of your baby can recharge your batteries, so take any offers of babysitting.

No matter how much you enjoy being a new parent, there are times when chores and a repetitive routine can take their toll. You are probably finding that you long for a little adult conversation and to get out of the house. Yet, parenting is a tricky business, and requires plenty of planning, negotiating, and agreement to keep everything afloat.

Equally, your relationship requires the same input and effort that it always did to keep it strong, so it is important that you and your partner spend time alone together. While there is no reason why you can't schedule "dates" at home, it's very refreshing to go out and focus on each other, without the inevitable interruptions and distractions that life with a new baby brings.

A grandparent or close friend whom you trust can care for your newborn for an hour or two. Choose a time when your baby is usually happy and fed, or likely to be asleep. Use this time to enjoy each other's company; don't let talk about your baby or the challenges of baby care dominate your time. Of course, you may want to discuss setting some goals, as parents, but talk about other things, and relate as adults in a relationship, not just tired parents. Your relationship will enjoy a new lease on life, as will you!

ASK A… PEDIATRICIAN

When will my baby sleep through the night? Most babies don't sleep through until around six months (and sometimes later). Your baby's tummy is tiny and digests feedings quickly, so needs regular refueling, even at night. Also, she needs the reassurance of being close to you. Comparatively, breast-fed babies sleep lightly and wake more often. Don't panic. Rest when she does, keep nighttime feedings quiet, and remember—this won't last forever.

YOUR BABY IS 4 WEEKS AND 2 DAYS

Enjoying sounds

Your baby is now starting to make sense of the sounds around her and will respond to loud and soft noises and, best of all, music!

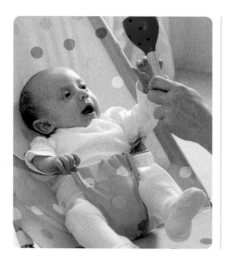

Your baby will begin to watch and listen carefully when she hears a sound that catches her attention. She'll be alert to new sounds and turn her head to find out what's causing them. Loud noises may startle her, and a lullaby may soothe her. Watch her response when you whistle or drum your fingers on the table. Play lively music and watch as she kicks her legs or listens with interest. Play a softer melody and she will quiet down and visibly relax. Some studies show that music can affect a baby's nervous system, lulling her off to sleep and easing anxiety.

Use music in playtime to stimulate her and add to the sense of fun. Play different types of music according to her mood—and yours—and show her the sounds that make up the world around her. Interestingly, she'll begin to associate sounds with the activities they denote, so she'll hear the bath running and eventually realize this means bath time. Fill her life with sounds and music and she'll become alert, interested, and in tune with what is going on around her.

Great shakes Your baby will be interested in hearing a variety of different sounds.

Night and day

Many babies don't have their body clocks set to your schedule, spending long hours awake at night, and sleeping through the day.

Daytime sleep To help your baby differentiate between daytime sleep and nighttime sleep, keep the room light during the day, and don't block out household sounds.

It can be very difficult to cope when your little one is regularly alert and awake when you are hoping for some sleep. Although it makes sense to sleep when your baby does in the early weeks, she does now need to be edged toward more practical sleeping arrangements so that you both get the rest you need.

Help your baby distinguish between night and day by making them feel very different to her. Handle her very quietly and efficiently when she does wake at night, and resist the temptation to play with her or talk. Put her back into her crib after she has been changed and fed, and make it clear that playtime is not at night. She may fuss a little, but she'll soon get the message.

In the daytime, put her to sleep in a carriage or Moses basket in a light room other than the bedroom and go about your daily business. The light entering the room will work on her pineal gland in her brain, which governs sleep and wakefulness, and she'll be much less likely to sleep for very long periods than in a darkened room. Also, she'll be more likely to wake at an appropriate time if there is a little background noise going on.

Stimulate her during the day so that she is tired enough to sleep at night. If she's napping and feeding all day, she's unlikely to be physically tired enough to sleep for longer periods at night. Wake her up from long naps with plenty of cheery chat, play, and songs, and find things to do together throughout the day. Babies do need plenty of sleep during the day, but by now there should be periods of activity between naps. At night, you'll aim for just the opposite.

DEVELOPMENT ACTIVITY

Mobile entertainment

A mobile over your baby's bed, floor mat, or even her changing table, if you have one, will be visually stimulating and encourage her to "track" objects (see p.81), which also strengthens her spatial perception. Choose bright colors, which will catch her attention, and, if possible, a model that can be wound up to move in a gentle, baby-friendly circular motion. Music is a bonus, too, since it can soothe, or stimulate, depending on what's best.

Her Moses basket or floor mat is a safe place for her to relax and play, and you can get to other household activities while she watches and listens to her new toy.

Around they go A mobile hung over your baby's crib gives her something to focus her attention on.

4 weeks

83

Feeling up and down

Having a new baby changes life dramatically, and it can be difficult to manage to begin with, which can leave you feeling a little low.

No matter how happily you anticipated your life with a new baby, the reality can be exhausting and, for some women, a little stifling. You may miss regular contact with friends and colleagues and feel lonely. You may be shocked by the fact that you can't manage to get anything done during the day other than caring for your baby, and long for the days when you could be spontaneous.

Don't feel guilty about these emotions—they don't mean you don't love your baby or enjoy being with her. This is a period of adjustment to a new

Down time Taking care of a new baby can be very tiring and it's perfectly normal to have mixed feelings in the early days.

way of life, guided completely by another person. Most of us like to feel in control of our lives to some extent, and life with a baby is about as far away from that as it gets. It can help to arrange get-togethers—with friends from your childbirth classes or other mothers in the area. Pop your baby in a carrier and take her to work to show her off. Get out into the fresh air and change your routine from time to time. Rest assured, soon, life will take on a more regular pattern and you can plan more.

Take some time for yourself. Ask your partner to take over for an hour and give you a welcome respite from baby care while you read a book, or even just paint your toenails.

You and your body

Even if you managed to keep your pregnancy weight gain to a minimum, it is normal for your body to change quite dramatically.

Couple the fact that your body will still be showing signs of a "pregnancy tummy" with your current inability to get near the shampoo, let alone a gym, before your baby needs you, you may be feeling slightly less attractive than you'd hoped. Many new moms glow with health, but the vast majority are likely to feel tired, a little downtrodden, and as if their bodies have taken a beating. It's also hard to feel beautiful when you have a perpetual patch of spit up on your shoulder!

Try to be realistic. It took nine months for your body to get this way, and it will take time for normalcy to be restored. Some women find their breasts remain much larger after breast-feeding, while others find they disappear completely. Your shoe size may have increased permanently, and even the best creams are unlikely to eradicate stretch marks. But with a healthy diet and just a little regular exercise, your body will return to its usual size, and you will get some time to spend taking care of yourself!

ASK A... DOCTOR

I'm breast-feeding and my periods have returned! Is this normal?
Although most women do not see the return of their periods until around six months, they could start as early as four weeks or as late as a year after the birth. For this reason, do not presume that breast-feeding offers you a reliable form of contraception.

Expressing milk

Expressing your milk allows you to buy yourself a little freedom and your partner to get involved with feeding your baby.

Special moments Dad will enjoy feeding his baby while you take a well-earned rest.

Some women start expressing around now with a view to continuing to breast-feed when they return to work, or because they want more flexibility and someone else to be able to give their baby a feed every so often. You can express milk using a pump (see p.28) or by hand (see box, right). The best time to express is when you are relaxed. You'll soon work out when in the day you have most milk—many women find that they have very full breasts first thing in the morning. Give your baby a feed from one breast, and either simultaneously express from the other or take a warm bath, pop your sleeping baby in her basket next to you, and express what's left.

When you express, your breasts will produce more milk. However, it can take a few days for your milk supply to catch up, so express small amounts and let your baby suckle at your breast often. You might notice that your breast milk looks watery in comparison to formula or cow's milk—but it's the perfect consistency for your baby.

If breast milk is frozen immediately, it will last up to four months. Store it in plastic feeding bottles with secure tops, or you can buy sterile bags made for this purpose. Write the date on the bottle or bag so that you know when you need to use it by. Freezing breast milk destroys some of the disease-fighting antibodies it contains, but its nutritional value is not affected.

Defrost frozen milk in the fridge overnight, or place the bottle or bag in a bowl of warm water. Don't use the microwave or the stove to heat milk, since this kills some of its nutrients.

Freshly expressed breast milk can be stored in the fridge up to five days at 39°F (4°C) or lower or in the freezer for three to six months at no higher than 0°F (-18°C).

HOW TO...

Express milk by hand

Some women find it easier to express by hand than they do being attached to a pump. Make yourself comfortable, preferably with your baby nearby. A warm bath first may relax you. Cup your breast with one hand and use the other to press the breast so the milk in the milk channels travels downward toward the areola. Now use your thumb and forefingers to squeeze the breast tissue to press out the milk. Keep pressing and releasing—you'll find a rhythm that is comfortable. It can take a few minutes for your milk to flow. If you are struggling, imagine your baby or even reach over to touch her to encourage the let-down reflex. Rotate your hands to reposition them from time to time, which encourages flow by stimulating the sinuses (see p.26).

Have a clean bowl or sterilized bottle ready to collect the milk. Express each breast until the flow slows down—for perhaps five minutes or so. You can go back and forth between them until your breasts feel empty. Label your milk with the date if you are putting it in the freezer.

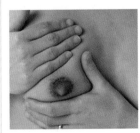  

Getting started Support your breast with one hand as you use the other to manipulate the milk along the milk channels toward the areola (left). **Press and release** Using your thumb and forefingers, press gently into your breast. Press and then release (middle). **Express and collect** Find a comfortable rhythm and catch the milk in a clean, sterile container (right).

4 weeks

85

5 weeks

AT BIRTH, A BABY'S EYES ARE ABOUT 75 PERCENT OF THEIR ADULT SIZE

Your baby may already have been making random cooing sounds but anytime between now and 3 months, she'll start to respond more specifically to sounds—first by turning her head and changing her facial expressions, and then by actually cooing and gurgling.

Listening and learning

Your baby's hearing faculty is quite sensitive. This makes her a great listener and means that sound is a good source of information for her.

Listening to mom Your baby is your most devoted audience; she loves to hear your voice.

Even before your baby was born she could hear your voice. Now that she hears it every day outside the uterus, and understands the link between that voice and her continued well-being, she finds it highly comforting. The same is true for her father's voice. Given that she likes to hear your voice so much, make the most of it—talk to her (see p.88) and sing songs to her. Hearing your voice around her helps her feel safe and secure.

Repetitive sounds Particularly when they are accompanied by repetitive actions, such as the "pop" in "Pop Goes the Weasel," or the tickle up the leg at the end of "This Little Piggy," repetitive sounds help babies learn expectation and predictability, because they learn to make a link between a particular sequence of noises and a particular effect. Some experts believe that repetitive sounds can help to improve babies' memories.

New sounds Unexpected sounds can make your baby startle—she might fling her arms in the air, bring her knees to her chest, or even cry. A sudden shout or bang may have this effect, although if she's used to noisy siblings, she may also learn to zone out all but the loudest of noises.

Reacting negatively to sounds affirms that your baby's hearing is working as it should. If you hear a dog bark or an airplane overhead, comment on the noise to reassure your baby and begin to teach her that noises have meaning.

Spotting a problem Your baby should be noticeably calmed or become distracted by your voice—although the pause in her activity may be only brief and you will have to watch for it carefully. In addition, if you clap your hands behind her head, she should startle. If you think your baby consistently doesn't seem to respond to your voice or loud noises, consult your pediatrician, who can arrange a hearing test to ensure everything is developing normally.

Often, though, babies simply learn to ignore the noises around them, especially if they feel secure; also, young babies can sleep through a large amount of noise. Full-term babies rarely experience hearing problems, unless there are other members of the family who have them.

DEVELOPMENT ACTIVITY

Playing music

Some studies suggest that babies who are exposed to many musical styles develop a good ear for sound and musical appreciation when older. Music, particularly classical music, may encourage neurological pathways to develop in the newborn's brain, improving thought processes and stimulating "alpha" brainwaves, which are associated with feelings of calm.

Bring different styles of music into your baby's life. Perhaps play lively, upbeat music in the morning, sing her nursery rhymes at playtime, and play her soothing classical music when you want to calm her down to sleep.

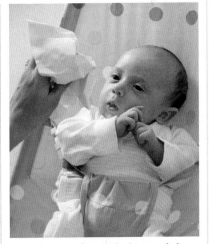

Exploring sounds Introducing your baby to new sounds, such as the sound of crinkling paper, is good for sensory development.

5 weeks

87

Baby talk

Constantly talking to your baby can help her develop her language and communication skills.

You may be surprised to find that you are, quite unexpectedly, speaking "baby talk" in a high-pitched singsong voice—and that your baby is responding. This is a natural, instinctive method of communication that parents use, known as "parentese" (or motherese), and it occurs in every language in the world. Studies have found that babies pay more attention to and prefer this type of speech. It encourages communication between parent and child and helps babies learn the rudiments of language. Using baby talk doesn't just interest your baby and hold her attention, but it helps her pick up words more quickly than without it, and contributes to her mental development.

You may feel uncomfortable speaking in a slow, high-pitched voice with a simplistic vocabulary (or even babble) and lots of repetition, but your baby will find it soothing and will actually begin to understand you—and the nuances of language. Talking to your baby has an incredible effect on her development, so don't hesitate to chatter away as you take care of her. Explain what you are doing as you go along. She won't understand the meaning of words at first, but over the coming months she will learn that these sounds are labels for your actions or objects around her.

Studies suggest that talking to babies helps them identify where words begin and end, and provides them with the clues needed for them to develop language skills. You'll find that most adults—and even children—adopt parentese when speaking to babies, and this is an instinctive way of speaking that will reap long-term rewards.

Sharing the load

Dads these days are much more hands-on, so if you plan to share child care, it's important to start out the way you intend to continue.

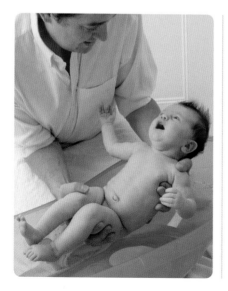

It's good to share baby care with your partner—it gives your baby equal time with both of you and ensures neither of you feel left out or less confident than the other. Your baby will enjoy his touch as much as yours, and sharing the care means she is as familiar with each of you, and both of you have figured out your own ways to care for and soothe her.

Talk to each other about how best to divide the workload of caring for your baby and running the home. Could he take care of the baby while you do the supermarket shopping, for example, or take charge at bath- and bedtime while you prepare dinner? Try to apportion less enjoyable chores fairly, so that neither of you feels resentful. When your partner is in charge of baby care, avoid criticizing if he does things differently. It's fine to offer a few "pointers" when you know how best to care for your baby, but try not to undermine him.

If you're bottle-feeding, you can share feedings (it's preferable that only the two of you feed your baby in the early days since this is prime bonding time). If you're breast-feeding, once you've settled into it, you can express some milk so your partner can give the feeding occasionally.

Dad's turn When you and your partner take an equal share in baby care, you divide the load and both learn new skills.

Bottle-feeding know-how

Whether you're using formula or you plan to start, or you've been expressing milk, here's how to ensure bottle-feeding goes smoothly.

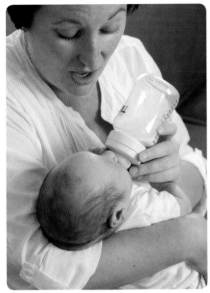

Angling the bottle To prevent your baby from taking in excess air, keep the bottle tilted so formula fills the bottle's neck and the nipple.

If you are breast-feeding, most experts advise against giving babies a bottle before about five or six weeks to avoid "nipple confusion." Sucking from a bottle requires less effort and babies can get used to drinking milk more quickly. However, if you can establish breast-feeding successfully over the first six weeks, your baby will develop the skills she needs and find it less daunting to switch between breast and bottle.

Remember that your milk supply is based on your baby's demands. If she is getting milk from a bottle, she won't be "demanding" it from you, and your supply will lessen. If you are planning to return to work, you should introduce the occasional bottle around now. Some babies will reject a bottle if you wait until it's too late. Once you

have expressed milk (see p.28 for more on pumps, and p.85 for information on manual expressing and storing breast milk), give her a bottle once a week or so to make the transition to bottle-feeding easier. Heat the milk so that a drop on your wrist feels just warm, and discard unfinished milk. Throwing away expressed milk may seem like a waste, but there's a risk of bacteria growing, which can lead to stomach bugs.

Sometimes even babies who have been bottle-fed from birth can experience problems. If your baby struggles when being fed, check the nipple flow. If it takes longer than 20 minutes to finish a bottle, she may need a faster nipple. If she chokes or splutters, the flow may be too fast.

HOW TO...

Introduce a breast-fed baby to a bottle

Choose a time when your baby is calm and not very hungry. Some babies take to bottles easily, while others are more resistant. If your baby is reluctant, try expressed milk rather than formula, and smear a little of your usual nipple cream around the nipple. Choose a slow-flow nipple shaped like a real nipple to mimic the breast-feeding experience, and open your shirt so she feels your skin and warmth. It may take a few attempts for her to accept it.

If you are having no luck, try asking Dad to take over. Sometimes babies smell their mom's milk and know that they are being offered something different—and possibly not as pleasant. If you aren't around, they may accept "different" because it is a whole new experience. If she becomes distressed, leave it for another day and breast-feed her as usual. The last thing you want is for the bottle to have unhappy associations.

Giving the bottle Gently stroke her cheek to elicit the rooting reflex and insert the nipple carefully into her mouth (left). **During the feeding** Talk to her and let her pause mid-feeding if she wants. Change sides to give your arm a rest (middle). **Removing the bottle** Gently slide your little finger into the corner of her mouth to stop her from sucking the nipple (right).

Downtime for baby

Raising a relaxed child partly depends on how relaxed you are, so it's important to include a little bit of wakeful downtime every day.

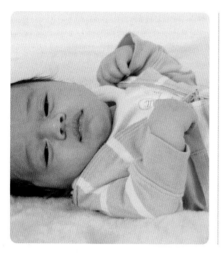

No newborn baby should ever be ignored, even for a short period of time, but that doesn't mean that you have to stimulate your baby during every waking minute of the day, either. It is healthy for her to spend some time each day looking around, taking in her world without you directing her. Otherwise you will have a irritable, overstimulated infant. It can be difficult to get the balance of active play and downtime at first, but as you learn to read your

Quiet time Give your baby quiet time on his back to explore his world on his own.

baby's signals this will become easier. Spend a little time every day—even if it's just 15 minutes—with your baby in the same room, but left to kick under her baby gym or on her mat with a few well-chosen safe toys just within her reach. Keep her on her back for this downtime, but make sure she has short bursts of tummy time every day, too. You can watch her quietly from a nearby chair, or take the opportunity to read a little. This kind of quiet activity allows her to explore her world, and to learn to love doing so. It also provides a little bit of rest for you.

Your social network

Meeting friends lifts your spirits, gives you a change of routine, and introduces your baby to the idea of social company.

Whether you meet with friends from your childbirth group or go to a mother-and-baby group, you'll build a helpful support network. Sharing stories and experiences, trading tips and advice, and giving yourself the chance to enjoy adult conversation can be invaluable. Parenting has its highs and lows. Having friends or acquaintances in the same boat can help you see the humorous side of some of your experiences and provide reassurance that your concerns are likely to be common—and shared. Best of all, you can explore solutions in the company of like-minded, or at least similarly placed, adults.

Your baby will also benefit from the experience, and be stimulated by adult conversation and the activities of the other babies. It will be a long time before she will play with other children, but she'll be fascinated by what's going on around her in this new experience.

Spend time with friendly, positive people who respect your philosophies. If you come away feeling as if you are not living up to collective expectations, it may be the wrong group for you. This should be an uplifting experience, which increases your confidence and gives you great ideas for approaching the minor problems of early parenthood.

ASK A... PEDIATRICIAN

My baby hates tummy time. Is there any way to encourage her?
Babies need about 30 minutes of tummy time each day to develop important muscles, but it doesn't have to be all at once. Plan three 10-minute sessions, and if your baby starts to fuss, distract her with a song or a toy to help get her through! As she becomes stronger, she'll get used to it. Choose a stimulating play mat, and get down on your tummy too, stroke her back, and talk to her.

It's bedtime

Now that your baby is almost six weeks old, she'll probably respond well to her bedtime routine and feel better about being left alone.

Sleep time Following a set bedtime routine will help your baby relax and fall asleep.

It will probably be some time before your baby sleeps through the night, and she will continue to wake up frequently to be fed or comforted as the weeks go by. No matter how tired or frustrated you may feel by these night wakings, try to stay calm and respond to her needs as quickly and quietly as you can. A baby who knows that her parents will come when she needs them is more secure, and that much more likely to develop self-soothing skills early on.

Good sleep patterns are dependent upon a gentle bedtime routine, which helps your baby unwind and anticipate the series of events that will ultimately lead to longer periods of restful sleep. Rowdiness with Dad on his return from work won't relax her, so keep things calm and quiet, giving her a wash, a lovely feed, and a lullaby before settling her

down to sleep. Babies love repetition, so sing the same song every night to help her understand what's coming next and anticipate it with pleasure.

Stay with your baby if she needs you and reassure her of your presence. Don't tiptoe around the house when she drifts off—let her hear the familiar sounds of your voice and normal household activities. She'll know you're there, and will get used to sleeping in noisier environments, so won't be startled awake by tiny sounds.

All babies need daytime naps, and babies who have regular naps find it easier to sleep well at night since they are well-rested and used to being put down to sleep. If you get your baby down at the first sign of sleepiness (see p.76), you'll miss her second wind of energy.

Finally, don't sleep train your baby yet or leave her to cry. At this stage, she needs a warm, loving routine that makes her confident enough to fall asleep and settle back to sleep when she wakes, knowing you're there if she needs you.

YOUR BABY'S HAIR

When your baby is born, her hair may be thick or thin, dark or light, standing on end, or neatly coiffed as if she's just stepped out of a salon. What a baby's hair will be like at birth is as unpredictable as anything else. Even if you and the baby's father have blond hair, she may be born with dark hair and vice versa. Very often, if your baby is born with hair at all, it will fall out over the course of her first few months of life, to be replaced by something more in keeping with the rest of the family!

Your baby may develop a bald patch on the back of her head, where her head rests when she's lying down; this is perfectly normal, and once her "real" hair comes in, the patch will disappear.

Thick hair Any hair your baby had at birth may fall out in the first six months and then grow back in a different color or texture (left). **Fine hair** Babies born with no hair, or very fine hair, may stay like that well into the first year (right).

6 weeks

BY SIX TO EIGHT WEEKS, MOST BABIES START TO SLEEP LONGER AT NIGHT THAN IN THE DAY

Around now, many babies have a growth spurt, making them hungry and demanding, so be prepared for extra feedings during this time. If you're lucky, your baby might just smile a real smile for the very first time this week. Many babies, however, don't manage to smile until around 8 weeks.

Time for a growth spurt

You can expect a rapid and intense period of growth any time now—sometimes it can seem as if your baby has become bigger overnight!

Meeting increased demand Feed your baby as often as she wants; the amount of milk you produce depends on how much she nurses.

Restlessness during sleeping, extended periods of sleeping, and, most obviously, an increased demand for food are all signs that your baby might be having a growth spurt, especially when they appear in combination. Many breast-feeding mothers mistake increased restlessness and feeding demands for signs that they are not producing enough milk—however, if these signs occur around the six-week mark, it is far more likely that a growth spurt is the cause.

During a growth spurt, it can be really difficult to establish a fixed routine of feeding your baby, and any routine you thought you'd established can seem to disappear since your baby constantly seems hungry. Your milk supply will respond to your baby's demands, so it's important that you feed her whenever she asks for food so that your body steps up the quantity of milk it produces to satisfy her. It's also important to encourage her to empty each breast fully, so that she gets plenty of fatty, filling hindmilk. Usually, her feeding pattern will settle down again pretty quickly as the growth spurt passes, often within only a few days.

If you are bottle-feeding your baby, it may be time to increase the amount you give, but only by 1 oz (25 ml) at a time. Consult your pediatrician if you are unsure.

NEWBORN SIZE UP

If your baby was over 8 lb (3.6 kg) at birth, she may not even have worn newborn sizes; however, the average baby normally outgrows the smallest-sized baby clothing between five and eight weeks—sometimes sooner. If things are starting to look a little tight (particularly at the feet), keep her comfortable by moving her up a size. Clothes designed for 0–3-month-old babies should get her through the month, but be prepared to be flexible. Take her along when you go shopping and hold the clothes up against her; allow for shrinkages in the wash and her upcoming growth spurt. When in doubt, go a size larger. She'll be into 3–6-month outfits in no time at all!

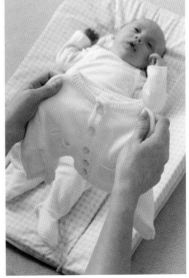

Make it roomy Factor in his growth spurt and go for a size larger when shopping for baby clothes.

ASK A... BREAST-FEEDING EXPERT

My baby seems hungry all the time. Can I give her a bottle of formula as well as breast-feed her? Although your milk supply should now be established, it will increase over the coming months to meet your baby's needs. Around this time, your baby will be undergoing a growth spurt, and want to feed more often to fuel that growth. Nursing will increase your supply to match her new demands, so it is important to put her to your breast as often as she wants. It's not a good idea to give extra bottles of formula at this stage because your breasts will not be stimulated to make enough milk for your baby. So if you want to continue breast-feeding successfully, try to avoid this. It usually only takes a few days for your breasts to catch up, so bear with it and feed her frequently.

Your postpartum checkup

When your baby is around six weeks old, you will visit your own doctor for a checkup. This routine examination is to check that you are doing well, and that you're coping with your new life as a mom. This is a chance to discuss any concerns you have.

ASK A... DOCTOR

My baby's belly button sticks out. Could there be a problem? Belly buttons come in all shapes and sizes, so how your baby's umbilical stump will detach and what her belly button will look like is entirely unpredictable. However, if it protrudes significantly, especially when your baby strains or cries, she may have an umbilical hernia. This harmless condition occurs when there is weakness in the muscles around the umbilicus, where the cord was attached. Most umbilical hernias clear up on their own in the baby's first year without medical intervention. Occasionally, however, babies need a simple surgery. It's a good idea to mention a protruding belly button to your doctor, so that, if there is a hernia, the condition can be diagnosed and monitored.

When will my hemorrhoids go away? Hemorrhoids are common in pregnancy, and can also occur as a result of pushing during labor. In many cases, they disappear within a couple of months of the birth, and you can encourage this by eating a diet rich in whole grains, fruit and vegetables, drinking plenty of water, and exercising regularly (including Kegel exercises, see p.65). Raising your feet when using the toilet can help when moving your bowels. If it's painful, not improving, or you have bleeding, see your doctor.

Asking questions Your postpartum checkup offers you a chance to ask questions about your health. Prepare a list of your questions, so you leave with all the answers.

The postpartum checkup, also known as the six-week check, is usually done by your ob/gyn in her office. By the six week mark, your body should have recovered from the birth. Your uterus should be back to its normal size, the lochia flow has likely stopped, and any stitches should be healed.

Checking your physical health

It is likely that, as with your prenatal appointments, the first checkups your doctor will perform will be to take your blood pressure and, possibly, to test a urine sample. Six weeks after birth, your blood pressure should have returned to normal levels (below 140/90), even if you suffered from either high or low blood pressure during your pregnancy. Your urine may be checked, especially if you had high blood pressure during pregnancy, have high blood pressure now, have any urinary symptoms, or if you had gestational diabetes.

If you are breast-feeding, your doctor will ask you about your breast health—whether you have any soreness or cracked nipples, and so on—and will perform a physical examination if you want one. He or she will also be ready to answer any concerns that you may have about breast-feeding.

Increasingly, doctors are conscious that mothers adopt good dietary and exercise habits after giving birth to speed their recovery and to help them achieve appropriate weight loss. For this reason, your doctor may weigh you and advise you, if necessary, about an appropriate diet and activity that will help you regain your pre-baby weight. It is advisable to wait until you have this checkup before embarking upon any significant exercise program, because your body will take at least six weeks to recover properly from childbirth.

Your doctor may ask if you would like him or her to check any stitches and healing in your perineum if you had a tear or episiotomy. He or she will ask if your vaginal bleeding or discharge has settled down and if you've had a period yet. You will also be asked whether or not you have had intercourse, and if so whether you experienced any pain. This is also a good time to talk about contraception, and whether you have any concerns. If you haven't had a pap smear test in the previous three years, the doctor will encourage you to have one done once the baby is over three months old.

Checking your emotional health

Your doctor will want to know how you are feeling emotionally following the birth. He or she will ask if you have experienced any low patches, how well you are sleeping, and how you are coping with the demands of being a new mother, including asking about your support network. None of these questions is intended to find flaws, and it's important that you answer honestly, voicing any worries or concerns you have (about any aspect, physical or emotional) about your own or the baby's well-being. Your doctor will be careful to look for signs of postpartum depression so that, if you do seem susceptible, you can receive the support you need as quickly as possible.

Questions about birth control

Birth control options depend on whether you are breast-or bottle-feeding. Bottle-feeding moms can use any form of birth control, but breast-feeding moms are limited to those that don't contain estrogen, since it can affect milk supply. Ask your doctor about the forms of contraception suitable for you. Condoms are a good option, as is an IUD.

It is likely that your six-week checkup will go smoothly and not bring to light any serious concerns. However, if your doctor has any worries about any aspect of the checkup, she will suggest appropriate follow-up appointments to make sure that any potential problems are caught and tackled, or dismissed, at the earliest opportunity.

CHECKLIST

Checks for your baby

Your baby also receives a checkup at around six weeks at the pediatrician's office. The examination is similar to the one she had at birth. You'll need to undress her, so dress her in clothes that are easy to put on and take off, and take a spare diaper.

■ **Bones, joints, and muscles** The doctor will lay your baby on her back and gently manipulate each of her legs to check that her hip joints have the full range of movement. He or she will straighten her legs to make sure they are the same length, and also check that her spine is straight and her other joints are functioning properly. The doctor will check that her fontanelles have a healthy appearance (that they aren't bulging or sunken; see p.99), and may check how the neck muscles and head control are developing, either by observing your baby as you hold her on your shoulder or by placing her on her tummy.

■ **Heart** Your doctor will check your baby's heart sounds and pulses to help rule out congenital heart problems.

■ **Reflexes** Your pediatrician may use some simple tests to check how your baby's reflexes are developing.

■ **Eyes** Looking into your baby's eyes with an ophthalmoscope will reveal any congenital problems, such as cataracts. The doctor will also check that your baby can track objects (see p.81).

■ **Other** Your doctor will feel your baby's abdomen to check for hernias. If you have a boy, the doctor will check that the testes have descended properly into the scrotum sacs.

Weight check Weighing your baby and plotting the reading on his growth chart will help make sure that he's gaining weight at an appropriate rate for his age.

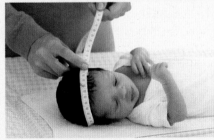

Checking her head Your baby's head circumference provides an indicator that his growth is normal and that there are no problems beneath his skull.

Heart check Listening to your baby's heart with a stethoscope enables a doctor to check whether there are any abnormal heart sounds or murmurs.

YOUR BABY IS 6 WEEKS AND 1 DAY

Little smiler

Your baby's first smile is one of the most precious moments of parenthood, as it shows things are on schedule and that she's happy.

Babies don't smile until they are ready to—even the most contented babies may not break out their first smile until about seven weeks old, sometimes later. However, evidence does suggest that talking to your baby, smiling at her, and making lots of eye contact with her helps the process along. Baby boys may be slower to smile than girls, but are equally open to encouragement. Once your baby does break that first smile, she'll be so thrilled with your reaction that she'll do it again and again.

First smile The more you smile at your baby, the more he'll try to copy you and smile back.

Your baby's first smiles will take place in response to familiar auditory stimulation, such as the sound of your voice. By two months, as her vision improves, she will begin to smile in response to things she sees—usually her favorite people: mom and dad.

Once your baby has learned to smile, she has reached the first milestone in her ability to communicate in a manner other than crying. This first smile seems a wonderful reward for all your work! Soon she'll be smiling at other familiar faces, such as siblings and grandparents. The bigger the fuss you make of her smiles, the more she'll repeat them.

YOUR BABY IS 6 WEEKS AND 2 DAYS

Gaining control

Your baby has little control over her movements yet, but she'll try to grasp if you give her something to reach for.

Your baby will automatically grasp anything that is placed in her palm, because her newborn grasp reflex is still in place. However, she's also becoming more aware of what's around her, so if she sees something that attracts her, she may try to stretch out or wave her arms and grasp it.

Instead of just watching that toy, she may lift an arm toward it in an uncoordinated motion. It will be a long time before she can actually open her hand and then close it around the object in a conscious movement, but she may well grasp something by

accident rather than by design, even if many of her movements are undertaken with a clenched fist. Now's a good time to make sure there's nothing within her reach that she could pull down upon her. She may also reach for dangling hair, jewelry, or scarves, so watch out!

Her kicks and arm motions are still a little jerky, but she will slowly become more graceful and intentional as her muscles and nervous system continue to develop. She may also start to kick and wave her arms in excitement or enjoyment.

Grasping hands Your baby will try to grasp things within reach, and may be successful!

Improving vision

By the time your baby is six weeks old, her eyesight has improved dramatically compared to how it was at birth.

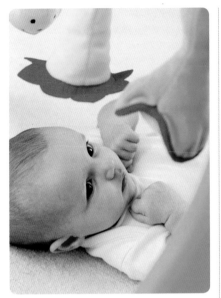

Seeing in color At six weeks, your baby's brain starts to decipher the colors red, green, and yellow, and, a little later on, also blue.

At birth, your baby could focus on objects that were about 12 in (30 cm) away—roughly the distance between your breast and face. She is now able to focus at distances of up to around 23½ in (60 cm). This significant increase is largely due to brain development, as her brain becomes more effective at interpreting data and processing it into clear pictures. You may also find that she starts to discover and focus on parts of her body, particularly her hands (see p.110).

By six weeks your baby has developed some special cells called binocular cells that help improve her ability to distinguish depth. However, she still can't move her eyes in perfect unison, and her ability to perceive depth properly is still a month or so away.

Color and shape It takes a while for the brain to distinguish different colors, and especially various shades of a single color, which is why babies tend to prefer black and white or strong light/dark contrasts when very young.

By the time your baby is six weeks old, her brain will begin to decipher the colors red, green, and yellow, with blue coming a little later. She prefers distinctive shapes to straight lines, and some research suggests that a special part of a baby's brain is acutely attuned to recognizing faces, which is why babies tend to love simple line drawings of a face and why they will fix on a face, and learn to smile in response to it.

Movement Your baby should be able to follow movement with her eyes, if only briefly (see Tracking objects, p.81).

TIME TO THINK ABOUT

Your baby's passport

Arranging a passport for your baby means that you are free to travel whenever you like—perhaps to take advantage of time off during your maternity leave, or to show off your baby to relatives abroad. You'll need to send with your application two identical photographs of your baby, certified by a guarantor, as well as proof of Canadian citizenship (birth certificate or certificate of citizenship). You may also need to provide proof of legal guardianship. Passports can take several weeks—or longer—to process, particularly during busy times, so plan well in advance so you can travel when you want.

ASK A... PEDIATRICIAN

My baby boy has an undescended testicle—will he have to have an operation? Normally, the testes (testicles) develop inside your baby's abdomen, then drop into the scrotum during the second half of pregnancy. By the time your baby is born, his testicles should have descended into his scrotum. Sometimes they remain in the groin, and this is known as "undescended testes." If they are not released into the scrotum, they will not be able to produce sperm later in life—and are at an increased risk of developing cancer. Try not to worry. In some cases, testes move down on their own, usually by 12 months. If your baby's testes don't, he may need an operation, known as an "orchidopexy," which is usually done by the age of two. Your doctor will monitor the situation, and talk you through the procedure.

Sometimes when I'm washing or changing my baby I notice he has an erection. Is this normal? Yes, this is normal. The penis is very sensitive and all baby boys have erections from time to time, some more than others. They have even been observed to have erections in the uterus.

Resuming intimacy

Sex might not be high on your list of priorities right now, but making time to be intimate together keeps you connected as a couple.

Between six and eight weeks after the birth, your body should have almost completely recovered. Any stitches or tearing should have healed, bleeding (lochia) should have stopped, and your vagina should have returned to its pre-pregnancy size. If you had a cesarean birth, your incision site should be on the mend.

However, the fact that your body has recovered doesn't necessarily mean that your desire for sex has returned. Indeed, for several weeks, even months, after birth, most women experience a significant drop in estrogen levels, which can lead to vaginal dryness. For most new moms, however, lack of desire has more to do with fatigue and adjusting to new parental roles than with hormones.

If you're worried that intercourse might be painful, talk to your partner and let him know what you are comfortable with. If you don't feel ready for full intercourse, consider foreplay instead. Be sensitive to each other's needs and patient with one another. If you want to have intercourse, take it gently at first and try using a vaginal lubricant to ease penetration.

Finally, be aware that sex can trigger your let-down reflex, so you may begin to leak milk during lovemaking. Also, you'll need to use some form of contraception if you don't want to get pregnant again, even if you are fully breast-feeding and have not had a period.

Peak period for crying

If your baby seems to be wailing nonstop today, take heart: studies show that crying is at its most fervent around this time.

Frequent crying At around six weeks, crying is often as bad as it will ever be. Your baby's crying will be more short-lived by 12–16 weeks.

There are many reasons why babies cry (see pp.68–69), but usually it's because they want attention (to be held perhaps), a feeding, or a diaper change. At six weeks, there are a few other likely causes.

Some doctors believe colic (see p.68) peaks at six weeks, causing particularly upsetting bouts of crying, often in the evening. If colic is the cause of your baby's increased crying, there's little you can do except to wait and reassure yourself that it is usually significantly reduced between 10 and 12 weeks old.

A growth spurt (see p.93) makes your baby more hungry and more liable to fuss. Some theories suggest that this is because crying triggers your body to manufacture more milk to meet the baby's increased demands.

Learning new skills, such as smiling, and becoming increasingly alert, can be tiring for young babies and crying provides a release for this. As your baby becomes more proficient at processing what is going on, crying will lessen.

Carry your baby in a front-pack carrier or rock her gently in your arms to reassure her. Take comfort that this phase will pass. Enlist the help of friends and family if you're struggling to get things done or need a break for an hour or so, so that you can get some rest or some fresh air away from the noise.

If you are finding it difficult to manage, your pediatrician can support you and, if needed, prescribe a gentle antispasmodic medication. Colic usually improves by 12–13 weeks.

Starting to exercise

If you were given the all clear at your six-week checkup, now might be a good time to start easing your body back into shape.

Making time for exercise Some postpartum yoga classes incorporate baby yoga, too. Yoga can help you regain strength in your back, stomach, and pelvic floor muscles, in particular.

First and foremost, remember that every body is unique and responds to pregnancy in its own way—so be realistic. If you were very fit and toned before becoming pregnant, and if you had an active pregnancy, you are likely to regain your fitness more quickly—but it isn't a foregone conclusion. Whatever your underlying fitness level, make your goals achievable and don't expect too much too soon—the truth is that you may never recover exactly the same body you had before, but you will, in time, and with a little effort, be fit, toned, healthy, and strong again.

Take it easy Because pregnancy and childbirth are the most natural things in the world, it's easy to forget that they have put your body through a major trauma. Ease yourself gently into exercising, taking things at a slow pace to start with. Your joints and ligaments will still be loose for around three to five months, so stick to low-impact exercise

and avoid anything too vigorous or jerky, which could potentially cause injury.

Spend some time both before and after exercising doing a few gentle stretches to warm up and cool down. If, at any point during your exercise session, something hurts, stop doing it immediately.

How much, how often? Initially, aim for about 5–10 minutes of toning exercises every day, and 20 minutes of gentle aerobic activity three times a week, if you can. You can increase both as you become more fit and your body feels stronger. Never push yourself beyond what feels comfortable or achievable.

You'll have to figure out ways of making time for exercise with a baby: perhaps exercising on the weekend when your partner is at home, or sharing baby care with a friend so that you can take turns exercising. You could even take your baby with you to a carriage-pushing exercise class, often held in local parks.

AS A MATTER OF FACT

The fontanelles

The two soft spots between your baby's skull bones are called fontanelles. They allow the skull bones to slide over each other as your baby's head passes through the birth canal. At the rear of her head, the posterior, triangular fontanelle will close when she is about four months old, while the one on the top of her head (the diamond-shaped, anterior fontanelle) takes between nine and 18 months. Your baby's brain is protected by a thick membrane, but it is important to be careful with these soft spots.

It is normal to see your baby's head pulsating in time with her circulation. Her fontanelles may bulge a little when she cries, and then return to normal. If they bulge more than usual, or become sunken, contact your pediatrician. A sunken fontanelle may indicate dehydration, which suggests she needs feeding more regularly. A bulging fontanelle needs investigating to find out if there is any pressure on her brain.

Don't forget to include your pelvic tilts and your Kegel (pelvic floor) exercises (see p.65) to help prevent postpartum incontinence.

Finally, one of the best ways to help tone your body is by doing yoga. Postpartum yoga classes adapt the yoga postures to take into account the fact that you have recently had a baby.

6 weeks

7 weeks

THE FIRST LANGUAGE SOUNDS BABIES MAKE ARE VOWELS, SUCH AS "AH" AND "OOH"

Even though your baby may smile and excitedly wave his arms when he sees you, he may not be so friendly with strangers. That's because he's beginning to develop the ability to remember people and objects. When they are unfamiliar, he may get a little anxious and need reassurance.

Thinking about safety

Now that your baby has a little more control of her movements, you'll need to keep anything that could harm her out of reach.

The following tips will help you make your home as safe as possible for your growing little explorer.

Make sure your baby is firmly supported, positioned, and held at all times, so that she doesn't suddenly jerk herself out of your grasp or roll herself off the bed.

Remove electrical cords and the cords of curtains and blinds from your baby's bed, play, changing, or feeding areas.

Never leave medicines, small objects she could choke on, household plants, or plastic bags within your baby's reach.

Always remember to fasten the harness on your baby's bouncy chair and car seat, even at times when she is sleeping and immobile.

Avoid leaving your baby alone, even for short periods of time, unless she is on a flat, safe surface (ideally the floor) or strapped into her seat or stroller.

Keep your baby's bedding tucked safely under her arms, so that she doesn't draw it up and over her face. Similarly, put her to sleep at the bottom of her crib so that she doesn't wiggle down under her covers.

COMFORT ITEMS

Your baby has the mental capacity to remember familiar objects, so now is a great time to introduce a comfort item. A soft toy or cuddly blanket are ideal—buy two, in case one gets lost. If you bring out her comfort item whenever you soothe her, she will associate it with comfort. This encourages her to learn to self-soothe by giving her a tool to encourage happy, positive, relaxing feelings.

Making new sounds

Your clever baby may have increased her vocabulary already, moving on to double-syllable sounds with the occasional consonant.

Cooing and gurgling—and even giggling—may be becoming second nature to your baby, and she'll be excited about communicating with you and Dad, and any other members of the family. Her babbling represents her first attempts at speech, and you'll notice huge leaps in her baby vocabulary over the coming weeks and months as she practices the sounds she has been learning to make.

Your baby is learning the basics of conversation and the art of listening and responding. According to linguists, babies can tell the difference between similar syllables, such as "ma" and "na," at about four weeks. You can support her learning by repeating the sounds she makes back at her. She'll love to know that you understand what she's trying to say, or the emotion that she's attempting to communicate. You'll find that she is most responsive when she is with familiar people, and when she is spoken to in parentese (see p.88).

Vowel sounds, such as "ah," "uh," "ooh," and "oh," are the first (and easiest) sounds babies make. These graduate to double vowel sounds, such as "ah-uh" and "ooh-ah," before a consonant such as "g" or "m" makes an appearance. "Ahh-gooo" may be your baby's favorite means of expressing pleasure, but you'll probably have to wait a couple of months before you hear that first "ma-ma-ma."

Make baby talk Encourage your baby's communication skills by "chatting" to him.

YOUR BABY IS 7 WEEKS AND 2 DAYS

Active baby

Your baby is beginning to practice her new muscle control—wiggling a lot more, kicking, and twisting her body from side to side.

This is the perfect time to introduce a baby gym, if you haven't already done so. Your baby's control over her body has improved to the extent that she'll enjoy batting at hanging toys—maybe even hitting them from time to time. She'll enjoy reaching outward to things, and may even manage to grab them, although she won't be able to close her fist around them for a while longer. If you put something in her hand, she'll happily hold on—and chances are, she won't let go, either.

Her arms and legs will wave furiously when she is excited—or even angry— and diaper changing will become much more trying. You may find that she responds to music by slowing down her movements when it's quiet and contemplative, and kicking up a storm when the music is more lively. She's now very in tune with her environment and eager to be as active as she can.

Her new interest in using her body may keep her awake at night as she works on honing her skills and inadvertently kicks herself awake. Some parents introduce a baby sleeping bag at this time, so that she stays warm throughout the night. If she has a low-hanging mobile, move it up a notch, since she may decide to bat it down.

ASK A... PEDIATRICIAN

Is it okay to let my baby have a pacifier? A pacifier won't harm your baby's health or development provided you use it responsibly, so if it helps to soothe her, there's no reason why not. But do be careful if you're breast-feeding that you don't give your crying baby a pacifier when what she really needs is feeding, as this could affect your milk supply. Try not to use a pacifier all the time, just when you're trying to settle or comfort her.

YOUR BABY IS 7 WEEKS AND 3 DAYS

Studying shapes and colors

Your baby is showing much more interest in complex designs and shapes, and is now able to distinguish more colors.

Your baby can now focus both her eyes on an object, and will show a preference for more complicated designs, colors, and shapes. She'll still love faces—both yours and those of family members and other babies—the most, but she'll be very intrigued by high contrast, colorful objects, which will be able to keep her mesmerized for many minutes at a time.

Colorful toys Your baby will try to reach out for anything that is moving, so surround her with interesting, vibrant objects to stimulate and entertain her.

Encouraging her to look at objects that interest her will help to strengthen pathways in her brain and develop her vision—but make it fun and don't overstimulate her. No homework allowed for newborns!

Your baby will be awake for longer periods, so has more opportunities to explore her environment. While she could once only focus on black-and-white and bright colors, she can now recognize interesting patterns and a wide range of colors, which is one reason why baby toys are manufactured in a rainbow of colors.

Your baby's vaccinations

An important part of preventative health care is immunizing your baby against illnesses that may seriously harm her later on in her life. Your baby will be given an immunization timetable, which is important to follow.

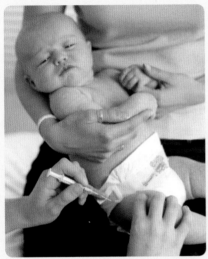

Take the sting out of it Hold your baby firmly while she is given an injection to reassure her.

While a baby's immune system develops life-long immunity against illnesses by acquiring them, many are dangerous, with a high risk of complications or death, so over the coming months, your baby will be immunized against serious illnesses to protect her. By immunizing her, you also help largely to eradicate diseases from the population.

Immunization usually begins at around six weeks and prepares your baby's body to fight diseases it may catch in the future. For example, the polio vaccine stimulates the immune system to produce antibodies against the polio virus, which later recognize the disease if and when it enters her body, and are ready to fight it.

In most cases, vaccines provide life-long immunity, although some need a booster every 10 years or so. It is possible to show symptoms of mild forms of some diseases by immunization, but the risk of complications is much lower than if your baby acquired the full-blown disease. It's natural to be concerned that combining several vaccines could overload your baby's system, but there is no need to worry. Your baby's immune system becomes more mature by the day, and is already capable of protecting her from a wide range of organisms causing infections that she comes into contact with all the time. Her system can very easily deal with the existing combined injections.

There is a small risk of side effects, such as a mild fever and some weak symptoms of the diseases against which she is being vaccinated. It is unusual for a baby to experience an allergic response, but natural to experience some tenderness, swelling, and redness at the site of the injection. She may be irritable and fussy, and sleep more than usual. A dose of pain medication and a quiet feeding should soothe her. Despite some media stories to the contrary, vaccines have a well-researched high safety record.

Keeping track Your baby's immunizations will be noted down on her medical chart, but you may want to keep your own record of the date and brand name of each immunization and any symptoms or side effects. Immunization programs differ by province or territory, so check with your baby's doctor for details specific to your area. The schedule on this page is an example of a typical program.

CHECKLIST

Typical immunization schedule

6 to 32 weeks:
- Rotavirus (Rot)

2 months, 4 months, and 6 months:
- Diphtheria, tetanus, pertussis (whooping cough), polio, and *Haemophilus influenzae* type b (combined into one vaccine known as DtaP-IPV-Hib)
- Pneumococcal disease (Pneu-C-13)

6 to 23 months:
- Influenza (to protect against the flu)

12 months:
- Measles, mumps, and rubella (MMR)
- Meningococcal disease (Men-C)

15 months:
- Varicella (to protect against chicken pox)
- Pneumococcal disease (Pneu-C-13)

18 months:
- Diphtheria, tetanus, pertussis (whooping cough), polio, and *Haemophilus influenzae* type b (DtaP-IPV-Hib)
- Measles, mumps, and rubella (MMR)

Making your baby comfortable Feed your baby before her shot to calm her. Stay calm and talk to her and reassure her in a soft voice, or distract her with a pacifier. It will be over in a few seconds, and she may not even notice it's happened. If she cries, hold her and talk to her gently. She'll be back to her usual, happy self in no time.

7 weeks

103

More regular feedings

Your growing baby should have settled into a pattern and be able to take in more milk at each sitting, and go longer between feedings.

Frequently fed Breast-fed babies usually need to be fed every two to three hours at this age.

Milk is still, and will be for the next few months, your baby's only source of nutrition and liquid, so it's important not to "schedule" her into a routine that leaves her hungry or thirsty. Breast milk is digested more quickly than formula so, if you are breast-feeding, your baby may feed more often than her bottle-fed peers, but the time between feedings will increase over time. Bottle-fed babies often sleep longer through the night than breast-fed babies, but that's no reason to make the switch to a bottle.

You'll ideally want to empty both breasts at every feeding, so that your baby gets the right balance of liquid and nutrition (see p.27); however, you may find that your baby is satisfied after just one breast. Make a note of the times you feed your baby and the breast from which she last fed to remind you which

breast to give first at the next feeding, and also see if there is a pattern to her feedings. If she is not gaining weight as expected, she may be snacking a little too often, rather than taking in a full, long feeding.

If you are bottle-feeding, keep a note of feeding times and the amount your baby drinks to help you to figure out how much she is getting in a day. At this age, most babies are having six to eight bottles of 4–6 oz (120–180 ml) in 24 hours, so if she is taking much more or much less, talk to your health practitioner.

There's no reason why you can't tweak your baby's schedule; for example, if you want to feed on demand during the day, wake her up before you go to bed to fill her up and buy yourself extra sleep before she next wakes up. You may also want to feed her before a long car trip, or to get her into a family routine, or to avoid feedings at less convenient times.

ASK A... PEDIATRICIAN

My baby seems to be uncomfortable after being fed, and she's suffering from diarrhea. Should I change her formula? If your baby has recurrent diarrhea or vomiting, and doesn't seem to be thriving on the formula you have fed her, it's most certainly worth looking at the potential causes. Some children are allergic to cow's milk proteins, and others are unable to digest the sugars (which is completely different, and known as lactose intolerance—see box, below). Your doctor may prescribe a soy, lactose-free or "hydrolyzed" milk formula, which contains all the nutrients your baby needs for normal growth and development without triggering an allergic reaction.

LACTOSE INTOLERANCE

Babies who are lactose-intolerant suffer digestive discomfort, such as diarrhea, vomiting, and colic, causing constant crying and distress.

Lactose intolerance occurs when there is a lack of the enzyme, lactase, which helps the body digest the sugars in milk (including breast milk). True lactose intolerance is very rare in Canada in full-term babies. Both parents would have to pass on the gene for this type of intolerance to their baby, who would suffer severe diarrhea from birth as a result of her inability to tolerate the lactose in her

mother's breast milk or in formula. Lactose intolerance is a little more common in premature babies because their level of the enzyme hasn't been able to build up as it normally would toward the end of the last trimester of pregnancy.

Sometimes, babies can develop lactose intolerance for a short period after suffering from a stomach bug. If this happens, your pediatrician can prescribe a lactose-free formula for your baby, which will give her relief from digestive discomfort while her stomach lining is healing.

Fun bath-times

If your baby has so far been reluctant to take a bath, a few toys and gentle splashing games may persuade her to start enjoying one now.

Making bath-time fun can bring your baby's day to a happy close, and put her in the right frame of mind for bedtime. She'll be much more interested in what's going on now, so you can add a few bath toys to the tub for her to kick and bat. She may be startled and excited by the fact that she can cause such an amazing series of waves by simply kicking her legs. Gently splash the water and use a small cup or bath toy to pour warm water over her—she'll love the experience, and be interested in the movement of the water.

Sing, laugh, and speak in a gentle, upbeat voice to encourage her to see bath-time as something positive. She's more likely to smile and enjoy herself if she sees your smiling face. Singing a song that relaxes her, or finding one she can begin to associate with bath-time, can help to keep her calm and happy.

Now she's a little more mobile, it's a good idea to use a nonslip mat for the bottom of your tub. Make sure you have a good grip on her, since she will be very slippery, particularly if she's determined to maneuver herself into a different position. If she's still in the sink or a baby bath and displacing most of the water before the end of the bath, it may be time to move her in to the tub!

If your baby still resists a bath, consider bathing with her. Get everything ready by the tub so you can step into a robe and get her dried off first. You may need your partner to hold her while you get into and out of the water. Remember that babies can't tolerate hot water in the same way we can, so resign yourself to a slightly cooler bath—no more than 99°F (37°C).

Sleeping well at night

Grabbing a nap when your baby sleeps may be your only option in the early weeks, but you will, over time, want a good night's rest.

Being woken at night can be frustrating, no matter how much you enjoy feeding your baby, and many women find it difficult to get back to sleep. If your baby is right next to your bed (or sleeping with you), you can feed her quickly and efficiently while still half asleep yourself. If her diaper isn't too wet, you can probably leave a change until later, too. It may sound difficult to believe, but you'll soon go on to "auto pilot" at night and feed her without even really waking up!

If you do wake up and can't get back to sleep, do some of the breathing or relaxation exercises you practiced during pregnancy, and try not to focus on how many hours of sleep you are not getting. Avoid alcohol or caffeine in the evenings, which can disrupt your sleep patterns. Try a glass of warm milk, a square of cheese, or even a little turkey breast before bed; these foods contain the amino acid "tryptophan," which will encourage restful sleep. If you are breast-feeding, it may enter your milk supply with a bit of luck, and your baby will sleep well, too!

Finally, about an hour before bed, take a warm bath (not hot, which can be overstimulating), and take some time to unwind. Running around the house doing chores is not an ideal pre-sleep routine!

Rest to recharge Easing the body into a good sleep routine is essential for all new moms.

8 weeks

THE "GRASP" REFLEX THAT BABIES ARE BORN WITH PERSISTS FOR THE FIRST FEW MONTHS

As her muscles become stronger, your baby may be able to push herself up a little when she's on her tummy. She'll "discover" her hands around now and find them endlessly fascinating. She'll want to reach out and grab things, but may not succeed for several weeks.

Your baby's immune system

Now that she's reached the two-month mark, your baby may need a little more help from you to protect her from illness.

When she's born, your baby has a rudimentary immune system that helps her fight off many bacteria and viruses. She has high levels of antibodies in her bloodstream that were passed from your own system during pregnancy, and if you are breast-feeding, you will be passing on still more. Once she reaches two months, however, your baby's "reserve" of antibodies begins to run dry, and she will be more susceptible to illnesses. This is the time when babies are old enough to receive many of the vaccines recommended on the immunization schedule for children.

If you are breast-feeding now, you will continue to protect your baby with the five most important types of antibodies. Breast milk also contains a type of white blood cells, called lymphocytes, that help your baby fight illness. The immunity your baby has now is known as "passive immunity," because it is passed to her rather than developed by her. Your baby will be protected against many, if not all, of the diseases to which you are immune. In fact, breast-fed babies have been shown to get sick less often, suffer from fewer ear infections, and experience less severe symptoms when they do become ill. Your baby's own immune system starts to kick into action in the first few weeks of life, but does not mature until much later in childhood, which is a reason why children get so many colds!

Hygiene Keeping her environment clean will help protect your baby against illness. This doesn't mean dousing the household in antibacterial solutions, but simply keeping anything that she could put into her mouth (such as bottles, teething rings, equipment for making up bottles, and pacifiers) scrupulously clean. This will prevent a buildup of bacteria that could cause stomach upsets, and also prevent the transmission of viruses from other members of the family.

Vet your guests Although it can seem absurd to turn away visitors who are suffering from a cold or another illness,

A close eye If your baby seems sick, monitor her and call your pediatrician if she worsens.

it is a good idea in the early weeks of your baby's life. Because your baby's immune system is so immature, something as simple as a cold virus can become much more serious, since she is less able to fight off the infection. Bacterial infections can also be very dangerous in little ones. Ask guests (and family members) to wash their hands regularly, dispose of any used tissues, and avoid holding your baby until they are healthy.

Taking these precautions can help to keep your baby well until her immune system is a little stronger. Sick babies tend not to feed well, and even a little weight loss can affect her overall strength and development. Any baby with a fever should be seen by a pediatrician as a precaution (see p.401).

ASK A... PEDIATRICIAN

How can I tell if my baby has an ear infection? It's difficult to know without seeing a doctor. Ear infections are common after a cold, but there aren't many specific symptoms. The ear won't be red, and although some babies will rub or bat their ear, many also do this when tired. Crying, irritability, high temperature, vomiting, and even diarrhea can all be due to ear infection (see p.411). There may be a discharge from her ear, which suggests that the infection has perforated her eardrum. At this stage your baby may appear better, but it's still important to see the doctor. Antibiotics aren't routinely given since many ear infections are viral, but the sicker the child, the more likely she is to get antibiotics, and this is often the case with babies. Ask your doctor what medicine is appropriate to relieve your baby's discomfort.

Dressing up

Spending a fortune on baby clothes isn't practical, but shopping for a special occasion will be fun and provide some priceless photos!

If you've managed to restrain yourself in the children's clothing department until now, a special occasion may give you just the excuse you need to buy something beautiful for your little one.

Before you head straight for the frills and ribbons, consider the nature of the occasion. If your baby will be passed around lots of people, or expected to get through a whole day outside her usual environment, it makes sense to be practical. Choose items that won't make her skin itch or feel uncomfortable, and make sure that it can be fastened and unfastened for quick changes. Small buttons, tight collars or waists, or anything that constricts your baby's movement or causes her to overheat probably aren't ideal.

Avoid anything too expensive, since it may end up in the bottom of your bag a few hours after it is worn, due to a leaky diaper or a lot of spit up. For this reason, too, always choose something that is washable. It may also be a good idea to go for separates that can be mixed and matched on the spot if a quick change is required. Bring along a couple of spare tops and/or bottoms, just to be on the safe side.

TWINS

Dressing twins

If you have to dress twins for a nice occasion, two outfits will obviously hit your bank balance harder than one, so look online or at twins' sales. Most special outfits only get worn once or twice before babies outgrow them, and nice clothes are often given as gifts and never worn, so you may be able to find something new or almost new, for very little outlay.

Developing memory

Your baby is developing her "recognition memory," which means that she can remember and identify familiar people and objects.

From birth, or shortly afterward, your baby was able to recognize your voice and smell, and soon showed a preference for familiar faces. Now, she will be able to make some general associations. For instance, if her older sibling always makes the same silly face, your baby may try to imitate it when she sees her. She may look expectantly at the rattle you produce, waiting for it to make its familiar shaking sound. Also, she will begin to associate you with milk and comfort.

Tuned in Your baby identifies objects and people and remembers more than you think.

Your baby is now building associations based on the repeated link between an action and a feeling; for example, you hold out your arms toward her and she anticipates a feeling of being comforted. Over the next few months, these associations build rapidly, and she will react with recognition to familiar stories and songs.

This type of memory is a natural, protective instinct that encourages babies to form strong attachments with their primary caregivers. Remembering and preferring familiar faces and objects is a method of keeping themselves safe from danger.

Healthy eating

Although you may be starting to get frustrated at carrying those extra pounds of pregnancy weight, there's no rush to diet.

Eating right It's important to eat lots of fresh fruits and vegetables that are nutrient rich.

All new moms need plenty of healthy, nutritious food. Dieting now, especially if you're breast-feeding, can leave you short of nutrients, making you prone to illness, fatigue, and mood swings. And if you're preoccupied with your weight, it will affect your enjoyment of motherhood.

Try to base your diet around fruits and vegetables, whole grains (such as whole-wheat bread and brown rice or pasta), proteins (such as lean meats, dairy produce, eggs, fish, nuts, seeds, and legumes), and healthy fats (olive and sunflower oil, avocados, and oily fish). Eating this type of healthy diet will provide the essential nutrients you need for optimum health. These, in turn enter your breast milk, so you'll enhance your baby's diet, too.

ASK A... NUTRITIONIST

How many more calories should I eat each day while breast-feeding?
Breast-feeding moms use up about 500 extra calories each day, but you don't necessarily have to replace them. If your diet is much the same as it was pre-pregnancy, you will naturally lose about 1 lb (450 g) per week without making any changes, since your fat reserves will be used. If you are exercising a little, you are likely to lose even more. It's best not to think about calories: if you focus on eating a healthy diet, the weight will come off without any real effort on your part.

BOOSTING YOUR ENERGY LEVELS

A good way of maintaining energy as you deal with the demands of early parenthood is to eat little and often. Low-fat cheese with apple slices, crackers with low-fat spread, or some dried apricots can keep you going between meals and keep your metabolism active. Try the following to help you feel healthier and fit:
■ Get a little gentle exercise every day. Walking, swimming, aerobics, and/or yoga (with your baby, of course) can help to build muscle, which burns fat and encourages your metabolism.
■ Stay hydrated. Thirst is often mistaken for hunger, and breast-feeding is thirsty work. You'll need about 2.8 quarts (2.7 liters) of water every day to make up for lost fluid.

■ Take all offers of meals made by friends, and get into the habit of batch cooking when you do get a moment in the kitchen. With a small baby, having some standby meals is always a good idea. If you've got a freezer full of nutritious soups, casseroles, or even delicious fruit-and-oat muffins, you are more likely to eat well, and you'll be less likely to rely on highly fatty or salty prepared meals. It's just as easy to make a quick salad as it is to make a prepared meal, and you will reap the rewards.
■ Keep plenty of healthy snacks. Cut some carrots, celery, or cucumber and pop them in some water with a squirt of lemon juice to keep them fresh. Buy salsa, low-fat dips, or hummus. If you long for something sweet, make a fresh

fruit smoothie, eat a couple of small squares of dark chocolate, or try a bowl of whole-grain cereal with fruit compote and yogurt.

Fruit boost Regular and nutritious snacks throughout the day will help keep your energy levels up.

Sleeping like a baby?

Your baby may now be going longer between feedings, and sleeping more soundly at night. You'll probably get more sleep as well.

One of the best ways to encourage your baby to sleep well at night is to ensure that she is comfortable. It's easy to fall into the habit of putting her in the same sleep suit and swaddle or sleeping bag. night after night, but it is important to note the temperature. A hot or cold baby wakes up frequently, even if tired. Keep her bedroom nice and cool, even in winter, keeping her warm with a swaddle or a baby sleeping bag, or even a combination of the two on a very cold night. Equally, if it's hot outside, it's fine to put her to bed in just a diaper and a onesie, plus maybe a pair of socks. A fan in the room, facing away from her bed, can help to keep air circulating and provide a gentle breeze to keep her comfortably cool. If you want a good night's sleep, check that she's comfortable before you go to bed.

If you really want to put a blanket over your baby, put her feet at the foot of the crib and tuck a chest-height blanket firmly under the mattress on three sides. She may be outgrowing swaddling, but if she is still waking herself up in the night with little jerks and startled movements, you might want to consider it (see p.53).

If you haven't yet used one, a baby sleeping bag might be useful now to keep her warm no matter how active she is. Choose a quilted cotton sleeping bag that zips up the front. It should be appropriate for your baby's age and size, and choose a weight that suits the temperature in her bedroom. Bags are available in different materials, heavier and lighter.

Fascinating hands

Your baby's favorite "toys" at the moment are her own hands, which entertain her as they move in and out of her line of vision.

Now that she is starting to open and close her own hands, your baby may stare at them in fascination for long periods of time, carefully bringing them toward her mouth or even aiming them in the direction of your face or breast. She may even attempt to bat at objects dangling from her baby gym, or at a rattle, if you hold it out to her and catch her attention—and she may move her hands together toward it to touch it.

Your baby is a tactile little person and will enjoy feeling new textures. She may unconsciously stroke her own face, your T-shirt or breast, her comfort

Increased dexterity Your baby now has better control of his hand movements.

blanket, or anything she comes into contact with. She may look up in amazement when you place something with a new and exciting texture under her fingers—a bit of soft fur or a textured teething ring, for instance. Everything is new and interesting, and her hands (and mouth) are her best tools for exploring it all.

Give your baby space to enjoy looking at her hands, and what they are capable of doing. Give her a rattle to hold for a moment (she is likely to drop it), and attach a wrist rattle to her arm to attract her attention. Although her hands are fascinating, she can become quite frustrated while learning to swipe or grab since her aim is not yet accurate.

Clothes for breast-feeding

If you have breast-fed since birth, you're probably ready to ditch the baggy T-shirts and functional nursing bras and update your look.

Nursing bra A basic breast-feeding bra does the job, but there are prettier styles to be had.

Nursing bras Most women who breast-feed start off by wearing plain, washable, no-frills nursing bras. There's not much point in buying anything else at first, especially while you're using nipple creams, leaking breast milk, and trying to get used to the mechanics of the breast-feeding process. While there's no reason to change or buy new bras unnecessarily, be aware that your breasts do change size during these early months. For this reason, it's worth your time to go for a professional re-measure every so often to be sure you are wearing the correct size. If you do need new bras, there's now a much wider range of colorful, feminine maternity lingerie to choose from, so this might be a good opportunity to treat yourself.

Breast-feeding clothes It's a similar situation with clothes for breast-feeding. At first, the most important

consideration is comfort, but once you start to feel more like your normal self again, you may want to shop for "normal" clothes in your favorite stores. You can still follow fashion when you're breast-feeding—just go for wrap tops, or low scoop-neck and loose-bottomed T-shirts that can be lifted up and tucked over your feeding baby. Choose cotton and other natural fabrics that won't cause you to get hot with a warm little feeder attached to you for long periods. Take the time to try on any purchases—your shape may have changed. There are also stores and websites selling stylish ranges made specifically for breast-feeding moms, so you may want to check these out, too.

DEVELOPMENT ACTIVITY

Fun with sounds

Rattles are wonderful toys for young babies, and as your baby becomes more interested in the world around her, she'll be mesmerized by the sight and sound of her favorite toy in action.

Whether you choose a rattle that attaches to her wrist or a handheld model that can be put in her hand, you will be providing your baby with a perfect first toy. She'll learn hand–eye coordination and develop her muscle control as she figures out how to operate it. Choose a brightly colored rattle that makes a sound easily. The idea is that she will be able to make the toy work herself—even if it is not through conscious effort. Most toys will end up in your baby's mouth, so choose something soft and easy to clean. The handle should also be easy for her little hand to hold. Be careful, too: her movements are still very jerky and she can easily bop herself on the head in excitement.

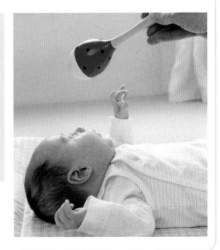

Sensory stimulation Your baby will want to taste her toy, too! (above). **Rattle fun** Give your baby a rattle that is light enough for him to hold (right).

111

9 weeks

BY 9 WEEKS A BABY SEES CONTRASTS WELL AND CAN EVEN SPOT A WHITE TEDDY ON A WHITE COUCH

You can expect your baby to gain around 6–8 oz (150–200 g) each week now. She needs her sleep in order to grow—research shows that 80 percent of growth hormone is secreted during slumber. If she's growing fast, you might want to help her start making the transition to a crib.

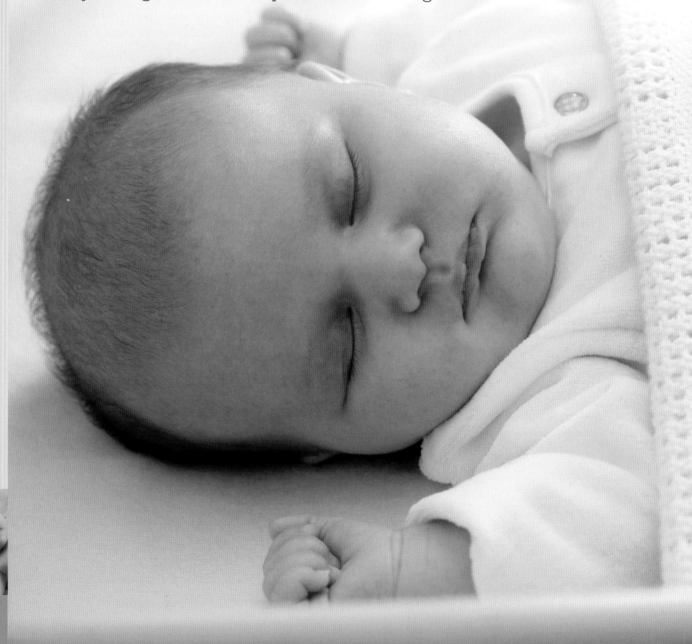

Getting used to a crib

Before you move your baby into a crib, putting her to sleep there in her Moses basket will help to familiarize her with this new space.

Your baby might be comfortable in her Moses basket until she's three months old but, equally, she might be touching the sides of the basket by now—and even waking herself up when she does. If this is the case, you'll want to move her into a crib. A big crib can be daunting for a baby who is used to a smaller and cozier environment, so it's a good idea to get her used to the crib gradually before you actually put her down to sleep in it for the first time.

If you've already bought a crib, it can be a safe place for your baby to play while you busy yourself with other things in her room—sorting her clothes or even setting up the ironing board to attack that growing pile. A mobile and a few toys scattered around, or a baby mirror fastened to the side, will capture her interest. She'll become accustomed to the space, so when it is time for her to sleep there, she will find it familiar.

Before you make the transition, put her Moses basket inside the crib (or nearby) for a few nights. If, when you do first move your baby, she seems distressed at the beginning, try putting her in her crib for daytime naps only. This way, she'll be able to see what's around her and grow more confident. When she's settling down nicely in the day, you can consider moving her at nighttime, too.

ASK A... PEDIATRICIAN

What do I need to consider when positioning my baby's crib? You should keep your baby's crib in your bedroom for the first six months to reduce the risk of sudden infant death syndrome (SIDS, see p.31). Also, position the crib so that it's out of direct sunlight and well away from windows, blind cords or strings, radiators, lamps, bookshelves, and hanging wall decorations or pictures.

Is a used mattress OK? Always buy a new mattress, even if your baby's crib is used. It should fit the crib snugly, so your baby can't slip between the crib and mattress. Check that it conforms to current safety standards and does not contain fire-retardant poly-brominated diphenyl ethers (PBDEs).

Moving to a crib Placing your baby's Moses basket in the crib for a few nights makes the transition easier for your baby to deal with.

CHECKLIST

Your baby's crib

If you haven't bought a crib yet, now's a good time to do so. It needs to be strong and sturdy, with no jagged edges or sharp points. Keep in mind:

■ If you are buying a new crib, check that it conforms to current safety standards. The distance between the slats should be no more than $2^3/8$ in (6 cm). Cribs with drop sides are not recommended due to recent safety issues and recalls.

■ It's better to buy a new crib than a used one, but if you get a used crib, avoid getting one which is more than 10 years old or that has been modified or broken. Cribs made before 1986 do not meet current safety standards. Furthermore, cribs made more than 30 years ago may have been finished with poisonous lead-containing paint, and so the paint would need to be stripped and the crib repainted. Make sure you buy a new mattress, even if your crib is used. The mattress should fit the crib snugly.

■ A teething rail is a protective covering—usually made of clear, nontoxic plastic—that lines the side rails of the crib. This helps to protect your baby's gums (and the crib) once she's teething and starts to chew.

■ When assembling, check that all screws and bolts are secure, so there is no danger of it collapsing. Also, badly installed screws could scratch your baby or even work themselves loose and pose a choking risk.

9 weeks

113

Post-baby health issues

If you can't seem to shake off the baby blues and still feel low or upset, it's possible that you're experiencing postpartum depression.

Long-lasting blues If you are still feeling upset, teary, or depressed, don't hesitate to ask your health professionals for advice.

The baby blues affect most moms about three days after the birth of their babies as a result of hormonal changes wreaking havoc on their emotions (see "Ask a… doctor," p.49). The baby blues should normally ease within a couple of weeks, so if you continue to feel low or exhausted, you may be experiencing postpartum depression (PPD).

What is PPD? Feeling distressed as the weeks go by, having a sense that other moms are managing when you are not, or becoming low during your baby's first year means it's likely you're suffering from postpartum depression. PPD can last for a few weeks or for months—but the sooner you get professional help, the more quickly you are likely to recover.

Typical signs of PPD include:
- feeling exhausted even when you've just woken up
- crying often; feeling empty and sad
- guilt and shame that you're not happy or don't love your baby enough
- being overly anxious in general or fearful for your baby
- feeling scared to be alone or go out.

One or two moms in every ten will suffer from postpartum depression. The important thing is to recognize that you aren't well and to get help as soon as possible. Your pediatrician and ob/gyn will recognize your situation and know how to get you help, often linking you into local services to support you. Your doctor may recommend medication, such as antidepressants, and may refer you for counseling.

Postpartum psychosis A very few women (about 1–3 in 1,000) develop a condition called postpartum psychosis, symptoms of which include severe depression, delusions (believing everyone is conspiring against them or they or others are possessed), hallucinations, and an inability to think clearly. It is essential if you feel this way to visit your doctor. Medication, such as antidepressants or antipsychotics, and therapy mean postpartum psychosis can usually be treated in a few weeks.

POST-BABY HORMONAL CHANGES

The pregnancy hormone relaxin softens collagen and elastin in the tissues. It remains in your body for up to five months after birth. If you are breast-feeding, prolactin, the hormone that produces milk, has a similar effect. As a result, your gums may soften and be prone to bleeding, which can lead to tooth decay. See your dentist to have your teeth cleaned and the state of your oral health assessed.

After pregnancy, hair follicles enter a "resting phase," causing excess hair loss (molting). This occurs any time between the 6th and 30th weeks after birth. Once your hormones return to pre-pregnancy levels, molting stops and your hair will regrow.

Breast-feeding affects your bones. Moms lose 3–5 percent of their bone mass while breast-feeding, although this is recovered within six months of your periods restarting or weaning your baby from the breast. This won't have any bad effects; in fact, breast-feeding prevents osteoporosis (thinning of the bones) in later life, but breast-feeding moms do need plenty of calcium in their diet—roughly 1,000 mg per day.

Oral care Cleaning and flossing fastidiously will help to protect your teeth and gums.

Embracing your wider family

Cherish your relationships with your extended family. They'll provide a support system for you and your baby for many years to come.

Over the past couple of months, you may have seen more of your relatives than ever before, as they flock to admire the new addition to the family and celebrate her birth with you. No matter how independent you have been until now, not relying on extended family, and maybe only meeting on special occasions, it is all about to change. You may already have found that your bond with your own parents is strengthened. Now you may realize how important other family members will be in your baby's life. The bond your baby develops with her relatives—close and distant— will enrich her life on every level.

Try to encourage these relationships and create frequent opportunities for visits. Relations can become strained when you have conflicting views on taking care of your baby, and you may be the recipient of plenty of unsolicited advice. Well-meaning family members, however, can be gently encouraged to respect your ideas and approach, even if they don't agree. Allowing them to establish a loving relationship with your baby is the most important thing.

If you are a single mom, your family will be more valuable than ever, for support and guidance, as well as love. It's hard raising a child on your own. You may feel you lack opportunities to talk about your baby's development or milestones, or even your worries. It can be a pleasure to share your baby's milestones with your family, since they also love her and are proud of her.

Staying close A strong bond with your extended family will enrich your baby's life.

Distracted baby

Your baby is fascinated by everything that's going on around her, and attracting her attention while feeding and changing may be difficult.

It's easy for your baby's attention to be drawn elsewhere at the moment, which could be a problem when you are trying to feed her. If she constantly turns her head while feeding and you are struggling to keep her on your breast, you might need to feed her in a quiet room that offers fewer distractions.

Turn off the TV when you are nursing, and talk to her quietly so that her focus remains on you—not what's going on around her. Cradle her head with your free hand to keep her in the correct position, and gently but firmly replace her if she turns her head away. Try to establish feeding times when she is genuinely hungry, and will want a good, long feeding. If she's snacking or feeding for comfort, she may lose interest, and you may find yourself putting her back to your breast over and over again.

You'll need to make sure your baby is on a safe surface when you change her clothes or her diaper, since she may wiggle and roll herself around in order to see what's going on elsewhere. Your baby may also resist being changed because her interest is somewhere else. Try to engage her by making diaper-changing time a bit more interesting: hang a mobile over her changing table, or fasten a rattle on her wrist, so that she has something to look at while you clean and change her. Talk to her, tickle her, and work fast so that you don't have to deal with the wiggling for long!

115

YOUR BABY IS 9 WEEKS AND 4 DAYS

Seeing in color

Your baby can now discern a variety of colors and is also starting to develop depth perception, marking the progression to seeing in 3D.

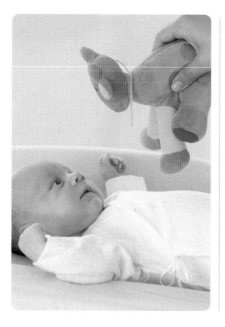

Her fascination with and ability to see a range of colors means that your baby will instinctively reach for toys—or even your T-shirt—if it's vivid enough to catch her attention. She is especially attracted to primary colors and will enjoy looking at pictures that are bold and highly contrasting.

Depth perception will not be fully developed for another four months (usually at least six months), but as her brain and her coordination develop, she'll be able to discern an object's position, size, and shape. This will eventually allow her to successfully reach out and grasp it. She'll also be

Colorful toys Fun toys in eye-popping shades grab your baby's attention instantly.

able to judge whether objects are closer or farther away than others. Before this can happen, her eyes have to be able to work together. What your baby can see now are individual features on your face, so you may find her reaching out to touch your mouth or eyes.

You'll notice your baby's depth perception slowly improving. Her eyes move together but aren't always coordinated in the early weeks, so it takes a while for her to see the world as a complete picture.

Depth perception will eventually help to keep her safe by preventing her from walking off the edge of the porch, for example, but you cannot rely on it to keep her safe since her curiosity will overcome almost anything.

YOUR BABY IS 9 WEEKS AND 5 DAYS

Hygiene and allergies

Good hygiene prevents illness but don't go overboard with the antibacterial wipes: some contact with germs is important for your baby.

Overuse of antibacterial cleaning products has now been linked with a higher incidence of allergies—probably because a baby's immune system will not be given the opportunity to develop properly without having things to fight. Allergies are a sign of a dysfunctional immune system, and anything that hampers its development in baby- and childhood could make your baby more susceptible. The general rule should be to keep things clean, rather than sterile.

This will ensure that your baby's environment is safe from harmful germs, yet suitable to allow her immune system to develop properly.

Hot water and ordinary bars of soap are perfectly adequate for cleaning your baby's toys (although you may choose to sterilize them until she is about six months old). Stick with natural cleaners wherever possible around the house. Filling your baby's environment with a host of chemical cleaners can also

trigger an allergic response, as well as overload her sensitive system. Normal cleaning products, soap, and water will be enough to keep your house clean and fresh the natural way.

Don't worry about a little dust settling; studies have found that early exposure to dust mites can prevent allergies to them, and it will take the pressure to clean off you. The same goes for pet dander (see also "Pets and your baby," p.128).

Relationship roles

Your lives have changed dramatically and you may feel unsettled and excited by the altered dynamics of your relationship.

No matter how much you adore your baby, if you worked before her birth you may feel baffled by how much your life has changed, and resentful that your partner is able to go out to work while you take on her day-to-day care. Your career may be on hold and, although it may make financial sense for you to stay at home until your baby is older, you may worry about taking time off from your career and the effect on your progress in the future.

What's more, because you're at home, it probably makes sense for you to take on more of the domestic chores. This can cause an imbalance in the way you perceive your relationship—and the equality within it. In addition, if you're not working, you may not enjoy the same financial independence, which can be difficult to adjust to.

It is important to establish roles. You may go back to work at some stage, and taking on the bulk of household labor and child care now may create an unsustainable scenario. Figure out a fair division of labor so that you both feel you are sharing the load. Partners can be unaware just how difficult life is with a young baby, and that days can pass without anything other than baby care being done. Talk about money, and how you can both have equal access to it. Express how you are feeling, so that grievances can be worked out before they become intransigent problems.

ASK A... DOCTOR

I had a cesarean and although the incision has healed, I'm still feeling low and tired. How long will it be before I'm back to normal? Every woman recovers from a cesarean birth differently, and although the visible scars may heal within six weeks, some women will take up to six months to regain their full energy. It's also quite common for numb areas on your skin to persist many months after the surgery. Try to take each day as it comes, as with any new mom, and rest if you feel tired. If you experience any pain in the pelvic area, or you feel low and tired, talk to your doctor: there may be a reason (such as anemia or postpartum depression) which can be treated.

I've noticed some very slight spotting of blood following intercourse. Should I be worried? Sometimes, just the manipulation of the cervix, which is still healing, or orgasm (which makes the uterus contract) can cause light spotting. It could also be related to hormonal fluctuations, or if you are using contraception, may be linked to the use of birth control pills. Occasionally, small skin tags form at the site of tears or incisions, which can bleed when rubbed against. Certain infections, such as chlamydia, can also cause spotting after sex. If you have any bleeding after sex, make an appointment to see your doctor.

Feeling valued It's important that you both feel that you are sharing the responsibilities of family life as fairly as you can, even though your roles may have changed.

9 weeks

SPOTLIGHT ON...
Planning child care

Going back to work may feel a lifetime away, but it's important that, sooner rather than later, you think about who will take care of your baby when you return to work. Deciding on the right child-care strategy is not something you want to feel rushed into.

The best way to begin your search is to draw up a shortlist by word of mouth—ask friends to recommend day-care centers, nanny agencies, and babysitters in your area. When you have your short list, you can then check any inspection reports, which are sometimes available online, to whittle it down. Your baby's well-being is paramount above all other factors. Also, child care may be your single biggest expense once you go back to work, so it's vital to get it right.

Nannies Hiring a nanny means you'll have someone to care for your baby in your own home. Use a reputable agency and interview each nanny on your shortlist. Have a list of questions ready, covering such topics as how they handle discipline and what kinds of games they would play with your baby. If you need them to be able to drive, ask about that too. Start by drawing up a full job description, describing every aspect of your baby's day-to-day care—and what you'd like to see happening in the future. Talk these through with each interviewee to make sure that her working practices, beliefs, ideas, and ethics match your own.

Make sure that you interview nannies with your baby, and watch how they interact. You'll want someone who is interested, playful, and affectionate with your baby. Check references and ensure that she has emergency first-aid training. Make sure she's licensed or accredited, do a thorough background check to ensure that she can safely work with children, and talk through issues such as nutrition, exercise, stimulation, and TV watching. Ask for an example of a daily routine, and assess how flexible she might be. If she has to leave on time every evening, you might find that that won't work for you. It's also worth asking where she sees herself in five years' time. If you are hoping for continuity over the coming years, it would be good to know now if she is planning to move to Australia!

You should draw up a formal contract of employment and meet your legal obligations as an employer, such as paying tax and making Canada Pension Plan and EI contributions.

Home day care A caregiver takes care of your baby in her home, probably along with several other children. Depending on the number and age of the children they care for, they may not be licensed. Once again, always take time to visit prospective caregivers in their own environment, and bring along your baby to see how she fits in. You'll need to go through all of the issues that you would discuss with a nanny, and ensure that your caregiver has plenty of experience with babies and very young children. Is the house clean and

Choosing a babysitter Your prospective babysitter should have plenty of experience with taking care of young babies and juggling their needs with those of older children in her care.

welcoming, with lots of suitable toys and books, and space to play outside? Is there a smoker in the house? Or a lot of TVs? Is your caregiver flexible? You don't want to end up with extra charges when you are running a little late. Consider the number of children she has in her care, and ask how she can balance the needs of differently aged children. A young baby needs a great deal of individual care, and you need to be certain that she'll get it. If both you and your baby feel comfortable in the caregiver's home, chances are your baby will be happy there.

Day-care center Day-care centers provide child care from three months old (although some take babies from as young as six weeks). Visit every day-care center on your list to get a feel for whether or not it has a loving atmosphere and an ethos compatible with your own. Ask about staff turnover, since long-serving staff suggests a happy, supportive environment. (For more tips on choosing a day-care center, see box, right.) The best day-care centers have long waiting lists, so it's never too early to start looking.

Other alternatives If a nanny, home day care, or day-care center doesn't seem right for you, brainstorm to see if you can find a creative solution. You may be able to plan your schedule so that both you and your partner can take on some of the child care, and get in extra help on the days you can't. You may decide to work at home, and try to juggle work and your baby—perhaps with the support of an au pair or a babysitter. An au pair is not permitted to have continuous sole charge of children under the age of two, but can help around the house or supervise older children. Ideally, use a recognized, approved au pair agency.

Sometimes grandparents are happy to step in and take care of children, but this is an arrangement that should be treated with respect, and carefully

Safe hands Knowing your baby's caregiver means you'll worry less about leaving her.

discussed in advance. Payment may not be necessary, but you should be flexible and also feel confident that your approach to child care is honored. It can work beautifully when you establish good communication. Equally, however, it can lead to resentment on both sides, so tread cautiously.

Finally, you may want to consider working part-time, or changing your hours so that child care is less frequently required; for example, if you can work from seven until three every day, and your partner takes over the early-morning care, you may be able to get away with just five hours of care a few days a week. Talk through the different scenarios with your partner, and make sure you are both in agreement. If you are a single mom, make sure that you have some backup support so that your baby will be cared for when you are running late, or she or your caregiver is sick. Being solely responsible for a baby can be overwhelming at times, so take any offers to help you out when you just can't be there for her.

CHECKLIST

Choosing day care

When selecting a day-care center, above all else, trust your instincts. If you see happy babies and warm, caring staff, you are probably on the right track. If it feels good, it may be right! Focus on centers with:

■ A high staff-to-child ratio. There are laws about the number of little ones that can be cared for by each responsible adult; you are looking for better-than-average ratios.

■ An arrangement in which younger and older children are separated, so babies get the right care without the distractions of older children.

■ A strong, fair discipline policy that matches your own beliefs.

■ Permanent staff members with good first-aid experience, and experience dealing with childhood illnesses and providing medical attention. If your baby has health concerns, check that caregivers can manage them effectively.

■ Well-trained, experienced staff who constantly update their knowledge, and understand child nutrition and development, and common issues of childhood.

■ Warm, loving staff with affection for and interest in the children.

■ A designated staff member for every child, to ensure that individual needs are met.

■ A sound policy and clear evidence of safety and security.

■ A good selection of clean, neat toys, and age-appropriate books.

■ Plenty of opportunities for your baby to be stimulated.

■ A quiet place for babies to sleep and a clean place for them to be fed.

■ A policy of updating parents daily on their babies' progress.

■ A good open-door policy, so you can visit at any time.

9 weeks

119

10 weeks

SINCE BABIES SLEEP ON THEIR BACKS, THEY NEED "TUMMY TIME" TO DEVELOP UPPER BODY STRENGTH

When something interesting, like a toy, catches your baby's attention, she will reach out for it. Although she won't yet be able to target objects accurately, this is the beginning of hand–eye coordination. Your baby is now more social, and may be starting to "talk" by cooing and gurgling.

Your baby's sleep cycle

Just when you think you've got your baby to sleep, she stirs and wakes up. What's happening as your little one settles down to rest?

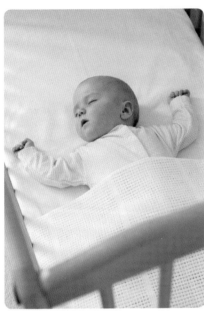

Sweet dreams Calming bedtime activities help to settle your baby down to sleep.

Babies, just like adults, experience two different types of sleep: deep sleep or "NREM" (non-rapid eye movement) and light sleep or "REM" (rapid eye movement). In deep NREM sleep, the body and mind are quiet, breathing is shallow, and limbs are relaxed and loose. In light REM sleep, the eyes move under the eyelids and the brain is more active, which is when dreams occur.

Sleep and brain activity Adults are able to fall into a deep sleep within minutes of going to bed, if they are tired and relaxed. Over an eight-hour night, adults typically spend 75 percent of the time in deep NREM sleep and 25 percent in light REM sleep, which occurs in cycles throughout the night. In the first few months of life, babies sleep for about 18 hours a day, half of which appears to be spent in light REM sleep. One theory is that lots of REM sleep is needed during the steep learning and growth curve of early life, to allow the brain to develop new and complex interconnections. Blood flow to the brain nearly doubles during REM sleep, when the brain is still active—even though your baby appears to be at rest. During REM sleep, your baby may be restless, with fluttering eyelids, facial movements, and her arms and legs may twitch and move, too.

Your baby is unlikely to adopt any kind of regular sleep pattern with identifiable NREM/REM cycles until about 20 weeks. At this point, she'll probably spend about 35 percent of her sleeping time in light REM sleep and 65 percent in deep NREM sleep.

What to do when If possible, even at this early age, it's a good idea to try to put your baby down just before she actually drifts into light sleep, so that she starts getting used to settling herself down. Once she drifts off, try to avoid moving her from one place to another, since she's likely to wake instantly.

If she looks as though she is about to wake up, try to resist the temptation to start patting her on the back or talking to her—chances are, you'll only disturb her. Leave her quietly, and she'll be more likely to drift back to sleep. When you're sharing a room, she'll be reassured by your presence anyway.

As your baby grows older and enjoys longer REM sleep cycles, she should sleep more soundly during these periods and be less likely to wake so readily.

ASK A... PEDIATRICIAN

Does my baby dream? There is evidence to suggest that babies not only dream from the moment they are born, but have been doing so for several months in the uterus. Dreams take place during REM sleep (see left), when your baby isn't sleeping quite so deeply and her brain is active, and because she has so many more hours of this type of sleep than we do, she'll be dreaming frequently. Her dreams will usually be based around her experiences of the day, which consolidates learning, emotions, and development. She may have upsetting dreams from time to time, but will be calmed by your soothing voice.

When can I sleep train my baby? Your baby will sleep as much as she needs to, whenever she needs to, and won't be ready to sleep through the night without a feeding for some weeks. Sleep-training techniques aren't generally started until babies are several months old, and involve encouraging them to sleep longer at night with minimal attention from their parents. This doesn't mean letting them cry, but helping them feel safe enough to fall asleep, knowing that mom and dad are close by. But it's not too early to adopt a calming bedtime routine, such as a bath, feeding, and a story or lullaby, so that your baby begins to associate this soothing sequence of events with drifting off to sleep.

10 weeks

121

Target practice

Your baby's hand–eye coordination is developing fast. She is working hard to get her arms and legs to go where she wants.

ASK A... PEDIATRICIAN

Why is my baby wheezing? This suggests a narrowing of the airways, but it is often difficult to tell where. Babies have narrow airways anyway, so wheezing isn't rare. Colds are the most common cause, but there are others, in particular bronchiolitis (see p.408), which is more serious. If your baby's wheezing persists, or she seems sick, has a fever, refuses feedings, or is fighting for breath, see your pediatrician immediately.

Until now, chances are that, when your baby batted her baby gym, it was a happy accident of her jerky newborn movements. However, by 10 weeks old, she will have started to realize that, when she hits something, it moves. She is beginning to make the link between cause and effect. Each time she reaches out to a toy, she is supplying important information to her brain about how her muscles and body move. She will now hit and grab with greater meaning.

Lay your baby on her tummy and put a toy a little away from her to encourage her to move for it, which teaches her she can move in order to get something she wants. Help her grasp the toy by placing it in the palm of her hand; her reflex will cause her fingers to tighten around it.

Place your baby under her baby gym and position her so that she can easily reach one or more of the hanging toys. She'll enjoy the experience much more if she is successful some of the time! When she's playing on her back, hold toys within her reach and attract her attention. In the coming months, she will be able to target them accurately and pull them toward her.

Tummy time

It is safest to put your baby to sleep on her back, but she needs dedicated time to lie on her front to strengthen her upper body.

At around 10–11 weeks, your baby will probably be able to lie on her front and attempt to lift her head to look up or to the side. She may begin trying to lift her head by using her forearms to push upward. She won't be pushing up confidently through her arms and hands for another month or two.

This important milestone in her development is the start of the motor skills that will lead to rolling over and, eventually, crawling. It is advisable for babies to have dedicated time to lie on their front when they are alert, since studies show that because babies sleep on their back, tummy time gives her

practice in looking and pushing up. Always stay nearby while your baby is on her front. Her neck muscles are still relatively weak and unable to hold up her head for long, so she may become anxious or distressed if left on her front for too long and will need you to rescue her. Put toys around her to encourage her to reach out and even begin to move (see "Target practice," above). If she objects to spending time on her front on the floor, you could ease her in gently by allowing her to lie on you with her chest on yours while you are on the floor. She's more likely to be happy if she can raise her head to see your smiling face.

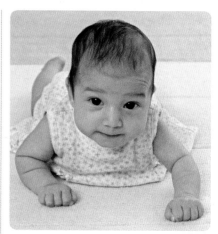

Developing muscles Your baby can probably lift up her head to see what's around her.

Out and about

Your baby can see quite well now and her sight is improving all the time, so give her lots of opportunity to explore the world around her.

Going for a stroll Babies are reassured to see mom from their strollers, as well as the exciting new world around them.

If you haven't used a stroller yet, you can now consider one that allows your baby to sit upright with support. Some strollers are designed to face outward, while other models face inward so that your baby can see you.

Some experts say that inward-facing strollers are best, since they allow your baby to continue bonding with you, learn from your talking and facial expressions, and be comforted by your visible presence. A stroller that faces outward, on the other hand, encourages your baby to look at what's passing her by. If she's daunted by your absence, talk to her as you walk, and reach over and stroke her face to remind her you are there. Occasionally, crouch down in front of the stroller and have a reassuring little chat. She's learning information about speech, content,

tone and rhythm as you talk, even though she can't understand the meaning of the words.

Stay safe Always fasten your baby's harness carefully, and check that she is comfortably upright, not slouched forward. Adjusting her bottom so that it is a little farther forward should help her to sink back in comfort. You may also want to invest in a headrest or neck support, to make her feel more secure. A good stroller will fully recline so that you can gently ease her down, ideally without waking her if she's asleep. Don't forget to put the brake on whenever you stop, even if there is no obvious incline. Accidents can and do happen. Avoid hanging heavy bags on the handle of the stroller; it can easily topple over. It's best to invest in a stroller that allows

you to store items under her seat, which gives it a good, firm base. Keep in mind that upright collapsible strollers with only one seat position are not appropriate until six months.

For moms of more than one, there are many double (and triple) strollers, some more practical than others. While some parents like the "one-in-front-of-the-other" (tandem) set-up (since it allows them to negotiate tighter spaces), these can be hard to maneuver and require brute force to turn them.

"Twin" strollers tend to be popular because your babies can see, hear, and communicate with one another easily. This form of "entertainment" may be invaluable if an outing takes longer than expected. The drawback to this type of stroller is that its width prohibits some entrances and aisles.

DEVELOPMENT ACTIVITY

Board and fabric books

Brightly colored books with faces of babies and/or animals are perfect for your baby's stage of development, and she will love to gaze at the pictures.

Sturdy board or fabric books are good, since they can often be easily cleaned and can double up as toys for your baby when she wants to entertain herself. Books that have a variety of different textures on their pages will appeal to your baby. Encourage her to reach out and touch them. Make up your own stories as you go, or repeat the name for the object on the page to help her learn.

Bright and fun Books that have a variety of colors and textures will appeal to your baby and keep her occupied.

Reading your baby's cues

Thrashing her legs? Wrinkling her forehead? Knowing what your baby is telling you can help to avoid too many tears being shed.

What do I mean? Sucking his fingers could signal tiredness, hunger, or watchfulness (left).
Winding down Your baby's yawn means that playtime is over and he is ready for a nap (right).

ASK A... PEDIATRICIAN

My baby doesn't pass a stool every day. Is he constipated? Babies' stools can vary, but a change from what is normal for your baby may suggest a problem. Babies can move their bowels anywhere from three times a day to once every other day.

Breast-fed babies tend not to get constipated since breast milk contains the right ingredients to keep the stool soft. Lots of babies strain when having a bowel movement. This is normal. Signs of constipation, however, can include hard, pelletlike stools, straining without producing stool, or painful bowel movements, sometimes with a tiny amount of fresh blood on the diaper due to a small tear in the anus. If bleeding occurs, consult your pediatrician.

Learning to read your baby's physical and facial cues and responding to them is the first precious form of two-way communication between you. As you repeatedly offer her what she wants as soon as you see the signal she gives, your baby learns that her needs will be met without having to resort to crying. She will build up a larger repertoire of cues and gestures to get her message across, and in the coming months will begin to anticipate your response and smile in anticipation. In this way, her communication skills are developing and her trust that you will come when she needs you is becoming established.

Looking for clues In these first weeks and months, your challenge is to learn to read and interpret your baby's cues. You can probably already recognize the different pitch and tone of a cry that means "I'm tired" compared to the one that tells you your baby is hungry. Now it is time to look out for more specific vocal and non-vocal signs. You should watch out for cues such as leg kicking, a reddened face, and fist waving because for your baby these signs or actions may mean she's overstimulated, frustrated, or in need of a diaper change. Look for mannerisms that suggest she's getting tired—perhaps she rubs her eyes, yawns, or puts her fingers in her mouth. Next time you notice these actions starting up, you can be ready to put her down to sleep. As you gain more understanding of your baby's signals, you'll predict ever more quickly what it is she needs.

To play or not to play? Your baby can also give you signals about whether or not she's in the right frame of mind to play, or whether she needs time to unwind quietly on her own. These are known as "withdrawal" and "approach" cues. If your baby becomes still, looks at your face, reaches out to you, moves her arms and legs smoothly, turns her eyes (wide and bright) or head toward you, coos, smiles, babbles, and raises her head, these are classic "approach" signals. She's letting you know she is in the mood for interaction!

If she turns away her head, arches her back, squirms or kicks, pulls away, turns her eyes away from you, wrinkles her forehead, hiccups, or frowns, these are "withdrawal" cues. They are a sign that your baby needs a break or a rest from what is going on. She may want to stop playing, feeding, or even being held. It may be time for a change in activity or even a nap.

Baby massage

Massage can relax and soothe your baby, help to ease the discomfort of gas and colic, and even promote restful sleep.

There are plenty of baby massage classes if you want to learn the right techniques (your doctor may be able to recommend one locally), but you can also use gentle strokes you practice every day as you rub her back to soothe her, or play with her hands or feet. The main goal of baby massage is for you to have fun together, and for your baby to enjoy your loving touch.

Try to choose a time when your baby is relaxed—so not just after a feeding or when she is hungry—and make sure that the room is warm and your baby is lying comfortably on a soft surface. Try stroking her arms and legs firmly to begin, then massage her abdomen lightly in a clockwise direction. Talk to your baby as you massage and watch her cues: if she seems unhappy at any point, stop the massage. Try a mixture of gliding, fluttering, and rotating strokes to see which she likes best.

Legs and feet Start by gently squeezing the thigh, and then rub the ankle and foot.

Your social baby

Your baby is smiling more and may be gurgling and cooing to "talk" to you. Your social baby is emerging.

Becoming social Encourage your baby to be social with grandparents and friends.

You and your partner have the greatest influence on your baby's social development. As you talk with her, wait for her to respond and then react to her. In doing so, you are teaching her how to engage in two-way communication.

Your baby's smiles are now becoming more frequent and you will find that she smiles not just in response to your smile, but even perhaps in response to your voice. She will also begin to smile at other willing adults who might grin at her. These are all signs that your baby is now widening her social network. Spend plenty of time throughout the day having face-to-face time. Look into her eyes, mirror back her expressions, speak and then wait for her reaction.

Around this age, babies become aware of who is familiar and who is a stranger, and may even begin to express preferences for certain people. You can help your baby to feel relaxed around trusted others by ensuring grandparents and friends get lots of cuddling time and opportunities to smile at and coo over her. Babies are also fascinated by other babies and often become mesmerized by another baby's face, perhaps even smiling at it. It will be a while yet (up to two years away) before your baby makes real friendships, but early interaction is good for long-term social capability.

10 weeks

125

11 weeks

A BABY'S MOUTH HAS MORE NERVE ENDINGS PER SQUARE MILLIMETER THAN ANY OTHER BODY AREA

Because your baby's mouth is supersensitive, he explores the world by mouthing anything he can get hold of. Your baby also learns by watching. He has "mirror neurons" in his brain, specialized nerve cells that enable him to imitate the facial expressions and movements of others.

Listen + watch = learn

Everything your baby sees and hears helps her learn how to adapt to her new environment, so what's fun for her is also good brain fodder.

Your baby was born with plenty of brain cells already connected so she could perform essential tasks such as sucking and swallowing right away. In addition, all her senses have been soaking up information from birth onward. Everything she experiences forges connections between brain cells, allowing her to learn. She's also primed to respond to you, copying your facial expressions and making a sound after you've spoken.

Imitating her facial expressions teaches your baby to express her feelings without words. If you imitate her expressions or noises, she learns that others can do what she can do—psychologists believe this plays a crucial role in developing a sense of self, others, and belonging. At 11 weeks of age, your baby is gleaning more and more information about what is going on around her, and creating a detailed picture of her environment. Whether she is watching her siblings dance to music or looking at a light, then turning away from it, myriad nerve impulses fire through her brain as she makes connections between, say, music and movement and light and dark.

Try to make her environment visually stimulating. Although bright colors stand out best at this stage, your choices don't have to be be expensive or elaborate. Put her next to a mirror (as long as she can't break it), or on a warm day, seat her in the shade beside a brightly colored paper windmill that spins in the breeze.

Mirror play Your baby will be fascinated by her own reflection in a mirror.

Time out as a family

A family outing can be a welcome change of scene and gives your baby the experience of different environments.

Now that your baby is increasingly interested in the sights and sounds around her, you may find a family outing is both refreshing for you while providing her with new sensations and stimuli for learning.

Seek out some family-friendly experiences to share—perhaps your baby is ready for her first visit to the countryside, to begin baby-swimming lessons with you, or visit her grandparents' home and backyard. Try to keep car journeys relatively short on these early trips so that she doesn't spend too much time in the car and is ready and in the right mood to enjoy her day out. Look for places that will give her new smells, sights, and sounds. She may have lots of fun watching you have a picnic and enjoy lying with you on a blanket under some trees watching the pattern of leaves and branches moving. Pushing her through the park or even along a quiet street offers new experiences for her senses that will truly fascinate her.

What's more, whenever you do things together as a family, at home or away, you are building up a reserve of shared memories and stories to tell relatives, especially details of your baby's cute or amusing reactions to new experiences. You are also beginning a tradition of family activities that will become a positive habit as the years pass.

Take plenty of photographs of these early experiences. As your child grows older, she will love to look through them and see what she did as a baby.

Pets and your baby

It's not only your own pets that you need to be careful about, but also friends' and family's animals, too.

It will still be a while before your child is old enough to build relationships with pets. In time, a sense of responsibility can be instilled in your baby regarding caring for pets, but for now, you should be aware of the fact that even the best-trained animals can become unpredictable, and with a vulnerable baby around, it is important never to take anything for granted between your baby and your pet.

Animals, and dogs in particular, can become jealous of the new kid on the block. If you have a dog, try to give him special attention when you can, so that he doesn't feel neglected. Make sure your dog still gets his routine walks and meals at normal times so that the baby's presence doesn't disrupt his life too much. Don't let the dog go upstairs if this is where your baby sleeps; install a stair gate if necessary to keep him away.

Now that your baby is almost three months old, she has grown used to being able to grab and pull the objects she can reach. When this is a pet's tail or ear, she risks a warning shot from the offended animal—usually a nip from a dog or a bite or scratch from a cat. For this reason, never leave your baby unattended around your pets, and keep the pets out of the room while your baby is free to play. Under no circumstances should any pet be allowed to sleep in your baby's bed. Cats, in particular, may go looking for warmth in a crib (or a carriage), which makes them especially dangerous. Always use a cat net to prevent this.

Health-wise, make sure your pets are regularly immunized and kept worm- and flea-free. Pets, especially puppies and kittens, may carry parasites that cause toxicariasis, so always maintain proper hygiene to minimize the risk of infection. Never allow either cats or dogs to lick your baby, especially on the face. If you're visiting friends who have pets, all the same precautions apply—keep your baby safe and don't let her out of sight.

DEVELOPMENT ACTIVITY

Dancing

Do you have a favorite song that you love to dance to? If so, why not make this song the anthem of a regular activity that you or your partner can share with your baby? Put on the favorite song, hold your baby securely, and sway with her to the music. You can make the movements rhythmic and gentle or a little bolder as the music dictates, as long as your baby is safe. She will love the feeling of being moved around in her daddy's strong arms, and she may even chuckle as you move around with her.

In time, she will learn to associate the music with a positive experience with Daddy or Mommy, and hearing it will make her feel good, even when you are out at work.

Song and dance Babies usually love being rocked to music—and at this age, they won't be embarrassed by your dancing!

CHECKLIST

Pet safety

■ If you own a cat, buy a cat net to cover the baby's crib and always use it.
■ No matter how trustworthy you think your dog or cat is, don't leave them unattended with your baby: the slightest movement or baby swipe could cause the animal to lash out.
■ Wash your hands after handling pet food or pet bowls to reduce the risk of spreading pet-food-related diseases, such as salmonella infection. Also, wash your pet's food and water bowls in a separate sink or bucket.
■ Reptiles are associated with a high incidence of salmonella infection which can be caught by handling them. Some experts recommend that they should not be kept as pets if children are under five years old.

Exploring by mouth

Your baby's mouth and lips are very sensitive, full of nerve endings and taste buds to give her information on flavor, texture, and consistency.

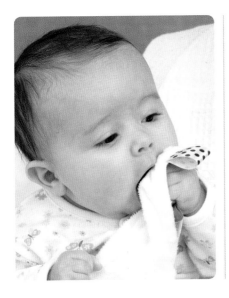

Your baby will by now be putting her fingers into her mouth and trying to grasp objects and bring them up to her mouth. She will enjoy exploring each item, discovering its taste, its feel, and the resistance to pressure as she bites down. She will probably go on exploring things by mouth until she's at least two years old or even longer.

Mouthing helps her to practice moving her tongue, lips, and jaw so that, over the coming months, she gains finer motor control of each. This will aid speech development, chewing, and swallowing.

Exploring her world Your baby will mouth objects to get a sense of their feel and taste.

Your baby will be indiscriminate about what she puts in her mouth, so just make sure that there's nothing within her reach you wouldn't want her to chew on. There are plenty of toys available that are specially designed for babies to chew—even cloth books these days often have hard, rubber edges that are perfect for your baby to get her gums into. Teething rings are good too, especially when they double as noisy rattles. They're narrow, too, so they're easy for tiny hands to hold.

You might find that your baby enjoys sucking on the corner of a soft toy or burp cloth—babies often do this for comfort, as a sort of alternative pacifier.

Caring for your baby's skin

Babies often suffer from dry skin, bumps, and rashes, so it's important to treat her skin gently and ensure that she's comfortable.

Babies' skin is thinner, more sensitive, and less oily than adults' skin, which makes it particularly prone to drying out, especially during winter when the air indoors can be dry and overheated.

If your baby's skin is dry, try not to bathe her too often (once every 3–4 days is fine, sponge bathing at other times) and avoid using soap or bubble baths. You can simply use plain warm water only, or just a drop of organic or hypo-allergenic baby bath if necessary. When you do bathe her, don't leave her in the water for too long, since this can

dry out her skin more. After a bath, pat her dry and apply a little hypo-allergenic moisturizer or emollient cream. Alternatively, if you prefer to go down the natural route, rub in a little warmed olive or grapeseed oil.

Keep in mind that laundry detergent residues can cause irritation, so use a baby-friendly detergent and fabric softener, and put her clothes through an extra rinse cycle. To help prevent skin irritation, avoid dressing your baby in wool or scratchy fibers, and synthetics such as nylon.

Tiny pimples on your baby's face are known as neonatal acne, which is common and can appear at any time between two weeks and six months. Even if this looks unsightly, leave it alone, or you risk making it worse. The condition will clear up on its own. If your baby has a bright red rash around her neck, armpits, or diaper area, she may have heat rash, especially if the weather is hot. Remove clothing to allow air to circulate and cool her skin. Sometimes a red rash is a sign of thrush (see p.405), which your pediatrician can confirm.

Keeping track

Your baby's weight gain is probably fairly steady now, but it's still reassuring to get her weighed at the pediatrician's office every so often.

Although every baby is different, most gain an average of approximately 6–8 oz (120–200 g) each week until they are about six months old. By this age, they have usually doubled their birthweight, and weight gain gradually slows down.

Breast-fed babies tend to grow more rapidly than formula-fed babies for around the first three months, but then they grow more slowly and, by the time they are 12 months old, breast-fed babies are on average just over 1 lb (half a kilo) lighter than formula-fed babies.

You'll have plenty of appointments at the pediatrician's office during the early months to find out your baby's weight and have it plotted on her growth chart. If she is following roughly the same percentile line, her rate of growth is perfectly healthy. Growth spurts or bouts of illness may lead her to jump up or down to the next percentile occasionally, but what you are looking for is a fairly regular pattern of growth overall. If your baby is doing well, the general advice is to get her weighed at

the pediatrician's office approximately once a month.

If your baby's weight gain does dip, or increase, significantly over an extended period of time, talk to your doctor. Weight variations can be due to a variety of reasons and she will be able to assess whether there is a problem. You may be asked to come into the office between regular appointments for weigh-ins, particularly if your baby doesn't seem to be gaining enough weight.

Toward sitting

Your baby's neck muscles are probably strong enough to support the weight of her head for a few seconds now.

Stronger neck muscles Carrying your baby so that he can look over your shoulder encourages him to lift his head and look around.

Being able to sit upright requires strength and balance. Your baby needs to be able to support her neck and back, and figure out how to use her legs to steady herself and her arms to stop herself from toppling forward—chances are that it won't all come together until she is about seven months old, but she can certainly start to practice.

Even if your baby can perform confident push-ups, she will need to develop greater neck stability for sitting. Tummy time is great for this, as is carrying her on your shoulder, where she can lift her head to look behind you.

We all need core stability for a strong back. You can help your baby develop this strength by propping her up in a

reclined sitting position. Make sure she is well cushioned at the back and sides so that, if she topples over, she doesn't hurt herself. Also, never leave your baby propped up and unattended. Be aware that she will easily tire of being in this position, so move her onto her back again as soon as she begins to show signs of discomfort.

Tummy time (see p.122) is perfect for strengthening baby arms, so try to make sure you put her on her tummy for a brief period each day.

Once your baby is strong enough to hold her head securely for prolonged periods, getting the balance right is really just a matter of practice—and lots of cushions to fall into.

Traveling with a young baby

Your baby's stronger now and she's also very adaptable, so if you've been thinking about going away, this could be a good time. With a little advance planning, there's no reason why you shouldn't all enjoy a relaxing, hassle-free break.

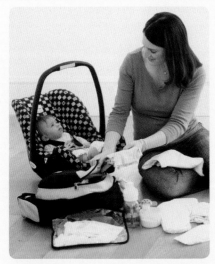

Packing Being prepared for every eventuality is the key to successful traveling with a baby.

Most new parents prefer to avoid traveling with a young baby, simply because it's enough to deal with attending to a newborn's needs at home, let alone while traveling or on vacation. However, now that your baby is almost three months old, she should be quite a good traveler. She's less fragile than she was and probably won't care too much where she sleeps. Also, she's still too young to have a set routine yet, so a little disruption to your usual schedule shouldn't disturb her too much.

Planning ahead If you intend to stay in a hotel and your baby sleeps in a crib, you'll either need to take your own travel crib, or reserve a crib for your room. If you are renting a car at your destination, it's important to reserve an infant seat when you make the reservation. If you're traveling internationally, you'll also need to have your baby's passport. If you plan to travel to a country where vaccinations are needed, check with your pediatrician to find out if your baby is old enough to have them. Some, such as yellow fever, are not safe for babies under six months.

Traveling by car In some respects, car trips are the most straightforward—if you have plenty of trunk capacity—because you can simply load up and take everything you need with you. It's a good idea to put in window shades to protect your baby's eyes and skin from bright sun. Hats and outdoor clothing should be removed when your baby is in the car. Make sure that the car seat is safely installed in the back seat and that the seat belts are properly threaded. If you have a long trip ahead of you, try to avoid traveling at rush hour, and consider driving at night, when your baby is most likely to sleep and go a bit longer between feedings.

ASK A... PEDIATRICIAN

When is it safe for my baby to fly?
It's safe from two days old but you're unlikely to fly with her so early. Many airlines suggest you wait until she is two weeks' old, so confirm with your airline see if this is the case. If you've had a cesarean, you will be unable to fly until 10 days after the birth. It's advisable to check with your airline to find out their policy.

Traveling by plane Check your airline's baggage policies before you travel. Diapers, creams, baby clothing, formula, feeding equipment, and other necessities add a lot of extra weight, and if you're not paying for an extra seat for your baby, you may find it worthwhile to book extra allowances in advance, rather than pay charges for being over your weight limit. If you can, try to weigh your luggage and carry-on before you go to make sure you're not over the limit.

You are not limited by the 3.4-ounce (100 ml) rule for liquids when bringing formula, breast milk, or juice for your baby in your carry-on luggage. You'll need to declare it for inspection at airport security. The contents of your container may be tested for explosives, but you won't be asked to taste it.

You can often take your baby in her stroller all the way to the plane door, at which point you'll need to collapse it so it can be taken to the hold. Or you can use a baby carrier.

Give your baby a feeding during take-off and landing: swallowing will help prevent ear discomfort due to changes in cabin pressure. Some planes have changing tables in the bathrooms and even special carry cribs so your baby can sleep during the flight.

MALARIA

The WHO advises against taking infants to areas with malaria. If you decide to go, seek expert medical advice on how best to protect your baby and yourself, especially if you are breast-feeding. Seek immediate medical help if your baby develops a fever during or after a trip to a malaria region, even if you have taken all the precautions.

---

11 weeks

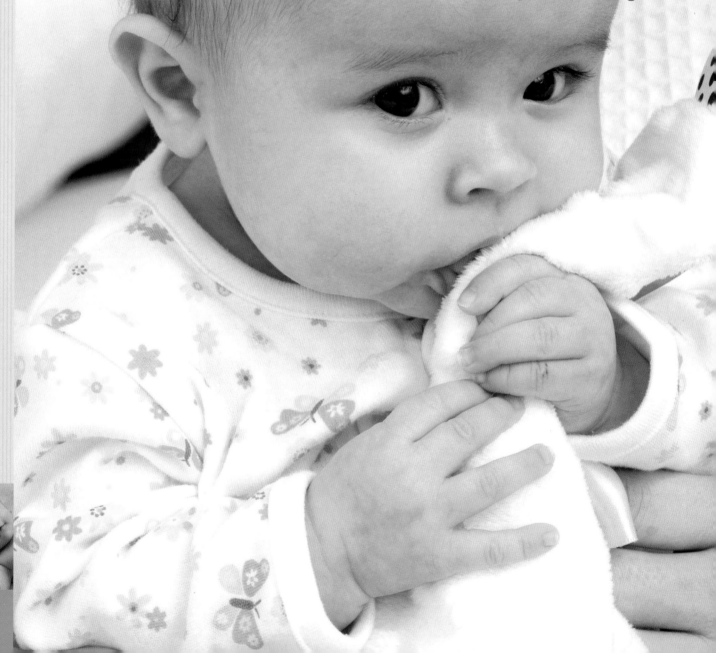

12 weeks

CHARACTER TRAITS PRESENT FROM BIRTH ARE PART OF WHAT MAKES UP YOUR BABY'S PERSONALITY

Your baby's eyes now work better together and vision is becoming more three dimensional. Her muscles are stronger, and she may be surprised to find that she can flip from tummy to back. She likes to kick, which strengthens her leg muscles in preparation for crawling and walking.

Another growth spurt

Your baby's due for a second growth spurt at around three months, so prepare for another feeding frenzy—and a restless night or two.

Supply and demand Your baby's frequent demands for milk are nature's way of making your body step up its milk production.

Six weeks ago, when your baby probably went through her last growth spurt (see p.93), you may remember spending long hours breast-feeding or giving her more formula to meet her increased appetite. You may also remember her being more restless, or sleeping more than normal —classic signs of a growth spurt, and tricky to deal with the first time around.

However, now you're more settled, the three-month spurt shouldn't come as such a surprise. Your baby may demand food as frequently as every two hours for a few days, which can be exhausting for you, but there's no fighting it, so as much as you can, try to go with the flow. If you're breast-feeding, stock up on healthy snacks, drink plenty of water, get a good book to read while nursing,

and prepare to be in demand for a while. Your body will increase milk production to meet her needs.

Formula feeding You may need to make up an extra bottle for your baby during the day, or increase the quantity of each bottle by 1 oz (30 ml). Be guided by your baby's appetite and be careful not to overfeed her. Your baby shouldn't have more than 5 fl oz (150 ml) of milk per 2.2 lbs (1 kg) of weight per day. So, if your baby weighs 13 lb 3 oz (6 kg), she shouldn't have more than 30 fl oz (900 ml)

over 24 hours. Keep some emergency cans of formula in your home, which can provide a good backup, too.

Sleeping You may find your baby sleeps more during the day and is restless at night, perhaps waking up more than usual. Or she may wake up earlier from naps because she's hungry. This sleep disruption may last a couple of days to a week but it will pass, and your baby's sleep patterns should return to normal, so try to rest when your baby sleeps to get you through this period.

TWINS

Dealing with growth spurts

To have two babies going through a growth spurt at the same time or one after another is utterly exhausting. Routines tend to be disrupted, so one baby may wake frequently for feedings (that is, has entered her growth spurt), while the other doesn't. To relieve the burden, express some breast milk so that someone else can give the baby who is going through a growth spurt an extra feeding.

Alternatively, when the twin demanding extra wakes to be fed, you wake the other one, too, even if it's for a smaller feeding. Many mothers find this simply means the less hungry baby eats little and often, but is generally perfectly happy. However, once the growth spurt is over, you may find that you have established a routine of frequent feeding in both babies that you then have to break.

Most importantly, sleep when your babies sleep, and enlist the help of friends and family to keep the rest of the household running smoothly.

Twice the work To feed two babies as they each experience a growth spurt will require plenty of patience on your part.

YOUR BABY IS 12 WEEKS AND 1 DAY

Looking farther afield

Everything your baby sees is new and exciting to her, and she'll begin to focus intently on objects that are farther away.

Your baby will be fascinated by mobiles, murals, and pictures on the wall, her older siblings and parents, and the family cat! By three months, her eyes are increasingly coordinated, and are working well together. She will not look quite so cross-eyed. She can also track an object with much smoother eye motions, as long as it's not moving too fast. Her depth perception is also improving, as the nerve cells in her eyes and brain mature, and her world is becoming more three-dimensional. Her distance vision is also beginning to develop, and she can now make out the shape of your face when you enter a room; in fact, you'll notice her watching things that are several feet away.

Giving your baby plenty of things to focus on and watch will stimulate her vision and entertain her. Hold her turned outward so she has a chance to see what's going on around her, and point things out to her. Call her from the other side of the room, and watch her delight when she makes out your familiar face. Shake noisy toys a little farther away than usual, so that she will turn and watch.

Up to around 12 weeks, many babies occasionally look cross-eyed as their vision develops. This is a normal phase of growing and nothing to be worried about. If your child continues to have crossed eyes after three months, you should tell your doctor. She may have a condition called strabismus, which should be diagnosed and treated in order to avoid vision problems later on.

YOUR BABY IS 12 WEEKS AND 2 DAYS

Doing the flip

Your baby may be about to flip over from tummy to back. Watch out! The acrobatics could soon begin…

Rolling over By three months, your baby's movements will become smoother. She may lift her head and shoulders high, perhaps to roll over and get closer to you or investigate a toy.

Tummy time (see p.122) helps your baby strengthen the muscles she uses to roll over. It's easiest for babies to flip from front to back, so this usually occurs first. In most cases, it won't be due to any conscious effort on your baby's part—it will just happen. It's unusual for babies to be able to do this at 12 weeks but it does happen. As soon as she flips over once, she'll be capable of doing it again and again in sequence. So be aware about where she might end up and what's within reach. Leaving her on the bed or changing table, even for a second, is definitely not an option now. Keep in mind that some babies never roll. Skipping this developmental milestone is nothing to worry about.

Your baby's personality

Your baby will have her own unique character, but knowing what type of personality she has can help you to bring out the best in her.

Sensitive soul Babies who are less eager to go to new people need extra reassurance (left).
At ease Some babies enjoy more interaction and cope better when visitors come along (right).

In her first few weeks and months, your baby's personality will start to show. She may be easy to please, excitable, or even a little grumpy and difficult to calm. If you have a child already, you may be surprised to find your new baby may have a very different temperament.

Your baby's personality is shaped by a combination of inherited traits, her present needs, and her environment—including your reaction to her. You may find it interesting to ask your parents whether you were similar to your own baby at this age: perhaps you were placid or difficult to comfort, just as your baby is. Your reaction to your baby and state of mind can affect how she responds on a day-to-day basis too.

If your baby is calm, responsive, and smiling, you may find her easier to parent and to respond to; however, if she is less calm, perhaps distressed because of difficulties such as colic, you may find you have to be particularly alert to her needs and spend more time soothing her and introducing activities such as baby massage (see p.125), which can relax and quiet her.

Some babies are less social and easily overwhelmed and overstimulated by groups of people and noisy, bright environments. If your baby has opportunities to meet new people in a warm and welcoming way, she'll soon overcome her natural fears.

Your baby may be energetic and enjoy physical exercise, or calm and laid-back, and take everything in her stride. She may be easily unsettled and need a routine to feel secure. All babies are unique. Getting to know and understand your baby's personality can help you adapt how you respond to her and decide which activities to offer. Try not to label your baby; embrace her for who she is and she'll flourish in your care.

SUN AND SAFETY

Babies need vitamin D from sunlight for strong bones and teeth, but their delicate skin can burn easily, and they can easily overheat. Health Canada recommends that you do not put sunscreen on a baby under six months' old. Instead, avoid direct sunlight and keep your baby inside when the sun is most direct (from 10 am to 3 pm). Dress your baby in a hat and lightweight, long-sleeved outfits with pants when outside to avoid exposing too much skin. For older babies, use sunscreen (SPF 30–50) on exposed skin that blocks the sun rather than filtering it, and is hypo-allergenic and water resistant. It should also protect against UVA and UVB rays. Try to keep her in the shade at all times, and offer her plenty of feedings if you're breast-feeding; bottle-fed babies may need a little extra water to stay hydrated.

Sun safety Use a sun hat and long-sleeved, lightweight clothing to protect your baby's delicate skin from the sun.

12 weeks

135

Working parent

If you need to return to work, you will undoubtedly have some juggling ahead of you. Remember that you don't need to be superwoman.

Back to work Returning to work is a big step; give yourself and your baby time to adapt.

Some parents have jobs that require their presence, no matter how much time off they may be entitled to take with maternity or parental leave, so they need to return to work while their babies are still very young.

If so, try to be as pragmatic about it as you can. Whenever you return to work, you are likely to feel guilty about it, no matter the circumstances, even if you had no choice. You will be reassured about her well-being when you have found excellent quality care for her and have confidence in her caregivers.

No matter if you've had a tiring day at work, you'll want to put her first as soon as you get home and spend time caring for her, playing, and having one-on-one quality time. These daily reunions will nourish the bond between you two.

Try to hold off on household chores until your baby is asleep. You may even consider getting in some paid assistance to help with the housework, even if it's only as you get settled into a work–home routine. Try not to worry too much about maintaining a pristine home; until your baby is a little older, your priority should be to focus on her needs.

Making compromises Figure out a system with your partner or even a helpful family member so that household chores are divided up evenly and fairly between you, and done to an acceptable standard without requiring too much effort on the part of everyone involved. Equally, don't worry about taking shortcuts. If you can't manage to put together a meal from scratch every night, look into some of the healthy, nutritious, ready-prepared meals that can be popped into the oven when you get home. Spending time with your baby can mean some compromising on your usual standards, but keep in mind that these are compromises from which you, your baby, and your entire family will ultimately benefit.

Above all, go easy on yourself. You may feel somewhat frantic at first, and worried that you aren't doing anything in your life up to your usual standards—you're certainly not alone in feeling this way. Over time, things will settle into a routine, and you'll find the best ways to manage both work and home life. Making time now for your baby and your partner will reap reward in years to come, and with a sturdy, healthy home life, you'll be well equipped to deal with additional demands.

TIME TO THINK ABOUT

Social Insurance Number

If you haven't applied for your baby's Social Insurance Number (SIN), think about doing it now. In some provinces, you can do this online. You'll need a SIN for your baby if you wish to start saving for her education with a Registered Education Savings Plan (see p.150), and she'll need it eventually to apply for jobs in Canada.

ASK A... DOCTOR

I'm still feeling very tired and low—could I be anemic? It's possible, but many moms feel tired and generally low not as a result of anemia due to iron deficiency, but because they are trying to cope with the challenges of motherhood on little sleep. It could also be a sign of postpartum depression (see p.114) or an underactive thyroid gland. Anemia can also cause the following symptoms:
- shortness of breath
- heart palpitations
- cravings for particular foods or substances, such as crunchy vegetables or ice
- food tasting different than normal
- sore tongue
- headaches.

If you have any of these symptoms or feel excessively tired, see your doctor.

Naps and nighttime sleep

Your baby may now be awake longer during the day, but she'll still need three naps and a good night's sleep to get the rest she needs.

By around three months, your baby will be sleeping about 15 hours in every 24-hour period. About 10 of those hours will take place at night (probably punctuated by one or two feedings) and the other five will be broken into three naps during the day.

Some moms complain that their babies don't nap, but if you put in place a good sleep routine, you'll find that your baby will eventually settle down into a good pattern of daytime naps and a long nighttime sleep. Babies who don't get enough rest during the day can become overstimulated and take much longer to settle down at night. Putting her down regularly during the day—even if she just kicks and plays in her crib—will get her into the nap habit, and she'll soon learn to accept that this quiet time is for sleep.

If your baby sleeps for more than 10 hours at night, you may want to wake her up in the morning to help "program" her body clock. This way, too, she'll be ready for her daytime naps, which will refresh her and boost her energy levels and mood.

ASK A... PEDIATRICIAN

My baby never seems tired—particularly around bedtime. How can I settle her down? It's normal for babies to get a second wind when it's time to put them down. This is a sign that they are overly tired and getting energy from adrenaline. Try moving her bedtime to half an hour earlier to catch her while she is genuinely tired, and look out for her sleep cues (p.124).

Little kicker

As your baby's legs get stronger and she becomes more coordinated, she'll enjoy kicking so much, she'll even wake up at night to practice.

Kicking and stretching her legs prepares your baby's leg muscles for crawling, walking, and even rolling over. To promote her leg development, offer her colorful toys just out of reach, and provide a safe environment for her to explore. Her natural curiosity will encourage her to become mobile in a few months' time, but she'll build up the skills and strength to do this by moving toward things that interest her now.

Tummy time mainly encourages the development of your baby's upper body, neck, and arms, and also provides her with an opportunity to bend her legs back from the knees, and to push forward with them later on. When she spends time on her back, she'll perfect her bicycle kick and a wide range of leg movements. You can encourage her to put a little weight on her legs by carefully holding her upright. When you do this, she'll naturally bounce, but no matter how steady she might seem, don't let go of her!

Babies kick with excitement and also when they are frustrated. Kicking in fact offers great exercise and stimulates your baby's development. Now is the time to be extra cautious; she'll wiggle more and use her legs to move herself around. She may even begin "creeping"—slowly and steadily moving herself from one place to another.

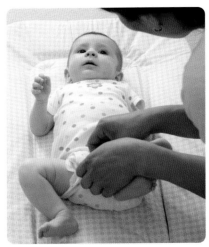

Kicking up a storm Your baby may try to kick away her clothes during her diaper change.

13 weeks

BABIES OFTEN GAZE INTENTLY AT OBJECTS OF INTEREST, AS IF MEMORIZING EVERY DETAIL

As your baby enters her fourth month, her social skills are flourishing, and she enjoys talking with you. Although your baby was born with a full set of primary teeth, they were underneath the gums. The first few may now be making their way upward, making her gums feel sore.

Babbling baby

Your baby's early attempts at speech represent her new way of communicating with you, so make sure you respond to her!

Little chatterbox Encourage your baby to use his voice by giving him opportunities to speak, and showing clear pleasure when he does.

Your baby will love to engage you in conversation, and you may notice her listening intently when you talk to her. But most of all, she will enjoy practicing all the new sounds she has been learning to make. Babbling is, in fact, an important stage of both your baby's overall development and her acquisition of language. She will experiment by voicing the sounds that make up the language or languages she hears around her, without actually creating any words that you can recognize. It's a bit like running through the alphabet phonetically! She's gathering together and consolidating all of her sounds so that she can effectively use them when she's ready.

When she was born, your baby's larynx (voice box) was high in her throat, to allow her to breathe while swallowing. Now it's on the move downward, and within her first year a "pharynx" will develop. This is part of the respiratory system in the throat, and it is important for vocalization. When the larynx is in place, she will be able to form all of the sounds used in human speech.

Encourage your baby to develop her own memory bank of sounds by talking to her as often as you can. She might not look as if she is listening, but she's absorbing it all. Give her plenty of opportunities to use her voice and lots of encouragement when she does. Smile, clap your hands, and praise her.

Teething and sleep

As your baby's first teeth start to emerge, she may wake up at night in discomfort and take longer to settle back down to sleep.

There is no doubt that teething is uncomfortable for the vast majority of babies, and you may find that your little one wakes up frequently at night, gnawing on her fist, batting at her ears, or just fussing. A breast-fed baby might want to nurse for comfort and may settle for nothing less, even if it is the middle of the night.

Although the jury is out on whether or not teething can cause a baby to suffer bouts of diarrhea, most parents find that their babies' stools are looser for short periods of time during teething, so more frequent diaper changes may be required.

First of all, if you know your baby is teething, it's important to ensure that she's comfortable before she goes to bed. Give her a warm bath and gently massage her face around the jawline and under her chin. This helps to relax the area and ease inflammation. You can offer her infant acetaminophen and rub a drop of teething gel into the affected area of her gums. (Follow the manufacturer's recommendations as to the amount and don't use more, since this could be dangerous for your baby's health.) Feed her before she goes to bed and make sure she gets as much as possible, so that hunger doesn't wake her up too early. If she does wake up at night, offer one more dose each of acetaminophen and teething gel—if the doctor allows it and enough time has elapsed since the last dose—and try massaging her jaw again. Cuddle her and be patient—this will soon pass.

YOUR BABY IS 13 WEEKS AND 2 DAYS

Peekaboo!

Gradually, it will dawn on your baby that an object she can't see may still be there—and peekaboo games help her to understand this.

The understanding that objects continue to exist even when they cannot be seen, heard, or touched is known as "object permanence," and is a major milestone in a baby's first year. The term was first used by child psychologist Jean Piaget, who believed that most babies grasp this concept between eight and 12 months old. However, all children are different, and some babies have been known to begin to develop this concept as young as four months old.

Now you see me... Your baby thinks you're gone when she can't see you—but she's slowly learning that you don't just "disappear."

Games of peekaboo now are great fun, because your baby will be pleasantly surprised each time you cover your face with your hands and then "magically" reappear again. They also test your baby's memory: she's learning to anticipate, so she will wait excitedly for your face to appear, and to hear you say "Peekaboo." If you leave your hands over your face for longer than usual, she may reach out to prompt you to move them! Learning that things—including you—can still be there when she can't see them is also good for her emotional security. When you vanish for a few moments, she won't feel so concerned.

YOUR BABY IS 13 WEEKS AND 3 DAYS

Easy does it

Your baby isn't ready to sit unsupported but she'll love to be propped or held in a sitting position to get a different view of the world.

Your baby is ready to start gaining the muscle strength and coordination that form the basis for sitting upright. If she can lift her head during tummy time and roll confidently, you can introduce some play ideas to build her readiness to sit. For example, prop your baby up securely so she has a stable position then give her noisy, bright rattles to reach for, or encourage her to stretch to grab a cloth draped over her legs. Each time she leans out she's refining her balance. She will topple over so be ready to hold her, and make sure there are plenty of cushions around to break her fall.

When you prop her up do not leave her alone even for a few moments. Until her muscles, coordination, and balance are improved she will tire easily and even become frustrated, so watch for signs that she'd rather do some less strenuous play. At this age, she may not be ready for this sort of activity at all and that's fine, too. The average age for sitting is six months, with some babies not reaching this milestone until around 10 months.

Good vantage point While she's sitting propped up, it's a good opportunity to hold up a book so that she can see it easily.

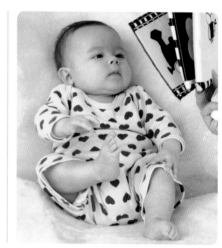

Baby dislikes

Even the most acquiescent baby will go through a stage of expressing not just her likes, but also her dislikes—and you'll know about it!

Changing tack If she dislikes her bouncy seat, has she been spending too long in it? She might be better off somewhere else for a change.

As your baby's memory develops, she will begin to make positive and negative associations. Soon, she will light up when you walk into the room, smile at her older sibling, and gurgle when she sees her baby gym. However, her car seat may produce an instant cry of protest; she may actively resist being laid down for tummy time, and your attempts to leave her alone in her bed at night may well end up in tears of frustration—and even anger! She's starting to know her own mind and express her opinion. In fact, browse any baby forum on the Internet and you'll see that 13-week-old babies have a wealth of dislikes, including their cribs, the family dog, bedtime, baby carriers, the bath, getting dressed, and even being burped. So get ready for a few disagreements!

Positive associations In the early days, the best way to deal with dislikes is to try to create positive associations. Maybe your baby has been stuck in her car seat too long in the past, so a few short trips with the nursery rhymes on and her favorite stuffed animal or board book next to her may make a difference.

Change your routine slightly if she's showing a dislike for the bath or bedtime. She may work himself up into a frenzy if she knows bedtime is coming, so make it feel different than usual. Perhaps take a bath with her, looking into her eyes and stroking her. If she dislikes being put into her crib, try staying close by, putting a containing arm around her while she lies there, or swaddling her. Make sure she doesn't overheat and loosen or remove the swaddling once she's down. Softly tell her stories, hum, or sing to reassure her that she is safe and secure.

Distraction often helps with daytime dislikes. Hang a mobile over her changing table; festoon her car seat with new toys; put her in a carrier facing outward; dress her in a different place and play "This little piggy" while you do it; or you could even put a mirror in her crib so he can see himself at bedtime.

Gentle guidance Ultimately, this is a developmental stage that you'll have to get through. Most activities to which babies object are necessary, and you'll have to guide her—gently, kindly, and patiently—through them. Talk to her quietly, make her laugh, maintain eye contact, and try to control your own frustration; there will be many times in years to come when you'll need to confirm that you understand the way she is feeling and why (which validates her emotions), but make it clear when something has to happen. Until she can express herself with words, negotiate, and understand why she has to do things she dislikes, you'll have to work your way through problem situations with as much creativity as you can muster!

ASK A... PEDIATRICIAN

My twins don't enjoy the same activities; how can I keep them both occupied and happy? Try to encourage solo play. Set each baby up with an activity he enjoys, putting one baby on each side of you. There will be some turning back-and-forth involved to keep them both occupied, but you'd probably be doing that anyway. It is good that your babies are expressing their individual characters, however hard it is to facilitate two very different sets of needs. If one hates the bath, sponge bathe him and put him in his baby seat while you bathe the bath-friendly sibling. If one resists bedtime, settle down the happy twin first and introduce a new element to your bedtime routine for the other. As they get older, they'll begin to look with interest at what the other is doing, and probably want to join in. Be as flexible and creative with your arrangements as you can, and keep in mind that this is just a stage.

13 weeks

141

Routines to suit you

At 13 weeks, your baby's sleeping and feeding patterns are more predictable, so try adjusting her schedule to work better for you.

Work and play Your baby may be happy playing with some toys in his recliner while you get busy with some housework nearby.

By now, your baby may be able to be a little more flexible than she was previously because she can go longer between feedings and, probably, sleep for extended periods of time. Many moms find this a positive development. It means that you are not quite so tied to your baby, and she will be much more amenable to getting into a routine that suits you a little more.

You can now anticipate when she's likely to be hungry, and squeeze in a good feeding before heading out for lunch with friends or a shopping trip. When she's usually alert and happy, you can set her up in his bouncy seat with a couple of board books, or in her baby gym surrounded by toys, in order to do some chores or make phone calls, or catch up on your email. Adjusting her routine slightly from time to time will help her become more flexible and buy you a little freedom. Routines are great for providing young babies with security, because they learn to anticipate what comes next; however, they can become overly binding—the last thing you need is to find yourself in a position where all lunchtime social engagements are put on hold while your baby has her nap. Don't hesitate to create a little time for yourself by involving others, too. If both you and Dad can take turns with the bedtime routine, you'll both develop a knack for settling her down—and she'll be equally happy in either scenario. Life will soon be getting much easier!

Months 1–3

Your baby day by day

142

AS A MATTER OF FACT

Colic

If your baby is still crying frequently and you are convinced she has colic, take heart that most babies outgrow colic around this time, and the distress, discomfort, and bouts of crying should soon stop completely.

In some cases, colic can go on for up to four months, or more. If your baby's colic continues much beyond three months, and nothing helps to make her more comfortable, see your doctor to ensure that nothing else is at the root of the problem, such as a reflux disorder.

DEVELOPMENT ACTIVITY

Playtime

Your baby will enjoy exploring her toys while held securely on your lap. Encourage her to reach for, grasp, and examine toys with different textures, sounds, and shapes. Noisy toys will get her attention, leading her to look, reach, and turn. Scrunch a crinkly toy, or shake a rattle a bit above and to the side of her and encourage her to reach and grab. These activities help hand–eye coordination, muscle control, and her ability to grasp by opening her hand and curling her fingers around a toy.

New game Your baby will be intrigued as you fill a container with toys then empty it, and will enjoy reaching out for toys himself.

Toys for three months up

Your baby is ready to play with toys she can grip, shake, and squeeze—she's ready for a new challenge!

Great shakes A rattle is an ideal toy now because it helps your baby learn that by shaking it, he can cause it to make a noise.

Your baby is losing her earlier reflexes and has more control over her arms, hands, and fingers. Her mobile, floor gym, activity quilt, and textured toys are still important to her development, but you can add toys with new textures, sounds, and even buttons that you can help her push. Give her a rattle or squeaky toy and she'll learn that she can make things happen. She will enjoy waving it, and squeezing and shaking it to make a noise, and over the coming months eventually will grasp the concept of cause and effect.

Toys with a variety of bright colors, lights, and sounds, such as musical crib projectors, or toys that make sounds when she pushes on a button, will be popular, too. Babies of this age also find toys with friendly faces comforting as well as fascinating. Your baby will respond well to a toy face, especially if you help her identify it by pointing out the toy's facial features, then your own, and then gently touch your baby's face as you name each part.

Don't box up old favorites. Babies benefit from being able to master a toy easily, along with learning about more challenging ones. If surrounded by unmastered toys, she may become dispirited and might stop enjoying play.

TOYS AND SAFETY

Always give your baby age-appropriate toys. Toys intended for children over three years old may have small parts that could come off and cause choking. Make sure stitching is firm in soft toys, and that labels are well sewn in.

Don't use string or elastic to attach toys to your baby's playpen or crib because she may trap her fingers in them. And remember that your baby can't yet tell a toy from a household implement, so make sure that you put anything that should not go into her mouth well beyond her reach.

If you have older children, store their toys separately, and try to teach your older children to keep their toys away from the baby so that she doesn't choke on something—but never take it for granted that they will always remember the rules.

Most importantly, never leave your baby alone when there is anything within her reach, or with anyone who is not responsible enough to make sure that she doesn't put something into her mouth that is a choking hazard.

CHECKLIST

Fun toys for now

Your baby's favorite plaything will always be you, and the time you spend with her is invaluable for her emotional development. But there are some toys that she will enjoy playing with, and that are great for this stage of her development.

■ Rattles are a perennial favorite and they help your baby learn to control her movements.

■ Textured fabric books are great fun, as are chunky board books with firm lift-up flaps.

■ Blocks with "surprises" in them will entertain your baby endlessly. Make sure they are chunky enough for her to grasp—eventually.

■ Stacking pots make a satisfying noise when banged together; and she'll enjoy learning to stack them.

■ Bath toys that squeak, leak, and float will make bathtime enjoyable.

■ Toys that can be clipped to your baby's stroller will keep her occupied when you're on the move.

■ A music box that responds to your baby's touch with nursery rhymes or lively music will delight her.

■ Toys that pop up when buttons are pushed, such as a jack-in-the-box, will provide endless entertainment and encourage your baby to develop her hand–eye coordination.

Your baby at 4 to 6 months

Grabbing hold Given plenty of practice, your baby should be able to reach out and grab things with much greater accuracy and ease.

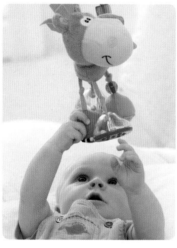

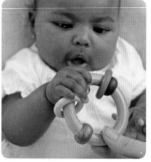

Young explorer Your baby will grasp and inspect any object that interests her, before instinctively putting it into her mouth for further exploration.

Did you know? A baby's mouth has a vast number of nerve endings, so it's perfect for exploring objects and learning about texture.

Seeing more clearly At four months, your baby's range of vision increases to several yards. Up close, he's attracted to colors and patterns.

Rolling over Your baby may learn to roll over any time between four and seven months. Most babies roll from tummy to back before mastering the more difficult back to front roll.

Did you know? Not all babies roll over—some skip this stage and go directly to sitting and crawling.

First laugh Your baby will probably delight you with a chuckle in her fourth month. You'll soon find lots of ways to make her laugh.

Your baby is exploring, laughing, and interacting more with you as well as gaining mobility and coordination.

Big bath time When your baby gets too big for the baby bath, it's time for the big bath. He'll enjoy the feeling of being in water while being held securely.

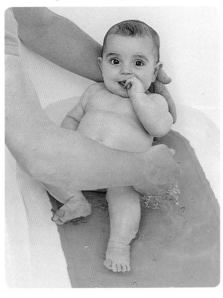

Babble and bubbles Your baby is developing her language skills by experimenting with new sounds, such as blowing raspberries.

Bedtime routine Your baby may be sleeping for about eight hours at night now, although many still wake up for a night feeding. A gentle bedtime routine helps calm him and encourage good sleep habits.

Solids begin By six months, your baby is ready for starting some solid food, which will complement her milk diet.

> **Did you know?** Some babies will bear weight on their legs now; others prefer to lie back and kick.

Sitting supported Toward the end of her fifth month, your baby can hold her head up well and is able to sit upright with plenty of support.

On the move Your baby may be preparing to move by about six months, pushing up into a crawling position or shuffling on his tummy to reach a toy.

14 weeks

BOLD PATTERNS ARE EASIER FOR BABIES TO SEE BECAUSE THEIR VISION ISN'T SHARP YET

Your baby is now sleeping for longer periods, making it easier to develop a more predictable timetable and giving you more time to think about yourself. At nearly four months after the birth, your body has regained strength, so why not get back to (or start) exercising.

Why it's good to get fit

So your baby may not be up and toddling yet—but when it happens, you'll need to be quick, agile, and full of stamina! Better start now...

It can be difficult to motivate yourself to exercise, especially if you've had interrupted sleep at night or little time to yourself. When you do have a spare half hour, the thought of putting your sneakers on and exerting yourself probably isn't very appealing. However, the sooner you can fit some kind of regular exercise into your routine, the better you will feel. Among the benefits of exercise for new moms are: healthier and stronger bones, muscles, and joints; lower body fat and better weight control; better balance, coordination, and agility; improved self-esteem, a more positive mental outlook, and less likelihood of suffering from postpartum depression, anxiety, or stress.

Even if you've never exercised before, having a child may make you think about how important it is for you to stay well, for his sake. Regular (even moderate) physical activity has substantial health benefits that are difficult to ignore.

What kind of exercise? 14 weeks after giving birth, your body regains enough strength to allow you to do some moderate aerobic exercise. Cycling, swimming, dance classes, Pilates, and yoga are all good options. Aim for a pace that makes you slightly out of breath but still able to hold a conversation. Don't push yourself beyond what feels comfortable, and if something hurts, stop.

Fitting in the baby Some gyms and local sports centers offer day-care facilities, and some will take a baby from three months old. The prospect of

Resuming an athletic activity A few quick laps of your local swimming pool, a stroller-jog in the park, or a game of tennis with a friend are all great ways of getting some exercise.

offering up your infant to someone else's care can be daunting, but classes often last only up to an hour. The feel-good factor of doing something for yourself can be a just reward for an hour's separation. If you can't get to a gym, you could join a park "stroller" walk, arranged by a local group, which enables you to meet other moms while you exercise.

If you are not comfortable leaving your baby in day care, try to find a class or use the gym when your partner gets home. This will give dad and baby some one-on-one time, so is good for them.

Alternatively, there are many classes for moms run in local community centers, as well as outdoors, to which you can take your baby along. Ask your pediatrician if she knows of any mommy-and-me type of exercise groups. Such classes also offer you a great opportunity to meet like-minded moms.

FEEL-GOOD FACTOR

It is very easy in the first weeks of having a new baby to become completely tied up with the business of motherhood and forget that you need taking care of, too. This week, agree on a time with your partner for him to take care of the baby so that you can go to the hairdresser, or have a pedicure, facial, or massage. If pampering isn't your style, perhaps there's an activity that you love, such as tennis (take it gently though); or lunch or a trip to the movies with friends might be fun. Whatever you choose, it should feel like a treat, enabling you to come away feeling great. Also, make sure it's something you need to book in advance, so that you don't get tempted to cancel it.

14 weeks

147

What a giggle!

Your baby has probably blessed you with smiles over past weeks, but any time now his first giggle will melt your heart all over again.

Finding something that makes your baby laugh becomes addictive. Babies respond best to eye contact, so looking him straight in the eye and smiling is the best way to start. To turn his return smiles into a giggle, you can try tickling his toes, under his armpits, or gently squeezing the fleshy, ticklish parts of his thighs. He will likely respond with a squeal or a giggle that lets you know he

Tickles Many babies giggle when tickled. Make a fun game of tickling your baby to get him to laugh with you.

finds it funny. In addition, because your baby is getting better at holding your gaze and having face-to-face interaction with you, try making a funny face (such as an exaggerated look of surprise) while you tickle his thighs or his toes, to add another humorous dimension to the game to help bring on the laughter.

Babies are more likely to be engaged and remember things if an experience stimulates more than one sense. So if you make a funny sound as you tickle your baby, he is even more likely to find it funny and let out a delighted giggle.

Forming attachments

Your baby can now identify your face, voice, and smell. When he hears you speak or sing, he will know you are just around the corner.

At birth, your baby's sense of smell and hearing were already well developed. At around 14 weeks, his sight improves dramatically, too. You may notice this week that, as you walk around the room, his eyes follow you more, because he now has greater muscle control in his eyes. As he becomes more aware of your coming and going, he may object or begin to cry if you leave the room, or simply if he can't see you any more.

Talk to him in reassuring tones as you move around. If you leave the room momentarily, tell him that you will be back in a second—although he may not understand your words yet, he will soon begin to make connections between

what you say to him and your actions. When you move back into his field of vision, smile to let him know all is well.

As babies begin to understand that they are a separate person from you, having something comforting to hold on to can help them feel secure. A comfort object can make life easier, especially at bedtime, but you may want to encourage your baby to use it only at bedtime or around the house (unless you are away overnight). It's wise to have two identical comforters, so if one gets grubby you can replace it while it's washed. He may also get attached to its odor, so an occasional wash is useful to ensure he doesn't reject it when it smells fresh!

ASK A... PEDIATRICIAN

Why does my baby drool? All babies will drool either a little bit, or a lot, from time to time—this is normal and nothing to worry about. Drooling is something they will grow out of over time. Most babies drool more when they are teething, or if they have a cold or a stuffed nose. Saliva contains protective proteins that provide a germ-fighting barrier against bacteria, so drooling can be helpful when your baby reaches the stage of automatically putting everything he picks up in his mouth.

Accidental rolls

It can happen that your baby will begin to roll as early as 14 weeks, but this is often by accident.

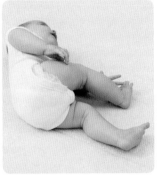

Tummy time to rolling All it takes is one stronger-than-usual push up with one arm and a slight rocking motion from side to side, and your baby will tip himself over onto his back.

Once your baby has achieved the flip from his tummy to back (see p.134), he'll be working on mastering the art of rolling over, every which way! Most babies can roll over by the time they reach six or seven months old, so it's unusual for them to be doing it now, but not unheard of.

Once he's done it once, that doesn't mean that he has mastered rolling: it takes muscle strength, coordination, and planning to make this happen each time he tries.

Encouraging rolls Your baby may be ready to try rolling, but don't worry if he is still working on the preparation. Short periods of tummy time and encouraging him to lift his head and push up with his hands are great practice for this milestone. Since it is much easier for a baby to roll from front to back, put your baby on his tummy. If he can support himself well on one arm, hold a favorite, easy-to-grab toy next to him, but slightly above him, just out of reach. With encouraging smiles, try to coax

him to tip his head back to look up at the toy and reach up for it. As he reaches, move the toy farther behind him and see if you can coax him to lean toward the toy, encouraging him to flip over onto his back. If he does, reward him with cheering, clapping, and lots of reassuring smiles, especially if he seems a bit confused by what just happened, and be sure to give him the toy. Encourage him to turn to both sides to prevent him from favoring one side.

Rolling safety Once your baby can roll over, never leave him lying on any raised surface. Change him on a changing mat on the floor rather than on a table. Keep one hand on him as you reach for things, to keep him stationary.

Also, never leave your baby unattended in a room that hasn't been babyproofed. You would be surprised just how much distance a rolling baby can cover. Keep all small toys and household objects high up and out of his reach, and remind older children not to leave their toys in harm's way.

Back-to-front rolls

The back-to-front roll happens only once the reflex that forces your baby's arm out as he turns his head is overruled by his improving coordination. He also needs enough muscle tone to support his head, body, and legs, and the coordination to be able to pull in his arms so they do not prevent the roll. To encourage a back-to-front roll, lay him on his back and place a toy next to him, just out of reach. Get him to reach for the toy. If he reaches far enough, his center of gravity will shift to bring him over onto his front. Once he's mastered the move, he'll combine it with the front-to-back roll, and will enjoy the freedom rolling across the floor gives him.

Reaching out Once your baby twists her body and leans over in one direction, she'll soon learn to take the movement all the way over into a back-to-front roll.

14 weeks

149

Your baby's financial future

It may seem early to be thinking about saving for your baby's future, but some early planning now really can pay off later on.

Do your research Whichever type of investment you choose to make for your baby, make sure you put some time into researching where to find the best deals.

ASK A... PEDIATRICIAN

My baby's bottom is sore and there is a red rash around her vagina. What is wrong? She may have thrush, a common yeast (fungal) infection that can be exacerbated by the warm, moist environment of her diaper. It can occur in girls and boys, and can be itchy and sore. Sometimes the rash is accompanied by small, white, raised bumps. Keep the area very clean. Dab at patches or spots with moist cotton pads rather than washing them (which can increase the irritation). Change her diaper frequently and give her bottom time to "air". If the thrush doesn't clear up in a couple of days, see your doctor. She may prescribe an antifungal cream, and will usually check your baby's mouth to make sure she doesn't have thrush there, too.

Why would you think about university costs, or even buying your baby's first car, when he's only 14 weeks old? It may seem precipitous, but saving now for your baby's future will make it far less burdensome financially than if you wait until later. A small regular investment now could grow into a significant sum by the time your little one reaches 18 years old—the sooner you start investing, the more time your money has to grow.

There's also the possibility that grandparents or relatives want to give you a lump sum to invest on your child's behalf, so you'll need to consider the best way to do this. While you could just save or invest money in accounts or funds you already hold, it can make sense to open up something in your child's name to benefit from special tax savings that may apply. If you are considering investing, it can help to talk to a financial adviser, or to look for financial advice online. You can also check your local bank branch to find

out what accounts and opportunities are available for children there. If you don't like the options, try a competing bank.

Savings accounts The simplest way to invest money for your baby is in a savings account. Options vary by the bank, but there are a few basic guidelines:
■ Your baby may need a Social Insurance Number in order to have an account so apply for one, if you haven't already.
■ A parent or guardian may need to have an account at the same bank where you wish to open your baby's account.
■ You can usually decide how much access your child will have to the account and set up a withdrawal limit for when he's older.
■ Shop around to find a plan that's right for your situation: an account with no minimum balance, a competitive annual interest rate, or another feature that's attractive to you.

RESPs A Registered Education Savings Plan (RESP) is a tax-sheltered savings plan that can help you save for your baby's post-secondary education. Having one will also allow your child to apply for a Canada Education Savings Grant. There are different types of RESPs, so do your research before you decide which one to pick.

Savings bonds Many babies receive Canada Savings Bonds as welcome presents from relatives. They're backed by the Government of Canada and have a guaranteed rate of return. They mature after 10 years (although they can be cashed out at any time) and can help toward paying education fees.

Structuring sleep and feedings

The days of constant feeding and unpredictable sleeping patterns should be over, and your baby will be settling into a regular routine.

Your baby's tummy can now hold enough milk to allow him to sleep for longer periods. This makes it easier to establish a more regular routine.

Don't be afraid to wake him up for his first feeding in the morning. If he wakes up when you do, he's more likely to sleep when you want to relax for the evening.

Most 14-week-old babies need six to eight feedings in a 24-hour period, including breakfast, midmorning, lunch, mid-afternoon, and evening. If he wakes up at night to be fed, try waking him for a feeding just before you go to bed. Keep stimulation to a minimum, which will help him settle back to sleep and sleep longer. In the daytime, introducing playtime after a feeding helps him distinguish between night and day.

On average, babies sleep for about 10 hours at night now and five hours during the day, but each baby is different. If it suits your baby, try a midmorning nap, an afternoon nap, and, if necessary, a short power nap in the evening. If you want him to go to bed at about 7 pm, try two longer daytime naps instead.

Good morning Waking your baby for his first feeding will help him adapt to your routine.

Physical play

Now that your baby's stronger, physical games such as knee rides and tickles encourage his confidence and physical awareness.

Studies suggest that a baby's time with his dad is often more play-focused than his time with mom, and dads often come into their own with physical play. Whether it's tummy time, tickles, or bouncy play, your baby will benefit from opportunities for big movements and activities that make him aware of his body.

With your baby on his front, roll a ball in front of him. He may move his legs and body to reach it. Sit on the floor with him and prop him securely in a baby nest, or

Fun faces Hold your baby close to your face as you make faces, funny noises, and rub noses—you may even elicit a giggle or two!

hold him safely between your legs, then build towers of soft blocks. He will try to reach out to bat them, and enjoy watching them tumble over his toes.

Your baby will love to be rocked from side to side if he is supported well. If he protests, stop, or continue more gently. If he can hold his head up, it's time to raise him up into the air, and "bump" noses as you bring him down again.

You could try water play. In a bath or paddling pool, sit with him firmly in your arms. Let him splash, and use a toy watering can to sprinkle water over his arms. Hold him throughout. Never leave him unsupervised near water.

14 weeks

15 weeks

UNTIL YOUR BABY IS SIX OR SEVEN MONTHS, REACHING AND GRASPING HAPPEN AT THE SAME TIME

Your baby's developing depth perception means that he now notices things that are farther away. Anything that is within reach, he'll make a grab for, but won't be accurate yet. He'll be chattering away to you, though he may be a little more bashful with unfamiliar people.

Feeding and teething

Although it might be a while before your baby's first tooth appears, this week he may start experiencing symptoms of teething.

Upset baby Many teething babies feel irritable and restless and, sometimes, pain as the tooth cuts through the gums.

Just as teething can affect your baby's sleep (see p.139), it can also disrupt his feeding. Many babies lose their appetite when teething because their gums are so uncomfortable and painful. If your baby has flushed cheeks, red gums, is drooling excessively, or chewing on his toys or fingers more than usual, or if his sleep is disturbed, he may have a tooth coming through. Some associate a low-grade fever with teething, but doctors are reluctant to make this link. If your baby does have a fever, or seems sick, do not assume this is due to his teething. Instead, ask your doctor to check him in case he has an infection that needs treatment.

Each tooth pushes up through the gum to become visible in your baby's mouth. You may be able to feel a hard, protruding bump in his mouth if you rub his gums with a clean finger, and the area may look sore and inflamed.

Some breast-fed babies respond to teething by wanting "comfort" feedings. Although the extra feedings can play havoc with your milk supply, you may find that this is the best way to settle your baby down. Other babies find being nursed uncomfortable, cry, and come on and off the breast, only to want it again later since they are still hungry. While this is frustrating for you both, keep offering your breast as usual. In many cases, he'll be fine in two or three days and normal feeding can resume.

Bottle-fed babies may also fuss when being fed or fail to drink as much formula as normal. A little teething gel before a feeding can ease the pain for long enough to get some milk into him. Use acetaminophen if needed. If you are concerned, see your pediatrician.

ASK A... BREAST-FEEDING EXPERT

My baby has a tooth and bites me when I breast-feed him! How can I discourage this? Often, babies bite when they are experimenting with their new teeth. If he does bite, release him from the breast while saying "ouch," then reattach him. He will begin to understand the meaning of the word. If your natural reaction is to shout in pain, this may shock him and be enough to stop him doing it again! He's more likely to bite if he's not hungry, so take him off your breast when he has had enough. Does he have a cold or congested nasal passages? If so, he may be clamping down with his gums and teeth to hold your nipple in place as he breathes through his mouth. Your doctor can help you to remedy this.

TIME TO THINK ABOUT

Teething rings

Invest in some non-PVC teething rings that can be cooled in the refrigerator, never the freezer. These are invaluable if your baby's gums are inflamed or sore. Although it may be a few weeks, or even months, until the first tooth emerges, getting him used to gnawing on a teething ring now can help prevent symptoms before they start.

Cool relief Keep a few teething rings in the fridge so there is always a cold one on hand to help ease your baby's discomfort.

In grandparents' care

If your parents or in-laws are willing and able, you may want to consider handing over responsibility and taking a whole night off.

An extended family Doting grandparents will enrich your baby's life, especially if his bond with them is developed early on.

Now that your baby's routine is more established, you've got expressing down pat (if breast-feeding), and taking care of his needs has become easier, you might want to think about indulging in some real grown-up time with your partner. If grandparents are able to babysit for the night, you can plan a trip to the theater, dinner out, or even a night away—a real break that gives you time to focus only on each other.

While some parents don't feel comfortable about leaving their baby early on, others find that the benefits to their relationship outweigh their anxieties. Letting your parents and in-laws help out allows your baby to begin to develop a loving and significant relationship with them. Your parents or in-laws will almost certainly relish the opportunity to spend time with your baby and bond with him. However, leaving your baby for the first time is a very personal choice, and in the end it comes down to what feels right for you.

If you agree that the time is right to get away, or perhaps you want to attend a wedding or special occasion, decide whether your baby will be staying at home or at his grandparents' house. At this age, your baby will probably sleep wherever he is. Then talk through every aspect of his care: when to feed him; change his diaper; put him down to sleep; and what to do if he wakes up. Make sure that they're aware how best to comfort him if he does become upset. It's important that you feel you have covered every eventuality. Once you have left clear instructions and contact numbers, there's no reason to worry. Ask your parents or in-laws to call you immediately if they have any concerns.

TIME TO THINK ABOUT

Recording your baby's voice

It may seem impossible to believe that you could ever forget the sound of your baby's gurgles and coos, but as he moves on in his life, each stage of his development will absorb you so much, you will lose track of those momentous, heart-warming attempts at communication. This week, make time to record him as he chatters to his heart's content. Perhaps you can continue to do so regularly, each time making a note of the date. Record him electronically and email the files to family and friends, or simply keep them safe for that trip down memory lane in the future.

LONG-DISTANCE GRANDPARENTING

If your baby's grandparents live far away, they may feel as if they need an invitation to visit, which you may not have considered! Keep them involved by talking to them via Skype with your baby on your lap, or send them weekly emails to update them on his development, with recent pictures attached. Don't forget to report all those amazing "firsts" to keep them in the loop. Ultimately, despite the distance, his relationships with his grandparents can be rewarding for your baby right into adulthood. Getting things right in the early days can ensure the relationships flourish.

In the loop Watching recordings of your baby can help his grandparents witness his development and feel close to him.

Encouraging social skills

Your baby will gurgle, chatter, and coo in your company, and be pleased to meet new people if introduced to them carefully.

Babies naturally favor their primary caregiver, and while there is simply no such thing as a bond that is too intense or strong, you can make things easier for your partner and other family members by encouraging your baby's social skills. At 15 weeks, he is ready for this—his social skills are developing apace, and everything you can teach him will help them to develop positively.

Make sure you set a good example by interacting positively with the people around you. After a busy day with just you for company, your baby will be eager to see and play with someone new. Give your partner a moment to get through the door, but don't keep your baby to yourself. A shared hug makes a nice handover as your baby transfers his interest to his other parent. Spend time together as a family as much as possible, so your baby witnesses how you relate positively to each other. You are your baby's first teacher, and he will learn and take his cues from you.

Studies suggest that if parents are social, their babies are more likely to be that way, too. A parent-and-baby group gives your baby contact with other babies and adults and lets you socialize, too.

Depending on your baby's temperament, he may be more or less willing to go to other adults. Be sensitive to his needs, and if he's reluctant, introduce new people gently and don't overwhelm him. If necessary, you may have to shorten visits until he builds his confidence.

Make sure you share child-care duties between you and your partner. If you stick roughly to the same routine, it won't matter if your techniques differ slightly. As long as your baby spends time with both of you, he won't mind if one of you changes his diaper or sings his bedtime song differently.

Reading as a habit

Developments in your baby's vision and comprehension mean that he is now able to enjoy books and stories much more than before.

Reading aloud to your baby teaches him about communication, encourages his listening skills, memory, and vocabulary, and introduces concepts such as "story sense" (which is essential for reading skills later on). Books will provide him with an exciting look at his world, full of colors, stories, numbers, shapes, faces, animals, and virtually everything else, in an entertaining and comforting way.

Sit down with your baby at least once a day to explore books. Encourage him to look and listen as you point at and talk about the pictures, and lift flaps so he can see what is underneath. Fill your voice with emotion and expression to capture his attention, and help him to experience positive social interaction with you during reading, which promotes his healthy emotional development.

Babies love repetition, so don't be surprised if he wants the same book over and over again. You'll be encouraging his memory skills by repeating the same stories, so go with it!

Most things go straight in the mouth at this stage, so choose books that can withstand a good chew. Sturdy, colorful books with rhymes, pictures of babies and animals, and interactive elements (such as lift-up flaps and textures) will engage him and involve him in the story.

Reading time Establish a reading habit that your baby can continue alone when she's older.

Reaching and grasping

Now that your baby knows his hands belong to him, he will start to practice his reaching and grasping skills in earnest.

Practice makes perfect With practice, your baby's attempts to reach out and touch or even grab things will become more accurate.

Your baby has been batting at and trying to grasp objects for a few weeks now. He has figured out that his hand is his own, and his goal now is to direct it toward an object without looking at his hand first.

Once your baby can confidently direct his hand toward an object, he will be able to reach out and grasp small, easy-to-grip, brightly colored toys or rattles. These will probably go straight to his mouth, although he may spend time looking at them, dropping them (usually by accident), and reaching for them again.

At this point in your baby's development, reaching and grasping occur at the same time. Your baby can't yet correct any mistakes while reaching. If he can't get hold of an object that he sees first time, he'll try again, reaching and grasping together. He'll close his hand when he sees that he's reached that interesting toy. With every attempt, he improves his hand–eye coordination.

To encourage your baby to reach out, surround him with light, sturdy toys that fit easily in one hand. Choose a variety of shapes, but make sure each one is easy to grip and has a shape, edge, or texture that would fit into your baby's palm. Offer your baby both still and moving objects—there are plenty of toys that vibrate, or can be rolled to draw his attention. Praise his efforts to reach and grab, and move toys a little closer if he's discouraged to avoid him becoming disheartened. Try not to intervene and do things for him, though. He needs to practice and learn from his mistakes in order to hone his skills.

Once your baby can grab things, keep hazards well out of reach. For example, remove your handbag (which may contain small items he could choke on); hot drinks or food; pets; strings or cords; hard or unhygienic items (which will end up in his mouth); electrical cords; plants; and medication.

DEVELOPMENT ACTIVITY

Clapping games

Although your baby will not be able to clap his hands until about seven to nine months, or later, clapping games, in which you move his hands gently to make a clap, give him the experience of bringing his hands together in front of his body. Sing songs while you clap his hands together. Let them fall, then clap your own hands, singing as you do so.

Encourage him to grasp your hands, one in each of his, then bring your hands together again—he's clapping your hands now! The song "If you're happy and you know it, clap your hands" is perfect for this activity. He'll associate it with the actions, and will be ready to join in as his ability to clap develops in the coming months.

Clap and sing Babies love the drama and dynamism of clapping their hands, and will enjoy having their hands clapped by Mom or Dad while singing songs and playing games.

What baby sees now

Your baby's vision is improving all the time. He's still drawn to bright colors, but can distinguish more subtle color contrasts now, too.

At almost four months, your baby's eyesight has sharpened and now he will be able to see and take notice of objects across the room, although he still prefers looking at people up close, so continue to give him plenty of eye-to-eye contact during feedings.

Your baby's eyes should move together smoothly and follow objects and people

Maturing vision At around this time, your baby will be able to see color and perceive depth more accurately than previously.

around the room. If you notice crossed eyes or any other vision problems, mention them to your pediatrician.

Your baby may now be able to distinguish between more subtle color contrasts, such as red and reddish orange, although subtle differences between pastel shades may still be beyond him. You may also notice that your baby's eyes are starting to change color. Lighter-colored eyes may go through several changes before settling on their final shade at about six months.

Changing friendships

Having a baby shifts your life and focus dramatically, and you may find that some friendships alter as your needs change.

It may be that many of your friends and family are perfectly happy to spend endless hours discussing the joys and concerns of new parenthood, and share your enthusiasm for your baby. Others, however, who are perhaps at different stages of their lives, may find your new focus bewildering and wonder where your common ground now lies. You may feel distressed that previously solid friendships are much less satisfying, and worry that they are coming to an end.

It is natural for friendships to wane and surge throughout our lives. You may well make a new set of friends among your baby crowd, and probably have more in common with them at this point. Equally, however, old friendships

are not dispensable, and you may need to make an effort to keep some of them going. Make time to go out with friends without your baby and show an interest in their lives. Keep talk of your baby to a minimum and focus on what you have in common. Your friends are no less worthy if they fail to share your passion—try to remember a time when you were not interested in diapers and teething yourself!

Your friendships will continue to evolve in the future, and you may one day find that you can play a supportive role when friends go on to have their own babies. Keep things simmering away for now, and remember that this is a phase that will eventually be resolved.

ASK A... PEDIATRICIAN

My baby has started to suck his thumb. Is this a problem? About 80 percent of babies suck their thumbs or fingers, which causes their brains to produce endorphins ("feel-good" chemicals) that soothe and calm. If he's sucking his thumb, this shows he is learning to comfort himself, which is a useful skill. There is no need to worry about his teeth, either. As long as you discourage the habit by the time his baby teeth fall out (at about five years of age), there won't be lasting damage. Most suck their thumbs much less by the age of three.

16 weeks

BABIES' BABBLING AT THIS AGE SOUNDS THE SAME, NO MATTER WHAT LANGUAGE THEY HEAR

Your baby should enjoy tummy time more now that she is stronger. If she hasn't already, she's about to push up on her arms and support the weight of her upper body—if only for a few moments. She'll be using a wider variety of sounds, and perhaps even joining syllables together.

Look who's "talking"

Your baby may start combining sounds and syllables so that they sound like "words," but they don't have any meaning just yet.

Conversation You can encourage your baby to talk by imitating her sounds and "words" as well as her facial expressions.

This week, you may notice that, as your baby practices his vocal skills, many different vowel sounds have crept into his "language," and that he is making more sounds when playing on his own. He may growl and gurgle, and even squeal and shriek unexpectedly. The occasional consonant may now sneak into his vocabulary, and he may create some peculiar words, such as "ibcooo" and "gipgooo." Your baby may also begin to recognize that the way your mouth moves affects the sounds you make, which is more or less lip reading!

You can encourage the development of your baby's verbal skills by answering him when he makes his little noises. He'll be learning the rudiments of language and conversation, which includes both speaking and listening.

He has been exposed to language since he was in the uterus, and he was born with a very basic understanding of speech patterns and different sounds. Now, he will attempt to replicate those patterns and sounds, and you may find that he mimics the high- and low-pitched voices you use when you speak to him, and also that his babbling and coos sound much more like language.

Bilingual baby If more than one language is spoken in your household, don't hesitate to use both languages regularly. Research suggests that being exposed to two languages early on affects brain development, making such babies receptive to new languages for a longer period. This is especially true if a baby hears both languages in the first year of life. Also, speaking more than one language helps your child's learning. Speak to your baby in whichever language feels comfortable to you. One of you may speak the first language while the other uses the second, community, language. Your baby will adapt and learn to use them individually as he moves between home and community.

Sometimes it's thought that children who learn two languages will have delayed speech. This isn't usually the case and such an assumption can mean that a speech problem is ignored. If you have any concerns about your baby's speech, consult your pediatrician.

DEVELOPMENT ACTIVITY

Rock, sway, and swing

The part of your baby's brain that senses motion and balance is known as the vestibular system. As this system matures, it helps him to keep his head upright and, eventually, to keep his balance when sitting and standing up. Rocking, swaying, and swinging your baby up and down, both gently and more playfully, will encourage the development of this system, and he will love the activity. There is good research to suggest that these types of movements help to improve a baby's sense of balance, his gross motor skills, and his perception of movement in advance of crawling and walking. Try to make movement part of your regular playtime.

Up, up, and away! Bouncing your baby up and down will help to improve his sense of balance and movement.

159

Your parenting style

By 16 weeks, you'll have developed your own ideas about raising your baby, but it's good to keep refining your thinking.

Whether to take others' advice is a tricky area for parents. One set of grandparents frowns on the use of a pacifier, the other thinks your baby should be toilet-trained pretty much from birth, while your best friend thinks that even young babies should be "sleep trained" to last through the night. Not your philosophy? Try not to worry. Instead, establish a culture of respect—you do it your way, I'll do it mine.

The basis of your parenting style should always be the provision of a warm, responsive, and loving family. It is too early to introduce rules or punishments right now, but it is the right time to discuss with your partner how you would like to parent together. Talk about how each of you was parented, since this will shape your attitude to parenting now. Discuss do's and don'ts: one of you may be easy with praise and rewards, while the other sees this as too much. Try to reach a compromise that suits you both.

You may find that other people are particularly vocal in expressing their disapproval of your methods—learn to negotiate these interventions with a dignified silence. It's always good to listen to the ideas of others, but if you and your partner are in agreement about how to raise your baby, you are perfectly within your rights to continue.

FOUR-MONTH VACCINATIONS

It's getting time for another set of your baby's immunizations (see p.103). At four months, he will likely be getting a second dose of the 5-in-1 vaccine to protect against diphtheria, tetanus, pertussis (whooping cough), polio, and *Haemophilus influenzae* type b. He may also be given a second dose of pneumococcal disease vaccine. If you haven't already made an appointment, contact your pediatrician now to ensure that your baby's immunizations are up to date.

Growing appetite

Your baby may be hungrier than usual this week, and he may demand the bottle constantly or spend long hours at the breast.

Your increasingly active baby needs more fuel to keep going, which may be why he's hungrier right now. If you are breast-feeding, feed him on demand. If you are bottle-feeding, when he begins to empty his bottle, this is your cue to give him an additional 1 oz (30 ml) of formula. If he drains the bottle and seems dissatisfied, give him another 1 oz (30 ml). Do not exceed 5 fl oz (150 ml)

More milk Your baby may feed more around now to fuel his increasingly energetic play and his rapid physical growth.

of milk per 2.2 lbs (1 kg) of weight per day. If you are unsure, speak to your pediatrician. You may want to give some cooled boiled water between feedings to make sure he isn't thirsty instead.

Your baby's nutritional needs are still being met by milk, so don't be tempted to introduce solids quite yet; his digestive system won't be ready for solids until 17 weeks at the earliest. If you are considering starting solids before six months, see your doctor, who can help you decide if he is ready (see pp.162–163 for more about starting solids).

The importance of play

Playing with your baby supports his development in so many ways, and promotes healthy communication with you in the years to come.

Noisy toys Babies love playing with toys that produce a lot of noise. The more sound the toy makes, the more fun he'll have.

Playing with your child supports his emotional health—for example, by encouraging self-esteem and trust. Play is an essential component of healthy development in babies and children, providing opportunities to develop motor, cognitive, perceptual, and social skills. It encourages creativity, imagination, and self-sufficiency, and it helps babies to discover new things, solve problems, and, above all, relax and enjoy themselves.

Play allows your baby to learn about the world around him. Whenever he hears, sees, touches, tastes, or smells something, messages are sent to his brain, prompting important mental connections to be created. So when you play with your baby, you're helping to shape his brain. Giving your child a variety of activities to experience will result in more brain connections being

made, and repeating these activities will make these associations stronger. Physical play (see p.151) encourages gross motor skills, spatial awareness, and much more; while books, shape sorters, rattles, cause-and-effect toys, and "conversation" promote cognitive development, hand–eye coordination, and fine motor skills. Mixing different types of play will allow your baby to grow into a healthy, stimulated child.

However, don't fall into the trap of thinking you need to stimulate your baby constantly, or make every play session a learning opportunity. Play should be relaxed, spontaneous, and fun. Your baby will learn just as much from a tickling game as he will from expensive, developmentally appropriate, high-contrast flash cards being dangled in front of him. Play never needs to be structured—just do what comes naturally, simply encouraging your baby to attempt new feats, enjoy your company, explore his environment, relax, and have fun. Most importantly, give your baby your time: you will encourage emotional well-being by simply being there for him.

DEVELOPMENT ACTIVITY

Playing with household items

Your baby doesn't need expensive toys; in fact, he may enjoy playing with the things you use and copying what you do. Plastic cups are great for stacking up, then knocking over. Give him a clean wooden spoon or spatula (keep it light so he doesn't get hurt if he bonks himself on the head) and an empty plastic mixing bowl to bang and "stir." Scrunch up a large piece of paper and let him investigate the texture and crunchy sound it makes. Even a cardboard box or plastic measuring spoons will amuse him! Avoid hazardous items, such as plastic bottles with screw-on lids that he could choke on, or painted wooden implements.

Fascinating new world Things we would consider ordinary are positively exotic to your baby. Almost anything can make a good plaything, as long as it is safe for him to play with.

SPOTLIGHT ON...
Starting solids

It's little wonder that new moms are often baffled by starting solids—differing opinions and contradictory advice about the process abound. So here's a straightforward guide to what it is, how to decide when to start, and what you'll need to get going.

Finger sucking A baby who is ready to move on to solids may demonstrate the classic telltale sign of sucking his fingers or fists.

CHECKLIST

Solids equipment

■ A high chair or a seat that clips onto your dining table. Look for a sturdy high chair, ideally with molded corners and crevices to make cleaning easy, a harness or five-point belt, and an insert to hold younger babies snugly. A detachable tray is a plus (see p.220).

■ A splash mat for under the chair.

■ Two or three small plastic bowls, preferably with a suction cup at the base for stability.

■ Two or three plastic or soft rubber baby spoons with a small, easy-to-use "scoop."

■ A plastic cup or sippy cup with a spout; choose a "slow flow" one.

■ Easy-to-clean bibs.

■ A food processor or hand blender. An electric grinder is useful for foods that become glutinous in a food processor and foods with tough skins, such as peas or soy beans.

■ A flexible ice-cube tray with a secure lid, and mini containers with lids to freeze larger quantities of your baby's favorite purées.

■ Stick-on labels so that you can note the type of purée and the date that you make it.

What does starting solids entail?

The gradual process of introducing foods other than milk into your baby's diet is also called complementary feeding because the foods, or "solids," are given alongside milk. It doesn't mean encouraging your baby to stop drinking formula or breast-feeding; milk will continue to be a mainstay of your baby's diet. However, as your baby becomes bigger and more active, he'll need the extra nutrients from solid foods to ensure his healthy growth and development.

What's the advice on when to start?

Over the next couple of weeks, your baby might start showing signs that make you think he's ready for some solid food. Perhaps he's consistently hungry and normal feedings don't seem to satisfy him, or he's started waking at night to be fed when he previously slept through. Perhaps other moms of young babies have started solids already, and you're wondering if you should too. Or your own mother may have told you that starting solids happened much earlier in her day, and it didn't do you any harm! All of these factors can prompt moms to start solids early—but is this really the right time—or should you wait?

The Canadian Paediatric Society and the World Health Organization (WHO) advocate waiting. They recommend exclusive breast-feeding (or bottle-feeding) for the first six months of life. The practical reasons to wait until six months are that it makes the process considerably easier if your baby is able to sit in a high chair, take food easily from a spoon, and/or pick up and hold food to feed himself.

However, some experts disagree that waiting until six months to start is a good idea. There is a growing body of evidence that this increases the risk of iron deficiency in babies, as well as the risk of allergies. It is known that babies' iron reserves begin to run down at six months, so if babies are only just starting on fruit and vegetable purées at this time, they're unlikely to get all the iron they need. Some experts believe that breast-feeding for six months is a desirable goal, and that starting solid foods should begin by six months at the latest, but not before four months (or 17 weeks). Also, breast-feeding should continue throughout beginning solids, particularly in the early stages. They also support research which indicates that introducing foods containing gluten between four and seven months while breast-feeding may reduce the risk of celiac disease, type 1 diabetes, and wheat allergy. Furthermore, high-allergen

foods, such as eggs and fish, don't need to be delayed until after six months. Other research suggests that babies who start solids before six months are more likely to enjoy a wider variety of tastes (including vegetables and fish) than those who started solids at or after six months because of their early introduction to solid food. The reason is that, up to six months of age, babies will readily accept new flavors, tastes, and textures; older babies show more resistance.

The right time Before you rush into anything, be certain that your baby is absolutely ready to take this step. Every baby is different, and your baby has to be physically and emotionally ready before you consider introducing solid foods. If he is healthy, happy, and growing well on his milk-only diet, there is no need to start solids for the sake of it.

The very earliest you should start to introduce solids is at four months, or 17 weeks. Before this time, your baby won't have the digestive enzymes required to digest and extract nutrients from solids; his jaw and tongue won't be sufficiently developed to "chew" and swallow food; and his kidneys will not be mature enough to deal with solids. He also needs to have lost his "extrusion reflex" (which causes him to push out anything that goes into his mouth with his tongue), and to have the motor capacity to move food from the tip of his tongue.

Once your baby is at least 17 weeks old, he may be ready for solids if he is doing some or all of the following:
■ sitting up unaided, which encourages digestion and helps avoid choking.
■ showing interest in your food, and perhaps reaching out to grab it.
■ hungrier than usual, and often dissatisfied after his usual feedings.
■ waking up at night for an extra feeding after previously sleeping through.
■ double his birth weight.
■ able to control his head movements.

■ attempting to put things into his mouth, and "gumming" them rather than pushing them out of his mouth with his tongue.
■ making "chewing" motions.
Talk to your pediatrician, who'll be able to reassure you whether it's the right time or not and give you advice.

The right pace If you start your baby on solids before six months, you can take the whole process at a relatively leisurely pace. If you wait until the recommended six months, you'll need to progress swiftly from vegetable and fruit purées and baby rice (see Your baby's first tastes, pp.190–191; Stage one solids, pp.234–235) onto dairy, meat, fish, eggs, and cereals and grains (Stage two solids, see pp.254–255). This is because by then, your baby will need the additional iron contained in protein-rich foods. By the time your baby is 10 months old, you'll have introduced texture (lumps and bumps) as he moves toward a balanced diet (Stage three solids, see pp.310–311).

SOLIDS AND A PREMATURE BABY

If your baby was born prematurely (before 37 weeks), it may be advisable to start solids later than usual. Some pediatricians recommend starting a premature baby on solid food four to six months after his original due date, rather than his actual birth date. The reason is that premature babies often have developmental delays, including swallowing difficulties, and a baby that cannot swallow solid food properly may have problems being introduced to solid foods early. In fact, some premature babies are given a special diet to follow by their doctor, based upon their needs, so it's important to check with your doctor before making the call yourself about the best time to introduce those first solid foods— and which solid foods—to your premature baby.

Gumming Frequent "chewing" on objects can be a sign that your baby is approaching the time when she is ready for solid foods to be introduced into her diet.

Sleeping through

By now, most babies' tummies can fit enough food to allow them to sleep longer at night, but your baby may have other ideas!

From around four months onwards, your baby may become capable of sleeping through the small hours without needing to be fed. If he still wakes up, it's likely he wants a little comforting. Make sure he has a good feeding and is burped before he settles down for the night, so you'll know he's not hungry if he wakes up, in which case he may nurse for a few moments before drifting off to sleep. While there's no harm in that for him, it will mean interrupted nights for you, which can take their toll.

To encourage your baby to break the habit of nighttime comfort feedings, give him some alternative comfort. Stroke his back, sing to him, and reassure him that you are there. This may be enough for him to settle back down to sleep. Because he has become accustomed to "snacks" at night, and to being picked up and held at regular intervals, he may be a little resistant to this approach at first. Pick him up and cuddle him, but don't feed him unless he appears to be ravenously hungry.

You can start to encourage him to self-soothe. Go to him when he calls so he knows he can trust you. (Leaving him to cry may exacerbate things—he'll learn not to cry eventually, but that doesn't mean he'll be secure and happy.) If he is secure that you are there and will offer him comfort if he needs it, he will begin to learn to settle himself back to sleep. See to his needs and, over the next few weeks, you can expect him to go longer between waking up until he sleeps through the night.

Feeling rundown?

A busy life and sleepless nights may have left you feeling lackluster. You may need to adjust your lifestyle to get back on track.

Healthy diet Try to eat three balanced meals a day, based on unprocessed meat, dairy, fruit, vegetables, and carbohydrates.

Lack of energy is often related to a lack of sleep, exercise, or decent nutrition, so if you're feeling under par, you may need to do something about one, or more, of these areas. Taking your baby for a walk in the fresh air will help you feel more energetic and could help you sleep better.

It's just as important to eat well. Many new moms are so desperate to fit into pre-pregnancy clothes, or busy with their babies, they don't eat properly. Eat healthy food that provides you with a sustained source of energy, such as a baked potato stuffed with tuna, or a vegetable soup with a whole-grain roll and butter. Eating well when breast-feeding is especially important since the quality of your milk is influenced by your diet.

Take time to unwind before bed, so you can get a good night's rest. If your baby is an early bird and wakes up at the crack of dawn, you might need to adjust your own schedule to fit in enough sleep. Perhaps go to bed an hour earlier and plan to get more done in the morning. Doing lots of chores in the evening will leave you drained and possibly resentful, which is not conducive to restful sleep. Take care of yourself, so you can take care of your baby. If exhaustion becomes debilitating, or you are finding it hard to cope, see your doctor. You may be suffering from low iron levels (causing anemia), an underactive thyroid, a low-grade infection, or, possibly, postpartum depression.

Getting ready to crawl

Although the average age to begin crawling is eight to nine months, your baby is practicing the moves now that he will need later on.

Precursor to crawling Tummy time helps to build up strength in the arms and legs in preparation for crawling.

Over the coming weeks, your baby will start to lift his head during tummy time, dig his toes in to see if he can propel himself forward, and push up with his arms. He'll also be getting ready to roll, and in a few cases may flip from front to back. Each time he moves, he is learning where parts of his body are and figuring out how they can move together.

During tummy time, he may move his arms and legs in a "crawling" motion, and, although he can't boost himself forward, he might rock forward on his tummy. This helps him develop the coordination needed to be able to crawl. He might wiggle his torso to achieve some movement, and will look around with his head raised and chest pushed up using forearms or hands. He is interested in the world around him, but though eager to be mobile, he won't crawl until he can sit well without support, some time after his sixth month.

The agile "one-arm-in-sync-with-one-leg" crawl is quite a sophisticated development in terms of coordination and gross motor skills, so most babies won't have this down pat until they approach their first birthday. Don't worry if your baby doesn't ever crawl—some babies skip this step entirely and decide to go straight for walking, and end up pulling themselves up on the furniture instead of shuffling around on all fours.

It's interesting to note that, since SIDS guidance that babies sleep on their backs came into play around 1994, crawling has begun much later in many babies. It's likely that, because they spend more time on their backs, they aren't getting as much practice time on their tummy, and so crawl later.

You can encourage your baby to spend time on his tummy and enjoy moving his legs by lying down with him and entertaining him during tummy time. Also, when he's on his back, dangle toys above him to encourage kicking, or gently "cycle" his legs. These activities will assist crawling when he has developed the balance, strength, and coordination to do so in a few months' time.

DEVELOPMENT ACTIVITY

Get that toy

Move a toy just out of your baby's reach when he is sitting upright or during tummy time to encourage him to practice his hand–eye coordination and the skills necessary for crawling.

Make sure you set it at an achievable distance; if he can't reach it, despite his best efforts, move it a little closer and encourage him to try again, so he doesn't feel frustrated and give up.

The power of determination Your baby's impetus to crawl may spring from his burning desire to get hold of something just beyond his reach. You'll be amazed at his perseverance!

16 weeks

17 weeks

AROUND THIS TIME, BABIES CAN WATCH (TRACK) AN OBJECT AS IT MOVES UP AND DOWN

With his muscles honed by lots of tummy time, your baby should now be less wobbly when you prop him up in a sitting position. He is much more skilled with his hands, and can now hold onto objects longer but hasn't yet learned to let go easily. He's starting to show preferences for certain toys.

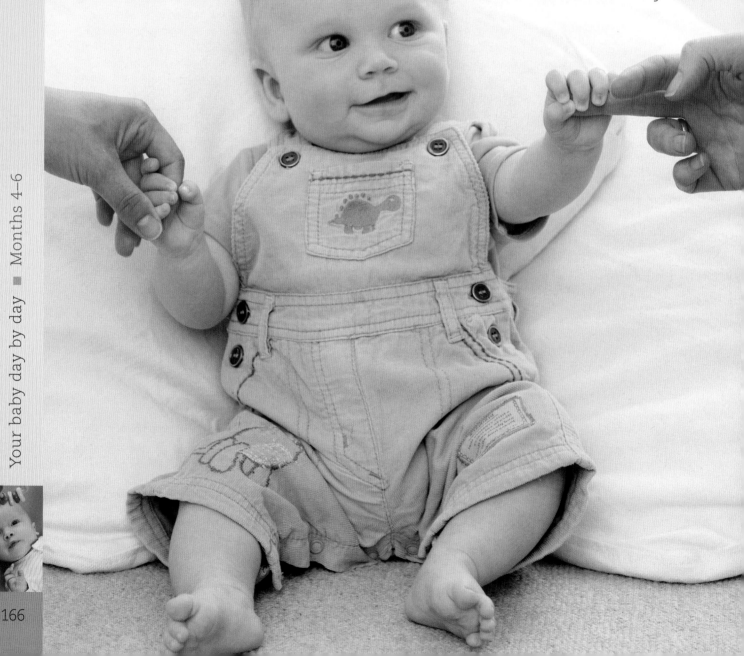

Baby gymnastics

Your baby now has greater strength and coordination, so he can bend his body to explore parts he couldn't previously reach!

Tasty toes Your baby's flexibility is innate, and as her strength and coordination develop, you may see her perform yogic feats of bendiness that would be difficult for an adult to achieve.

Babies are born flexible; their pliable bone structure and cartilage means that they are able to curl up in the uterus and move through the birth canal prior to birth. Up until now, he hasn't had the strength or sufficient control of his gross motor skills to do anything much with this innate flexibility. However, around this time, you'll notice that his ability to perform circus-like contortions develops swiftly. You can encourage his flexibility by playing a version of "peekaboo." Hold his legs together, then gently move them apart and say "peekaboo." Stretch his arms up as part of the game, too.

Strength and coordination Your baby's muscles are significantly stronger now: his neck muscles are fully supporting his head, and his chest and back muscles are enabling him to sit with support for up to 15 minutes at a time. Interestingly, studies show that babies learn to control the muscles closest to the torso first. For instance, your baby learns to move his arm at the shoulder before he figures out how to bend it at the elbow, then at the wrist. Skillful manipulation of the fingers, or fine motor skills, comes last. At this time, your baby will probably be reaching out and grabbing an object with both hands. He'll wrap his hands around it, study it, and most likely put it right into his mouth.

Now that your baby has stronger back and neck muscles, he will love "pony ride" games. Sit him on your knee and sing nursery rhymes about horses from Mother Goose or play a game of "This is the way the lady rides" with a big but gentle "Gallopy, gallopy, whee!" at the end. These games support the healthy development of his muscles.

TIME TO THINK ABOUT

Vitamin D

This vitamin is very important for your baby's healthy development, and it will also protect him from certain illnesses (such as rickets) now and later in life. The best source of vitamin D is sunlight on bare skin. However, long Canadian winters with low levels of sunlight mean that we don't get enough exposure for significant stretches of time. To deal with this issue, certain foods sold in Canada are fortified with vitamin D. Your baby isn't able to have much or any of this food at this time, and he won't get enough sunlight over the winter, so he may be at risk of a deficiency.

Formula contains enough vitamin D for your baby. Breast milk also contains vitamin D, passed on through the mother's diet of vitamin D–rich foods such as oily fish and fortified cereals. However, breast milk does not contain enough vitamin D, so if you are exclusively breast-feeding, Health Canada recommends giving your baby a daily vitamin D supplement during his first year. The recommended amount is 400 IU of vitamin D per day. However, if you live at a latitude of 55 degrees (on par with Edmonton) or higher, or if your baby is dark-skinned, you should give him 800 IU per day between October and April. If your baby is premature, speak to your baby's doctor about how much is recommended for him.

YOUR BABY IS 17 WEEKS AND 1 DAY

Building self-esteem

Even at four months, your baby is building up a self-image that will affect how he views himself and the world for the rest of his life.

> **ASK A... PEDIATRICIAN**
>
> **I need to go back to work. Can I breast-feed part-time?** Yes, you can. You may even be able to continue exclusive breast-feeding if you have access to a pump at work and can get your milk home in a cooler. Or substitute formula for the feedings you can't give, and nurse your baby at night and in the morning. Your milk production will adapt as needed. See page 179 for more information on breast-feeding while working.

At this age, the most important way in which you can let your baby know that he is loved and valued is by responding to his needs as soon as you can. If he is hungry, feed him; if he is cold, wrap him up; if his diaper needs changing, do it right away. Let him know that if he is lonely, you'll come to him and cuddle with him; and if he is bored, you'll play with him. Although some parenting advice advocates letting a baby cry, overwhelming evidence suggests that babies whose needs are met quickly grow up to become secure and self-assured individuals.

Your baby needs to know that all the minuscule things he is learning to do every day are important and worth celebrating (and, therefore, doing again). When he bats his baby gym and makes a sound, cheer and smile in appreciation so that he knows he did a good thing. If he manages to pass an object from one hand to another, tell him how smart he is. Kisses, cuddling, clapping, and cheering for even seemingly minor achievements let him know that he is a successful little person who can do things worth celebrating, which will help him develop a sense of self-worth.

YOUR BABY IS 17 WEEKS AND 2 DAYS

Playing alone

It's important for your baby's development that he learns to occupy himself for short periods, so try to encourage this.

As much as your baby enjoys and benefits from your company, he also needs a little time on his own to help him gradually start to understand that he's independent from you.

Look for occasions when you can place your baby under his baby gym or on a blanket or rug on the floor with some soft toys within easy reach. Leave him there for a short time so he can explore his environment and learn to be alone and amuse himself for a short time. Over a few weeks, try to stretch the amount of time he has to himself. Keep watch and read his signals: you should try to pick him up before he

starts fussing or crying. For safety's sake, keep your baby within sight. He can just as easily learn to amuse himself while you sit nearby. Being able to sense your presence is likely to make him feel happier playing by himself, and willing to do so for a longer period of time.

Learning to occupy himself paves the way for a much easier time in toddlerhood (and beyond), when he will be more able to find a toy and play with it without always needing your help or participation.

Developing self-sufficiency Give your baby lots of opportunities to play on his own.

Nature versus nurture

Being aware of how your baby's character is shaped by environment as well as by his genes can help you give him the best possible start.

Natural ability Whether your baby seems naturally curious or particularly active, positive interaction with you on a daily basis can help him to thrive and develop new skills.

Whether or not your baby's character and development are predetermined by his genes, or influenced by his everyday experiences and environment—nature versus nurture—is an age-old debate. Whereas in the past, views tended to be fairly polarized, today it's more widely accepted that it's the interaction of genes and upbringing that determines how we develop. Your baby's environment and everyday care therefore are crucial components in how he interacts with you and others, and learns new skills. This is especially true in the early years, since it's thought that the care and stimulation a baby receives can affect how his brain develops. As his primary caregiver, source of food, love, comfort, and stimulation, your vital role in your baby's positive development is undisputed.

While your baby's genes may favor him having certain traits, for example being particularly dextrous, or, say, musical, he needs to be in a stimulating and secure environment provided by you for these traits to flourish. At this stage, he is learning new skills at a rapid rate, and his senses are constantly bombarded with new information. Your job is to help him make sense of each new experience and ensure that he is sufficiently stimulated without being overwhelmed. It's thought that positive interaction with your baby on a daily basis actually enhances his brain development, and responding to his needs will help him thrive. On the other hand, failing to respond to your baby and/or limiting the time you spend interacting can make him feel less secure, and more likely to act out negative character traits.

While talking to, playing, and interacting with your baby are crucial nurturing skills, it's important, too, not to overload him. Nurturing also requires you to be in tune with his needs, recognizing when he has had enough, and letting him develop at his own pace. That way, he will have time to process each new piece of information, and consolidate each new skill, knowing that you are there to provide support whenever he needs it.

17 weeks

169

Tooth care

Some time between four and seven months, your baby will cut his first tooth. As soon as he has it, you need to start taking care of it.

Early brushing Use a special infant toothbrush or a piece of dampened gauze to keep your baby's first teeth clean.

Your baby's first tooth might come through any time now, and it will usually be one of the two lower front teeth, which tend to appear first (followed by the upper front teeth). Although baby teeth eventually fall out (a process that usually begins at around six years of age), they are important because they enable your baby to speak and eat (chew) properly. For these reasons, you need to take care of them as soon as they appear to avoid infection and promote good dental hygiene habits that will hopefully last throughout your baby's childhood and into adult life.

There is no need to use toothpaste while your baby is so little. Instead, use a little water on a very soft infant toothbrush or piece of clean gauze, and sweep it lightly over your baby's tooth in the morning and evening.

Change your baby's toothbrush or gauze regularly. In addition, avoid allowing your baby to fall asleep with a bottle in his mouth because formula and breast milk contain sugars that will remain on his teeth all night and can lead to tooth decay. Offer cooled, boiled water as a supplementary drink rather than diluted fruit juice, which contains high amounts of sugar.

Picking things up

Not too long ago, your baby could only just curl his fingers around objects, but now, at 17 weeks, he holds onto them confidently.

Your baby is able to grasp objects fairly confidently now. While he still uses the broad "palmar" grasp, a reflex present from birth that causes him to grasp anything placed in his palm and which remains until around six months of age, he is able to hold onto objects longer now and shake a toy as he holds it. Giving him rattles, cups, and other objects will help him develop his handling skills. Blocks are great for learning to pick up and hold. He might love to hold a ball and then release it on the floor and watch it roll away (make sure the ball is too large to fit in his

mouth). Many baby balls have specially designed grip holes that he will be able to fit his fingers into.

Interestingly, babies at this age are not as competent at letting go of objects as they are at picking them up, and will release something they are holding only when they feel the object is up against a hard surface, such as the floor.

Whatever your baby picks up will end up in his mouth, so ensure choking hazards are kept well out of his reach.

Developing skill As your baby's grasp develops, she can hold onto objects for longer.

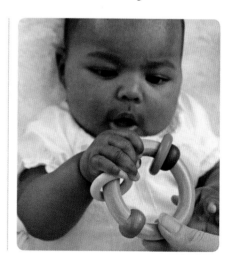

Fun baby classes

Babies have great choices these days—from the age of about four months, there's a class for every infant. Some might be fun to try...

If you're looking for some structured activity that gets you out of the house and puts you in touch with other moms and babies, why not try a baby class? There are plenty to choose from, so take a look online or in local magazines to see what's happening in your area. While some can be expensive, others, such as singing sessions at the local library, are often free of charge. Among the offerings you might find are:

Baby gymnastics Although most programs start from six months old, there are some that start as early as four months. Baby gyms are becoming increasingly popular and classes are designed to build up babies' core body strength, using exercises such as forward rolls, before they even start crawling.

Sensory development Baby sensory development programs aim to give babies a wide range of visual, auditory, and tactile experiences to encourage learning and development. Fiber-optic light shows, bubbles, bells, musical fun, baby signing, and puppet shows are among the attractions available for moms and babies who sign up. There are lots of different activities, so this might be good for babies, or moms, who are easily bored!

Music There are lots of groups designed to introduce young babies to music, most of which involve singing songs and nursery rhymes, dancing, and playing percussion instruments. Babies do enjoy listening to new sounds, but at this age, they have a short attention span, so mom might enjoy them more than baby.

Baby yoga Yoga classes are said to be great for helping babies to sleep. A typical session involves stretching and movements such as swinging, rolling, and lifting that will all help strengthen a baby's muscle tone and encourage coordination and flexibility. Some classes enable moms and babies to exercise together.

DEVELOPMENT ACTIVITY

Up and down

Your baby is now able to follow objects with his eyes as they move vertically. To hone his ability, move a brightly colored toy up and down in front of him. Hold the toy still to begin with, until you see him focus on it, then slowly move it down, watching his eyes as he tracks the movement. Once you have reached the bottom of his field of vision, slowly move the object back up again. Describe what you are doing as you go. Move slowly at first, so that his eyes have a chance to keep up with the object.

Vertical tracking Being able to watch an object as it moves up and down is a skill that develops after horizontal tracking.

DADS GET THE BLUES TOO

While postpartum depression (PPD) in women is well documented, it's less well-known that around 1 in 10 men suffers depression after the birth of a baby. Although the hormonal triggers are not present for men, many of the other triggers that contribute to PPD in women are relevant, such as sleep deprivation, isolation, and changes in their relationship. In men, these factors can be compounded by additional financial responsibilities, and worries about combining the demands of work and fatherhood. Dads may also feel resentful if partners, maybe unwittingly, undermine their baby-care skills. Symptoms can include exhaustion, anxiety, irritability, poor concentration and appetite, and worries about the future. It's important for men to seek professional help from their doctor if feelings persist, and to talk to family and friends about their feelings.

171

18 weeks

SUBTLE CHANGES IN BABIES' HEARING MEANS THEY CAN NOW DETECT CHANGES IN TONE OF VOICE

Your baby is reaching out more to grab and investigate anything that catches his roving eye. He's busy listening also: he knows where certain sounds come from and makes associations with the sounds he hears, such as a nursery rhyme and the movements that go with it.

Running commentary

Tell your baby what you're doing and describe what goes on around him to help him connect your words with objects and concepts.

As you go up the stairs, count the steps; count the toys as you put them back in the basket, and count your baby's chubby little toes when he is in the bath. Show him the cat's tail and the leaves on the house plant. Point out his tummy, eyes, fingers—and yours. Give him the names of all the things around him. Every single thing you say to your baby will be filed away in his brain, and it won't be long before he will have the developmental ability to access and use it.

Repetition is by far the best way to cement your baby's learning. If he has heard you count 1, 2, 3, 4 as you climb the stairs dozens of times, he will find counting that much easier when he is older, largely because he remembers what comes next. Every time you dress your baby, give him the names for all of his body parts. You may find that he starts to imitate the basic sounds of the words you use. He won't understand the words just yet, but he is a great mimic and has begun already to associate sounds with objects.

Learning words Point to your nose and your baby's and say the word "nose." Bring his little hand to your nose, repeating the word. Eventually, he will point to it himself when you give him a cue.

Talking to your baby about what you are doing throughout the day not only supports his language development, but also helps him to understand how things work, the order of events, and how activities such as cooking, cleaning, and shopping unfold. Tell him what you are preparing for dinner, show him the ingredients, and explain what you are doing. Show him the faucets that fill the bath tub, and the light switch on the wall, and demonstrate how it works. Explain what you are doing as you tidy up and put things away. Talk to him about what you are going to do each day, and who you'll see.

Describing emotions Give your baby a head start on gaining emotional intelligence, too, by making faces and giving them names. You can also describe the emotions you think he is feeling: if he is crying, say "sad." If he is laughing, say "happy." Many of his emotions are felt as physical sensations in his body. Make sure, therefore, that you hold and soothe him when strong feelings are evident, because this will help him learn that you and he can deal with these feelings together.

ASK A... CHILD PSYCHOLOGIST

My baby wants to be picked up all the time. Is this normal? Your baby is used to plenty of physical comfort in your arms and still needs that comfort and reassurance from you. However, you can begin to teach him that he can cope for a few moments without you holding him. Gently encourage him to play with his toys, for example, get down on his mat with him, and spend time showing him how things work. Move a short distance away, but come back if he wants you, stroke his back, then move away again. Over time, move farther away, talking to him as you go, so that he is reassured by your voice. He'll soon realize that, even if you aren't in his immediate vicinity, you are still there and will come when he needs you. If he gets distressed and you can't pick him up right away, reassure him with your voice. In a soothing tone, tell him you are there: he'll start to cope better longer and need fewer pick ups.

173

Milk matters

If your bottle-fed baby seems ravenous all the time now, you might consider using a formula specially designed for hungry babies.

Flu shots

The Public Health Agency of Canada recommends that all children, from six to 23 months get a seasonal flu shot annually. Young children have a higher risk for serious complications from the flu. Babies under six months old have the highest risk, but the flu vaccine is not approved for such young children.

If you're bottle-feeding, your baby will have been on first-stage formula up until now. This type of formula is specially designed to reflect the composition of breast milk closely and be easily digestible. It's fine for your baby to stay on this formula for his entire first year. However, if your baby is no longer satisfied after a feeding, even when you've offered him some more, you may want to consider using a special "hungry baby" formula. Check with the manufacturer of the formula you use to see if this is an option, along with formulas targeting gassiness and frequent spit up and ask your pediatrician what she would advise before making any changes to your baby's formula.

If you do change to a "hungry baby" formula, make sure you follow the manufacturer's instructions exactly. Be aware, also, that the transition may cause your baby to be constipated. If your baby does become constipated, try giving him some previously boiled, cooled water in addition to his usual formula feedings.

Action rhymes

Action rhymes provide a fun way in which to enhance your baby's coordination, memory, language—and even social—skills.

Singing to your baby helps him to identify and respond to different sounds, timbers, pitches, and patterns of language, and it will engage him in a way that speech may not. "Itsy bitsy spider," "The wheels on the bus," "If you're happy and you know it," and "This little piggy" are all ideal rhymes to teach your baby, as they encourage him to sing along and practice the actions. Show him how to move his hands in time with the song, and repeat the rhymes to help him remember them.

Rhyme time Get a friend or relative to recite a favorite rhyme—it's familiar to him, but also novel because someone else is doing it.

Making sense of sounds

Your baby is now able to make connections in his brain between what he sees and what he hears. He's recognizing more sounds every day.

Linking sound with action Games that involve words and actions will help your baby learn that the two often work together.

At 18 weeks, your baby is making and becoming familiar with more sounds. He is accustomed to the noise of his rattle, the sound of your voice, and the creak of the door opening and shutting. He is also beginning to associate objects and sounds, and the ability to anticipate is just emerging: he may respond with squeals when he hears your voice since he knows your arrival will follow.

His hearing has been good since birth, but he may have now made the leap to processing what he hears and linking it to what he knows about his world in a more complex way. He may expect you to sing "Patty-cake" when you set him up for his clapping game, because he has learned to associate this song with the movements that always accompany it, and may be surprised if you clap but don't sing to him when he's

expecting to hear the familiar words. He will also watch your tongue and lips intently now as you speak: he is starting to link the sounds you make with the movement he sees in your lips. Let him see your face when you talk to him and sing to him to encourage this skill.

While loud or sudden noises may distress your baby, he will be soothed by familiar sounds, so you can calm him in bustling, noisy environments he finds disturbing by quietly singing a familiar song; he will be able to focus on your voice and relax more easily. It is likely that your baby associates his favorite lullaby with rocking, so if you want to calm him by singing him the familiar lullaby, you'll need to rock him, too.

Interestingly, recent subtle changes in his hearing mean that your baby also understands more about the tone of your voice. When you are happy, he will respond in kind; if you are stressed, he will pick up on this and may become anxious. Using positive body language—turning to face him and making plenty of eye contact when you talk to him—will enhance your communication.

DEVELOPMENT ACTIVITY

Animal noises

Nothing fascinates a baby more than unusual sounds, and animal noises are ideal for stimulating your baby and helping him understand that different animals make different sounds. Show him pictures in a book and explain that the cow goes "moo," the sheep says "baa," the chicken says "cluck," and so on. Exaggerate your voice and let him see your lips so that he can see how you shape your mouth to form sounds. Point to the picture of the animal—or show him a plastic or soft-toy version—so that he makes the association. While he won't repeat animal noises until he's into his first year, he will have fun listening and learning in these early months.

Seeing and listening As you mimic the sound of an animal, show your baby a toy or picture of that animal, so he can make the association between the animal and the sound it makes.

Bundle of laughs

First your baby got the giggles—now he's really ready for a laugh. The simplest of things can make him chuckle over and over again!

Pop-up toys, silly faces, gentle tickles under his chin or arms, and even hiding your face behind your hands before revealing yourself with a "boo" may well invoke a fit of laughter, and the more you do it, the more hysterical he will find it! Your baby is just gaining the cognitive ability to anticipate, whereby he begins to predict what happens after a certain event. As this ability emerges, he may, for example, laugh the moment you put your hands over your eyes, or when you press down on his pop-up toy.

Fun and laughter Incorporate fun into your daily routine so that your baby has plenty of opportunity to enjoy laughter with you.

Some babies start to laugh at 8–10 weeks, and most give small laughs of pleasure and surprise by about 12–14 weeks. This marks a developmental milestone that shows your baby's socialization and language are developing. He has learned to communicate by crying, cooing, and grunting, and is now learning to interact by laughing. Encourage this with plenty of opportunities for a good chuckle. Sometimes the best way to distract him from fussing is to bring out a silly hat or pop a favorite toy out from a blanket.

On a physical level, laughing produces chemicals in your baby's brain that will lift his spirits and make him feel happy and secure.

Falling asleep by himself

If your baby is used to being rocked or fed to sleep, you'll need to teach him how to go to sleep by himself.

Many parents don't manage to establish the ideal bedtime routine when their babies are small, preferring to rock them to sleep before laying them down. With this approach, your baby will associate you with sleep and be unable to settle down himself. When he wakes up in the middle of the night, he will be alarmed to find you gone, and will need your presence in order to drift off again. If you encourage him to get back to sleep without you there, he will quickly drift back off by himself whenever he wakes and, therefore, will have a better sleep.

This does not mean you should let your baby cry. It just means that you should try to put him down while he is still awake, allowing him to begin to associate his bed with falling asleep.

Lay him down after his feeding or a story and ensure he is comfortable. Dim the lights and stroke him. Say goodnight in a calm voice, or choose a phrase you will always use to settle him so he learns to associate Mom and Dad saying "sleep tight" with sleep. Leave the room and see how it goes. If he resists, return and stroke him again, speaking to him

gently to reassure him of your presence. Come to him every time he calls, but, if possible, try to comfort him without picking him up and rocking him to sleep. Eventually, he'll get the message that it is safe to sleep, secure in the knowledge that you will come when he needs you. However, if he really isn't settling down and just continues to cry, then pick him up and give him a reassuring hug before settling him back down.

If he cries each night having previously been easy to settle down, he may be in pain or sick. Consult your pediatrician.

Diaper leaks

A leak every so often is to be expected, but if you're mopping up on a regular basis, you might need a different diaper.

Diaper incidents are part of life with a baby (exploding poops are a rite of passage for all parents). However, when leaks happen all the time, you may need to look at changing the size, brand, or type of diaper you use to find something else that might work better.

First, check that your baby is wearing the right diaper size. Diapers are sized by weights, but these do overlap and vary between brands, so you may need to experiment to find the right fit. The right diaper should fit well around your baby's legs, without digging into his flesh, and fit snugly around his waist with no ruching or gaps. If his diaper is leaking urine, you may need to go down a size; if it is leaking feces, his diaper is probably too small.

Second, check that you're changing your baby's diaper frequently enough. He will probably need changing every two-and-half hours during the day now,

so a little less often than a newborn. However, if he looks uncomfortable or his diaper feels full, change him more regularly. A diaper holding a bowel movement should be changed immediately so that the acid it contains doesn't harm his delicate skin.

Nighttime poses more of a challenge for diapers. Your baby's bladder is larger now, so it can hold a lot of urine and, as a result, he urinates regularly at night. If he is filling his diaper every night to the point where he is waking and has soaked his sleepsuit and the bedding, you could try adding a booster pad to the diaper (disposable or reusable) to absorb the excess urine. Alternatively, you could try using ultra-absorbent "nighttime" diapers. Also, if you use disposables, it may be worthwhile to try another brand, if only just for the night, to see if it prevents leaks more successfully.

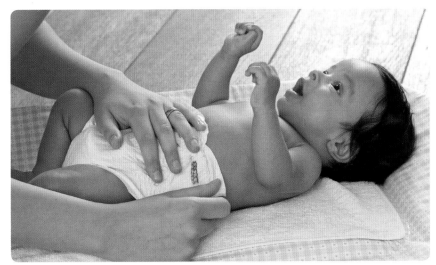

The right size As your baby grows and requires progressively larger diaper sizes, make sure his diaper fits him snugly around the leg and waist, without either ruching or digging into his flesh.

ASK A... DOCTOR

My baby has diarrhea. How can I help him? Diarrhea in babies can have a number of causes, the most common being gastroenteritis and, less often, milk intolerance. It can also be a temporary problem after antibiotics. Diarrhea can be dangerous in babies, quickly causing dehydration. See your pediatrician if your baby has a few loose stools in a day, especially if he vomits or refuses to be fed, has a fever, is floppy, sleepy, or passes blood in his stools. Your doctor will decide on the best treatment and whether he needs a stay in the hospital if dehydrated. Meanwhile, breast-feed on demand, and give cooled, boiled water if he is bottle-feeding: it's important that he gets as much fluid as possible.

My baby coughs a lot at night—what should I do? The most common cause of a cough is a cold. Secretions from the mouth trickle down the back of the throat, causing irritation and a cough. Raising the head of his mattress a bit may bring relief. Another cause of a recurrent cough that is often worse at night is narrowing of the airways caused by an infection such as bronchiolitis. Some babies need a short stay in the hospital to help their breathing. See your pediatrician if he struggles for breath, rejects feedings, has a fever, is sleepy, sick, or coughs for over a week. Follow your instincts: if you're worried, take him to the doctor.

18 weeks

177

19 weeks

BABIES WILL COPY FACIAL EXPRESSIONS, WHICH HELPS THEM LEARN HOW TO EXPRESS EMOTIONS

Your baby has become a bundle of energy and will love all kinds of physical games, such as being bounced on her legs. But she'll also enjoy quieter activities like playing by herself in her crib. Getting to know her body language will help you to understand what she's in the mood for.

Breast-feeding while working

Returning to work doesn't have to spell an end to breast-feeding. With careful planning, your baby can still receive your nourishing milk.

If you are returning to work soon and hoping to express your breast milk, you will need to plan for this at least several weeks before you return. You should inform your employers in writing before you return to let them know your intention so that they can provide a safe environment for you to express your milk. Employers are advised to provide a private, clean, comfortable area for you to express (bathrooms are not suitable), and to help you plan dedicated time out during your day for you to do so. How often you will need to express will depend on the age of your baby and the frequency of his feedings, so discuss this with your employer when planning your working day. They should also ensure there is adequate refrigerator storage space for your milk.

Try to start expressing your milk at least several weeks before your return so that you can practice and perfect your technique. You will also need to make sure that your baby is comfortable taking your milk from a bottle. Again, introduce a bottle gradually several weeks before your return date.

If you are planning to partially breast-feed, and for your baby to receive formula from his caregiver during the day, you will need to reduce your breast feedings gradually to avoid having your breasts become engorged. Drop one feeding every four to five days until the remaining feedings fit around your working day. You may need to stick to this routine as much as possible on the weekends and holidays so that your milk supply remains consistent.

Getting organized In addition to your pump, you will need sterilized bottles or bags to store your milk, and ice packs to transport it home.

TIME TO THINK ABOUT

Creating a memory box

Your baby's hospital wristband, a lock of his hair, pictures from your pregnancy scan, a recording of his coos and giggles, a book noting down his "firsts," and even a print of his hands or feet—such items can form the basis of your baby's memory box, which you can build over the years to produce a perfect record of all of those memorable moments. Pop in anything that will evoke memories, such as his first onesie or rattle, when he's outgrown them. Keeping special mementos in one place will allow for a wonderful trip down memory lane in years to come.

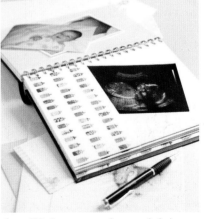

Collecting memories Start a collection of items that will help you remember your baby's infancy. Include a scrapbook in which you can jot down accounts of memorable milestones.

Your baby and infections

Babies do get sick, but symptoms are a sign that your baby's immune system has kicked into action and he's getting stronger all the time.

Signs of illness Disruption in your baby's usual patterns of feeding, sleeping, and responses will alert you to any changes in his state of health.

Every time your baby gets a virus, such as a cold, his immune system is stimulated to fight it off, producing a series of side effects (such as coughing, a runny nose, and even a fever) that we recognize as symptoms. His body is working hard to rid itself of the infection—although it's important to keep a close eye on him while he is sick. With every infection, his immune system becomes more mature and efficient and, in the future, he'll be far less likely to suffer so frequently.

It's normal for babies to become more prone to infections in the first year since the immunity they gained in the uterus wears off after the first few months. Breast-fed babies have immunity longer from the antibodies in breast milk.

Babies' own immune systems are immature at birth and develop over the first year. Try not to worry if your baby seems to catch one infection after another. As long as he continues to gain weight, is happy, content, well between illnesses, and developing as expected, he should be fine. If you're concerned, talk to your pediatrician.

The very best way to prevent illnesses is to avoid large groups of people, where he is likely to catch one infection after another, and to make sure that all family members and friends wash their hands before playing with him. Also, don't smoke, and don't allow anyone else to smoke near your baby.

If you are breast-feeding, continue as normal. Breast milk boosts your baby's immunity while providing him with your own antibodies.

Restful sleep is also important for a strong immune system, so don't be tempted to skip the naps or keep him up too late; he still needs at least 15 hours of sleep in every 24-hour period.

Finally, when your baby begins solids, make sure that everything you give him is fresh, healthy, and nutritious. He'll only be getting little tastes in the beginning, but every vitamin and mineral he gets through his diet will contribute to his overall health and well-being.

Signs that your baby is sick If you think your baby is sick or you aren't sure how to take care of him, consult your pediatrician who can advise you on a wide range of common symptoms. If he stops feeding, develops a rash, or has a fever, do not delay in seeking help since babies can deteriorate quickly.

Keeping up with exercises

It can be tempting to let your Kegel exercises slip, but it's worthwhile continuing them to keep these important muscles in shape.

If you're still regularly practicing those Kegels (pelvic floor exercises) and pelvic tilts (see p.65), well done! Continuing to strengthen your pelvic floor and increasing your abdominal exercises will really benefit you now. Carrying even the smallest baby for long periods can strain your back and cause discomfort, but you are less likely to suffer if your abdominals are strong.

If you haven't exercised yet, it's not too late to start these exercises now, which will not only help to improve your posture and reduce minor back pain, but will also improve your circulation and help your pelvis "knit" back together where it meets in the front. Your ligaments, including those in your pelvis, became more elastic during pregnancy to allow for the birth of your baby, and regular exercise is necessary to bring your core muscles back in line.

Kegel exercises should be practiced every day to strengthen the muscles supporting your uterus and bladder. This will get you back in shape for subsequent pregnancies, and help to prevent urine leaking when you laugh or cough. There's no time limit on how long you should continue these exercises; in fact, once you're in the habit, it's worthwhile continuing Kegels indefinitely.

Continue to practice your pelvic tilts too, to help your abdominal muscles to get back into shape. Similarly, sucking in your tummy and holding for a few seconds before releasing will help to flatten your tummy and encourage correct posture—which helps to avoid back pain. Why not use your baby's playtime to exercise? Pop him on the floor under his baby gym and perform the pelvic tilt exercise eight to 10 times once or twice a day.

Touch and feel

Your baby's senses are continuing to develop, and his sense of touch, in particular, will teach him a great deal about his environment.

Show your baby how to stroke his soft toys, feel the crunch and crackle of scrunched-up paper, and experience warm water running through his fingers from the faucet. Books, play mats, and toys with different textures come into their own at this age, and he will love to feel the rubbery duck, the fluffy feathers of a chick, or the smooth skin of the snake that appears in his book. Let him roll in the grass, and feel the texture of his soft blanket. Use words to describe what he's feeling: soft, rough, hard, smooth, and so on. This helps him to learn more about his world.

Stimulating your baby's sense of touch can improve his curiosity, memory, nervous system development, and his attention span, as he takes an interest in his surroundings. He'll also develop confidence in unfamiliar situations, since his curiosity rather than his fear is piqued by the things he can feel around him. Soon, he'll be introduced to solid food—a whole new world of textures. If he's had experience of textures in the lead-up to this, he'll feel less daunted by a squishy avocado or a dry cracker.

Water play Wash your baby's hand under a running faucet. She'll enjoy the feel of water flowing over her hand and through her fingers.

19 weeks

YOUR BABY IS 19 WEEKS AND 4 DAYS

Taking a tumble

No matter how careful you are, accidents can and do happen. If it's a minor tumble, try not to worry—babies are remarkably resilient.

There are times, inevitably, when your attention is elsewhere for a second, or you are holding your baby and you trip or fall, and an accident happens. No matter how minor, most parents feel mortified when their babies take a tumble, and suffer paroxysms of guilt and anxiety over the damage they might have caused to their beloved child.

Fortunately, however, most babies emerge from such incidents almost entirely unscathed. So, while not downplaying the importance of keeping

Kiss it better A comforting hug and plenty of kisses will help your baby get over the upset of a minor accident more quickly.

your rolling baby safe at all times, and being careful when you hold or carry him, try not to feel too mortified if your baby has a tumble.

If he cries right away, or almost right away, all is likely to be fine, especially if he smiles soon afterward and returns to his usual self.

However, injuries can occasionally be more serious, so get medical advice if your baby has a sizeable bump after a fall, especially on the head, or has trouble moving a limb. If he vomits or becomes unusually sleepy, or you have any other concerns about the severity of the fall, consult your doctor urgently.

YOUR BABY IS 19 WEEKS AND 5 DAYS

Team Mom and Dad

Adopt a team mentality to tackle the sink full of dirty dishes, towering laundry pile, and caring for your baby's every need.

The simple truth is that you and your partner are probably never going to see eye to eye on every parenting issue that comes up and, equally, you may struggle to find a perfect arrangement for the division of household labor. But what you can do is develop a strategy that gives you both an opportunity to shine at the things you like and are good at, and allows relaxation time for all.

Different parenting styles are not grounds for a clash. Everything that you and your partner bring to Team Mom and Dad will provide important gifts

and opportunities for your baby. Don't be critical when your partner does things differently—if there is one thing you'll learn as parents, it is that there is no single "right" way to raise and take care of a baby. Respect, cherish, and celebrate your differences and be prepared to compromise from time to time. You will both learn from the experience and have a more positive relationship.

Attack that to-do list together. Make a list of everything that has to be done around the house and to care for your baby. What do you enjoy? Are you an

early bird and find the dawn playtime acceptable? Do you hate doing dishes or vacuuming? Can you take turns cooking several nights a week and agree on a prepared meal on the other nights? Can you give each other a day without child-care duties once in a while? There are solutions to common problems partners face, as long as you are willing to communicate and plan. Resolve these issues now to avoid any buildup of frustration, which could affect your relationship. As a team, you can give your baby the best possible home life.

Body language

Until your baby is able to communicate verbally, you can rely on the way he moves his body to figure out what he's trying to tell you.

Body talk Understanding your baby's body language will help you to establish what's wrong, and how best to make it right.

With every day that goes by, you and your baby are getting to know each other a little better, and not only is his body language becoming more clear to you, you are getting better at interpreting it, too. Learning to read your baby's cues (see p.124) can be an invaluable method of anticipating his mood changes and diverting his attention before he has a meltdown.

Yes, I am bothered Babies can get annoyed and frustrated just as much as adults can. They may narrow their eyes, lower their eyebrows, and grimace or purse their lips into a square shape. If your baby's facial expression seems to darken, think about what may be bothering him. You may be offering the wrong set of toys or playing the wrong game; equally, he may think that it is not the right time for a diaper change or to

undress for a bath. A little distraction and the usual tricks that make him laugh should be enough to ease him gently out of his mood.

Babies also sometimes wrinkle their noses to show an aversion. He may not want that silly rattle game again; he may not want to be held by someone unfamiliar; he may not want what you just had for lunch via his breast milk. Watch his nose!

If he arches his back and flexes his fingers and toes, with his eyes open wide, he may be in pain. Burp him to see if trapped air is the culprit. Or, if he's bottle-fed, think about his last bowel movement—it's possible that he could be constipated (see p.403).

Party on or party over? If your baby is purposefully averting his gaze, fidgeting, and turning his head away when you are playing, he may simply need time away from stimulation and interaction and is ready for a break. This is a good moment to try a quieter activity to help him unwind: pop him into his crib under a mobile, or on the floor under his baby gym, and let him have a little "alone time." You may also notice that he covers his eyes with his hands, which is his way of avoiding excess stimulation and loud noises— he hasn't yet figured out that covering his ears will muffle sounds!

If he's kicking up a storm, however, and breathing rapidly, he's probably excited and happy, and boisterous games and tickle time will definitely be appreciated! Similarly, if his hands are clasped at the front of his chest, he is ready for playtime.

DEVELOPMENT ACTIVITY

Do what I do

Your baby is a natural mimic and he will learn emotional expression and control of his face, mouth, and tongue muscles by copying what you do. Stick out your tongue at him, then put it back in slowly. Repeat, and watch him try to do the same. Make sure you applaud his efforts—he may not even know he's succeeded. Open your eyes wide and make a funny face. Continue to repeat it until you see that he's trying it, too. Your baby will soon start this game on his own when he settles down to play with you.

Copycat Make faces and expressions and watch as your baby tries to copy them.

20 weeks

A BABY MAY BE READY FOR SOLIDS NOW IF HIS NORMAL FEEDS AREN'T SATISFYING HIM

If your baby clearly prefers you over others, try not to worry. It's a sign he has bonded with you, and feels safe in your arms. Some babies are happy to be held by and to gurgle to anyone around them, while others are more reticent. Allow your baby's unique personality to express itself.

Competitive parenting

Child rearing isn't a competitive sport even if some parents treat it that way. All babies grow and advance at the right pace for them.

Enjoying groups Being with other parents and babies can be valuable for you and your baby, as long as you don't feel bad if another baby sleeps for longer or reaches a milestone earlier.

Being with other parents whose babies are a similar age gives you access to support and parenting tips, as well as providing an opportunity to socialize and a welcome change of environment. These settings are usually positive; however, occasionally, a hint of competitive parenting emerges. It is natural to talk about and compare milestones, and positive for a parent to be proud of their own child, but watch out if there are suggestions of superiority if one baby is a little ahead of the others. Avoid being drawn into this atmosphere; remember that your baby will develop in his own time with your nurturing and affection.

Choose friends well, avoiding those who undermine confidence, or make you feel your baby is not as good as theirs.

Seeing and hearing about other babies' development can be a help, though, if you are worried about your own baby's milestones. If there is a clear, consistent difference between your baby and others the same age, seek advice from a health professional. Usually you will be reassured; however, for the small number of babies whose development is delayed, getting help early is most effective.

Your baby is unique; he will develop, learn, and grow at a rate that is right for him, and shine in some areas more than others. Moreover, early crawlers or talkers don't necessarily go on to be "early" achievers later on. Celebrate your baby's individuality and personal milestones, and he'll become a happy, well-adjusted child with the confidence and ability to fulfill his potential.

PREMATURE BABIES AND TWINS

Consider your premature baby's corrected age when reviewing whether or not he is meeting his milestones at appropriate times. Little ones who had an early start can take much longer to catch up, but that doesn't mean they don't! In the vast majority of cases, premature babies catch up by school age, and go on to succeed at the same level as their peers.

Similarly, try not to compare your twins to each other; it's common for one twin to leap ahead a little on the developmental front, which is the legacy of sharing resources and space in the uterus. Again, celebrate their unique characteristics, personalities, and achievements, and give each of them the support they need to be the best they can be at the time that is right for them.

Individuals It's easy to forget that twins pick up skills at different rates. Enjoy their individual achievements.

Are you listening carefully?

By 20 weeks, your baby may be using sounds to try to tell you something. You just have to figure out what it is...

It's common for babies to create their own sound vocabulary in advance of real words, and it can be a challenge to figure out what they mean. Sometimes your baby might be experimenting with sounds by copying. For example, if you always say "Gooood baby" when changing his diaper, he may start to make an "oooo" sound when he's being changed. At other times, he may use a sound to say that he's tired: grunting is common, as is a slightly whiney, fussing sound. He may try to let you know he is hungry by smacking his lips and plaintively "babbling" while trying to maneuver himself into a feeding position. If he's in the mood for fun, he may coo, gurgle, or squeal to attract your attention.

He's using his voice and his ability to create different noises to let you know what he wants and needs, and it is important to respond by listening, replying, and seeing to those needs.

Getting the message In addition to the different sounds your baby makes, his tone and body language will also tell you if he wants to keep playing or is getting tired or hungry. When you respond to him quickly and "read" his sounds, expression, and movement, he will be reassured that you understand his communications. Respond with words of your own and wait for him to react: he is learning the turn-taking and listening skills vital to conversation. Listen carefully to his babbles and you will hear sounds repeated over and over: respond and encourage, and he will want to communicate even more.

If sometimes it's hard to figure out what your baby is communicating, look at his body language, follow his gaze, and point at things he might want, then watch for a change of expression. For example, if he's looking frantically at his comfort toy and using the same sound, repeat the sound and hand it to him. If you've got it right, you are bound to get a smile of appreciation. Name objects, activities, and even feelings as you go about your day.

You are filling your baby's memory with words that he'll retrieve when his verbal skills develop, and he is already attempting his own interpretations of those words. These first conversations are an important step in his cognitive and speech development, and, as he reaches the 12-month mark, you'll be rewarded with his first words.

---

10 GOOD THINGS ABOUT BEING A PARENT ...

When you're feeling exhausted, remind yourself of some of the reasons why being a parent is so fantastic!

■ The immense pride you feel at having created a life from a single moment.

■ That lurching feeling when your baby first returns your smile.

■ Reliving your own childhood. Even while he's so young, it's exciting to anticipate all the things you can share.

■ The realization that this is forever—scary, but amazing too! Putting another's needs first is liberating.

■ That intoxicating baby smell, and that incredible cuddling!

■ Looking at things as though for the first time through your baby's eyes.

■ Rediscovering the art of giggling—you never realized how infectious your baby's giggles could be!

■ Enjoying a new sense of closeness with your partner.

■ Watching your parents fall in love with your baby, too.

■ The first time your baby says "mama" or "dada"—that's you!

Baby love Raspberries, gurgles, and giggles—a baby's endearing attempts to communicate are enough to melt any grown-up heart, but particularly those of her parents.

Daytime play

The more your baby enjoys his playtimes during the day, the more he'll learn and the stronger your bond will become.

Built-in fun Every good routine has a little time set aside for playing together.

The older your baby gets, the more important his daytime play sessions become. They expend some of his exuberant energy, and encourage him to use his muscles, practice coordination, and increase awareness of how his limbs move. They also provide opportunity for learning and development in a relaxed, fun way. Plus, they're a wonderful way to nourish and support your bond.

Your baby will anticipate your play times with pleasure. Think of different ways to keep him entertained and stimulate or challenge him a little; for example, you could sway and dance with him in your arms, hold toys out for him to bat or kick, or blow bubbles for him to swipe at (make sure they don't pop in his face). Try giving him some different smells to sniff—rubbing a little lavender or cinnamon on your hand, for example.

Keeping playtime fun and upbeat is important, since he will learn best in a calm, happy environment. Some parents worry that their baby is not reaching developmental milestones as quickly as others, and use playtime to push their babies to achieve skills before they are ready. Avoid falling into that trap. Play should be about stimulation and fun in a supportive environment.

Your baby's role models

Adults are not just your baby's first teachers, but also role models who set an example and help him learn positive lessons for life.

As parents, you are already sensitive to your baby's needs and tuned in to recognize when he wants to be held, entertained, or to have a feeding or a diaper change. You provide both the day-to-day care and unconditional love that is the cornerstone to healthy emotional development. In addition, the other adults in your baby's life—his grandparents, aunts, uncles, godparents, and close family friends—provide extra role models. You and his other role models provide a positive influence, and, over time, your baby will learn to mirror your habits, views, and actions.

While it may seem too early to be setting a good example for your baby, and you will not see the results until he is older, he is learning all the time, so it's important to start demonstrating now all the qualities you want to see in him as he grows older. By setting a good example for your baby, all of the adults in his life can teach him fundamental qualities such as empathy, good manners, fostering a positive outlook, responsibility, and healthy social interaction. Your baby will observe positive characteristics and, eventually, copy these in his own life.

If you are a single mom, call upon a close family member or friend to play a role in your baby's life. It's great to know that there is someone else looking out for him, and good to have someone with whom you can share your concerns and your baby's achievements.

Your baby is learning all the time, and absorbs the most about his world—and how to interact within it—from the people around him. Supplying him with strong, responsible, and loving role models will give him a support network and influences that will guide him through childhood and into adulthood.

Daytime naps

Some babies may be ready to drop a nap now—probably the late-afternoon one—while others continue happily with three naps a day.

You may have noticed that your baby hasn't been settling down quite as easily for his late-afternoon nap. Perhaps he has been playing and fidgeting rather than nodding off. If he does fall asleep, you may find that he won't go to bed in the evening quite so readily, and takes longer to wind down.

Your baby still needs around 15 hours of sleep in every 24-hour period, broken into naps during the day and including his longer nighttime sleep. At this stage, he may well be ready to have two longer naps during the day, rather than three or four short ones. He's probably going longer between feedings, too, which means that his naps can now last a little longer. Usually, the late-afternoon nap is first to go, and babies of this age often manage well on a midmorning nap followed by a longer sleep after lunch. However, babies are naturally more playful at this age, so don't assume that he's ready to drop the nap just because he's harder to settle down to sleep. He may simply need a nice pre-nap routine to encourage him to go to sleep. If your baby is not really sleeping, but playing, he probably doesn't need to be asleep. There's no reason why he can't spend some quiet time in his crib; in fact, a little gentle solo play will relax him and give him (and you) a break.

When you first drop a nap, you may find that he struggles to reach bedtime without dozing off or becoming cranky, so it's a good idea to push his bedtime forward by half an hour or so, until he makes the adjustment.

Giving and receiving affection

At this age, your baby loves attention from you—but is also learning how to return your love and affection. Enjoy!

The simple exchange of physical affection between you and your baby is a potent way to express your growing relationship. At first, affection is largely one way as you offer cuddling, hugs, massage, and stroking. Now, though, as your baby gains control over his body, he will respond to the attention you give him. Give and take will begin as he puts his arms around your neck when you hold him, or squeals in delight when you tickle him. Very soon, he will reach out his arms to invite you to pick him up or give him a hug. This early gesture

Reaching out Your baby loves to be held close and will begin to reach out for you—if you're wearing jewelry, he might want that, too!

is important in his developing ability to communicate. Responding to his gesture right away shows him that he has successfully communicated his need, and will encourage him to continue communicating with you.

Your baby also displays affection when he snuggles into your body, and, in turn, feels safe when you hold him firmly against you. Support his head and let him nestle into your shoulder, which allows him to take a good look at his world from the security of your arms.

Keep interacting with your baby positively, giving him plenty of attention and responsive communication. In return, you'll receive his warm affection, which strengthens your bond each day.

Using his initiative

Your baby needs brief periods each day for experimentation on his own to play without your direction and explore at his own pace.

Satisfying toys To make solo play fun, give your baby toys that are easy to use, such as textured fabric books that squeak easily.

It is certainly time to give your baby brief periods when he can play unaided. Your role is to make his toys available, whether attached to his stroller, or beside him on his rug, then supervise, but don't interfere for a few minutes. Solo play allows your baby to direct his attention without prompts, so he can spend as little or as much time as he wants feeling, mouthing, and watching his toys or mobiles. This should not be his main form of play, however, since he gains most when you talk to him about his world, and play and interact together.

When he does play on his own, set him up so that he is either well supported by cushions, lying on his back on the rug, or securely strapped into his stroller or bouncy seat. Place a selection of toys within reach, but not so many as to overwhelm him. He may enjoy a basket of small, easy-to-grasp, noisy toys so he can grip them and explore texture and sound as well as bring them to his mouth. Provide toys that he can work himself, such as pop-up toys and fixed items, such as those on a baby gym, that won't roll out of reach and frustrate him.

When he plays without your intervention, he'll keep trying to reach his goal, whether kicking upward to hit a toy dangling from his play gym, or pushing buttons on a stroller toy. He may try a bit longer when you aren't there to help, but he can also get frustrated, so intervene if he needs you. If he becomes distressed or gets into an awkward position, be ready to help out immediately. Solo playtimes should be of short duration, and you need to be nearby and attentive, even though you are not involved.

HOW TO...

Calm an overstimulated baby

It's important to help your overstimulated baby gain some peace when he needs to have the volume on life turned down. You'll have to follow his lead to figure out what he needs to calm him. Sometimes "alone time" can be just the thing. Try lying him in his crib on his back. Turn on his mobile and let him watch it go around, or put a few easy-to-manage (or chew) books in his crib and let him lie quietly.

Alternatively, your baby may need some comfort. Hold him on your lap and sing his favorite nighttime song or recite a familiar rhyme that has calming associations. Speak quietly and stroke his back. Physical touch has a calming impact on his nervous system, so a gentle touch is always soothing.

Babies who are overstimulated often respond positively to a cool, dark environment. Pull down the blinds and turn down the heat, open a window, or undress him a little to help him cool down (but keep checking him since he can quickly become too cold).

Signs of overstimulation Your baby may avoid eye contact, arch her back, or squirm in your arms if she needs some quiet time.

189

Your baby's first tastes

So you've decided that the time is right to start your baby on solids? Going about it the right way from day one will help make the whole experience more enjoyable for you and your baby and encourage him to try new flavors.

CHECKLIST

Good beginnings

All babies start with simple fruit and vegetable purées, as well as a little cereal, such as baby rice, which can be mixed with your baby's usual milk. Start with vegetables—babies who begin on fruits tend to resist anything more savory and develop a sweet tooth. Try different colored vegetables—orange, yellow, and green are all good to try.

■ **Vegetable purées:** potato, carrot, butternut squash, parsnips, turnips, pumpkin, sweet potato, spinach, broccoli, avocado.

■ **Fruit purées:** apple, pear, banana, peach, nectarine, mango, papaya.

■ **Baby rice or oatmeal** (can contain gluten after four months).

■ **Consistency:** first purées should be liquid, then gradually thicken them as he gets used to puréed food.

■ **How often:** once a day for the first week or two if starting solids earlier than six months, or for the first few days if after six months.

■ **Best time:** after a milk feeding so he is calm and not ravenous.

■ **How much:** 1–2 tsp at first; you can give more once your baby becomes accustomed to purées and if he wants more (see pp.234–235).

New flavors Choose healthy and tasty foods for your baby, using a hand blender or food processor to purée them.

Choose a time when your baby is alert and not too hungry, which may cause him to become upset when his usual milk doesn't appear. About an hour or so after being fed is usually a good time to start. Put him in his high chair or bouncy seat, and have everything prepared well in advance so that he isn't sitting on his own for too long. His fruit or vegetable purée should be lukewarm; check the temperature by testing a little on the inside of your wrist, as with milk.

Offer the spoon Use a spoon to scoop up a little purée and, coming from the side as you might feed yourself, put the spoon against his lips. If he opens his mouth, gently insert the spoon. In the beginning, your baby will "suck" the food from the spoon, rather than use his lips to remove it. Hold it there until he has sucked off the contents; if he doesn't do this, gently scrape the spoon against his upper gums so that the purée is left in his mouth. Don't be surprised if he looks a little shocked, or spits the food back out again. (If he does this repeatedly, he may not have lost his "extrusion" reflex, whereby his tongue pushes out when something is placed on it, in which case you may have to wait a couple of weeks and try again.) If he doesn't open his mouth, rub a little purée on his lips. His tongue will eventually appear to lick it up.

Clean up any purée that has dribbled onto his chin with the spoon and scoop it back into his mouth. Then start with a fresh spoonful. Most babies will only have one or two spoonfuls on the first few occasions, so don't expect him to eat a whole meal. If he seems reluctant, stop. The important thing is to take your time and enjoy the process together.

Social mealtimes Talk to your baby as you offer him the spoon, and open your own mouth to show him what to do. You may even take a taste yourself from a different spoon to make it clear that it's delicious. Most babies are active mimics and will follow your lead. Let your baby play with his food—although messy, this is part of the developmental process involved in learning to eat. He may dip in his fingers and suck them, or try to scoop up some of his food and eat it himself. It may take some time before he actually gets any food in his mouth.

At the beginning, offer your baby just a spoonful or two per day, usually in one sitting. Offer him a new food every three days. If he doesn't like something, just introduce it again a little later. For more information on how to progress with the first stage of solids, see pages 234–235.

Baby-led eating Some moms skip the spoon feeding stage entirely and encourage their babies to take the lead by feeding themselves. However, this is not for babies under six months, who don't have the ability (or the motivation) to feed themselves. (See pages 234–235 for more on baby-led eating.)

Keeping a food journal Make a note of every new food you introduce to your baby, when you introduce it, and any reactions your baby might have to it. It's a good idea to introduce new foods in the morning or at lunchtime, since this makes it easier to monitor your baby's reaction to it during the rest of the day.

(See pages 234–235 for more on baby-led eating.)

HOW TO...

Make purées

To make first purées, steam your chosen vegetable or fruit until it is soft. (Vegetables such as carrots can be boiled, or cooked in the microwave.) Use either a tiered steamer pot, or a steamer basket that fits in a regular pot. (Some purées, such as ones made with very ripe peach, papaya, mango, and banana, don't need to be cooked.)

You can purée a large batch of baby food in a food processor, or use a small bowl attachment for little amounts. Alternatively, use a hand blender or food mill to achieve the correct consistency. First foods should be semi-liquid and almost milklike in consistency to make them easy to swallow. You can add your baby's usual milk or a little cooled, boiled tap water to thin purées if they are too thick.

Prepare batches of purées, then chill them right away, and freeze them in portion-sized, freezer-safe containers. Ice-cube trays produce ideal baby-sized portions. Batch cooking helps you give your baby a variety of tastes every day, and provides you with a series of great stand-by purées when you're busy. To preserve nutrient content, cover ice-cube trays or freezer pots. Fill them almost to the top and put them in a freezer at -0.4°F (-18°C) or below within 24 hours. You can keep purées in the freezer up to a month.

Light steaming Peel and dice your chosen vegetable and put it in a steamer basket inside a pot containing a little boiling water, or in a tiered steamer pot, and steam until the dice is soft (above). **Puréeing** Put the steamed dice in a bowl to cool, then blend with a hand blender, food processor, or food mill to achieve the correct consistency (top, right). **Freezing** Divide the purée into portion-sized containers, cover, label with the date and contents, then freeze (right).

Can I give my baby fruit juice when starting solids? No. Bottle- and breast-fed babies do not need juice before they begin eating solids. Until one year of age, their main drink should be their normal milk or plain water. Drinking juice won't help them learn to chew while swallowing, nor will it help in the development of the jaw and tongue muscles. Furthermore, juice given in a bottle can damage a baby's emerging teeth because it "swirls" around his mouth before being swallowed. If you do give juice after your baby has begun to eat solids, make sure you dilute it to a ratio of 1:10 parts water to reduce the natural sugar levels, and give it in a cup.

Is there anything my baby shouldn't eat under the age of six months? It's best to avoid foods that cause most food allergies, including cow's milk, eggs, soy, shellfish, tree nuts, and peanuts. Some pediatricians recommend introducing wheat after other grains because younger babies can have allergic reactions. Research has shown that breast-feeding for four months can reduce the risk of allergies in high-risk babies. But don't delay starting solids beyond six months if you're worried about food allergies; it's best to introduce solids between four and six months, since research shows that delaying can increase the risk of allergies. (See pages 234–235 for foods that should be avoided under a year.)

Can I reheat purées in the microwave? Yes—but stir it carefully before serving since it may have hot spots. You can also use the microwave to defrost foods. Defrost thoroughly, then heat them well in a little boiled water and allow to cool to the right temperature.

20 weeks

191

21 weeks

BY AROUND FIVE MONTHS, BABIES ARE OFTEN HAPPY TO SPEND MORE TIME PLAYING ON THEIR OWN

While you may be amazed at the sophisticated skills your baby has learned to master, he may well be frustrated at what he can't yet do. As you support him through the ups and downs, don't forget to take care of yourself, too. Eat well, get enough rest, and make time for some exercise.

Introducing a cup

If your baby can sit steadily with support, you might want to let him experiment with a sippy cup now so that he doesn't resist it later on.

Introducing a cup sooner rather than later can make the process of starting solids easier. This is because the longer a baby drinks from a bottle, the more difficult it tends to be to get him to drink from anything else. Sippy cups can also be useful for breast-fed babies who refuse to drink from a bottle, since they are often more willing to take expressed milk or formula from a cup. While the advice is to start babies on sippy cups at six months, some babies readily accept them at five months, while others show no interest until much later (although bottles should be discouraged after a year). The main prerequisite is that your baby is able to sit up with support. If he's not sitting

properly upright, there is a risk that he may choke on the fluid. Giving your baby a cup doesn't mean giving up the breast or bottle entirely; it is simply an additional means of giving him fluids.

The right cup Choose a sturdy plastic cup with a lid that won't break when your baby throws or drops it on the floor. Try experimenting with a few different cup styles until you find a combination of handles and spout that your baby is comfortable with. Some babies prefer to hold a cup with no handles between their palms; others like a handle to grasp. Babies who have been bottle-fed sometimes prefer soft spouts, which are more like bottle nipples, while breast-fed babies often prefer the harder, flip-up spouts, which release liquid more easily. Many babies become quickly frustrated with spouts that require a strong suck. Keep in mind that a slow-flowing spout is a good way to start on a cup, since the first few times he uses a cup, your baby may gag.

What to put in the cup When your baby moves onto solids, he might welcome a drink of water with his meals. You don't need to start expressing milk into a cup; nor do you need to switch to giving your baby his formula in a cup if you are bottle-feeding him. Instead, put a little cooled, boiled water in and allow your baby to sip on it briefly—just a few sips at a time. Once he starts on solids, you can offer a cup at mealtimes and stick to the bottle or breast for his milk feedings. Babies don't need juices, or fruit drinks, because the sugars can damage newly erupting teeth.

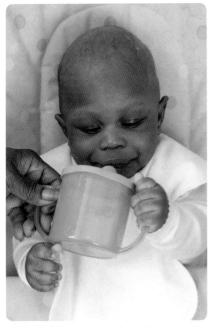

Taking hold You will need to hold the cup for your baby at first, but as she becomes more dexterous, she will be able to hold it herself.

CHECKLIST

Cup know-how

■ Put only tiny amounts of fluid in the cup to begin with, because your baby won't be able to take too much at a time. It will also make it easier for him to learn how to handle the cup.

■ Teach your baby how to bring the cup up to his lips and tip it back to enable him to take a sip.

■ Put a bib on him. Your baby is likely to swallow only tiny amounts of the liquid he takes into his mouth, and the rest will run down his chin and onto his clothes!

■ If he can't hold the cup for himself effectively, give him a helping hand, supporting the bottom as he takes his tiny sips.

■ Once your baby turns his head to indicate that he doesn't want any more, don't force the issue. Put the cup away and try again tomorrow or next week.

■ If your cups are dishwasher safe, the best way to clean them is in the dishwasher. Be sure to take all of the parts apart, including valves and straws, and put them in the dishwasher separately. If the cups become scratched or cracked, throw them away and replace them.

■ Never leave your baby unattended while he is learning to drink from a cup, in case of choking.

21 weeks

193

Safe rolling

Some five-month-old babies can roll—often at speed—right across the room. Now is the time to baby-proof your home!

If your 21-week-old baby can roll himself along the floor, you might be surprised at how much ground he can cover within just a few seconds. Make sure there is nothing that could harm him along the way.

Most importantly, check your floors thoroughly and remove anything that you don't want him to put in his mouth, either because it is dirty, or because it presents a choking hazard or another danger. Also, remove anything that, if grabbed, could topple over on top of him and hurt him, such as loose wires attached to floor lamps or telephones.

Keep in mind that your baby's perspective is much lower than yours—get down on your tummy to see what dangers lurk beneath coffee tables and sofas that would otherwise pass under your radar. Remind your older children not to leave small toys lying around.

When you change your baby's diaper, dry him after a bath, or get him dressed, do so on the floor so he can't roll off an edge while you reach for something. If you have no choice but to put him on a raised surface (say, when using a changing table in a public bathroom), keep one hand on him at all times.

ASK A... PEDIATRICIAN

Do I need to sterilize my baby's toys? You may be choosing to sterilize bottles, nipples, and pacifiers, and you can decide to sterilize mouthed toys, too. However, since your baby needs exposure to some germs to build his immunity, common sense is the key. If the dog has licked a toy, or a sick sibling or adult has touched it, clean it in a hot dishwasher or washing machine, or in a sterilizer before letting him play with it again.

Frustrated baby

Some babies are determined to get ahead in life—and want to do more than they are physically capable of. No wonder they're frustrated!

While some babies are content to sit back and watch the world go by, others really do want to run before they can walk! If yours is the type of baby who wants to be on the move, then you are going to have to be patient while he goes through the difficult stage of learning to be more mobile.

Expect tears of frustration when your baby sits up and reaches forward to support himself on his arms, but then collapses. Anticipate a meltdown if he becomes "stranded" on his tummy.

Striving and success Your baby's frustration will be alleviated when he achieves his goal.

Although it might be difficult to witness on a daily basis, just accept that this is an essential part of the learning process—without it, your baby would be content just to sit still. You simply have a baby who will generally be much happier once he is able to crawl.

Of course, there are times when you will have to be on hand to help your baby calm down when he needs it. If he begins to get very upset, sometimes it's best to step in. If he is reaching for a toy, gently stretch him toward it so that he can grab it himself; if it is being stranded on his tummy that is upsetting him, move in and reposition him.

Feeling connected

Parenting is both wonderful and stressful. At times, the road ahead seems tough, but there are lots of resources you can tap into.

Sharing experiences Online forums offer you a chance to connect with other parents at a time that is convenient to you.

Connecting with other parents can be invaluable, not just for new parents, but also for parents with older children. By sharing experiences and advice, you can find and offer reassurance on parenting issues and concerns that can be difficult to deal with in isolation.

If you are a new parent, and not many of your existing friends have started families yet, local parent-and-baby groups are a great way to meet other families. Groups are often run at community centers, places of worship, or libraries, so take a look at notice boards in your area, or at your pediatrician's office for details. You can also search online (see also the resources section of this book,

pp.416–417). If you attended a prenatal class, contact some of the other attendees to see if any other new parents would like to get together and socialize.

Community-run family services
Many local places of worship and community centers offer help and guidance to parents. Some may offer advice on different aspects of parenting, from the health and well-being of your baby to self-care. Others may offer free classes for moms and babies, so you can meet and socialize with parents who have babies the same age as yours. Check your local resources for the type of free classes that may be given. Some might be mom-and-baby exercise classes, where you use your baby as resistance, while others might be playgroups or story time at libraries.

Some national chain gyms offer fun classes for moms and babies, where you can introduce your baby to different types of movement, rhythm, and group participation. Mommy and Me, Gymboree Play & Music, and The Little Gym are a few names that you may recognize, because there are franchises around the country. You'll need to register and pay for classes, but you might enjoy interacting with your baby in a social group of like-minded moms.

Internet resources Social networking has boomed in recent years, and among the many chat rooms and blogs lie invaluable and resourceful parenting websites. Many facilitate live chat and give advice on topics from feeding to sleeping, and information about local groups and activities.

BabyCenter.ca, CanadianParents.com, and TodaysParent.com all provide local listings, advice, and opportunities to log on and share experiences. Above all, they can provide a sense of community in motherhood and, if your baby does something that worries you, you will find other parents who have gone through the same thing and can offer practical advice, or a reassuring and empathetic voice. If you don't have a computer at home, libraries often provide internet access.

AS A MATTER OF FACT

Single parents

From advice on finding appropriate child care to arranging contact with your baby's father (or mother), single-parenting websites help you to negotiate the particular twists and turns of taking care of a baby on your own. Many provide extensive advice on rights and benefits, in addition to case studies and guidance on how to deal with the challenges of juggling work and taking care of a baby on your own. Downloadable fact sheets, help lines, and email advice are just some of the services they provide, and, if you become a member, all tend to offer an online chat forum so that you can share your concerns and successes with other single parents. SingleParent.ca, ParentsWithoutPartners.org, and SingleMommyhood.com are three sites that may be useful.

Your baby's developing brain

Your baby's experiences build up to create trillions of neural networks in his brain, forming the basis of his understanding of the world.

Babies are born with a full complement of brain cells to last them throughout life but, at first, there are only a few connections between them. With every passing week, however, whatever your baby sees, hears, touches, smells, or tastes creates a unique connection or neural pathway, building up thousands of connections in the first few months alone. These complex connections lay the foundation for thinking, feelings, and behavior, and are responsible for your baby's many mental milestones, such as color vision, a pincer grasp, or

his strong attachment to you. Your baby's environment and the care you give him play into how these connections are formed. The more experiences you provide for your baby, the more his brain will absorb. For example, talking to your baby helps develop language pathways in the brain. Similarly, attending to your baby's needs helps to develop the emotional parts of his brain, providing the basis for healthy relationships in later life. So you, and members of your family, really are crucial to your baby's brain development.

AS A MATTER OF FACT

Brain cells

Babies are born with more than 100 billion brain cells, or neurons; they don't grow or need any more. The brain is shaped by experiences taken in by the baby's five senses which help to form connections between these cells. By the age of three, a baby's brain has formed about 1,000 trillion connections.

Diversion not discipline

You can't explain anything to a baby, so if yours is doing something he shouldn't, the best tactic at this age is to divert him.

Diversion tactics Occupy your baby with a favorite toy to keep him calm and cooperative when doing less than welcome tasks.

Your 21-week-old baby does not yet have the capacity for naughtiness—the mistakes he makes are merely the result of his supremely inquisitive mind and his investigations into cause and effect. There are certain lessons in safety you'll want to reinforce, but at the moment, one of the most effective ways to do that is through diversion. If he picks up something he shouldn't and chews it, offer him a safer object and remove the original object from his grasp.

Similarly, if your baby reaches for something you don't want him to have, for example, your coffee cup if you're holding him at the table, simply move the object away from him and divert his

attention with one of his toys. Babies are fickle—you'll probably find that he switches his allegiance with barely a moment's thought.

With every diversion, offer him a firm, but calm, "no" so that over the months, the meaning of "no" sinks in. Be consistent about activities that elicit a "no" from you, so he doesn't become confused.

Finally, never become angry with your baby and, above all, avoid physical discipline. He is more likely to learn in a safe, loving, nurturing environment, and listen to you if he trusts you. If you yell, he will cry, but if you are calm, consistent, and firm, he will begin to understand the boundaries.

Instant energy fixes

It's important to keep your energy levels up, so if you're feeling drained at the moment, here are some fast fixes to try.

Get out and about Taking your baby out for a brisk walk in the park in his stroller is good exercise for you, and stimulating for him. Arrange to meet a friend there if you need more impetus to go!

Eat breakfast Try to make time for breakfast every day—a bowl of oatmeal, yogurt, or a smoothie all keep hunger at bay. If you don't have time to eat at home, pack a banana or muffin to eat on the go.

Drink plenty of fluids Aim for eight glasses a day (more if breast-feeding). In addition to water, fresh juice (no more than one glass a day), milk, decaffeinated drinks, soups, and fruit and vegetables all count.

Get some exercise A brisk 30-minute walk (at a pace that gets you breathing hard) will push your heart rate up and boost your circulation and energy.

Take some deep breaths Deep breathing allows a more efficient intake of oxygen, making you feel energized.

Sit back on your heels and rest your hands on your knees. Keeping your back straight but relaxed and your head facing forward, breathe in slowly and deeply through the nose, then slowly exhale, forcing the air out of your lungs. Repeat these deep, slow breaths in and out three to five times, then return to normal breathing.

Take a cold shower If you can bear it, try alternating the shower temperature between hot and cold. This is said to speed up your metabolism and boost circulation, increasing the oxygen flow to the body, making you more alert.

Sustained energy Avoid high-sugar snacks; instead, have a bowl of muesli, or plain yogurt with fruit to provide a more sustained release of energy.

ENERGY NAPS

Being a mom is a great excuse to revive the siesta! Research shows that the body is designed to have a short rest in the afternoon, and that doing so improves energy levels and cognitive function significantly. When you put your baby down for his afternoon nap, take the opportunity to take a nap yourself. A longer nap of about an hour or an hour and a half should put you through a full sleep cycle, which has excellent restorative effects on your energy levels for the afternoon. However, if you also have jobs to do while the baby is sleeping, try to take a 20 minute nap, which will be enough to refresh you, but not send you into such a deep sleep that you wake up feeling groggy. Set an alarm so that you don't have to worry about judging the time.

Quick rest If you have been feeling tired, it's a good idea to take a nap when your baby sleeps to restore your energy levels.

21 weeks

22 weeks

BABIES DEVELOP THE STRENGTH TO SIT UP BEFORE THEY CAN BALANCE AND AT FIRST NEED SUPPORT

Your baby can now hold her head up well, and sit upright with lots of support. She is starting to understand that animate objects (like you) can move on their own, while inanimate objects (like her teddy bear) only move when carried, pushed, or pulled by someone else.

Milk still rules

Even after your baby starts on solid food, milk should remain the mainstay of his diet throughout his first year.

Your baby's diet is about to change during the next month or so as you begin to introduce him to new tastes, textures, and foods. This coincides with his ability to master the skills necessary to chew, swallow, and digest them. However, that doesn't mean that milk feedings become any less important. In fact, milk should still constitute the most important part of his diet.

When your baby first starts on solids, he'll have only a few spoonfuls of very liquid purées (see pp.190–191). Although these should be nutritious and healthy, your baby will rely on his usual milk to supply him with key nutrients, fats, proteins, and carbohydrates.

As your baby progresses from his first tastes toward regular meals (see pp.234–235 and pp.254–255), you can slowly reduce the number of milk feeds you give him, or the amount of time you spend feeding him (and, therefore, the amount of milk he receives during each feed). But you'll also need to play it by ear—if he's hungry, he'll need to be fed.

Until they are a year old, babies need at least 16–20 fl oz (500–600 ml) of formula or breast milk per day, and that means regular feedings still. Keep in mind that formula or breast milk added to purées will count toward your baby's overall milk intake, too.

Comfort feedings Aside from needing the nutritional value of his usual milk, your baby also enjoys the familiar comfort that sucking offers.

At 22 weeks and beyond, babies still require lots of physical touch to nurture their emotional development. Also, by continuing to breast-feed or bottle-feed your baby, you are helping him to establish positive associations between nurturing his body with food and feelings of love and security.

There's no doubt that some babies are a little reluctant when eating solids commences as it is such a different experience from feeding from the breast or bottle. However, they soon begin to accept the difference and enjoy the new tastes and textures. They will feel reassured that milk—their old favorite—is still available.

It's better to wean your baby gradually from the breast or bottle since this helps both mother and baby adjust physically (if breast-feeding) and emotionally to the change. As you reduce the number of feedings, you might consider which is usually the smallest and easiest to drop—perhaps the lunchtime one. Most mothers like to keep the morning feeding and the bedtime feeding for as long as possible.

Staple diet Milk, whether in the form of breast milk or formula, continues to constitute the greater part of your baby's diet.

ASK A... PEDIATRICIAN

When will I be able to tell whether my baby will be right- or left-handed? You'll have to wait until your baby is at least 18 months before you notice any marked preference, and, particularly if your child uses both hands equally, it might not be until he is five or six years old that he makes a final choice. Right- or left-handedness is determined as one or other side of the brain becomes dominant; if the right side prevails, your baby will be left-handed, and vice versa. However, babies rarely show a preference for using a particular hand in the first year. They tend to grab with the hand nearest to what they want, rather than twist to use a preferred hand.

About 10 percent of people are left-handed, a trait that is thought to be influenced by genetics. If both you and your partner are left-handed, your child has a 45 to 50 percent chance of being left-handed, too. Try not to influence a preference since this may affect his psychological well-being and interfere with writing later on.

22 weeks

Little wiggler

With so many things to do and new skills to practice, it can be difficult for your baby to stay still. It's time for a little distraction!

Distraction skills A bit of fun is often all it takes for your baby to forget for a while that he dislikes having his clothes changed!

Changing your baby's diaper or clothing and even feeding him can become more challenging as he is starting to wiggle a bit more, and becomes distracted by his surroundings. This isn't only a normal development, but one that can last for a good few months unless you can make the activities he dislikes more fun.

Try catching him unawares. Change him or get him ready for the bath in a new spot. A little break in routine may intrigue him, and he may forget to try his escape techniques. Put a mobile over his changing table and a few toys nearby to attract his attention. Sing and talk to him, keeping eye contact, as you get him ready. Count his toes, tickle his tummy, blow a raspberry on his neck, buy a new bath toy, talk about the colors of his clothing, and, meanwhile, do your job as quickly and efficiently as you can!

If he wiggles when you feed him, move to a place with no distractions. Set up a "feeding association" that imparts pleasure, comfort, and relaxation, such as a new lullaby. Sing it to him every time you settle him down for a feeding; he'll soon realize that it signals the time to be calm and enjoy a feeding and close, quiet time with mommy. When he is eventually reintroduced into noisier, more stimulating environments, his feeding lullaby will help him to concentrate on the job at hand.

Weight-gain checks

It is normal to be concerned that your baby is putting on the right amount of weight, and growing at the right rate for his age.

With the current focus on childhood obesity, you may worry that your baby is too chubby and may go on to have a weight problem; or if he is small, you may be concerned that he is underweight and will always be small. Most parents are reassured by regular weight checks, and, generally, if your baby remains on, or close to, the "percentile" line (a line showing the expected pattern of growth) on which he was born, he's doing well.

If you are breast-feeding, your baby is far less likely to have weight problems— exclusively breast-fed babies tend not to be overweight. If he seems too small or thin, the chances are that his regular weight checks would have picked up potential problems. As long as he is alert, active for periods during the day, sleeping well, and feeding and filling his diapers normally, all is well.

If your baby is bottle-fed, he may be more prone to weight gain, simply because he can be overfed more easily. When you wean him, ensure that you reduce his milk intake appropriately. Keep in mind that babies can be reliant on milk for comfort as well as nutrition and hydration. Cutting out feedings should therefore be done slowly and gently over the next few months so that your baby has plenty of time to adjust both physically and emotionally.

If you're concerned about your baby's weight, your pediatrician can check his weight and height. Your baby's growth patterns can shift in the first year, but will generally follow the percentile lines of expected growth. Some babies lose their chubby appearance as they get more active, while others with a slim build fill out later in childhood.

Early rising

Just when your baby begins to sleep through the night, and you think you may get some rest, he begins to wake early—to play!

If your baby wakes up early regularly, you could assess his overall sleep patterns and needs to see if there is anything you can do to adjust his hours. Do be aware that babies this age vary in the amount of sleep they need, with a few managing 11 hours a night, some eight hours, and many still waking for a night feed. If he's going to bed at 6:30pm, and rising again, fully alert, by 5am each day, you could try putting him to bed a little later. Don't be tempted to cut down on his daytime naps, though, as this will not encourage him to sleep longer at night, and your baby still needs two to three naps during the day. However, you may want to time his naps to ensure that he doesn't sleep past 4pm, as this could interfere with his ability to calm easily at night.

Think about whether he is waking early because he is being disturbed by something in his environment. Is the morning sunlight waking him? If it is, consider installing a blackout blind. Are other members of the family getting up early and rousing him? In that case, try to keep noise to a minimum.

Make sure your baby is physically active during the day, with plenty of playtime and stimulation. If he's regularly sitting in his chair or in the back of the car for too long, he simply may not be physically tired enough to sleep for long periods. (Also, it's not good for babies to sit in chairs or car seats for long periods.) A good balance of stimulation and rest will ensure he is tired enough to fall and stay asleep and take regular naps that will keep his

energy levels stable, and will also give him more information to "consolidate" when asleep.

If he's happy to play on his own for a short period when he wakes up, leave something for him to look at such as a cloth book or soft toy. Make sure that anything you leave is safe, with no long ties or straps that pose a choking risk.

However, if he wakes up and needs your attention, go to him and give him the meal, diaper change, or playtime that he needs. If you think he's stirring rather than waking, try your usual techniques to get him off to sleep, such as rocking, stroking, singing, humming, or just patting him as he calms himself.

If all else fails, take turns getting up with him and enjoy his energy, even if you would rather be under the covers!

Early riser If your baby is waking up earlier than usual, you may need to make some slight adjustments to her routine to encourage her to wake up at a more sociable time!

TWINS

Wake-up call

Even if both twins are sleeping through the night now, at some point in the next few weeks or months you can expect one of them to wake up earlier than the other, and disturb the other. Perhaps one twin needs more sleep, or has adapted more readily to a regular sleep pattern. Although it is important for them, and for you, to synchronize their sleep patterns as much as possible, if one of your babies is waking up a lot earlier, it's easiest to separate them. If your twins are still sharing a crib, it might be the time to explore separate cribs.

22 weeks

Small is beautiful

As your baby's eyesight improves, he'll take an interest in the tiniest things—dials, knobs, little flowers, and even your smallest earrings.

This week, you may find your baby looking with interest and excitement at the polka dots on his pants, the eyes on his teddy bear, or the clip that fastens your diaper bag. In fact, the smallest items will now capture his attention, and he will naturally reach out to touch them and try to pick them up using a whole-hand grasp. At this stage, he won't be able to use his index finger and thumb to pick up a small object—this pincer grip develops between eight and ten months—so his efforts may be a little clumsy. However, he is practicing hard, and this develops his fine motor skills. By now, your baby can also stretch out with one hand to grasp toys and other objects, and can hold them, examine them, and will probably lift them up to suck.

Encourage your baby's curiosity by giving him lots of different objects to look at and pick up. Transparent plastic balls with "surprises" inside, toys with fine design details, and activity boards with buttons, dials, and knobs will all fascinate him.

At the same time, however, beware of his new skills. Keep everything that is smaller than his fist out of his reach to avoid a choking accident, and watch him carefully. Ensure that buttons are firmly sewn onto clothing (his and yours), and avoid leaving your bag or anything that may contain potential choking hazards near your baby.

Fast learner

Your baby's development continues to surge ahead. You'll be amazed at your 22-week-old's ability to learn and remember new things.

You may have noticed that your baby repeats tasks and makes certain sounds over and over again. Repetition is the best way for him to learn about his physical and social environment. Also, developing the ability to reason (a skill that involves working out patterns for things and learning about how the world operates) requires repetition for your baby's neural pathways to process information well. While social interaction is best for stimulating his senses and building emotional security at this stage, your baby will also enjoy some independence to explore things at his own pace, fathom how things work, and experiment. If you pick up his toy each time he drops it, for example, he'll expect you to do it each time. If you give him a chance to do it himself, he'll learn a number of valuable skills, including hand–eye coordination, fine motor skills, and, perhaps most importantly, some self-sufficiency.

Encourage your baby by giving him toys he can play with on his own without too much help—it won't speed up his development to give him toys intended for older children. In fact, mastering skills with familiar toys helps to reinforce new pathways in his brain and will give him the confidence to move on to more complicated toys when he's ready.

Ring ring Your baby won't make a connection between pushing buttons and hearing noise yet but he might if he does it many times over.

Into the big bath

If your baby is getting too big for his baby bath, it might be time to introduce him to the full-sized tub.

 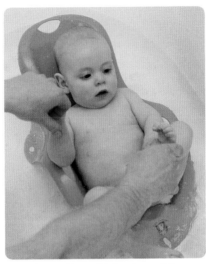

Nonslip mat A rubber mat prevents your baby from slipping and keeps his head out of the water. **Bath support** A bath support leaves your hands free to wash your baby.

Some babies take to a big bath right away and enjoy the freedom of being able to splash about; others are daunted by the expanse of space so may need to get accustomed to it gradually. You know how your baby is likely to react, so if you think he'll be fearful, pop his baby bath into the big bath a few times before taking the plunge fully. Or you may want to get into the bath with your baby to help get him used to it.

When you do put your baby in the big bath on his own for the first time, make sure that he's safe. Use a nonslip mat for the base of the tub. Get the water temperature right, around 98°F (37°C)—run the cold water first, then add hot water until the temperature is just warm. Keep a small washcloth over the hot faucet while your baby is in the bath to catch drips and prevent him from being scalded. Always supervise him in the bath—don't leave him even for a second.

Make bath-time as fun and relaxing as possible: place his favorite bath toys within easy reach, and add some exciting new ones. Show him how they bob on the water or how the water runs through them. Speak quietly and gently, as your voice will probably echo around the bathroom, and if he shows any sign of distress, sing a familiar song.

Bath supports You may want to use a bath support suitable for young babies, which holds your baby securely, leaving your hands free to wash him. Sit-up bath seats aren't suitable for babies under six months old, as babies need to be able to sit without support in them so that they don't slip down in the seat. Look for ergonomic bath supports that recline and are molded to support a baby's head, shoulders, and back, which are suitable for babies who can't yet sit upright very well.

HOW TO...

Wash a reluctant baby's hair

If your baby, like so many babies, does not like having his hair washed, squeeze warm water over his head during bath-time so he becomes used to the sensation, and distract him with a toy as you wash his hair unobtrusively. While supporting him with one arm, place a drop of shampoo on his hair, then press a damp washcloth to his forehead to prevent water or soap from entering his eyes. Massage the shampoo into his hair and scalp, then wet a second washcloth or sponge and squeeze it over his head. Continue until the suds disperse. If he still resists, consider buying a special rinse cup, which has a lip to prevent water from reaching his face or eyes. While you wash his hair, make soothing noises to help him relax.

No tears A rinsing cup prevents water from streaming down your baby's face.

22 weeks

203

23 weeks

AROUND NOW, BABIES BEGIN TO BE ABLE TO DIFFERENTIATE BETWEEN PASTEL COLORS

Your baby can now remember what comes next in a sequence of events and recognizes a range of familiar faces. He is good at mimicking your facial expressions and is learning to imitate sounds now; he may study your mouth intently to try to copy your inflections.

Learning through imitation

Your activities fascinate your baby, and he mimics what you do. He'll enjoy having his own versions of objects and tools you use regularly.

Babies learn by imitating their parents and carers, and enjoy age-appropriate toys that mimic common household objects they see being used in front of them day to day. Toy keys, mixing bowls and spoons, pots and pans, cell phones, and even a baby guitar can provide endless hours of entertainment and, better still, your baby will be learning as he plays.

Show him how to stir his bowl. Have a pretend phone call, each on your own phones. Teach him how to bang a drum like his big brother, or jingle toy keys. He is making sense of his world, and these activities provide the opportunity to experiment in a safe environment.

Choose toy versions, or real household objects, such as bowls and spatulas, that are very clean and easy to handle, so that your baby doesn't hurt himself or come into contact with germs. For example, your keys may delight him, but they will inevitably end up in his mouth, which is dangerous because they will harbor plenty of germs and may be sharp enough to cause harm.

The more you repeat activities and sounds, the greater his understanding of the world will be, and the larger his memory bank—and his ability to retrieve information from it—will become.

Vocal imitation From around five months, babies have the ability to imitate not just movements and facial expressions, but also sounds. You may find that your baby hums while he "stirs" his bowl with a spoon, as you do when you are cooking; he may make noises that are louder and more excited than usual when he is "talking" on his

It's for you! Activities such as having a pretend phone conversation will encourage your baby to act out what he sees in real life, which stimulates his imagination and enhances his creativity.

phone; he may even "sing" when he bangs on his drums or baby guitar.

Your baby's vocalizations take on a similar tone and energy to yours when you perform certain activities. You may notice these imitations throughout the day: for example, he may coo in a quiet, melodious way at bedtime, when he is used to your gentle voice and his favorite lullaby, shout and squeal during playtime, or murmur a little in the bath if he's used to you soothing him while he's in the water.

Interestingly, too, you'll find that your baby is beginning to mimic your tone, so his vocalizations with you will differ from those with his deeper-voiced father as he copies each of you. Imitate the sounds your baby makes so that he will, in turn, imitate you.

ASK A... CHILD PSYCHOLOGIST

Should I say "no" to my baby? Yes, you can say "no," but use the word judiciously—and only when you pair it with an action. Babies reach an understanding of the concepts of "yes" and "no" when they are around 9–12 months old. Start using these words now and you are preparing him well to reach this milestone. As you pair the word "no" with an action, such as holding your baby back from touching the hot oven, you teach him that the word "no" means he should stop. He wants your approval, and "yes" and "no" will soon become clear signals as to what you do and don't want him to do.

23 weeks

205

I remember that!

Your baby's memory is developing quickly. He remembers sequences of repeated events, and anticipates with smiles or cries what comes next.

You'll notice that your baby's face lights up when he sees a familiar book, and he may even try to turn the page, or encourage you to do so, in order to see the rest of the story. He may start to remember sequences of events and become excited, for example, when he sees his toys coming out, and may even look for one that interested him on an earlier occasion. He may become quieter when you snuggle up with a book at bedtime as he recognizes this as part of his evening routine.

The things your baby will retain first are those that are most frequently repeated and those that most engage his interest or attention. He will remember and imitate actions that he's seen you do many times. Through repetition, he'll know where his toys are, how to activate the music on his baby gym, and which button to press to make his toy pop up. Repetition is the most effective way of encouraging your baby to remember and learn; don't expect him to recall things after just one try.

Your baby's memory skills are still rudimentary. At this stage, the strength of his memories is dependent on how often he has had the same experience. He may show recognition and anticipation with a very familiar story, but not with one he has heard only a few times, and will master more quickly a regularly presented toy. This need for repetition means he may look with delight on his grandmother who regularly cares for him, but be less willing to accept a cuddle from a relative who visits less often.

Emotional baby

Your baby won't hesitate to express his emotions, and you may find that he's capable of picking up on and expressing your moods, too!

Your baby may throw a toy in frustration, or become angry, tearful, and anxious when you leave the room. He may be excited and happy one moment, giggling and squealing as he plays with an older sibling or is tickled by Dad, then annoyed and angry the next, when the games stop or he's had enough. It's important to realize that he isn't able to control or understand his emotions: they are simply there and can feel overwhelming. Knowing this can help you feel less frustrated by his emotional outbursts.

High emotions Your baby can't understand or control her emotions yet, and may be happy one minute, and crying the next.

From a very early age, your baby has been sensitive to your emotions, too, and often responds to things in a way that's similar to your responses. If you are stressed and anxious, you may find that he becomes tearful or fractious; if you are happy, he may exhibit a sunny, smiley demeanor.

It is important therefore to try to keep calm. Research suggests that children not only pick up on stress, but also become stressed as a result. If your baby is regularly stressed by your emotions, his ability to learn and remember can be affected and he may become over-sensitive to adverse experiences, making it hard for him to respond well to stress in later life.

Good nutrition for babies

Your baby's nutritional requirements are different to yours—so it's good to know the basics before you begin to introduce food.

Natural goodness A variety of different-colored fruit and vegetables is an important element of a baby's healthy diet.

Now is a great time to think about what the essentials are for your baby's diet, in preparation for the time when you begin to introduce foods. Your baby's healthy diet, however, will be different from your own, as he has particular needs to ensure that he has adequate nutrients and energy to grow and be healthy. There are four main components of a healthy diet for your baby in the second half of his first year: fats; carbohydrates; vitamins and minerals; and protein.

Fats Your baby has high energy needs in relation to his size, so breast milk or formula provides a high proportion of fat, which is a concentrated source of energy (calories). As you introduce first tastes (see pp.190–191), it is often a good idea to combine them with your baby's usual milk, not only because the flavor is familiar, but also because it contains more energy from fats and the sugar lactose found in milk. During the last couple of months of your baby's

first year, you can begin introducing dairy foods: these need to be full-fat because he has only a tiny tummy and high energy needs. While your baby needs dietary fat, that doesn't mean fatty or deep-fried foods, such as chips, fries, cakes, and cookies, but rather simple foods in which fat is naturally present.

Carbohydrates Lactose, or milk sugar, is the main carbohydrate in breast milk, which is why it is sweet. Formula also provides lactose. As your baby's diet widens, he will encounter starches and other natural sugars in fruits, vegetables, grains, and potatoes. Although not as concentrated a source of energy as fat, carbohydrate-rich foods contain different vitamins, minerals, and protective plant substances (phyto-nutrients). Your baby's diet will gradually become lower in sugars and higher in starches as more foods are introduced and milk plays a less dominant role.

Proteins Every cell in the body contains protein, and milk is a great supply. However, it's important to introduce other protein-rich foods into the diet as they also provide important minerals and vitamins. Red meat, for example, provides essential iron and zinc. Vegetarian sources of protein, such as tofu, are easy to mash or purée and are a good source of iron and calcium, too.

Vitamins and minerals These are essential. Fruit and vegetables are excellent sources—the more colorful, the better. Include green vegetables such as broccoli and spinach early so your baby gets used to their flavors.

CHECKLIST

Baby's balanced diet

Below are foods from each of the four main groups to include in your baby's diet after beginning solids.

- **Fats** Especially for babies 10 months and older: vegetable oils (such as olive and canola); fish (such as salmon); cheese, yogurt, and butter (after nine months); and egg yolks.

- **Carbohydrates** Baby rice; potatoes; yam and sweet potato; cereals and foods containing gluten such as wheat, rye, barley, and oats (usually after nine months); followed by pasta, bread, and unsweetened breakfast cereals.

- **Vitamins and minerals** Fresh or frozen vegetables, including cooked (soft) carrot sticks, green beans, and baby corn. Fruit may be fresh, frozen, or canned in natural unsweetened juice. Good choices are sliced banana, pear, avocado, soft summer fruits (peeled and cut into bite-sized pieces), grapes, and blueberries (after nine months; both halved to avoid choking).

- **Proteins** Lean red meats (cooked through); chicken or turkey (opting for the darker cuts, which contain more iron); white fish fillets and oily fish such as salmon, or canned fish in oil; lentils, beans, and peas cooked as dhals; low-salt hummus; egg yolks (egg whites are best avoided until your baby is one year old).

23 weeks

Playing alongside others

Although it will be a long time before your baby is able to play properly with other babies, at 23 weeks he will play happily side by side.

Your baby is fascinated by faces, and will probably watch other babies and children with amazement, even though he won't interact with them yet. He'll be interested in the sounds they make and the things they do, and will learn new skills by watching and mimicking them. In fact, one study found that babies of this age copy other babies, for instance by picking up a rattle or a book if that's what another baby is doing. Your baby may cry when another baby cries, and smile and "talk" to other babies. Regular play dates with other babies or play with older siblings will provide him

with opportunities for social interaction, which builds the foundations of his future social relationships. Although it is far too early for him to absorb social skills, he is learning as he sees all sorts of relationships in operation.

Your baby is likely to absorb himself in his own play while with other babies, and you may wonder if he is a little shy. However, this simply reflects his developmental stage. Furthermore, new faces and experiences involve a period of adjustment. Once social experiences become familiar and he remembers them as fun, he'll be keen to repeat them.

Play date Playing alongside other children helps your baby discover new activities and toys, and she may get her first view of sharing.

Who's that baby?

It will be many months before your baby understands the concept of "you" and "me." For now, his identity is inextricably linked to you.

ASK A... PEDIATRICIAN

Should I discourage my baby from sucking his thumb? I'm worried it will become a habit he won't be able to break. Thumb-sucking is very comforting for babies and gives them a convenient way of soothing themselves without your help. There's absolutely no harm in it, so let him suck away. Most children do grow out of the habit and, provided that it ceases by the age of five, there's no evidence that it does any harm to the alignment of teeth.

Your baby is experimenting all the time with how his body moves: he is able to copy you and others in simple ways and is deeply interested in his interactions with you, even though he does not yet recognize, or see, himself as a separate person. Put him in front of the mirror and you'll find that he's excited by the "new baby" that he sees, completely unaware that it is a reflection of himself, even if he recognizes you and knows that he is in your arms—just as the other baby is. You may find him looking back and forth between you and your reflection, and wanting to reach out and touch both.

It will not be until around 16 months at the earliest that your toddler will begin to recognize himself as a separate individual, a stage of development called differentiation. This is when your baby finally realizes and recognizes that he is a separate individual from you, able to make his own choices, and even to disobey you!

As he reaches this stage, at around 16 months to two years old, you may begin to experience the so-called "terrible twos" as he strongly asserts his will and personality. His favorite word and response to your every request at this stage will be "no."

You're not only a mom

No matter how much you love and enjoy caring for your baby, it's normal to need a little time without him to just be yourself.

All parents need a little time to themselves to pursue their interests, enjoy some adult interaction, and re-establish a sense of self outside of parenthood. In fact, creating a satisfying life alongside your life with your baby will not only make you more relaxed and happy, but will probably make you a better parent, too. It won't be helpful for you or your baby if you feel isolated and never take the time to recharge your batteries.

While it is important not to overload yourself with new projects and activities that can leave you tired and frustrated, it is beneficial to achieve a balance in life that allows you some space to follow your own interests and maintain your identity as an individual.

Your baby is approaching six months and you can certainly leave him with a trusted babysitter, family member, or friend for short periods of time. In fact, if he's been introduced to solids, he'll probably be able to go a little longer between feedings and will happily take a bottle or a spoonful of purée to keep him going while you are out.

You may enjoy reading, and simply need some time to curl up with a book and relax, or maybe you want to plan some regular trips to the gym. If you have career aspirations, or are thinking about changing careers when you return to work, you may want to consider investigating the opportunities available to acquire new qualifications. Even time out with friends whose focus is not on babies and children can be rewarding and remind you that, while your role as a parent is paramount, there are other aspects of your life that are valuable and need to be nurtured.

Talk to your partner about making time for each of you to pursue your interests. You could also discuss things you can do together without your baby to help to cement your relationship. It isn't selfish to ensure you are appropriately stimulated. Ultimately, you are a role model for your baby. If you show him how to live a balanced, satisfying personal life, in which individual interests and family both play an important role, he is much more likely to follow your lead as he grows, and develop friendships and interests.

ASK A... CHILD PSYCHOLOGIST

My baby makes a big fuss when I pay attention to my other children. Is this normal? You are the center of his world and, at this stage, he will naturally think you belong to him. He won't understand that you have other responsibilities or grasp the concept of sharing for some time yet. Involve him when you are with your other children; talk to him and encourage them to as well. As long as he is getting attention, he'll probably be content. If you are playing with another child, set him up with some toys nearby so he can have fun while you're occupied. Show affection to all of your children regularly so your baby becomes used to it. Sharing you will become natural to him in time.

Alone time Having time to yourself to relax and see to no one's needs but your own will refresh you so that, when you return to your baby, you'll be that much more ready for action!

24 weeks

AS THEIR MEMORY IMPROVES, BABIES INCREASINGLY ANTICIPATE WHAT'S COMING NEXT

If your baby lost her hair in the first few months after birth—which is very common—it may look patchy for a while once it starts to grow back. Bald patches on her scalp may be the result of sleeping in the same position, but the hair will grow back once she's sitting up more.

Story time

At this age, your baby begins to anticipate story time with pleasure and will want to become actively involved in the process, too.

Your baby will love familiar stories and shows anticipation about what comes next. He may pat or try to grab the book to show his interest, and show his unhappiness with a frown or crying if you stop reading or put the book away. In addition to the enjoyment he gets, reading to your baby introduces him to a wider vocabulary, different tones and pitches of speech, his first experience of looking at letters and words, and following a sequence of events. All of these will assist his speech development, and are good preparation for the future when he starts to read himself.

If you've got twins, you can probably manage to read to both of them from time to time while they're settled on your lap. However, it's good, too, to read to each baby on his own, to give both an opportunity to have one-on-one time with you and develop their own reading preferences. Prop up one baby on the floor with his own books and toys while you read to the other, or ask your partner to read to one while you read to the other.

While it can be tough for over-stretched parents of multiples to allocate reading time for each child, this really will benefit their language and learning skills, particularly if they were born prematurely.

Involved reader Encourage your baby to explore books by getting him to help turn the pages, lift flaps, and stroke textured areas.

Trial and error

When your baby finds a task difficult, resist the temptation to leap right in! Give him a chance to learn by trial and error.

It's natural to want to jump in to help and comfort your baby when he finds his physical limitations frustrating. However, babies learn best through repetition, trial and error, and your guidance through new activities as they slowly but surely master the skills necessary to achieve their goal.

It can be difficult to get the balance right of helping out, but not stepping in too early to give assistance. Your baby may repeatedly drop a toy, or be unable to get his little fingers into just the right position to make his pop-up animals pop, and he may fumble as he tries to turn the pages of his book or lift the flaps. However, try to resist doing everything for him. On his first attempt at a new movement or activity, guide him through the actions: you might hold his hand or support his body in the right position as he tries. Next time, give him less, or no, help as he tries independently. Make positive sounds of pleasure when he attempts something new, and a cheerful "not quite" or "uh-oh" when he doesn't quite manage it. If he becomes frustrated, do step in and help, and check whether he's trying to do something he is not ready for developmentally. If that's the case, your help is needed for a little longer.

If he gets attention for trying, and is frequently encouraged from the sidelines to carry on trying, he is much more likely to continue his efforts. His problem-solving skills will be enhanced, and so will his confidence, effectiveness, and, of course, pride.

211

SPOTLIGHT ON...
Your baby's teeth

Your baby's teeth started developing in his gums in early pregnancy—now the first of his 20 primary baby teeth may begin to come through. Some babies experience discomfort, while others sail through teething with barely a dribble.

Cleaning her teeth Make brushing fun for your baby, and start to get her into the habit of brushing each morning and evening now, so that it becomes a familiar part of her routine.

ASK A... PEDIATRICIAN

Is it normal for my baby to have diarrhea when he is teething?

Although there is no reason why your baby should experience a runny tummy, some parents do report that their babies tend to have looser bowel movements during teething. If the diarrhea is short-lived, there shouldn't be anything to worry about. However, it should never be assumed that teething is the direct cause of diarrhea. If your baby's diarrhea becomes persistent, he seems at all unwell, or has a temperature, take him to see your doctor to rule out any other causes for concern.

Rarely, babies are born with teeth, but most babies begin teething between the ages of four and eight months, with the average age being six months, although some can start as late as 12 months.

The bottom incisors (bottom front teeth) are the first teeth to come through, followed by the top incisors a month or so later. Next, at 9–12 months, come the top lateral incisors (either side of the top front teeth). The bottom lateral incisors emerge about a month later, then the canines (the pointy teeth on either side of the bottom and top front four teeth) at about 16 months. Molars (back teeth) might appear before the canines, and second molars, at the back of the mouth, may not appear until after 20 months. By the age of two and a half to three, he will have all of his baby teeth.

Caring for your baby's teeth As soon as your baby cuts his first tooth, clean it regularly (see p.170). By the time he has three or four teeth, move on to a children's toothbrush. You'll want a toothbrush that is specially designed for babies, with super-soft bristles and a small head that can reach comfortably into the corners of your baby's mouth. It's not necessary at this young age to use toothpaste, but if you do, use only a pea-sized amount of fluoride-free toothpaste. Babies tend to eat toothpaste instead of spitting it out, and swallowing fluoride can be problematic for babies and toddlers. Wet the toothbrush with water, which in most communities contains safe amounts of fluoride.

Wait at least half an hour after feeding before brushing to allow the antibacterial properties of saliva to get to work first. Brush gently in a circular motion, cleaning the area around the gums in particular, as this is where plaque can build up.

If your baby resists having his teeth brushed, make a game of it. Count his teeth when you brush them, and give him the toothbrush after brushing so he can experiment on his own. You'll need to brush his teeth for him until he is about seven years old, so it is something he will have to get used to.

Seeing the dentist Your dentist will let you know when your baby should have his first visit; this is normally between six and 12 months old, but if the teeth are coming through and look healthy, you can probably wait longer. Take your baby with you to your appointments, so he becomes familiar with the process. It may help him create positive associations with the process if the dentist has a peek on one or two occasions before his first full appointment.

Mom's a cry baby

It's often said that once you're a mom, tears tend to flow at the slightest provocation. Read on and don't weep.

A story on the news, a poignant picture, a children's cartoon, even an episode of your favorite soap—it may seem that these days, just about anything can have you reaching for your box of tissues. Feeling extra-sensitive, particularly in all matters concerning children, seems to come with the territory of being a mother. Perhaps this change has to do with becoming more empathetic as a mom. Feeling intense love for your own child makes you more aware of other people's suffering and makes you highly aware of the vulnerability of babies and children. If you talk to other friends who are moms, you'll probably discover that they are just as sentimental as you are.

However, if your propensity for tears is accompanied by severe premenstrual syndrome (PMS), and you are currently in the process of weaning, the way you are feeling will probably be a result of hormonal changes. When you stop breast-feeding, there can be a shift in your hormone levels—specifically in prolactin, the hormone that stimulates milk production and which also has the effect of making you feel calm and relaxed. When production of this hormone declines and progesterone and estrogen levels increase, you're likely to experience symptoms. The feelings of aggression, anger, or low moods associated with PMS should lift once your hormones settle. If your low mood persists, see your health practitioner—you may be experiencing postpartum depression and he or she can offer help.

Hands free!

Once your baby can sit propped up, he'll be able to practice using his hands more, and will soon use them more effectively and efficiently.

Being able to use two hands, since he no longer needs to rely on his hands to keep him stable, allows your baby to practice his hand–eye coordination more readily. Over the next few weeks, your baby will develop the ability to pass a toy from hand to hand. He may also choose a toy for each hand and bang them together, or examine them both with interest before dropping one to concentrate on the other.

The ability to use both hands together to manipulate an object is known as bilateral coordination, which usually evolves and develops throughout your baby's first year. Any two-handed activities will help your baby to practice this skill. Toys with dials that need turning, strings to pull, and buttons to push, as well as busy boxes, activity boards, shape sorters, stacking blocks, and toy rings are all ideal—and may now become playtime favorites.

Not every baby develops this skill quite so early, so if at six months, your baby can grasp an object and put it into his mouth, bring his feet to his mouth, hold smaller objects, and even release objects purposefully from time to time, he's right on track with the developmental milestones necessary for bilateral coordination.

Two-handed exploration Give your baby toys that require her to use both hands to develop her "bilateral" coordination.

That looks yummy, mommy

Your baby is looking longingly at your food and reaching out to grab a taste, but can he have it yet?

Tempting, but not for you! It's best to delay introducing adult foods, such as cookies, for as long as you can.

Watching you eat and looking interested in foods is one of the developmental signs that your baby is ready to start solids, or "complementary feeding." However, not all the foods that you eat are going to be suitable for your baby in the early months, and some are best avoided for much longer. One aim of this is to introduce your baby to family foods, but you will need to adjust your meals to ensure they are suitable and safe for him to eat. This is because adult food often contains ingredients that are not appropriate for babies.

Too much salt Many foods—especially highly processed foods—contain salt. Babies' kidneys are not fully developed, so can't cope with more than 1g of salt (sodium chloride) per day before the age of one year. That includes the salt naturally found in vegetables and grains, and through your breast milk. An average bag of chips or savory snacks contains at least 0.5 g of salt, and a few baby-sized pieces of pizza could easily exceed your baby's recommended daily amount.

Too little fat Your low-fat yogurts are great to help you with weight control, but do not contain sufficient fat, and therefore calories, for your baby to grow and be active. Full-fat dairy products, which you may begin introducing once your baby is nine months old, are important until at least the age of two, with a gradual reduction after that up to the age of five.

Too much sugar Your baby is born with an innate preference for sweet food, hence the importance of introducing vegetables and savory foods early on. Foods with added sugar can encourage a baby to eat sweet foods over savory, which not only causes a dietary imbalance, but also increases the risk of tooth decay once teeth have erupted.

Too much bulk Snacks such as baked beans on wholemeal toast and apple slices are healthy for you, but you need to avoid giving your baby too many high-fiber foods. It's fine to encourage your baby to eat plenty of fruit and vegetables, but not to the exclusion of other higher-calorie foods. Vegetables, fruit, and grains tend to be filling, so it can be easy for a baby to be filled with food without having many calories. This is one reason why it is a good idea to mix your baby's first tastes with his usual milk, and move onto other higher-calorie foods as soon as the first tastes are accepted. You'll probably know if you are giving too much fiber as you'll notice the number of diapers you deal with will increase.

Sweeteners Sugar substitutes have been developed to help adults and older children reduce their intake of added sugar and decrease the risk of tooth decay. They are not suitable for babies or toddlers, so drinks and foods that contain them should be off limits.

Alcohol Some adult desserts may contain alcohol. Be very careful not to allow your baby to taste these.

ASK A... NUTRITIONIST

Will starting solids early make my baby more prone to allergies? Most babies' digestive systems can cope with basic food from about 17 weeks, but starting solids is generally recommended at six months; if you do plan to introduce solids earlier, you should talk to your doctor first. Current advice suggests that common allergenic foods, such as wheat, egg, peanuts and tree nuts, shellfish, and soy, should be avoided until babies are at least six months old, as introducing these earlier may increase the risk of allergies. That said, there is controversy about this advice. New research suggests that babies should be given solids earlier to induce tolerance and lessen the risk of allergies. Studies into this area are ongoing. See pages 162–163 and page 241 for more information on foods and allergies.

Repetitive sounds

You can encourage your baby's recognition of sounds and words by talking to him constantly, and naming everyday objects.

At this age, your repetition of words and sounds is a vital component in your baby's language development. He will be playing constantly with his vocalizations, babbling, and running strings of sounds together. Your baby is busy improving his control of his mouth, lips, and tongue to form sounds. Your job is to keep talking to him, to show natural gestures, and to be responsive to him by listening to his babbles, repeating them back to him, then waiting and listening while your baby responds with more babbles.

You can gradually develop your baby's understanding of language by regularly demonstrating in your everyday speech that words can be labels for an object or person. So repeatedly saying "teddy" when a teddy bear is held out, or saying "daddy" when his father walks into the room, is an excellent way to build the connection between something or someone and the name for them.

Familiarizing him constantly with sounds now will assist him with word recognition later on, helping him to take the next developmental leap.

ASK A... PEDIATRICIAN

Is it safe for my baby to play in the playground sandbox? As long as he is supervised, he will probably enjoy this experience and learn a lot from watching other children, feeling the texture of the sand, and seeing how it moves in his hands. Choose one that is protected from dogs and cats and cleaned regularly. Ensure he doesn't put sand in his mouth, and that he washes his hands after play.

Nature trail

Whether he's lying on a rug in the garden or enjoying a wildlife tour in your arms, your baby will love outdoor sights and sounds.

The big outdoors can be a source of fascination for babies. Pop your baby on a blanket in the shade in your garden, or in a safe area of your local park, and let him experience the fresh air and the wealth of textures and activities that surround him. Point out a squirrel leaping between trees, a bird in the sky, a duck in a pond, and even a tiny ladybug perched on a leaf.

Encourage your baby to touch the soft blades of grass, the delicate petals of a flower, some gritty sand from the

Environmentally friendly Help your baby to explore all the exciting sights, smells, and textures of the great outdoors.

children's sandbox, and the coarse bark of a stick. Take off his socks and hold him upright so that he can feel the grass or the sand between his toes.

All the while, continue to add to your baby's memory bank of words. Tell him the names for everything around him, and give him words such as "rough" or "soft" to describe the different textures he encounters.

Feed your baby's interest by giving him an increasing number of things to see, smell, and touch from the outside world. These activities will stimulate his senses. Each new experience increases his knowledge of the world and will also entertain him.

25 weeks

BABIES USE A WHOLE-HAND GRASP UNTIL 8–10 MONTHS, WHEN THEY DEVELOP A PINCER GRIP

Your baby may be increasingly mobile and will make good use of his developing hand skills to reach out and grasp objects. He is also experimenting with cause and effect, and is learning fast that when he pushes a ball or a rolling toy he can make it move away.

New adventures

Now that your baby is more interested in his surroundings, and feedings are easier to plan, you might enjoy venturing farther out.

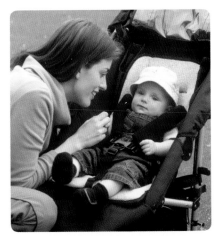

Young traveler Make outings fun for your baby with lots of stops to allow him to look at all the things that catch his attention.

ASK A... PEDIATRICIAN

A friend has come down with chickenpox. We saw her recently—could my baby have caught it? It's possible, but unusual, for young babies to contract chickenpox. This is because most babies get antibodies against the virus from their mothers while in the uterus, giving them immunity for the first few months. After being exposed to chickenpox, symptoms usually appear within three weeks and last for between five and 10 days. If your baby has caught it, he may be tired, off his food, and a bit feverish. You may notice small red spots, typically on the trunk, and sometimes on the face. Chickenpox in babies tends to be mild, so is not usually a cause for concern. If you think your baby has chickenpox, consult your pediatrician.

As your baby edges closer to six months old, he's more aware of what's going on around him and is very receptive to new experiences. For your part, it's probably much easier to anticipate what he needs and when he needs it. This means that you can be a bit more adventurous and enjoy longer outings occasionally, because you'll know when to take a pit stop to feed or change him while you are out and about. So perhaps now is the time to visit that friend or relative who lives a bit farther away, organize a day out with other moms and babies, or spend a day at the beach with the family.

Visits to grandparents help your baby get to know them better: the more familiar they and their homes become, the easier it will be to plan short stays for him with them in the future. Also, you will both enjoy the company of other moms and babies, so why not plan a baby group reunion at a nearby historic site and make a day of it?

Babies at this age love the great outdoors and so will be fascinated by parks, playgrounds, and beaches (as long as they have some shelter from the sand, heat, and sunlight). Your baby will also enjoy activities where there are other children to watch, such as soft play areas where there are separate designated areas for babies.

If you are planning to use public transportation with your baby, it's probably worth checking in advance what the facilities are for strollers. For example, check if you will be able to push your stroller onto a bus rather than having to fold it up; and whether there are elevators at the station.

BEING PREPARED

Outings with your baby can be great fun for both of you, especially if you are prepared for every possible situation. Nothing can spoil an outing more effectively than running out of clean clothes for your baby if his diaper leaks, or not having enough toys to distract him if he becomes cranky. Ensure you are armed with everything you'll need for your outing, and a little more, in the event of an unexpected change of plans. Make sure your diaper bag is fully packed, and that you have enough diapers, baby food (if you are starting solids), formula (if you are bottle-feeding), toys, a comfort item to help to soothe him, and changes of clothes for you both.

Quick change Clothes that are easy to take off and put on make for hassle-free diaper changes when you're on the run.

Legs bearing weight

Your baby may love to bounce when held upright, which strengthens his leg muscles in preparation for crawling and walking.

Learning to stand Bounce your baby on your lap to help her develop balance and build her lower-body strength.

Your baby may be able to bear most of his weight on his legs now when held upright in a standing position. This is good practice for standing because it helps strengthen his bones and muscles. It's important not to force a baby to stand before he is ready, but by about seven months most infants enjoy standing (and bouncing). It's worth noting that some babies don't like to bear weight and prefer to shuffle on their bottoms. These babies tend to be later walkers.

Many parents are confronted by a few common concerns when they first start to hold their babies upright, such as whether by encouraging him to stand, you'll make your baby bow-legged. (At least that's what grandma may have told you!) Here, you'll find some answers to issues that might arise at this point.

Bow-leggedness Holding your baby as he stands and bouncing him won't give him bow legs. Most babies have legs that curve outward from the hip, then in again around the ankle, giving them a "bow-legged" appearance. In the uterus, the legs take on this shape to make the most of the space they have available for growth.

When your baby begins to stand, and then, eventually, to walk, new bone grows and is remolded in order to support his weight. The result of this is stronger, straighter legs. By the age of three, your baby's legs should be as straight as they will be in adulthood. If you have any concerns, or if the curvature appears on only one side, speak to your pediatrician, who can help to rule out any problems.

Slender legs Parents of slim-framed babies with slender calves and thighs often worry that their babies' legs are not physically strong enough to bear their weight. There's no cause for anxiety: if he's able to support his weight on his legs, held by you, he's just fine. Leg muscles develop through movement and play. To encourage this, cycle his legs when he's on his back, and hold his hands so he pulls himself up and bounces. Tummy time helps him bend his legs back from the knees and propel himself forward.

Flat feet All babies appear to have flat feet, partly because of "baby fat," which masks their foot arch, and partly because the arches don't develop until about the age of two, once they have been walking for about a year.

ASK A... PEDIATRICIAN

One of my baby's legs looks shorter than the other, and I can't get her to put any weight on that leg when I hold her upright. What could be the reason for this? Your baby could have a condition known as developmental dysplasia of the hip (DDH). This occurs when there is an abnormality in the shape of the head of the femur (thigh bone), or in the hip socket or its supporting structures. The abnormality may be mild, where there is incomplete contact between the femur and the hip socket, known as subluxation; or it can be more severe, where there is no contact, known as dislocation. DDH affects 1–3 percent of newborns, is more common in girls, and runs in families. It also occurs more in breech and multiple births, and in babies with clubfoot (talipes).

All babies are checked at birth for DDH, and at 6–8 weeks, and those at high risk are also given a hip ultrasound. However, as it can develop after eight weeks, consult your pediatrician with any concerns, including if your baby won't take weight on one or both legs by about seven months; if her legs seem to be different lengths; or if she always turns one foot outward when taking weight on her legs. After four months, a pelvic X-ray can be used to confirm a diagnosis of DDH. If treatment is given early enough, the prognosis is excellent, and most babies with DDH do not walk late.

Sensing something's wrong

Your baby is affected by your feelings, so it's important to try to shield him from negative emotions and accentuate the positive.

You may find that your baby watches you carefully if he hears a note of sadness or frustration in your voice; if you make an angry phone call, he may stop what he is doing and turn to check that everything is okay. If he sees that you are sad, distressed, stressed, or angry, he may cry and hold out his arms to be held. He doesn't understand your change of moods, but wants you to be happy because it makes him happy. He still feels very much an extension of you, and your emotions will guide his. When you are sad and anxious, he will become clingier and in need of reassurance and comfort. Of course, this is a paradoxical situation because the very last thing you need when you are feeling dispirited or distressed is an irritable baby; however, what he is doing is reminding you that he's there. Some experts believe this "antenna" is a primitive instinct that helps a baby ensure his mother doesn't become too preoccupied and ignore him!

Your baby is becoming more sensitive to your moods and in tune with them as he learns about his world. He's watching you and picking up clues about how to react in each new situation. If you become angry or frustrated in different situations, he'll learn that this is the correct and appropriate response. If you are happy and cheerful, and sociable with others, he will be more inclined to adopt this frame of mind, too. Although no one can be even-tempered all of the time, try to make an effort to keep your voice and your facial expressions bright and positive. Your baby will feel much more secure as a result, and will learn to react positively in difficult situations.

Into everything

It's exciting to see your baby's interest in exploring his world, but ensure you keep potentially dangerous objects out of his reach.

Fascinating objects Your baby may be drawn to dangerous objects such as scissors and keys that have sharp or pointed edges.

Purses are a particular favorite for babies. Your baby regularly sees you rummaging around in yours for all sorts of interesting things, from drinks, pacifiers, and car keys, to your cell phone and, probably, the odd toy or two. He will set his sights on investigating this fascinating treasure trove for himself as soon as he is able to! Be aware that he'll soon be in a position to get hold of your unattended purse.

Do you have any low cabinets with cleaning products, or low drawers containing objects unsuitable for your baby to get hold of, such as scissors, gardening shears, string, and glue? Your baby will want to mimic what he sees you doing and try things out for himself, but more than that, he'll want to satisfy his natural curiosity and develop his understanding of the world.

He may think it is a great idea to eat the soil around your potted plant, push his rattle into your DVD player, or perhaps to yank down an iron by its cord. There is an endless set of new things to discover!

Supervision is now more important than ever, and you may also need to rethink how your home is baby-proofed. It will be many years before your baby understands what is and isn't safe, so you'll need to take every precaution to ensure his home is safe and secure.

YOUR BABY IS 25 WEEKS AND 4 DAYS

Mama, Dada

At 25 weeks, your baby repeats sounds and uses more consonants. He'll begin to try out sounds such as "ma ma ma" and "da da da."

Much as you may want it to be, your baby's first "mama" or "dada" will not be said with meaning: he just happened to get certain sounds in the right order. But your excited response will encourage him to repeat it, and when you answer his call, he'll eventually (in three or four months' time) learn that Mama is you!

Don't be surprised if "Dada" is your baby's first recognizable word. Hard consonants, such as D and B, are learned before soft ones, such as N and M, so Dad may get the honor of being named first.

Mama! The first time your baby says "mama," it will be accidental, but she'll repeat the sound when she sees it gives you so much pleasure!

He'll love it when you repeat his babbles back to him, and benefits when you name objects and people, as this strengthens the concept that they can be represented by words, something he'll start to grasp over the coming months. At this point, speaking is a game, and your baby is experimenting with using his vocal cords, tongue, and teeth to make many sounds. Babies have similar patterns of speech development and babbling vocalization regardless of their native language, so around the world there are babies making sounds like yours! He'll make sounds that he finds interesting and fun, and repeat them when he provokes a response, or just because it feels good!

YOUR BABY IS 25 WEEKS AND 5 DAYS

High chairs

Your baby's high chair will help him master his eating skills, and make him feel part of the family as he joins in the fun of eating together.

A high chair can be a considerable investment, so be armed with a list of requirements before you buy one.

Practicality Your baby's chair should be easy to clean (a detachable tray is easier to wash and dry than a fixed one) and suitable for the size of your kitchen. If space is tight, you may prefer a model that folds, or one that can be pushed up against a table and, therefore, doesn't require a tray. Some models can be raised and lowered, which can be useful if, say, you don't have a kitchen table, in

which case you can lower the chair and push it up to a coffee table. Or you may prefer a model that adapts to become a table and chair for toddlers.

Comfort The seat should preferably be padded or able to hold a padded insert that supports your baby in an upright position. Removable, washable padded inserts are best—buy two, so there's always one available while the other is being washed. A chair with an adjustable footrest and seat heights may prove useful as your baby grows.

Safety Make sure the base of the chair is wide, so it can't topple over without considerable force. The high chair should also have a five-point safety harness, which should be used each time your baby is in it—babies have an astonishing ability to slither out of high chairs. Finally, ensure that a foldable seat has a safety latch and won't trap your baby's fingers or collapse while he's in it. Secondhand chairs are perfectly fine, but ensure their restraint systems have been approved by the Canadian Standards Association (CSA).

Changing your baby's feedings

You might be thinking about stopping breast-feeding, or you may wish to mix breast- and bottle-feeding or try a new formula now.

If you have been breast-feeding and are going back to work, you can arrange to express and store your milk during your workday (see p.179) if you don't want to switch your baby onto formula. Or you may decide to mix bottle- and breast-feeding in a way that works for your schedule and your baby's needs.

If you have difficulty getting your baby onto a bottle, try smearing the nipple with a little of your usual nipple cream, or mix formula and expressed breast milk to make it more palatable. You could also trying changing nipples, or give him formula in a sippy cup. If you are going straight to formula, you may need to experiment with different brands to find one that appeals to your baby.

A new formula It's not necessary for your baby to move on to follow-up or "hungry-baby" milk as he can remain on his first formula until the age of 12 months. However, whether you have been breast-feeding and are moving onto formula, or have been bottle-feeding, and he seems to be hungry even after a good feeding, another type of formula may be more appropriate. The idea of follow-up milks is that there is more nutrition in a smaller amount of formula—in particular, there may be more iron, which babies will increasingly need.

However, your baby will be slowly and gently weaned off his regular milk as he eats more solid foods, and, if you are careful to provide him with a variety of healthy foods, he'll undoubtedly receive an increasing amount of vitamins and minerals from solids and become less dependent upon milk for nutrition.

That said, if your baby is fussy and slow to take solids, consider milk designed for older babies—not only because it often contains more calories and is, therefore, more satisfying, but also because it's designed to provide more iron, omega oils (EFAs), and vitamin D.

Whatever milk you choose, it should satisfy your baby and he should continue to put on weight as normal. Cow's milk (full-fat) is not appropriate as a drink for babies under the age of 12 months, but your baby will have plenty of time to try other dairy products in a few months, beginning with baby yogurt and cheese.

PLANNING TO STOP BREAST-FEEDING

If you have a date in mind in the next few weeks for stopping breast-feeding, you may wish to start replacing a session with a bottle-feeding now. This is because it's not a good idea to stop abruptly, as your baby is likely to be distressed by the withdrawal of his main source of comfort and sustenance, which will only upset you. Also, stopping suddenly can cause your breasts to become engorged and may result in mastitis. Instead, you need to cut down the number of breast-feedings your baby has and slowly replace them with bottle-feedings over a period of a few weeks. The advice is to drop one feeding every four to five days.

You may want to start by dropping the early evening feeding. If your partner or another carer can feed the baby in another room so that he won't smell your milk, so much the better. Usually the last feedings to go are late evening and morning, which your baby will associate with security, cuddles, and contentment.

If you do have to stop breast-feeding suddenly and your breasts become uncomfortably engorged,

you'll need to express some milk. Express just enough to relieve the discomfort; if you express too much you will produce more. It can take up to a couple of weeks before your milk completely disappears. (For more information about stopping breast-feeding, see pages 274–275).

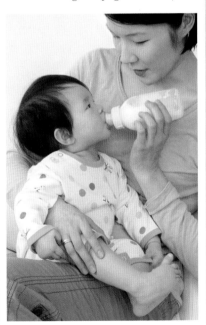

New experience Switch from breast to bottle slowly so your baby has time to adjust.

26 weeks

YOUR BABY'S EYES ARE WORKING TOGETHER TO FORM A THREE-DIMENSIONAL VIEW OF THE WORLD

Your baby needs his daytime naps more than ever now—whichever method he's using to help him move about will use up lots of energy and leave him worn out! He may be able to bear some weight on his legs if you hold him upright in a standing position, but don't force him to.

On your mark, get set…

Your baby is about to get going! Whether rolling, commando crawling, or crawling on his hands and knees, he's entering a new mobile phase.

ASK A… PEDIATRICIAN

Is it OK to use an activity center?
Activity centers foster fine motor and problem-solving skills, imagination, and independence. A sturdy activity center, in which your baby is seated and surrounded by dials to turn, flaps to lift, shapes to sort, and buttons that produce sounds, can stimulate and amuse him. Stationary activity centers are appropriate once your baby can sit unassisted, and many adjust to different heights to ensure that he can reach the activities while sitting upright. Once he starts to stand or walk, these centers are no longer safe.

When my baby starts crawling, can I put her in a playpen when I want to keep her safe? Once your baby is mobile, a playpen prevents her from doing what she really wants to do: get around and explore; so she's likely to protest loudly at being confined. It's important to give her as much freedom as possible to investigate and move physically at this stage of her development, so try to make sure that she has a baby-proofed area where she can scuttle about freely (under your supervision, of course). On the other hand, there are times when you can't watch her every second, and if you want to make sure that she's safe when your attention is focused elsewhere—while you make a phone call, for example—and you have plenty of space, a playpen can be useful.

On the move Once your baby begins to experiment with creeping or crawling, carpets or rugs on the floor provide soft cushioning during practice sessions.

It's still early for babies to roll or crawl at the moment—some don't attempt it until eight or nine months, or even later. This is common in premature babies and multiples. However, some babies do start to become mobile this early—so it's just as well to be prepared.

Babies learn to maneuver themselves in different ways. While there is a series of developmental steps involved in progressing from sitting to crawling, and crawling to "cruising" and then walking, many babies have their own agendas and simply choose the easiest way to get around.

Some babies rock on their hands and knees to move forward or backward; others develop an efficient bottom shuffle and never make it onto their hands and knees. Some babies roll across the floor, wiggle on their bellies, or pull themselves along with their tummy to the ground. Some babies crawl backward rather than forward; others skip the crawling stage altogether and pull themselves up on furniture and try to walk. If you have twins, you may find they move in different ways and, of course, in different directions!

Road to independence The way in which your baby moves is not as important as the fact that he does move. Mobility is a step toward emotional and physical independence, and a developmental milestone that must, obviously, be reached before your baby is able to walk. It allows him to explore his environment at his own pace, satisfy his curiosity, entertain himself, and develop coordination, balance, and muscle strength. What's more, it exercises his heart and lungs, lifts his spirits, and promotes deep, restful sleep.

Encouraging your baby to be mobile helps him to enjoy physical exercise, understand how his body works, and, ultimately, have fun as he pursues what interests him.

26 weeks

223

Learning to eat solid foods

When you start to give your baby foods other than milk, keep in mind that it takes time to learn to adapt to food coming on a spoon.

New tastes and textures Eating solid food from a spoon is an entirely new experience for your baby, and she will need time to adjust to it.

Tips for success

To help the process of introducing solids get off to a smooth start for you and your baby, try the following:

■ Find a time when your baby isn't too tired or too hungry—a good time is often after a small milk feeding.

■ Be relaxed and happy yourself.

■ Expect a mess, be prepared for a range of reactions, and don't allow yourself to become flustered.

■ Give praise and encouragement for each mouthful.

At the outset, your baby will have very liquid purées of baby rice with milk, cereals, fruits, or vegetables. In fact, the purées will be very much like milk in consistency, and he'll suck them from the spoon. As he becomes accustomed to taking purées from a spoon, you can make them a little thicker by adding less of his usual milk, or by adding a little baby rice. Baby rice on its own is also a good starter food because it is bland, easy on your baby's digestion, and most brands are fortified with vitamins and minerals.

Depending on when you start the process and how well your baby receives foods, you'll probably find that for the first few days your baby will only try one or two spoonfuls at one meal a day.

However, if your baby seems to want more, allow him to eat more. He'll turn his head away, get upset, or close his mouth when he's had enough. If he is reluctant to try altogether and makes a big fuss, simply stop and wait until the next day to encourage him again.

It is important to make meal times pleasant and upbeat so that you establish a healthy association with food right from the outset. Ensure, too, that you give your baby a variety of foods, even ones you don't enjoy. Don't be tempted to add salt or sugar to foods to make them taste better. Salt is dangerous for your baby and extra sugar unnecessary. Rest assured that he will enjoy the simple flavors.

Healthy start The fact that these early meals are just "tastes" doesn't mean they don't have to be nutritious. One of the most important parts of introducing solids involves introducing your baby to the flavor and texture of healthy foods. The earlier he learns to eat vegetables, for example, the more likely he is to continue to eat them throughout his childhood and into adulthood. So giving in and offering your baby his favorite apple purée because he won't touch his broccoli purée is not going to teach him how to enjoy broccoli. Don't forget that he may respond to your cues about food, so if you don't like broccoli he may pick this up. Offer your baby one new food every three days and, if he rejects it, try it another day. It can take up to several encounters for a baby to consider a food to be familiar, and it may well take that long for him to take to something that he doesn't seem to like initially.

A room of his own

If you're planning to move your baby into his own room, start getting him used to the space now, before you make the transition.

From the age of six months, it's safe for your baby to sleep alone. Help him make the transition from your room to his own room slowly. Settle him down in his room for naps only at first, so he can become familiar with the feeling of falling asleep in this new environment. Slowly increase the number of naps he takes in his room before you take the plunge and put him there for the night.

You may find that your baby sleeps better in his own room at first because he won't be disturbed by your night-time coughs and movements. Alternatively, he might wake more often because he misses the rhythmic sound of your breathing, and may feel a little lonely and frightened at first. If he cries in the night, go to him and soothe him so that he learns that you're still there and will continue to see to his needs.

Give him a comfort object (see p.345) to help him settle. Being able to see, touch, and smell something familiar can help him to soothe himself to sleep. Don't leave objects in his crib overnight.

You may wish to invest in a baby monitor for your own peace of mind. Many parents experience sleepless nights when their babies first sleep in their own rooms. You may find yourself waking repeatedly to check on your baby. If you can hear his cries and his breathing, you will feel reassured that it's safe for you to fall asleep. If you can find a monitor that allows your baby to hear your voice, too, he may also sleep better with a few whispered words from mom or dad from time to time.

Tip and tilt

Gently tipping your baby or changing his position gives him a whole new perspective on familiar surroundings.

While rough-and-tumble games come later in his development, your baby benefits from the sensory feedback when he is held in different positions. Tip him backward while firmly supporting his neck and back so that he can look at the ceiling; lay him on his back over your knee; and tickle or blow raspberries on his tummy or neck so that he tips his head backward. He may wiggle with pleasure or become still as he takes in this unusual perspective. As long as you hold him firmly by his body, rather than his limbs, he will feel safe and secure.

A new perspective Holding your baby so her body is tilted slightly gives her different sensory feedback about how her body moves.

Also, try carefully leaning the seat of his stroller back when you are out so that he can look up toward the sky and see the clouds and the trees.

This type of play encourages your baby's vestibular system (which controls balance) to improve as he learns how his body operates in various positions. Also, he'll rely on different muscle movements, and different coordinated efforts of muscles, to maintain his balance and support his head and neck.

Seeing things from a new perspective when you hold his body in different positions benefits both your baby's muscles and his neural development. Make sure, though, that he's securely supported, or he will find it unsettling.

Eagle eyes

At 26 weeks, your baby's eyesight has greatly improved. He'll watch you like a hawk, and notice the subtlest of changes around him.

Babies first develop depth perception between the ages of three and five months, and by now your baby's brain can efficiently interpret the images from each eye to create a sophisticated three-dimensional view of the world.

Depth perception requires visual experience, good eye–muscle coordination, and sufficient maturity of the nerve cells in the eyes and brain. At this stage, your baby's level of vision is approaching that of an adult's, and by the time he is about eight months old it will be almost perfect. Although objects at close range will interest your baby most, he can now see and recognize things from across the room. He'll notice the curtains stirring in the breeze, a toy lodged under the sofa, and your purse tucked away in the corner. Once he can make out these objects, he'll be determined to get to them because now he's attracted by novelty, whereas previously he was probably more interested in looking at familiar objects.

AS A MATTER OF FACT

Studies of depth perception in babies involved a "visual cliff"—a glass surface with patterns creating the illusion of a drop. Babies crossed the "shallow" side, but most reacted with fear of the "deep" side, suggesting that most babies who can crawl have depth perception. This won't keep them safe though, so precautions, for example baby gates, are vital.

Sunshine and vitamin D

Vitamin D is important for you and your baby. It is needed for the development of bones and teeth, and for immunity and cell growth.

Widespread use of sunscreens means that more people are now deficient in vitamin D, which is made by the body when the skin is exposed to sunlight (as well as obtained through diet, see p.167). Ideally, we should all get at least 10 minutes of sunlight a day (without sunscreen) to maintain vitamin D levels.

This may sound confusing, as the last thing you want is your baby's delicate skin to burn; however, natural sunlight in the shade (under a tree, for example) is as effective as direct sunlight. In the warmer months, go outside for a few minutes of shady play without

Outdoor play Ten minutes per day in the shade allows your baby's body to produce vitamin D.

sunscreen each day if you can, avoiding the hours between 10 am and 3 pm in summer, when the sun is strongest. For the rest of the day, your baby should be well in the shade or indoors.

Many babies are vitamin D-deficient in the winter, so maintain safe exposure then, too. As well as manufacturing vitamin D through sunlight, it is also obtained from our diet. A suitable dose of vitamin D supplements is advised for breast-fed babies, and for breast-feeding moms. Supplements are also advised for babies with darker skin, for example those of African, African-Caribbean, and South–Asian origin, because their bodies are not able to make as much Vitamin D (see p.167).

Separating gently

If you plan to go back to work, try to ease your baby into the idea of separation, and give him confidence in the fact that you'll be back.

Happy goodbyes Make the separation as easy as possible for both of you by ensuring your baby is familiar with her surroundings and the people who are caring for her in your absence.

Whenever you return to work, there will be some fussing and distress when you leave your baby. This will be somewhat worse if separation anxiety has set in, from around eight months onward (see p.283). Use the following strategies to make the parting easier on you both.

Introduce your baby to his caregiver, and have a few sessions with you there so your baby can familiarize himself with his new caregiver in the security of your presence. The first time you leave your baby and his caregiver alone, do so only briefly (say, for 15 minutes).

For the first attempts at separation, avoid leaving your baby if he is tired, hungry, or unwell. The happier he feels, the more likely he is to settle quickly. To help him feel secure, give him a comfort object (see p.345) to hold on to while

you are gone. Make it an object you have played with together or, if he is being cared for away from home, something that reminds him of home.

Adopt an exit ritual so that your baby learns to anticipate what's happening—he'll find security in the routine. Give him a hug, a kiss, and a firm goodbye. Keep your tone positive and expression happy. If he cries, reassure him that you'll miss him, but will soon be back. (Later, you can provide a marker for your return, such as "after lunch" or "after your nap.") Say goodbye again and leave. Avoid the temptation to return to soothe any crying. Instead, put yourself out of earshot. If you are worried, call the caregiver after about 15 minutes to see if your baby has settled down—in most cases, babies are easily distracted.

CHECKLIST

Dehydration

This occurs when a baby isn't getting adequate fluid, for example through poor feeding because of illness, making him sleepy, breathless, or uninterested in feeding. It also occurs when a baby loses too much fluid, for example through vomiting and/or diarrhea, as in gastroenteritis, or through sweating, caused by a fever or overheating.

Dehydration is a potentially dangerous condition, and your baby should be seen immediately by a doctor if you suspect he's dehydrated. Continue to feed him as often as possible, offering bottle-fed babies some cooled, previously boiled water alongside regular feedings. Rehydration solution, which replaces lost fluids and body salts, may be necessary to maintain his body chemistry.

If left untreated, dehydration can develop into a medical emergency causing brain damage, so if your baby shows signs of lethargy or drops in and out of consciousness, call an ambulance, or, if quicker, take him to an emergency department at once. Signs of dehydration include:

- A sunken fontanelle
- Listlessness
- Sunken eyes
- Dry mouth, eyes, and lips
- Strong-smelling urine
- Clammy hands and feet
- Fewer than six wet diapers per day.

26 weeks

227

Your baby at 7 to 9 months

WEEK	1	2	3	4	5	6	7	8	9	10	11	12	13	14	15	16	17	18	19	20	21	22	23	24	25	26

Solid diet Eating solids will be underway now, so your baby will have fewer milk feedings as he gets used to eating more solid food.

Passing skills There's quite an art to passing an object from hand to hand, since your baby needs plenty of hand–eye coordination and to be able to open and close her grip efficiently. Once she's mastered this skill, she may spend lots of time honing it.

Sitting unsupported Many babies can sit unaided by 6–7 months, and may be able to sit and play with a toy without toppling over.

Did you know? Babies usually use their arms to pull and push themselves up to a standing position at first, before they learn to successfully push up with their legs.

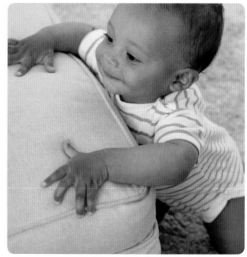

Reaching for toys Reaching forward from a sitting position is a tricky maneuver, but as your baby's balance improves, it won't phase him.

Pulling to standing Your baby may be able to pull himself up to a standing position, using a piece of furniture for support.

From sitting to standing to doing simple puzzles to trying new foods, your baby is a busy little person.

Problem solving Your baby's problem-solving and fine motor skills are fast developing and she'll be mesmerized by simple shape-sorting puzzles.

Separation fears Around eight months is when your baby is most likely to become anxious about strangers or separating from you and may need extra reassurance.

Side-stepping baby Once your baby can pull up to a stand, she'll start to move one leg or the other and may practice taking steps while she's holding on.

Copy cat Your baby will want to copy the sounds you make and her comprehension is improving. She is learning about facial expressions by watching you.

Finger foods Your baby will enjoy feeding herself with simple finger foods now. These give her the opportunity to learn how to chew properly and to explore new tastes and textures at her own pace.

Did you know? Everything a baby sees, touches, tastes, smells, or hears helps to form connections between the 100 billion nerve cells in the brain.

27 weeks

EATING A WIDE RANGE OF FOODS IN THE FIRST YEAR IS LINKED WITH A HEALTHIER DIET LATER

The apple of your eye is likely to have doubled his birth weight—and is ready to start making the most of thicker foods as an important part of his diet. He should be sleeping for 8–10 hours at night. If he's still waking at night, you may want to try breaking this pattern.

Six whole months

Can you believe how grown-up your baby seems? She's on a roll now—or rather onto much more purposeful moving around.

Your baby is already halfway through her first year, and probably bears little resemblance to the tiny newborn who came into this world. You are most likely very different parents, too, having settled into your roles and grown more comfortable and confident with the responsibilities of parenthood. Can you even imagine now what you did with your time before your baby was born?

Your six-month-old baby is more sociable than ever, and loves to be with people. She'll be smiling and laughing with gusto in company—but may be a little more selective about whom she wants to engage one-to-one with. Take advantage of her sociability to introduce her to a variety of people when you're out and about and encourage her to say hello and wave goodbye.

There is a sudden burst in awareness of her surroundings. Your baby is very curious and wants to explore everything. She also appears to make decisions when choosing which toys to play with. She will love playing face to face with you, and her sense of trust and confidence is growing. She'll enjoy studying your face and other people's faces, touching, poking, and pulling them as she tries to understand her separateness from other people.

Big and beautiful Most babies have doubled their birth weight by six months so, having filled out nicely, she's probably looking particularly healthy now. If you haven't done so already, it's definitely time to start solids now (see pages 234–235 and pages 254–255 for more guidance). You may be thinking about introducing supplementary bottles of

Giggle all the way Your baby will enjoy games that involve an element of surprise or silliness. Hide her under a blanket and then "discover" her. She'll be amused and burst into peals of laughter.

formula, or expressing extra milk, if you are breast-feeding, stopping breast-feeding (see pp.274–275), or changing to follow-up formula (see p.221).

Your baby may be able to sit without support now, and be capable of bearing some weight on her legs when held upright (she'll love bouncing in this position, too). She may even be able to stand if she's lifted and supported, and she'll be rolling, or even creeping or crawling, to maneuver herself around.

She'll also be using her entire hand to rake over a small object with her fingers and then pick it up. She will be much more purposeful about grasping, shaking, and banging items she can get hold of. If she drops things, it probably won't be deliberate yet—babies only start doing this purposefully at around nine months.

BABY WALKERS AND BOUNCERS

Baby walkers have been banned in Canada since 2004 due to the high number of accidents involving them. Moreover, your baby needs to learn to sit, roll, crawl, and play on her tummy to gain the skills she needs to walk, and baby walkers prohibit these activities. If someone gives you a second-hand baby walker, remove the wheels before disposing of it. There is some thought that baby bouncers put too much pressure on bones, joints, ligaments, and muscles at too young an age. Also, accidents can result if they're not attached properly. If you choose to use one, make sure it is properly installed and that you don't leave your baby in it for long periods.

27 weeks

231

Showing a preference

Your baby is becoming more aware of herself, you, and other people. She may even indicate who she prefers to have looking after her.

While both parents have a role in their baby's life, whoever is the primary caregiver is likely to be the one whom your baby prefers when she feels insecure. Equally, the parent who comes home and focuses on play carves a special place in her affections. Try to keep the baby care as balanced as you can when you are at home together. For instance, take turns to put her to bed so that she feels equally comfortable with either one of you doing it.

Wary of strangers Your baby may feel shy with less familiar people, and may "nestle in" to mom for some comfort and reassurance.

One of the concerns of some parents who have to leave their baby with a caregiver for parts of the week is whether or not their baby will come to love the caregiver more than them. There is nothing to worry about on this score. Babies know instinctively who their parents are, and, as long as the time you spend with your baby is spent happily (with lots of play and interaction), your baby will never switch her allegiance from you.

Try to remain thankful that your baby loves her caregiver, because it would be much harder to leave her if she didn't, and was crying for you.

Sleep at six months

In theory, your baby should enjoy 8–10 hours of blissful sleep each night. In practice, a good night's rest may still be a distant dream.

Babies vary widely in the amount of sleep they need, although on average most will sleep 12–14 hours out of 24, and for twice as long at night (8–10 hours) as during the day. However, if your baby is still waking for regular feedings, your nights will be interrupted. Now might be a good time to try to encourage her to break the pattern of nighttime waking. If your baby is still sleeping with you in your room, you might be disturbing her when you come to bed or if you stir or make a noise during the night. You could consider moving her to her own room now (see

p.225); this may prove disruptive while she gets used to it, but better for you all in the long term.

If you're breast-feeding and you think your baby is waking in the night because she's hungry, you could try giving her extra feedings, known as "cluster feedings," in the early evening before she goes to bed. You could also try rousing her very gently, but without waking her completely, if possible, for a drowsy nighttime feeding just before you go to bed, so between 10pm and midnight. You could also try this late feed to help a bottle-fed baby sleep

longer at night (but cut out a daytime bottle-feeding to ensure she does not become overweight). There are no guarantees that these tactics will work, but they're worth a try.

At six months, your baby might be showing the first signs of separation anxiety (although this generally happens at around eight months), so she may wake up and worry that you're not there. If this is the case, you will need to go in to reassure her and help her settle back down, so that she feels secure enough to go back to sleep. For more strategies, see pages 352–353.

Dad's shift, mom's shift

Whether dad stays at home full-time, or you share your baby's care, switching traditional roles can present challenges for parents.

According to a recent survey, about 30 percent of eligible fathers take advantage of parental leave benefits. Many more fathers take on caretaking responsibilities during mornings, evenings, and weekends. Most dads who take a more active role in childcare find it enormously rewarding, but there are stresses that can develop as a result of these changes to parents' traditional roles. When mom becomes the main breadwinner, she can feel guilty and resentful at being separated from her baby, while a stay-at-home dad can feel isolated if he doesn't know any other fathers in the same situation.

Even if both parents work flexibly and split baby care more or less equally, it's common for moms to feel that they're still shouldering most of the domestic burden as well as trying to manage a job.

When the boundaries of your roles become blurred, it's all too easy to step on your partner's toes or feel resentful that one of you is pulling less weight. For this reason, it's important to do whatever it takes to make sure you are comfortable with your roles and responsibilities. Talk about every aspect of your baby's care so that you both know exactly what's happening and

when. Apportion the household chores fairly; plan your baby's menu for the week if she's starting on solids; make sure you're both consistent about naps and bedtimes; discuss what to do if she's upset or won't eat her food; and check that you're in agreement when it comes to setting boundaries that keep her safe. It's important to make sure that you both are equally involved in these decisions. Provided your baby has loving care and consistent routines, she won't mind which parent takes main responsibility for her; although she'll always need quality time with you both.

Hands-on dad Many dads are spending more time at home, honing their baby-care skills, building strong bonds, and enjoying the rewards of playing with and watching their baby develop.

AS A MATTER OF FACT

Studies show that babies who have spent quality time playing with and interacting with their fathers in the first five to seven months of their lives achieve more in school and find it easier to form strong relationships.

Interestingly, it doesn't seem to be the amount of time a father spends with his children that has the most influence in this way, but his immersion in the activity with them during the time he has.

Even if you have only evenings and weekends to play with your baby, studies suggest that if you give her your full attention, she'll grow up to be more self-assured. In addition, your enthusiasm for fun and physical play develops her trust in you and her own confidence. In the coming months, rough-and-tumble play promotes mental and physical strength in both sexes.

27 weeks

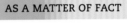

233

Stage one solids—first tastes

If you have waited six months before introducing your baby to solid foods, now's the time to start doing so in earnest. If your baby has already enjoyed her first tastes, now you can start expanding her repertoire.

CHECKLIST

Simple starters

As soon as your baby accepts simple single purées, you can blend them to create new flavor combinations.

Fruit and vegetable blends Such as carrot and parsnip; pea and cauliflower; lentil and butternut squash; peach and banana; apple and pear; avocado and banana.

Vegetables and meat/poultry Try carrot and chicken; broccoli and beef; peas and ham; sweet potato and lamb; turkey and sweet potato.

Starchy foods with fruits Try stewed puréed apricots with baby breakfast cereal; mashed banana with wheat biscuits; baby rice and oatmeal (mixed with breast milk). (Slightly older babies can try multigrain and wheat in the same way, but rice and oatmeal are best for younger babies.)

Consistency Semi-liquid purées quickly progressing to thicker purées and mashed foods.

How often? 1–2 meals a day, progressing to 3.

How much 4–6 tsp (more if your baby is hungrier) of 2–3 different foods at each sitting.

Milk At this stage, your baby won't need to drop any milk feedings.

From six months on, breast milk or formula alone isn't sufficient to meet all your baby's nutritional demands as she needs calories and nutrients from other foods. Additionally, your baby is more likely to accept new flavors, tastes, and textures between five and seven months, so if you've waited until the recommended six months, as soon as she accepts food from a spoon, move on quickly using lots of variety.

How to start To begin with, offer your baby single flavors of vegetables, fruits, or baby rice each mixed with her usual milk. Try each food on its own so that you can tell what your baby likes or dislikes and make a note of it. Your pediatrician will recommend that you wait about three days after introducing a new food to see if your baby has an adverse reaction before you introduce yet another new food. Wait until your pediatrician gives the go-ahead before introducing any potentially allergenic foods, including egg whites, cow's milk products, wheat, peanuts, or tree nuts (see page 241 for further information). Your baby is more at risk of a reaction if she has a family history of atopic conditions—for example, if either your or the baby's other parent or any siblings have a food allergy, eczema, or asthma. If this applies to your baby, it's a good idea to keep breast-feeding while starting solids as this seems to provide some protection against developing these conditions. If you have been using infant formula, don't give any of these foods under six months.

What next When your baby is happy with a few single flavors, you can begin to offer blends (purées with more than one fruit or vegetable blended together). The more tastes to which you introduce your baby during the first days and weeks of starting solids, and the more combinations you offer her, the more likely she is to "develop her palate" and enjoy different foods.

What if she refuses? Some babies find it hard to adjust to the concept of food coming on a spoon, especially if they are

First tastes Gently place the spoon with some puréed food in your baby's mouth. She may take a while to get used to taking food from a spoon, and may push out more than she takes in to begin with. Simply scrape it up with the spoon and try again.

Baby-led feeding is a different approach to introducing solids that involves skipping purées and spoon-feeding and allowing babies to feed themselves from the outset.

Some babies who start solids this way may find the transition to lumpy foods easier and manage family meals much earlier. And because they are given an element of choice, some people think that babies who start solids in this manner enjoy the process of eating more than other babies, and are less likely to be fussy eaters. There is a risk of choking with this approach, so babies must be supervised when eating.

Some health professionals are concerned at the lack of clinical trials that properly assess the adequacy of nutrition using this method of starting solids or confirm claims that babies eat better as a result. The Canadian Paediatric Society recommends introducing solid foods by spoon-feeding basic foods like rice cereal mixed with breast milk or formula in a 1:4 or 1:5 ratio, then introducing different fruits, vegetables, and other flavors gradually (waiting two to three days before introducing a new ingredient to check for food

Helping himself At first, a baby may simply play with his food, grabbing chunks of whatever is in front of him, and sucking it.

sensitivities or allergies). It's a good idea to wait until a baby is eight or nine months old before offering finger foods that she can feed to herself without choking.

It's also important that the foods babies eat are highly nutritious (see p.207). Finger foods tend to be bulkier than purées and babies may fill up without having adequate calories, so introducing the right foods is key.

still under six months old. However, if you feel your baby is ready, but spurns feeding, be patient, and try again the next day. You may want to let her suck some food from your clean finger. Keep offering different foods at regular times, but if she doesn't want it, don't force it. It might be that she'd prefer to be more in control and feed herself (see Baby-led feeding, above), or that she just needs to take things at a slower pace.

Expanding the menu As soon as your baby is happy eating vegetables and fruit, you can introduce other foods such as

puréed or blended meat and poultry. If you're worried that puréed meat will be unappealing to your baby, try serving it mixed with fruits or vegetables that she's already familiar with to make it more pleasant. Chicken is an ideal first meat as it is mild-flavored and tender. The dark cut of the meat contains twice as much iron and zinc as the breast, so try to give your baby some dark meat, too. You can also start to introduce well-mashed lentils, split peas, chickpeas, or other legumes; and within a few months, full-fat dairy products, such as yogurt and cheese.

Foods to avoid

Foods listed below are not suitable for babies until they are over 12 months old.

Some types of fish Shark, marlin, and swordfish can contain high levels of mercury that could damage a baby's developing nervous system.

Salt Don't add salt to your baby's food—season your family meal after taking out your baby's portion. Avoid salty and processed foods, such as bacon, ham, olives, sausages, ready-made meals, and pizzas.

Egg whites To reduce the risk of an allergic reaction, avoid egg whites until your baby is one year old. Cook egg yolks until they are firm.

Honey Because of a tiny risk of a potentially serious food poisoning bacteria (*Botulinum*), it's safest not to give honey to babies under one year.

Unpasteurized dairy products All dairy produce should be pasteurized because of the risk of bacterial infection. Cow's milk as a beverage should not be served to babies until after their first birthday.

Artificial sweeteners and food colorings These ingredients are not designed for use in foods for babies, so keep them off limits.

Adult foods It's important to avoid deep-fried foods, chips, fries, or oily dressings; sugar and sweetened foods, such as grown-up desserts; tea and coffee, which contain caffeine and can interfere with your baby's ability to absorb iron; and low-fat or diet foods (see also p.214).

Whole nuts These are not suitable for children below age five because of the risk of choking.

27 weeks

235

Diaper news

On her milk-only diet, your baby's poop was yellow and mousse-like in consistency. That changes with the introduction of solids.

Your baby's digestion is still immature, which means that her gut can't yet absorb her food fully. This manifests itself in the form of multicolored poop! If you give your baby broccoli, you are likely to find that her poop is slightly green; give her carrots, and its waste product will arrive in her diaper bright orange. This is all normal and will settle down as her digestive system develops.

Consistency Even though your baby's first foods are likely to be very runny, her poops will start to firm up when she starts on solids. Expect to find some soft lumps in her diaper from now on. If, however, you find that the lumps are dry and hard, it indicates she isn't getting enough fluids and may be constipated (see 403). If your baby is eating finger foods, you may find chunks of these make their way through her digestive tract almost undigested, emerging more or less intact at the other end.

Smell The poop of a baby on solids begins to smell more like adult poop, unfortunately! Where possible, shake the loose poop into the toilet so that you can flush it away. If you don't already have a dedicated diaper pail with a lid, now might be the time to invest in one—or, put the soiled diapers straight out into the main trash outside. You may want scented diaper bags, too.

Unhealthy poop Look out for stools that are too hard or too loose, which might indicate constipation or diarrhea respectively, and talk to your pediatrician if you see mucus or blood in your baby's stools. Some believe that babies who are teething have slightly looser stools, but if your baby is also unwell or has a fever, consult the doctor.

Having fun with mirrors

Your baby is developing socially all the time. She is a natural mimic, and you will often see your expressions reflected in her face.

Your baby is still too young to recognize herself in a mirror—most experts agree that self-recognition doesn't happen until around 14 months. However, she loves looking at faces—her own and yours—and will respond to the different expressions she sees you make, often copying them. This behavior shows she is developing all the time as a social being. She is learning that she can increase her interaction with you by responding to your expression with one of her own—when she responds to your smile with one of her own, she will see that you smile even more and that she is able to hold your attention.

Build on this interaction by holding her up to a mirror and interacting with her reflection. Make a range of faces and expressions—silly faces to make her laugh; a sad face; a happy, smiley face; and a surprised face. Exaggerate your expressions to help her read emotions; for example, raise your eyebrows when you smile, or open your mouth in mock surprise. As well as watching you, she will see the delighted response of the baby in the mirror, too!

Here's looking at you Hold your baby in front of the mirror so that he can see you both. Say his name and point to parts of his face.

Vitamins for babies

Vitamins are vital for your baby's healthy development—which is why supplementation may be recommended.

Babies need vitamins for the healthy growth of bones, teeth, brain, and blood supply. Most babies will get the vitamins needed from diet alone, but infants need supplemental vitamin D, because they should stay out of the sun, and the skin makes vitamin D by sun exposure. Formula is already fortified with vitamin D, so formula-fed babies shouldn't need supplements unless they live in a northern community. Breast-fed babies, however, do need this supplementation.

Some pediatricians may recommend other supplemental vitamins. Supplements can be bought over the counter in pharmacies, but these may contain other vitamins or ingredients, so talk to your pharmacist about which supplement would be most appropriate for your baby.

It's important to remember that having too much of some vitamins is as harmful as not having enough. Do not give your child two supplements at the same time.

Vitamin A This vitamin is essential for the normal growth of different cells and tissues, and plays an important role in the development and maturation of your baby's lungs. A lack of adequate vitamin A can lead to a susceptibility to infection as well as the poor functioning of the lungs and other tissues. Food sources include: egg yolk; butter or spreads; oily fish such as salmon; yellow and orange fruits; and leafy green vegetables.

Vitamin C Vitamin C is important for general health and the immune system. It also helps the body absorb iron. Good sources of vitamin C include kiwi fruit; strawberries; broccoli; tomatoes; sweet potatoes; and butternut squash.

Vitamin D Important for the bones and teeth, inadequate vitamin D can lead to rickets, which weakens bones. It is mostly made in the body by the action of sunlight on skin. Few foods contain vitamin D—oily fish, eggs, and butter among them—but some breakfast cereals and margarines are fortified with it.

Iron The manufacture of red blood cells and the development of the nervous and immune systems rely on iron, which is best absorbed by the body from animal foods. Red meat is the best source, but dark poultry meat, and oily fish, such as canned sardines, are also good.

Tofu, chickpeas, legumes, and dark green leafy vegetables are all good plant sources of iron.

DEVELOPMENT ACTIVITY

Playing with water

Your baby will enjoy playing with water. She'll splash about, soaking herself in the process. Ensure that she is supervised at all times: play alongside her, and keep her body stable and well supported so she can safely lean forward. Half-fill a large bowl with warm water, put in some bath toys or safe kitchen utensils, and encourage your baby to fill and empty cups, bob her ducks, swirl the water with a spoon, or simply to splash with her hands. She's used to water at bath time, but this activity teaches her how water works in a confined space, and how her actions can cause it to ripple, pour, bubble, splash, and seep. She will also learn how things float and sink. Encouraging water play helps to increase her confidence in water.

Water play Babies are fascinated by water and relish opportunities to get their hands into it and learn how it behaves when poured, splashed, or sprinkled. It's a whole new world of fun!

28 weeks

EARLY BABBLING IN BABIES USUALLY CONSISTS OF ONE SYLLABLE REPEATED, SUCH AS "MAMAMA"

Your baby may now be able to sit up on her own without support. This means that her hands are free so that she can take full advantage of her increasing dexterity. She wants to play constantly, and enthusiastically explores anything within her reach and beyond!

One hand to another

You'll notice that your baby has more control over her hands, and seems quite enthralled by passing things between them.

RAISING AN AVID READER

Make books a part of your baby's daily life to support the development of her verbal skills, her understanding of language and pleasure in listening, and to promote a habit that may one day become a passion. Select age-appropriate books and get her to turn pages and lift flaps. Use an expressive, exaggerated voice that will appeal to her, and don't hesitate to read the same book frequently. Repetition will spark her memory and help her to learn. Look for chunky books that will withstand her attempts to explore them. Simple stories are ideal, and books with peep holes will stimulate her curiosity. Keep a selection of books around the house, and in your handbag or the stroller to pass the time when you are out and about.

Book fun Make reading part of your routine so your baby anticipates it and develops a positive association with books.

Improved grasp Your baby can now scoop things up with one hand and transfer them to the other. Give him plenty of objects, such as soft blocks and toys, to help him practice this skill.

Your baby is beginning to grasp objects with both hands, and even hold an object using both of her hands together. She is also developing the ability to transfer objects from one hand to the other, and to place them accurately in a container in front of her. She will visually explore whatever she is holding in her hand, becoming more "creative" about her examination. For example, she might hold it at a distance, then pass it from hand to hand, which helps her to find out about its properties. This enables her to learn that objects don't change size when moved closer or further away, even though they look bigger or smaller.

Manipulative movement Suitable toys and opportunities for play will support the development of your baby's manipulative movement. This involves the controlled use of her hands and feet—grasping, opening and closing her hands, and waving are all examples of manipulative movement. This type of movement develops not only over the first year of her life, but also throughout childhood, and involves fine motor skills and hand–eye coordination.

Give her different sized toys and objects to hold and handle, as well as items with varying textures, so that she is encouraged to explore with her hands as much as possible. Small, soft bricks and blocks are ideal at this age—while she certainly won't be stacking or building for a good while yet, she will be able to grasp them with her fist and pass them between her hands, and will enjoy exploring the shape—feeling the defined edges and smooth surfaces. You may find, sometime between seven and nine months, that she starts to clap on her own, as you do, when she hears her favorite action rhyme, or if she does something well.

While your baby is keen to discover the world around her and practice her growing bank of skills, she will also continue to imitate you, so showing her what to do is as important as allowing her to try it herself.

Let me investigate

Your baby will attempt to do everything she sees you doing to find out all about it, and want to investigate anything that looks exciting.

Her curiosity is boundless! Your baby's growing ability to perceive depth and see at a distance allows her to spot new things constantly, and she'll make an effort to get to them. She may become fixated on objects, such as the potted plant you moved out of her reach, or your car keys, and become quite vocal in her attempts to get to them. She may stretch, reach, and wiggle toward what she wants, so make sure dangerous

Learning touch Your baby's explorations and experiments teach her about the properties of different objects.

items are put away out of reach. Watch out for your cup of coffee on the table, fragile ornaments, and small parts from toys left lying around by older siblings. You may need to do another sweep of your home to ensure that anything potentially dangerous is out of reach.

Curiosity leads to learning and babies find everything interesting. They respond to sensory experiences with a desire to find out more about the world. Playing with and exploring different textures, tastes, and consistencies all give valuable feedback to her brain about the world in which she lives.

When's a good bedtime?

Your baby doesn't have to be in bed at 7pm; provided she gets enough quality sleep, you can adjust bedtimes to suit your lifestyle.

Many parents feel a bit disappointed to find that their babies have already gone to bed by the time they arrive home from work. In this situation, they are forced to rely on weekends to spend time playing with and caring for their babies. But is this necessary? Consistent bedtimes are, indeed, important for your baby because they help to set her body clock and form part of a good sleep routine. However, putting her down to sleep at 8pm instead of 7pm is certainly possible, and gives working parents more opportunities to spend some quality time with their babies. If you do go for the later-bedtime option, ensure

her room is dark enough to allow her to sleep a little later in the morning. She will still need at least 8–10 hours of sleep a night, regardless of when it starts and stops.

Avoid the second wind If your baby becomes overtired, she may get a second wind and find it difficult to settle. Giving her a late afternoon nap can help to prevent this. You may need to experiment a little to work out how much sleep she needs in the late afternoon to last until mom or dad comes home. When whomever's been out all day does get back, make sure

that they don't over-stimulate the baby with exciting fun and games right before bedtime. While it is a happy occasion for all of you to share this time together in the evening, activities prior to bedtime should be low key and relaxed.

Early bedtime If you prefer to have some time to yourself in the evenings, and your baby naturally tires at around 6–7pm, then put her down to sleep at that time and get the rest you need to refresh yourself. The habits you establish now should not be hard to alter later. Babies are generally quite adaptable up until the age of about 12 months.

Food allergies

It's natural to worry about allergies when starting solids—knowing what the symptoms are, and where to turn, means you're prepared.

Food allergies are on the increase, but they are still relatively uncommon in babies, and are very often outgrown in childhood. Your baby is more likely to develop allergies if there are family members with a history of eczema, asthma, hayfever, or food allergies.

If this is the case, when you start solids (see pp.234–235 for more information), you should introduce milk, eggs, peanuts, tree nuts, wheat, soy, fish and shellfish (the most common allergenic foods) one at a time. This is so that you can watch for any reaction. Don't introduce any of these foods before six months if you are bottle-feeding.

Some food allergies are fairly easy to spot, particularly if a reaction occurs soon after the food is eaten. If your baby

Food diary If there are allergies in your family, it's a good idea to record each new food, when you introduce it, and any reactions that occur.

displays any of the following symptoms after eating, see your pediatrician:
■ Flushed face, hives, or a red and itchy rash around the mouth, tongue, or eyes. This can spread across the body.
■ Mild swelling, particularly of the lips, eyes, and face.
■ Runny or blocked nose; sneezing.
■ Sore, red, itchy eyes.
■ Nausea, vomiting, stomach cramps, and diarrhea.

Very rarely, foods can cause a severe allergic reaction called anaphylactic shock (see p.404).

In some cases, reactions to certain foods are not so easily identified because the symptoms are less obvious and may not appear for up to 48 hours after the food has been eaten. These used to be called food intolerances, but they are now known as delayed food allergies because they do involve the immune system. Common culprits are milk, soy, egg, and wheat, and symptoms include eczema, colic, reflux, diarrhea, and constipation.

If an allergy is suspected, your pediatrician may refer your baby for a skin prick test and/or a blood test for a definite diagnosis. Sometimes you may be advised to eliminate the suspected food or foods for at least two weeks to see if the symptoms subside. It may then be possible to reintroduce foods slowly, or you may need to adapt your baby's diet to include alternative foods.

Always consult your health professionals and don't be tempted to cut out food groups from your baby's diet without their support, as this could put your baby's health at risk. (See page 261 for further information.)

ASK A... NUTRITIONIST

I'm worried that my baby might be allergic to peanuts. Should I avoid giving them to her? There's no reason to avoid foods containing peanuts, or any other nuts or seeds for that matter, after six months, unless you know that there's a history of allergies in your family or your baby has already been diagnosed with a food allergy or suffers from eczema. In these cases, your baby has a higher risk of nut allergy, and you should talk to your pediatrician before giving your child food containing nuts (such as peanut butter) for the first time. You may be advised to wait until your baby is much older before introducing these foods.

Can I arrange for my baby to be tested to diagnose a food allergy? It's very important to see your pediatrician in the first instance to rule out any other possible cause for any symptoms your baby is experiencing. Your pediatrician will likely refer you to a pediatric allergist or dermatologist, who will be best equipped to decide how to test your baby for allergies. Your child may be given a skin-prick test or a blood test to check for suspected allergens. Seeing an allergist for a definitive diagnosis is best. Commercial allergy-testing kits, which can be purchased online or at some health food stores, are not recommended by pediatricians.

28 weeks

241

Less vital statistics

If you are still struggling to return to your pre-pregnancy weight and fitness levels, cut yourself a bit of slack.

It's important to be realistic. Most women put on weight quite steadily over the nine months of pregnancy, so it makes sense that it could take time to lose it after the birth. While exclusive breast-feeding can encourage continual weight loss, some women testify that their weight stubbornly refused to shift until they actually stopped breast-feeding. Losing weight seems to depend quite a bit therefore on your individual build and metabolism, and there's no "one solution" easy fix for everyone. Some women's bodies change completely during pregnancy and never return to their pre-pregnancy shape. You may find, for example, that while you've lost the weight, your waist is thicker, your breasts may be smaller or heavier, and your hips may be broader or rounder. This is all part and parcel of motherhood—and there are very few women who escape with their figures entirely unscathed!

If your weight and shape concern you, take a look at your diet to see if there are areas where you can make healthier choices. Cut back on sugary or fatty foods, for example; reduce overall portion sizes; and switch to low-fat versions of milk and cheese spreads. You can also increase the bulk of your diet by eating more vegetables and whole grains.

Exercise helps weight control, as well as firming muscle and skin tone, all of which can help you feel better about your body. If you can't manage to get out on your own to exercise, find out about mom-and-baby classes, or take lots of long walks with your baby. Do some stretching and toning floor exercises at home, or work out with an exercise DVD. The more active you are, the more calories you'll burn.

Sound combinations

Speaking is a complex process that requires lots of nerve and muscle control, which is one reason why speech comes slowly.

When we speak, we must coordinate many muscles from various body parts and systems, including the larynx, which contains the vocal cords; the teeth, lips, tongue, and mouth; and the respiratory system.

At 28 weeks, your baby has established some of the groundwork for speech acquisition. At the moment, she is using a combination of vowels and consonants: lip consonants with vowels that are generated in the center of her mouth, with her tongue flat ("mama," for example); tongue-front consonants in front of vowels that come at the front of her mouth (such as "dada"); and tongue-back consonants in front of vowels that are created in the back of the mouth (for example, "gaga").

Your baby is starting, therefore, to create some interesting sounds that begin to sound more like adult speech in that some of the basic sounds are starting to be formed. At this stage, though, it's still baby babble. Nevertheless, you should always respond to her babbling and be very interactive and positive.

Words of praise Encourage your baby with praise when she tries to communicate with you and uses her "words."

Not so silent nights...

Your baby's sleep may not be quiet. You may hear her snort, breathe irregularly, bang her head, and rock herself to and fro as she sleeps.

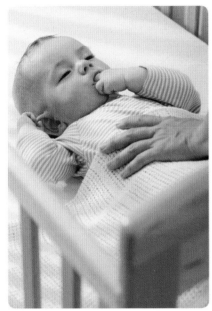

Comfort habit Your baby can find it soothing to suck his thumb or fingers, which can help him to settle and fall asleep.

If the prospect of sleeping like a baby sounds like heaven at the moment, you might want to think again. Not all babies sleep in utter tranquillity—many snore and sniffle, have irregular breathing patterns, or even rock or bang their heads as a way of soothing themselves. Most of the time, this is nothing to worry about and babies grow out of whatever peculiar sleep habit they happen to adopt, but occasionally you may need to take action.

Snoring and snuffling Babies often snore, snort, or snuffle when they have a cold or a blocked nose. Try using a vaporizer in her bedroom to add moisture to the air, which can ease breathing. This is particularly helpful if your home is very dry in the winter. You can also raise the head of your baby's crib a little to help mucus clear from her nose. Talk to your pediatrician if you see a noticeable change in your baby's habits, for example, if she starts sniffling much more than usual, if she has difficulty breathing, has a fever or seems unwell, or has difficulty feeding due to congestion.

Irregular breathing Lots of babies experience changes in their breathing patterns while they are fast asleep. For example, your baby might breathe rapidly for a while, then her breathing will slow down, and even pause for several seconds before she starts breathing again. Her breathing may also change as she becomes excited or frightened by her dreams. These pauses in breathing should start to happen less frequently now, but if they continue and you are at all concerned, consult your pediatrician. If she seems clammy or blue, get emergency medical attention.

Very occasionally, a pause in breathing may be caused by an episode of sleep apnea. However, this is a condition that is more common and recognized in babies who are one year or older. Your pediatrician will need to diagnose sleep apnea and will recommend treatment depending on the severity of the condition.

Head-banging and rocking After the age of six months, some babies adopt rhythmic activities, such as head-banging and rocking, to soothe themselves. From their time in the uterus, they are used to rocking as

---

ASK A... PEDIATRICIAN

I've heard of something called ALTE. What is this? Rarely, babies stop breathing for a longer period than a few seconds, which causes oxygen levels in the blood to drop. This can give the skin a white or blue appearance, and the baby can also choke or gag, and/or become floppy or stiff. Such an episode is called an Apparent Life-Threatening Event (ALTE), which used to be called a "near miss crib death." This should be treated as an emergency, and the baby may need resuscitation. Even if a baby recovers fairly rapidly on her own, an ambulance should be called and she should be assessed in hospital, and her condition prior to the episode assessed. Monitoring over the weeks following ALTE is important to ensure that the baby is recovered fully.

---

well as being in a head-down position, so may feel comforted by rhythmic pressure on the top of the head. If your baby isn't harming herself, leave her to it. Most children outgrow this by the age of three, and many stop long before that.

There is no indication that rocking or head-banging is a sign of an emotional disorder. Sometimes babies bang their heads to distract themselves from a sore throat, teething, or an ear infection. If you think this is what is causing discomfort, call the pediatrician to see if a baby painkiller is appropriate and take her to the doctor if her condition doesn't improve within 24 hours.

28 weeks

243

29 weeks

AT THIS AGE, A BABY'S LEVEL OF VISION IS NEARLY AS GOOD AS AN ADULT'S

Your baby loves all types of music now, and with the right instruments, he'll be able to make his own! The idea of object permanence—that an object is there even if not visible—begins to develop around this time. So, too, does separation anxiety—not wanting to be away from you.

Where did it go?

Your baby's grasp of the concept of object permanence is maturing. She will delight in games of hide-and-seek and may hide from you!

What's in the box? The understanding that objects exist even when he can't see them will increase your baby's curiosity.

Your baby's cognitive development is continuing steadily, and she will now show that she's beginning to gain the concept of object permanence—that an object exists even when she can't see it. This means that she may continue to look for a toy if it is covered with a cloth or has fallen out of sight, and will delight in games that involve the disappearance and reappearance of an object, face, or toy.

She will apply this understanding to other parts of her life, too, for example, pulling the covers away from your head when you are sleeping to check that you are still there, and moving toys to find something underneath.

Emotional implications Your baby is approaching the age when separation anxiety starts to set in (see p.283). This development, coupled with her increased understanding of object permanence, may make your baby much clingier than usual. While once she may have played happily on her own, oblivious to your presence even when you popped in and out of the room doing chores, she will now start to wonder where you are when she can't see or hear you. After all, you are not in sight, so you must be there somewhere. It's no longer "out of sight, out of mind," and she may shout and cry to bring you back. Reassure her by responding to her when she cries out so that she begins to feel confident that you are nearby even when she can't see you, and that you are still there to answer her needs when she calls out.

DEVELOPMENT ACTIVITY

Peek-a-boo

Your baby will be a big fan of peek-a-boo games now and will love to play them with you—and she can join in, too! She may think she's invisible when she can't see you, and find it great fun to "reappear," even though she's been there all along.

Playing peek-a-boo at this age can reinforce her understanding of the concept of object permanence. With lots of chances to rediscover that "missing" things are not gone forever, but eventually reappear, she will eventually learn to cope more effectively with feelings of anxiety when you are not able to be with her.

Surprise! As your baby gets used to this game, you can make her enjoy it even more by using a range of silly expressions.

ASK A... PEDIATRICIAN

How can I reduce the risk of my baby getting asthma? If one of you, or another one of your children, has asthma, breast-feeding your baby for as long as possible will reduce her risk of developing it. You can also reduce her risk by both you and your partner avoiding smoking during and after pregnancy. Replacing old carpets and rugs with laminate, wood, or linoleum flooring, and replacing old bedding and cushions reduces your baby's exposure to dust, which in turn reduces her risk of getting asthma. Some children experience increased symptoms with certain pets, so research this before introducing a pet into the home.

29 weeks

YOUR BABY IS 29 WEEKS AND 1 DAY

Where's mom?

Your baby is approaching the age at which separation anxiety sets in, which can be difficult not just for her, but also for you.

In the coming weeks, you may notice that your baby experiences anxiety when separated from you. Suddenly, your happy, independent baby may cry each time you leave the room or put her down. She may hate to be alone, and spend more time looking for you than engaging in the activities she usually enjoys.

This behavior is completely normal, even if it is a little frustrating. She doesn't want to be without you, and she will do what she can to prevent your departure.

At this age, your baby is learning to develop trust, so to support this it is important that you recognize her fears and emotions, and do whatever you can to help her feel secure.

Go to her whenever she calls you. Do what you can to reassure her that you are there, and give her a little cuddle to help her feel more confident. Talk to her when you are out of sight, so that she knows you are there, and return to her frequently so she understands that you will always return.

While frequently stopping whatever you are doing to reassure your baby can be time-consuming at the outset, she needs to learn to feel safe and to anchor an understanding of the fact that you will always be there for her, even when she can't see you. When you leave, she must learn that you will always come back. These feelings are the foundation of trust and emotional well-being, so constant reassurance at this stage will go a long way toward encouraging confidence and independence later on.

YOUR BABY IS 29 WEEKS AND 2 DAYS

Hands together

Your baby is now aware that both of her hands belong to her, and she's beginning to learn that she can operate them simultaneously.

Your baby may reach for a toy with one hand and thoughtfully peruse it or place it in her mouth. Suddenly, her attention is captured by another toy. She knows that one hand is busy, so she'll put the other to work to grasp what she sees. She may look at both toys with interest, or perhaps drop one as she focuses on the other. She may see something else and the process will begin again. She can use both hands, but she hasn't quite worked out how best to use them together for even better results! She may pass a toy from hand to hand, and

Better grasp Your baby may have more control over her hands and fingers, but she's just getting the hang of using her hands together.

bang toys together if they make a satisfying sound, but her actions are likely to be uncoordinated and slightly clumsy as they are probably not intentional at this stage. She may manage to place two hands on the same object, pick it up, and turn it over, but when her attention is caught by something else, she'll forget that she's holding something at all, and drop it.

If you guide her, your baby may be able to hold a cup with both hands, but she's likely to let go unexpectedly and may find it difficult to pick it up and guide it to her lips. Babies develop their hand skills by touching, reaching, exploring, and grasping, so give her plenty of opportunities to do just this.

Your baby's drinks

Are follow-up formulas beneficial for your baby, and what else should she be drinking—or not—in the second half of her first year?

Mastering a cup Encourage your baby to start drinking from a cup after six months.

Now that your baby has passed the six-month mark, you may question whether the milk she has enjoyed since birth still meets her nutritional needs, or if there are other types of milk that might suit her better. Also, you may wonder what to give her—alongside her usual breast milk or formula—to quench her thirst now that she has started, or increased solids.

If you're breast-feeding, breast milk is the ideal drink for your baby for the first six months and, together with an increasingly varied diet, can form the basis of her nutrition up until one year.

If your baby is formula-fed, you are mixing breast and formula, or thinking of weaning her off breast milk, you may wonder which type of formula is suitable after six months, and whether you should switch to one marketed for older babies.

Formulas contain two types of protein: whey and casein. First formulas, suitable from birth, are whey-based, which is easy for your baby to digest. Follow-up and

"hungry baby" formulas marketed at babies over six months, are casein-based, which takes longer to digest and is thought therefore to keep babies satisfied for longer. However, there is no significant nutritional difference between these formulas, and first formula is suitable for your baby for the whole of her first year.

Soy formula is not suitable before six months. After this, some choose soy if they wish to exclude animal proteins from their baby's diet. Soy is also promoted as an option for babies allergic to cow's milk formula. However, these babies can also be allergic to soy milk, and there are more suitable formulas, known as fully hydrolyzed formulas, that pediatricians prescribe for babies with an allergy. Soy also contains glucose, which can damage your baby's teeth. Talk to your pediatrician before giving soy formula milk.

Goat's and sheep's milk and oat drinks are also promoted as an alternative for babies with a cow's milk allergy. However, these are not suitable under one year as they contain insufficient iron and other nutrients. Goat's milk also contains

lactose so isn't a good low-allergenic alternative. Full-fat cow's milk should not be given until one year.

Quenching thirst Up until now, your baby's needs have been simple. If you've breast-fed her, she will have received all the fluids she needed from the watery, thirst-quenching foremilk. If she has been bottle-fed, you may have supplemented her feeds with cooled boiled water to prevent dehydration.

Once she's on solids, you can supplement feedings with another drink. Tap water is best, and there's no need to boil it unless you have well water or you know of issues with the water in your town's supply. Bottled water is also suitable for babies. Fruit juice contains vitamin C and it's fine after six months, but to protect your baby's teeth, give it only at mealtimes, in a lidded cup, and diluted to a ratio of 1:10. Fruit drinks and flavored milks should be avoided under one year, and limited or avoided after this; and carbonated drinks, and other caffeine-containing drinks, shouldn't form any part of a young child's diet.

ASK A... MOM

My baby cries and spits out all the solid food I give her. What can I do?
Offer her some breast milk on a spoon to get her used to the idea of the spoon itself. Mix her vegetable purée with breast milk to make it seem more familiar, then slowly reduce the amount of milk you add. Give her her own spoon with a chunky handle and a little purée in a bowl. Let her use her hands and spoon to play with her food; most will probably end up in her hair, but her instinct will be to put some into her mouth. This may be an easier way for her to make the transition to new tastes and textures. If she still resists, rather than force the issue, leave it a while. You can try again later when you know that she's hungry and in a more receptive mood.

YOUR BABY IS 29 WEEKS AND 4 DAYS

Using the right words

Your baby is too young to understand instructions, but it's valuable to begin using the words "yes" and "no" to introduce these concepts.

The word "no" can be overused when it comes to children, and it can become ineffective over the years as children "tune out" to this instruction. However, while your baby will not yet understand the concepts of "yes" and "no," do use them to start teaching her the meaning of these important words. It is helpful to use "no" paired with a firm tone and an action such as a shake of the head or finger if your baby is in danger, for example, if she reaches out to a hot radiator or pulls at a fireplace screen.

When you say "no" like this, you will also need to act quickly as she won't stop on your say so at this age. Child-proofing your home will minimize situations when you need to say "no."

As your baby grows, it is most helpful to tell her what you want her to do: for example, "Hold the teddy bear," rather than "No, don't drop it." Children respond more quickly when they know what you want, rather than what you don't want.

When you want your baby to stop doing something such as wiggling on the changing table, or stiffening her body when you dress her, try to distract her by entertaining her with a new toy, pulling funny faces, or waiting while she calms down. It's not appropriate to introduce discipline now, as scolding at this age is more likely to distress her than have a positive, calming effect.

Equally, don't hesitate to say "yes" when she responds to a request. Praise, a big smile, and a positive, cheerful "yes," while you nod, will encourage her to continue in the same vein.

YOUR BABY IS 29 WEEKS AND 5 DAYS

Enjoying music

The best way to teach your baby musical appreciation is to fill her life with all kinds of music and enjoy it with her.

Your baby may display a preference for certain types of music. There may be a calm song that always soothes her if she is frustrated or helps her fall asleep, and some favorite playtime music that makes her giggle and has the power to entertain even when she is unsettled.

Music encourages the development of speech, and research suggests that babies exposed to lots of music are better able to understand the patterns of speech and grammar, and language development is enhanced. Also, studies show that soothing music can reduce the stress

Making music Take out the baby musical instruments and create music together. Dance along as she shakes and rattles.

hormone cortisol, while lively music will engage your baby, but may overstimulate her if she's tired or ready for quiet play. One study on the effect of music on young children found that soft music (in this case, lullabies) relaxed restless children. Your baby will enjoy it when you sing lullabies as you put her to bed, and this helps her settle as she prepares for sleep.

Whatever the long-term effects, there is no doubt that your baby will enjoy listening to and making music. Sing along and hold her in your arms or on your lap as you move to music. Keep in mind that she can learn from all types of musical genres. It isn't only classical music that works on her brain's neural pathways—any music will do the same.

Practical babywear

Now that your baby is bigger and more mobile, you may need a few more items of clothing that allow her to move about comfortably.

I have always put my baby to sleep on her back to lower the risk of SIDS. But now, she's started to flip over and sleep on her stomach. Should I turn her back? There isn't much point in turning her onto her back again once she's learned to roll over. If she prefers sleeping on her stomach, that's where she'll end up. While you keep putting your baby to bed on her back until she is one year old, the high-risk period for SIDS is generally passed by the time a baby can turn over. Just make sure that your baby's crib is safe and continue to follow the guidelines for preventing SIDS, such as avoiding pillows and duvets (see p.31). But try not to worry if her position changes during the night.

My baby's hands and feet are very cool at night, but she is sleeping well. Does she need more layers? Her hands and feet will always be cooler than the rest of her body. A better gauge is to put your hand under her neck and feel her face. If these are warm, she's probably dressed appropriately; if they feel cool, try a baby sleep sack or pop on a pair of bed socks. Sweating around her face, head, or neck is a sign that she is overheating—it is very important to avoid this. Provided your baby's room is kept at a temperature of around 60.8–68°F (16–20°C), ideally 64.4°F (18°C), she shouldn't become too cold or too hot.

Loose clothing Choose garments that do not restrict your baby's movements (left).
Snaps Vital for quick changes, snaps make dressing easy to manage (right).

Comfort over style Choose garments that are a little on the large size to give your baby space to maneuver. She'll be on her hands and knees a lot, so patches, reinforcements, or padding on the knees will help to keep her comfortable (and the pants intact). Long-sleeved shirts can protect little forearms and elbows as she shuffles across the floor. Practical should always win over style!

As your baby's clothes bunch up when she moves, T-shirts and vests with easy-to-fasten snaps at the crotch will keep her cozy. She's probably impatient with diaper changes now with so many new things to investigate, so choose clothes with snaps and elastic waists, which are excellent for quick changes, and avoid fiddly fasteners that will leave you both frustrated.

Change is inevitable Eating is a messy business and, no matter how many bibs you have, you can expect several changes of clothes a day as your baby attempts to get more food in her tummy than on her clothing. Go for a mix-and-match set of clothes (in which all of the tops and bottoms are interchangeable). Clothing should also be washable, kind to her skin (there will be a lot of chafing going on as she learns to crawl and to walk), and not require ironing. Don't spend too much on her clothing at this stage; it will be stained and worn, and then outgrown before you know it!

Feet first Your baby may be rolling, bottom shuffling, or trying to crawl across the room, so she'll need to get a grip on the floor. Socks with little grip pads on the soles are ideal for this. If the weather doesn't call for socks, let her go barefoot, which will give her the best grip. Babies need socks and booties only for warmth; they don't need shoes to learn to walk and should not, in fact, be fitted for their first pair until they are cruising or walking confidently.

29 weeks

249

30 weeks

AT THIS AGE, BABIES RESPOND MORE TO HOW YOU SAY SOMETHING RATHER THAN TO WHAT YOU SAY

Your baby is beginning to understand more of what you are saying just by watching your facial expressions and listening to your tone of voice. She's very sensitive to her emotional environment so try to deal with any domestic disagreements calmly to give her the security she needs.

Talking with gestures

Your baby is beginning to understand how words and gestures go together. Activity rhymes can encourage this development.

Giving clues Help your baby learn simple concepts such as "hungry" or "tired" by pairing hand gestures with your words.

TIME TO THINK ABOUT

Using a cup

Once your baby can hold onto things and starts to eat finger foods, you can introduce a cup for drinking water. Choose one with a spout, preferably soft, and a large handle she can easily get hold of. It will be dropped, so look out for one that will bounce without the lid falling off! Learning to drink from a lidded cup is important, as by now she should be giving up bottles with slow-flowing nipples. If you choose to give diluted fruit juice, it should only be given in a lidded cup at mealtimes so that her emerging teeth are not bathed in sugars for longer than it takes to finish a drink (see also p.247).

Your baby may begin to make gestures, such as raising her whole hand toward something she wants, which will rapidly develop into pointing over the next couple of months. You may hold up toy after toy before realizing that she is gesturing to you, and wants a hug!

Encourage your baby to pat or touch things in her books by saying "Where's the cow?" or "Where is the dog?" and point to them to help her make the connection. When she looks at and gestures to her favorite soft toy, bring it to her so that she knows her signal is understood. She may direct you to what she wants with her gaze, as well as babble and wave her open or closed hand.

Until she learns to point, your baby may gesture with her fist rather than her finger: she may ball up her hand and stretch out her arm. At about nine months (and, in some cases, a bit earlier), she will learn instrumental pointing, which involves an outstretched arm and an extended index finger.

Imitating gestures At 30 weeks, your baby may be able to imitate some of the hand movements in her activity rhymes and songs, and copy you when you bang on her drum or pat her soft toy. Say, "soft, pat-pat" when you stroke the kitty, "bye-bye" when you wave goodbye, and "kiss" when you blow her a kiss, so that she understands that actions and gestures are associated with words, too.

Two U.S. studies have revealed that babies who are encouraged to gesture in advance of, and then in conjunction with, speech, actually learn to speak more quickly and experience faster cognitive development.

ASK A... PEDIATRICIAN

My baby is constantly teary-eyed. Will this clear up? Newborn babies have tiny tear ducts in the corner of each eye. When tears start being produced, at around one month, they drain away through these ducts. Occasionally, the ducts in newborns are blocked and the tears are unable to drain away. Rest assured that this is not great cause for concern, and most blocked tear ducts resolve themselves by the end of the first year. Your pediatrician may show you how to massage them to help unblock them. If the eye becomes crusty, use cotton pads dampened with cooled boiled water to clean it. If you notice any redness in the eye or a yellow discharge, consult your pediatrician as your baby may need antibiotic drops.

Should my baby be vaccinated against the flu? Yes. Health Canada recommends that all children aged six months and older receive an annual flu shot, so if your baby is old enough, you should have her vaccinated. Visit fightflu.ca for more information.

Is it normal for my baby to pull up her legs and grimace when she does a bowel movement? She's just helping her bowels move. Drawing up her legs gets her into a squatting position and makes it easier—she's not in pain. As long as her movements are regular and there's no blood in her stools, she'll be fine.

30 weeks

251

YOUR BABY IS 30 WEEKS AND 1 DAY

Emotional awareness

Your baby's emotional antennae are sensitive. She'll pick up on stress in her immediate environment and will be affected by it.

Research tells us a lot about how babies experience stress, and why. We know that if they are hungry and not fed, or not given physical comfort when distressed, they experience symptoms of stress. As babies are still developing their sense of security, and are not equipped physically or emotionally to deal with high levels of stress, this can have a profound effect on their physical and emotional well-being. Your baby needs you to reduce her experience of stress by meeting her needs for food, warmth, and love, and by soothing her when emotions overwhelm her. When you respond rapidly to calm and contain her emotions, she learns that feelings need not be overpowering. As a result, she will learn to develop trust and will have a sense of security, which will help her learn to self-soothe efficiently when she does experience stress.

Studies have shown that babies have sensitive social barometers and pick up on parental stress and emotional upheaval, causing them to feel unsafe, afraid, and even unwell. If an argument becomes heated, even if raised voices aren't directed at her, she'll be startled and upset. When conflict occurs, work hard to ensure discussions are calm and respectful; agree that if they get heated, you both take a break to cool off. Your baby doesn't understand the context of your disagreements, so heated debate can cause distress. As she grows, show her how you calmly resolve differences, and she'll understand that disagreements can be sorted out in a healthy manner.

YOUR BABY IS 30 WEEKS AND 2 DAYS

Gentle guidance

Your baby certainly knows her own mind, so if she's veering in an unsuitable direction, you'll need to steer her gently elsewhere.

Guiding your baby toward appropriate objects, activities, and behaviors is a technique all parents will need to adopt. Babies may be single-minded, but they are also easy to distract as their memories are still fairly short and their interest in new things is limitless.

When your baby wiggles while being changed, heads for the potted plant for the 25th time in a row, or tries to eat her outraged siblings' snacks, it's time to employ some diversion tactics. Keep toy stashes dotted around the house so you can grab a toy when you need to capture her attention. Change the toys frequently so they always seem new. Choose a song or activity rhyme your baby enjoys that requires her involvement, and launch into it when she's heading for trouble. Pick her up and move her to a different room, tickle her toes, or point out a bird or airplane in the sky.

Your baby is too young to reason with, or to understand why she can't have or do what she wants. Instead of facing a battle with her, quickly divert her to interrupt undesirable behaviors. Over time, your baby may begin to realize that she won't be allowed to get to the potted plant or wiggle away from you while she's being changed—but it still probably won't stop her from trying!

Look at this! If your baby is doing something unwanted, divert her attention by grabbing a toy that you know will distract her.

Toys for seven months and up

At seven months, your baby will be ready for new toys that stimulate her reasoning, coordination, and gross- and fine-motor skills.

Working it out Puzzle toys such as shape-sorters will occupy your baby now, even if he isn't yet able to fit a shape into the right hole.

Toys don't have to be expensive to entertain your baby and promote her development. In fact, many household items can keep her occupied. There are, however, some great toys for this age.

Balls and toys on wheels encourage mobility and promote hand–eye coordination. Rolling a ball back and forth encourages motor skills and coordination, not to mention a sense of fun! Also, go for a toy on a sturdy string that you can pull just out of her reach, or that she can pull toward her.

Toys that make your baby think will sharpen her reasoning skills. Look for toys with features that hide behind or inside part of the toy. Very basic puzzles with chunky handles for lifting and moving will stimulate your baby. Ensure they are not too difficult or she will become frustrated and give up.

Toys that help your baby explore different shapes and sounds as well as cause and effect nurture her thinking and motor skills. Shape-sorters, noisy blocks, toys that ring, rattle, and crinkle when you squeeze or touch different parts of them, and stackable toys that fit inside one another will all entertain her. Musical instruments designed for her age, such as a baby rainmaker, can intrigue her with the sounds they make.

An activity board attached to her crib or the back of a chair will help her to practice her coordination, and she'll love learning that she can open doors, twist, squeeze, shake, and pull things to get a good reaction. Blocks that can be piled, knocked down, banged together, and dropped in and out of containers are a good investment, as they'll be put to different uses over the coming years.

Finally, don't forget books! If books form a regular part of playtime, she'll develop an avid interest in stories and reading, and her vocabulary and speech will continue to improve.

ASK A... CHILD PSYCHOLOGIST

Does it matter that my baby boy seems more interested in toys for girls? The truth is that toys are toys, and they really should be considered genderless, even if they do come in lurid pinks and rough-and-tumble blues! Boys may well enjoy playing with dolls and safe kitchen utensils in imitation of mom, while girls may get pleasure from cars and balls. Toys are designed to stimulate development (which includes emotional development) as well as entertain. Until they are three or four years old, children will have no real understanding of gender differentiations in either themselves or the toys they choose, so encourage your baby to play with whatever interests him.

DEVELOPMENT ACTIVITY

Treasure box

Fill a basket or box with a selection of baby-friendly objects, and encourage her to investigate the contents one by one. The box doesn't have to contain toys—household items such as a comb, and clean kitchen utensils, such as a whisk or spatula, are ideal. Your baby can rummage through the box and touch, bang, chew, smell, and study the items. This type of game encourages hand–eye coordination, imagination, speech development, and, above all, a sense of fun!

Box of fun Place an assortment of child-safe items in a box for your baby to investigate.

30 weeks

253

SPOTLIGHT ON...
Stage two solids—lumpier foods

As soon as your baby is enjoying a variety of puréed foods, she's ready to move on to the second stage of solids. Now you should introduce her to a greater range of foods as well as new textures and some finger foods.

A TYPICAL DAY'S DIET

To give you an idea of what your baby should be eating at this stage, below is an example of a day's food intake for a 6- to 7-month-old baby. Your baby should still be having around 24 fl oz (720 ml) of breast- or formula milk each day. At first, some parents prefer to feed their baby at breakfast and lunch to give them time to digest their meal before sleeping at night. A simple, easily digestible meal can then be introduced in the evening.

■ **Breakfast** Breast milk or formula, cereal, and mashed fruit. You can offer a variety of fresh or canned fruits or applesauce, and toast can be plain or served with a spread that is sweetened with fruit juice (not artificial sweeteners).

■ **Lunch** Meat, poultry, or lentils with vegetables and mashed potato or baby pasta shapes or sweet potato; soft pieces of fruit; water to drink.

■ **Mid-afternoon** Breast milk or formula.

■ **Dinner** Vegetables and starchy foods like mashed baked potato. Also, fresh fruit, vegetables and cereals/grains, including mixtures of these products (such as peaches and oatmeal); water to drink.

■ **Bedtime** Breast milk or formula.

Expand your baby's diet Once your baby is happy with solids, it's important to introduce a variety of textures and combined flavors.

As your baby starts this next stage, she will begin to cope with soft lumps in foods, as well as mashed foods rather than runny purées. She doesn't need to have teeth to deal with lumps, but she does need to learn to chew rather than just suck and swallow.

She will start to learn to move foods around in her mouth, and this will be a different sensation for her. So it's important to vary the textures of your baby's food to get her used to chewing and moving food around, which will also help to develop the muscles used for speaking.

Moving on from purées Your baby will be familiar now with the taste and consistency of her usual purées, so it's important to alter the texture of her foods, doing so fairly quickly if you have waited until the recommended six months to start solids. You can adjust the texture of these familiar foods as well as adding new foods to them. For example, you can add finely chopped, mashed, grated, or ground "new" foods to her purées. This will provide a different texture and flavor as well as improve their nutritional value.

Start by adding very tiny, soft lumps to familiar foods. Don't be surprised if the lumps reappear—simply scoop them back up again and spoon them back in. Try well-cooked, baby-sized pasta shapes, mashed potato, or some soft cooked vegetables, which you can gently mash with a fork.

Introduce her to some finger foods—a little bowl of bite-and-dissolve foods such as baby bread sticks, soft cooked carrots, eggplant and potato cut into fingers, slices of banana, pear, and cubes of melon, papaya, or avocado. She will investigate these foods and over time will learn to chew or "gum" them, and then swallow. Make sure you stay with her in case she chokes.

Larger lumps After this, it's time to introduce slightly bigger lumps and textures, and some different new foods. For example, coarsely blend cooked chicken breast so it is not a smooth purée and stir into mashed potato with puréed peas. Offer a cauliflower purée; and mash banana into baby rice.

If you are bringing up your baby as a vegetarian, try lentils or chick peas ground up with puréed carrots or apples, or add to sweet potato or carrot purée to thicken the texture.

The idea is to introduce a much wider variety of foods over the next few weeks, mixing them with her favorite fruits and vegetables, while increasing the number and size of the lumps until she is able to move toward eating a similar texture of food to the whole family.

The atmosphere around mealtimes is really important, so give your baby plenty of encouragement and praise and don't press her to eat if she obviously doesn't want to. If she is really reluctant, check how much milk she is having and perhaps avoid giving a milk feeding in the hour or two before mealtime to see if this helps.

How much? Most babies won't eat much more than a tablespoon or two of a purée at the beginning of this stage, but this can dramatically increase as her milk feedings start to decrease a bit. Your baby needs a diet that contains protein, carbohydrates, and fat as well as a range of vitamins and minerals. To achieve this balance, she needs to be given foods from the four food groups (see p.207). You'll be able to work all these foods into two or three small meals per day.

Checking for reactions If your baby has not reacted to foods up until now, you may just prefer to jot down what she likes and keep on trying the foods she seems to dislike. However, if your baby has reacted to foods, it is likely you'll have discussed this with your pediatrician, who can advise you how to introduce other potentially allergenic foods.

IDEAL FINGER FOODS

- Vegetables steamed or cooked in the microwave until soft, then cooled: carrots, sweet potato, baby corn, green beans, broccoli, or cauliflower florets.
- Plain cooked potatoes cut into wedges, steamed new potatoes, slices of eggplant.
- A few pieces of chicken, with a vegetable purée for "dipping."
- Toast fingers or puffed baby snacks, sold at grocery stores nationwide.
- Miniature, unsalted, and unflavored rice cakes.
- Puréed fruit, vegetables, or beans spread on pita bread fingers, or baby crackers.
- Small cubes of ripe avocado.
- Soft ripe fruit, such as sliced pear, melon, banana, peach, nectarine, and berries (halved).
- Cooked pasta shapes served plain or with a small amount of sauce or a little olive oil drizzled over.
- Some snacks are intended for older babies who are sitting up and/or crawling. These should only be given to babies whose development skills match the description on the package.

Happy meals Babies love to grab food and some may be happier if allowed to feed themselves. Learning to feed herself is a huge step in your baby's physical and intellectual development, so encourage all her efforts and don't worry about the mess.

CHECKLIST

New flavors and textures

It's time to introduce new flavors and meals with lumps by adding mashed, ground, and coarsely chopped ingredients.

- **Meat, poultry, eggs, and legumes** Once thicker purées are going down well, add small chunks or ground pieces of cooked poultry or meat to get your baby used to lumps. A casserole with vegetables can be pulse-blended to keep some texture. Add to mashed potato, couscous, or baby pasta shapes.

- **Fruit and vegetables** Introduce a wider variety of fruits, including berries and dried fruits, and offer green vegetables such as spinach and broccoli.

- **Carbohydrates** Provide a range of cereals: unsweetened breakfast cereals can be softened in milk and used as finger foods. Try pasta, couscous, sweet potato, rice, and potatoes, as well as baby crackers, toast, or pita bread.

- **Temperature** There's no reason why your baby can't eat her food warm, chilled, or at room temperature. However, it's important to be sure that whatever you're serving isn't too hot.

- **Consistency** Mashed foods at first with tiny lumps and progressing to larger soft lumps.

- **How often?** 2–3 meals a day.

- **How much?** 4–6 tsp (more if she is hungry) of 2–3 different foods at each meal, with at least 2–3 vegetables and one fruit each day, plus some foods from the other food groups.

Growing up fast

The way your baby looks is changing as she grows, and you may also find that her little rolls of fat are starting to disperse.

Million-dollar smile Your baby may now have four to eight teeth, just two, or even none, but her cute smile is still irresistible!

Some babies look a little leaner as they become more mobile—all the activity burns off fat stores so that they begin to lose some of their chubby rolls of dimpled flesh.

Your baby's fontanelles are closing over, and, as she begins to bear weight and then walk, her feet will begin to flatten. Although she will continue to bounce up and down when held upright, she will straighten her legs at the knees for longer periods of time. Her head is becoming more rounded as she spends far less time on her back, and, as her body grows, it looks more in proportion to the rest of her body than it did previously. She may have a full head of hair by now or a just few delicate wisps covering her head.

Your baby will continue to grow at a tremendous rate in the lead-up to her first birthday, but that rate will now slow down a little. She will probably put on about 1–1¼lb (450–600 g) per month, and grow about 2¼in (6 cm) before she turns one.

Your baby's base eye color will have reached its final color by now, although very subtle changes may continue into adulthood.

Kitchen hygiene

Preparing your baby's food requires scrupulous hygiene; her immune system is still immature so she's susceptible to food-borne illnesses.

Hygiene is really important to keep your baby well, so read on for tips that will help protect your baby from germs. To prevent cross-contamination, use one cutting board and set of knives for meat and another for vegetables and fruits. Keep raw and cooked foods separate (and on different shelves in the refrigerator). Cook meat and poultry until it is well done, and wash fruits and vegetables or peel them before puréeing.

Use your baby's food immediately or freeze it for future use. If you store leftover food in the refrigerator, keep it in there for only two or three days, then discard it if unused. If you think she's going to eat only a little of a jar of food, pour some into a bowl for serving, and refrigerate the remainder for later use.

Wash all your baby's spoons, bowls, and food containers in hot, soapy water or in the dishwasher to kill any germs. You don't need to sterilize them, as her body is accustomed to swallowing a good share of bugs! After all, your baby always seems to have something in her mouth, even when it's nowhere near feeding time—but there's no need to add more germs to her system. Also, wash your hands (and your baby's), clean surfaces frequently, and change dish towels fairly regularly.

YOUR BABY'S FEEDING AREA

Clean your baby's high chair after every meal with hot, soapy water and, if you wish, a little disinfectant. Pay particular attention to crevices around her tray and seat, where she may have dropped bits of food. Mop the floor around her chair and look for food that she may have fired across the room; she'll undoubtedly spend some time on the kitchen floor and put anything that looks interesting straight into her mouth, even if it is a week-old meatball.

Coping with chaos

Babies are messy! You may find that your once-tidy kitchen is in shambles, and your living room looks like a cyclone has hit it!

Baby corner Keep an area for your baby's toys, and pop them back in a basket after use.

Try not to let the mess get to you. You may have to lower your standards and expect things to look less tidy than usual. Time with your baby is precious, and it's much more important to spend it interacting with her than it is to follow along behind her cleaning up.

Having said that, you can put into place a few routines to help keep things a little more organized. Clear away the toys at the end of every play session. Make this easier by keeping them in baskets or boxes placed on open shelves, or screening off an area of your sitting room in which toys are piled out of sight.

Create baby areas in several rooms in your home, each with a large basket or a shelving unit in which to keep all your baby's things together. At the end of the day, do a sweep-up, gathering the single socks, dropped toys, bibs, wet towels, and books, and put them back into their homes, or give them a wash. Take a few minutes to refill your changing bag, so you are ready to go out on impulse. It may seem like one extra thing to fit in, but you'll be able to relax more if things are ready for the next day.

When you wash up after dinner, give your baby her own little bowl of warm water at her high chair, with a little baby shampoo to make it bubbly like your sink, to buy yourself a few extra minutes. Protect the floor around her high chair with a mess mat, and buy a bowl with a suction-cup base to prevent her from hurling the contents around the kitchen.

If you can afford help with cleaning, don't hesitate to organize it—if some of the heavier cleaning is done regularly, it's easier to stay on top of the general tidying. If a cleaner isn't right for you, spend some dedicated time each weekend cleaning with the help of your partner while your baby sleeps.

DEVELOPMENT ACTIVITY

Clean-up time

Encouraging your baby to become involved in cleaning up her toys at the end of a play session will help to establish good habits, and she'll soon accept it as part of her routine. Show her how to pile her toys back into the basket and put her books on the lowest shelf of the bookcase. Demonstrate how to neatly line up her soft toys and put everything in its place. Explain what you are doing, and repeat the fact that you are making things "nice and neat" to establish a positive association with the activity rather than making it sound like a chore! Praise her when she manages to put a toy in the basket. Your baby will enjoy this activity because it's with you, and as she notices your pleasure, she'll be more likely to join in next time, too.

The clean-up game Make a game out of putting away her toys so that your baby learns what to do after playing with them. This is a great way to introduce the idea of cleaning up.

31 weeks

DISCIPLINE AT THIS AGE IS NOT APPROPRIATE AS BABIES DO NOT UNDERSTAND "YES" AND "NO"

If he's not yet crawling, give him plenty of tummy time to develop the strength and coordination he needs to get started. His curiosity is boundless, so make sure he's got plenty to do, but in a safe, secure area. Listen to his chatter, which is starting to sound like real words now.

Strong emotions

Your baby will be unable to control her emotions, and may end up in tears of frustration or become sad when you need to leave the room.

A young baby has highly changeable emotions, one minute squealing with delight, the next upset or frustrated. While these changes may be difficult to predict at times, each is an important communication from your baby to you, telling you about her needs and wants. Try to remember that what she is doing is communicating with you, and that this is a good sign.

In her first year, your baby will experience strong emotions as physical feelings in her body—her task is to separate out these emotions gradually, and, eventually, with your help and guidance, to label each one.

At first, strong feelings can be frightening for your baby, and she will need your help to tolerate the sensations and to return to a calm, regulated emotional state. According to "attachment" experts (who study the deep relationship between a child and their main caregiver during the first few years of life, and the profound influence this has on a baby), your role is to show her you accept her feelings, that they don't scare or overwhelm you, and that she doesn't need to feel out of control or afraid of them.

One way to do this is through "mirroring," which involves reflecting your child's emotions, but in a milder, less intense version. You may naturally tilt your head during mirroring to signal your understanding. Holding her while a feeling grips her can also reassure her that she is safe. You can mirror your child's emotions no matter how young she is, and your steady reaction will give her confidence that feelings need not overpower her.

Reassure, comfort, and calm Your baby can't handle her emotions and will look to you to calm her down when she's feeling angry or frustrated.

Help your baby also to put a name to her feelings by talking about what is going on. For example, when you say "You look angry" or "Is that a sad face?", you are helping her to name and separate her emotions.

Good role model How your baby perceives your reactions will also influence how she manages her own emotions. Be a positive role model for your baby by showing her how you are able to manage your own strong feelings and recover from them when you are feeling upset.

However, if you find yourself struggling to cope with a prolonged period of distress from your baby, do seek help in soothing her from your partner, or a trusted friend or relative, while you take a break and regain your patience and equilibrium. It's important to be realistic about your own limitations and needs, and to recognize when you need time out yourself.

ASK A... PEDIATRICIAN

Why has my baby suddenly developed regular bouts of diarrhea, even though she doesn't seem ill? A change in your baby's diet may cause diarrhea and/or constipation, as her digestive system makes the transition to solid foods. Sometimes, new foods can appear undigested in the runny stools as they're introduced in the diet, a phenomenon known as "toddler" diarrhea (although this is more common after one year). If this is the reason, your baby will be otherwise well, and the diarrhea should settle down as the bowels get better at digesting new foods. Make sure that your baby drinks plenty of fluids—give cooled boiled water on top of her usual milk feedings—and if you are giving any fruit juice, ensure that it is well diluted.

31 weeks

259

Is she a bottom shuffler?

Not all babies like to crawl, so don't be surprised if your baby seems determined to stay on her bottom and move in her own sweet way...

Learning to move around can be frustrating for babies, which is probably one reason why they all have different approaches. Some crawl before they walk, some don't crawl until after they walk, and others don't crawl at all. Instead, they shuffle on their bottoms, sometimes using a hand behind and a foot in front to propel themselves. As bottom shuffling involves being able to sit and wiggle forward on their buttocks, it typically develops two to three months after a baby is able to sit unsupported.

Around nine percent of babies are bottom shufflers and it is thought to run in families, so if you or your partner were shufflers, there's a chance your baby will be one, too. Many bottom shufflers walk a bit later than usual, often because they are so successful at scooting around on their bottoms that there's less incentive to stand up. As long as your baby can get around, it doesn't matter how she does it.

My way Babies who favor bottom shuffling are often highly efficient at moving around.

I want you!

From time to time, your baby may express a strong preference for one parent, and even cry or hide her face from the other. What's going on?

Showing favoritism Many babies go through phases of "preferring" one parent to another, so try not to take it personally.

As your baby develops, she may at times show a preference for one of you over the other. Try not to be disheartened by this favoritism—it will swing around to you again at some point, and is not because you have made a mistake, or because she hasn't bonded with you. Most often, your baby will show a degree of preference for the person most tuned into her needs and communication, and who knows all the best ways to soothe her. This is usually the parent who spends the most time with her, and who therefore has more opportunity to "read" her signals and gain confidence in responding to her.

The opposite can also be true on some occasions. For example, a fresh face may be what she wants at the end of the day. So if you are returning from work, you may be the one getting the squeals of delight and a greeting of raised arms ready for a hug.

Balance her preferences by taking turns to care for her. Each establish your own special activities with her when you are together, and don't be disheartened when she does show an unashamed preference for the other parent. She doesn't know it may feel hurtful, and she is definitely not doing it deliberately to upset you.

Coping with a food allergy

Having a baby with an allergy can present a number of challenges. Thankfully, many babies outgrow their allergies with proper care.

Whether your baby shows mild discomfort after eating certain foods or is in danger of an anaphylactic reaction (see p.404), it is essential to scrupulously avoid the foods that cause her problems. If you haven't yet had a suspected allergy confirmed by an allergy specialist, ask your doctor to refer your baby for a skin-prick or blood test so you can find out exactly what to avoid.

You may discover, for example, that she's fine when she eats egg whites, but yolks will cause problems. You may also find your assumptions are wrong. For instance, a rash you had attributed to an allergy to peanuts in a peanut butter sandwich was actually caused by an allergy to the seeds in the bread.

If you are still breast-feeding, you will need to cut out the offending foods from your diet. It's worth continuing to breast-feed, because your antibodies will help to support your baby's immature immune system, which, in a baby with allergies, is under particular duress. Also, since babies with an allergy often have necessarily limited diets, your breast milk will help fill her up with important nutrients she may otherwise miss out on.

Talk to your pediatrician about whether you need an antihistamine that's appropriate for babies. If your baby's allergy is severe, you may need to carry an auto-injector (which administers medication in the event of an anaphylactic shock). Anyone else who spends time with your child should also know how to administer any medication.

Ensure that anyone else who feeds your baby knows what to avoid. Prepare her food using kitchen utensils that have been carefully washed in very hot soapy water to avoid cross-contamination, and learn to read labels on foods that you buy for her extremely carefully.

Maintaining a food diary Keep a food diary to help you identify foods that may have caused a reaction in your baby. If you think that you need to cut out some food groups, such as dairy, for example, you'll need the help of a nutritionist to ensure she gets all the nutrients she needs from her diet, and a food diary will help you keep tabs on her overall intake.

You may feel anxious about the possibility of an allergic reaction, but it's important that you don't pass these feelings on to your baby, as that could make her nervous about eating, trying new foods, and relaxing during mealtimes. She may come to view food as the enemy rather than something that can enrich her life on all levels.

DEVELOPMENT ACTIVITY

Washing-up time!

Babies like nothing more than joining in with mom and dad's activities, and a little help with the washing up can provide an opportunity for fun. Give your baby a washing-up bowl of warm, soapy water, set her up on her mess mat on the floor, and allow her to "wash" her own dishes using a big sponge and a clean dish towel. She'll love being involved and doing things she sees you doing, and she'll also learn a helpful skill, develop her hand–eye coordination, and enjoy the sensation of playing with water.

Soapy fun Set your baby up with a big bowl of soapy water, a sponge, and a few "dishes" to wash, and let him enjoy doing what the grown-ups do.

Bed sharing

Your baby may be sharing your bed—perhaps it's time to encourage her to sleep in hers.

Most parents confess to bringing their babies into bed when they wake up in the night, as it sometimes seems the quickest and easiest way to get some sleep. While, in the short term, this is not usually a problem, being in your bed can, over time, become a habit that your baby is reluctant to give up. Unless you plan to co-sleep with her for an indefinite period of time, you may need to get her used to her own bed again.

Try to resist the temptation to bring your baby into your bed when she wakes up. Instead, stroke her, sing to her, and snuggle with her, then leave the room. Return whenever she calls to reassure her that you will come whenever she really needs you—if you leave her to cry, she'll simply become more insecure.

Implement this new policy for the first time on a night when you don't have to wake up early the next morning. Be calm and patient and remind yourself that even if it takes an hour or so for your baby to fall back asleep, only to wake up again an hour or so later, it's worth the effort in the long run as you will all get more sleep.

Over the coming nights, she'll whine and complain for shorter and shorter periods of time about being on her own, until the fact that she isn't going to be invited into your bed, no matter how much she argues, becomes clear.

If you need more advice about encouraging your baby to get to sleep on her own, ask your pediatrician. For more on sleep strategies, see pages 352–53.

Time-saving strategies

Most moms feel that there are never enough hours in the day, but there are ways to save time and buy a little more freedom for you.

Now that life has settled into some sort of routine, you may really want a little spare time in which to pursue an interest or hobby. Or you may simply want to be able to flake out on the sofa once your baby is asleep and not feel that you have to start attacking the chores. To gain yourself a bit more freedom, start by taking an objective look at how you prioritize your day and how much time each activity takes up. This can be a really good way of taking control of your time and assessing where too much is devoted to unimportant things, and too little to what really matters, such as your relationship, friendships, and health. Then try to find ways of reducing time spent on what you least enjoy, such as household tasks. If you iron regularly, for example, think about hanging out your laundry as soon as it's done to prevent creasing, and then smooth out and fold the items before putting them away. Or tumble-dry clothes on a low heat for 5–10 minutes and then fold them. If you're cooking a family meal, double the recipe and freeze the leftovers. Arrange to receive and pay bills online to avoid having to mail them, and shop online, especially for bulky items, if this is more convenient for you.

Going online Doing your grocery shopping, arranging insurance, and banking and paying bills online can all save you time.

Pulling up to standing

Your baby may start to pull herself up and stand with support, but she probably won't find it so easy to sit back down again.

Pulling up A favorite toy positioned on an armchair provides your baby with an incentive to pull himself up. From there, he can cruise around, using the chair as support.

Over the next few weeks or months, your baby will start to pull herself into a standing position using anything that is convenient, from the bars of her crib to the nearest chair or coffee table, to your leg. At first, she may need your help, but eventually, she'll realize that by putting one hand above the other, she can haul herself upward. From this fascinating new vantage point, she'll be able to see lots of exciting new places, which will only increase her motivation to get moving.

Unfortunately, at first, what goes up doesn't always come down easily: your baby might well find that she is stuck! She hasn't worked out how to move her hands and feet to inch along the edge of a piece of furniture. She doesn't know how to walk. Neither does she know how to lower herself back down to the floor—so she will probably become frustrated and cry out for you. You may need to help her sit back down gently and reassure her many times before she feels confident enough to plop down safely on her own, but eventually she'll understand that she won't hurt herself. She may even begin to have as much fun dropping down with a thump on the floor as she did pulling herself up in the first place.

While she's standing, leaning on furniture for support, she'll be practicing maintaining her balance, supporting her weight on her legs, and shifting her weight to enable her to lift one foot or the other. Once she's mastered the art of standing and balancing, she will at some point take a step while holding onto whatever she has used to pull herself up. This development is called cruising and is a precursor to walking (see p.269).

Update your baby-proofing Once your baby starts to pull up to standing on her own, look around the room— what can she now reach in her upright position? Also consider whether there is

ASK A... PEDIATRICIAN

My baby's feet are curving inward. Is this normal? When your baby is born, her feet turn inward and her legs bow slightly, which is a result of living in the small confines of your uterus for many months. As she grows and develops, her legs become straighter and her feet flatter, to aid her ability to walk. Later on, as she approaches the age of three, her flat feet will probably develop arches.

At about 31 weeks, your baby's feet should sit quite flat on the floor when she is held upright. She may balance on the outsides of her feet from time to time to establish her balance, and then adjust her position. Sometimes a baby's feet, or even lower legs, may be slightly misaligned, and turn or even twist inward (known as intoeing). Your doctor will be able to check if there is a problem. Be reassured that in virtually all cases, intoeing will correct itself naturally, and will not hinder your baby's ability to walk.

any furniture with sharp corners that could hurt her if she pulled up onto it and fell back down again. If she climbs onto the sofa and takes a tumble off it, will her fall be broken by cushions or a soft rug? Is your bookcase securely fastened to the wall? Can she reach high shelves if she climbs onto the back of the armchair? Your baby is intrepid and curious, and she will be out of sight in no time, so make sure that you are prepared and she is safe.

31 weeks

263

32 weeks

TOYS THAT ENCOURAGE EXPLORATION OF DIFFERENT SHAPES STIMULATE A BABY'S MIND

Shape-sorting and stacking toys test motor and cognitive skills and encourage problem-solving. Help your baby to learn about sequences and sizes by demonstrating how these toys work. Your baby's speech is more complex now, and she's getting better at imitating the pitch of speech.

Babies and antibiotics

Antibiotics are not a cure-all for every illness or infection—you may like to know why they may or may not be prescribed.

Should your baby become sick, her illness is likely to have been caused by one of two main types of germs: bacteria or viruses. Bacteria are organisms that can be found inside and on the body (such as on the skin) and can cause infections including tonsillitis or strep throat and ear infections. However, not all bacteria are bad—some help to keep your baby's body in balance, such as the beneficial bacteria in her intestines that help her use the nutrients in milk and food.

Viruses are organisms that cause disease by invading healthy host cells in the body. Viruses can cause chickenpox, measles, flu, and many other diseases. Antibiotics are used to treat bacterial infections, or infections that are very likely to be bacterial. They have no effect on viruses, so will not work for coughs, colds or flu, or sore throats (not strep throat) or runny noses.

Taking antibiotics for viral illnesses won't only be ineffective, but also produces an unwanted side effect: over time, this practice helps to create bacteria that are more difficult to kill. Frequent and inappropriate use of antibiotics encourages strains of bacteria that can resist treatment. This is called bacterial resistance. These resistant bacteria require higher doses of medicine or stronger antibiotics to treat. Doctors have even found bacteria that are resistant to some of the most powerful antibiotics available today.

Doctors are now well aware of the drawbacks of unnecessary antibiotics and are unlikely to prescribe them unless they're needed. If you are concerned, you can always discuss each prescription with your pediatrician.

More complex chatter

Your baby's chatter is changing all the time, and she now has a greater variety of sounds than she did in her first six months.

Moving on to solid foods encourages your baby to develop lip control as she learns to keep her lips sealed when she chews and swallows. Her chewing takes on a circular motion, which in turn helps with tongue control. These changes allow her to start to create more complex vocalizations.

Your baby's babble now contains more syllables and different consonants and vowels. She's moving beyond repeating a syllable, such as "mamama," to combining them, for example, saying "digabu," "apaba," or "babamado."

She's also becoming more accomplished at imitating the pitch and intonation of the speech she hears around her, and maybe even imitating individual sounds. So at a lively gathering, she may babble more loudly and in a higher-pitched voice, and when you read to her at bedtime, she may murmur and use a softer tone of voice, just as you do. This is known as echo "talk": instead of simply imitating the tone and vowel sounds of your speech, as she has been doing over the past few months, she starts to pay much more attention to pitch.

Early speech Your baby's communication skills are more consistent and understandable now. It won't be long before she says her first word!

Spoiled by grandparents?

Grandparents are a wonderful part of your child's life, lavishing love, attention, and gifts. Just keep an eye that treats aren't over the top!

It is very normal for grandparents to want to "spoil" their grandchildren, and it can give them great joy to provide your baby with things that you may not be able to afford yourself.

While it can be a godsend to have some of the more expensive items provided by your baby's grandparents, you may feel it conflicts with your desire to be independent. In extreme cases, you may fear that this is the start of spoiling your baby so that in later childhood she will come to expect lavish gifts. There may also be an inequality between what different sets of grandparents are able to offer, which can lead to resentment.

On a different note, you may find that grandparents are more relaxed about behavior and household rules than you are, which can be confusing for a baby or young child.

Talk to your baby's grandparents about your concerns. Explain that, while you appreciate their generosity and the fact that your baby can have toys and equipment that might otherwise be beyond your reach, you would prefer that expensive gifts were approved by you first. Talk about how you understand that, as grandparents, they wish to provide gifts and thank them for this. Explain, too, that as she grows up, you want her to value their love above their gifts, and to realize that sometimes she must wait for what she wants.

Share with them the lessons you want to teach your child. Whether these are about valuing relationships over material goods, working for what they want, or about cultural or religious values, this will help you understand each other.

Taking turns

This is a good stage to begin teaching your baby about cooperation by taking turns when you do things together.

My turn When you take turns playing with toys, your baby learns the give and take of communication and social interaction.

Roll a ball to your baby and encourage her to push it back to you. Push the button on her toy telephone (my turn), then ask her to do it (your turn). Opportunities to teach her about taking turns are virtually limitless: she can lift the flaps or turn the pages of her book, then you can; she can "wash her face" with the wash cloth in the tub, then you can, or she can hold her teddy bear and hug him, then you can, too.

This is a great way to show her how to do things and give her the chance to try them out herself; it also helps to ensure you get a chance to do things properly, such as wash her face, after she's had a chance to try.

Your baby will begin to experience satisfaction when she has an opportunity to experiment and become involved in activities, which over time will build her self-confidence.

However, she won't begin to understand the concept of sharing for a while yet, even when taking turns playing with toys. In fact, it won't be until she is around three to five years old that she'll begin to understand this concept and start to put it into practice.

With twins, while it's a good idea to set up both babies with their own toys, you can also start to encourage them to play "together," taking turns with toys—although you'll need to supervise.

Healthy food on the go

As well as your baby's regular meals, it's a good idea to also have a supply of healthy snacks and drinks on hand.

Healthy snacks Bananas are the perfect convenience food, whether you're at home or out. They don't need preparation, are easy to digest, and contain important nutrients, including vitamin C.

It is a good idea to get into a pattern of giving your baby a healthy morning and afternoon snack, including a drink, in addition to her three main meals. This helps to prevent her from grazing throughout the day, which can lead to her being too full to eat a proper meal, increase the exposure of her teeth to food, and can override her innate capacity for appetite control.

Watch how much your baby drinks, too. If you are using formula milk, make sure that you don't let her drink more than the recommended amount, and use a fast-flowing nipple or cup so that she can finish the drink quickly. If she constantly has a bottle of milk in hand, her appetite may be poor for other foods. Setting up good patterns in your baby's first year is essential.

A snack can be a useful way of adding important nutrients to your baby's diet. So instead of a fruit juice and a sweet cookie, which provide calories, some sugar, and fat, instead opt for some mashed beans, a baby bread stick, or puffs and a few peeled, cut-up grapes, which supply essential calcium, vitamin C, as well as calories, sugar, and fat.

Keep a few essentials in a cool bag to which you can add fresh foods. Pop in a bowl, lidded cup, bib, baby wipes, spoon, a fork for mashing, and a sharp knife. Dried foods such as mini rice cakes, baby puffs, and baby-friendly bread sticks, will not spoil quickly. Add a fresh banana, avocado, and other cut-up fruits, as well as cooked vegetables or mashed beans when you go out, along with a bottle of water.

ASK A... NUTRITIONIST

Won't regular snacking make my baby overweight? Nutritious snacks are part of your baby's healthy diet, helping to ensure she gets the nutrients she needs throughout the day. It's important to look at snacks as part of her overall diet, rather than as treats, to help you choose nutritious foods. Try to avoid feeding her snacks to distract her when she is bored or unhappy. While it may seem like a good quick-fix solution, she may learn to use food to alleviate boredom, and to associate food with comfort. This may increase her long-term risks of becoming overweight. Offer her regular snacks when she seems hungry, and at regular intervals, leaving a good break between snack and mealtimes, to ensure she develops an appetite. Water is the best drink at snack time as an alternative to milk (see "Your baby's drinks," p.247).

Meals on the run If you're going to be out at a mealtime, pack a suitable purée for your baby in an insulated bag. Find out if you can heat up your baby's meal, making sure it is piping hot throughout, then let it cool. Alternatively, keep it hot in a wide-necked thermos. You can also carry some foods that can be puréed, mashed, or cut into chunks on the spot, such as bananas, melon, papaya, avocado, carrots, and ripe pears or peaches. Chunks of soft chicken, canned turkey, and fingers of pita, baby crackers, or bread can all be eaten cold.

32 weeks

267

YOUR BABY IS 32 WEEKS AND 5 DAYS
Fidgety baby

Your mobile baby is less content to sit and watch the world go by—so you may need to adapt your routine to give her a bit more action.

ASK A... NUTRITIONIST

I'm trying to move my baby on to lumpier foods but she gags. What can I do? Rather than backtrack to familiar purées, give her some finger foods or a spoon to hold to help her feel in control. Or let her explore the food with her fingers before offering it on a spoon: put a little on her high chair tray so she can investigate. If all else fails, have a couple of days on familiar purées then try smaller pieces of whole, mashed foods.

Now that your baby is older and more mobile, you may find that she's less keen to be confined to her stroller or car seat for even short periods of time. Whereas once she might have dozed off during the supermarket shop, or slept while you met other moms and chatted over coffee, now she's more restless and likely to become irritable if expected to remain still for too long.

It can come as a bit of a shock to realize that your baby is now setting the agenda and that life has to be planned around her needs in a different way than before. However, this is all part of growing up, so your best bet is to adapt your routine a little to suit you both. For instance, you might want to arrange to meet friends at a soft play area where you can grab a coffee and chat while you watch your babies crawl, climb, and explore. You could take turns with other moms to host get-togethers in each other's homes (your babies will love to discover an entirely new range of toys) or, in the summer, arrange picnics in the park. If you dread shopping with a wailing baby, go alone when your partner is at home and can take over. Just a few small changes can make a difference.

YOUR BABY IS 32 WEEKS AND 6 DAYS
Night-time acrobatics

Your baby isn't only active during the day; she may turn while she sleeps and roll over onto her tummy.

Roly poly Although she may roll over in her sleep, it's important to still place your baby on her back when you put her in her crib.

Babies can be restless in their sleep. If you've heeded the advice always to place her on her back to sleep to reduce the risk of SIDS (see p.31), it may worry you that she flips over onto her tummy in her sleep. If she is strong enough to roll onto her tummy on her own, you don't need to worry about her sleeping on it. At this age, the risk of SIDS is greatly reduced, as some 90 percent of cases occur before a baby is six months old. It's important that you don't restrict your baby's movements or try to force her to sleep on her back.

It is also suggested that you avoid swaddling at this point. Confining her will disrupt her sleep and possibly encourage her to develop negative sleep associations.

Another thing that might alarm you is finding that your baby's tossing and turning has caused her to kick off her blankets. Firmly tuck in her blankets at the base of her crib at bedtime to prevent them from covering her face as she moves about in her sleep. Alternatively, invest in a baby sleeping bag appropriate for her age. Start her off on her back at night (the position she will probably find most familiar) and continue to avoid using pillows and covers, and placing soft toys in the crib.

SPOTLIGHT ON...
Learning to walk

From standing and balancing to cruising around the living room holding on to the furniture, your baby's progression toward walking may occur any time from now on, so make sure you are prepared!

All babies learn to walk at different ages, from as early as nine months, right up to 18 months, so if your baby is in no hurry to walk, there is no rush. Follow her lead. Help her to develop strength in her legs by holding her hands and bouncing her up and down. Continue to give her some tummy time to strengthen her back and neck muscles and improve her coordination and balance, and offer her a good, sturdy toddle-truck that will tempt her to get up onto her feet and push it along when she is ready.

On her feet Practicing to walk in her bare feet is best for your baby as it encourages good balance, coordination, and grip.

Before your baby can walk, she'll need to master getting herself up into a standing position while holding a support, then bending her knees and sitting down. It can take many months for her to develop the techniques required to achieve this developmental milestone, or she may seem to acquire it almost instantly. When she can stand for short periods without support, she may be ready to take her first steps.

First steps Your baby's first steps represent an enormously important milestone in her physical development as she puts together balance, gross-motor skills, control, coordination, and especially courage!

In advance of walking unaided, she will spread out her feet to increase her balance, giving her a slightly waddling gait. She may launch herself in the direction of something stable, such as a table or even you, and probably throw out her arms to protect herself from an inevitable tumble.

Over the coming weeks, your baby will learn to take a single step at a time, stopping to regain her balance before continuing. One thing she won't be able to control for a while is speed; when babies first walk unassisted, they tend to hurl themselves forward, then lean too far back to in an effort to regain balance, resulting in a series of stumbles and falls. Brush her off and help her back onto her feet. She'll learn through her mistakes and realize soon enough that she really must learn to walk before she can run.

> **CHECKLIST**
> # Walking safety
>
> Check that your baby's environment is safe for her walking. Although she'll take many tumbles, you can help to cushion the blows.
>
> ■ Tape down loose rugs or carpets, so she doesn't trip over the edges.
>
> ■ Watch out for obstacles around the room that may trip up your baby as she concentrates all her efforts on keeping her balance and just staying upright.
>
> ■ Erect baby gates at the top and bottom of the stairs.
>
> ■ Install guards or locks on windows.
>
> ■ Secure or remove any furniture that is unsteady and could tip over when your baby grabs it for balance.
>
> ■ Consider padding sharp corners or edges on furniture (such as tables), or remove the piece of furniture.
>
> ■ If you have a glass-topped coffee table, consider temporarily replacing the top with Lucite or acrylic.
>
> ■ Keep drawers shut—your baby may use open drawers to climb up onto unsuitable surfaces.
>
> ■ Cover heated surfaces, such as radiators, and install a fire screen if you have an open fire.
>
> ■ Ensure the toilet seat is kept down; get a clip to lock it into place.
>
> ■ Position pot handles facing inward on the stove.
>
> ■ Keep dangling electrical appliance cords out of your baby's reach.

33 weeks

STUDIES SHOW THAT BABIES WHO GESTURE MORE DEVELOP A LARGER VOCABULARY

Your baby is getting better at expressing herself all the time as she uses a greater range of gestures and her babbles become increasingly complex. If your baby is now eating a range of puréed foods, you can start giving her lumpier textures and introduce some finger foods.

Is fresh always best?

Using a mixture of homemade and bought baby food can increase the range of flavors your baby experiences and gives you more time.

You want what's best for your baby, especially when it comes to her food. Many parents feel they should provide exclusively homemade food, and feel guilty about using commercially produced baby foods. However, while nutritious and wholesome homemade food is ideal, there's no doubt that jarred baby food is getting better by leaps and bounds, and there are now nutritious and appetizing foods available that are salt-, sugar-, and additive-free. In fact, giving your baby a mixture of homemade and quality store-bought foods may introduce her to a wider variety of flavors. It's also undeniably convenient to have a pouch or jar of store-bought baby food on hand when you're out, or simply don't have time to cook. Rest assured that combining homemade and store-bought baby foods provides a nutritious and varied diet.

ASK A... NUTRITIONIST

Which is more cost-effective— store-bought or homemade baby food? Commercially produced baby food is a relatively expensive way to feed your baby. Making food at home allows you to freeze several batches of meals from just one or two ingredients. Also, it's easy to give your baby a portion of your own meal by putting her portion aside before seasoning and then puréeing it to the desired consistency. So while store-bought foods are very convenient and largely nutritious, the bigger outlay is another reason why a balance is desirable.

When shopping for baby foods, it's important to compare ingredient labels closely, because some brands add sugar, water, and fillers to their foods. Whenever possible, it's best to serve your baby food that contains no extraneous ingredients—nothing but peas, for example, if the label says "peas." You may also want to factor in whether foods are grown organically when making your decision. Even the size of the jar or container may matter, since some babies eat less at each sitting, and you may prefer to serve your baby right out of the jar, rather than pouring half into a bowl.

In addition to store-bought meals, make sure that other commercially produced food you give your baby is suitable. For example, your baby needs "baby" cereals since these are fortified with vitamins and minerals and don't have added salt or sugar; and baby yogurts are made with whole milk and contain no artificial sweetener, colorings, or other additives found in regular yogurts. They also come in baby-sized containers so there's less danger of overfeeding.

Measuring nutrients Some baby foods are sold at room temperature, which means they have been treated at high temperatures to ensure they keep safely on the supermarket shelf. This can destroy some of the vitamins, but these are often added back in. On the other hand, some baby foods are frozen at high speed, which ensures that a high proportion of vitamins is kept.

When making your baby's food, look for the freshest ingredients and steam

or lightly boil vegetables to make sure that your baby's purées have the optimum nutritional content.

Ultimately, home-cooked food tastes different than store-bought, and it's important that commercial foods do not become the mainstay of your baby's diet so that she gets used to the tastes and varied textures of homemade meals.

CHECKLIST

Using store-bought baby foods

■ If you are out, a jar or pouch of baby food that doesn't need to be kept cool can be extremely helpful, and wait staff should not object to you bringing your own baby food into a restaurant (See page 267 for more ideas on healthy food on the go.)

■ When buying commercially produced baby foods, make sure that your baby doesn't stay on thin purées for too long. Make sure the progression of textures and tastes that you make for her at home is reflected in the store-bought foods that supplement her diet.

■ If your own diet is restricted in any way through choice or intolerance, commercial baby foods are a convenient way to give your baby flavors you don't tend to eat. However, try to make sure that you also cook foods at home specially for your baby, so that she doesn't develop an aversion to homemade foods.

YOUR BABY IS 33 WEEKS AND 1 DAY

Mini Mom or Dad?

Your baby's personality is beginning to unfold, and you might notice certain traits that seem very familiar—and a few that are unique.

Different personalities Your job as a parent is to support and respect your baby's personality.

Your baby is her own little person, with her own likes, dislikes, and foibles. If these don't match yours, it's important to accept this and allow her the space to grow in her own way. It can be easy to regard your baby as a "mini-me," but don't be surprised or frustrated if she doesn't behave as you expect. If she is an extrovert, who loves attention and being around others, but both you and your partner are shy, try to give her lots of opportunities to socialize. (This may change in the coming months as she experiences separation anxiety—see page 283.) Equally, if she is shy and from a family of extroverts, don't force her into situations that cause her anxiety. Let her play on your lap while you talk; she will probably get bored and, in time, choose to investigate what else is going on at her own pace.

Likewise, if you are fairly laid back and tend to go with the flow, it doesn't mean that your baby will enjoy this; on the contrary, she may crave routine. As her parent, you need to try to structure her day so that she feels comfortable and secure, even if you are not the sort of person who relishes routine.

YOUR BABY IS 33 WEEKS AND 2 DAYS

Caring for your baby's hair

As your baby gets more active and makes more of a mess at feeding times, you will find regular hair care becomes essential!

If your baby was born with a full head of hair, by now she may need her first hair cut. Be gentle and—if you are doing this at home—very careful, combing the hair first, and making sure that cut hair doesn't go into her eyes or ears.

Baby hair doesn't need to be washed every day: twice a week is usually enough. However, you will inevitably find bits of food in her hair as she gets more involved at mealtimes, so you may need to wet sponge it after she's eaten. Before you wash her hair, gently tease out any tangles with your fingers or a fine-toothed comb. Start at the tips and work your way up to the roots to avoid tugging the roots. Use a baby shampoo that doesn't contain harsh chemicals (such as parabens and sulphates) or perfume that could sting her eyes, and has a balanced pH of between 4.5 and 6. If your baby has very curly hair, you might want to comb conditioner through to help keep it soft and loose. Sponge it off with water.

Hair care Using a sponge or wet washcloth to rinse the shampoo from your baby's hair will stop soapy water from trickling into her eyes.

All sorts of sounds

As your baby hears words repeated regularly, many will start to sound familiar to her and she will be stimulated to babble even more.

Noisy boys and girls Toys that make sounds can help language development. "What noise does a train make? Choo-choo!" **Where's the ball?** Give a running commentary as he plays.

Although babbling seems nonsensical, studies show that the way babies babble is modeled on how we talk, in that they use the right-hand side of their mouths slightly more in the same way that adults talk (watch yourself in the mirror!). Research shows that the left brain, which controls the right side of the body and is responsible for understanding and language, is therefore also instigating babbling, confirming that babbling is important in language development. Psychologists believe that babies begin meaningful talk long before we realize (as early as between eight and 10 months) —we just don't recognize the words!

While most babies won't utter their first comprehensible word until close to a year, or older, babies are like sponges, soaking up sounds, so keep talking. Your baby watches your mouth intently as you talk, so face-to-face talk helps

speech development, as do games that involve distinctive sounds. Point to animals in books with phrases such as "What does a cow say? A cow says mooo!" Even if she doesn't make the sound, she might copy the shape of your mouth. Use every chance you find to play sound games, for example, talking about her toys ("an airplane goes wheeeee!"), and talk to her constantly during everyday tasks such as dressing and bathing.

Naming people and objects all the time, including using your baby's name, helps her word recognition. Although a baby's recognition of her own name is usually around nine months, there are clear indications that before this, babies grasp that words have associations.

If your baby isn't babbling by now, or doesn't respond to loud noises or a parent calling out of their range of vision, consult your doctor.

DEVELOPMENT ACTIVITY

Song and speech

Studies suggest that babies who are sung to a lot learn to speak more quickly than those who are not. Singing separates out syllables in words, breaking them down so that they are easier to pronounce, and listening to songs helps to improve attention spans in young babies. There are lots of musical and singing activity groups for parents and babies, but simply singing to your baby at home is enough. Don't worry if you think you're tone deaf; your baby won't mind and will enjoy being held by you as you sway and move to a song. Sing nursery rhymes and introduce your baby to songs with actions to help her get involved. Feel free, too, to play music that you enjoy—your baby won't be picky and will enjoy hearing you sing along.

Sing along Singing to your baby can help speed up her speech acquisition and encourage her to develop a love of music.

33 weeks

273

SPOTLIGHT ON...
Stopping breast-feeding

Many moms continue to breast-feed throughout the first year—and beyond. However, if the time is right for you and your baby to stop, take things slowly and drop one feeding at a time to make it a painless experience for you both.

ASK A... NUTRITIONIST

Our family has a history of allergies. Should I wean my baby onto soy or goat's milk formula instead of cow's milk formula?

If you are concerned that your baby has a higher risk of being allergic to cow's milk formula, it's essential to talk to your pediatrician before deciding how to wean her off breast milk; she will be able to give you unbiased advice on the pros and cons of different types of formula. She may also advise you not to make any assumptions before you have started weaning.

Goat's milk also contains proteins that your baby may react to, so is not a good alternative. Most importantly, though, goat's milk isn't advised for babies because the level of proteins are too concentrated, and there have, in the past, been concerns about hygiene.

Soy is sometimes promoted as an alternative for babies allergic to cow's milk. However, a significant proportion of babies who are allergic to cow's milk also react to soy milk formula. If, while weaning your baby, you notice that she develops a rash or is experiencing stomach upsets, for example, talk to your doctor, who can prescribe a special type of formula called fully hydrolyzed formula (see p.247) in which the proteins are broken down so that they are easier to tolerate.

Some babies naturally lose interest in breast-feeding, preferring instead to drink their milk (either expressed breast milk or formula) from a bottle or a cup because it's easier for them. If they enjoy formula, this allows you to wind down breast-feeding fairly easily. Other babies continue to enjoy the comfort of nursing and breast milk long past the point at which mom has had enough, and it can be a hard task to wean them.

The length of time you breast-feed is a personal decision based on your needs and those of your baby. Common reasons for reducing, or stopping, breast-feeding are that you want to allow other caregivers a chance to feed your baby or if you are going back to work (you can still express milk, mix breast milk and formula, or you may want to stop entirely). Whatever the reason, it is gentlest to your baby, emotionally, and better for you physically, to drop feedings gradually, one at a time.

A successful transition means planning ahead and carefully timing the dropping of feedings. Try to avoid times when your baby may feel unsettled, for example, if she's just moved to her own room, or she is feeling sick, because changing her feedings during these times may add to her distress.

It's important to be aware that milk, whether breast milk or formula, remains the most important source of nutrition for the first year of your baby's life. When she starts on solids, although she starts to drink a little less milk, and

Breast to bottle Giving your baby formula allows your partner and other relatives to get involved in her care, helping them strengthen their bond with your baby.

eventually solids will start to replace some of her milk feedings, milk still forms the bulk of her calories, while she gets used to new textures and tastes. Weaning from breast milk in the first year therefore involves substituting formula (not cow's milk) for breast-feedings.

You can begin to substitute one breast-feeding at a time for formula in a cup or bottle. While there is no set timetable, it's recommended that you drop just one feeding a week to start with—or allow a minimum of four to five days in between dropping feedings, to give your baby and your breasts time to adjust. Make the first feeding you switch one where she isn't ravenously hungry, for example, mid-afternoon.

Many moms like to continue the evening feeding for as long as possible, since it's a relaxing way to unwind before bed and often a cherished part of the bedtime routine. Your baby may also be more resistant to losing this feeding, especially if you've been at work. There's no reason why you can't continue to give your baby one or two breast-feedings a day for as long as you both want.

When your baby resists If your baby is finding it hard to give up breast-feeding, ask your partner or a friend to give her her formula feeding in a bottle or cup, so it is less confusing for her, and you are not tempted to give in. If you feed her, she is more likely to protest and want to be breast-fed. Try changing your routine slightly so that she isn't as aware that her bedtime breast-feeding hasn't materialized. Distract her with a book away from the place that you usually feed her, and offer her a cup of formula before the story instead of after, or the reverse. Or have her dad or grandparent put her to bed instead. Try to keep your baby away from your breasts, and avoid changing in front of her. Not only will the sight of them remind her that she would probably like some milk, but she will also be able to "smell" your milk.

You could try enticing her onto a bottle or cup by giving her expressed milk at first so that it's a familiar taste.

Dealing with discomfort A slow approach helps prevent your breasts from becoming engorged or leaky, since it can take a week for your breasts to adjust to missing one feeding. If they feel full, a cold washcloth can be soothing, and make sure to wear a supportive bra. If your breasts are very full and the excess milk does not leak naturally (in the bath or shower), try expressing a tiny bit extra, at feeding times only, to relieve the fullness without stimulating them to make more. Taking off small amounts of milk can decrease the milk you make so your body adjusts. If it doesn't and you become feverish or suspect mastitis (see p.59), see your doctor.

Weaning can be difficult for you both; rest assured she won't starve herself, and will be happy if she continues to get the comfort and affection she is used to.

Bedtime hugs Make sure you still have a lot of cuddling before bed so that you continue to feel physically close to each other.

ASK A... BREAST-FEEDING EXPERT

My friends are stopping breast-feeding, but I want to keep going. Is it a good idea to continue?

There is absolutely no reason why you can't continue to breast-feed for as long as both you and your baby enjoy it. This could be for her first year, or much longer. Plenty of research suggests that breast milk continues to offer antibodies well into toddlerhood, which can help your little one to resist infection. It also contains protein, essential fatty acids, vitamins, and minerals, complementing a healthy, varied diet. There are also health benefits for Mom: breast-feeding beyond infancy has been shown to lower women's risk of developing certain forms of cancer, for example.

Breast-feeding offers emotional nourishment and comfort, and can play a strong role in a healthy mother–child relationship. If you are worried that returning to work means an end to breast-feeding, it may reassure you to know that many working moms keep it up with a little organization (see p.179). You can express and freeze milk so your baby can be fed in your absence. This can be a comfort for her and means you keep up your supply of milk. Of course, many working moms keep just the evening feeding to enjoy that reassuring bond at the end of the day.

It's important to focus on what's best for you and your baby, and try not to be swayed by the actions or opinions of others. In retrospect, the time you spend feeding your baby can seem all too fleeting, so follow your instincts and enjoy this special bond with your baby for as long as you want. (For more on extended breast-feeding, see page 361.)

YOUR BABY IS 33 WEEKS AND 4 DAYS

Encouraging good behavior

Although your baby is only 33 weeks old, establishing patterns of good behavior now will help her grow into a kind and helpful child.

YOUR FRUSTRATED BABY

As your baby grows, she becomes more aware of her needs, yet has a limited ability to convey them—and no concept of patience! Pay attention when she's frustrated, and help her cope by communicating all the time. Even if you can't get over to her immediately, respond to her babbles and cries, talking to her and vocalizing what you think might be wrong: "Are you hungry/tired?" Knowing you're paying attention helps to calm her.

Your baby is highly inquisitive, which sometimes means that she does things you would prefer she didn't do. While she doesn't understand "good" and "bad," you can start to set boundaries, which in turn forms the foundations of good behavior later on. She is testing your responses, too, so make lots of positive noises when she does something you approve of, and don't make too much of a fuss if she does something you would prefer she didn't do! If she passes you a toy or offers some of her food, praise her. Likewise, if she lets you wash or dress her without making a fuss, tell her "Good job!" and give a great big hug for being so helpful! Gently patting animals is also worthy of praise.

Babies at this age don't intend to hurt others or be naughty, so it's important that your response to unwelcome behavior is appropriate. For example, it is perfectly normal for them to grab toys from another child. Gentle admonishment—holding her hands, making eye contact, and saying "No, you shouldn't grab" is adequate to establish boundaries. If she repeatedly grabs, gently move her away so that she senses her actions are not welcome.

YOUR BABY IS 33 WEEKS AND 5 DAYS

Regular "me-time"

Now that you and your baby have a more predictable routine, you might want to schedule "appointments" to pursue your own interests.

Taking care of your baby and making sure she is entertained, stimulated, and content leaves very little time for relaxation. However, by now, you and your baby have probably settled into some sort of routine, and this allows you to plan some regular time off to do something for yourself.

Rather than feel overly anxious about how your baby will manage if you're not there, reassure yourself that regular "me-time" will recharge your batteries and help you maintain a balance between self and family that will allow you to tackle motherhood with a clear head and a sense of calm.

Take the pressure off yourself and trust your other half or a grandparent to take care of your baby for an hour or so. Ideally, join a weekly class so that you make a commitment to the time off. Alternatively, reading the newspaper in a local café for half an hour, going for a swim, or just settling down with a book, will all give you rewarding and rejuvenating time off. Your baby will be in good hands with her caregiver and you will be a more relaxed, happy parent.

Time for you Give yourself a little space—take a yoga class, go for a run, or just indulge in a long soak in the bath. You deserve it!

Your monthly cycle

If you've recently stopped breast-feeding your baby, you may find that your periods have returned and you are fully fertile again.

All the hormonal changes that your body experiences during pregnancy and breast-feeding can affect your body in a number of ways.

You may find that problems such as PMS are no longer as debilitating as they were before you became pregnant, or that you now experience stronger symptoms. Your previously regular cycle may be all over the place now, or the opposite may be true—some women who have never had a reliable cycle find that everything goes like clockwork once they've had a baby.

If you do find that having a baby has brought on some uncomfortable symptoms, such as heavier and more painful periods, talk to your doctor. He or she can discuss ways in which to relieve pain or discomfort and check your hormone levels if necessary.

Still breast-feeding If your periods have returned and you are still breast-feeding while your baby moves toward solids and therefore starts to drink a little less milk, you may find that your cycle becomes a little unreliable. You may skip periods for a month or two, and sometimes experience only spotting at the time when your period would usually appear.

If it's usual for you to experience some breast tenderness just before your period, it can make breast-feeding uncomfortable. Although easier said than done, try to relax during feeding, since any tension will increase the discomfort. To help ease the pain, hold a warm cloth on the side of the breast from which your baby is feeding, and massage the milk downward. If all else fails, try a mild analgesic, such as acetaminophen, to ease discomfort.

Return of fertility Once your baby is over six months, or you begin to reduce the number of breast-feedings she has, or as soon as she starts on solids, breast-feeding stops contributing toward contraception. In fact, ovulation may occur at any time, so it's possible to become pregnant again before your period returns. You may want to discuss contraceptive options with your doctor. If you are still breast-feeding, the combined oral contraceptive pill is not recommended since it can interfere with your milk supply. Your doctor may suggest the progestin-only mini-pill, or talk to you about other forms of contraception, such as an IUD.

277

34 weeks

MOST BABIES CAN PULL THEMSELVES UP TO STANDING AT BETWEEN EIGHT AND 10 MONTHS

Your baby is developing a greater sense of self all the time, which means she is also becoming more aware of her personal likes and dislikes—and won't hesitate to express them! This new awareness, however, is accompanied by an increased anxiety whenever you leave her.

Scaling new heights

When your baby starts to negotiate her way around, it's time to make some changes to your rooms. Everything moves upward!

As soon as your baby can pull herself up to standing, from around eight months, she will realize that she can use her new-found technique to climb. The first step is often the stairs! Negotiating the stairs requires a great deal of both brain and brawn, so it marks an important stage in your baby's development. Her brain has to be able to coordinate her movements so that her hands, legs, and feet move in synchronicity to keep her weight stable with each upward movement. The hoist she needs to push herself up comes from the coordinated efforts of one arm and the opposite leg, which alternates with the opposite arm and leg at each step. Climbing therefore requires her to have fairly sophisticated control of her limbs, and considerable strength in the major muscles.

Babies know danger only because we alert them to it, and although scaling stairs is potentially risky, it is an activity that, with constant, close supervision, helps to develop a baby's confidence. Some babies will cry when they first get to the top of the stairs and look back at the precipitous height they've reached, while others will get half-way up and freeze. Some babies, of course, will get to the top and be ready to do it again!

Allow your baby her foray into the danger zone of the stairs, but stand right behind her; she will have a surge of self-confidence, especially with you there praising her every effort.

Safety considerations Never leave your baby unattended on the stairs. Although going upward is a fairly foolproof adventure, the slip of a hand or knee can make a tumble likely.

Getting up It's very tempting for your baby to use any furniture she can pull herself up on just like a jungle gym.

Furthermore, coming down requires a completely different skill set and, at this age, it's important to teach your baby to descend in the least risky way possible. Feet first and on her tummy is best, since this allows gravity to do the work and minimizes the risk of toppling forward, as she might if she bumped down the stairs on her bottom, facing forward.

Install stair gates at the top and the bottom of the stairs and shut them when you are not there to help her. If you have large gaps in your banisters, consider investing in mesh to fill them for the time being. Now is also the time to take a fresh look at the rest of your home and make sure it's safe for your baby.

Our home isn't ideal for safe climbing. What can I do to help my baby climb safely? You can encourage your baby to climb in a completely safe environment by making regular visits to a local soft-play toddler gym. Most gyms have areas that are cordoned off for babies which are furnished with small, baby-friendly play equipment designed for their little limbs, and with soft spongy mats to break their fall when they tumble. Your baby will learn from watching other children as they move themselves up and down the play equipment, and will enjoy the social nature of this kind of play. However, your child will still want to practice climbing at home, so if your home isn't safe, you will need to be extra vigilant.

Mini mountains It's not just stairs your baby will want to climb. Onto and over sofas or chairs, cribs, and low tables are other common options for infant explorers. Try to babyproof these mini mountains as much as you can. Keep sofa backs against walls so she is less likely to try to climb over the top, and try gently to steer your baby away from unstable items of furniture that might topple as she climbs them.

If she is trying to climb out of her crib (she'll manage to get her leg over the side with increasing agility), adjust the base of the crib so that it's at the lowest height and remove anything inside the crib that might give her a leg up.

34 weeks

279

A flexible routine

Planning a day out or a short break can play havoc with your baby's routines, but by using familiar cues you can help her adjust.

A certain amount of predictability can make a baby feel secure, and most respond well to having a routine to their day. However, it's not a timetable; your baby notices and understands a series of events, not the hands of a clock.

So if occasionally it is better for you to shift your baby's nap time up by half an hour, this is fine, as long as she isn't fussy. She is unlikely to expect to have a nap until you take out her sleepy-time story and settle her into her crib. It is the elements of the routine that trigger her expectation of the sleep that comes next, and she will probably offer up no more or less resistance than she would have done had she been put down for her nap at the usual time.

Thinking of her routine as a sequence of events allows you to be flexible, for instance when you go on vacation or want a spontaneous day out. Implementing a familiar routine on trips and visits can help calm her. As much as possible, do the same things, so if it is a quiet game, bath, book, then lullaby, do it in the same order as usual and keep it up while you're away. She'll recognize the cues and realize what's coming, whatever the time or place.

AS A MATTER OF FACT

How strictly to schedule your baby's day is a subject of debate. Some experts recommend precise scheduling, but most suggest a degree of routine, with mealtimes, play, and sleep being predictable to help your baby feel secure. It's up to you to tailor the day to you and your baby's individual needs. Of course, no routine should stop you from taking care of your baby's immediate needs for food, comfort, or rest.

Question time

Your baby is beginning to understand that objects (and people) have names. Have fun with simple questions that reinforce this learning.

Where's daddy's nose? Asking simple questions as you point to dad's nose is a game she'll enjoy. Soon she may point to it herself!

The more you read to your baby, sing songs to her, and talk to her, the quicker she will learn that everything has a name. Brightly colored board books with clear pictures can help you teach her the names of objects. Ask her "Where's the ball?" and guide her hand toward it; in later months, she'll surprise you by pointing to it herself. When Daddy gets home, ask her "Where's Daddy?" and she may turn her head toward him. You might even find that when you tell her "No," she stops to listen.

One of the best ways to teach your baby names is through song—try "Head, shoulders, knees, and toes," putting your hand on the different parts of your baby's body, then follow up with a game. Ask her "Where is [her name]'s nose?" Then touch her nose yourself, saying "Here it is," and move her hand to touch it. Use the third person, because her language skills are not developed enough to understand possessive pronouns and adjectives (such as her, his, your, my).

You can also help your baby learn how to respond to questions that are requests. She'll want to please you, so if you ask her something simple like "Bring me the book" while pointing to it, she'll enjoy getting it for you.

Using a babysitter

You and your partner may want to go out and leave your baby with a sitter, but how do you find someone you feel confident in?

Getting to know you Give your baby and babysitter the chance to get used to each other before you leave them alone for the first time.

Family and friends who have spent time with your baby are an obvious choice for babysitting, but that is not always an option. So who do you trust?

If you are back at work, you might consider asking someone from your baby's day-care center. Your baby and the sitter are already familiar with each other, and the sitter is a qualified child-care provider, so has experience of calming and distracting a crying baby and knows what to do in an emergency. Or can friends recommend a babysitter?

A professional babysitting agency that specializes in finding caregivers, and who will check their credentials, is a good option. Or if there is a parents' babysitting circle in your area, your local library or community center may have details. If not, perhaps you could set up your own babysitting circle with moms from your childbirth class or other families you know well.

Grown-up, or teenage, children of neighbors are a traditional option. You may feel comfortable with an older teen who has taken a babysitting course. You may also want to gauge carefully whether you think they are mature enough to care for a baby.

You should always feel confident in your choice of babysitter. Talk to them and find out how they would calm your baby if she woke up and how they would handle an emergency. Find out if they have any references from moms that you know. Ask a new babysitter to arrive at least half an hour before you put your baby to bed, so he or she isn't a total stranger, if your baby wakes up.

34 weeks

Getting creative

It's time to get arty! Your baby will enjoy trying a new activity and she might even create something to treasure.

Encouraging your baby's creative side can be a fun way to spend an hour or so. Don't expect her to create a masterpiece, though her efforts will certainly brighten up a wall, the fridge, or a scrapbook!

Simple painting activities that don't involve holding brushes or creating neat lines are easy to arrange with your baby. The secret is to prepare an area first. An ideal place on a warm day is outside on grass; otherwise, clear a space on the floor, or a low table, and put newspapers or old towels down to soak up spills.

Have water and cloths at the ready to wipe her clean afterward.

Nontoxic paints are available at toy stores, craft supply stores, or even big supermarkets. Check that the ones you buy will not stain your baby's skin or clothes, and make sure she is wearing something old, or just a diaper! You'll need large sheets of blank paper or a roll of craft paper—it will all get used up over time! Spread the paper flat on the floor, pour some paint into an old dish or saucer, and get creative.

Daub her hand in paint or let her put her hand in it, then help her press onto the paper and make prints. You can do that with her feet, too. (This will also be a great one to try when she is walking, so she can toddle up and down the paper to make tracks of footprints.)

Her first attempts will probably be splotches, but you should at least get one lovely hand print to frame or put in a book. Remember to date them! It's a great way to see her growth and her reactions to painting each time.

Baby won't go to bed

Resistance at bedtime needs careful handling to prevent bad habits from forming. What should you do when your baby wants to stay up?

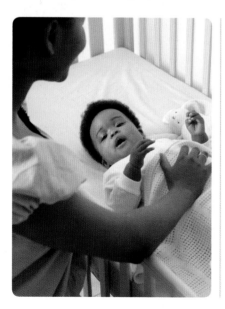

It can be unsettling for everyone if your baby suddenly starts to create a fuss about going to bed, especially if previously she easily settled down. Many babies go through a phase of resisting bedtime at about this age. Your baby has realized that events in her life follow a predictable sequence, and she will begin to know what's coming next. She is also increasingly aware that sleep time means separation from you. Separation anxiety (see page 246 and opposite) is a normal developmental stage, and can lead to tears when you

Resisting bedtime Being firm about sticking to the bedtime routine will encourage a reluctant baby to settle down for the night.

try to leave her at bedtime, or when she wakes up and you're not near. How you react now can affect her future routine, so do your best to get her back on track.

Make sure she has had an active day so that she is physically tired. There's no need to cut back on naps, but stimulate her with trips to the park or a soft play area. Stick to her bedtime routine, making sure it's an enjoyable experience that she wants to take part in: say goodnight to the pictures on the wall or her soft toys, read a story, or sing a song. Finally, be firm that this is bedtime; don't be tempted to let her play a bit longer. Be reassuring when you settle her, and return if she calls, but try not to pick her up. Eventually, she will settle down again.

Separation anxiety

Your baby's growing independence reminds her that she is separate from you, and she may become anxious about you leaving.

See you later! Make sure you stay calm and upbeat as you hand over your clingy baby, no matter how you feel inside.

From around eight months, your baby is very likely to experience separation anxiety. This milestone signals her deep attachment to you and her recognition that you are her primary source of care and protection. At the same time, she is gaining the concept of object permanence, becoming aware that when not in sight, you have gone away. The source of her safety and care has left her and she's unable to understand that you'll be back. She'll show how she feels through genuine distress, tears, and tantrums.

Reassuring your baby When you leave the room, keep your voice calm and positive, and tell her you'll be back in a moment. If this phase coincides with your return to work, try to leave her for short periods only to begin with, getting her used to the fact that you always return. When you leave her with her caregiver, talk about what you're doing, "Mommy is going to put you in the car and strap you in." Avoid sounding anxious, and don't be impatient—she is more likely to be calm if you are calm, even if you have to be firm. Leaving a transition object, such as a comfort toy, blanket, or piece of clothing smelling of you, will help soothe her while you're apart.

When you drop her off, don't prolong the agony by spending too long cuddling, or telling her you wish you didn't have to leave—at her age, this sends a mixed message because the outcome will be the same. Talk to her while you hand her to her caregiver, tell her that you love her and will see her soon (or after lunch/her nap/at dinner time); give her a big kiss, a wave, a smile, and leave. Wait until you are out of sight and earshot before you burst into tears, if you need to!

Like most things in a baby's life, this is a passing phase (although one that often lasts, albeit in a milder form, up until three years old). If, however, you think she is genuinely unhappy with a caregiver, you may want to consider other child-care options. Keep in mind, though, that a change may not make a difference. You may just have to ride out the storm and build her self-confidence so she learns to separate more willingly. Visit play areas with her so she gets used to being around other babies, and grows in confidence while in your company.

DEVELOPMENT ACTIVITY

Tickling games

Now that your baby has a greater sense of anticipation, she will squirm and giggle with excitement and expectation long before the moment at which a tickling rhyme actually becomes a tickle! Among the traditional favorite tickling rhymes is "This Little Piggy" (in which you say the rhyme while wiggling each of the toes on your baby's foot in succession, then, at the last "piggy," tickle her feet and run your fingers all the way up her leg to her armpit for "wee, wee, wee, all the way home!"). There are a host of other tickling rhymes that she'll enjoy and she will learn to anticipate the part when she's tickled.

Tummy tickling You can tickle your baby on his tummy to squeals of delight. His reaction will probably make you giggle, too!

34 weeks

283

35 weeks

BY AROUND EIGHT TO 10 MONTHS, BABIES LEARN TO USE THEIR INDEX FINGERS TO POINT

Your baby's pincer grip—the ability to hold or pick up things with the finger and thumb—is starting to develop, making it easier for her to manipulate objects. Give her plenty of opportunities to practice by giving her toys or household objects of all shapes and sizes to play with.

Post-pregnancy weight loss

Usually it takes at least six months to lose any weight gained during pregnancy, and often the last few pounds are the hardest to lose.

Motivating yourself Being active quickly becomes a habit, but to get started requires a little bit of self-motivation.

Feeling good about yourself helps you give the most to your baby. If you are overweight, losing extra pounds can help boost your self-esteem. It's important, though, that you have a nutritious diet rich in vitamins and minerals, especially if planning another baby in the future. Also, if you're breast-feeding, you need a slightly higher caloric intake so shouldn't actively diet unless advised to. Keeping fit also helps you to stay trim, as well as enabling you to keep up with the demands of parenthood, which can be a physically demanding job.

Getting active The key to reaching your weight-loss goal lies in motivating yourself to get active. You may already

feel that your baby never lets you sit down, and this constant activity is definitely beneficial. However, you may need to do more to increase your heart rate to fat-burning levels. Whenever possible, walk your baby in her stroller to places, rather than drive. Try to walk to any activity within a mile. If you walk at a fast pace (enough to raise your heart rate a little), a mile takes 15 minutes. You could go to a local gym that has baby care and sign up for an exercise class. You'll be amazed at how quickly a simple change affects your body shape.

Resisting temptation There's something inexplicably tempting about finger foods. Now that your baby is on solids, you might find you are "picking" more than you used to. Try to resist the temptation to finish off her leftovers. As a rule of thumb, you should eat your own lunch when your baby eats hers, so that you aren't hungry for her leftovers. If at times it's not practical to eat together, have a healthy snack (see box, below) and a cup of coffee while she eats her dinner. That way you avoid grazing, and keep her company.

HEALTHY EATING

While you may be eager to shed the extra pounds gained during pregnancy as soon as possible, it's judicious to avoid trendy diets and quick-fix solutions. Instead, concentrate on maintaining a nutritious diet and moderating your portions. This will help you lose weight steadily and instill healthy eating habits that will enable you to maintain a constant healthy weight, rather than yo-yoing up and down. The following tips can help to keep you on track.

■ **Eat regular meals** Eat three meals a day and ensure that each meal contains at least one vegetable portion, as well as fruit.

■ **Choose foods that give a sustained release of energy** This will help you feel full longer and resist snacking between meals. Try oatmeal and whole-wheat toast for breakfast along with some fresh fruit. Lunches and dinners should contain whole grains,

lean meat or fish, and, ideally, two portions of vegetables.

■ **Opt for low-fat dairy products** Fat contains twice the amount of energy as carbohydrates and proteins, so choose reduced-fat milk, dairy spreads, yogurts, and cheese, and measure out oils, mayonnaise, and salad dressings with a spoon. It's important, though, not to eliminate dairy entirely since it plays an important role in your diet. There's also evidence that calcium has a part to play in weight loss.

■ **Include protein** All meals should include some protein, which helps to keep hunger at bay.

■ **Maintain your fluid intake** Drink water regularly; this helps to keep you hydrated and can stop you from mistaking thirst for hunger.

■ **Eat healthy snacks** Keep cut-up carrots, celery, and cucumbers in the fridge for quick, healthy snacks.

285

A little silence

Your baby's brain is not yet mature enough to stream sounds, which means that she cannot select what she hears by focusing on it.

Adults can filter out background noise in order to listen to someone speak or listen intently for something. Babies are less able to do this and can easily be overwhelmed by the cacophony or lose concentration. This is one reason why babies startle so easily at loud noises—everything is heard at full-blast and in conjunction with the other sounds in the environment.

Try to keep things quiet from time to time to allow your baby to concentrate on her activities and focus on your voice. She is learning all the time, but this learning can be hampered if she is subjected to constant background noise. This doesn't mean that your household has to be completely silent, but keep in mind that televisions, blaring radios, loud talk, and the food processor whirring will distract her from her activities. Turn off the television when you are reading or playing together, and turn off or turn down the volume of any music during playtime. Try to tone down the overall noise level of your household at your baby's bedtime, but don't try for total, or almost total, silence because falling asleep with a little background noise means your baby is less likely to wake at normal evening sounds.

If your baby is struggling to reach some of her developmental milestones, give her some peace and space in which to try again. If the room is noisy and she is constantly distracted and attempting to make sense of the sounds around her, she'll find it much harder to master new skills. Your baby will grow to appreciate regular "quiet" time, and will recognize this as a time to relax and enjoy some undisturbed play time with you.

Problem solving

While learning through play, your baby develops skills that enable her to look at a problem and find solutions on her own.

Studies show that, once they reach eight months, babies' cognitive awareness has developed enough to enable them to understand cause and effect ("If I want to drink from my cup, I need to tip it"), and that one problem might have several solutions.

To encourage these important skills, you don't need to do anything more complex than allow your baby to play with toys that require her to move objects around or press a button and see what happens. Sorting cups (which you can stack, and she can enjoy knocking over), shape sorters of different kinds, and toys with lids that need replacing or removing (ideally to discover something hidden inside) are all fantastic toys for encouraging her problem-solving skills.

Watch as your baby uses her ingenuity to solve problems such as reaching a toy that isn't at hands' reach—she might crawl to it, or protest until you get it for her, and by nine months, she may start to point at it! These are all signs of her developing cognitive skills. As always, offer your baby plenty of encouragement and praise her efforts.

Think and play Shape-sorting toys help to improve your baby's problem-solving skills as she tries to fit the pieces into the right slots.

Your baby and television

Is it okay for your baby to watch television briefly, or is any screen time bad for her development? There are arguments for and against.

Popping in a DVD or finding an educational children's program can seem like a blessing when you need a little distraction for an irritable baby, or to keep her amused while you take a breather or deal with something close by. However, there is much debate about whether television time is helpful or unhelpful to your baby's overall development.

The information available can be confusing, since some programs indicate that they are instructive and promote development, while research suggests that watching TV actually impedes the development of language as well as children's ability to concentrate.

Who's right? The Canadian Paediatric Society recommends limiting TV watching to less than one hour per day for children under two years old, because research hasn't shown that babies have the capacity to understand what they're watching, so it isn't really educating them; human interaction is much more educational. Studies show an increased prevalence of attention disorders such as ADHD and obesity. This is all highly speculative, but there's little doubt that watching a screen eats into your baby's time to play, observe, and explore the real world, and to be stimulated by physical games, reading, and creative play. Research has shown that television can't match the educational value of time spent with you. For example, studies show that language is acquired most effectively through face-to-face interaction rather than from passive observation of TV shows.

Instead of banning television, the best solution is probably to use it mindfully and for brief limited periods only.

STAYING HYDRATED

Babies can become very attached to their bottles, so the longer you wait before introducing a cup, the more difficult it could be to persuade your baby to give up her bottles. If you haven't already done it, introduce a cup of water after, or between, feedings or meals. Your baby's tummy is small, so if she fills up on liquid at mealtimes, she's not likely to eat much. You could also offer her diluted fruit juice (10 parts water to one part juice), or milk at the end of a meal. Diluted fruit juice contains vitamin C, which will help her body absorb the iron from the food she eats. But limit it to mealtimes to protect her teeth. Don't give her undiluted fruit juice, which will encourage a sweet tooth.

Thirsty work Drinking water or diluted juice after a meal will keep your baby hydrated.

Keeping it interactive Make sure that your baby is not in front of the TV for too long (at the most, watch just one program or a brief part of a DVD), and turn the television off after the show to allow your baby to engage with a book or enjoy some playtime.

Interact with your baby while she watches television to bring any learning to life. Point to objects in the program and name them as they are shown, and repeat rhymes from the program afterward to reinforce the rhythm, as well as acting out any actions that go with them. Keep in mind that you are beginning to establish your child's viewing habits, so try to keep the television as an occasional help rather than a dominant presence in the home.

AS A MATTER OF FACT

When you shop for food, be wary of cheap processed foods that might contain partially hydrogenated vegetable oils (HVOs). These are used to prolong the shelf life of processed food. However, since being identified as contributing to the development of diseases such as diabetes, cancer, and cardiovascular disease, some countries and cities have banned them. But because they're still widely available, if you're in any doubt, read food labels. Food for babies and toddlers should not contain these ingredients, but check the labels to be safe.

35 weeks

Testing your reactions

When your baby does something repeatedly, you may notice that she's watching you carefully to see how you will react.

This usually works to your advantage as she'll repeat sounds, actions, and behaviors that make you smile, or give her praise, attention, or a hug. However, if she gets lots of attention for something you don't want her to do, this can encourage her to do the same thing again.

No baby is willfully naughty, she's simply motivated to get your attention. She doesn't know that it's not nice to be rough with the cat, or that it hurts you if she pinches your skin or tugs your hair, but you can begin to teach her that these things are not okay. Calmly saying "Stop, that hurts" and showing in your expression that it's painful, can be enough. You can go on to show her how to be gentle, for example moving her hand to stroke your arm and saying "Let's touch gently."

Your baby needs plenty of attention, and this is best given when she is playing nicely, being gentle and loving, and showing off her new skills, language, and learning. When you need to respond to her being rough, keep your reaction in check and remind yourself that her actions are not deliberate or meant to upset you. Ignoring negative behavior is not a recommended strategy at this age since you need to stop her if she is doing something potentially harmful to herself or others. Instead, respond to her calmly in the spirit of teaching her how to be kind and gentle.

If your baby receives the most attention for the positive things she does, she will repeat those actions. So if she pets the cat gently, eats her food without throwing the bowl, and copies you by putting a toy in a box after playtime, praise her, clap your hands, and give her plenty of attention. In this way, you will begin to teach her the boundaries of acceptable behavior.

Great communicator

Your 35-week-old baby is open to learning, so explain things to her and respond to her communications to support her development.

Talk to your baby to describe your activities throughout the day so she develops an understanding of the world. Everything is new and exciting to a baby, so stop and look at the cracks in the sidewalk and the butterfly perching on a pretty flower. Lie on your backs in the grass and look up at the clouds and show her the leaves on the trees.

Also, listen and respond to your baby's communications as if you are having a conversation. Show an interest when

Running commentary Explain to your baby what you are doing around the house, and what comes next in his daily routine.

she babbles to you, repeat her sounds and intonation, and allow her to respond. Pay attention when she shouts, laughs, gurgles, or gestures toward something she wants. While it can be frustrating to figure out what she wants, responding to her needs and efforts to communicate will help her to become confident about expressing herself. She'll also get an early grasp of the subtleties of social interaction and manners. You are your child's first teacher. Everything you help her to understand in these formative months forms the basis of her curiosity, self-belief, memory, vocabulary, imagination, and much, much more.

Going swimming

Swimming with your baby is fun and relaxing. It also promotes a healthy respect for water and encourages her development, too.

Water supports your baby's weight, which means that she's able to move around freely in a swimming pool even if she's not yet particularly mobile on dry land. This gives her a feeling of freedom and independence, and allows her to work her muscles while kicking and splashing around. It also helps her build her confidence in the water so that she doesn't feel afraid of it.

Before you go To avoid unwanted accidents in the water, you'll need to buy swim diapers for your baby (ordinary disposables will disintegrate in a pool). You can choose between disposable or reusable diapers—just make sure that whichever you choose fits snugly. You may also want to invest in some inflatable baby arm bands or a swimsuit with buoyancy inserts, to help keep your baby afloat.

If you're using a public pool for the first time, check the water temperature beforehand. If it's below 86°F/30°C, your baby may find it too chilly. Avoid peak hours if possible; it's best to plan your visit for when the pool is not too busy or noisy or your baby may be frightened by the echoing sounds.

Make sure that you feed your baby at least an hour beforehand—don't go swimming just after a meal—and take a drink and snack for afterward.

Getting started Take things slowly so she doesn't feel overwhelmed. Introduce her to the water slowly, holding her close to you and giving her time to get used to the sensation of the water and being in the pool before you start to play. Once she is comfortable, splash

Free movement Once your baby learns that she can kick her legs and splash around in the water, she'll love the freedom of movement that being in the pool gives her.

gently, sing, and kick her legs for her so that she realizes the range of movement she can achieve in the water. Make a game of showing her how to blow bubbles. This is an important skill, because exhaling (blowing) means she won't inhale water.

Keep your first session reasonably short—20 minutes or so to start with—to make sure that she leaves the pool happy and having enjoyed herself, rather than having overdone it. If, at any point, your baby seems cold, or if her skin or eyes are irritated by the chlorine, stop and remove her from the pool.

It goes without saying that babies need to be supervised at all times both in and around a pool. Give her a warm shower after her swim and dress her before you dress yourself to make sure that she is comfortable.

ASK A... PEDIATRICIAN

My baby has eczema. Is it okay to take her swimming? While chlorine can be a potential irritant to children with eczema, taking a couple of precautions can help make sure it's an enjoyable and stress-free activity for her. You can apply a barrier cream first to protect her skin from the chlorine. However, since this can make her slippery in the water, you might want to put her in a UV swimsuit or baby wet suit after applying the cream so that you can hold her securely during the swim. After swimming, make sure that you shower her to wash off the chlorine, then pat her dry, and apply her usual emollient cream.

35 weeks

289

36 weeks

ABOUT 12 PERCENT OF BABIES ARE WALKING BY NINE MONTHS

Now that she is increasingly active and alert throughout the day, your baby may be tired enough at night to sleep through until morning. This shift in her sleep pattern may also affect her daytime naps. What remains the same is that when awake, she'll be eager to play and learn.

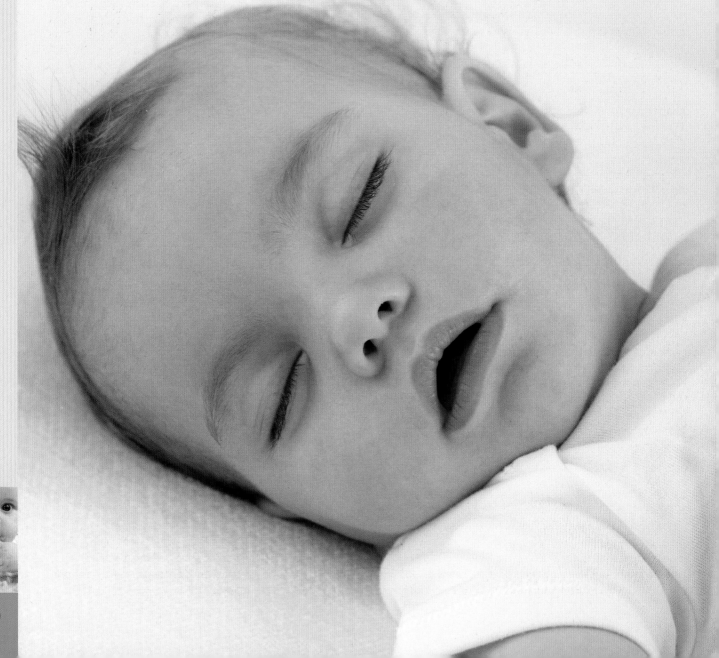

Going cruising

Once your baby pulls up to standing, the next step is to start edging her way around the furniture—it's time for cruising.

Baby steps Your baby may spend weeks pulling herself up to a standing position before she is willing to step out and cruise between items of furniture. Let her do this at her own pace.

Over the next few weeks, or months, as your baby experiments with her new ability to stand upright and step, she will be cruising from one piece of furniture to the next.

To help her move around safely and easily, try to arrange your furniture so that she can move from one piece to another while holding on. As she becomes more confident, you can create small pieces in between so that she can test her walking skills.

Make sure that the furniture is sturdy and will support her weight, and move any items with sharp edges out of the way. Your baby will soon become adept

at moving around furniture at high speed, so don't leave her alone.

Cruising is a developmental milestone of its own, and it can be accompanied by quite a few bumps, bruises, and tears, as well as plenty of celebrations as your baby begins to master the skills required for walking without support. Keep in mind, though, that some babies never go through a cruising stage at all, preferring instead to bottom shuffle (see p.260).

There are several defined stages of cruising. A first-time cruiser uses both hands to hold onto her support and will keep her body close to it. Later, she'll

stand a little farther back from the support, holding on with one hand only, and then—at some point—she will try letting go. Your baby may also develop an interest in climbing—over cushions, up the stairs, and even up onto the sofa. Keep an eye on your baby-proofing and make sure she can't get into danger when she does this. Once she's feeling confident about her balance and control, she will enjoy walking while holding your hands and may even attempt a step or two on her own. Take off her socks so that her toes can grip the floor and help her balance more effectively.

ASK A... PEDIATRICIAN

How many milk feedings does my baby need at this age? At nine months, most babies need 2–3 milk feedings a day, along with 2–3 meals of solid foods. It's recommended that they have approximately 20 oz (600 ml) of breast milk or formula each day alongside a varied diet until they are one year old, at which point they can drink cow's milk. If you're in any doubt, be guided by your pediatrician who will be able to advise if she's getting too much or too little.

My baby is cruising on his tiptoes—is this normal? Don't worry—quite a few babies do this and before long he should start to use his whole foot to support himself while moving around. If it continues, mention it to your doctor.

If you cry, I will too

Your 36-week-old baby is sensitive to other people's distress. Her cries in reaction to your tears are a forerunner to her later empathy.

By now, you have noticed that your baby is mimicking some of your facial expressions and tone of voice, and engaging in exchanges of babbles and sounds. She has also been noticing your emotional reactions and reacting with distress if you are upset. This is known as "reflexive" crying. You may have noticed this when, for example, your baby is calmly settling in at day care, but then starts to cry when another baby cries. Soon several more babies in the room start to cry.

Your baby may also reach out for you if you cry. This gesture of comfort is probably copied from you and, although it is not truly empathic, such gestures will gain genuine meaning as your baby moves into the toddler years.

The development of empathy is vital to your baby's relationships with, and understanding of, others. However, it won't be until her toddler years onward that she will really start to identify emotions. Over the coming years, she will gradually gain an understanding

of others' perspectives and recognize the effects of her behavior. To help her develop an understanding of emotions, it's important not to hide your own feelings; but you also need to make sure that if you are showing strong feelings, she sees you manage them rather than become overwhelmed.

When you soothe your baby, you are teaching her to comfort herself. This is an invaluable life lesson, and she will use methods such as stroking or hugging to show her empathy for others.

Changing sleep patterns

If your baby is sleeping through the night, she may be ready to drop her morning nap and make it through the morning in a good mood.

Don't assume that your baby is ready to give up her morning nap at this stage. Some babies will need two naps a day well into their second year of life, and need more sleep during periods of growth and activity. But if your baby is happy and playful in the morning, and resists attempts to settle her down, she may be ready to switch to one nap a day. Play it by ear. Settle her down for her morning nap and encourage her to relax in her crib: If she plays quietly instead of sleeping, she'll still get a little respite from her busy day and will benefit from the quiet time. There will, however, come

A long nap Your baby's afternoon nap may last longer when you drop the morning nap.

a point when she resists being put down, and shows no signs of being tired.

For a smooth transition from two naps to one, alter your routine a little to give your baby her lunch and midday feeding a little earlier and put her down for her afternoon nap an hour or so earlier than usual. Watch for signs that she is going "past it" and becoming overstimulated. Without a morning nap, she may sleep longer in the afternoon, so if she doesn't stir, wake her after a couple of hours or so, or she won't be tired enough to sleep at bedtime.

If she seems tired the following day, you may find that she'll need two naps again, then just one longer one the day after. Let her be your guide.

Keeping love alive

Parenting a baby is tiring, so while being intimate together may seem like too much effort, it will help keep your relationship strong.

Falling into bed (and right to sleep) well before your partner; feeling a little resentful that you've been trapped at home with your baby all day; being too busy to make time for each other—these are all common reasons why sex can end up on the back burner in early parenthood. The physical closeness you share with your baby, and the affection you lavish on her, can also leave you feeling as if you need space rather than comfort, and if you're breast-feeding you may feel that your body isn't your own.

It's natural to feel underwhelmed about sex, no matter how much you love your partner. In fact, both men and women find that life with a new baby can turn off, rather than on, feelings of arousal. A healthy relationship can withstand a period without regular sex, however it is a powerful way of expressing feelings, and it can also lift your mood and help you to relax. Eventually, it will play a stronger role in your relationship, and help keep it strong; for now, being more affectionate with each other will help revive your physical relationship over time.

Romantic moments Try making a few "appointments" to spend time together. Curl up together in front of the TV or, better still, switch it off, light some candles, and give each other a massage. Share a warm bath or just snuggle up in bed and talk. Chances are that you'll drift off to sleep before anything sexual happens, but simply savoring the warmth of each other's bodies and becoming familiar with them again is a good stepping stone toward regaining a sex life.

Staying close Make time to be physically close with your partner. Even if it doesn't lead to sex, the intimacy will help you both to feel more connected and in tune with each other.

Make sure that you respond positively to each other's overtures. Even if you aren't in the mood for sex, a positive response to gestures of tenderness will reassure both of you that you are still lovable and attractive. A little foreplay or even some passionate kissing can help you feel more in the mood and rekindle a little sexual excitement.

Equally, however, sex may not be a priority at the moment, and if you are both happy with the situation, it's absolutely normal and acceptable to show your love and affection in other ways. If your sexual desire does not match at the moment, and one or both of you is feeling pressured—or lonely, frustrated, and isolated—try to come to a compromise that suits you both. Expressing your love for your partner should be an important part of your relationship, whether you do this sexually or through words and actions.

ASK A... DOCTOR

Sex is still painful after my baby's birth. Is this normal? If you had a difficult birth, your body may still be recovering, and you may feel emotionally bruised. The anticipation of pain may be making you tense, which will increase discomfort. Using a lubricant can help, especially if you are not becoming aroused due to fear or pain. Take things slowly and experiment with positions. Practice Kegel exercises (see p.65) to tighten up the area and encourage circulation, which may help. Occasionally, episiotomies or tears cause long-term discomfort. A yeast infection may also cause discomfort or pain. If you continue to feel pain, consult your gynecologist or obstetrician right away.

36 weeks

293

Good combinations

Although it can be tempting to feed your baby exactly what she likes, it is important to expand her menu to include new foods.

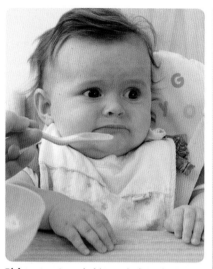

Picky eater Some babies actively resist trying new foods. It's worth persevering, but you may need to try some new tactics.

Even if she resists, don't give up trying to broaden your baby's diet. Keep offering her a new food, using different accompaniments to alter the flavor, texture, and appearance of the meal to help her accept it.

If you've gotten into the habit of batch cooking, it's easy to adjust your baby's diet, since you can rely on a ready supply of one or two foods she likes and use these as a base for many new meals. So if she loves mashed sweet potato, you could stir in some ground chicken, or a few small or finely chopped chunks of chicken and some peas—you'll have an instant casserole, packed with nutrients, with her favorite food as the star flavor to tempt her. If she's a fan of potatoes, mix mashed

potatoes with finely chopped chicken or beef and chopped spinach for a healthy "chicken pie." If she likes mashed carrots, blend it with equally sweet foods such as sweet potato, parsnips, and butternut squash to introduce her to new flavors while packing her meals full of nutrients.

Dippers are a good option, too. Show your baby how to dip healthy finger foods, such as carrots, cucumbers, or strips of toast, into her favorite mashed foods. This helps her to get used to different combinations of flavors and textures. If she loves carrots, mix some chopped spinach in with the mashed carrot and give her some pasta pieces to dip into the blend, with a few cucumber sticks to gum on the side.

Getting dressed

Your baby may be far too busy for anything as trivial as getting dressed! Distraction tactics will help get her clothes on her.

When you want to dress her, catch your baby off guard! If she gets dressed at the same time or stage of her routine each day, you can alter things occasionally so that she doesn't begin to resist as soon as she anticipates what's coming next. Alternatively, if your baby thrives on routine and always likes to know what's coming next, make sure you dress her at the same point each day, since this type of personality will probably resist less if she knows what's coming.

You may find it easier to dress your baby on your knee, so you can hold her firmly to stop her from wiggling away. This change in routine might also surprise her into cooperation. Or, as long as she will be warm enough, dress her in stages, letting her play between adding layers. She might not resist just one item of clothing being slipped onto her body.

Do your best to make dressing fun for your baby. Give a commentary to distract her—for example, "Here are your pretty

red leggings and we'll pull them up over your legs and around your tummy! Now it's time for your striped T-shirt. Arms up, over the head, good girl!" Tickle her when you pull down her T-shirt, encourage her to help you put on her socks, play "This little piggy," or sing one of her favorite songs. If she's engaged and having fun, she'll forget that she doesn't like getting dressed. Whatever you do, practice speed and efficiency, and it will be over before she knows it!

Successful child care

Whether you leave your child with a family member or paid caregiver, it's important to build a good relationship with them.

Trust, understanding, and mutual respect are key when it comes to sharing child care, whether you are paying your baby's caregiver or relying on the generosity of a family member. When you hire someone, of course, the arrangement is more formal, but, nevertheless, whoever takes care of your child, good two-way communication will help everything run more smoothly.

Paid-for care If you employ a nanny or babysitter to take care of your baby, you should try to maintain a good professional relationship. You don't need to be best friends, but you do need to be a good boss. Listen to her (or his) concerns, pay her on time, keep to the agreed hours, and be willing to oblige if she needs you to be more flexible from time to time. You'll definitely need the same from her, too.

Remember that she isn't just an employee. You may be paying her, but she is the most important "other" person in your child's life, so make time to get to know her, remember birthdays, and ask about things that are important to her.

Communicate with your baby's caregiver as fully as possible. Pass on information about what's happening at home, for example, was your baby up all night teething? Is she crying without her comfort blanket? Her caregiver needs to know about these things. Similarly, she must report on all developments, no matter how minor, at the end of the day so you can be kept in the loop.

Share your philosophy on child care. Rather than lay down rules for your baby's caregiver to stick to blindly, take time to explain why you want your baby to eat the food she eats, or why you'd rather she didn't watch television, and how you are maintaining her routine at home. If your caregiver feels involved, she's more likely to follow your lead. Show respect for her experience and expertise, though, and open your mind to new ideas—you may actually learn some important tips from her.

Set up regular reviews so that any concerns or tensions can be aired before they become big problems. Working together as a team is always the best approach. Show sensitivity to her needs and she's likely to do the same in return.

Family affair If a family member is taking care of your baby, show them your appreciation regularly. It is not easy taking care of a young child all day, and if no (or little) money is changing hands, the situation can become a breeding ground for resentment. Talk through any problems as soon as they arise, and show willingness to shoulder extra responsibilities if he or she is finding it difficult to cope. Understand that anyone caring for small children needs a break from time to time, as well as some adult company and conversation. Show your appreciation and that you do not take them for granted.

A harmonious arrangement Grandparents are often caregivers; make sure your baby's grandparent feels valued and respected.

36 weeks

37 weeks

REPETITION OF EXPERIENCES CEMENTS THE NERVE CONNECTIONS IN YOUR BABY'S BRAIN

Your baby continues to explore objects with her mouth and she is more alert than ever, constantly making connections between words and objects. She's also more mobile, so make sure that your home is as safe as possible. Be prepared, however, to deal with the occasional bump!

Talking to herself

Your baby will happily babble away whether you are listening or not, and she'll start to experiment by turning up the volume.

Range and volume As your baby goes about the important business of playing, he may hum, blow raspberries, squeal, make burring noises, and laugh as he entertains himself.

At 37 weeks, your baby will be practicing her speech patterns and inflections by talking, chattering, singing, and even shouting to herself. This is an important step in the development of her language skills, and her repertoire of sounds and words will increase almost daily. Don't be surprised if she practices a single sound for a long time, before confidently combining it with another. She'll also be eager to experiment with volume, and emit some amazingly loud, high-pitched shouts that may make her laugh at her own capabilities. Listen for her blowing raspberries and other funny noises as she practices her vocal range!

She's used to hearing you talk to her and will think it's absolutely normal to give a running commentary of babble as she goes through the day. As your baby approaches nine months, she continues to respond to you by mimicking the sounds you make, including the pitch and inflection. This copying helps to cement the rhythm and cadence of language in her brain. You may notice that your own speech patterns are echoed in her babbling, and that she ends some of her "sentences" with a higher-pitched sound somewhat like a question mark, or even an exclamation. Repeating what she says back to her will help this process. Your baby will watch your mouth closely to try to understand what you're saying, but her understanding comes from association, so keep pointing to things and explaining what you are doing.

DEVELOPMENT ACTIVITY

Bye-bye!

Waving goodbye as someone leaves is one of our most common gestures, and one that babies love to watch and copy. Most babies give their first meaningful wave between 10 and 12 months. Some do earlier; especially if Mom or Dad has held their arm to wave from an early age—or might do so later if this gesture is not used very often. If your baby isn't waving by herself, you can show her how as you say "bye-bye." After plenty of repetition, she'll start to respond. Soon she will automatically raise her hand and wave unprompted when leaving friends or at buses and in stores!

Waving By 37 weeks, your baby may be linking the action of waving to hearing the words "bye-bye."

37 weeks

297

YOUR BABY IS 37 WEEKS AND 1 DAY

My baby's weight

Although she's more hungry these days, your baby's weight gain slows down at this age because being mobile burns lots of calories.

It's normal to be worried about your baby's weight. Maybe those dimpled thighs and chubby arms are causing you to question if she is overweight, or perhaps your slender baby, with not an ounce of spare flesh, seems to be on the brink of being underweight.

If your baby's weight continues to follow the same percentile line on the medical chart at her pediatrician's office, she'll be doing just fine. Continue to have her weighed regularly, around once every two months, to keep tabs on her progress and, if nothing else, to give you a little reassurance.

Your baby's growth rate rapidly slows down during her first year of life, reaching a near plateau by 12 months. Breast milk and formula are more caloric than the foods your baby will be tasting and eating now, and it can take time for her to be able to eat enough to make up the difference in calories. Don't panic if she doesn't seem that interested in solid food at first; many babies take a while to show an interest. Be reassured that milk still provides the basis of her nutrition at the moment, and that your baby needs time to get used to and accept new tastes and textures.

ASK A... PEDIATRICIAN

My baby's fontanelles are still soft—is this normal? It can take up to 18 months for a baby's skull bones to fuse together. By 11 months, the smaller gap (the posterior fontanelle, toward the back of the head) has usually closed, leaving only the larger gap (the anterior fontanelle, at the top of the head) still soft. So there's no need to worry for seven months or so, but if it looks sunken or bulging, see your pediatrician immediately.

YOUR BABY IS 37 WEEKS AND 2 DAYS

Into her mouth

Now that your baby is able to hold on to toys without dropping them, she can move them around her mouth to explore all of their surfaces.

Your baby's jaw and tongue movements are now quite coordinated, and her "mouthing" skills are sophisticated, allowing her to extract sensory information from whatever enters her mouth. She will explore toys and other objects with her tongue, lips, and jaw to find out about their size, shape, texture, and weight. She also uses this skill to find out all about the food she eats.

Your baby will also begin to mouth and even gnaw on things to ease the discomfort of teething. Biting, chewing,

Tool for discovery Your baby's mouth is often the first port of call when investigating objects.

and exploring toys orally will help to soothe her gums, and you can also help her by offering cold non-PVC teething rings to chew.

Interestingly, your baby's mouthing prepares her for chewing and swallowing solid food, and for speech, since the muscles of her jaw and tongue are used.

Now that your baby is becoming more mobile and is in the throes of mastering her pincer grip (see p.339), you'll need to be very careful not to leave small items around that she could potentially choke on. Equally, make sure that anything dangerous or poisonous is on a high shelf or in a locked cabinet.

Crib safety

Once your baby is able to pull herself up to stand in her crib, you'll need to take some steps to make sure she remains safe in there.

Safe height By now, the base of your baby's crib should be set at its lowest height. Ideally, she will be completely behind the bars, even when she is standing up.

Make sure your baby's crib base is set at its lowest possible height. If she is able to sit—and most definitely when she is able to stand—she could pull herself up on the bars and topple out if the base of the crib is too close to the top bar.

Once she can stand up in her crib, your teething baby is likely to chew on the top rail. If the crib is painted, check that the paint doesn't contain lead. You may be able to purchase a plastic teething rail that sits over the top rail, which will not only protect your baby from paint and splinters, but will also keep your crib looking a little nicer, too!

Remove mobiles and adjacent wall shelves that your baby could reach and hold on to for balance as she maneuvers herself up and out of the crib. Make sure cords for lamps, blinds, or curtains are tied up away from the crib.

Check that the mattress fits snugly. Now that your baby can work her way around the crib, she could become trapped if her foot gets lodged in a gap between crib and mattress. For the same reason, cover cut-out designs or other spaces in which her arms or legs could get caught. They may be pretty, but they certainly aren't safe. If the crib you are using isn't new, check that the spacing between the bars conforms to current crib safety standards. There should be no more than 2 ⅜ in (6 cm) between the bars to prevent a baby's head from becoming lodged between them.

Finally, as a precaution, place a thick, soft rug on the floor by your baby's crib. With an intrepid baby, where there's a will, there's a way, and if she wants to climb out of her crib, you may find that nothing can stop her!

ASK A... CHILD PSYCHOLOGIST

My baby wants to be picked up all the time. When I put her down, even for a couple of minutes, she cries. It makes life very difficult—what can I do? Some babies feel more insecure than others (perhaps as a result of separation anxiety, see p.283). Your baby feels safe in your arms and that's where she wants to stay. However, carrying your baby around the clock not only prevents you from getting things done, it also stops your baby from practicing new skills such as creeping and crawling, that will eventually enable her to get around without being carried. Nor does it allow her to learn how to entertain herself for short periods.

Babies also cry to be picked up because they want comfort and attention, or because they need something. So ask yourself whether you are spending enough one-on-one time with her. Is her diaper dirty or is it time for lunch? If her needs are being met, then try to lengthen the time between pick-ups. Give her enough toys to keep her entertained and leave her to her own devices for a short time. If she starts fussing, play with her for a few minutes, and then move away. If she cries to be picked up, try distracting her by engaging her in an activity. Be realistic—all babies need lots of cuddling and carrying around. Once she starts crawling and gains a sense of independence, she's less likely to want to be held all the time.

37 weeks

Brain power

Your baby's brain is developing faster than at any other time in her life. What's going on in there?

Stimulation and repetition While your baby's brain is developing, experiencing repeated stimuli will encourage the development of neural pathways, which is how information is stored.

SOFT PLAY AT HOME

Safe, soft play areas are not the province of toddlers only—babies love them, too. Set up a soft-play gated area in your living room—your baby will be fascinated by the transformation of the room, and playing in it will encourage the development of her gross motor skills. Collect as many quilted or fleecy blankets and comforters as you can and cover the floor with them to give her a soft landing whenever she falls. Use cushions and upturned plastic boxes to create obstacles to climb over, and a cardboard box (open at both ends) to make a tunnel to crawl through. Don't leave your baby alone while she explores this fascinating play zone and, if she needs it, help her negotiate the ups and downs of your homemade adventure course.

Your baby's brain grows more during the first year of her life than at any other time. By 12 months, her brain has doubled its volume and reached about 60 percent of its adult size. Your baby was born with her full complement of nerve cells (called neurons), but as she grows those used most frequently grow stronger and branch out to make more connections and pathways, which enable your baby to think and to learn new skills. By the end of the first year, your baby's brain will have made millions of new connections—and the more connections it makes, the more advanced her mental development will be. In addition, each of your baby's neurons has a coating called myelin, which insulates and protects it, and helps messages move faster.

Repetition Neural pathways are formed as your baby's brain processes her experiences of the world. Repetition in words, actions, and play is vital to cement these connections, and is much more beneficial to your baby's neural development than a single experience, because it's through repetition that neural pathways become entrenched.

Building skills Your baby's development occurs in logical stages, with each milestone or developmental achievement providing the building block for her to go on to reach a more complex or demanding milestone. For example, mastering the ability to lift her head and push up provides her with the skills she needs for rolling to occur, and also enables her to practice the movements she will need for crawling. Once strength and balance are added to her repertoire, she will be able to combine all of these separate skills and start to crawl in earnest.

Stimulating her senses Your baby's brain development relies on information from all her senses. All of her experiences—what she smells, tastes, sees, each voice, song, or noise she hears, and each texture she feels—is translated into the firing of neurons in her brain, which in turn forge connections between cells and create learning.

At the same time, pathways that are rarely used fall away and can be lost. In this way, her brain is "pruning" itself—keeping and strengthening some connections and letting go of those that are less important. You can help your baby by giving her plenty of stimulation and different experiences, and keep repeating these experiences so that her pathways grow strong.

Testing times

Your adventurous baby is pushing the limits of her ability, and sometimes she is going to get stuck!

Being endlessly curious, your baby may manage to pull herself up to a standing position, then feel unsure how to get back down. She may crawl up the stairs, then look back to see that she's gone a bit too far, and realize with dismay that she's not sure how to get back down. She may cry when she hears a dog barking or another loud noise, and even express a sudden dislike of her dark room at bedtime. These reactions are a form of self-protection. They may

encourage her to be cautious, but this is often overpowered by her curiosity and hunger to learn or practice emerging skills. There may come a time when your baby has really overreached and is afraid and in need of your support, reassurance, and comfort.

Show her how to climb and descend the stairs and sit down from standing. Encourage her to repeat the actions until she beams with new confidence. Explain that the loud noise is just a silly

doggy, and, at bedtime, make soothing sounds or repeat her favorite lullaby when you switch off the lights. No matter what situation she's gotten herself into, stay calm. If you're frantic, she'll quickly grow alarmed. Help and reassure her, then let her try again with your help. Don't show her your fear of dogs or accidents, and be confident in unfamiliar situations. Set up opportunities for playtime success to boost her confidence and praise her when she does well.

Bumps and falls

It is inevitable that your baby will end up with bruises and bumps as she becomes more mobile and interested in doing things herself.

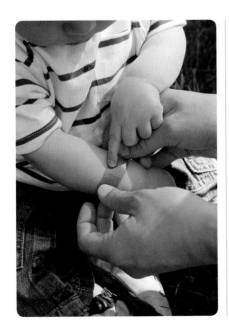

Be careful not to overreact when your baby takes a tumble, even if she hurts herself. She'll gauge your reaction before deciding how to respond, and if she sees you panicking or becoming anxious and distressed, she'll do the same. Instead, brush her off with a cheerful "uh-oh," and encourage her to try again. If she becomes fearful of new experiences because she associates them with being hurt, she'll be much less likely to engage in healthy experimentation and exploration. If you teach your baby that making mistakes—and bumps and tumbles—

Baby tumbles Take the sting out of falls and minor cuts with some fun bandages and lots of attention and cuddling.

are all a normal part of life, she'll take them in stride and continue trying.

If your baby becomes distressed after an accident, comfort her, put a cold cloth on bruises or swelling, and check her carefully. Being positive doesn't mean ignoring her or adopting a cavalier approach to her well-being. You'll need to be vigilant to make sure she hasn't hurt herself badly. For example, any bump to the head, awkward fall, or cut that bleeds for longer than a few minutes should be discussed with a doctor, particularly if your baby seems woozy or distressed. Consider contacting an organization such as the Red Cross (see pp.416–417) to learn first aid so you feel confident about when to seek medical advice and what to do in an emergency.

37 weeks

301

38 weeks

BABIES LIKE TO PLAY BESIDE OTHER BABIES BUT WON'T PLAY WITH OTHERS UNTIL ABOUT TWO YEARS

Your independent baby will love to make music by himself, so encourage this as much as possible. His memory is also improving, and he will recognize familiar objects and people more frequently. He loves to play sitting alongside "friends" and will learn from watching other babies.

Your baby day by day ■ Months 7–9

Let's play some music …

… and dance! Stimulate your baby's natural sense of rhythm and encourage her enjoyment of listening to music—and making it.

Musical life Make listening to music—and making it—a part of your baby's everyday life. It will stimulate him on every level.

Music can have a significant impact on your baby. Soothing music can calm her, while lively music can lift her spirits, and is an excellent distraction when she's tired or irritable. It's a great trick to change the mood or amuse her on a long car trip. Listening to and making music supports the development of your baby's sensory coordination and memory. Singing nursery rhymes promotes her language development and teaches her a lot about rhythm.

Toy musical instruments help to develop your baby's fine motor skills. Baby keyboards, xylophones, and tambourines are ideal for babies, since they are easy to hit and make interesting sounds. She'll enjoy adding musical accompaniment by banging on drums or shaking rattles, too.

Dance practice Whether your baby is prepared to stand with your support, or happier to be held upright on your lap, encouraging her to move in time to music will help her develop a sense of rhythm, improve her coordination and body awareness, and express herself creatively. Put on a tune you know she likes, and she'll instinctively move her arms and legs to music when she's little, and bounce and sway as she gets older.

Hold her hands to support her and "dance" with her, lifting her up for a twirl in time to the music. Or put on a waltz or a tango and glide around your living room—ballroom style—with your baby in your arms. Your baby will love to be swayed and twirled across the floor!

AS A MATTER OF FACT

Research suggests that babies are born with a predisposition to move rhythmically in response to music. In a study of 120 babies between five months and two years old, researchers played recordings of classical music, rhythmic beats, and speech to them, and videotaped the results. They found that the babies moved their arms, hands, legs, feet, torsos, and heads in response to the music much more than to speech. The reason for this ability isn't clear, though dance and music making were important to our ancestors for social cohesion.

DEVELOPMENT ACTIVITY

Homemade band

Your baby will enjoy making lots of noise with safe household objects. Make a shaker from a plastic bottle full of pasta or rice. But make sure that the top is securely sealed and taped so that nothing can escape to create a choking hazard. Use pots and pans and plastic bowls and containers together with a spatula or a wood spoon to create a homemade drum kit. Use her rattles as maracas. If you have a keyboard or piano, let her bang away on that, too. Make music together, but also leave room for her to make her own sounds. Play lively then quiet music and watch how your baby reacts to each; does her banging slow down when the tempo changes?

Improvised instruments Anything can be a musical instrument, as long as your baby is able to make plenty of noise.

303

Comfort objects

If your baby has a comfort object, she's probably become very attached. It may be difficult for her to settle down at night without it.

At this stage of her babyhood, when separation anxiety sets in (see p.246 and p.283), a comfort toy can ease your baby into new situations by providing a link with the familiar. With her "comforter," she'll find it easier to sleep at Grandma's or sit on a stranger's knee. If you are going back to work, her comfort object can help her feel more at ease with her caregiver, and she can use it to soothe herself when she is distressed.

Special toy A comfort object can help your baby feel more secure when you're not around.

If your baby doesn't have a comfort object already, it's not too late to set her up with one. Choose a toy that she likes with a soft, smooth texture she can rub or chew, or a blanket that's light enough for her to carry herself. Pick one that is easy to clean or machine wash, and safe for her to handle—and, ideally, something that's easy to replace if lost! Tuck it under her arm when feeding, and make sure she has it with her when she goes to sleep. Use it to soothe her when she's tired and grumpy, and she will soon associate it with comfort.

Your social baby

Your baby is fascinated by other babies. She will chatter away to them, imitate their actions, and enjoy playing alongside them.

At 38 weeks, your baby will engage in parallel play—she'll sit alongside another baby and do her own thing as he does his. They may chatter to one another and look over to see what the other is doing. They may even tussle for the same toy or copy each other's activities, but they are largely interested in their own activities. In fact, they may even forget the other is there.

For your baby, her little friend is like another toy or interesting thing to watch. She loves to see others who are just her size. These early interactions allow her to become used to the company of other children. She'll learn things by watching other children, and make "friendships,"

which, at this age, means other babies become familiar and, therefore, favorites. She'll gravitate toward babies she knows when you enter a playgroup or meet up with friends.

Don't be surprised if your baby wants to examine her companion and give his hair a good tug or poke at his face as she would with a new toy. She may enjoy getting a good reaction when she bashes him on the head or climbs on top of him. Be patient; this is experimentation, not aggression. Show her how to pat other people gently, then distract her.

Parallel play Your baby will play alongside others but won't share for a couple of years yet.

Dropping things is fun!

You'll have to pick things up a lot over the coming weeks as your baby discovers the fun in dropping things, and does it over and over again.

Pick and drop Your baby may decide that dropping objects is lots of fun, and will spend plenty of time playing this fascinating new game—if you'll help her!

So far, your baby hasn't had the motor coordination needed to be able to open her hands to release an object she is holding purposefully. At around seven months of age, she begins to make the transition from involuntary release to intentional release. At first, this is almost forced—in passing an object from one hand to the other, the giving hand has to let go as the receiving hand pulls the object free. In addition, when your baby feels the object she is holding pressing against another surface, she learns to let it go. Over time, she learns to extend her fingers and thumb to release an object deliberately. Although it seems obvious to us, for your baby this is a fascinating new skill that she wants to practice.

At around the same time, your baby has an increasing understanding of the concept of object permanence (see p.245). She soon realizes that if she drops something over the side of her high chair, it hasn't disappeared, but is now to be found on the floor. In addition, she is learning to point—so she can also tell you that the object is down there, and "request" that you pick it up, which, of course, you do.

Dropping objects also compounds lessons in cause and effect. When an object hits the floor, it makes a noise. Your baby will want to hear that noise repeatedly, each time reinforcing the connection between the drop and the thud as it hits a surface. The delay between the action and the noise teaches her important lessons about timing and space.

Dropping objects is an important game, as irritating as it might be to repeatedly pick things up. Humor your baby for as long as you can bear to, reminding yourself that dropping something, looking for it, and pointing to it are all important developmental milestones. Once she gets a little bit older, you can adopt the "rule of three"— once it's been thrown on the floor and you've picked it up three times, the fourth time means it stays on the floor!

DEVELOPMENT ACTIVITY

Play catch

Your baby is definitely interested in dropping her toys, and is about to find out about throwing. She's learning to let go of objects, so play catching games with her. Put her in her high chair and throw a soft beanbag toy onto her tray. She will pick it up and, with any luck, go to drop it from the chair. When she does, catch it and gently toss it back onto the tray. Before long, she will get the hang of the idea that she is to pick it up and drop it again, perhaps even copying your movement and giving the beginnings of a throw herself. You could follow the same principle when rolling a ball along the floor to her—now that she can let go purposefully, she'll eventually learn to bat or roll the ball back.

Ball games Roll a soft ball gently to your baby so he can pick it up and roll or bat it back to you.

YOUR BABY IS 38 WEEKS AND 4 DAYS

Nap time

Your baby's naps, now down to about two per day, continue to be important for her well-being, whether she thinks so or not!

Your baby may be difficult to settle down at nap time. She may not want to miss out on any fun and resists all attempts to stop her activities. But that doesn't mean she doesn't need to sleep. In fact, her rapid development and all the activities she enjoys will make her very tired, even if she doesn't admit it!

If you are having trouble calming her, try putting her down a little earlier. Set up a short pre-nap routine with a milk feeding, a wash, and a comforting lullaby. She may begin to anticipate these activities with pleasure and unwind enough to sleep. Some babies are happy to sleep in broad daylight, while others need silence and good black-out blinds. See how she settles down best and work your arrangements around her needs.

She may have already dropped a nap, and may not be coping with the extra hours of being alert. If she's flagging but resisting her nap, give her plenty of quiet time. A nice long walk in her stroller may help her to relax and recharge her batteries, or quiet time on the sofa while you read to her can be enough to keep her going longer.

Figure out a daily routine so that you can get out and still fit in her important naps. Schedule playdates, shopping, or social visits for when your baby is alert, but stay tuned in to signals that she's tiring, and settle her down if needed.

There will be times when she falls asleep in the car and you will have to transfer her to her crib, or she may doze off in her stroller. There is no right way to encourage her to nap—as long as she has one, she'll be fine. Use her nap time not as an opportunity to do housework, but to regroup and relax.

YOUR BABY IS 38 WEEKS AND 5 DAYS

Recognition

As her memory improves, your baby may turn her head when you call her, and start to show she recognizes familiar objects you name.

Your baby may be starting to point when she sees something that she wants, and she shows excitement and recognition of familiar places such as the park, even getting enthusiastic as she identifies that she's on her way there.

She will now recognize people she hasn't seen for a few weeks, and will therefore be happier to be put down at night with a familiar babysitter. She will recognize the toys she enjoys, and maybe even vociferously request them with an urgent "uh-uh-uh" and a dramatically pointing finger.

I know that! Your baby may be able to gesture to things that you name in his favorite book.

Encourage her attempts to communicate by trying to figure out what she is saying and what she wants. It may involve a lot of holding up objects and saying "This?" but she will appreciate your efforts to understand her, and when you get it right you will be rewarded with a very big grin.

If you generally keep to a daily routine, your baby will come to recognize the stages of the routine. She understands much more of what you say now, and will love to become involved in what is going on. She may even adopt a bold grin when you hold up your camera! She recognizes what comes next, and she's game to do what is required.

Preventing tooth decay

The enamel on your baby's teeth is weaker than yours, and even a little sugar or inadequate oral hygiene can put her at risk of tooth decay.

Applying toothpaste Rub your baby's teeth with a little children's toothpaste to prevent buildup of bacteria (left). **Brushing teeth** Let your baby try brushing her teeth (right).

The most important thing to remember is that your baby doesn't yet have a full diet of solid food, and therefore she has less of the saliva that builds up when she eats (saliva helps to protect the teeth and make them stronger). For this reason, it is important to take steps to guard against tooth decay, and to give her teeth every opportunity to become strong and healthy.

Encourage your baby to eat foods that contain lots of calcium, which will help both her baby teeth and the next set of teeth develop properly. Leafy green vegetables and soy are the best sources, so try to include these in her daily diet. Of course, she will be getting plenty of calcium from her regular milk feedings too, but establishing healthy habits now allows her to become accustomed to eating the foods that will create strong teeth.

You should also clean your baby's teeth regularly and effectively (see p.212). Even if she doesn't have many teeth yet, rub or brush them with a little children's toothpaste and try to encourage her to spit it out. This will keep her teeth clean enough to prevent bacteria from building up, and will encourage strong enamel.

If you offer your baby an occasional sweet treat, do it at mealtimes because when she eats, saliva builds up to protect her teeth. Similarly, fruit juice should only be given with meals, to reduce the impact of the natural sugar in the juice on her teeth. In fact, anything that contains either natural or processed-and-added sugar should be given with meals, not between them. Snacks should be accompanied by water when at all possible, or milk, since the protein and calcium content of milk will help keep your baby's teeth healthy.

FLUORIDE AND BABIES

Fluoride is a natural mineral found in many foods and in drinking water. Fluoride promotes good dental health because it strengthens tooth enamel, making it more resistant to decay. It reduces the amount of acid that bacteria on your teeth produce. It can also prevent grooves from forming in teeth, reducing areas where plaque can collect. For these reasons, it's added to adult toothpaste to help make brushing more effective.

Fluoride has been added to water in some areas in Canada in an effort to improve dental health. Water fluoridation has been proven to reduce decay by 40–60 percent. However, it is not added in every area, so you'll need to check with your local water authority if you want to find out whether your supply is fluoridated.

When choosing a toothpaste for your baby, pick one that doesn't contain fluoride so it's safe for babies to swallow. Swallowing fluoridated toothpaste contributes to an elevated level of fluoride in the body, and babies and toddlers don't have the ability to spit out toothpaste. For this reason, experts recommend against using a fluoride toothpaste for children under two years old.

Too much fluoride isn't good for children either, and can cause discoloring of the teeth. For this reason, you should seek a product with "fluoride-free" on the label.

38 weeks

39 weeks

BABIES' GUMS ARE FAIRLY HARD, SO THEY CAN CHEW FINGER FOODS EVEN WITHOUT TEETH

Your clever baby will focus on your instructions and may even do what you ask if the request is simple and familiar. She'll understand much of what you say and has her own way of communicating with you. Her ability now to categorize allows her to compare new things with previous experiences.

Growing up fast

In nine months, your baby has evolved from a helpless newborn to an active, curious infant, trying out sounds ready for her first word.

Your baby may be two or three times the size that she was at birth, and the dramatic developments in her physical and cognitive skills are increasingly evident. Her milk-only diet has made way for a variety of foods as she progresses toward feeding herself. She is increasingly independent and happy to play on her own at times, and learns from her experiments and explorations on a constant basis. She's a willing communicator and likes nothing better than a good "chat" with Mom or Dad—or, indeed, anyone who will listen. While crying was once the only way for your baby to express her needs, signals, gestures, increasingly sophisticated sound combinations, and even an

occasional "real" word make up her new repertoire of communication skills. What's more, her ability to interact and respond to people shows a huge leap in her social competence, which has been fostered by her sensory awareness.

Your baby's gross motor skills have developed to the extent that she has learned to hold up her head and sit unassisted, and also discovered how to roll over, crawl (possibly), and perhaps pull herself up to stand. Her hand–eye coordination improves as her fine motor skills continue to mature, she can manipulate objects with both hands, and may be able to use her fingers efficiently.

If your baby seems slow to reach her milestones, you may wonder if she's

developing at the right rate. If she hasn't yet achieved the same social, language, cognitive, and gross and fine motor skills as her peers—or your other children—don't panic. All babies develop at different rates. However, if you are concerned that your baby doesn't seem to be reaching her milestones, speak with your pediatrician for reassurance or help.

If your baby was born prematurely, you can expect her to lag behind on some developmental tasks. This is entirely normal. Use your premature baby's adjusted age when you assess her development, and as with any developmental issues, seek advice if you're concerned.

DEVELOPMENT ACTIVITY

Puppet time

Your baby will love to watch a puppet show, and probably want to take part herself! Make a sock puppet using a felt-tipped marker to make eyes, or purchase an animal hand puppet. Make the puppet play hide and seek behind a cushion, and laugh, cry, and even tickle your baby! Pop your baby's hand in the puppet and show her how it works. Finger puppets are ideal for playtime, and can easily slip onto your baby's little hands. Make your finger puppet dance, whisper, giggle, shout, and jump up and down, and ask your baby if her puppet can do these things, too. Puppets encourage creativity and imaginative play and help concentration and visual skills.

Was that a quack? Puppet games are great fun for your baby, and he won't even notice if your skills as a ventriloquist aren't up to snuff.

Stage three solids—a varied diet

As soon as your baby is enjoying a variety of puréed foods, she's ready to move on to the third stage of solids. Now she'll be introduced to a greater range of foods as well as new textures and some finger foods.

CHECKLIST

Three meals a day

It's time to introduce more lumps, and new textures, flavors, and finger foods.

■ **Protein** Your baby should have at least three servings of protein each day. One serving is approximately 1¾ oz (40 g). Sources include egg yolks, meat, fish (check for bones), tofu, legumes, and seeds.

■ **Fats** About half her calories come from fat, some from her milk. Include healthy fats such as avocado, olive oil, and full-fat dairy products (no cow's milk until 1 year).

■ **Fruit and vegetables** Aim for five servings per day.

■ **Carbohydrates** Your baby should have approximately three servings a day. Include cereals, bread, pasta, couscous, potatoes, rice, pita.

■ **Consistency** Mashed, chopped, and ground foods with larger lumps.

■ **How often?** Three meals a day, plus snacks.

■ **How much** Be guided by your baby; she may be hungrier on certain days. Start with a small amount so she isn't overwhelmed, and give her more if she wants it. Keep in mind that she's not likely to be hungry if she's having more than two milk feedings a day (see p.291).

Expand your baby's diet Once your baby is happy with solids, it's important to introduce a variety of textures and combined flavors.

The third and final stage of introducing solids basically involves continuing with all the good work you've done so far, but adding more texture to your baby's meals—in the form of bigger lumps and foods she needs to chew—as well as a wider range of flavors.

Your baby will now be familiar with a range of different tastes and should be able to eat some finger foods as well as enjoy mashed meals. She may also be able to drink water from a lidded cup.

In this third stage, which is generally from about nine months, you can introduce finely chopped or ground foods as well as finger foods since she'll be able to bite and chew more confidently. Some babies will also be very happy trying to feed themselves at this stage even if the result is quite messy. Although she will be happy holding a spoon, the dexterity required to find her own mouth without spilling the contents comes later on in her second year, so don't expect success overnight. Some babies like to eat meals composed of finger foods, which they can hold more easily than a wobbly spoon that seems to have a mind of its own. However, it is good to let your baby experiment with a spoon since it's an important skill to master.

Your baby should now be eating three meals a day, plus snacks, and sampling a wide variety of different foods. If you're still mostly spoon-feeding, you shouldn't need to do much more than roughly mash the food with a fork first; by nine months, you should really only be chopping up or food processing the bigger lumps.

Whether you're spoon-feeding or taking the baby-led solids approach, you can also now take advantage of your baby's fast-developing pincer grip (the ability to bring her thumb and first finger together to pick things up) to give her smaller finger foods, such as peas, and halved cherry tomatoes or grapes. Or something altogether squishier.

Good eating habits for life At this stage, it's important to introduce your baby to more complex recipes that combine different flavors, as well as herbs and spices. Simply adding a sprinkle of mixed herbs to spaghetti marinara, for example, can turn a bland meal into something new and exciting for your baby. Hot spices may be difficult for babies to manage, but other fragrant options, such as coriander, cinnamon, lemongrass, thyme, and basil, are all good options. And broadening your baby's palate now can help to make her less fussy about her food in future.

Meals like chicken pot pie, tuna salad, and casseroles provide an appealing mix of flavors, as do mixed fruit desserts, and fruity breakfasts. Dishes that contain different combinations of ingredients add variety to your baby's diet, and help to educate her taste buds.

Just remember, as you start to mix up the menu and offer your baby more family meals, that your baby's nutritional needs are very different than those of an adult. Unlike you, your baby still needs plenty of fat in her diet because she is growing so fast and fat is the most concentrated source of energy. Also, she shouldn't have too much fiber—a low-calorie, bulky material, it will fill her stomach, but it won't give her all the calories she needs. (For more information on good nutrition for babies, see page 207.)

Following your lead Of course, the best way for your baby to learn to eat and enjoy new foods is by copying you. This is one reason why it's a good idea to sit down and eat as a family so that you can lead by example and spend valuable time together. Your baby is much more likely to try a new food if she sees you or one of her siblings eating it. She'll also learn something about table manners as well as enjoying the social aspects of mealtimes. Try to keep mealtimes fun and enjoyable, and don't push your baby to eat or try new foods if she really doesn't want to. Praise her for eating, even if she only manages to eat a small amount, and if she rejects a particular food or doesn't want any more, take it away without commenting on it.

Studies show that children who eat with their parents regularly have a much better idea of which foods are healthy and are more likely to be adventurous eaters.

MEAL IDEAS FOR OLDER BABIES

Breakfast
- Oatmeal or unsweetened cereal with breast milk or formula and banana
- Toast, sliced into "fingers," with hard-boiled egg yolk and slices of fruit, such as peach or pineapple
- Puréed apple, organic yogurt, and unsweetened cereal

Lunch
- Baked potato with yogurt and grated zucchini
- Small bites: for example, sliced cherry tomatoes, pita bread, cucumber sticks, and hummus
- Low salt-and-sugar baked beans and toast
- Mini sandwiches: for fillings, hard-boiled egg yolk or chopped chicken and a little mayonnaise or yogurt instead
- Spaghetti with tomato and basil sauce
- Homemade tomato soup with soft bread sticks
- Pita with chopped cherry tomatoes and cucumber
- Fish (check for bones) or chicken fingers with carrots and tomato sauce mixed in or for dipping the chicken
- Bread sticks and vegetable crudités with fresh dips

Dinner
- Ground or chopped meat, mashed potatoes, and carrots
- Fish sticks, peas, and mashed potatoes
- Chicken casserole and rice and peas or broccoli
- Vegetable risotto or pasta
- Beef or lentil burgers, zucchini, sliced tomato, and boiled potatoes
- Baked chicken with cooked carrots and rice
- Meatballs with broccoli and carrots
- Poached salmon with rice and vegetables
- Chicken and vegetable kebabs

Happy meals Baby oatmeal with milk, yogurt, and banana (left); fillet of fish with cheese and vegetable sauce (center); and pasta with Bolognese sauce (right) provide the proteins, carbohydrates, fats, and vitamins and minerals that your baby needs as part of her daily diet.

Feeling displaced

If you're back at work, you may be a little envious that your baby's caregiver is able to witness your baby's milestones before you do.

The relationship between you and your baby's caregiver is important, and you will need to nurture it, no matter how you are feeling about her (or his) relationship with your baby (see p.295). If she is an experienced and professional caregiver, she will be aware that you may be struggling with a variety of emotions, so it's a good idea to express how you are feeling. To help you feel close to your baby, ask your caregiver to keep you up-to-date with everything that occurs in her day, even if it means calling you at work to celebrate a new achievement.

Make it clear that you respect and appreciate the efforts your baby's caregiver makes and comment positively on what she has taught your baby. If you begin to feel a little left out, remind yourself that your baby is with you many more hours than she is with a caregiver.

Don't be surprised if your baby fusses or even cries sometimes when you come to pick her up. The transition moments between her caregiver and parent can be stressful for her, no matter how much she has anticipated your coming to get her. You may be interrupting her play or

a nap; she may be feeling comfortable where she is, and doesn't want to be wrapped up and moved. Take your time at the changeover, hold her while you ask her caregiver how the day was, and get into the habit of waving goodbye to mark the end of her time with her caregiver.

Once you've picked her up, try to spend some one-on-one time together, even if there are other jobs to do. She'll appreciate some mom or dad time now. Be reassured that most parents feel some degree of guilt about spending time away from their baby; you are not alone.

What's that word?

You may find that your baby has her own words for familiar objects. For example, point to her comfort item to see what she calls it.

What's that up there? Ask your baby to tell you his words for everyday objects.

If your baby repeats a sound each time you show her an item, chances are she's developed her own word for it. It's common for babies to blend some of the sounds from the name for an object to create an identifiable "word." She may call her bottle a "baba" and call you "mop;" she may say "mi-mi" for milk or "dob" for the dog. Encourage her to name things, and applaud her efforts. Listen carefully for patterns in her speech—do the same "words" crop up regularly? What is she trying to tell you?

Your baby may become frustrated when she tries to communicate with you, pointing and repeating her words to try to get her message across.

To ease her frustration, hold up familiar items such as her plate, her blanket, or her cuddly toy to hear what she calls them. Repeat her words and give her the correct word as well. For example, say "Yes! Dob! This is the dog!"

Give your baby opportunities to practice her new words. Ask her to point to different objects in a picture book. Give her the correct words and see how she responds. If you've been practicing your animal sounds together, she may actually use the noise that an animal makes rather than attempt to say its name. Celebrate the fact that she is linking words and sounds with objects, and encourage her to continue.

Family vacations

Vacations with your older baby can be fun. As long as you are well prepared, she'll love having an adventure with her family.

Go prepared Pack your baby's essentials in a diaper bag that you can carry with you.

Many babies feel unsettled in a new environment, so it is a good idea to take a few of your baby's familiar toys when you go on vacation, to comfort her and keep her occupied at your destination. Pack some toys and books into your hand luggage, too, to distract her while you are in transit. If you are staying in a hotel that provides a crib, or taking a travel crib with you, take your baby's usual sleeping bag—she may find it easier to sleep in a different place if there is something familiar about it. Let her play in her new bed before you settle her down, so that when she wakes up at night she will know where she is.

Milk and food If your baby is bottle-fed and you are going abroad, take a supply of her regular formula in case you can't find the same brand at your destination.

You might also worry about which solid foods she's going to be able to eat while on vacation. If she's used to jars or pouches of food, take a few with you so she still has some familiar meals as she adjusts to a new place and different food. These also serve as a standby in case of emergencies. Individual containers of fruit purée usually appeal to most babies, and if there is a fridge at your destination, you can chill some of these treats for her.

Pack a few favorite snacks, too, such as baby bread sticks and rice cakes. Small boxes of baby breakfast cereal may also be useful.

You should be able to buy bread, fruit, and vegetables wherever you are. Also, rice, noodles, or pasta (served plain, if requested) are usually easy to get hold of in most restaurants. Between local supermarkets, markets, and Mom and Dad's plates, it's usually fairly easy to cobble together enough for your baby to get by on. Fresh fruit and vegetables purchased in their country of origin are also particularly delicious—and you may be able to tempt a fussy baby to expand her palate by offering her tastes of fresh local produce.

Sensible precautions Wash the fruit and vegetables carefully with bottled water, and peel fruit when possible. If you buy bottled water for your baby, make sure it's low in sodium. If you order a poultry or meat dish from a restaurant, always check that it is thoroughly cooked before letting your baby try any.

On arrival at your accommodation, check for potential hazards. If your baby is crawling, starting to stand, or even

cruising, look to see if there are any steps she might fall down, wires or cords that she may grab, accessible electrical outlets, unstable furniture, or anything else that could lead to an accident. If you are concerned about your baby's safety, speak to someone in charge. If there's a bona fide safety issue, your hosts should take it seriously. Finally, don't forget to take your travel insurance details, including emergency phone numbers, along with passports and other travel documents.

On page 131, you'll find lots of tips

> **CHECKLIST**
>
> ## Useful extras
>
> On page 131, you'll find lots of tips for traveling with a young baby. Now that she is a little older, you may want to include some additional items when packing, such as the following:
>
> ■ A sunshade for the car, and a shade or umbrella for the beach
>
> ■ A first-aid kit with some infant acetaminophen and teething gel
>
> ■ A baby monitor or night-light
>
> ■ A canopy for her stroller
>
> ■ A baby backpack carrier
>
> ■ Stroller books and stroller toys
>
> ■ A universal bath plug that fits all plug holes so that a shower can be turned into a bath
>
> ■ Some laundry detergent to clean her clothes after messy meals.

39 weeks

Shining locks

From a fine downy covering to a mass of unruly tangles, babies' hair grows very differently and so needs caring for accordingly.

During their first year, most babies lose their soft downy hair as new, thicker hair grows. However, as with all things baby related, there's huge variation. Some babies might still have very little hair at nine, or even 12, months; others may have a mop of unruly curls, or hair down to their shoulders. If your baby is still lacking in the follicle department, don't worry—the hair will grow, and at least for the time being, it's easy to take care of. A wash with a gentle shampoo a

This is the way ... we brush our hair. Make routines more fun by involving your baby and making her an active participant.

couple of times a week, and a brush with a soft-bristled brush, is all that's needed.

For parents of babies with lots of hair, particularly if it's curly, taking care of it can be more of a challenge. Use a small amount of conditioner after a shampoo and rinse, and then comb through with a fine-toothed comb to ease out tangles.

Thick, coarse, curly, or wavy hair requires special care because of its texture and curl pattern. It needs to be treated gently because the hair can be dry and prone to breakage. Overwashing can also strip the hair of its oils, leaving it brittle and frizzy, so it's best not to wash it more than once a week.

Hot and cold

Your baby's body is now better able to regulate its temperature, but you still need to make sure she doesn't overheat or become too cold.

At 39 weeks, your baby will be good at letting you know if she is uncomfortable. She may pull at her clothes or become irritable if she's too hot, or climb onto your lap to snuggle up with her favorite blanket if it's chilly.

In cold weather, dress your baby with the same number of layers you put on yourself. When she's in her stroller, she'll be less active than you and will probably feel cold more easily, so pop a hat on her head and tuck a blanket around her. Padded booties or a double layer of socks will keep her feet warm inside her stroller blanket. She's not likely to enjoy

wearing mittens since she will want to practice her hand skills all the time, but if it's cold enough for you to need gloves, she should have them too. Choose a jacket with attached mittens that she won't be able to unfasten herself.

When it's hot, allow your baby to play outdoors in just a hat, onesie, and diaper, or dispense with the onesie. If she's in the shade and wearing sunscreen and a hat, she doesn't need to be fully covered. If her face is red, she seems damp and clammy, or pokes her tongue in and out frequently, she may be too hot. Give her a drink and remove a layer of clothing.

AS A MATTER OF FACT

Key temperatures

The temperature of your baby's bedroom should be kept somewhere between 61°F (16°C) and 68°F (20°C). Your baby's bath water should be at a temperature of about 98.6°F (37°C). A "normal" temperature for a healthy baby is 98.6°F (37°C) when taken in the mouth. This can be up to one degree lower when measured from the armpit.

Your baby's memory

Since birth, your baby's memory has come a long way. She remembers many things and retains information for increasing amounts of time.

I know that face! Your baby's face may light up when he sees someone he remembers, particularly if it is someone he likes!

Your newborn baby operated primarily by reflex, and while your smell, touch, and voice would be familiar, out of sight was, quite literally, out of mind. From there, her memory has developed gradually.

One of the first things your baby remembered was your face, which allowed her to form a strong bond with you. Before she was six months old, she began to remember things that were significant to her on a short-term basis. This was evident in her ability to anticipate certain actions and events, indicating that she was drawing from her memory. For example, she would know what was about to happen next when her book was brought out or you sat her down in her high chair for a meal, and she may have shown excitement at seeing her comfort object or a favorite toy.

By the time your baby was six months old, she recognized you and your partner as the most important people in her life, and by now she turns if you call her name, indicating that she remembers that this sound refers to her. She will recognize familiar objects, too, and will remember where her toys are stored, or where her snacks are kept, and will recognize familiar faces and everyday routines.

There are, of course, some disadvantages to her developing a memory. For example, she may remember that she hates having her hair washed and begin to fuss and wiggle the moment she hears the bath water running.

Developing long-term memory The development of your baby's memory is such that she has a steadily increasing ability to store and recall new information. The more she sees and experiences something, the more likely she will be to recall it.

She is also gradually increasing the amount of time she can hold a memory. For example, if she sees her grandparents infrequently, she may recognize them immediately if she sees them again within a month, but will probably take a moment or two and/or need a reminder if it's been a longer break than this. How much your baby remembers can depend on various factors, such as familiarity and the reminders she receives about certain pieces of information.

DEVELOPMENT ACTIVITY

Messy play

Your baby is interested in textures, consistency, and generally getting her hands dirty. You'll already notice she wants to put her fingers into her food, stirring it around, squeezing it, and patting it on the high-chair tray. She may also enjoy smearing it on her face and clothes. This playfulness with different consistencies is all part of understanding the properties of familiar items in her world so that, eventually, she'll be able to predict or anticipate how things feel. Give her some sloppy oatmeal or springy jelly; let her pull the leaves off brussels sprouts or push her hands into pliable pastry dough—it's all about learning how things look and feel.

Flour power Making lots of mess with foodstuffs is not only fun but teaches your baby about texture and form.

39 weeks

315

Your baby at 10 to 12 months

To the point Your baby is refining her hand movements and will begin to use her index finger, rather than her whole arm, to point at things.

Self-feeding Your baby won't have the dexterity to be able to feed herself with a spoon for a while yet, but she'll enjoy giving it a try.

First words There might be one or two words that your baby says regularly now—whatever the sound is, if she uses it often, with meaning ("bah" for her bottle, for example), it counts as a word. You might hear "dada" and "mama" said with meaning now, too.

Did you know? Your baby will recognize her name—but it may be a while before she can say it herself.

Upsy daisy Standing with support is fine but your baby may land with a bump if you let go. Once she gets a feel for balancing on her legs, she'll stand alone momentarily.

Emotional outbursts At this age, babies may cry from frustration at not being able to master something. Emotions often feel overwhelming, so calm, patient handling is key.

Turning the page Your baby may be able to turn the pages of a chunky board book now, and will enjoy looking at clear, simple pictures as well as lifting flaps.

Your baby is now a social little person with a host of new skills and the beginnings of control over her body.

Using a crayon With your help, your baby will be able to hold and move a chunky crayon across a piece of paper to create his first marks.

Complex play Through activities like stacking, sorting, and opening, babies learn about the world, including how objects relate to each other, balance, fall over, and move.

Understanding "no" Your baby is beginning to realize what "no" means but he won't always cooperate. He's more likely to think it's a game!

Did you know? A few babies take their first independent steps during their first year, but for most this happens during the second year.

Clap hands Your baby can make her arms and hands work together and flatten her palms to clap, and she'll do this to express enjoyment.

Social baby Your baby sees her peers as objects for now and wants to know how they look and feel.

Standing alone Standing for a moment without any support is a huge breakthrough for your baby.

40 weeks

SEPARATION ANXIETY IS USUALLY STRONGEST BETWEEN THE AGES OF 10 AND 18 MONTHS

Your baby can use both hands simultaneously with confidence, and is proud to show off her skills to you. Give her plenty of praise for her achievements. She's now eating a wider range of more solid foods and, naturally social, she will enjoy and benefit from family meals together.

It's just baby's way

As your baby grows up, there are occasions when he might be less cooperative than you would like. Patience will be required…

Hats off! You put the hat on. Your baby takes it off. It's a great game for him and a test of patience for you—especially if you're about to go out and want to keep the sun off his head!

Gone are the days when your baby was more or less an extension of you, easily carried around in a baby carrier or popped in the stroller fast asleep. Now he has a mind of his own and, although he won't be striving for his own independence just yet, he's certainly capable of objecting to or taking an instant dislike to something you are trying to do. Life can suddenly seem bumpier, and you may find yourself getting irritated when your baby isn't doing what you want him to do.

Perhaps you want him to have his hat/socks/booties on and he keeps taking them off, or he's objecting to having his diaper changed or his coat put on, or he keeps emptying his food bowl all over the floor. There may be days when you feel that your patience is being sorely tested. However, it's important to keep a sense of perspective and remember that your baby—even

though he seems to have developed quickly all of a sudden—is still very much a baby and doesn't mean to be difficult.

Allowing extra time Try to build some time into your routine so that if your baby doesn't cooperate right away, you don't become flustered because you're under pressure to be somewhere.

Try to respect his wishes when you can—if he doesn't really need his socks on and you can cover his feet with a blanket, let it go. If he prefers a cozy cardigan to being buttoned up in a coat, take the easy option. If he becomes frustrated, offer help; if he pushes you away, let him experiment and try to achieve whatever he's trying to do.

Above all, don't get angry with him. He won't understand and he'll be upset by it. Try to see the funny side and don't expect too much of your baby—after all he is only nine months old.

DEVELOPMENT ACTIVITY

Pick it up

At around 10 months, your baby's pincer grip (see p.339) is fully developed. You'll find he uses his fingers to "rake" small items that he wants to hold until he has positioned them so that he can pick them up between his thumb and forefinger. Mealtimes provide the perfect opportunity for practice— a small piece of soft fruit or lightly cooked vegetables put on his tray are tempting treats to pick up. Place two or three pieces at a time on your baby's tray and let him pick them up and release them into his mouth by himself. He'll enjoy dropping everything onto the floor from his high chair. This activity is also known as "casting," and to your baby it's great fun.

Pincer grip Your baby may now be adept at picking things up between finger and thumb, and will use this skill repeatedly.

Consistent nap times

One of the keys to ensuring that your baby sleeps through the night is to give him consistent nap times during the day.

Although at 10 months babies can manage with little shifts in their routine for the occasional day out, it's important that, by and large, nap times are consistent and that your baby gets a good quality sleep when he naps. If he is overtired by the time you put him down at bedtime, he'll be harder to settle down and may become upset at night.

Most babies at this age need at least one long nap a day, usually after lunch, or sometimes two—a shorter one in the morning and a longer nap in the afternoon. If these naps are well-scheduled (timed to coincide with your baby's signs of sleepiness) and of a good length (two to three hours in total), your baby should be able to make it through to bedtime without becoming overtired, then sleep well at night.

A consistent nap-time routine that is similar, but not identical, to your baby's bedtime routine is also important. For example, dim the lights and sing a lullaby, but perhaps leave the bedtime story for the evening. Keep the same pattern every day so your baby learns to anticipate that nap time is coming and prepares for it, so that he's more likely to settle in happily and fall asleep quickly.

Good-quality naps Your nine-month-old baby needs one or two good naps every day.

Going naked

Our ancestors would be amazed at how we wrap up our babies. When cold isn't a factor, it can do a baby good to go naked at times.

AS A MATTER OF FACT

The babies of our ancestors had very little in the way of clothing—in the Middle Ages, for example, cloth was considered a luxury. Babies were usually swaddled in linen strips until they were old enough to sit up on their own. Then they were often simply naked, or wrapped in blankets if it was cold. They may have been clad in simple gowns. It wasn't until the 18th century that baby boys were dressed in jumpsuits and girls in simple shift dresses.

Your baby will love some diaper-free time every day if you can manage it. For obvious reasons, summertime is best to do this, although just before bathtime in the safety of a well-heated and tiled bathroom is good at any time of year. If you have carpet throughout your home, you could invest in a waterproof mat, covering it with a couple of towels so that accidents are soaked up quickly.

Giving your baby two or three short diaper-free periods each day will help prevent, or clear up, diaper rash. It will also enable your baby to become familiar with the sensations of urinating and a bowel movement, which means that, in time, he will learn what it feels like just before he needs to go. He will love the sensation of being unencumbered by the trappings of his diaper, and if he is without his clothes, too, all the better.

Some experts believe that diaper-free time every day does hasten the process of toilet training. Although that might be a happy end-product of daily diaper-free time, don't make it the reason. Toilet training will come in good time. Your baby is still very young, and his diaper-free hour should be nothing more than an opportunity for him to get a sense of freedom in his body, and for his bottom to get a good airing!

Eating as a family

Your 40-week-old baby will benefit from regular family meals. This will encourage good eating habits and a willingness to try new foods.

It might not be practical to sit down as a family to eat all the time, but try to do it a few times during the week and also when you have more time on the weekend. Babies are social and they tend to be less choosy in their eating habits when everyone is around the table together. If your baby sees his family eating foods he hasn't tried, he'll be more willing to try them himself. Offer him appropriate foods from your plate, and if you can, make meals that you can all eat.

Your baby will see you using cutlery, drinking from cups or glasses, and perhaps using napkins. He'll notice that you don't throw your bowl across the room, and that family members may ask to leave the table and help with the dishes. Although he won't develop these types of social skills for years, you are providing him with an excellent example of how people eat together and the kind of behavior and manners that are expected. Keep mealtimes cheerful. It's best if you don't use the time for heated debates, and remember that your baby is a great observer, so if you set different rules regarding eating for different children, he will notice.

Involve your baby in social or larger family meal gatherings—perhaps on holidays or festive occasions, anniversaries, or birthdays. Even though he may be naturally wary of strangers, the more opportunities he has to meet new people and experience new environments, with you at his side, the more confident he will become. Different people, exposure to a variety of foods, and conversation will be stimulating and fun for everyone, baby included.

Social mealtimes Family meals offer a good opportunity for interaction. Your baby will observe your table manners, and when she sees you eating something she's more likely to want to try it.

CHECKLIST

Family meals

There are many family meals your baby can eat too, remembering that he shouldn't have salt and sugar added to his portion, or hot spices and some condiments, such as strong mustard or vinegar, which may upset his tummy. Make sure the texture is right for him by puréeing, mashing, or finely chopping. Ideas for baby-friendly family meals include:

■ Chicken pot pie with vegetables and a crust on top.

■ Thick vegetable or lentil-based soup with toast cut into strips.

■ Baked chicken or fish with spinach or peas and potatoes.

■ Homemade meatballs in tomato sauce with noodles or rice (if you blend the meat finely and make the meatballs small enough, he can eat them as finger foods).

■ Broccoli, carrots, or cauliflower and tofu with a puréed red pepper dipping sauce.

■ Pasta with tomato sauce.

■ Lamb burgers with avocado (form his patties into small, firm balls and mash avocado, or leave in slices).

■ Meat and bean pie—be careful with stocks, which are high in salt.

■ Mashed lentils with rice (avoid spices and pastes that contain salt).

40 weeks

YOUR BABY IS 40 WEEKS AND 4 DAYS

Wary of strangers

It's common for even the most social of babies to become fearful and uncomfortable in the presence of strangers around this time.

Your baby's anxiety about strangers and separating from you may become more intense now. He understands that his relationship with you is special, and that other people need to be treated with caution. This is a perfectly normal and important part of his social development. Instead of beaming with pleasure when he sees the lady at the supermarket check-out counter, he may cry, cover his eyes, and cling to you.

This can be a tricky time for close family and friends, who may feel rejected by your baby's sudden refusal to go to them. Try not to be embarrassed if your baby fails to be sunny, cheerful, and social. Reassure them that this is a normal stage of development called separation anxiety (see p.283), which can last, in some form, until age three.

Let your baby go at his own pace. Introduce him to social situations slowly, and reassure him constantly, using a low, gentle voice. Give him time to warm up around strangers before you pass him to someone to be held. If he really doesn't want to go to someone, don't force the issue. If you feel the need, explain to strangers that he's not comfortable with people he doesn't know right now, and not to take it personally. Show them a few tricks that always make your baby laugh, to relax him and help him make positive associations. Even if he only wants to be held by you, let him meet new people—he may feel fearful and uncomfortable at first, but he needs to get used to noisy environments and new faces. As long as you are there, reassuring him, it will help to build his confidence. Above all, be positive and social in the company of others. If he sees that you are relaxed and having fun, he'll soon realize that there's nothing to worry about.

YOUR BABY IS 40 WEEKS AND 5 DAYS

Lots of laughing

Laughter is a developmental milestone—it shows your baby can respond positively to stimuli and is developing a sense of humor.

Socialization depends upon your baby's ability to interact with others. His finding something funny is the clearest sign you have that he enjoys the company and actions of those around him. He has probably been able to let out at least a little giggle since he was about three months old (some babies' first laugh comes as young as eight weeks) but, at 40 weeks, his giggles may have actually turned into full-blown belly laughs.

All sorts of silly behavior will leave your baby in helpless laughter—blowing raspberries on him, tickling his thighs, or pretending that his feet are very smelly (which is often a winner). Since he is now better able to read other people's expressions and feelings, he will love it that his feet have made you make a face and groan in horror. You'll probably find that he thrusts them into your face for you to repeat the act over and over again. And when you find something that makes your baby giggle uncontrollably, you'll want to repeat it, too—because, for most parents, your baby's laughter is among the most wonderful, uplifting sounds in the world.

Stinky! Try tickling your baby's funny bone by pretending that his feet are really smelly—he may find it hysterical!

What's my baby eating?

Your baby can now eat food that is more like your meals. He may eat three meals a day with snacks, and can tolerate lumpier textures.

Now is the perfect time to introduce a wider range of finger foods into your baby's diet. Other than finger foods, the rest of your baby's food will be mashed, and you can progress to giving him cut-up chunks of food (see Stage three solids, pp.310–311).

Your baby will probably have a few teeth by now, and his jaw and tongue have developed enough to allow him to "gum," chew, and swallow food efficiently. The more lumps, bumps, and different textures he is given, the less likely he is to become a fussy eater.

Mashing together vegetables, rather than using a food procesor, is a good way of providing plenty of texture. Babies seem particularly to enjoy mashed root vegetables. You can also mash well-cooked and raw fruits, or several vegetables and/or fruits together. Finely grinding foods such as meat also produces pieces that have a little bite, but are soft enough to be chewed and swallowed by your baby.

Once ground and mashed foods are acceptable, finely cut and chop your baby's food. As he becomes accustomed to eating food in pieces, gradually increase their size. Some babies prefer large identifiable chunks to smaller lumps that take them by surprise.

Variety of textures Work toward the point at which, at mealtimes, you can give your baby a dish made up of all sorts of different textures for him to enjoy. For example, you could mince chicken, mash his potatoes and carrots, and give corn pieces as finger food. Or try blending together some spinach with some nutmeg, and serve this alongside

baked or poached chicken or fish, pasta shapes, and lightly steamed green beans or broccoli florets for your baby to pick up and chew.

By the end of your baby's first year, he will be eating three meals a day, although the amount of food he eats at each meal can vary considerably. If he finds breakfast difficult to manage, you may want to feed him less milk first thing in the morning so that he has more room in his tummy for breakfast. If he still has a milk feeding during the day, give it after a meal, and not before, or he won't be hungry enough to eat what you're giving him.

Try to encourage your baby to eat three nutritious meals a day now, with a couple of healthy snacks between meals. Don't worry if he doesn't eat everything at every meal. As long as you give him balanced meals and snacks throughout the day, he will be getting the nutrition that he needs.

Changing diet Solid foods now become more important in your baby's diet, and the food she eats is much more like your own food.

ASK A... PEDIATRICIAN

My baby won't breast-feed. What should I do? As he gets older, he's likely to be more easily distracted from feeding by all the things going on around him, and may feel impatient with how long a feeding takes. Usually, the problem is temporary. Try the following tactics to get your baby interested in feeding: feed him away from the action, since he may settle down once the distractions are removed; feed him when he is sleepy and less likely to be distracted; offer a little skin-to-skin

contact to encourage him to recall positive early bonding experiences; feed him when he is most relaxed and when he is in his favorite, familiar spot. Continue to give feedings around the usual times, working around his mealtimes, and begin a session by rubbing a little breast milk on his lips. He may just need to be reminded about how nice it all is. If all else fails, offer him breast milk in a cup or bottle and express regularly to keep up your supply. Eventually, you'll be able to coax him back.

40 weeks

323

41 weeks

WHEN CRUISING, YOUR BABY MAY LET GO OF HER SUPPORT FOR A FEW SECONDS!

Your baby can entertain herself for longer periods, giving you a welcome break! However, her increasing independence also means that she will try to test you. While protecting her from danger, be firm about what she can and can't do. Always praise her for good behavior, such as giving up a toy.

Breast-feeding and your body

Breast-feeding doesn't change the shape or size of your breasts—it's pregnancy that's to blame. But there's good news for your breasts…

Accepting changes Embrace the changes caused by pregnancy and breast-feeding and respect the body that has nurtured your baby.

During pregnancy, a surge in hormones causes your breasts to increase in size. They stay like this throughout pregnancy, and if you breast-feed, will stay this size more or less until you're baby is weaned. (If you don't breast-feed, your breasts will return to their pre-pregnancy size a few weeks after giving birth.)

Your breasts don't contain any muscle, but are attached to the muscles of your chest wall by thin ligaments. As your breasts increase in size, these supportive ligaments may stretch, which happens regardless of whether or not you breast-feed. If you gained a lot of weight during pregnancy, and go on to lose it, this can have an effect on your breasts, too. It's important to wear a properly fitting nursing bra when breast-feeding to support your breasts.

Your breasts are made up of fatty tissue, so if you gain weight your breasts will grow larger, and if you lose it, they shrink. The amount they shrink should be in proportion to your weight loss, so if you become slimmer than you were prior to pregnancy, your breasts are likely to be smaller than they were, too.

Your breasts might be a little less firm when you stop feeding, but there is some good news. In the six months or so after stopping, fatty tissue will gradually replace the milk-producing tissue in your breasts, which leaves your breasts feeling fuller. Exercising your pectoral muscles (see box, below) can help your breasts become firmer and more lifted. Well-hydrated skin has more elasticity and looks smoother, so drink plenty of water and use moisturizer to keep your neck line feeling soft and supple.

Get re-measured by a professional bra fitter when you stop nursing in case your breast size has changed.

STRENGTHENING YOUR PECTORALS FOR A FIRMER BUSTLINE

A pair of handheld weights or a couple of small bottles of water will help you get the best results with some of the techniques below.

Push-ups If you're new to push-ups, place your hands on the floor, extend your legs out behind you, and rest your knees on the floor. Cross your ankles. Support yourself on your arms, keeping your back straight. Bend your elbows to lower your upper body so that your nose touches the ground, then straighten your arms to raise yourself again. Repeat 10 times, rest, then do another 10 times. If you are concerned about straining your abdominals or uterus, try an inverted push-up. Stand facing a wall with your arms outstretched and palms placed on the wall at shoulder height. Gently bend your elbows to move your body toward the wall, then straighten them to return to the starting position.

Chest press Lie on your back with your arms above you, elbows slightly bent, and a weight in each hand. Slowly and deliberately lower your arms out to the sides, keeping your elbows bent, until your fists hover over the ground. Raise your arms to your starting position. Do 15 repetitions, rest, then do 15 more.

Overhead press Stay on your back with a weight in each hand, arms above you, elbows slightly bent. Gently lower your arms over your head until you feel the weight, touch the floor behind your head, then bring your arms back up to the starting position. Do 15 repetitions, rest, then do 15 more.

Chest stretch To wind down, stretch the muscles you have been exercising. Sit with your back straight and hold your hands behind your back, bringing your shoulder blades together to open up your chest. Hold for a count of 10, then release.

Shopping with your baby

Any parent knows that supermarket shopping with baby in tow can be a trial, so here are some ways to navigate the aisles without tears.

Write a shopping list before you go. If you know the supermarket layout, you can write your list in the order of the aisles you visit so that you're super efficient when you get there!

Plan your shopping around meal and nap times so that your baby isn't either too hungry or too cranky. Try to avoid going at peak times, so that you don't have to negotiate long lines at the checkout counter. Take a snack, such as some rice cakes or a bread stick, that he can munch on as you're walking around. If you're putting him in the baby seat of the shopping cart, make sure the harness is safely fastened. Bring a couple of his stroller toys, too, that you can attach to the shopping cart to keep him amused. Also, park as close as you can to the supermarket entrance and cart bay, so that you only have to cover a short distance to return the shopping cart after loading the car. This could be a lifesaver if your baby is not being particularly cooperative. Last but not least, try to make the experience fun and interesting for your baby by involving him. For instance, pick up a pineapple, explain what it is, and let him touch it before you put it in the cart. Keep talking to him as you walk around the supermarket, and praise him, touch his hand, and make plenty of eye contact with him to let him know that you're happy that he's sitting nicely in the shopping cart.

You can let me go...

If your baby had already started to move around gingerly while holding onto furniture, he may begin to cruise more confidently now.

I'm almost off Once your baby learns to walk, his feet will be set fairly far apart to provide stability, causing him, quite literally, to toddle.

Long before your baby is able to set off and take those first momentous steps, he needs to be able to stand confidently, eventually standing all by himself without support. Once he's mastered this balancing act, he'll feel more confident about putting one foot in front of the other.

The average age for babies taking their first steps is 13 months. Before this time, your baby will be concentrating on spending lots of time pulling up to a stand, and becoming an increasingly confident cruiser. By now, he may be very happy working his way around the room holding onto furniture, and may stand more upright, leaving a larger gap between his body and the furniture as his confidence grows. At some point, he may even let go momentarily and stand with no support at all.

While you will want to wait until your baby is really walking to buy his first pair of sturdy outdoor shoes, there are plenty of soft shoes available that can be ideal for your baby around now, especially when he is outside (see p.328).

Try not to worry if your baby seems to prefer other methods of getting around, such as bottom shuffling. As long as he is showing an interest in being mobile, then he is fine. Many bottom shufflers are so proficient that they show less interest in walking than other babies.

Home safety checks

With your increasingly mobile baby often on the prowl, it's a good idea to reassess your babyproofing to make sure he is safe from harm.

Safety locks Cabinet locks help to keep little explorers away from hazardous substances.

The best way to keep your home as safe as you can for your baby is to get down on your hands and knees and look at it from his height. If there are loose wires, tuck or tape them away; buy safety plugs to fill outlets; and look for any head-height edges and corners that might cause bumps or cuts. Babies often use the space between the door and the frame on the hinged side to hang on to, because their little fingers can fit in the gap—if the door swings closed, fingers get squashed. Invest in doorstops to hold doors open to prevent little fingers from getting trapped.

Leave floor spaces clear by removing rugs, if you have them, for the time being. It might also be a good idea to put away your coffee table temporarily. Not only will it have sharp corners and edges but, inevitably, drinks will be left on it, presenting spilling hazards and, in the case of hot drinks, the possibility of scalding.

Buy a cover for your oven door if your baby can reach it, and put child locks on cabinets that contain items such as knives and chemicals. Also, unplug hair dryers or straighteners and avoid leaving them lying around to cool.

Keep the washing machine, dryer, and dishwasher doors firmly closed so that he can't open them and climb in. Internal glass doors should contain safety glass; if yours don't, you can arrange to have a special film put over them to make them safe. If you have pets, keep their food and water shut in a room that your baby can't get to, or put them out only when he is out of the room.

DEVELOPMENT ACTIVITY

Making faces

Your baby was born with the ability and motivation to copy you, so if you make faces at him, he'll do the same in return. Making faces to each other is important to his social development; he is mirroring your expression and you are reflecting this back to him. He is learning social turn-taking, and these facial movements eventually have meaning for him as in later years he connects the raised eyebrow to questions, or a frown to anger. Pairing an expression with a label such as "angry" or "happy" is the very beginning of teaching your baby the labels for different emotions. He won't make the connection right now, but it's a good idea to start this emotional education early.

Making faces also helps to develop your baby's facial muscles, which, in turn, helps to develop his speech.

Copying faces Your baby can learn a lot from copying the faces that you make to amuse him, and will have lots of fun with you at the same time.

YOUR BABY IS 41 WEEKS AND 4 DAYS

Sweet tooth

Your baby may prefer sweet foods over savory, but avoid giving him processed sugary foods that could harm his emerging teeth.

Natural sugar Fruit is full of sweetness and flavor, and will appeal to a baby's sweet tooth.

Many studies suggest that a sweet tooth is a learned phenomenon and that, although they have a preference for sweet things as tiny babies, older babies are far more accommodating and can have their need for sweet foods satisfied easily with healthy foods.

Sugar is naturally present in many foods, including fruit, vegetables, and milk. Sugar in whole foods is less damaging to teeth than extracted sugar, such as that found in fruit juice, which acts on teeth in the same way as table sugar. As your baby's teeth are emerging, his sugar consumption needs to be monitored. Avoid giving refined sugar products such as cakes, cookies, candy, and chocolates. A treat in the form of grated apple or a mashed banana is sweet enough. Restrict dried fruit (puréed only) such as prunes to mealtimes since they can lead to tooth decay. For a drink, give primarily water. If you give juice, dilute it one part juice to nine parts water.

While your baby is still fairly suggestible, encourage him to eat savory foods as much as possible. Even if he rejects a food initially, keep presenting it (blended with foods he likes, if this helps). Babies usually learn to accept, if not love, many foods they have previously rejected.

YOUR BABY IS 41 WEEKS AND 5 DAYS

Shoes for cruising?

Once your baby starts cruising confidently, you may wonder whether his feet need support and protection.

Once your baby is cruising and, later on, learning to walk independently, going without socks and shoes allows him to figure out how to use his toes to balance. So, as much as possible, let your baby practice walking in bare feet. His feet are going through an important phase of development, and walking barefoot also helps build the arches and encourages the ankles to strengthen.

You may be concerned, though, about whether a standing baby's feet need more protection, especially when he is outdoors or moving around on slippery surfaces. Many outlets sell shoes specially designed for "cruising." While there is some debate as to whether or not these are a good thing for babies, proponents of cruising shoes state that they provide support for toes and heels, which gives a baby confidence on his feet.

Soft "cruising" shoes give complete flexibility, allowing your baby's feet to bend, making sure that he can still feel the floor. Choose ones made out of natural material such as leather, and make sure you have them professionally fit at the shoe store by a trained fitter used to working with babies.

ASK A... MOM

Even "cruising" shoes are expensive. Can I buy a used pair? It's not a good idea to buy used cruising shoes because they mold to the shape of the previous owner's foot, which isn't advisable when your baby's feet are developing. If he'll be wearing them regularly, it's a good idea to buy a new pair. You could make an exception if you want an "occasional" pair for special events that won't see much action.

A real personality

Your baby's personality is increasingly evident now as he learns more ways to express himself and has distinct behavior patterns.

A real character Celebrate your baby's personality and find good ways to channel it.

Many aspects of your baby's eventual personality have already emerged, and seasoned parents know that, for example, a relaxed, happy baby often carries these same characteristics into older childhood and adulthood. You will identify many elements of his personality as he grows. He may be strong willed or easy to please; he may be calm and quick to laugh or a little more highly strung and sensitive.

Whatever the case, avoid labeling him. Calling him "easy" or "difficult" can influence his personality, and your label becomes a self-fulfilling prophecy. If your baby grows up thinking he is "the picky one," he's more likely to define himself, and act, in this way. This is particularly important if you have twins or other multiples, which makes it easier to compare and label.

Celebrate your baby's individual characteristics, even when they are at odds with your own personality or, in the early years, somewhat frustrating.

A nonstop, highly energetic baby may be exhausting for new parents, but keep in mind that these qualities will be admired when he is older.

Some characteristics may be a little extreme, and you can work to ease them a little during these formative months. For example, if your baby is relaxed to the point that he doesn't respond much to his surroundings, play lively music often and encourage him to be physically active. If he's easily frustrated when things don't go right, show him patiently how it's done, or distract him with another activity until he's calm. His temperament may not change, but he'll develop the ability to tolerate frustration.

Keep in mind that it is possible to stifle your baby's natural characteristics by trying to impose your own. For instance, if you are quiet, you may find his noisy, ebullient personality exhausting. However, actively avoiding noisy play or situations in which these characteristics shine through could leave your baby slightly confused, without an outlet to express himself.

Try to celebrate your baby's unique personality traits and look for ways in which to channel them appropriately. If you see characteristics that you don't like, be positive about their long-term benefits. With guidance and a loving, happy home, even the trickiest babies become settled, happy, well-behaved children and adults, with personalities that reflect the individuals they are and the upbringing they've been given.

DEVELOPMENT ACTIVITY

Making moves

Wiggling, swaying, bouncing, clapping— these are all dance moves that your 10-month-old can achieve with very little effort. If he is comfortable with standing and holding on to something, you can put on some music, hold his hands or lightly grasp his waist to keep him steady on his feet, and dance with him. The bouncing in his knees will encourage him to bend and straighten his legs, which is another step on the road to walking, and will also build strength in his legs.

Dancing together Get your baby moving to some music. Doing it on a bed allows for soft landings when things get rowdy!

42 weeks

YOUR BABY MAY SEEM TO CATCH ONE COLD AFTER ANOTHER IN HIS FIRST YEAR

Your little one's fine motor control is improving all the time and he's becoming adept at manipulating objects accurately. He is also more interested in trying to use items, such as a spoon or phone, for their intended purpose.

Constant colds

Your active, social baby contracts lots of germs from many people and environments. It may seem as if he has a constantly runny nose.

Danger signs

If your baby has a cold and shows any of the following complications, contact your pediatrician.

Fever A temperature of 102.2°F (39°C) or higher, or one above 98.6°F (37°C) that persists for more than two days, should be checked by your doctor.

Drowsiness We all feel a bit more sleepy when we are trying to beat infection, but if your baby is hard to rouse from his naps, or floppy or unresponsive, seek medical help.

Dehydration Babies need fluids to fight infection, so if he has refused his bottle, the breast, or water for more than eight hours, seek advice. See page 395 for signs of dehydration.

Rash While some rashes are relatively harmless nonspecific rashes that accompany a virus, any rash is worthy of medical attention since there may be a specific cause that requires treatment.

Ear rubbing If your baby is rubbing his ear and seems very unhappy, he may have an ear infection.

Persistent cough If he has a cough that lasts more than a week, he may have a chest infection, especially if he also has difficulty breathing.

Labored breathing If your baby is struggling for breath at any time, go immediately to the doctor.

Sniffles and sneezes Babies do tend to suffer a lot from colds during their first year—but each minor illness helps to build their immunity so they can fight off similar viruses in the future.

Your baby's immune system has yet to encounter and build immunity to certain infections, which makes him more susceptible to common viruses such as colds. While a cold may disturb his sleep, contracting relatively harmless bugs is an important part of building his immunity. Your baby will inevitably be exposed to germs through toys at the homes of friends or at play groups, especially since he will be putting everything into his mouth. This is fine, and there is certainly no need to carry antibacterial gel around with you.

However, it's best to avoid obviously very ill children, especially those with infections such as croup or a chest infection. Ideally, you don't want your baby catching anything more serious than a common cold.

Treating colds There is no antidote to most viral infections. All you can do is make your baby as comfortable as possible. Take his temperature—if it is above 98.6°F (37°C) he has a fever; call the pediatrician's office to see if you should give him infant acetaminophen or ibuprofen, and if so, what the dosage should be based on your baby's age and weight. You may feel sorry for your baby and think about giving him over-the-counter cold remedies, but those drugs are intended for older children and adults.

Give him plenty of fluids to help prevent dehydration, and make sure he gets lots of time to rest and sleep when he needs to. Don't force him to eat if he doesn't want to—babies often lose their appetite if sick. Offer him small amounts of food often.

42 weeks

YOUR BABY IS 42 WEEKS AND 1 DAY

Was that "dada"?

Studies suggest that babies are most likely to utter their first word at around 10 or 11 months. But what will it be?

Since he was about two months old, your baby has been making cooing sounds that are his first attempts at talking. Now he has developed enough control over his vocal cords to be able to make sounds purposefully. Inevitably, you and his father will vie for "mama" or "dada" being his first word—a friendly competition that can only help your baby's speech development as you both concentrate on getting him to talk.

"Dada" is the most common first word, followed by "mama," most probably because the "d" sound is easier

My Dada More babies say the word "dada" before "mama," but that has more to do with how speech develops than relationships.

for babies to utter than the "m" sound. So don't be surprised if your baby says "dog" or "duck" before "mama." Other popular first words are "cat" (although it will probably come out as "tat") followed by "milk" ("mah") or "ball" ("bah"), while less popular but frequent contenders include "juice" (usually pronounced "juh"), "shoe," "dog," "bye," and "nana."

Words with easy-to-form consonant sounds (p, b, d, m, n, s or sh, g, and so on) tend to be the basis for first words, with words that are made up of trickier sounds (k, j, th, l, for example) following on much later. Whatever your baby's first word is, encourage him by talking, reading, and singing to him, because more will follow.

YOUR BABY IS 42 WEEKS AND 2 DAYS

How your baby grows

It now seems inconceivable that your newborn baby was ever that small—just look at the size of him now!

Between now and 12 months, your baby should weigh somewhere between two and three times as much as when he was born. Keep in mind, however, that these figures are guidelines and all babies gain weight at slightly different rates. He should also have grown by about 10 in (25 cm) by the time he reaches his first birthday.

If you notice slowed growth or a drop in weight, it could be due to illness—a couple of days of not eating, especially if combined with vomiting or diarrhea,

can lead to weight loss that will be regained when your baby recovers. Or it could happen if your baby is crawling, cruising, or walking, since these all burn calories, so weight gain might slow a bit. If your baby is alert, happy, feeding well overall, and filling his diapers normally, all is likely to be well. If there's any cause for concern, see your pediatrician.

If you are worried that your baby is too plump, get his weight checked by your doctor. He or she will tell you right away if there's a risk of him becoming

overweight. It's also important never to withhold feedings from your baby, although you should pay attention to cues that he is full.

If your baby is a little overweight, it's important to make sure that his calories come from nutritious sources—like fruits, vegetables, healthy fats, and cereals—rather than candy and processed food. Play with your baby to encourage physical activity, making sure that he has a safe space in which he can practice becoming more mobile.

Balancing work and baby

It's not easy to balance work and home life: add a baby to the mix and you'll need to put all your organizational skills into practice.

Nobody is perfect at everything, so don't try to be superwoman or superman. If the housework slides or your baby doesn't get her bath one night, the world won't end. Making things easy at home is the secret to survival. Babies are hugely resilient creatures and their needs are very basic. As long as your baby is loved, cared for, and stimulated, she'll be just fine. Don't feel you must offer constant stimulation for your baby. Sometimes she'll be glad just to be in your presence, so take a break and relax with her.

Also, learn to say no. Your baby, family, and job are your priorities. Maintaining these will sometimes be all you can manage. Work out the parts of your life that you enjoy—the things that stimulate and relax you and make you happy. Say no to anything or anyone that doesn't add something positive to your life.

Similarly, don't succumb to guilt. If staying at home with your baby is not an option financially, embrace your situation and find ways in which you can make it healthy and happy for you, your partner, and your baby. In other words, think positively. How can you get the most from the time you have with your baby? Focus on the things you can do, rather than the things you can't, to relieve some of the emotional pressure.

Establish boundaries at work You may once have been a 24/7 employee, but this will be hard now. It helps for your work colleagues to know your needs when you return to work. You may wish for more flexible or part-time working arrangements; don't be afraid to ask for these. Most workplaces value their employees and are willing to try to accommodate your needs so you can achieve the work-life balance you hope for. If you are in charge yourself, consider delegating some of your workload to give you more time.

Take care of yourself An exhausted, underfed, emotionally drained parent isn't any good to anyone! You'll be able to keep more balls in the air if you eat well and sleep well.

Time alone for both yourself and your partner is also important for a healthy emotional life. Sometimes both home and the office can feel like hard work, but even if there isn't much time to spare, you both need to be able to take time out without guilt and with support.

Different individuals

Your twins' personalities will be emerging in earnest now, and no matter how alike in some ways, they will probably have different character traits, even if they are identical. You may find that one wants to crawl, and the other isn't interested, or one is relaxed and placid while the other is easily frustrated. The challenge with twins is to avoid comparing or labeling them. A label can stick, and one child being labeled the "shy one" and the other the "loud one" could put each child into a category that is difficult to change later on. As your babies grow, it's important that they feel valued as individuals as well as having a close relationship as twins.

Same but different One twin may be more dominant or gregarious early on, but that doesn't mean it will always be so—the dynamics of the relationship will change as they grow.

YOUR BABY IS 42 WEEKS AND 4 DAYS

Troublesome teeth

A new set of wide, square teeth will emerge at the back of your baby's mouth soon as he welcomes four first-year molars.

Emerging molars Your baby might rub the side of her face or put her fingers in her mouth where it's feeling tender.

First-year molars often surface toward the end of a baby's first year. These blunt, square teeth, used for grinding and chewing, can cause much pain as they erupt through the gums. You may be able to see their upward transit as a large bulge in the gums. Sometimes a flap of gum loosens to reveal a new white tooth, and your baby may rub the side of his face or ear, worry the area with his tongue, and dribble or drool more as saliva in his mouth is increased. Teeth often appear in pairs, so both sides of your baby's mouth may be affected. Girls tend to teethe earlier than boys, too, although this isn't always the case.

Your baby may want to chew to ease the discomfort. Offer hard foods such as breadsticks, rice cakes, toast, or apple slices. Very cold smoothies can help to soothe inflammation.

ASK A... DOCTOR

My baby's milk teeth look mottled and almost striped. Is this normal?
It is normal for a baby's teeth to have mild ridging and appear bluer rather than white. If there are distinct marks on his teeth, there may be a few possible causes. Certain antibiotics, in particular tetracycline, shouldn't be prescribed in pregnancy as they can cause baby teeth to become mottled, as they form in your baby's mouth early in pregnancy. There may also be problems with his enamel if it has formed unevenly. Ask your dentist to check his teeth if you are worried, but rest assured that most problems will not affect your baby's permanent teeth.

YOUR BABY IS 42 WEEKS AND 5 DAYS

How clean?

Your baby is exposed to many germs during his daily activities, so is there any need to sterilize his feeding equipment now?

The simple answer is, for the most part, no. Your baby's mobility means his hands make contact with the floor wherever he goes, and if he goes to play groups or has siblings, he frequently plays with toys handled by other children. He puts his fingers and toys in his mouth all the time, so there seems little point in being overly concerned about keeping everything sterilized.

However, do wash plastic toys in warm, soapy water regularly and put cuddly toys through the washing machine on the hot cycle from time to time.

Wash plastic spoons and bowls in hot, soapy water, or in a normal dishwasher cycle, but don't worry about sterilizing them now. You may want to sterilize bottles and cups that have had formula or breast milk in them, as the fatty deposits on the insides of the bottles can be hard to remove from washing alone, and residue can cause tummy upsets.

Keep your floors clear of debris and wash wood and tile floors regularly. Also, wash your baby's hands before meals and after handling pets. Try not to be neurotic, though—your baby has to be exposed to a few germs to build his immunity.

Encouraging independence

You can support your baby's development by allowing him some freedoms that enable him to take more control over his world.

When your baby is around 10 months old, he may be showing signs of separation anxiety (see p.283). To help ease this, give him the opportunity to explore a little further afield at home without you by his side. Ensure that wherever he can go is safe, of course, and free from hazards, but then let him travel from room to room—he may be very keen for you to follow, in which case you can go with him. If he seems intent on staying close to you, try leaving the room yourself—only briefly at first, and keep talking to him while you are gone so that he is reassured that you are not too far away. Slowly, his confidence in the idea that you will come back and in the fact that he is okay without you for a little while will grow, along with his independence.

Playtime leader Give your baby a basket containing a few suitable toys and let him choose what to play with. Once he has selected one, engage with him in his play to show him that you are interested in the choices he makes and that you will follow his lead.

There are certain toys that are particularly good for encouraging independent thinking. Shape sorters, stacking cups, and building blocks will all help your baby look at problems and try to solve them on his own.

Self-feeder At mealtimes, allow your baby to have a spoon of his own so that he can try to feed himself, even if you have another spoon so you can ensure some of the food actually finds its way into his stomach! Finger foods are great for independent feeding.

What to eat As your baby gets older, you will relish the days when you could choose his food without him making any objection. You can give him a little independence by offering him two healthy choices for a snack, encouraging him to point to the one he prefers.

Whatever he chooses, he gets to eat. If he then wants the other snack, too, give him this, as the exercise should remain fun. This will help him to feel as if he has a degree of control over his own life, which, in turn, helps him to understand the advantages of independence.

DEVELOPMENT ACTIVITY

Hide and seek

Your baby has understood the concept of object permanence (see p.245) for some time now. Playing peek-a-boo (see p.140) has helped him to realize that you are still there even when he can't see you, and hide and seek is the perfect progression for a mobile baby, as it encourages trust in your presence and absence. Play it in one room only and do it as a family first to allow your baby to get the idea of how it works. Dad hides while you and your baby count, then you go off together to find him. Next time, you and he hide while Dad counts. Your baby will love it when Daddy pretends he can't see him (until he gives himself away with his giggles). Once he understands the concept of the game, you and he can play it together. You hide in the room, calling for him from your hiding place to give him a clue and, importantly, to reassure him that you're there; then you give him time to hide (inevitably in the same place!), pretending for a while that you don't know where he is.

Here I come, ready or not! Your baby will love playing hide and seek with you, and it will encourage her to have faith in the fact that there's no need to panic when she can't see you.

43 weeks

BE WARNED—BY 10 OR 11 MONTHS, FOOD, CUPS, AND TOYS ALL BECOME POTENTIAL MISSILES!

Your baby wants to do everything herself. Although she won't be physically coordinated enough to be very efficient, let her try; for example, give her her own spoon at mealtimes. With her growing independence, it's more important than ever that you show her how much you love her.

Showing caution

Your baby's life is full of new experiences and not all are to his liking, so he'll naturally show caution and even distress at times.

Building confidence If the height of the slide is an issue, help him come down it slowly and reassure him that you've got him and it's safe.

Just a couple of weeks ago, your baby may have been fearless in his curiosity and exploration but now, after a few tumbles and one too many startling discoveries, some babies will be a little more cautious in their exploration. Separation anxiety can also mean he's more easily distressed in new situations, especially if he thinks you may be leaving him. This is a natural progression as he learns about his world and may vary from day to day or week by week as he gains confidence in each situation.

Gently encourage your baby to keep exploring and engaging in new situations. Stay by his side while he scans the room or begins to investigate a new toy or play equipment, for example, or push him in a ride-on car, but keep talking so he knows you are there, even if he can't see you.

You may find he startles easily at loud or unfamiliar noises; these often can't be avoided so handle this with plenty of cuddling and reassurance, and very simply explain, "Oh, that's the noise of a car going 'beep beep.'" Gradually, he will become accustomed to most sounds as he experiences them but, of course, being startled is a natural response to keep us safe, so it's bound to occur occasionally when there's an unexpected noise. Don't make fun of your baby's wariness or reluctance to do something, or use the phrase "Don't be silly!" It's important to keep reassuring him until he feels more comfortable in any new situation.

ASK A... CHILD PSYCHOLOGIST

My baby doesn't seem to like the dark. How can I help him get used to it? For some babies, being in total or almost total darkness can be frightening (even some adults prefer to sleep with some light at night). A small night-light may be enough to reassure your baby that all is well if he wakes up, and allow him to recognize his surroundings quickly. This reluctance to be in the dark does not need to be changed or "treated"—trying to force him to sleep in total darkness is more likely to cause distress than teach him that darkness is okay. If your baby insists on bright light at night, however, then use a dimmer switch to turn the light down slowly over a period of a week or two.

FEAR OF STRANGERS

Your baby has now learned who takes care of him and whom he can trust. Quite naturally, when someone he doesn't recognize comes along, he will be wary of them, even if the new person is someone you would like him to get to know. Don't push him. Instead, sit together in a room, with your baby on your lap, and allow him to size up the stranger as you talk to him or her. When your baby is ready, allow him to make the first move with the new person, and welcome his overtures with lots of encouragement. However, don't expect too much, too soon—he may make a tentative gesture by passing over a toy, but then return to your lap for the rest of the session (see also p.283).

Wary of strangers It's natural for your baby to be suspicious of new people at this age. Let her get to know them at her own pace.

Eating out

It's never too soon to get your baby used to being in a restaurant with you, but certain things can help make the experience easier.

A good indicator of a baby-friendly restaurant is that it has high chairs, baby-changing facilities, a children's menu, and kiddie activity packs. If you're not sure, call ahead to check that the establishment welcomes children—having wait staff or other diners scowl each time your baby squawks is stressful. A restaurant that has appropriate food for your baby gives you a break from preparing food, but if you want to bring your own, ask before you go. Also, it's a good idea to reserve a table by the window so your baby has distractions if necessary.

Take plenty of tabletop activities with you. A few building blocks, board books with flaps, and a small shape sorter will keep your baby occupied while in his high chair. Time your reservation to coincide with your baby's lunchtime so that he is preoccupied with eating while you are (even if you have to feed both of you simultaneously). This should also give you plenty of time before he becomes tired and needs his nap.

Finally, remember that talking, playing with, and involving your baby throughout the meal will make this an experience he'll want to repeat.

ASK A... PEDIATRICIAN

How do I clean my baby's ears?
The ear is self cleaning—ear wax removes dust and debris from the inner ear. It may look unsightly but it's beneficial, so don't remove any lumps of wax while they are still in your baby's ear cavity. You can wipe away wax from his outer ear with a damp cotton pad. Never put a cotton swab in his ear. Even if your hand is steady, he is liable to move and you could damage his eardrum.

Learning through touch

Your baby's senses teach him everything he needs to know; now that he is more aware, capitalize on his ability to learn through touch.

There is much that your 10-month-old baby can learn through the sense of touch, and you can support this learning by giving him different textures to feel and experiment with.

Put your baby in his high chair and present him with two or three bowls of different textures to get his fingers into. Make sure they are safe for mouthing. Some mashed-up banana, a bowl of cereal loops, some pasta shapes, and a bowl of cooked rice are all interesting

Exploring textures Books that feature a variety of textures allow your baby to explore and learn through the sense of touch.

textures for him to explore with his fingers. Babies also love sticking their fingers in jelly! Keep an eye on what goes into his mouth (to prevent choking) and be ready with a clean burp cloth to remove the goop from his fingers.

Give your baby books that feature a variety of fabrics and textures. There are many fantastic books available that are designed for teaching babies the meaning of words such as silky, soft, squishy, rough, and so on. Sit with him and read these books together, and encourage your baby to touch the different textures in the book and say the words that describe them.

Using objects correctly

Your baby can associate objects with actions and anticipate sequences of events, which inspires him to use objects as he sees you doing.

Who to call? As your baby gains control over his hands and fingers, he'll be eager to employ them "correctly" when using objects.

Your baby now understands that his cup holds water or juice, and is able to bring it to his mouth. He knows what his toothbrush and washcloth are for, and he may try to use his spoon and his toy telephone correctly. It will be many more months (and, in some cases, years) before he can independently use many everyday objects but, now that he's so much more skilled with his hands, he will enjoy practicing the skills involved on a regular basis.

Let your baby take a turn at brushing his own hair, or yours. Let him brush his teeth alongside you, put your socks on together, and let him stir the cake batter with the wooden spoon. He will love feeling important and involved, and trying it himself will enhance his understanding of the relationships between objects and activities. Every part of his day offers opportunities for this type of learning by association, and if you prompt his understanding by giving him the words for the objects used and the things you do with them, he will soon point to named items, and even retrieve them.

Ask your baby to pass you his washcloth in the tub, or his cup when he's finished drinking. He may look puzzled at first but, if he hears an instruction and the correct words often enough, while watching you point to and use objects, he'll soon make the links necessary to understand your requests.

THE PINCER GRIP

The pincer grip is a fine motor skill that begins developing from around eight months of age, and becomes increasingly sophisticated as your baby grows older. To perform it, he uses his index finger and thumb together to pick up and hold items. It is this grip (or grasp) that will allow him to button his shirt, use a pencil, play musical instruments, and operate a mouse on a computer in years to come. Being able to perform the pincer grip is a developmental milestone that indicates that your baby's brain, nervous system, and muscles have become much more coordinated and synchronized. It also opens up a world of possibilities for him. With a pincer grip, your baby can stack blocks, feed himself, manage a shape sorter and puzzles, and much, much more.

You'll notice that your baby began to pick up objects by brushing his hand over a toy, then curling his palm and fingers around it. Then he'll grasp things using all four fingers and thumb, which is still a bit awkward. As he approaches 12 months, the ability to hold something between his forefinger and thumb in a pincer grip enables him to pick up and maneuver objects much more easily and precisely. To encourage the refinement of your baby's pincer grip, give him small things to pick up from his high-chair tray at mealtimes, such as cereal loops and vegetable puffs, or give him a simple lift-out puzzle to tackle. Avoid small objects that might pose a choking hazard if he puts them into his mouth.

Better grip Give your baby toys that fit in his hand to help him improve his whole-hand grip and, eventually, his pincer grip.

43 weeks

339

Encouraging self-feeding

Your baby loves to put his fingers in his food and transfer it to his mouth. Although messy, this is the start of him feeding himself.

Many babies want to be independent and feed themselves but, at this age, most lack the hand–eye coordination to get food onto a spoon and into their mouths. Finger foods come into their own at this point since they allow your baby to enjoy more independence, yet expand his dietary horizons.

Try to introduce a wider variety of tastes and textures now: crunchy foods, such as soft breadsticks, rice cakes, toast, and dry breakfast cereals are all ideal finger foods. Also try cucumber sticks, cubes of mild cheese, and cooked pasta shapes. As your baby gets better at feeding himself, you can introduce a daily meal of "small bites"—for example, mini sandwiches, pita bread, or toast cut into strips with cheese; veggie sticks with hummus; chunks of cheese or finely grated cheese; cooked vegetables; some chopped grapes, apple, pear, or banana. Make sure that your baby's finger-food meals are balanced and healthy (not too low in fat or too high in fiber, see Good nutrition for babies, p.207).

Always go at your baby's pace and try to introduce new foods when he's happy and alert and not when he's tired or feeling irritable. If he's grumpy, you're better off sticking to old favorites. You could encourage him to try new foods by adding just one new item to his finger-food meal among others you know that he likes.

All this practice with finger foods is great for his fine motor skills and coordination, which will help when he starts to use a spoon (see p.369).

Fun with animals

Young children adore animals and soak up everything to do with them, whether looking at animal pictures, or meeting the real thing.

Your baby will be fascinated with animals. While he may be wary, or even scared, on his first contact with them, learning about animals is a natural part of his development. Familiarize him with animals early on by looking at pictures in books, and watching TV programs about animals. Talk about the animals, pointing out each one by name with the noise it makes. Sing nursery rhymes, too, that have animal noises, like "Old MacDonald had a Farm."

If you have a yard, consider putting up a bird feeder and let him watch the birds eating. Or point out regular visitors such as squirrels; he'll be delighted by their antics. On outings, point out birds, cats and dogs, and ducks and geese in ponds or rivers. Or take him to a zoo or a children's petting zoo, which offers an accessible and safe way to let your baby experience animals at close quarters. While he may be too young to pet the animals, his senses will take in everything, and he will build his confidence around them. Hygiene is of course essential to remember when handling animals. Wash his hands well after being with farm or domestic animals, and make it routine to wash his hands after playing in the sandpit or yard and before mealtimes.

Family pets Contact with pets increases your baby's confidence around animals. Supervise animals around your baby at all times.

The importance of affection

Showing your baby love and attention is probably second nature by now and he will thrive on as much physical affection as you can give.

Secure and happy Consistent love, comfort, and protection from parents and caregivers helps babies develop good mental health.

Some of the most important work on babies' need for affection and attention was done by psychologist John Bowlby in the 1960s and it has defined our way of nurturing and creating security for children ever since.

His attachment theory taught us that the bond between parent and child is the foundation for your baby's security and creates a positive pattern he will repeat in the relationships he goes on to make.

A baby who has been brought up in a secure, loving environment where affection is given and received freely through hugs and kisses, pats and snuggles, is more likely to grow up to be an affectionate adult.

There have been plenty of different ideas about the "best" way to raise your baby, from the old adage that children should be "seen and not heard" through to schedule-based and more baby-led methods. Whichever approach you prefer, there's no doubt that fundamentally your baby needs your love, attention, and affection in order to develop his sense of security, stability, and confidence. When you comfort him, go to him when he cries, give lots of physical affection, and show that you enjoy his company, you are creating this security. He also needs your consistency, so that he can predict what reaction he will get and what pleases you. As he gets older, it will be important for him to know what behavior is preferred and what is unacceptable.

Undivided attention Laughing with your baby, tickling him, giggling, and giving him undivided attention is another way to show him how much you love him. Studies have shown that if you are watching him playing but doing something else too, such as reading or talking on the phone, his play will be less complex than if you watch him with your full focus.

Follow his lead at playtime—sometimes he will want to be held, at other times, to get down because he wants some freedom. Sometimes all he needs is a gentle stroke on the cheek or head to know that you love him. By responding to, and respecting, the peaks and valleys in your baby's need for affection, you show him that you value his feelings, which means that he learns to value them himself.

BEING GENTLE

A 10-month-old baby doesn't have any real sense of his strength, and still lacks the necessary coordination to monitor how hard he pats or holds on to things. However, it is never too early to teach him to be as gentle as he can be. Encourage your baby to stroke his cuddly toys or dolls, gently holding his hand so that he gets a sense of the lightness of touch. Choose one special toy, perhaps a teddy bear, and give it a hug in front of your baby, then encourage him to do the same, saying "Ahhhh, teddy bear." Gently put the bear down, cover him in a blanket, and give him a kiss, then encourage your baby to do the same. Such role play reinforces a baby's understanding of the need to care for others and treat them with kindness.

Learning to be kind Teach your baby how to be kind and gentle by showing her how to take good care of her stuffed animals.

43 weeks

341

44 weeks

MANY BABIES HAVE A FAVORITE COMFORT OBJECT THAT THEY WANT TO TAKE EVERYWHERE

As your baby becomes more mobile, she develops greater self-confidence and she'll be very clear about what she does and doesn't want to do. Be patient but firm about the limits you've set. From her first smile at about six weeks, your baby may have progressed to fits of full-blown laughter. Enjoy!

Letting your baby help

Your baby might enjoy giving you a little "help" with some small tasks and will think it's fun to be just like Mommy.

Tidy up time Ask your baby to perform simple tasks, such as putting her clean bowls and plates away.

The simplest and most useful thing that your 10-month-old baby can do for you is to help you put his toys back into the toy boxes at the end of the day. If you make this activity part of his end-of-day routine, you may also find that, by the time your baby reaches toddlerhood, this behavior has become second nature and you will have a helpful baby at hand.

Place a toy box in the middle of the room and encourage your baby to collect toys to put into it. Turn it into a game as much as you can—"Can you find the rabbit? Clever boy! Now put the rabbit in the box." Give him lots of praise and even take turns—"Now Mommy can find the train. Here it is! Into the box." Use the time as an opportunity to reinforce colors, shapes, animals, and so on in your baby's experience and learning. Slowly, but surely, the tidying up will be done.

Cleaning Although it will be a long while yet before your baby can earn an allowance by doing the vacuuming, you can let him join in as you clean by giving him a clean duster and letting him wipe the surfaces he can reach as he cruises around the house. Even if wiping down the sofa is not altogether very helpful, give him lots of praise and encouragement for helping out. Similarly, give him a damp cloth after mealtimes and ask him to help you wipe the table—although his wipes will be in one area back and forth in front of where he's sitting, he'll get the idea, and his efforts are worthy of much praise.

DEVELOPMENT ACTIVITY

Stacking fun

Stacking helps to develop your baby's hand–eye coordination, encourages him to work out logic puzzles, and reinforces what he has learned about cause and effect. Good stacking toys include cups that fit inside one another and also sit on top of one another if turned upside-down (plastic measuring cups will do the job just as well), colored bricks, and rings that go over a central cone.

To stack cups and rings appropriately, your baby has to work out their shapes and relative sizes and pass the objects from one hand to the other. The bricks require skill with balance, fine motor skills, and the gentle touch that's needed to get items of the same size to rest securely one on top of the other. With either type of toy, these tasks introduce your baby to the beginnings of mathematical problem-solving, which gives him a head start with mathematical skills for later in life.

Start your baby off by showing him how the stacking is done, then tell him it's his turn. Watch as he carefully tries to work out which item goes next and give him a hand if he needs it. If the toy topples over, that doesn't matter—it's all part of the learning process, and he will love building things back up again.

Early math Stacking toys introduce your baby to math skills, all in the name of fun.

Meeting other children

Your baby's still too young to play constructively with other children, but it's good experience for him to be in a social group.

Your baby will benefit from growing up in the company of children of all ages. He will probably play in parallel with babies his own age, while older children can engage him in a variety of games such as peek-a-boo, hide-and-seek, dancing, singing, and nursery rhymes. Older children will enjoy reading to him and crawling around pretend "forts" in a way that adults might find awkward. Your baby might find it easier to engage with children, with whom he can play nearby, rather than with new adults who may want to interact, or interfere with his play. Children may also love the chance to "look after" your baby and—given clear guidelines—can be surprisingly good helpers. Even though you have to be there, it will help your baby feel more independent and give you both a bit of space. Of course, if he has older siblings this will already be happening. If not, you may need to engineer it so that your baby has time with other children.

Using a child-care center means he'll meet other children of varying ages in a safe environment (and even if you're not going back to work, sessions with other children will prove beneficial).

If you have nephews and nieces, ask them to visit or supervise a visit to their home. Meeting regularly, if practical, can build close ties, which are a loving support to your baby and yourself as he grows up.

If it appeals, you could consider going on vacation with friends with children. However, make sure there's enough space within your accommodations and you know the other family well enough to be able to speak freely about your wishes for your baby and yourselves.

Time to yourselves

You and your partner need some time to focus on each other, and to pursue some of your favorite individual activities again.

Just the two of you You and your partner need time away from your baby to relax and enjoy being on your own together.

You and your partner will benefit from having some regular time away from your baby. This might mean getting a babysitter for the evening and going out together, or booking a night or two away. Of course, it depends on having child care you can trust and afford. An alternative is to set up a babysitting circle between you and your friends with babies so you can take turns looking after each other's babies once in a while. However you manage it, your relationship will thrive on having time to enjoy each other's company, taking in favorite activities, or treating yourselves.

You can also give yourselves "permission" to resume individual activities you used to enjoy. You may want to restart a sport you have put on hold, such as running, aerobics, cycling, or hiking. Seeing friends socially can be a boost; whether it's shopping, going to a movie together, grabbing a coffee, or attending organized activities, this gives you time to recharge your batteries. Whatever the activity, the important thing is that you both have some time and space to do the things you enjoy and that make you each feel special, together and individually.

When baby can't let go...

There's no doubt that a comfort object is helpful, especially when your baby is anxious, but what if it starts running your life?

Inseparable friends Babies may not want to give up their comfort object—if she wants it 24 hours a day, it's unkind to take it away.

Your baby encounters new experiences every day. Even if the events are the same, he'll start to see them from a new perspective as he begins to cruise; he may suddenly feel at sea even in familiar surroundings because he has newfound independence. The bombardment of experiences, learning, and understanding comes fast and furiously at 10 months, and the whole process can be both exciting and unsettling. So it's hardly surprising that comfort objects (sometimes called transitional or security objects) provide a constant. They represent your love, they smell of home, and they have positive, safe associations. He'll need his comfort object when you are not nearby, when he experiences something new, or he feels ill or tired. Sometimes, he may rely on his comfort object so heavily that he just can't bear to let it go.

This is all very well, but can start to fray the most patient parent's nerves after a while. It's difficult enough to remember everything you need when you go out, but simply frustrating if you're halfway down the road with baby safely in the car seat before he starts wailing—because you've left his "best friend" behind! Plus, you are saddled with the huge responsibility of looking after—and never, ever losing—your baby's most precious possession.

Go with the flow There's little you can do about this situation other than accept it and make contingency plans. Once your baby has formed an attachment to a particular thing, taking it away will make him feel insecure and upset. So ideally, he should be able to reach his comfort object whenever he needs it, wherever he happens to be. Eventually, he'll either grow out of it, or you'll need to help him let go of the object gradually, but not until he's older. For the time being, do all you can to protect it. If possible, buy a couple of spares in case it gets lost. If your baby is attached to an irreplaceable blanket, consider cutting it in half so that you can wash one half, while the other is being used. Try to wash it before it becomes too deeply embedded with your baby's scent so that he doesn't reject it when clean.

DEVELOPMENT ACTIVITY

Tunnel time

Babies of this age love playing in toy tunnels. Nylon tunnels are readily available from most good toy stores. However, a tunnel made from three cardboard boxes taped together with their ends open can work just as well. Customize it with peepholes along its length so your baby can peek out for you. Encourage him to crawl inside the tunnel, perhaps by placing a few toys inside, and play peek-a-boo as he emerges from one end. Or surprise him yourself by appearing "magically" at the opposite end. If he seems confident within it, you could hang a blanket over one end for him to peek out of. Don't force him to play with the tunnel if he seems nervous about going inside—just leave it on the floor until he is ready to explore.

Tunnel play Playing in a toy tunnel helps to develop your baby's gross motor skills and his powers of anticipation.

Story and rhyme sessions

As well as enjoying books at home, it can be fun to join in with story and rhyme activities with other babies and parents.

Many libraries now offer membership to children from birth, and actively encourage babies and toddlers to make the most of their facilities. You may find that your local library has a regular activity session for babies, using rhymes, stories, songs, and possibly pictures and puppets, to help keep little ones entertained and interested. Alternatively, your local parent and baby group may have a story-time session that you can join in. This can become a favorite regular outing for you both, and allows your baby to experience new books and be part of a group of parents and babies.

This also provides an opportunity for you to meet other parents and, even if your baby doesn't want to join in and sit and listen, you can explore the wealth of books available at the library. Many libraries stock a good range of board books for babies, as well as a selection of toys and games.

Visiting the library from an early age and encouraging your baby to explore and enjoy books will set him up for reading activities as he grows older.

AS A MATTER OF FACT

Babies laugh much more frequently than adults: an average baby laughs around 300 times a day, compared to an average adult, who laughs around 20 times a day—although how much we laugh also depends on personality. Between nine and 15 months, babies understand that when Mom puts a diaper on her head or "moos" like a cow, she's doing something unexpected—and that it's funny.

Quality time

If one or both of you are out at work all day, it's important to make sure that you have some one-on-one quality time with your baby.

Babies derive and learn different things from their mothers and fathers, so it's important that your baby gets individual time with each of you if at all possible. This can be difficult to manage when one or both of you works away from home, especially if that involves long hours or unsociable shifts, but there are many benefits to your child.

Moms and dads have different styles of relating: mommy is often a source of comfort and peace, for example, while daddy represents excitement and fun.

Daddy's way Dads often approach story time in a different way than moms, so your baby's father has his own unique influence on her.

Love and attention from you both helps promote your child's social, emotional, and intellectual development.

If you're both at home in the evenings, try to organize your routine so that one of you does bathtime, and one of you reads the bedtime story, then you both get to kiss your baby and say good night. Or try to plan things so that at least one of you gets to sit down and have breakfast with your baby before you go out in the morning. When you do have time off together, make sure that you play individually with your baby, as well as together, so that he can enjoy the different ways in which you both stimulate him.

On the way to walking

By 10 months, your baby will probably crawl, possibly pull himself up to standing, and may even cruise—but when will he walk?

Enjoying mobility As long as your baby is moving around, it doesn't matter whether he does it on his bottom or his legs for now.

It's natural to look forward with excitement to witnessing your baby's first steps—after all, as he totters unsteadily toward your waiting arms for the very first time, he's making huge strides on the road to independence.

If your baby is by now cruising reasonably confidently along the furniture, it's possible that he may take his first independent steps at any time. However, since the average age for babies to take their first steps is at 13 months, it is unusual—though not unheard of—for them to start walking this early.

Walking depends on the development of gross motor skills, coordination, and build (a baby with a long body and short legs, for example, might find it harder to get his balance). If your baby was late to hold his head up or sit unaided, he's likely also to be late to walk—his gross motor function is taking a little longer than average to reach each milestone. There's no apparent correlation between early walkers and athleticism or intelligence—some babies simply do it sooner than others.

Slowly, slowly Your baby's first steps are more likely to be a side-to-side shuffle that gradually inches him forward rather than a striding march. Only once he has developed much better coordination and balance (often not until the age of two) will he pick up one foot to place it in front of the other.

Until then, he will take lots of little steps, barely raising his feet from the floor at all. Babies also keep their feet wide apart and bend their knees, making them look bow-legged, and they tend to walk with a slightly arched back and toes pointing inward. Early walking may not look elegant, but it'll seem miraculous to you.

Once your baby starts walking, patience will be your biggest virtue. He'll need you to hold his hand and match his snail's pace as you walk to the car, or to fetch something from another room. Progress can be frustratingly slow, especially when you're in a hurry. But try to avoid scooping him up too often—he needs all the practice he can get now.

DEVELOPMENT ACTIVITY

Cruise control

If your baby is at the stage where he's pulling himself up but not quite cruising yet, you can encourage him by putting a toy or teddy bear a few feet away from him so that he has to side-step to get it. The more stepping he does, the better his stability and coordination will become.

All this movement is good exercise for his leg muscles, making them stronger, and good stepping practice, as he's lifting his feet and planting them as he cruises. Once he's more competent at cruising, you can place his toy a little further away, or on the next chair, to encourage him to move between pieces of furniture.

Nearly there Your baby will derive a real sense of satisfaction from being able to move and get to something he wants.

45 weeks

A 10-MONTH-OLD BABY SHOULD BE ABLE TO SLEEP MOST OF THE NIGHT WITHOUT WAKING

Your baby's problem-solving abilities are developing rapidly, and she'll enjoy and show remarkable determination in tackling all sorts of challenges. Now may be the time to take her along to a local playgroup so that she can start to learn important socialization skills.

Parenting with confidence

As you race toward the end of your baby's first year, reflect on just how much you've learned—and be proud of yourselves as parents.

Happy family Being confident in your decisions and abilities as a parent will help you, your partner, and your baby enjoy family life that much more.

You are not alone. Your baby's father, your own parents, and your friends are all there to offer advice if you need it. Your partner, in particular, is there to share all the decisions about how to raise your baby. Make them together and lean on each other when one of you feels unsure. Confident parenting isn't a solitary exercise.

Be confident Your baby will look to you for guidance—now, and in the decades to come. Don't put so much pressure on yourself that you believe you have to get it right every time, but do have confidence that the decisions you make are made with the best intentions.

Also, remember that confidence and arrogance are not the same thing. It is important to believe in your decisions, but also to be able to abandon them if you realize you've made a mistake. It is

a sign of strength to be able to admit when you are wrong, take responsibility for the error, and move on. No parent gets it right every time.

Be firm Your self-confidence as a parent shines through in your ability to be able to set boundaries for your baby. No matter how much he protests something you have good reason to say no to, or to prevent him from doing, hold firm. Your baby is more likely to grow up into a confident individual if he sees that you mean what you say.

Be happy Finally, love the job you're doing. Every day, as you watch your baby grow and learn something new, be proud of him, but also give yourself a bit of praise. He will feed off your own delight in the successes you achieve together, which means he will be happy.

CHECKLIST

Confident parenting

Do...
■ Take the positives from your own upbringing and repeat the good practices your parents had, and learn from the best aspects of other parenting styles you see around you.
■ Think about the negative parenting traits your parents or others might have had—and avoid repeating them.
■ Treat your baby with respect, which doesn't mean giving in to him all the time—but instead gently setting firm boundaries.
■ Talk to your baby as you would like to be spoken to, listen to him as you'd like to be listened to, and be there to comfort him whenever he needs you.
■ Always show love—tell your baby how much you love him, and let your actions speak louder than your words.

Don't...
■ Be hard on yourself if your plans go awry—if your baby is growing and happy, you're doing fine.
■ Be critical of your partner—always discuss your differing approaches and keep an open mind to the specifics of your parenting styles. Remember, you both have your baby's best interests at heart.
■ Be afraid to ask for help: there are lots of resources available to you—use them if you need to.

45 weeks

349

More gibberish?

Listen very carefully—your 45-week-old baby might well be saying actual words, only you don't know it!

In some cases, it's not always easy to recognize the words your baby says, but at other times, they may be obvious. Perhaps if he likes trains, he might say "choo-choo," or he might say "meow" when he sees a cat. His increased vocabulary doesn't necessarily have to be full of the actual nouns that we attribute to objects.

Consider, too, that your baby's words might lack an ending. It is perfectly normal for babies to be unable to make the hard sounds at the ends of words when they first begin to talk. In which case, a horn noise might be more a "too" than a "toot," a cat might be a "cah," and a dog, a "doh."

Although your baby might be closer to two years old before he has a real knack for finishing his words, you can move the process along by keeping background noise (such as the radio or television) to a minimum when you talk to him, so he can hear you clearly. Also, be careful to finish your words. From time to time, feel free to exaggerate the hard sounds at the ends of words a little to help him focus on them.

What a clever girl! Your baby loves to babble, but if you listen carefully to what she's saying, you might hear some actual words!

Sheer determination

Babies are remarkably resilient and steadfastly tenacious when it comes to achieving something they have set their minds on doing.

The utter determination of babies is what drives them to learn new skills and develop the ones they already have every single day. He's not quite ready to build a block tower, but he'll love stacking simpler toys and will keep trying long after you might have given up.

Of course, if there is a downside to your baby's will to try it again and again, it is that he might be unwilling to let you help him, which can mean that some practical tasks—such as putting on a hat so that you can go out, for example—take significantly longer than they might if you stepped in.

"Stickability" is a buzz word in schools these days, with teachers increasingly reporting that if children struggle, they are unwilling to go back to a task to see it through to its conclusion. Try to encourage stickability in your baby by praising his willingness to keep trying, and giving him lots of chances to keep trying all sorts of things. Allow him to continue until he has had enough and either turns his attention away naturally, or allows you to help him. Above all, give him lots of praise for his continued efforts and, of course, a cheer of delight when he succeeds.

ASK A... MOM

My baby has started biting me and it hurts. How do I stop him? Your baby has no idea he's hurting you and is just being playful. However, it's not a habit that you want to encourage! Make sure you don't react too strongly but do say "Ouch, that hurts" and give a matching expression. Sit him on the floor for a minute and distract him. He'll soon get the message that this is something you don't like.

Time for playgroup

Helping your baby to socialize will teach him important life skills, from communicating with peers to learning to be kind.

Now is a good time to start taking your baby to a playgroup, because he'll enjoy playing near other children and playing new games and with different toys. The closer the playgroup is to home, the better, as your baby can make friends with children who live nearby, and who one day might even go to school with him. Some groups are run by community centers, others by local churches or a group of dedicated moms (who will pass the baton as their own children head off to school). Try out a few in your area, finding one (or more) that feels the friendliest and that your baby seems to enjoy the most.

What to expect Much of what happens at playgroups depends upon their size. A small playgroup might have a room or area for toddlers, with a few climbing toys and arts-and-crafts activities, and a separate room or area for babies. Larger playgroups will have whole rooms dedicated to aspects of play—perhaps a room for painting (or other messy play), a room for babies, and a room for active play for toddlers. Some offer cups of tea and coffee, and light snacks, as well as drinks and snacks suitable for the children. At the end of the session, there is usually a circle time, when everyone joins together to sing some songs, celebrate birthdays, and give notices about activities that are planned in the coming weeks.

As a rule, playgroups are informal and relaxed, and moms are free to play with their children and talk to other moms as they wish. Some groups will ask for a small contribution each time you visit (or periodically) and some will ask if you would be willing to help out one week—perhaps by serving snacks or doing some at-home preparation for an upcoming activity. Getting involved is a great way of meeting other moms and to begin to feel part of a community.

Baby doesn't want to play The noise levels and frenzied activity at some playgroups can be quite daunting for some babies, and if your baby doesn't want to get off your lap the first few times he goes, don't despair. Find an activity that the two of you can do together, or simply find a book and read to him. Once you have been several times, his natural curiosity will get the better of him, and he'll go off to explore. However, bear in mind that, at only 10 months, he will be happy playing alongside other babies, but won't necessarily want to play with them.

DEVELOPMENT ACTIVITY

Flour painting

Find a shallow tray that is ideally of a dark color. Sprinkle some flour over the tray and rock the tray back and forth so that there is an even covering across its surface. Now show your baby how to trace his finger through the flour to "draw" patterns and shapes. This activity is far less messy than using paints! Flour "painting" is a great way of bringing out the budding artist in your baby, and it will help him to develop his fine motor skills, which are so important for drawing and writing later on in life.

Budding artist Flour painting is a good way of introducing your baby to the concept of mark-making. He'll enjoy drawing shapes as well as the tactile quality of this activity.

SPOTLIGHT ON...
Sleeping through the night

If your baby isn't sleeping through the night yet, don't worry, you are not alone. However, a 10-month-old should be capable of a good night's rest, so it's worth considering whether some of the ideas below might help you both get the sleep you need.

Your baby needs sleep so he can process the events of his day, and in order to grow. You and your partner need sleep, too. Generally, having too little sleep makes us irritable, impatient, and uncompromising. If both parents are feeling this way, that is not a recipe for family harmony. If this is the case with your family, then it's time to take some action. While it may seem hard to tackle your baby's night-waking now, any bad habits he has established will become even harder to break as he gets older, so it's best to address these issues sooner rather than later.

Assuming that his nap times are working well, at night a 10-month-old baby should be able to sleep for a good stretch, perhaps 10 to 12 hours. By this age, he should be eating 2–3 meals a day, possibly with snacks in between, so he shouldn't need any nighttime milk feedings. The sooner he learns to settle himself without help from you if he stirs at night, the happier you'll both be.

Reasons for waking If your baby isn't used to settling himself back to sleep during the lightest phase of his sleep cycle (which, as adults, we don't notice),

he will rouse fully and call out for you for comfort or for milk. This can become a habit, and your baby will be unable to soothe himself back to sleep without a cuddle or a feeding. Babies who are between nine and 12 months often also suffer from separation anxiety, which can become acute when they wake all alone in the darkness of night. Other reasons for waking might be that your baby is getting too much sleep in the daytime, napping too late in the afternoon, or he might just be struggling to reestablish good habits after a bout of illness or teething pain that disturbed his usually peaceful slumbers.

There are different strategies you can use to try to regulate your baby's sleeping patterns so that you can all get some well-deserved rest. The key thing is to decide which approach or approaches you feel comfortable trying, and stick to your guns. Keep in mind that if your baby has been consistently wakeful in the night (that is, you've never had a period during which he's slept through), breaking the habit can take up to three weeks of persistent effort. Don't give up!

Bedtime basics Your baby will benefit from a strict but loving bedtime routine and a happy environment. He needs plenty of positive and soothing signals that it's time for bed. Spend the last hour of the day engaged in quiet interaction together. This way, he'll get plenty of positive attention that will encourage him to feel calm and relaxed by bedtime. Give him a bath, get him dressed for bed, and read him his bedtime story. Saving one story specifically for bedtime is an unequivocal signal of what is coming next.

When the time comes for him to sleep, cuddle and kiss him, put him in his crib, settle him down (with his teddy

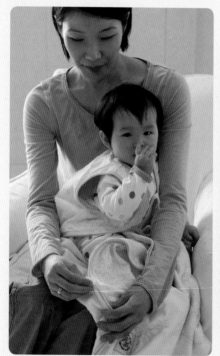
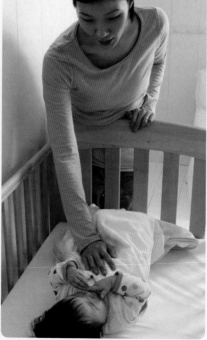

Cosy bedtime routine Keep the last hour of your baby's day restful as you prepare her for bed with lots of reassuring cuddles and kisses. Encourage her to soothe herself to sleep in her crib.

bear if he has one), say good night, then leave the room. You can leave a nightlight on if you wish, and perhaps soothing music. Ensure his crib is a happy place to be. Avoid using it as a convenient place to confine him while you do something quickly. Instead, make it a place where his favorite cuddly toy sleeps, where he keeps his comfort object when he isn't using it, and where he sees a big smile from you last thing at night and first thing in the morning.

Midnight mayhem If your baby has a tendency to wake up and want to play, you need to convince him that night time is really boring and there is little point in asking for interaction in the wee hours because nothing of any interest happens. If he is crying, soothe him calmly, but don't chat with him or engage him. If your baby's nap times are too long, or he is still having a late afternoon nap, he may not be tired enough at bedtime to sleep through the night. You could try moving his afternoon nap forward by 15 minutes, and making it 15 minutes shorter, too. You don't want your baby to be overtired when he goes to bed, but he needs to be ready for sleep.

Waking for a feeding If you're in the habit of giving your baby a nighttime breast- or bottle feeding, this can be hard to give up, especially if there is a part of you that enjoys the closeness that you share in the still of the night. Even if it's not a special time for you or you resent being woken up, your baby may have other ideas. If you're starting to question whether your baby really needs this feeding or is simply waking out of habit, you may want to take steps to drop this feeding. You can try gradually reducing the amount of milk you are giving, either by reducing the time you spend breast-feeding or by gradually decreasing the amount of formula in the bottle over several nights. Or you could start offering your baby water instead of milk when he wakes; over time he may not consider this worth waking up for. Also, you'll be more confident that he is not actually hungry if you know he has eaten well and had a milk feeding before bedtime.

Waking for a cuddle If your baby is determined to have your reassuring presence in the night, it can be hard to keep getting out of your warm bed and going to him. However, be aware that if you take him into bed with you (see box, opposite), he will not learn to settle in his crib—and that when he is a toddler he will take up a lot of room in your bed! If you prefer to have him sleep in his own space, it is best to soothe him by going to him when he calls and patting him in the crib, talking calmly to him or singing to him, rather than lifting him out to cuddle him. Some babies need to have a short wind-down cry before they go to sleep, so be careful not to mistake this for a summons.

Sleep "training" You may have heard other sleep techniques mentioned, for example gradual withdrawal or controlled crying. Gradual withdrawal is the gentler method that involves soothing your baby to sleep in the usual way, but then laying him in his crib just before he drifts off, and sitting in the room (without engaging with him) until he falls asleep. Eventually he should learn to go to sleep with you at the other side of the room, and then with you out of the room altogether.

Controlled crying involves soothing your baby in the crib by stroking and patting him when he wakes, but each time he cries leaving him to wait a little longer before you go to him, the idea being that eventually he learns to soothe himself back to sleep. Many experts, though, feel controlled crying is not advisable on the grounds that it is stressful for babies and parents.

With all the different methods, consistency is essential.

Restful sleep Babies need a good night's sleep so the brain can consolidate the day's learning and the body can recharge for more action.

IN BED TOGETHER

There's little doubt that a baby in his parents' bed is less likely to wake up crying or be difficult to settle at night. However, even if at this point you are all getting a good night's sleep, as your baby gets older your nights are likely to be less peaceful. As your baby gets bigger (and stronger), he'll move more, kick, and make a noise at night. There are also risks associated with co-sleeping, and it is not advised in certain circumstances (see pp.30–31). If you or your baby are not co-sleeping as soundly as before, you may wish to think about moving him into his own bed sooner rather than later. Some babies make the transition easily, others need to get used to the idea—you may have to keep your baby's crib in your room for a while, for example. Even if your baby moves out, your bed can still be a great place for cuddles in the morning!

Toys for 10 months up

Choosing appropriate toys for your baby can be mind-boggling. Observe him at play to help you select toys that will interest him.

At 45 weeks, your baby's thinking and problem solving are geared to fun and discovery. Books, balls, building blocks, and stacking cups are all great for honing his ability to understand cause and effect and shape and size, and to develop his problem-solving skills. Make sure items are of a size that your baby can hold and pass from one hand to the other easily.

Any toys that encourage movement, or support your baby as he pulls to stand, are also appropriate at this age.

Fun with learning Toys designed for this stage of your baby's development will help him enjoy and be enthusiastic about learning.

If you are buying a new toy for your baby, check that it is suitable for his age—most state this on the label—and take into account your baby's stage of development. All babies develop at different rates, so a toy should suit his individual level of mobility, dexterity, and understanding.

You don't need to spend a fortune on store-bought toys—make good use of anything appropriate you might have lying around the house. For example, the inner tubes of paper towel rolls or wrapping paper rolls make wonderful "trumpets," and a cardboard box is fantastic for climbing into and out of, or to use as a goal for a thrown ball.

Shapes and sizes

You can start to introduce new concepts such as large and small now, but don't expect him to identify these all by himself yet.

Your baby is working hard to make sense of his world; you can help by commenting on familiar objects and describing their properties using words such as "bigger," "smaller," "soft," and "hard." Familiarity with these ideas will assist in his development and he'll grasp them in the months to come.

Introduce shape sorters, toys of different sizes and textures, and simple puzzles and he'll be acting out concepts such as in and out and large and small without realizing it as he puts together these actions and ideas. Play story

games with his soft toys or teddy bears, talking about little baby teddy and big mommy or daddy teddy. Then you can show him the toys and ask, "Show me the big one." Soon he'll be experimenting with these ideas intentionally. Make use of stories that contain themes about shapes and sizes, especially those with "touch and feel" panels. In your daily chats, talk to your baby about big, small; round, square; high, low, and so on, bringing shape and size into conversations and observations on a regular basis.

AS A MATTER OF FACT

Don't be surprised if your baby's eyes are still changing color. Although base eye color is usually established between 6 and 9 months, subtle changes in tone may be noticed later as more dark pigment is produced in the iris (green eyes turning more hazel, for example, or hazel eyes becoming deeper brown). Eye color can keep changing into toddlerhood, and sometimes even in adulthood.

Going away, minus baby

You're bound to have mixed feelings about a night away from your baby. Leaving him with caregivers you trust will make it easier.

Now that you are so accustomed to being responsible for your baby's welfare, it can be quite difficult to "let go" and hand him over to someone else, especially for a whole night. For this reason, it's important to be comfortable with whomever you choose to look after him while you are away. And so that your baby doesn't feel too unsettled, it helps if they're very familiar to him and have an idea of his routine and his preferences.

Preparing your baby Ensure that, in the week leading up to your absence, your baby spends lots of time with the person or people who'll be looking after him. Ideally, have them come to stay with you, so your baby has the security of his own home as he familiarizes himself with them. If you can invite the caregivers to stay for a few days before you leave, all the better. Ask them to do some feeding, nap time, bedtime, and waking routines so your baby is used to their care by the time you leave.

Preparing the caregivers By familiarizing themselves with your routines before you leave, your baby's caregivers will be well attuned to his patterns. Encourage them to stick to your routines, and ensure they know which foods he can eat (leave meals prepared for him if you can) and which snacks are permissible. While, no doubt, you'd prefer they kept to your schedule, let them know they should make changes in order to do what's necessary to keep your baby happy.

If your baby is staying with his caregivers for the duration of your absence, ensure he has a crib, his comfort object, and plenty of food, diapers, and changes of clothes to see him through until you return. Plan for a day longer than your planned absence to guarantee he will be short of nothing. Ask the caregivers to do a quick baby-proofing check with you before you leave, as you may be more aware of certain hazards than they are. Finally, don't forget to leave emergency contact details.

Preparing yourself Agree on times to call before you go so you can check on how your baby is doing. When the time comes for you to leave, make it clear to your baby that you are going and be cheerful about it. If you sneak off, he may worry that you won't be back. Be brave, give him a wave, and hit the road.

ASK A... CHILD PSYCHOLOGIST

Will my baby get out of his routine if he's with another caregiver overnight? It can be unsettling for your baby to be in a different environment, and his routine is bound to change, at least a little bit. However, your baby is able to tolerate brief variations to his usual schedule as long as his routine at home is well established. Once he's home, quickly settle him back into the usual pattern and don't be tempted to keep him up late or change things because you want extra time or want to "treat" him because you've been away.

Preparation for your absence In the week before you go away, make sure your baby spends plenty of time with whomever will be taking care of him during your absence.

46 weeks

BABIES LEARN TO SHAKE THEIR HEADS TO MEAN "NO" AT AROUND 10–12 MONTHS

Your baby can now probably pull herself to standing and may even have taken her first steps. She's babbling away and well on the road to saying her first word. It's time to stop using "baby-speak" and talk to her in adult language so that she will learn to say things correctly.

Anything you can do …

… your baby will want to do, too! By watching and copying you, your baby is just starting to learn about you as a role model.

Hello and goodbye Wave to your baby and he may wave back (left). **Grandma's calling!** Toy phones allow your baby to practice making and answering calls, just as she's seen you do (right).

Your baby may not have uttered his first word yet, but may be shaking his head to say "no," pointing at items he wants or wants you to notice, and waving bye-bye. These are all actions we use as we communicate with our babies every day, and he has picked them up from you. If your baby isn't waving yet, don't worry—some babies don't do this until well into their second year.

Capitalize on his copying behavior by pointing things out, or expressing your meaning with actions as well as words. If you're telling him something is big, open your arms wide. If you are telling him it's lunch time, make an eating action.

Mimicking chores Your baby will also want to play with the things he sees you hold and use, from a harmless measuring cup to a dangerous kitchen knife. (Hazardous items should all be locked away by now, but it's always good to double-check you haven't become complacent and left anything lying around the house.)

Give your baby toy versions of grown-up tools. A toy telephone can keep the real one on the hook (and ensure that your baby doesn't make any "accidental" phone calls), while a toy iron allows him to be just like Mommy, but without the danger of burns.

You are the ultimate learning tool
Maximize on your baby's wonderfully suggestible nature. If he sees you respond happily to a given situation, he is much more likely to respond happily in a similar situation, too. And if he sees you using utensils to eat your food, he'll want to use his spoon, too. Even if he doesn't mimic you immediately, he may well have processed what he's seen and do it another time—psychologists call this deferred imitation.

All this does put parents in the spotlight—observing your behavior takes precedence over any other kind of learning your baby will experience at this age. So whatever you do, be good!

TWINS

Twins' talk

Do your twins give the impression that they understand each other's babbling? Most experts agree that twins don't share a "language" as such, but rather a "code," or series of shortcuts that they develop when conversing with each other. This usually starts in infancy, when twins copy one another's immature speech patterns, such as jumbled sounds and made-up words. Because both twins are developing at the same rate, they often reinforce each others' communicative attempts and increase their own language. Although "twin talk" may be cute, you should help your children learn to use correct language when speaking. You can do this by speaking to your twins individually rather than together, and reading to them so they hear plenty of words.

Say something then! Twins often like to copy each other's babble.

Time for grown-up talk?

At 10 months, you might want to use a bit less "parentese," start to lower your pitch, and make your intonation more adult in style.

At this stage in your baby's development, it is important to encourage all forms of communication between you, and to promote his confidence in his ability to "talk" to you. Whether these are words you can understand or not, give your baby the space to say what he wants to say to you, even if it appears to be complete gibberish.

When your baby pauses for a moment in his babbling, respond to him with adult language. At this point of his speech development, what he needs to hear back from you is the correct way of saying things.

Try to refine your understanding of what he is saying. For instance, you could ask him, "Are you asking me for a drink? Would you like to go out? What are you trying to tell me? Would you like the teddy bear?" Don't worry if you can't always tell what he means; keep trying and you may get a smile to show you've got it right. Listen and respond to his sounds and first words, and show your delight so he'll know he's on the right track. Allowing him to speak, and then listening and responding to him, encourages him to develop his language skills and builds his confidence.

ASK A... PEDIATRICIAN

My 10-month-old wakes during the night and wants a bottle of formula. How can I discourage this?
Your baby shouldn't be hungry during the night now; he should have taken in all the calories he requires during the day. Often, the only reason babies of this age demand a feeding at night is for comfort. Make sure he has a good last feeding before bedtime and offer him water if he wakes in case he is thirsty.

Muscle development

Your baby's fine and gross motor skills have come a long way, but there's still plenty you can do to encourage his development.

The muscles of your baby's legs and arms continue to strengthen with each physical challenge he encounters. You can promote this development by encouraging your baby to climb over and under soft pieces of furniture (with a soft landing), up stairs (with supervision), and in a soft-play environment. Playing games such as "Row, Row, Row Your Boat" helps to develop good upper-body strength as you pull and push each other in the rowing action. Also, try dancing with

Gripping a crayon Scribbling is fun and improves your baby's fine motor skills.

your baby by holding his body or his hands as he stands and bounces, which is great for developing his leg muscles.

Your baby is now more able to control his smaller muscles, such as those in his fingers. Get him used to paint and paper by making handprints, or guiding his paint-covered fingers across paper to create his first painting. You can try giving him a fat crayon if you think he'll hold it and guiding his hand to make a mark across the paper. It might be a bit early for him to grapple with this yet, but you'll probably find that he has quite a strong grip—if you try to take the crayon away, he may not let go willingly!

Encouraging healthy eating

Help your baby to develop a taste for healthy foods before he starts to develop any particularly strong likes or dislikes.

FINGER-FOOD DUNKERS

Your baby loves to feed himself, so encourage this developing skill with finger-food dunkers. He'll enjoy this fun way of eating healthy foods. Below are ideas to get you started, but be warned—they are messy!

■ **Homemade baby guacamole** Mix chopped tomatoes with mashed avocado and a teaspoon of lemon juice; serve with whole-grain toast.

■ **Tomato sauce and pasta** Make a simple tomato pasta sauce and offer your baby a few very softly cooked pasta twists (chopped into smaller chunks, if necessary) to dunk in it.

■ **Cheese fondue** Make a cheese fondue: gently heat in a pan 1oz (25g) butter, 1oz (25g) cream cheese, and 2oz (50g) grated mild Cheddar cheese until melting. Serve with chunks of bread or toast and lightly steamed vegetables for dipping (halved new potatoes are good).

■ **Pancake dippers** Strips of pancake or pieces of banana can be dipped into plain yogurt.

■ **Meatball dippers** Dip meatballs into a fresh tomato sauce.

■ **Yogurt dippers** Dip chunks of steamed fish (check for bones) or chicken into a minty yogurt dip made of Greek yogurt and chopped fresh mint.

■ **Homemade fish fingers** Dip in a homemade tomato sauce.

Helping Mommy Spark your baby's interest in his meals by talking to him about how they are made and getting him to "help" you (left). **Fun faces** Babies love finger-food faces (right).

Although your baby is too young to stir or chop, he can sit with you as you prepare his food and talk him through the process of what you're doing. If you can spark his interest in what he's eating and make him feel part of the preparation process, he's more likely to be open-minded about enjoying it.

Allow him to experience the textures of what you're feeding him before and after cooking and talk to him about the colors of the foods. For instance, say to him, "This is a carrot—look how orange it is! Should Mommy peel the carrot?"

Make it visually appealing If you were presented with a plate of food in a restaurant that looked unappealing, it's unlikely you would want to eat it. Your baby's response to food is no different. Babies love bright colors, different shapes, and, once they can cope with small, soft lumps, a variety of textures. Use these facts to make the healthy foods you offer your baby look interesting and appetizing.

Arrange different types of foods in little piles on your baby's plate—for instance, put softly cooked vegetables that he can pick up with his fingers in one area, and his chicken casserole in another. Try serving his meals on plates that have separate compartments—these are often brightly colored and decorated to appeal especially to babies and toddlers.

If you are feeling artistic, you can use finger foods to create fun faces, or make a train out of mini sandwiches. Use shaped cookie cutters to make shaped sandwiches—your baby will love eating a star or flower!

Another good trick is to create swirls or other shapes of colorful fruit compote in a bowl of otherwise bland-looking breakfast oatmeal.

46 weeks

YOUR BABY IS 46 WEEKS AND 4 DAYS

Work and home bonuses

There are positives to being back at work and staying at home, so it's a good idea to remind yourself of these occasionally.

As well as giving you more financial stability, being back at work can have other benefits:

■ You will quickly relearn all the important information and skills you need to do your job and this will allay any worries you had about forgetting these while you focused on family life.

■ Being at work can be an important confidence boost after months of meeting the needs of a young baby.

■ It can make a change to dress up in your work clothes and even take the opportunity to refresh your wardrobe!

■ Work allows you to socialize and see the friends and colleagues whose company you enjoy but who may have been missing from your life during your baby's early months.

■ Being away from your baby, even for a day, can remind you of what a wonderful addition he is to your life and make you all the more grateful when you get home to him each evening.

Some benefits of staying at home are:

■ You're around to marvel at your baby's progress and witness every milestone.

■ You can avoid office politics.

■ You have a chance to make friends with other parents with babies and become part of local daily life and culture, which you might not have known about previously.

> **TIME TO THINK ABOUT**
>
> ## A new car seat
>
> Your baby may outgrow his infant Stage 1 car seat when he reaches 22 lb (10 kg). But don't be in a hurry to move to the next stage, since a rear-facing seat is safer for young children. Only move to a front-facing Stage 2 car seat when your baby exceeds the maximum weight and height limit of the seat. A Stage 3 booster seat will not be needed until your child is around 45 lb (20 kg).

YOUR BABY IS 46 WEEKS AND 5 DAYS

What's that noise?

Your baby is interested in all the sounds he hears around him, so help him to learn about the different noises in his world.

You can have lots of fun teaching your baby about the many different noises he's likely to encounter. From cars to animals to the telephone or doorbell ringing, there's plenty of scope to hone your skills of imitation or engineer it so that your baby hears the real thing.

Play with toy animals with your baby and demonstrate the noises they make. If barking, mooing, and meowing all gets a bit much, think about buying, or borrowing from the library, an animal

Say it out loud Sound out the noises of objects and animals in your baby's picture books.

sounds book so that you can help your baby push the animal buttons to hear "baas" or birdsong. Or you can download an app designed to teach babies about animal noises.

You can teach your baby about everyday household noises, too, so that he isn't startled when there's a knock at the door, or you switch on the vacuum cleaner. Help him to push the doorbell so that he can hear the noise it makes; when the phone rings, explain what the noise is and take him with you to answer it. He'll soon start to remember who or what makes the noises he hears.

Extended breast-feeding

Extended or long-term breast-feeding means breast-feeding beyond your baby's first year—so is it for you?

Still breast-feeding While it's more unusual in the West, breast-feeding older babies and toddlers is normal in many cultures.

The longer you breast-feed your baby, the longer he will benefit from the goodness in your breast milk. Breast milk becomes more concentrated in its nutritional benefits when your baby is feeding less often, and continues to provide him with vitamins A, C, B12, and large amounts of folate, calories, protein, and calcium. However, it is also true that by the time your baby reaches his first birthday, his primary source of nutrients will be the food that he eats.

The World Health Organization (WHO) has identified benefits in breast-feeding up to the age of two years. Toddlers between the ages of 16 and 30 months who breast-feed have been found to have fewer illnesses, as well as illnesses of shorter duration than non-breast-feeding toddlers.

Extended breast-feeding has benefits for moms' health and well-being, too. The longer you breast-feed your baby, the more you reduce your own risk of developing certain cancers, including breast, ovarian, uterine, and endometrial cancer. The WHO also suggests that it may reduce the risk of osteoporosis.

Making the right decision for you

How long you choose to breast-feed should be entirely dependent on what feels right for you and your baby, as the experience of breast-feeding is a very personal and individual one. You may encounter negative opinions about the benefits of breast-feeding beyond six months or a year. If you wish to continue, take heart that breast-feeding is a natural way to feed your baby, and as long as you are both enjoying and benefiting from the experience, there's no reason to stop. Those with positive feelings about extended breast-feeding counter that babies who are given the opportunity to breast-feed for a longer period of time are often more confident and independent as children.

If you do experience negative comments, simply explain why you are continuing to breast-feed to those family members and friends whose opinions matter to you, giving particular emphasis to the benefits for your baby.

As your baby becomes a toddler, you may feel more conscious about where you breast-feed. Bear in mind that as your baby has a varied diet now, he will be able to wait for a breast-feed until you get home or can find a quiet spot,

if you prefer. If he's thirsty when you're out, you can also offer water from a sippy cup. Many mothers of older babies continue to partially breast-feed—offering breast milk in the morning and evening as a comforting start and end to the day. This can be ideal as your baby shouldn't need to nurse during the day if he is properly established on solids.

46 weeks

361

47 weeks

NATURAL COPYCATS, BABIES WILL TRY TO MIMIC WHATEVER PEOPLE AROUND THEM ARE DOING

Your baby's muscles are stronger and she's better coordinated, enabling her to learn new skills such as sitting down from standing. She may be burning off more calories with her constant motion. She's looking more like the toddler she'll soon become!

Upside down

Your baby's increased coordination allows him to maneuver himself into different positions to gain new perspectives on his world.

Safety outdoors

Once your baby is on the move, he will want to explore the great outdoors—starting with your yard! Plenty of outdoor play is hugely beneficial for your baby's health and well-being, but before you let him on the loose, take a good look around any outdoor space and ensure it's safe for your inquisitive, mobile baby. The following guidelines will help to keep your baby safe:

■ Check that there are no poisonous plants your baby could reach. If you're unsure whether something is poisonous—perhaps flowers were planted by a previous owner—take a cutting or photo to your local garden center to see if they can identify it.

■ Keep potted plants out of your baby's reach so that he isn't tempted to eat the soil or pebbles, which are also a choking hazard.

■ Watch your baby all the time near water. Be careful around bird baths, water tables, wading pools, and swimming pools.

■ Make sure any play equipment is sturdily built. If you are assembling it yourself, follow the instructions exactly. Keep play equipment away from fences and walls.

■ Cover the sandbox when not in use to prevent cats from using it as a litter box. Check the rest of the yard for cat and other animal feces.

■ Most importantly, supervise your baby at all times in the yard.

At this age, your baby will probably pull up to standing, but getting down is more problematic as he still hasn't worked out how to bend his knees. If he sees a toy on the floor that he wants, he will either bend down from the waist with legs straight to grab it, or will simply sit straight from standing with a thud (although slightly less of a thud than before!). When leaning down from standing, he may peek between his legs and try to reach through them to grab toys and other objects. In fact, he has no real sense of his own abilities and limitations, and will try all sorts of approaches to get what he wants. For this reason, he may look surprised or become distressed when he lands on his bottom or finds himself in an unexpected position.

Help your baby to practice his balance and coordination by encouraging him to bend forward and pick up toys on the floor from a standing position.

He may also push himself up on his legs when he's in a crawling position, and peek backward. Every new position provides your baby with a new angle from which to view his environment, and he's also developing spatial awareness and an understanding of the shapes of things from different perspectives. Encourage him to point to things that he sees from his new vantage point, and watch him giggle with delight when he sees his favorite items upside down.

While it's important to install baby gates, you should teach your child how to move both up and down the stairs. Now that your baby is probably a very competent crawler, you can help him to master descending (far harder than going up); demonstrate how to hold the rails on the staircase if necessary. The same movement is used for sliding off the sofa or furniture, that is, on his tummy, feet first, and sliding backward.

A different view The world looks different from various angles, and your baby now has the maneuverability to try out new positions as she straightens her legs and pivots down.

YOUR BABY IS 47 WEEKS AND 1 DAY

Getting his attention

Your busy baby may be so intent on exploring at times that he doesn't pay attention to your guidance or warnings.

Usually your baby will hang upon your every word, keen to interact, listen, and respond. Of course, he'll also spend time engrossed in play and it'll be more of a challenge to get him to listen, especially if you're asking him to stop or want to divert him onto something else. If you need to interrupt him, you'll get his attention most effectively if you get down to his level and make eye contact. Say his name first and then give a short, simple statement. For example, if he's annoying the cat and you can see a scratch coming, say, "Tom, stop prodding the cat" and guide him away to reinforce the instruction. Avoid long sentences or multiple requests and always guide him gently to move if he needs to. There's no point listing dangers to him as he can't imagine the possible hazards that come so readily to your mind. Instead, if there's a problem, mime the consequences, for example if you need to show him your drink is hot, then mime touching the cup and say, "Ouch, hot, don't touch" while waving your fingers as if they're burned. It will take many repetitions to teach this danger awareness so don't expect him to remember this for quite a while.

If he consistently doesn't respond when you talk to him out of his range of vision, it's worth asking your doctor to check his hearing.

YOUR BABY IS 47 WEEKS AND 2 DAYS

No more bottles

At 47 weeks, your baby is able to master a sippy cup and drink milk this way. Dropping the bottle early can help to protect his teeth.

Drinking from a cup Get your baby into the habit of drinking her milk and other fluids in a cup to prevent tooth decay.

It's easy to continue offering your baby a bottle, particularly at night, as it is comforting for him, already part of his routine, and you can gauge how much milk he drinks in a bottle.

But the longer your baby drinks from a bottle, the harder it will be for him to move onto a cup and fall asleep without sucking. The sucking action causes milk to swirl around his mouth, bathing the teeth in the sugars contained in milk, and allows milk to pool in his mouth when he is asleep, causing tooth decay. If you transition him onto a cup early on, he won't be as likely to associate milk with comfort, so is less likely to encounter problems with comfort eating later in life.

If your baby is used to always using a bottle, he may resist being offered a cup instead, so try to make the transition fun. Start by switching the nipple on his bottle to a spout so he becomes used to drinking rather than sucking. Buy colorful cups and let him choose which one he'd like to drink from. Habits can be established quickly in babies under a year, and if he feels he has a choice, the disappointment of not having a bottle will soon be forgotten. Things can sometimes go awry when he's upset or ill, but you can comfort him by snuggling up with a book and warm milk in the cup of his choice.

If you are breast-feeding, continue with your regular feedings, but move toward one or two smaller feedings a day and offering expressed breast milk in a cup to make up the difference. Suckling breast milk does not cause tooth decay.

Your child's first teacher

You are your baby's first teacher. Your guidance and actions are his benchmarks for understanding the world around him.

Setting an example As well as being sociable occasions, family mealtimes offer the perfect opportunity to model good table manners.

ASK A... CHILD PSYCHOLOGIST

My baby has temper tantrums already! Is this normal? While your baby is not yet emotionally capable of a true "toddler"-style tantrum, babies can appear to lose their tempers. This is a sign that they are frustrated at being unable to express their needs. Try to remain calm and patient yourself. Many babies respond to being held and comforted when feeling out of sorts; sing a familiar song to calm him and try to distract him from the situation. Speak quietly so your baby is reassured that everything in his world is not out of control, and show him how to master whatever it was he was trying to do, or gently move him to another room where the trigger will no longer upset him.

You've probably been chatting with your baby since he was born, explaining your daily activities and showing him how everything from light switches and faucets to doorbells and toys operate. For the next few years, your baby will continue to turn to you for guidance and information and will learn how to behave, interact, and negotiate his world by watching and listening to you.

For this reason, it's important to do your best to model the type of behavior you want your baby to learn, and present your family ethos and values to him through your actions. While he is still too young to display any table manners (and digging in and making a mess is an important part of his learning to eat), you can exhibit good manners yourself. Sit and eat with him whenever you can, and try to enjoy regular family meals. Studies show that the more frequently families eat together, the better their

relationships. He'll also learn that mealtimes are sociable, and will see how you and your partner listen when others are speaking and wait your turn to talk. Let him see a healthy, respectful relationship between you and others. How you interact with family, friends, and acquaintances teaches him about relationships and acceptable behavior.

Work out healthy ways to control your frustration and anger when things go wrong or you're stressed; babies who grow up hearing shouting or seeing you lose your temper will mimic this behavior and consider it the norm. It certainly isn't always easy to cope with a single-minded baby, and you may find your nerves get frayed, but how you cope with your emotions sets the standard for how your baby copes with his.

There's no doubt that setting a positive example for your baby is beneficial; when he sees you socializing, reading, being organized and active, and enjoying fulfilling relationships, he will be likely to absorb these qualities, too. However, while the example you set is important, it's also healthy to recognize that there's no such thing as a "perfect" parent, and that parenting is a constant learning process. Don't be too hard on yourself if you don't manage to get everything right, whether leaving a messy kitchen, ignoring a phone call, letting routines slip, or being petty with your partner. Babies can cope with things not always being ideal. As long as you're in tune with your baby's needs, put these first, and give consistent care, then you're being a "good enough" parent. Providing a secure, understanding environment is the best thing you can do for your child.

Growing appetite

The more mobile your baby becomes, the more his appetite increases. He may need more food and regular snacks to sustain his energy.

Giving your baby a balanced diet of nutrient-rich foods ensures he has the energy to grow and develop, and sustains his energy for longer periods of time. Milk forms the basis of his nutrition for the first year, but his intake of solids is steadily increasing, and by now he's eating two or three meals a day. He should be getting plenty of whole-grain carbohydrates, fresh vegetables and fruits, lean meats and fish, egg yolks, dairy products, and beans. While some babies can become picky eaters at this age, continue to serve a variety of

healthy foods, revisiting the foods that have been rejected every few days or so until they become familiar.

Don't offer your baby unhealthy snacks between meals. Snacks should contribute to his overall diet and make up for any shortfalls. If he learns to satisfy his hunger with fruits, whole-grain toast, yogurt, squares of cheese, strips of fresh vegetables, a hard-boiled egg yolk, or a few spoonfuls of tuna, he will develop healthy eating habits and associate good, fresh food with mealtimes and snack times.

Encourage your baby to taste new, appropriate foods from your plate. Show him different foods when shopping or preparing meals, and let him touch, smell, and taste them so he gets familiar with them. Let him eat until he feels full; he may eat lots at each sitting for a few days, then seem to want less for a while. Allow his hunger to decide how much he eats: while it is important that he gets regular, healthy meals, it is also acceptable for him to eat smaller or larger quantities on occasion, as long as his weight remains stable (see p.298).

A different approach

Instead of racing to do the chores when your baby is asleep, slow down and let him join in. You may be surprised to find you both have fun.

Little helper Unpacking the groceries doesn't have to be quick when it's this interesting.

When your baby begins a play session, you may have a few minutes to make a phone call, check emails, or make a list before he demands your attention. You may also be able to get a few things done while he naps. However, you're unlikely to be able to cram everything you need to get done in your day into these small windows of opportunity.

Although it may take much longer, letting him join in your practical activities will keep him occupied and teach him about the way in which a household runs. Let him sit on a pile of laundry while you sort the clothes and name the different colors; or make a

game out of refilling your diaper changing stations and repacking your changing bag, letting him handle the items. He may do more unpacking than stocking up, but he'll be entertained while you work.

You might even want to include him in some of your other daily routines, for example taking a bath together. If you read your book or your emails out loud when he is happily playing on the floor, he'll love the sound of your voice as you catch up with your reading. You may get less done than you would like, but you'll have the satisfaction of working with your baby, not in spite of him.

Outdoor play

It's important that your baby has plenty of outdoor playtime to ensure he gets fresh air, sunlight, and lots of exercise.

Outdoor fun Playing outdoors allows for exuberant fun and a change of scenery.

Babies need time and space to explore and get moving away from the confines of the home, car seat, or stroller. Gross and fine motor skills, coordination, balance, and the imagination are developed when children are given plenty of opportunities to climb and play, and to respond to the natural world with its multitude of textures, smells, activities, and possibilities.

Being outdoors is also helpful in letting your child experience a different field of vision and new sensory stimulation. Seeing into the distance, feeling the wind on his skin, and noticing changes in the light all offer his senses new information.

Time spent outdoors in a natural environment is known to improve adults' moods, so taking your baby outside regularly will probably give you a boost and start a habit for your baby that will be good for him as he grows.

Time spent in sunlight also encourages the production of vitamin D in your baby's body (see p.226), which helps him build healthy bones and teeth. Be sure to take steps to prevent sunburn

Make an effort to get outside at least once a day, and in nice weather, let your baby sit in the grass, crawl in the park, or amuse himself in the sandbox in your local playground. Push him on the baby swings, play ball, point out the squirrels, and take a bag of stale bread to feed the ducks. Give him a safe place to explore; hold his hands so that he can stand supported and splash in puddles; and let him crawl and get his hands dirty. Once he is on his feet, hold his hand and enjoy "mini" explorations of your local park or neighborhood, letting him take his time and stop to examine nature along the way. Have his stroller at the ready so he can rest when he gets tired.

Spending quality time outside with your baby will do wonders for your perspective and it will give him a new view of the outdoors, your neighborhood, and the world.

DEVELOPMENT ACTIVITY

Rainy-day fun

Your baby needs some time each day to move his body freely so that he can make those gross motor movements that teach him so much about what he can do with his body.

If you can't venture out due to rainy days or cold weather, think of ways in which you can keep him active at home. Encourage him to crawl up and down the stairs next to you, and have a crawling race across the living room floor. Hold his hands and dance to lively music; and set up an obstacle course with cushions, pillows, folded towels, and toys for him to climb up, over, and around.

You could make a drum kit with kitchen pots and pans and wooden spoons, or play a game of tag, chasing him as he crawls around the living room, and playing action rhymes when you catch him.

As long as he gets a little out of breath and, ideally, is giggling too, he'll be using up energy and, of course, having plenty of fun.

Doing the crawl Get down on your baby's level and enjoy seeing the world from his point of view.

48 weeks

AT FIRST, BABIES BELIEVE THAT THE IMPORTANCE OF A POINTING FINGER IS THE FINGER ITSELF

Your baby's manual dexterity has come a long way and she is now adept at using her index finger to point to items of interest. She's also getting better at using a spoon to feed herself, but as her hand–eye coordination is not yet fully developed, mealtimes are bound to be messy!

I'm feeding myself

It'll be a while before your baby can successfully feed himself with a spoon, but he'll enjoy trying to eat with one, just like mom and dad.

By now, your baby may want to feed himself, even though he doesn't yet have the motor skills and coordination to bring a spoon easily to his mouth. However, there's no harm in giving him a spoon of his own to practice with. To make it easier for him, give him a short-handled plastic spoon rather than a long-handled infant spoon. A shorter handle is much simpler to maneuver. Give him a bowl, preferably one with a suction ring on the base to prevent him from knocking it off his tray. This type of base also holds the bowl firmly in place, making it easier for your baby to experiment with dipping his spoon into it.

As he negotiates his spoon and bowl of food, offer him spoonfuls from a second bowl that you're holding. When he watches you feed him, he will eventually learn the art of picking up and holding a spoon, filling it with food, and placing it in his mouth.

Forget about etiquette To begin with, your baby is likely to hold the spoon in one hand and use his other hand to scoop what's in front of him into his mouth. At this stage, let him do exactly as he pleases. If he wants to grip the spoon and eat with his fingers, that's fine—he'll get around to spooning it in when his coordination has improved. Give him a bib (a wipe-clean one will save on washing), and you may also want to put some newspaper or a splash mat on the floor under his high chair.

Even if most of the food ends up in his hair, don't discourage him from experimenting with his spoon. You can hold his fist as he grips the spoon and

Self-feeding with a spoon Be prepared for a good portion of the contents of your baby's bowl to end up in her lap, on the floor, and all over her face—even in her hair!

help him move it to his mouth, but remember that he doesn't yet have the coordination or the flexibility in his wrist to be able to do this himself. Don't underestimate the importance of providing your baby with guidance and a model to copy. Sit down to eat with him at mealtimes so he sees how you operate your own cutlery.

The most important thing at the moment is that your baby is encouraged to get his food into his tummy in the easiest way possible and that he enjoys himself at meal times.

Successful self-feeding is a big developmental step for your baby. At the moment, he's growing in confidence, but he will be unlikely to be able to feed himself a full meal without any help until he is about three, so he'll need plenty of guidance and help from you in the meantime.

ASK A... NUTRITIONIST

Why isn't my baby hungry at mealtimes? How much breast milk or formula is he still consuming? By now, he needs no more than 16 fl oz–1 pint (500–600 ml) a day. While it's still too early for cow's milk, small amounts of cheese or yogurt are acceptable. Offer him solids before milk feedings so meals start on an empty stomach. Also, cut down daytime bottles or milk feedings. He can now manage on a feeding in the morning and at night, with a little milk alongside meals. Ensure he doesn't have constant access to other drinks, especially juice. It's good to avoid offering too many snacks: a couple of healthy ones a day is enough.

48 weeks

369

Patting, poking, and pinching

Your baby's hand–eye coordination is improving constantly, and he is now capable of pointing and poking, and may even pinch, too!

Being gentle Teach your baby how to treat her siblings with gentleness.

Your baby will begin to test his own strength and abilities and you may find him prodding, poking, pushing, and even pinching pets, toys, and people. In fact, any activity that offers a resounding reaction will attract his interest and he'll want to repeat it.

Your baby's unwelcome behavior is nothing more than an exercise undertaken to satisfy his curiosity and gauge the response he gets. He's not being malicious, but is trying out his skills and experimenting. When he does poke or hit, show him how to interact more gently with everything and everyone around him. Show him how to pat your family pet and stroke his siblings. Provide words for these actions, such as "Nice cat, pet the cat," so he learns to understand the terminology for the actions you want to see. Soon enough you will be able to say simply "Pet-pet" to get him to stroke rather than hit.

If he continues being too physical, distraction is the key. He will learn what is expected of him, even if that doesn't happen immediately! Find opportunities to put your baby's skilled little fingers to better use. Give him an activity board with buttons to push, dials to turn, and strings to pull.

He won't go to bed!

Your baby equates bedtime with being away from mom and dad—and all the fun—and he may resist attempts to settle him at night.

As your baby approaches the end of his first year, he may be more reluctant to settle at night if he doesn't want to miss out on any of the fun! If he starts to put up a fight at bedtime, make sure that his evening routine continues to be relaxing and comforting so that he looks forward to this time and continues to associate it with the chance to enjoy close, quiet time with you.

Bear in mind that babies do need less sleep as they get older (see p.376) and during times when they are less mobile, so if your baby still has two daytime naps, this may be a good time to try to drop one of them (see p.292).

Throughout the day, ensure your baby gets plenty of physical exercise and stimulation so that he is tired enough to go to sleep at bedtime, and consider moving his nap time to an earlier slot, or his bedtime to a slightly later time, so that he is ready to settle down at night.

Try not to become frustrated or angry, which will make him anxious and more distressed. He may also find that his reluctance to go to bed is a good way to get attention. Simply settle him in his crib as usual and return when he calls you. Stroke him and pat him, sing his familiar night-time song or say the usual "good night," then leave. Be upbeat and positive so that he doesn't feel as if bedtime is a punishment. Keep household noise to a minimum during this phase so that your baby isn't distracted by what's going on elsewhere.

If all else fails, at bedtime put your baby in his crib with a few toys and his usual comfort items, and allow him to occupy himself quietly until sleep descends, then remove the toys.

Limits and boundaries

As your baby's first birthday approaches, you may be wondering what you can expect of his behavior, and what parenting style to develop.

Clear explanations Let your baby know when she has done something wrong, and explain why it is wrong clearly and kindly.

Most parents are concerned about what sort of parent they will be, and most aim for a middle ground focused on being warm and loving, and firm, but fair, when it comes to guiding their child's behavior. The challenge is often to get the right balance between giving your child the freedom to explore the world, yet ensure that they grow up to be well-behaved individuals with a real sense of right and wrong.

You are already setting boundaries, by moving your baby away or distracting him if he snatches toys from another child. You probably also hold his hands firmly and say "no," if he does something he shouldn't. So by 10 months, your baby may have worked out that "no" means "stop," but he hasn't grasped the abstract ideas of right and wrong, and may not heed your instructions simply because curiosity has got the better of him.

Types of discipline Discipline tends to fall into two main categories—that needed for safety and that needed for good behavior.

When it comes to safety, it's important to remove your child physically from danger. If, for example, he goes to touch the oven door, or grab a lamp from the table, move him away, hold his hands firmly, and, kneeling at his eye level, tell him "No" and explain why—"The oven is hot, it will burn you. Ow!" or "The lamp is heavy, it will bump you." Once won't be enough with explanations, but repetition and consistent responses will help your baby get the message.

When it comes to good behavior, don't expect too much. Your baby still considers himself to be the center of the world and has only the shakiest idea that he could upset others. At this age, he learns by watching, and you are his key role model. When you show good manners and speak calmly, he'll absorb this and start to show this behavior too as he develops. He doesn't understand the concept of saying sorry yet, but it's not too early to demonstrate how it's done so that he gets to know what's expected.

Whatever parenting style you develop, there are some key points to remember. Your child will be more responsive if you are consistent; spend more time and energy praising and encouraging rather than scolding him; and, when the time comes to use discipline and consequences, you do so calmly and without anger.

DEVELOPMENT ACTIVITY

Soft and hard

Help your baby to understand the different properties of the objects he encounters each day. Give him different textured toys and household items to hold and handle, and describe each one, talking about whether it is smooth, hard, soft, or furry, as well as what color it is. Talking to him in this way helps to expand his vocabulary and understand that not only do things have names, but they also have different characteristics. This in turn helps him start to make connections and comparisons. He's not ready to name all these items himself, but you are helping him to understand.

Exploring through touch Fill a basket with different textured toys and objects, and encourage him to dive in and explore.

48 weeks

371

YOUR BABY IS 48 WEEKS AND 4 DAYS

In your baby's own time

It can be tempting to want your baby to meet the same milestones as his peers, but remember that every baby is different.

Milestones are designed to give you a rough idea of when your baby will be physically, mentally, and/or emotionally ready to master challenges or skills that are acquired across infancy and childhood. They are not, however, tests to establish his intelligence or define his future prowess in different areas. In fact, his achieving milestones such as walking or sleeping through the night early is no indication that he will continue to "achieve" at a high level, nor do everything else early. It's important to realize, too, that, just as milestones act as a guide rather than a rule, the order in which they are reached can vary from baby to baby. Some leap ahead physically and are slower to talk. Others gain hand–eye coordination earlier, while walking happens further into the second year. So while your friend's baby of the same age may be busy climbing stairs, yours may be far more preoccupied with making different sounds.

Your baby is unique, with his own personality. He will meet his milestones when he is ready, and unless he is obviously lagging well behind his peers of the same age (see pp.412–13), there is no reason for concern. It can be helpful to compare him to other babies as this will usually reassure you that he's on track, or, very occasionally, alert you that there could be a problem you should check with a health professional. However, while comparing is okay, avoid getting into a milestone competition. Stimulate him and encourage him to develop the skills necessary to meet his milestones in a playful, supportive, and loving environment, and celebrate every single one of his achievements.

YOUR BABY IS 48 WEEKS AND 5 DAYS

It's me!

Your baby is developing a sense of independence, and in the coming months, his self-awareness will grow.

Security Although more independent, your baby craves closeness to you as much as ever.

Your baby is showing signs that he's beginning to understand that you are separate from him. The earliest signal of this was a few months ago, around the time he realized that you aren't always there and that you sometimes move out of sight. This is when he grasped the concept of "person permanence:" the idea that you exist even when he can't see or hear you.

As he discovered his own body, his self-awareness grew, alongside his increasing control over, and consciousness of, how his body moved. He is also developing a mental picture of himself and others. At around 12 months, he'll be able to tell the difference between a photograph of himself and that of another baby, and from 15 months comes the revelation that the image in the mirror is a reflection of himself.

Your baby's involvement in some basic fantasy play is another sign that he's aware of himself and others. When the two of you act out cuddling a teddy bear, or pretending to give it a drink by putting a cup to its mouth, he's copying others' behavior.

As he moves through his second year, his awareness that he's a separate person from you will grow, so watch out for him asserting his personality. Soon, "no" will be his favorite word!

Working parent

Juggling work and parenting can be stressful, and you may feel that you aren't able to give 100 percent to either. These feelings are normal.

Quality time Ensure that the time you spend with your baby is fun, and that you are focused on him when you are with him.

Despite any concerns you may have as a working parent, be assured that you can most certainly raise a healthy, happy baby and enjoy your work. The secret is to be organized and flexible, and to get your priorities right. If you put your job first when you are at work, and your baby and family first at home, you are bound to get things right. The other parts of your life that surround this, including household chores and socializing, may need to move to the back burner for a while—certainly until you establish a routine that works for everyone—and it is equally important that you lower the expectations you hold for yourself. If you are just about keeping all of the balls in the air, then well done!

Achieving a "work–life" balance

While it's undeniably tricky to keep work and family life running smoothly, there are several things you can do to help your days go well. First, get organized. Make sure you know what needs to happen when, and stick to the same routine each day so you can streamline events and your baby knows what's going on, which will help him to feel secure. Set out everything required for the morning the night before so that you can relax knowing that everything is ready, no matter what happens the following morning. Batch-cooking and bulk-buying are other organizational godsends that save you a great deal of time in the long run—and probably some money, too.

It's important to have backup plans, too, in case your baby is sick or your caregiver is away. Try to organize a support network that you can turn to for dealing with the unexpected.

If at times you feel overwhelmed, focus on the positives. Feeling guilty for not being there to see all of your baby's "firsts" or tend to his daily needs won't help you. Instead, celebrate the fact that your baby is healthy and happy and you're able to go out and earn a living. Concentrate on the most important areas of your life and only agree to things that enhance your life. An exhausted, unhealthy, and emotional mom isn't going to be effective in any area of her life.

Lastly, don't feel guilty about relaxing work ambitions for the time being if you find a young family isn't conducive to a go-getting mentality. There will be plenty of time to chase those goals when your baby is more independent.

DEVELOPMENT ACTIVITY

Homemade fun!

Your baby will be just as excited by a big, empty box into which he can crawl or tip over as he will be by the latest and most expensive new toys. Scrunch up paper into balls to fill the box, then encourage him to tip the contents out and reload the box. Drop in a few toys for him to discover while he plays. Similarly, a sturdy laundry basket makes a great toy car or train—your baby will enjoy playing the part of the driver or passenger when you push him around.

These games will help to stretch your baby's imagination and improve his gross and fine motor skills. What's more, they'll keep him occupied for stretches of time!

Improvised toys Even a piece of paper taped into a cone shape will be "useful."

49 weeks

AN 11-MONTH-OLD BABY NEEDS ABOUT 14 HOURS OF SLEEP IN A 24-HOUR PERIOD

Ensure that your baby is getting a wide range of colorful foods to provide her with the nutrients she needs. Your baby may be shyer than usual now and even clingy—a sign that she is increasingly aware that she is separate from you, so ease her into new situations gently.

Working it out

Your baby now shows an increased ability to solve problems, and enjoys creative activities and toys that test his developing skills.

Analyzing Your baby's ability to work out what fits where, and his developing fine motor skills, allow him to solve more complex puzzles.

Toys such as shape-sorters, simple first jigsaw puzzles, musical instruments, and building blocks will help your baby to improve his analytical thinking, which, in turn, will develop his ability to work out how things in his environment operate.

By playing with these types of toys, your baby will learn to discriminate between the different parts of the toys, so in the coming months and years he will be able to identify their shape, size, color, and use, and will begin to reason, deduce, analyze, and use logical thought to assess how his toys work before putting his ideas to the test. He is also learning to find solutions when his ideas do not work immediately. For example, if he has chosen a slot in which to fit his wooden puzzle piece and it doesn't fit, he may persevere for longer to find a solution to create the right match. Although they can become frustrated, most babies enjoy a challenge and repeat things over and over again until they get them right.

To encourage your baby to develop and hone his problem-solving skills, give him puzzles and activities he can master before moving him on to more challenging toys. With early successes, he'll become confident about his abilities, and will remember his successes when things get harder. If he is struggling to master a toy, rather than let his frustration build, bring back simpler toys that he's successfully mastered in the past to rebuild his confidence first.

Observation and imitation Your baby will solve problems by observing and copying. This is one good reason why it's worth spending lots of time playing with him and showing him how things work. Demonstrate new toys first and and then let him have a try and applaud his efforts with them.

Give him a chance to play alongside other children on a regular basis, if possible. Seek out local playgroups, or a community playgroup or local mothers' group, so that he gets used to playing alongside other babies—and you may get some time to yourself. Or arrange a regular get-together with local moms and babies you've met, perhaps rotating houses. All of these provide opportunities for your baby to mix in an environment where other children are trying things out in different ways, allowing him to observe and learn.

Arts and crafts

Encourage your baby's creativity as well as his hand–eye coordination and fine motor skills with regular arts-and-crafts sessions. Purchase some chunky nontoxic crayons, tape a large piece of paper to the kitchen floor, and show him how to make marks with his crayons. Create patterns and scribbles. Talk about the colors you are using and guide your baby's hand to make straight lines or circles, naming all the different shapes you make. Every couple of months, save one of his creations in a scrapbook or art portfolio so you can see how his skills progress over the coming years. In the summer, go outside and use chalk to create pictures and scribbles on the pavement or deck.

Free flow Your baby will enjoy being expressive with colors and shapes.

49 weeks

375

Planning your baby's birthday

You may wish to celebrate your baby's first birthday with a party. But don't be surprised if he doesn't show much interest in the proceedings!

Plan to keep your baby's first birthday party simple—you can't celebrate his transition to toddlerhood if you are busy serving appetizers or clearing up spills, and he will prefer to have you by his side, particularly if there are more people than usual in your home.

Limit the number of guests—most babies experience separation anxiety at this age, so a big gathering may distress him. Choose a few people he knows well.

Forget about themes and party games—your baby will have no interest in them. Balloons may be fun, but tape them out of reach to prevent your baby from popping them (the scare could ruin the day!) or choking on them once they've deflated. Or use helium balloons and cut the strings so the little ones can't reach them.

Keep the party short—an hour or 90 minutes is probably the full extent of your baby's attention span. Aim to start the party half an hour after he wakes from his nap so that he's refreshed, but not too grumpy, and ensure he has something to eat and drink before the guests arrive, as he'll be too excited to eat much once they do. Keep an eye on what he's eating, as some foods put out for the adults may not be suitable. Supervise him as usual while he eats, and ensure he gets some healthy treats and not too much cake.

Don't go overboard on gifts. He's likely to lose interest if there are too many to be opened, and he'll probably find the mountain of colorful paper more fun than the gifts themselves! If guests ask for gift ideas, a good choice is books. This will build up your baby's library, and it's affordable for most people.

How much sleep now?

Your baby may resist settling down at bedtime and need much less sleep than before, but it's important he gets enough to stay healthy.

Routine A consistent bedtime ritual helps your baby to prepare for impending sleep.

As he approaches one year, your baby needs about 14 hours of sleep in a 24-hour period. He may have one long nap of around two hours, or two short naps totaling two to three hours, and may sleep for 11–12 hours at night.

If your baby resists going to sleep at night, stick to a regular bedtime routine—he'll be less likely to resist if these bedtime events become habit and he operates on autopilot. He'll benefit now from having a comfort object, which will help him to soothe himself if he wakes in the night or early in the morning. You can also place a few toys at the end of his crib: he may resist going to sleep, but remain happy to be settled in his crib if he can see something fun to keep him occupied! You can be fairly confident that he'll fall asleep mid-activity!

Work out the best nap system for your baby. A late-afternoon nap might make it hard for him to settle at night—a quiet, gentle playtime instead may relax him. One longer nap around lunchtime may keep him going all afternoon, as long as he's in bed early.

Consistency is key with bedtime. Be aware, though, that if you settle him down before 6pm, he's going to rise before 6am the next morning! If you're a night owl rather than a lark, you may need to adjust his bedtime accordingly.

Outdoor pursuits

Now that your baby is almost one year old, you can start to enjoy some new outdoor activities together.

Easy rider Baby carriers are a great way to enjoy walking with your baby—and she gets to see the world on your level.

Your baby is old enough to enjoy taking part in some of the outdoor activities you enjoy, and which you may have neglected somewhat since he was born.

There's a range of relatively inexpensive equipment that enables you to include your baby in outdoor pursuits. If you like to walk or hike, you can purchase a baby backpack carrier. Take your baby with you to buy it so that you're happy that you both find it comfortable. It needs to have adequate back support for you, with a sturdy, front-closing strap, and to be the right size for your baby, with sufficient head support if he falls asleep. Most are waterproof with sun and rain shields, and have a pouch to carry essentials such as a drink, snack, diaper-changing kit, and sunscreen. Ideally, walk with at least one other adult so that someone can check on your baby and help get the carrier on and off, as well as share the carrying. A sturdy, thick-wheeled stroller also allows you to enjoy longer walks over uneven terrain.

Cycling as a family If you're looking to get back on your bicycle, you can fit a bike trailer to your bike. Popular cycling trails often hire out bikes with all the necessary equipment to transport your baby safely. The age at which a baby can sit in a trailer is determined by the strength of his head and neck development, and the weight of the helmet. Ideally, he should have been sitting well without support for at least two months, which is usually at around 10 to 12 months. Some countries have laws that state babies must be at least one year old before riding as a passenger on a bike, and make it compulsory for babies to wear helmets, including when in a trailer. Avoid putting your baby in a bike seat until he is at least one year, as he won't have sufficient muscle strength and development before then to support his head while wearing a helmet.

Your baby will thrive on the new experience of seeing the world up at your height in a backpack, or watching the sights whiz past from a bike trailer; and you'll both benefit from the fresh air and sharing these new experiences.

To get your baby used to the sensation of being in a trailer, and help you to adjust to carrying him behind you, start with short rides on smooth paths to avoid jolts, and steer clear of roads. Take your partner or a friend with you at first, and build up to longer trips as you and your baby grow in confidence.

Don't put your baby in a backpack or a trailer if it's very hot or cold as it will be difficult to regulate his temperature. On longer trips, take frequent breaks to check him, and take him out at intervals so he can move freely. When you purchase equipment, check that it has been tested for babies, and inspect all the straps and fixtures regularly for wear and tear.

ASK A... NUTRITIONIST

Should I encourage my baby to eat everything in front of her? It's best to let your baby's appetite be the guide. Encouraging her to finish up her plate may lead to negative food associations and increase resistance. At this age, the appetite of some babies wanes slightly. In the first year, your baby tripled her birthweight, but she gains weight more slowly in her second year, so while more active, she may not need to eat as often. Keep in mind, too, that she still gains a proportion of her calories from milk. Also, as she is more mobile, it may be harder to get her to stay still long enough to finish every last morsel. On the other hand, if your baby is less interested in her milk now, you may find that she wolfs down her food. Either way, as long as you offer her a variety of healthy foods (ideally concentrated around mealtimes), she will gain the nutrients she needs to thrive.

49 weeks

Mind those Ps and Qs

This is the ideal time to demonstrate good manners to your baby by showing him the polite responses you would like him to mimic.

We can't all be on our best behavior all the time of course, but since your baby will pick up on phrases you use regularly and start to understand their meaning, being polite and considerate toward your baby and other people can only have a positive effect on him.

Say "Thank you" when you hand your baby a toy, and "Please" when you ask for something from him so that he gets used to the sounds of these words. It doesn't matter that he won't be saying "please" or "thank you" himself for a while, just hearing them as part of your daily conversation will help them begin to make sense. Say "Excuse me," "You're welcome," and even "I'm sorry" appropriately as you go about your activities. He'll grow up understanding that these words are part of normal behavior, and will adopt them more easily when he starts to talk more.

Be polite to people around you, too, including your partner. Be generous with praise and appreciation, and always show empathy for others. On those occasions when you can't be a perfect example, just be aware that your baby may be listening—the odd rude remark here and there probably won't register—but do it too often and he may pick up on your language!

As your baby's vocabulary expands throughout his second year, you will be able to prompt him to say "please" and "thank you" by asking "What do you say?," or "What's the magic word?," and repeating either "please" or "thank you" so he gets into the habit of using them.

Dressing for the weather

While your baby's clothing needs are fairly modest, there are a few wardrobe basics that will equip him for all weather conditions.

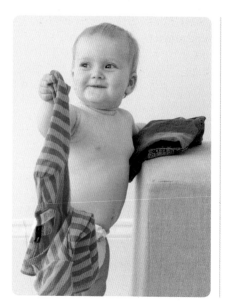

The key to ensuring that your baby is appropriately dressed for the weather is to layer clothing so that you can adapt what he's wearing as conditions change, or he moves between inside and outdoors.

In colder months, dress him in several layers, including a onesie, top, and then warmer fleece or sweater. He'll need a warm outer jacket (waterproof if it's wet) for outdoors, as well as mittens and a warm hat. All-in-one snowsuits are perfect for especially cold days. If he's sitting in his stroller, he'll need a fleecy cover or blanket to keep him cozy.

Comfortable clothing Opt for simple styles that are easy to add or remove to keep her the right temperature in all weathers.

If you go into a store, remove his blanket and hat, and remove layers and hats at home so that he doesn't overheat.

In the warmer months, a couple of light layers are sufficient, with a summer cardigan to put on and remove as needed. His clothes play an important role in sun protection. A sunhat is essential: opt for a floppy one or Legionnaire-style hat with a brim and back flap to cover his neck. It's important, too, to protect his shoulders from the sun, especially in exposed areas such as the beach. Keep a long-sleeved T-shirt on him, or better still, buy a baby lycra swimsuit that covers him and blocks most UVA rays. When he's indoors on a hot day, a diaper may be all he needs.

Too sick for child care?

It can be tempting for working parents to dose up an unwell baby with medicine and send him to daycare, but he should be kept at home.

Feeling unwell An under-the-weather baby should remain at home until she's better.

A child's immune system gradually builds up antibodies to unencountered infections; meanwhile, your baby may well catch whatever bug is going around at his child-care center, and may well succumb again a short while later. For this reason, parents have an obligation to keep children who are ill away from that environment until they are no longer contagious, or it will become a veritable breeding ground for infections.

Also, your baby's immune system is already hard at work fighting off an infection at this point, so he'll be in danger of acquiring a secondary infection if he's in contact with another set of germs.

If your baby is ill, be honest about it. The staff will know when your baby is under the weather, and you can set up an embarrassing situation if you try to pass him off as being perfectly healthy when he's not.

Set in place a contingency plan for times when your baby is ill, with a list of family members or friends who can step in; or see if you can work from home, or change your hours temporarily.

Ensure your baby is comfortable at home and gets plenty of fluids to flush out infection. Expect some crankiness, tearfulness, and irritability, as well as a few hard nights, and be patient. In a calm, relaxing environment, he will be back to himself in no time. When in doubt, call your pediatrician who can assess the situation, reassure you, and provide guidance.

ASK A... PEDIATRICIAN

When should I keep my baby at home?

Keep in mind the following points:
■ Most babies and children suffer from regular colds (you can expect anywhere between one and six a year in the early years). If nasal discharge is thick and sticky, your baby may be more susceptible to further infections, including ear infections. It's best to keep him at home until the cold has cleared completely.
■ If your baby has a fever, he should stay at home for at least 24 hours after it has broken. Not only will he be irritable, sleepy, and uncomfortable, making the child-care experience distressing, but he will need plenty of rest and fluids to recover.

■ If your baby has a rash, you will need to get him checked over by your pediatrician. Rashes have many causes, including infectious diseases, which will need to be eliminated.
■ Flu and other respiratory illnesses can become serious in babies if they are not monitored, so take your baby to the doctor if he has flu symptoms (see p.408). These illnesses can easily spread around a child-care center, so a baby with the flu must stay home.
■ A baby with diarrhea or vomiting should always be kept at home. Your baby will be sent home if he experiences these symptoms at the child-care center. He'll need to stay at home for at least 48 hours after the last episode, no matter how well he seems to feel.

■ Bacterial eye infections, such as conjunctivitis (see p.402), are highly contagious. Keep your baby at home until symptoms clear and he has been taking antibiotics for at least 36 hours.
■ Keep your baby at home if he catches whooping cough, or another childhood illness such as measles, rubella, or mumps. Although in the early months whooping cough is routinely vaccinated against, it's still possible to catch, but is less severe. Keep him at home, too, with chickenpox, roseola, scarlet fever, and hand, foot, and mouth disease.
■ If your baby has impetigo or another contagious skin disease, keep him at home for at least 48 hours after starting antibiotics. Scabies needs to be treated before your baby can return.

49 weeks

50 weeks

BABIES UNDER A YEAR ARE NOT EMOTIONALLY MATURE ENOUGH TO HAVE A TRUE TEMPER TANTRUM

Your baby may now spend longer periods of time on more complicated toys. While a routine can help him feel secure, altering things from time to time helps him learn to be flexible. He's likely to work toward walking if he isn't doing so already, so ensure your house is toddler-proofed!

My little reader

Your baby will have definite favorites on the bookshelf now, and will love having the same stories read to him over and over again.

Books make wonderful gifts for your baby. They are great "toys," as they can keep him occupied for long periods of time as he peruses the pages, then turns them over to see what's next. However, they offer your baby much more than just a way of passing time. The world of books will enhance his vocabulary, language acquisition, and concentration. Also, as the months pass, he will be more able to follow a story—a skill that will eventually help him to read on his own.

Babies love to have familiar stories read to them. Research has found that every time you read the same story to a baby, he picks up new information from the narrative, and his memory is improved. You may find that your baby "follows" the story with you when you read a familiar book to him, as he anticipates what is coming next and begins to respond to what is about to happen. If you miss a page—or even a sentence or a word—he'll probably look perplexed!

Old and new While reading old favorites will encourage your baby's development, it's important, too, to introduce him to a variety of books and, once he is able, to encourage him to choose his own stories.

Keep his books on a safe, low shelf in an accessible bookcase or basket, so that he can dig them out himself and select the ones he would like to look at. Pack a few books too for long car rides and shopping trips. Give your baby as many opportunities as you can to use books to distract himself and keep himself occupied.

When reading with your baby, engage him in the story. Ask him to point to different elements in the pictures, and make animal and vehicle noises to match the pictures as he goes along. At this age, he'll enjoy books with single words on a page that encourage word recognition. If he is reluctant to look at books, give him interactive books with flaps to lift, textures to stroke, or buttons to push.

Board books are ideal for little fingers as they're more likely to withstand chewing and rigorous play sessions.

Consider creating a special book for your baby full of photographs of his favorite people, places, toys, and activities. You could laminate the pages and sew them together. As he gets older, encourage him to tell stories about what he sees in his special book.

DEVELOPMENT ACTIVITY

Splish, splash, splosh!

Once your baby is on his feet, it's time to invest in some rubber boots. Babies love nothing better than a good splash in a puddle on an outdoor walk! Or get a baby pool out in the summer and supervise him while he learns about how water moves in response to his actions, and how things float. Playing with water makes swimming fun for your baby and develops his senses and confidence. Best of all, it allows him to explore his environment while making a splendidly satisfying splash! However, never leave him unattended near any pool, no matter how shallow.

Summertime fun Older babies love to splash around in small pools in warm weather. Make sure, though, that you never leave him unattended in the water, even for a few seconds.

Making savings

Having a baby is an expensive business, as you certainly know by now, but there are ways to save money as you go along.

If you have paid out a small fortune on baby supplies and equipment over the past year—you might think twice in your baby's second year about buying things you won't use for long. Items like the bassinet, clothing, blankets and sheets, and baby bathtub are probably no longer useful to you. If you're thinking about extending your family, they may come in handy the next time around; if not, you might want to think about giving them to a friend or relative with a new baby or donating them to charity, possibly a group like Goodwill or the Salvation Army. Buying secondhand often makes sense when it comes to clothing in particular, which often isn't worn for long. Thrift stores and secondhand shops are also excellent sources of books and toys for babies. If buying new, look for a sale, even if you won't need the item for another six months. And collect coupons and offers that come with baby products for future purchases—they can add up to considerable savings.

AS A MATTER OF FACT

Your baby grows more in his first year of life than he will ever again. How he continues to grow after this time is partly influenced by genetics, namely the height of you and your partner, but also by his environment. So if he is well nourished, loved, and cared for, he will almost certainly reach, and quite possibly exceed, his growth potential.

Sibling support

Older siblings may feel a little sidelined by a baby who is demanding of your attention, so make sure they get special time with you, too.

If you have older children, their place in the pecking order will have changed. They may adore their little brother and be thrilled to be involved in looking after him and playing with him. However, as he gets older and more interested in their toys and games, they may find him a nuisance. At times, they may become irritated with him or even try to hurt him. If this does happen, intervene right away and explain firmly to your older child that this type of behavior (hitting, pushing, grabbing, or biting, for example) won't be tolerated.

See how it's done Older siblings will enjoy helping their new brother and sister to play, but do supervise them when they're together.

It's important to be aware that as your baby demands more, his sibling's needs will also increase. The closer in age they are, the more difficult they might find it to have to share your attention. However, even much older siblings can feel left out, but may not express it as obviously to you.

Make time to be with your baby's bigger sibling on a one-on-one basis. When your baby has a sleep, do not rush around getting jobs done. Instead, spend time playing with his sibling. Regularly arrange a time when someone can look after your baby, and plan a treat or activity with your older child in advance so he can look forward to his special time with you.

Toys for 12 months up

As your baby approaches his first birthday, he'll be ready for some exciting new toys that will stimulate him in the coming months.

Puzzles Chunky puzzles with simple shapes will appeal to your one-year-old baby (left). **Making it fit** Sorting shapes challenges your baby to combine fine motor and reasoning skills (right).

Your baby may have outgrown many of his old toys by now. If you are having a party to celebrate his first birthday, you may be thinking of gift ideas and, no doubt, you'd like to get him one or two age-appropriate toys yourself. There are many toys on the market that are suitable for one-year-olds, so you've plenty to choose from. Try to give him a variety of toys to help him develop different skills.

Toys that encourage physical activity are a good idea, as your baby's motor skills are developing rapidly. He'll make the most of push-along baby walkers, which support him as he pushes them around. These get him used to standing and moving, although watch that he doesn't become too reliant on them for walking. Balls are also a good choice; he will enjoy traveling in search of a ball, and may pass one back and forth to you.

This is also a good age for sorting toys, such as shape-sorters and stacking cups, which help him to hone his problem-solving skills and explore how smaller objects fit into bigger ones.

Very basic and sturdy wooden puzzles with knobs to lift the pieces in and out of position will appeal to your older baby, and he may spend a long time turning them to try to make them fit into their holes. Choose simple shapes and show him how they work.

Toys with a string to pull will also delight him as he can grasp and pull quite easily now. Try a toy that climbs up its own string, or makes a sound or plays a song when its string is pulled.

If it's warm outside, water or sand tables or sandboxes provide endless enjoyment as your baby fills buckets, empties them, and makes a mess! Never leave him unsupervised near water.

TWINS

Playtime for twins

Entertaining two babies is definitely challenging, but not impossible. Make sure you put out enough toys for both of them. This doesn't mean dragging everything out (which would be overwhelming) or going overboard purchasing twice as many toys, but ensuring there are enough toys to keep both occupied. Toys that can be easily split, such as soft blocks, are perfect, too. It's important to treat them as individuals. Be aware of each twin's likes and dislikes, and provide toys to suit their different needs. Lastly, enjoy one-on-one time with each baby. Don't assume that because they have each other, they have less need for you. You are their number-one playmate and teacher, so it's vital that you both spend quality time with each baby.

Side by side As with other babies this age, your twins will be happily preoccupied in their own pursuits.

Finding a balance

Happy, fulfilled parents are good for babies, so you both need to have time and space for all those aspects of your lives that are important.

See you later It's important to find a routine that works and makes you feel that you have a life both with and away from your baby.

ASK A... MOM

I keep having to get up at night to replace my baby's pacifier. Is now a good time to wean him off it? Yes, it is generally recommended that babies stop using pacifiers by the age of one, partly because habits are less ingrained before then and partly because of concerns that relying too much on pacifiers when babies start babbling could affect their speech development. Start by limiting its use: let your baby have it to fall asleep, then take it out of his mouth so he gets used to it not being there when he wakes. When you get rid of the pacifier, offer another comfort item, such as a blanket or toy, to distract him. Your baby might object for a night or two, but most adapt quickly.

By now, you and your partner may both be back at work, on a full- or part-time basis, having arranged additional care for your baby. Or one of you may have decided to stay at home to look after your baby while the other one works. Or you may both be working part-time and juggling the sharing of child care between you. Whatever you have decided to do will probably be the result of planning and discussion between you.

There's no doubt that life now is different from your life before your baby. If one of you is looking after your baby at home, you may be thrilled with your new role of raising him the way you want, sharing activities with him each day, and proudly watching him grow and develop. However, you may also miss some aspects of your life from before you had your baby.

A different person If you have given up work, you may miss the feeling of achieving tangible tasks by the end of each day, adult conversation and interaction, and the routine of getting out of the house. You may feel that your image of yourself has changed and that you feel like a different person than before. It's easy for your confidence to falter, even though you are doing what you chose to do and recognize the valuable role you are playing. It's important that you don't give yourself selflessly over to what you think your baby needs. You need to develop a new life for yourself in which you find a routine that works for you and to feel confident in your parenting.

Take some time for yourself each week, perhaps asking your partner or a relative to watch your baby for a morning or a few hours on the weekend so you can do something you enjoy. You may decide to hire a babysitter or employ a part-time nanny to give yourself a break. Never feel guilty about this. Being happy and fulfilled as a person will make you a better, more evenly balanced parent.

Most of all, nurture friendships with other parents with babies of a similar age. You will be an invaluable support to each other, and these friendships often sustain you through life. If you feel isolated, use local playgroups or support networks to meet parents. Your pediatrician may be able to put you in touch with these resources. Your local library may also have details.

If you have gone back to work, you may miss your baby or feel cheated out of being able to care for him. Avoid feeling guilty as your baby will not suffer because you're at work as much as you might think. Create special times together, perhaps tied in with relieving your partner. If your partner is the main caregiver, make sure you have time to talk each day. Your partner will need to tell you everything your baby is up to; this will boost your partner's sense of achievement and ensure you feel part of your baby's development.

At this stage, it's best not to be too rigid in your plans. You may find that one or the other of you does not have the work or child-care options they expected, or changes their mind about working or staying at home. Always be prepared to discuss anything that doesn't feel right for either of you, and be open to making changes.

Changing tastes

Your baby's palate is becoming more sophisticated, so this is the ideal age to expand his diet and get him interested in family meals.

If your baby shows an interest in what the rest of the family is eating, by all means, let him partake in your meals. This is one of the best ways to encourage healthy eating habits. If you start him off on family meals at this age, he'll learn to enjoy the flavors of the food he will grow up on, and will also enjoy feeling part of the social experience of eating as a family.

Although your baby is still learning to feed himself, offer him a plate of his own with a selection of foods customized from your meal. (Separate his portion before adding any salt when cooking.) He can pick up food with his fingers or use a soft spoon.

Soups, casseroles, pasta, meatballs, and family roasts are perfect for older babies. If your baby is a picky eater, you can hide a selection of vegetables in sauces and soups to ensure he's getting as many nutrients as possible.

It's now acceptable to cook with herbs, spices, and wine when preparing food your baby will eat. If using wine, ensure that you cook it off long enough for the alcohol to evaporate. Leave salt and whole nuts off the menu still, but you can add new seasonings and cheeses to flavor his food.

If your baby is still reluctant to eat very lumpy foods, continue to offer him finger foods alongside his meals, and get him to try his regular foods in a lumpier form. For instance, if you give him finely chopped poached chicken with mashed vegetables, also supply chunks and strips of each to encourage experimentation.

When your baby sleeps

At this age, your baby begins to dream a little less than he used to, but his brain is still consolidating what it has learned during the day.

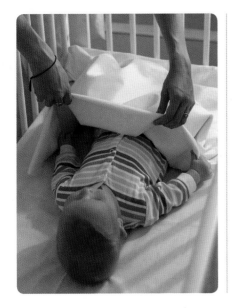

As your baby approaches one year of age, some changes take place in the way he sleeps. He will have less "REM" (rapid-eye movement) sleep (see p.121) than before. This is the lightest stage of sleep, and it is characterized by flickering eyelids, irregular breathing, and changing facial expressions. It is during this phase of sleep that your baby's brain works hard to process and consolidate information acquired during that day. (Premature babies still have more dream sleep than babies born at full term, and continue to need more

Sleep tight Throughout the night, your baby has periods of deep, restful sleep, and phases of lighter sleep, during which he dreams.

for several more months.) When your baby dreams, his central nervous system enters an "active" state and his temperature may rise a little, while his brain-wave activity and his heart rate both increase. During this lightest stage of sleep, he may wake up briefly, or seem restless in his sleep.

Try to avoid responding too quickly if he cries slightly or sounds disturbed in his sleep, as he will usually settle himself. Periods of dream sleep are followed by phases of deep sleep, and most babies have about five periods of each type of sleep, occurring in a cycle, throughout the night. In deep sleep, your baby's breathing will be regular, and he may sigh and make sucking motions.

51 weeks

IT'S NEARLY TIME TO CELEBRATE YOUR BABY'S FIRST BIRTHDAY!

It's hard to believe that your baby has progressed from being a dependent infant to a chatty, self-sufficient toddler. Offer her plenty of supervised freedom to explore her environment and practice new skills; she'll love to be independent, safe in the knowledge that you are just around the corner.

Becoming more mobile

Mobility is a part of every toddler's development, and even the most reluctant crawlers or walkers will make a move in the coming months.

Early walkers may now move on to running. However, most babies are still working toward taking their first tottering steps.

Once you baby does start to walk, he will test his skills by trying to walk backward, sideways, and up and down the stairs, before lurching himself forward at full speed—and usually taking plenty of tumbles on the way.

Try to spend some time outdoors on grass, which will cushion your baby's falls and help him to develop balance on a slightly uneven surface. He will have no sense of distance, nor will his depth perception be mature (so he may walk off the end of landings and porches), so keep a close eye on him.

Multiples mayhem This can be an interesting time for parents of twins or more as their babies head off in different directions. Give them a safe environment to practice walking.

In most cases, there's no reason why multiples should not develop as well as singleton babies. If they were premature, they may take longer to achieve certain milestones, but they should catch up, usually in the first year. They may develop at different rates; for example, one may crawl earlier. This simply reflects different developmental traits.

Full steam ahead! Your baby may find it difficult to stop once she gets going, so ensure your home is fully toddler-proofed!

Sleep at one year

Over the coming months, your baby will need slightly less sleep. Let his needs, not his routine, dictate how much sleep he gets.

Depending upon how active your baby is, you may have already moved from two long naps to two shorter naps, or even just one. Over the coming year, your baby will need to sleep for between 10 and 13 hours in a 24-hour period. Whether this requirement is met entirely during the night, or is divided between daytime and night-time sleeps, will be determined by your baby's individual needs. However, very few babies manage a whole day without at least one restorative nap.

You may also find that your baby is more tired on some days than he is on others, and will need a morning nap just a few hours after he wakes up. He may also develop a habit of sleeping through lunchtime, so you'll need to tweak your routine to ensure he gets a good meal before he settles down for his nap so that he doesn't wake up early because he feels hungry.

Moving to a single afternoon nap is fine. If your baby is showing signs of being sleepy, settle him down and wake him only if he sleeps past 4 pm—the point at which daytime sleep usually interferes with a good night's sleep.

If your baby fares better with a nap during the day, ensure he gets some physical activity beforehand to help him settle well, and continue with your usual pre-nap routine. Beware that at this age, he's more likely to wake up and want to play after his nap, and may make an attempt to escape, too, so ensure that his crib is safe (see p.299), with the base on its lowest setting.

Cow's milk as a drink

Your baby is now officially old enough to have cow's milk. Choose full-fat milk until he's two, after which you can give low-fat milk.

Up until now, breast and formula milk have been the most suitable to meet your baby's particular nutritional needs. The sodium, potassium, and chloride levels in cow's milk were too high for your young baby's tiny kidneys. Also, formula and breast milk contain important vitamins and minerals required for the rapid growth and development that occurs in a baby's first year, which cow's milk notably lacks.

Now that your baby is a year old, though, it is safe for him to drink cow's milk, which will provide him with healthy fats, protein, calcium, vitamin A, and essential fatty acids (EFAs), along with other key minerals.

If you are bringing up your baby as a vegetarian, or if he is a particularly fussy eater, you may want to consider a "growing up" formula aimed at toddlers at first, which contains additional iron and vitamins. Aim, though, to expand his food repertoire so that, eventually, his regular food alongside full-fat cow's milk meets his nutritional needs.

All dairy products are high in the nutrients contained in cow's milk, so don't panic if your baby doesn't take to it. Simply increase his intake of other dairy products and calcium-containing foods, such as leafy green vegetables, beans, tofu, and soy.

Babies need a great deal more fat in their diets than adults, so give your baby full-fat milk. This provides the energy and fat-soluble vitamins needed for growth. Under the age of two, fats should make up about half the total calorie intake. After that, as long as your child has a varied, nutritious diet, you may consider changing to low-fat milk.

Baby still wants to breast-feed

Whether or not you have other ideas, your baby may want to continue breast-feeding and show no signs of being ready to stop.

Still natural For a one-year-old, breast-feeding still feels natural and comforting.

There's no right time to stop breast-feeding. Many moms find that their babies often "wean" themselves around now as they get distracted by the world around them. Others seem happy to continue. This is fine, too—unless you would like to stop, in which case you may both face a difficult transitional period as breast-feeding is removed.

Take your time weaning your older baby off the breast as this is a well-established habit for him that provides much comfort. Give him cuddles and reassurance. Replace breast-feedings with formula (until he is one year old, at which point you can switch to cow's milk) as he still needs 17–20 fl oz (500–600 ml) of milk a day, even once he's on solids. However, he'll probably get what he needs in two feedings a day, plus some milk with meals if necessary. If you want to keep the morning or evening breast-feedings, this is good for you both on every level (see p.361).

For an older baby, breast milk can be a valuable source of nutrients. One study found that in a baby's second year, just 15 fl oz (450 ml) of breast milk can provide 29 percent of a baby's energy needs; 43 percent of his protein; 36 percent of his calcium; 75 percent of his vitamin A; 94 percent of his vitamin B12; and 60 percent of his vitamin C needs, each day.

First times

Your baby will face many new experiences in the coming months. A little preparation will help him negotiate them comfortably.

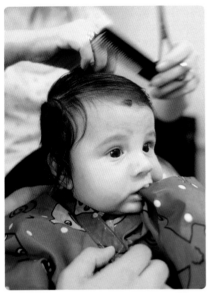

Hair raising His first haircut shouldn't worry him if he's already visited the salon with you.

At some point over the coming year, your baby will have his first visit to the dentist or hairdresser, or perhaps his first sleepover at Grandma's if, up until now, he's been babysat at home in familiar surroundings. Some babies happily adjust to new experiences; others need a little warming up before they accept them. Either way, if your baby knows what to expect from a new situation, he'll feel more secure about it.

If you need to go to the dentist, doctor, or hairdresser yourself—or are taking an older sibling—take your baby along, too, to get him used to the surroundings and what goes on. Of course, it's best to do this when you're not likely to be too long, such as when you're going for a routine checkup or a quick trim, so that your baby doesn't become bored and restless.

While the hairdresser is cutting your hair, hold your baby on your lap and explain what's being done in an upbeat tone of voice, so your baby learns that this is all very normal. Let him see the dentist examining your teeth, or the doctor taking your blood pressure, while you sit back calmly to show that there's nothing to be concerned about.

If you think your baby might be fazed by a new upcoming experience, borrow a library book that features the new situation he is to encounter—seeing a favorite character visiting the dentist, for example, will make the experience much easier for your baby.

If he's going to stay at Grandma's on his own, plan a trip or two in advance for both of you so that he gets used to being there with you first (see also p.355).

On the day When the time comes for your baby's first haircut or other new experience, make sure he's not hungry or tired, and give him his comfort object or a toy or book to distract him if he looks a little worried. Explain very simply where you are going and what's going to happen. Remind him of the story you read (about the scenario he's going to encounter), or recall that just like Mommy had her hair cut last time, now it's his turn to look handsome! Let him know that afterward you plan to wrap up the experience with something fun, such as a trip to the local playground. This will help to create positive associations with the event. Above all, stay calm and upbeat yourself—if you show a fear of the dentist, for example, your baby will quickly pick up on this.

ASK A... PEDIATRICIAN

When does my baby need his first dental appointment? It's a good idea to have your baby's teeth checked at around six months, or whenever the first teeth emerge, so that he becomes accustomed to the experience of visiting the dentist, and to check that all is well. He won't need a full checkup until around his first birthday. Your dentist will give you plenty of advice about your baby's oral health, including brushing and fluoride, and will check that there are no signs of early decay.

Treat the first appointment like a social occasion, getting your baby used to the new environment and different smell. At first, and maybe for the first few appointments, your baby can sit in your lap while the dentist looks at his teeth. Your baby will probably love the attention. Try not to panic, though, if this isn't the case and he creates a fuss; you can always reschedule an appointment for a later date.

My baby was distraught after having his shots. Does this mean he'll be terrified of future vaccinations? Your baby won't remember his first sets of shots, so rest assured that he won't have developed a fear of the pediatrician! However, it may be in his nature to react loudly: some babies do scream loudly, while others are fairly easily comforted.

51 weeks

389

Words with meaning

By 12 months, many babies have a small repertoire of words that they can use with meaning, and a rapidly increasing vocabulary.

First words tend to be those that have the most meaning for your baby, such as "mama," "dada," and "bottle" (which often comes out as "baba"). Your baby may not be able to say many of these words accurately, but by now you should have a good understanding of their meaning. Don't be surprised if your baby changes his words for various people and items. He may call his bottle a "baba" one week, only to move on to "bobo," or even "mik" (milk), the next.

Your baby learns language by listening to it being used and, at this point, he'll understand far more than he can say. Continue to chat with him and offer him the correct words for items—repetition cements words in his memory. However, being able to repeat certain words doesn't make him able to use them meaningfully. Listen carefully and watch him when he speaks—his intonation and gestures may give you a clue about the meaning intended by the words he is using.

Some babies don't use their first words until well into their second year, but by around 20 months, you can expect your baby to have 30–40 words in his repertoire (usually nouns, and simple phrases such as "bye-bye"). These will be mixed in with a stream of babbling. After 20 months, he'll begin to pick up words at an amazing rate—sometimes one or two a day—and you'll have no doubt about what he's saying—and what he wants!

Mom's the word

So have you loved the past year—or just about survived it? All moms are different and some are more "ga-ga" about babies than others …

Apple of your eye Your baby is adorable, of course, but he can be hard work at times, too!

Now you have almost 12 months' experience under your belt, how do you think you would describe yourself as a mom? Have you emerged as a natural earth mother type, who's relished every aspect of baby care and breast-feeding, is knowledgeable about all things baby-related, and a dedicated follower of BabyCenter.ca? Or perhaps you've found the entire diaper-changing, feeding, and routine nature of baby care just a little bit laborious and dull?

You probably sit somewhere between the two extremes, but if you haven't enjoyed the past year as much as you had hoped, try not to feel guilty or disheartened. It doesn't mean that you don't love your baby, but for some women, looking after a little one simply becomes more interesting and rewarding as babies grow and become better able to communicate and interact. As your child develops and his personality really begins to emerge, you'll probably find that you are far more engaged and feel less fettered by the practicalities of caring for a young baby. Although it's a cliché that's repeated by every single parent, babies really do grow up incredibly fast—one day you have a toddler, the next thing you know he's starting first grade—so try to appreciate every moment. There will always be trying times and no parent is perfect, but the bond you share with your child is precious and unique—wherever you happen to be on the mothering scale.

Your baby is one today

Congratulations—your baby is officially a toddler! You have many exciting changes to look forward to in the coming year.

Your baby's first birthday can be a time of mixed emotions for you—he is becoming more independent, and will depend less on you for feeding and even getting around. He may have clear ideas of what he can and wants to do, and for the first time you may find yourself locking horns with a contrary little person. As he heads toward the age of two, you can expect him to become much more reluctant to accept your intervention—even if you are only trying to keep him fed and dressed!

Paradoxically, separation anxiety continues well into your toddler's second, or even third, year, and he will constantly seek out your comforting presence and find security in his regular routines. Continue to reassure him with regular physical affection and continue to enjoy plenty of activities with him—reading books, singing songs, and playing—to remind him of your close relationship.

His speech will develop dramatically in the coming year, and you will soon have a knack for working out what he's trying to say. Reading to him, singing, and chatting with him about your day will continue to support his language acquisition. Over the next year, he'll begin to string together short sentences and, with a combination of gestures and words, make his needs easily known.

Your toddler's safety will remain one of your top priorities, and you will have to check his environment and activities continually to ensure he isn't putting himself in danger as he explores his rapidly expanding world. Make sure he understands the basics of stair safety, and keep an eye on him constantly when you are out and about.

Happy birthday! Your baby's birthday marks the end of a miraculous year of development, and you may choose to celebrate this wonderful journey with your family and closest friends.

Continue to support his developmental skills with games and pursuits that keep him entertained and stimulated. Although he'll be more likely to want to play for longer periods on his own, he still needs plenty of interaction with you, and your input remains crucial to his development.

Your baby will hold his own at the dinner table now, and the more often you can arrange to eat together, the better his table manners and social skills will eventually be—and he'll be more likely to eat a wide range of foods. Try not to pass on your own dislikes; the world of food is a joy for your baby to explore, and a varied diet will give him the best chance of good health and development.

Above all, take time to stop and enjoy the small things with him—write down his amazing firsts, capture his activities on film, save his first artistic creations, and record his attempts at speech. The coming months, and even years, will pass with lightning speed, and you may be astonished to find that your baby is on the road to independence much more quickly than you ever imagined.

You've created this wonderful, unique little person with a world of opportunity in front of him. Take pride in his achievements—and yours—and rest assured that all of the hard work you've put into parenting and creating a family has produced the best possible results.

 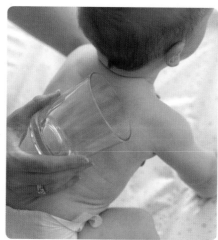 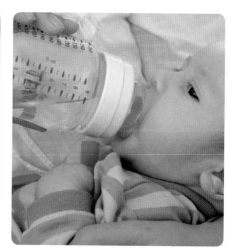

The health and well-being of your baby are prime concerns, and the more informed and confident you feel about recognizing and treating illness when it happens, the easier it is to manage. Most babies experience at least one bout of sickness in their first year, so this chapter clearly explains all the common illnesses and how best to treat your child. Of course, there's no substitute for a parent's instinct, so if you are worried about your baby's health, always call your doctor right away.

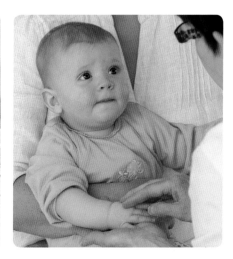

Your baby's health

Your unwell baby

THE BETTER INFORMED YOU ARE, THE MORE CONFIDENT YOU WILL FEEL CARING FOR YOUR SICK BABY

Your baby's immune system is still developing, so she is susceptible to a number of illnesses during this first year. Most of these will be minor, but occasionally a more serious illness may develop. It's vital that you know what to look out for so that you can take the right action.

When your baby is ill

As a new parent, it can be hard to tell if your baby is sick, but as you get to know her, you'll recognize when something is wrong.

Babies often cry, but prolonged crying can be a sign that your baby feels sick or is in pain, especially if you can't pacify her. Listen, too, for a hoarse cry or one of a higher pitch than usual. It's also worth knowing that a very ill baby may cry much less than usual, so always take note if your baby is unnaturally quiet and subdued, especially if she has other symptoms as well (see checklist, p.396).

Your baby may lose interest in feeding when she's not feeling well, or she may take in less than usual. Vomiting is a common symptom too,

and it doesn't always mean the problem is with your baby's tummy.

Once your baby starts smiling, she's likely to smile a lot of the time. If your baby looks grumpy or won't smile at you when you talk to her, there may be something wrong. In much the same way, older babies often lose interest in playing when they're not well. Instead, your baby may become more clingy, hanging onto you when you are nearby and not wanting you to leave the room. If your baby's breathing is noisier or faster than usual, there's likely to be something wrong. A slightly ill baby

may also sleep more than usual. However, you should be able to rouse her; if she's unresponsive, call an ambulance or take her to the hospital yourself if you can get there quickly.

Dehydration

Many common illnesses cause serious fluid loss, and fever compounds the problem. Babies can quickly become dehydrated, which is a major concern, so it's vital to recognize the signs.
■ At first, dry lips may be the only symptom.
■ As dehydration worsens, your baby's diapers may be drier than usual. Her skin may feel dry and loose. Your baby may be a bit lethargic. You may also notice that her fontanelle (the soft spot on the top of her head) looks slightly sunken. Contact your doctor immediately.
■ With severe dehydration, your baby's eyes may appear sunken too, and she may not urinate for 12 hours. Call an ambulance or take her to the ER yourself if you can get there quickly—at this stage, there is a risk that she could lapse into shock or a coma.

To avoid dehydration, give your baby plenty of breast milk or formula. She will need extra fluids to replace those lost through illness, especially if she has diarrhea or is vomiting. It may help to give her smaller amounts more frequently. If she is formula fed, you can also offer her boiled and cooled water between feeds. Ask your doctor about giving an oral rehydration solution, which is easier for babies to keep down if they're vomiting. Rehydration solution not only replaces fluids, but also the sugars and salts lost due to vomiting or diarrhea.

HOW TO...

Take your baby's temperature

Fever is the body's normal response to infection, so a raised temperature can help tell you if your baby is ill. Normal body temperature is 98.6°F (37°C) and about 1°F (0.5°C) lower when taken in the armpit. The best way to take your baby's temperature is

from the ear or armpit, although the latter can be problematic if you have a wiggly baby because you need to hold her still for at least a couple of minutes to get a reading. Oral thermometers can't be used for babies because they might bite them.

Ear thermometer Hold your baby firmly and place the thermometer in your baby's ear, following the instructions to make sure you position it correctly (left). **Under-arm thermometer** Place your baby on your lap and hold her still to get a more accurate reading.

Getting medical help

If your baby is ill, you may need to take her to the doctor's or—if you are seriously concerned about her health—to the hospital.

When to call the doctor

As you get to know your baby, you'll find it easier to recognize when you need medical advice. There are some symptoms you should never ignore, but seek advice if you think your baby may be sick, even if there are no clear symptoms. Very young babies can become critically ill very quickly. Call your doctor if your baby:

■ Runs a fever of 102.2°F (39°C) or higher or 100.4°F (38°C) for babies under 3 months

■ Refuses feedings

■ Vomits persistently

■ Screams as if in pain

■ Seems listless or unwell

■ Seems dehydrated (see p.395)

■ Has more than two watery stools in 12 hours

■ Has blood or mucus in her stools

■ Is bleeding from anywhere

■ Has had a discharge from her ears, eyes, or genitals in the past 24 hours

■ Appears to be breathing more rapidly than usual

■ Has a rash

■ Has a seizure (convulsion)

■ Has a minor burn or scald.

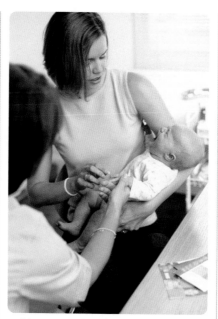

Making an appointment Talk to your doctor if your baby is showing signs of illness, or you are not sure of her condition.

Seeing the doctor

Parents see their baby's doctor on average six times during their baby's first year, so it's good to know how to get the best from these visits.

Don't worry about taking your sick baby to the doctor. Taking a feverish baby to the doctor's doesn't usually do them harm, and you will get seen more quickly. When you call, make sure the receptionist knows how young your baby is. Many practices fit sick babies in between appointments, and make an effort to avoid your waiting. If your baby has a rash, mention this, so you do not spend time in the waiting room potentially putting others at risk of infection. Giving this information will also benefit you since the doctor is likely to see your baby more quickly.

Take a spare diaper with you, since you will probably want to put a clean one on after the doctor examines your baby. If your baby has diarrhea, it can also be useful to take a dirty diaper with you in case your doctor needs a stool sample for testing.

Getting the most from your visit

Describe your baby's symptoms clearly, not forgetting the details of her temperature and any medicines or home remedies you have already tried. Always tell your doctor what's on your mind, whether you're concerned about a cough or worried about the possibility of meningitis. This will ensure you are both on the same wavelength.

Make sure you understand any instructions as to what to do, and how to give any medicines. Your doctor should also tell you what to look out for and what to do if your baby doesn't improve, and when to return for follow-up. Don't worry about being a bit of a nuisance; occasional false alarms are inevitable when you're finding your way as a parent. Many doctors have children themselves and can identify with your situation. They should understand your concerns about your precious little bundle, and will know that one or two unnecessary consultations are far better than letting things go unchecked for too long.

If you feel you can't communicate with your doctor, perhaps this isn't the right doctor for your family. Every professional has different interests and skills, and after a few consultations you may decide you would be better with a different doctor, either within the same practice or an entirely new one.

If you just want advice

Depending on where you live, you may be able to get 24-hour advice from your local Telehealth Services. Try your pediatrician for issues such as breastfeeding and minor health concerns like colic, or your pharmacist for advice on treating minor ailments such as diaper rash. Many areas have walk-in clinics, where you can drop in any time during office hours and see a nurse or doctor, but before you go, check that they have facilities for babies. If you need to see a doctor when the office is closed, call your doctor and his service will arrange an appointment or have the doctor call you.

Going to ER

Taking your baby to an emergency room is a daunting prospect, but it's an experience that most parents have to deal with at some point, so it's good to be prepared. In the majority of cases, there's nothing seriously wrong, and parents and baby can go home once they have been seen. Occasionally, if there are concerns about a baby's condition, she may need to stay in the hospital (see below).

No matter how worried you feel, try to stay calm. When you arrive at the hospital's ER department, find your way to the main ER reception. You may be redirected to a special children's ER if there is one; otherwise there may be a dedicated children's nurse, who will assess your child. Be as clear and concise as you can when explaining what has happened or describing your baby's symptoms. The nurse will assess the severity of your child's illness, and you will either be seen by a doctor immediately or asked to wait.

If you aren't seen immediately by a doctor, it can be difficult to predict how long you will have to wait since priority in an ER is given to the most urgent cases. However, as a general rule, young babies will be prioritized and seen within a few hours at the most. Because you may be waiting some time, don't forget to take your baby's comfort object, a pacifier if needed, plus any milk, bottles, or diapers.

CHECKLIST

When to call 911

Call 911 for an ambulance, or take your baby to the hospital yourself (if you can get there accompanied quickly) if your baby:

- Is unresponsive

- Is severely dehydrated (see p.395)

- Has a high-pitched cry

- Has a bulging or sunken fontanelle (spot on top of her head)

- Develops mottled or blotchy skin

- Has trouble breathing or turns blue

- Can't move one of her limbs

- Has a head injury

- Has an extensive burn or scald, or an electrical or chemical burn

- Suddenly develops a swelling in the groin or testicle.

STAYING IN THE HOSPITAL

Fortunately, children's hospital units are now much brighter, friendlier, and less formal places than they used to be. You'll find that the staff has a genuine interest in their little patients as well as the right professional skills. Pediatricians rarely wear white coats and are often the most approachable of all hospital specialists.

Staying with your baby If your baby has to stay in the hospital, you can almost always stay too, though expect facilities for parents to be basic in many units. From your baby's point of view, the most important thing is that you can be there to reassure her throughout most tests and procedures. If she has to have blood taken, an anesthetic cream is usually applied first to make the test painless. If your baby needs a surgery under local anesthesia, your presence is usually welcome. You won't be allowed in for procedures under general anesthesia, but you can be there holding her right until she is fast asleep. Bringing in your baby's favorite toys, comfort object, or a blanket can help your baby to feel more at home.

Planned hospital admissions If an older baby needs to go into the hospital, there'll be time to warn her. Tell her a little about it so that it doesn't come as a huge surprise. Babies are very aware of their parents' moods and emotions, so try to stay positive no matter what's happening. If you have negative feelings about hospitals or needles, do your best to keep them to yourself. Use a soft voice to help calm your baby. You can also sing her favorite songs or nursery rhymes.

Being informed Understanding the treatment your child is being given will help to prevent unnecessary anxiety. If you're not sure what's happening, ask, and never feel intimidated. There are usually doctors and nurses on hand who will be happy to answer your questions. It can be useful to write down any questions you have, since it's easy to forget when there is so much going on.

When it's time for your baby to go home, make sure you understand the discharge plan and have contact details if you need to seek help.

Taking care of your sick baby

Your baby is likely to need all your attention when she's feeling ill. Knowing what to do can make all the difference in her recovery.

You can expect babies who are sick to be demanding and to need your presence. Prioritize things so you can spend time cuddling your little one, or at least sitting with her. A good babysitter or trusted relative can fit the bill, but your baby will prefer to have the reassurance of a parent.

A sick baby may still want to play simple games, or to hear you tell a favorite story. Often this is the same story told over and over again. Now more than ever, there's real comfort in what's familiar. She may also enjoy listening to recorded stories and rhymes, though it's your voice that has special significance for her.

Keep an eye on your baby's temperature (see p.401) and check it as necessary. There's no need to treat every fever, but try to lower it if she is uncomfortable, her temperature is very high, or your doctor has advised you to do so. Infant acetaminophen or ibuprofen may be appropriate, depending on your baby's age (read the instructions). Use one of these medicines or the other, not both.

Your baby generally needs extra fluids when she's ill, especially if she's feverish. Fever is a normal response to infection, but it contributes to dehydration. This in turn can make

---

Your baby's health ■ Your unwell baby

CHECKLIST

Your home medicine cabinet

Stocking a cabinet with essential medical supplies will enable you to deal with common ailments quickly and effectively. Keep medicines out of your baby's reach, ideally in a cool, dark place, and check expiration dates. Make sure medicines are right for your baby's age.

- Liquid baby acetaminophen

- Baby ibuprofen

- Calamine lotion, for bites and rashes

- Rehydrating solution/sachets

- Antibacterial ointment for cuts and scrapes

- Infant topical pain-relief gel, to relieve teething discomfort

- Medicine syringe and/or spoon

- Thermometer

- Adhesive bandages

HOW TO...

Administer drops

In all cases, wash your hands, make sure the dropper does not come into direct contact with your baby, and sterilize it between uses.

Nose drops Lay your baby on her back on your lap, tilting her head back gently if she is an older baby. Be sure to support your baby's head and drip the nose drops into each nostril.

Eye drops Lay your baby down on your lap and hold her head steady with one arm. Gently pull down the lower eyelid and squeeze the bulb so drops go into the space between the lid and the eyeball. Then wipe the excess drops off her cheek. If you have trouble managing this, get another adult to help hold your baby.

Ear drops Warm the ear drops by holding in your palm for a few minutes, then lay your baby down on her side on your lap. She needs to be comfortable since she will have to stay in this position for a little while. Hold her head firmly, yet gently, and let the drops fall from the dropper into the ear. Keep her still for a few minutes since you don't want the drops to spill out right away. When your baby sits up again, a little excess may leak out, so have a tissue ready to catch it.

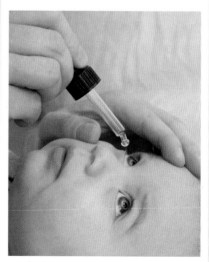

Putting in eye drops Holding your hand steady, squeeze the bulb of the dropper to infuse the medication behind the lower lid.

Give your baby medicine

There are several techniques for giving a baby medicine by mouth, whether it's a prescription from your doctor or an over-the-counter remedy. Wash your hands before you start, and check the correct dose. An overdose can be dangerous, especially for young babies. When giving medicine, hold your baby so that she is slightly upright. Don't lay her down flat because there's a risk that she may inhale the medicine into her lungs.

Using a syringe This is probably the best method for very young babies, who haven't learned to swallow from a spoon, and for medicines for which small, precise doses are needed. For a baby under six months, sterilize the syringe before use. Fill the syringe with the correct dose from the bottle, then pick up and hold your baby in the crook of your arm. Put the mouthpiece of the medicine syringe on your baby's lower lip and gently push the plunger so the medicine goes into her mouth.

Using a dropper Sterilize first, for a baby under six months, then draw in the right amount of medicine in the dropper before picking your baby up. Lean your baby back slightly, and place the tip of the dropper in the corner of her mouth, or just inside the lower lip. Squeeze the medicine out, making sure the dropper empties completely into your baby's mouth.

Using a spoon This is the most common method for babies over 12 weeks or so of age, especially if the dose is at least 2.5 ml. Measure the dose before picking up your baby. Holding your baby upright, touch the lower part of the spoon to her bottom lip, then gently tip the spoon up so that the medicine goes into her mouth.

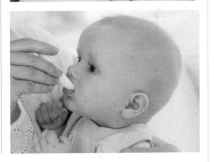

Syringe For very young babies, you'll probably find it easiest to give medicines with a syringe (top). **Dropper** When using a dropper, make sure all the medicine goes into your baby's mouth (middle). **Spoon** Babies over 12 weeks can usually manage a spoon (bottom).

fever worse, so it's something of a vicious circle. If you're breast-feeding, continue with this. She may or may not need water as well—check with your pediatrician. Older babies can need encouragement to drink more. Make sure there's always a drink within reach.

If your baby is on solids, don't worry too much if she won't eat much while she's not well. Right now fluids matter more than food.

There's no need for your baby to be in her crib when ill, though it may be convenient to keep her in nighttime clothing since this is often simpler to change in and out of. At night, it's a good idea to keep your baby close by. If she already sleeps in her own room, you might want to move her crib back into your room as a temporary measure. This makes it easier to attend to her if she needs anything during the night, and you may sleep more easily knowing that she is near you.

While your baby is ill, you could skip bathtime in favor of sponge bathing, or a simple cleaning with a washcloth. It all depends on how sick she is and how much she enjoys a bath. Some older babies relax in the bath. You can then put her into fresh clothing, which could make her feel a lot better. Lukewarm sponging is no longer recommended as a treatment for fever.

It can be tiring taking care of a baby who is sick, so put your feet up and rest when she sleeps. Don't waste precious time rushing around doing chores. If you need help, don't be afraid to ask friends or relatives to take over for a little while so that you can get some rest. However tired you are, never fall asleep with your sick baby on the sofa.

Giving medication If your baby has been prescribed medication, such as antibiotics, it's very important to give the correct dosages and to finish the course as directed. This applies to topical treatments, such as steroid creams, too. You'll need to give any medicines to your baby in liquid form and there are several different methods for doing this (see above).

399

Illnesses & injuries

AN ILL OR INJURED BABY NEEDS LOTS OF COMFORT COMBINED WITH THE RIGHT ACTION

When your baby isn't well or has fallen and bumped herself, it's important that you know when it's fine to treat her at home, which measures are appropriate, and when you need to seek medical advice. If you're confident about what to do, you'll be calmer and more effective.

Common conditions

When your baby isn't feeling her best, it could be any one of a number of conditions. Babies often can't signal what's wrong.

In babies over six months old and young children, a high fever can lead to a seizure, which is also known as a febrile convulsion.

Fever can be stressful for a baby or child's brain and can temporarily disrupt the signals between brain cells, in some cases triggering a seizure. This usually occurs at a time when body temperature rises rapidly. Your baby is more likely to be affected if there is a family history of febrile convulsions or other types of seizures.

A seizure can be frightening to see even though it usually lasts less than two minutes. The baby loses consciousness, stops breathing momentarily, and tends to wet or soil herself. The limbs and face may twitch and the eyes often roll upward. When it stops, the baby regains consciousness, but may be very sleepy.

During a seizure, lie her on her side and don't try to restrain her, but make sure she is safe and cannot fall. If possible, note the time of onset of the seizure. Call an ambulance if your baby's seizure lasts over five minutes: any seizure lasting longer than this is likely to be more serious than a febrile convulsion.

If your baby has had a seizure, call your doctor. If this is her first seizure, she is likely to need hospital tests to rule out a serious cause. For any subsequent seizures, she should still have a checkup to find the cause of her high fever.

Fever

Fever is not an illness in itself, but it is a common symptom. It is the body's normal response to infection or inflammation, so always take note of a fever, especially if your baby is under six months old.

Causes include the flu, chest infection, gastroenteritis, urinary tract infection, and infectious diseases such as roseola (see p.406). A fever can also occur after a routine immunization.

You may suspect your baby has a fever from touching her, especially if the back of her neck feels hot or sweaty, but take her temperature to confirm (see p.395).

Dealing with fever Fever can make your baby uncomfortable and can also have a dehydrating effect. That's why it's important to give plenty of fluids when a baby or child is feverish, and to look out for any possible signs of dehydration (see p.395).

Don't overdress your baby since this makes it harder for body temperature to drop back down to normal. When indoors, a diaper and a onesie may be enough, depending on room temperature, but make sure she doesn't then get too cold, since young babies aren't good at controlling their body temperature.

There's no point in sponge bathing your baby or giving her a bath since it is likely to make her miserable. You can relieve fever in babies over six months with baby acetaminophen or ibuprofen if your doctor says it's okay (ask her for the proper dosage). Do not give both at the same time. Don't give aspirin (ASA) to feverish children because it can lead to Reye's Syndrome, a serious condition that can cause liver and brain damage.

When to see the doctor In young babies, fever is less common and therefore more significant. As a rule, the younger your baby, the more quickly you need to get medical attention, but use your instincts, too. In older babies, their actual temperature or how long they have had it often does not indicate how sick they are. Contact your doctor if:

■ Your baby has a temperature of 102.2°F (39°C) or more (100.4°F/38°C or more if she is under three months)
■ Your baby seems unwell, even if the fever is mild
■ There are any worrying symptoms such as vomiting or trouble breathing
■ She is unresponsive.

Your doctor may ask for a urine sample because a urinary tract infection is relatively common in babies yet does not cause any of the typical symptoms adults get (see p.409).

Get medical attention urgently if:
■ Your baby has a rash that doesn't fade with pressure (see p.410)
■ Your baby has a seizure
■ Her general condition worsens.

Reflux

Gastroesophageal reflux disease (GERD) is a condition in which the stomach contents flow up the esophagus and cause symptoms. It's estimated that around half of all babies under three months have it, but few have severe symptoms. Both breast-fed and formula-fed babies may be affected.

Reflux occurs because the valve at the lower end of the esophagus is lax. However, this corrects itself in time.

Symptoms include:
- Bringing up large amounts of a feeding
- Vomiting
- Coughing
- Irritability
- Feeding poorly
- Rarely, blood in the stool or vomit (seek urgent medical help).

You may suspect reflux in your baby if she screams during feedings as if in pain, or she spits up a lot. However, many babies spit up without having reflux. Occasionally, reflux has more serious effects such as breathing problems or poor growth because a baby is unable to keep down feedings.

Giving smaller, more frequent feedings can help reflux. Burping and holding your baby upright for 20 minutes after being fed can also relieve symptoms.

Your doctor may prescribe a thickened formula or a thickener that you add to feedings, and also an infant antacid, which helps the action of the valve in the esophagus. If neither of these approaches helps or your baby has severe symptoms, your pediatrician may suggest tests or a different prescription.

Tongue-tie

There is normally a strip of tissue between the floor of the mouth and the underside of the tongue (this is called the frenulum). In tongue-tie, this strip is shorter and often thicker than usual, which can restrict tongue movements. Most cases of tongue-tie are mild, but in some babies it may prevent successful breast-feeding.

It's debatable whether tongue-tie can hinder learning to speak. Most experts don't think so, mainly because it has often improved by the time speech starts. However, if you think your baby has tongue-tie, see your doctor. A few babies need a minor procedure, using a local anesthetic, to release the tie.

Conjunctivitis

This is inflammation of the lining of the eyeball and/or eyelids, also called pink eye. It can be bacterial, viral, or allergic. Bacterial conjunctivitis is the most common type in babies under six months. They often get conjunctivitis because their tear ducts are still immature, so germs can easily collect and set up an infection.

You may notice that your baby's eyelids are crusty in the morning or after a nap, or there may be a blob of pus in the corner of the eye. Your baby's eyes can also become bloodshot and the eyelids may be swollen.

If symptoms are mild, and the white of the eye isn't red, wipe your baby's eyes with cotton balls dipped in cooled, boiled water or your own breast milk. Wash your hands before you begin, and then wipe from the nose toward the outer side of the eye, using a clean cotton ball for each eye. Be careful not to touch her eyeball.

If pus accumulates again, consult your pediatrician. Your baby may need a prescription for eye drops or ointment containing antibiotic. Conjunctivitis can affect one eye or both, but it's usual to treat both eyes if you are prescribed drops.

If your baby has frequent episodes of conjunctivitis, your pediatrician may show you how to massage the tear ducts to help the flow of tears.

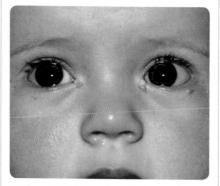

Conjunctivitis Blobs of pus in the corner a baby's eyes, as seen here, are often a sign of conjunctivitis caused by bacterial infection.

Vomiting

All babies spit up—bring up a little milk—but in vomiting the stomach contracts, and the amount brought up is much greater. Vomiting is most often related to a problem with feeding or something affecting the stomach or intestines, as in:
- Overfeeding
- Gastroenteritis (see opposite)
- Allergy to food (see p.404)
- Reflux (see p.401)
- Pyloric stenosis (see below)
- Bowel obstruction (see right).

However, vomiting doesn't necessarily mean that the trouble is anywhere near the tummy. Babies can also vomit when they're sick with an infection, especially a serious one like a urinary tract infection (see p.409), meningitis (see p.409), middle ear infection (see p.410), or chest infection (see p.409). Whooping cough also causes vomiting, most often at the end of a bout of coughing.

If your baby is sick and only vomits once, you may not need the doctor. However, babies get dehydrated easily and can become ill quickly, so as a rule consult your doctor if your baby vomits more than once or twice. Specific treatment depends on the cause.

Pyloric stenosis In this condition, there is overgrowth of the muscle of the pylorus, the valve at the stomach outlet. As a result, the outlet is too narrow for stomach contents to pass through and instead they are vomited out. Around one baby in 400 develops the condition. It's most common in boys between four and six weeks old.

Vomiting occurs right after a feeding and can be so forceful that the regurgitated feeding shoots across the room—so-called projectile vomiting. The baby is usually hungry and may appear well, but dehydration sets in as the condition progresses. Pediatricians sometimes check for a lump in the stomach area after a feeding, but ultrasound scanning is a much more reliable test for pyloric stenosis. Treatment is a small operation to release the overgrown muscle. This can sometimes be done laparoscopically.

Bowel obstruction This is not common, but it is very serious. Normally vomit looks like milk or food, but in bowel obstruction the vomit is bile stained, so it looks green. If your baby's vomit is green, contact your doctor immediately or go to the ER.

Gastroenteritis

This means inflammation or infection in the stomach or intestines, and can be caused by bacteria or viruses. It causes vomiting and often diarrhea too, though some infections, such as norovirus ("winter vomiting disease"), cause vomiting without diarrhea.

Rotavirus infection is the most common cause of gastroenteritis in babies. Bacterial causes include E.coli, salmonella, shigella, and campylobacter. In general, gastroenteritis is more common in bottle-fed babies. Possible symptoms are:
■ Vomiting and/or diarrhea
■ Stomach ache, especially before a bowel movement
■ Fever.

Always talk to your doctor if you think your baby has gastroenteritis, since babies can become dehydrated very quickly. Seek help urgently if your baby has had any blood in her stool. This can occur with some types of gastroenteritis, but it is also typical of intussusception (see right), a form of bowel blockage in babies under a year. In an episode of gastroenteritis, it isn't usually essential to know which bacteria or viruses started it off. However, occasionally your doctor will ask you to provide a sample for analysis.

The main goal of treatment is to replace lost fluids and, in many cases,

---

INTUSSUSCEPTION

In this condition, part of the bowel telescopes into itself, as if being swallowed. This creates a blockage. Symptoms include:
■ Screaming from pain (often intermittent)
■ Fever
■ Vomiting
■ Dehydration or shock
■ Blood and mucus in the stool (often described as looking like red jelly).

It's a rare condition that affects babies 3–12 months old, sometimes just when they're recovering from gastroenteritis. However, it's worth knowing about since it can be very serious if untreated. It is often possible to treat without surgery, but some babies need an operation.

---

your doctor will tell you to treat your baby at home, especially if she's an older baby. Your doctor will probably advise you to give your baby an oral rehydration solution, which contains the right balance of salts and sugar to prevent dehydration. Give small sips at a time, or your baby won't keep it down. If you're breast-feeding, you can continue. If your baby is bottle-fed, use rehydration solution instead of formula.

It's advisable to keep plenty of paper towels on hand, and possibly a bowl for an older baby, since you can't tell when she might vomit again. Maintain good hygiene, and keep away from other people. Most causes of gastroenteritis are very contagious. Keep a close eye on your baby's progress. If she doesn't improve, a hospital visit may be needed.

Diarrhea

Every baby has loose bowel movements sometimes. Breast-fed babies often have loose stool, and this is normal. Diarrhea

---

means the frequent passing of stool that is looser than usual. In some cases, the motion will be very runny and may leak out of the diaper. Causes include:
■ Gastroenteritis (see left)
■ Allergy or milk intolerance (see p.404)
■ Cystic fibrosis.

The most common cause of diarrhea is gastroenteritis, but in babies almost any feverish illness, even an ear infection, can trigger diarrhea. Some antibiotics can cause diarrhea too, since they can kill off some of the beneficial bacteria in the intestinal tract. As with vomiting, diarrhea can make your baby dehydrated very quickly, so call your doctor if your baby has more than four to six runny bowel movements in 24 hours, or has other symptoms that concern you. Watch for signs of dehydration (see p.395), keeping in mind that when a baby in diapers has diarrhea, you can't tell if she's urinating or not. You'll probably be advised to:
■ Give rehydration solution. You can continue breast-feeding. If your baby is bottle-fed, you may also be able to continue, but this depends on how bad the diarrhea is. Your pediatrician will guide you.
■ Keep a close eye on your baby.
■ Take strict hygiene precautions and keep away from others.
■ Avoid taking your baby to a swimming pool for 14 days after the last episode of diarrhea.

Constipation

This means the passage of hard, infrequent stool. Breast-fed babies can pass stool less often, but if the bowel movement looks normal, then it's not constipation. The most common causes of constipation in babies are:
■ Starting on solid food
■ Lack of fiber in the diet
■ Lack of fluid (for example, during an illness)
■ Incorrectly made formula.

In very young babies, constipation can be caused by a rare congenital condition called Hirschsprung's disease in which there is an abnormal segment of bowel.

When a baby is constipated, she may only move her bowels two or three times a week. The motions may be hard and pelletlike or much bulkier. They can be painful to pass, and may even tear the edge of the anal canal, causing bleeding. As a result, the baby avoids bowel movements, constipation worsens, and pain can develop.

Consult your pediatrician if your baby is constipated. Avoid home remedies or laxatives for older children or adults, which are often unsuitable for babies.

Hirschsprung's disease may be suspected if your baby did not pass meconium (black sticky stool) in her first day of life. More tests and surgery may be needed. However, in most cases, the cause is more likely to be dehydration or a diet low in fruit and vegetables. Your doctor may prescribe a mild laxative to begin with, but the long-term answer is for your baby to have a well-balanced diet.

Jaundice

Jaundice means a yellow tinge to the skin and the whites of the eyes caused by a buildup of a chemical called bilirubin in the blood. Bilirubin comes from the breakdown of red blood cells—it's the reason why bruises go through a yellow phase.

Normally the liver clears bilirubin from the bloodstream, but the liver is immature in newborn babies and they also have more red blood cells. That's why over half of all babies develop slight jaundice during the first week after birth. In most cases, no treatment is needed and the jaundice gets better on its own within a few weeks. Premature babies are more likely to become jaundiced because their livers cope less easily with bilirubin. This can

occasionally cause problems, so if your baby is born prematurely, she may be placed under a blue light (phototherapy) which speeds up the removal of bilirubin. Breast-fed babies are more likely to get jaundiced. This seems to be due to factors in the milk that block enzymes in the liver, and it can run in families. It does not need treatment.

Jaundice can be serious:
■ If it begins before 24 hours; causes include bleeding due to a difficult delivery, infections, and blood group incompatibility. Urgent treatment in a neonatal intensive care unit (NICU) will be needed.
■ If it lasts longer than two weeks. See the doctor promptly to rule out a possibly serious liver problem. Watch, also, for pale stools and dark yellow urine because these are also very significant symptoms.

Allergy

Although allergies are common, they are probably not quite as common as some parents think. If there are allergies in your family, your baby is more likely to develop them. However, there's more to it than genetics, because even identical twins don't necessarily have the same allergies.

Eczema (see p.407) is the most common allergic reaction in babies. It often starts around 3–12 months. In one in 10 children, eczema is linked to an underlying food allergy even though the food allergy may not be obvious yet.

The most common food allergy in babies is cow's milk allergy (specifically to cow's milk protein). About 2–7 percent of babies under a year have it. A reaction can occur immediately after ingesting cow's milk, or it can take several days to develop, which makes the condition difficult to diagnose.

Various symptoms may occur, but fortunately, not every baby gets all of them. Reactions include:

■ A flushed face
■ A rash or worsening of eczema
■ Nausea and vomiting
■ Abdominal pain
■ Diarrhea
■ Rarely, anaphylactic shock (see below).

See your doctor if you think your baby may have an allergy to cow's milk. Tests can help diagnose it, but they don't always. You may be advised to change your baby's formula, or, if you are breast-feeding, to avoid dairy products yourself. Babies usually outgrow this type of allergy by their third birthday. However, some do not and will need to continue to avoid milk products.

Milk intolerance is not a true allergy. It is actually intolerance to lactose, the type of sugar in milk, due to an enzyme deficiency. Symptoms can include diarrhea and vomiting (but not breathing difficulties). It can occur after gastroenteritis and is usually treated by prescribing lactose-free milk for a month, after which your baby should be able to resume normal milk.

Other true food allergies include reactions to eggs, peanuts, tree nuts,

ANAPHYLACTIC SHOCK

This is a severe, overwhelming allergic reaction. Luckily, it is rare in babies. Possible triggers include foods such as milk, nuts, and eggs, as well as insect venom and drugs. There could be vomiting or a rash at first, then:
■ Noisy breathing or wheezing
■ Swelling of the tongue
■ A hoarse cry
■ Collapse
■ Widespread rash.

However, anaphylaxis is difficult to spot in the very young, and your baby may just become very floppy. Immediate hospital care is vital. If you have been prescribed an adrenaline (epinephrine) injection for your baby, give it right away.

wheat, soy, and shellfish.

■ Symptoms of food allergy can be severe and affect breathing or cause anaphylaxis (see opposite).

■ Other possible signs include reflux, colic, eczema, diarrhea, and failure to gain weight.

If your baby is allergic to eggs, speak to your pediatrician as certain vaccines contain eggs and special precautions may need to be taken. There is no known way of preventing allergies from occurring but current advice is for your baby to start solids no earlier than four months, to introduce wheat at around six months, and to delay introducing eggs (particularly the whites) or any form of peanuts until your pediatrician gives the go-ahead.

Diaper rash

Even with modern, highly absorbable diapers or the softest terry cloth, diaper rash is still common. Affected skin will be sore, inflamed, and may look pimply.

A wet or dirty diaper is the main cause of diaper rash, so the longer you can leave her diaper off, the better. At the next diaper change, let her have some diaper-free playtime. If she is already on the move, put towels on the floor and wear old clothes yourself. You'll find that letting air get to the rash soon makes it look less irritated. Try to do this a couple of times a day for 20 minutes or so, or as long as you can manage. Apply a little barrier cream before putting a clean diaper on and change it often.

Get advice from your pediatrician if the rash looks very angry, is weeping or blistered, or has small spots outside the main area of redness.

Chickenpox

Chickenpox is more usual in toddlers, but babies under a year can get it too. The varicella-zoster virus that causes chickenpox is very contagious and spreads from someone else who has the illness, or from someone with shingles (herpes zoster). The incubation period (time to develop the illness) is 14–21 days, and one episode usually gives immunity for life.

Your baby may feel sick for a day or so before the rash. Spots then appear as small red dots, mostly over the torso. They quickly develop into blisters. More crops of blisters may appear over a few days, but they all crust over and then begin to fall off. Chickenpox is extremely itchy and your baby may be irritable and feel ill, especially if she also has spots inside the mouth. These are ulcers rather than blisters, and they can make feeding very uncomfortable for her. Your baby is contagious until all the spots have crusted over and no new ones appear.

Diagnosis is usually easy since the rash is distinctive. But it's still wise to get medical advice when a baby has the infection, particularly if she refuses feedings. In most cases, you'll be able to treat your baby at home. The following measures may help your baby feel more comfortable.

■ Soothe itchy skin with calamine lotion.

■ Keep your baby's skin cool since this can help prevent more spots.

■ You can try bathing your baby in lukewarm water with a tablespoon of sodium bicarbonate (baking soda).

■ Keep your baby's nails short to reduce damage from scratching.

■ If your baby has a sore mouth, give cooler feedings than usual, or else soft foods if she is on solids.

■ Treat fever with baby acetaminophen or ibuprofen if necessary.

■ If your baby is exposed to chickenpox at under four weeks, talk to your pediatrician since she may need specialized treatment to stop her from developing severe symptoms.

Keep your baby away from anyone who hasn't had it. Chickenpox can be very serious for adults who have never had the infection.

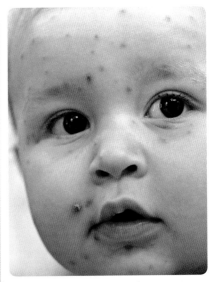

Chickenpox A chickenpox rash starts as small red dots. These turn into fluid-filled blisters with red bases, which then crust over.

Thrush

This is caused by a yeast called *Candida albicans* (also known as monilia), which is normally present in the lower bowel. Most of the time, it causes no symptoms, but if it's present in larger amounts than usual then it can cause thrush.

In babies, the most common areas for thrush are the diaper area and the mouth. That's because these areas are warm and moist, so they encourage the growth of Candida. Recent antibiotic treatment is also a factor, since some antibiotics suppress the beneficial bacteria that normally keep Candida in check. Candida can infect your nipples if you breast-feed, causing stabbing pains, but this is not a reason to stop nursing. In the diaper area, you may see:

■ A red rash, often with a glazed appearance

■ A scattering of small spots (satellites) outside the main area of rash.

If your baby has thrush in the mouth, there may be:

■ Soreness when feeding from the breast or bottle, and poor feeding or crying during feedings

■ Redness of the inside of the mouth

To protect her against measles, mumps, and rubella, your baby will be offered the MMR vaccination at around 12 months and then again at 18 months.

Measles (see below) is a highly contagious viral infection that can lead to serious complications, including pneumonia and brain damage. Before a vaccine became available, this infection was almost universal in childhood and caused the death of many children.

Mumps is usually a mild viral infection if contracted during childhood (it's rare in babies under two years old), but it can have serious complications, including deafness. In adults, the illness is usually much more severe and can lead to inflammation of the testes in men or ovaries in women.

Rubella (German measles) is usually a mild illness. However, immunization is important to protect pregnant women, since if they contract it, the unborn baby can be seriously affected.

■ White or creamy patches on the mouth or gums.

In most cases, thrush responds quickly to antifungal drops or gel prescribed by your pediatrician. Sometimes your baby needs a swab first to make sure that Candida is the right diagnosis.

Measles

Measles is one of the most serious infections in babies. Caused by a virus of the paramyxovirus group, it is very contagious and spreads from person to person in moisture droplets in the air. Your baby will get protection against measles when she has her first MMR (measles, mumps, and rubella)

vaccination (see left) around her first birthday. Until then, she has some immunity from your own antibodies, but babies occasionally still develop the illness. The incubation period is 10–14 days.

The first symptoms to appear include:
■ A high fever
■ Runny nose
■ Small spots inside your baby's mouth.

About five days after development of the initial symptoms:
■ The typical measles rash appears, with blotches on the face and neck spreading over the torso.
■ By now, your baby may be very miserable. Her eyes may be red and puffy, and she may have a cough.

Always see your doctor if you think your baby may have measles. There is no specific treatment for it other than giving fluids, controlling fever, and keeping your baby comfortable. Keep her away from others. Watch your baby closely for any deterioration. Measles can cause complications, including ear infection, chest infection, and even encephalitis (inflammation of the brain). Call your doctor again if your baby:
■ Becomes listless or unresponsive
■ Has trouble breathing
■ Won't take feedings
■ Appears dehydrated.

Roseola

This viral infection usually affects babies who are over six months old and is caused by herpesvirus 6. Its other names are roseola infantum, exanthema subitum, sixth disease, and three-day fever. Although it's common, not many parents know about it. It's very contagious and has an incubation period of 5–15 days.
■ The first symptom is a high temperature, often over 104°F (40°C). There can be febrile convulsions (see p.401), but despite this your baby may seem remarkably well.

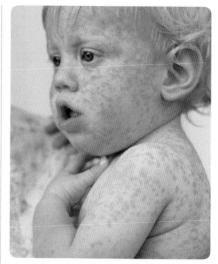

Measles The flat, blotchy measles rash appears first on the face and spreads to the rest of the body before starting to fade.

■ After three days of fever, a rash of pale reddish spots appears over the torso and then spreads to the arms and legs, and sometimes the face. The spots may have a lighter halo around them. Because the rash may last only for 12 hours, it can be easy to miss.
■ Your baby may also be irritable and tired, and have mild diarrhea and decreased appetite.

There's no specific treatment for roseola other than keeping your baby comfortable, giving fluids, and controlling fever. Most babies recover quickly. However, if your baby doesn't, talk to your doctor.

Rubella

This viral infection, also known as German measles, is a mild, short-lived illness and is not dangerous for your baby. However, rubella is of great concern if contracted during pregnancy because it can cause serious problems in the unborn baby. For this reason, it is very important that your baby receives the MMR vaccination at around 12 and 18 months (see left), which protects against measles, mumps, and rubella.

Symptoms of rubella appear after an incubation period of 14–21 days.

■ The first symptom is usually a rash, often appearing as small pink patches on your baby's neck, face, torso, and limbs.

■ Your baby may seem unwell and run a fever.

■ She may also have enlarged lymph glands high up at the back of the neck.

Talk to your doctor if you think your baby has rubella, and keep her away from anyone who might be pregnant. Warn any adult with whom your baby has been in contact over the last three weeks. There's no specific treatment other than keeping your baby comfortable.

Hand, foot, and mouth disease

This is an infection caused by a type of coxsackie virus. It has no link with foot-and-mouth disease in animals. The illness is very contagious, but not usually serious. The incubation period is about 10 days. Because there are several coxsackie viruses that can cause this illness, it can recur.

■ The typical rash appears on the palms, soles, and buttocks as small red spots, which can be flat or raised. Sometimes, there's blistering.

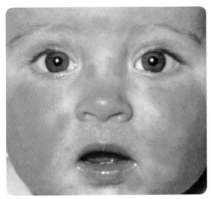

Fifth disease A bright red rash on the cheeks is characteristic of this viral infection, which is sometimes accompanied by a mild fever.

■ There may be ulcers in the mouth, which make feeding difficult. The spots can take two days to develop.

■ Your baby may also feel unwell and run a fever.

The infection is easy to diagnose from the rash. There's no specific treatment other than keeping your baby comfortable, but it is wise to speak to your doctor, especially if your baby is very young.

Fifth disease

Also called parvovirus, slapped-cheek disease, and erythema infectiosum, fifth disease is usually mild. It's caused by parvovirus B19 and is very contagious. School-age children are more likely to get it, but it can occur at any age. The incubation period seems to be 13–21 days, and it's no longer contagious once the rash appears.

■ The typical rash is a red facial rash with a sharply defined edge on one or both cheeks.

■ There may also be a fine lacy rash on the arms and legs.

■ Sometimes there's a mild fever.

In general, a baby or child with fifth disease will seem well. However, someone with sickle-cell disease can get very ill with parvovirus. The infection can also be dangerous if caught during pregnancy, with a small chance of miscarriage in the early stages. In adults, parvovirus can also cause joint pain, but this symptom is usually transient.

Eczema

This is a common skin condition in babies. It's also known as atopic eczema, atopic referring to the tendency for the immune system to overreact. Babies affected by eczema usually have a relative with eczema or another atopic condition, such as asthma or hay fever.

Eczema can clear up completely in time, but sometimes it becomes chronic.

Common sites for eczema are the ankles, elbows, wrist, face, neck, and back of the knees, but it can appear almost anywhere. The skin can look dry and cracked, or raw and weepy.

Your baby is likely to find her skin itchy, and may scratch a lot, especially at night. Keeping her nails short will help. Otherwise put scratch mittens on her before bedtime. Simple emollients are almost always needed for eczema. You can apply these direct to the skin, and there is also the kind you put in the bath. They make the bath much more slippery, so be careful. It's best to avoid soap and other bath-time toiletries, and use a soap substitute instead. Try changing to a hypoallergenic laundry detergent to see if this makes any difference. Your baby may also need a mild steroid cream prescribed by your pediatrician. Eczema can become infected because bacteria easily enter through small cracks. If your baby's eczema gets worse, this is a possibility, so see your doctor.

Heat rash

Also known as prickly heat, this is common in babies during warm weather. It's caused by excess sweat and is a sign that your baby is too hot. The typical small red pimples can appear almost anywhere, but most often on the neck, arms, face, torso, or near the diaper area. Your baby can find them irritating or itchy.

Cool your baby down by taking her clothes off, or changing her into lighter, cotton clothes. You can also apply calamine lotion if the rash seems to irritate your baby. The rash of prickly heat subsides within a day or two. Contact your doctor if it doesn't clear up quickly, or your baby seems unwell.

Colds

Babies often have colds because they are born with little immunity to the 200 or so different cold viruses. Acquiring resistance to them is a matter of gradually becoming exposed to the range of these viruses. Colds have a short incubation period of around two days. Your baby is most likely to have a cold in the winter, when more people spend time indoors with each other—and with their viruses.

Symptoms in babies are much the same as in older children. Your baby is likely to sneeze and have a runny or stuffed up nose, which makes feeding more difficult. Be patient during feedings and give your baby plenty of time. Your baby may also have a slight cough. This isn't usually serious, but it can develop into a chest infection (see opposite) or bronchiolitis (see right).

You can help your baby keep her nose clean by wiping it gently for her. Cotton balls or pads may be softer than a tissue. Safely raising the head of her crib at night can help keep her nasal passages clear.

Antibiotics do not treat colds since they are viruses. Don't give your baby any over-the-counter cold remedies; she's simply too young for them, and some can cause serious problems. A moist atmosphere makes it easier for your baby to breathe; put a humidifier in your baby's room.
See your doctor if your baby:
- Seems unwell
- Refuses feedings
- Coughs a lot
- Has trouble breathing or becomes wheezy
- Runs a fever, especially if it's high.

These are possible signs that a more serious infection has developed or that your baby has the flu instead of a cold.

COUGH AND COLD MEDICINES

Over-the-counter cough and cold medicines should not be given to babies or children under six years old, according to the Canadian Paediatric Association.

Research has demonstrated that over-the-counter cough and cold medications are not very helpful for such young children, but in certain situations, they can actually be quite harmful.

Cold and cough medicine usually contains more than one active ingredient, so there's a danger of your baby or child overdosing if you give her, for example, baby acetaminophen after giving her a combination cold medication that also contains acetaminophen. Instead, it's better to stick with simple pain relievers and fever reducers, such as baby acetaminophen or baby ibuprofen, and give your baby plenty of liquids and love and attention.

Contact your pediatrician if your baby's symptoms worry you.

Bronchiolitis

This is an infection of the tiny air passages (bronchioles) in the lungs. It almost always affects babies and can be serious, especially in the very young. The most common cause is respiratory syncytial virus (RSV), but other viruses (such as adenovirus and flu virus) can cause the same symptoms. It is very contagious and often spreads in day-care centers.
- Bronchiolitis usually begins like a cold, then quickly progresses to coughing, wheezing, and rapid breathing.
- Your baby's breathing may sound crackly or bubbly.
- A mild fever is usual.

Many babies with bronchiolitis seem well, but some become very ill. One sign to watch out for is indrawing of the chest between the ribs (or below the rib cage) during breathing. This suggests that your baby is fighting for breath. In severe cases, a baby may turn blue from lack of oxygen.

Always consult your doctor if you think your baby has bronchiolitis. Get medical help urgently if your baby is turning blue or she is fighting for breath. In many cases, it is possible to take care of your baby at home, with your doctor's advice, but sometimes a baby with bronchiolitis needs to go to the hospital, especially if she:
- Is very distressed
- Is not taking fluids or becomes dehydrated
- Is working hard to breathe
- Has a very rapid respiratory rate
- Turns blue.

Wheezing

Babies can wheeze and cough during or after viral infections. They may start with a cold but then develop a wheeze, cough, or noisy, rattly breathing that lasts a week or more. These symptoms occur as a result of inflammation and

Treating wheezing Drugs to relieve symptoms by widening the airways are given to babies via a face mask and spacer attached to an inhaler.

narrowing of the airways. Babies have narrow airways making them more likely to wheeze. It can be hard to tell the difference between this and bronchiolitis (see left). Seek urgent medical help if your baby is fighting for breath or looks blue. Wheezing may be treated with drugs given through an inhaler to open the airways. It's too early to tell if wheezing might lead to asthma because asthma is a chronic, long-term condition that may not be diagnosed until babies are over one year old.

Chest infection

This means any infection affecting the large air passages (bronchial tubes) leading to the lungs or the lung tissue itself. It includes pneumonia and bronchitis. Doctors often use the term "chest infection" when they can't be sure exactly where the problem lies. Both bacteria and viruses can cause chest infections. There are various symptoms that can accompany a chest infection, including:

- Seeming unwell
- High fever
- Rapid breathing and distress
- Shortness of breath
- Cough (though many babies with a chest infection do not have a cough)

■ She may be feeding almost normally, or she may reject food and drink, at the risk of becoming dehydrated.

Always see your doctor if you think your baby might have this. It usually needs antibiotics and she may also need oxygen and fluids in the hospital.

Croup

This is a form of laryngitis that affects babies over six months. It is very common in the winter, and is usually due to infection with para-influenza virus. Like bronchiolitis (see opposite), croup usually begins with cold symptoms and then progresses to wheezing and a typical barking cough. Your baby's voice may be hoarse. She may also have stridor—a noise when breathing in, which suggests the airways are partly blocked.

If you think your baby has croup, talk to your doctor. A baby with mild croup can usually be kept at home as long as you give plenty of fluids and watch her closely. Your doctor may prescribe an inhaler and steroids, and may suggest you steam the room to help reduce swelling in your baby's airways. Always call your doctor again if there are worrying symptoms (as for bronchiolitis).

Urinary tract infections

Urinary tract infections (UTI) are surprisingly common in young babies. Most are bacterial and get into the system from the urethra—the opening that leads from the bladder to the outside. But symptoms in young babies are very different than in adults. A baby with a UTI may experience the following:

- Fever
- Irritability
- Vomiting
- Refusing feedings.

Young babies can just have prolonged jaundice, or may not put on weight.

Always see your doctor if your baby has these symptoms. There is usually nothing to suggest the trouble is in the urinary system, except for the fact that your doctor will be unable to find a focus of infection when examining your baby. Only a urine sample can determine whether it's a UTI.

It's vital to get a clean sample of urine for testing. You may be able to catch some urine in a sterile bottle when your baby urinates. However, this can be difficult with small babies. Your doctor will give you a special urine collector, which needs to be taped carefully over the penis or vagina until the baby urinates again. Very sick babies may have urine removed by catheter by the doctor. Make sure you deliver the sample to the doctor without delay.

UTIs need prompt treatment with antibiotics to avoid kidney damage and other complications. In most cases, a specialist will suggest a scan to rule out any abnormalities of the urinary system that could have led to infection. The doctor should give a follow-up test to make sure the infection has been eliminated after the course of antibiotics.

Meningitis

This means inflammation or infection in the meninges, the layers of tissue that wrap the brain. It can be due to viruses or bacteria. Bacterial meningitis is more serious than viral. Many of the germs that can cause meningitis live harmlessly in the back of the throat in healthy people. It's not certain exactly why they cause disease in some babies and children, but factors include overcrowding and passive smoking.

Since Hib, pneumococcal, and meningococcal C immunization, many of the worst forms of meningitis have become less common. Still, meningitis is a very serious disease and it often goes hand in hand with septicemia (blood poisoning). By the time a baby has

Rashes are common in babies, and it can be hard to tell simply by looking at one if it's the rash linked with meningitis and septicemia (see p.409). However, the rash of meningitis and septicemia does not fade when you press it, and a good way to check this is to do the glass (tumbler) test. Press the side of a glass firmly against your baby's skin where you see the rash. If you can still see the rash through the side of the glass, your baby may have meningitis/septicemia and needs urgent hospital treatment. It is harder to see on dark skin so check against paler areas.

The glass test Press a glass firmly against your baby's skin where you see a rash. If the rash doesn't fade, call an ambulance.

reached this stage, treatment is vital to save her life and you must not waste a minute. That's why every parent needs to know how to recognize it and what to do. Symptoms in a baby can include:

■ A high-pitched cry or moan
■ Refusing feedings
■ Irritability
■ Drowsiness
■ Limp or floppy limbs
■ Having a fever, but with cold hands or feet
■ A tense or bulging fontanelle (soft spot on the top of the head)
■ Pale, blotchy, or clammy skin
■ A rash of small red or brownish pinprick spots, which can turn into large bruises and purplish marks. If you see this rash, it could be septicemia. Do the glass test (see left).

Call an ambulance immediately if your baby is ill with any of the above symptoms. Never wait for all the symptoms to develop. The rash and other skin changes are signs that a baby is already critically ill. Treatment is much more successful when it's given in the early stages. Tell the 911 operator as well as the ambulance and the hospital, that you suspect your baby may have meningitis.

Otitis media with effusion is also known as glue ear. Normally, the middle ear space contains air. In otitis media with effusion, there's a buildup of sticky fluid instead. It occurs after repeated episodes of middle ear infection (see right), though there's no agreement on how many infections cause it. Some babies are more likely to develop it than others, and there can be a family history of the condition.

The most obvious symptom is hearing loss. Your baby may fail to hear you clearly, may not turn to look at you when you speak, or may look surprised when you suddenly appear

over the side of the crib because she hasn't heard you approach. Babies are learning all the time, and hearing is vital to most of their development. If untreated, otitis media with effusion can lead to problems with speech and behavior. Always see your doctor if you think your baby may have this or any other hearing problem.

Treatment may involve minor surgery to put in tympanostomy tubes. These tiny tubes let air in and equalize the pressure on each side of the eardrum. After a few months, the tubes usually fall out, by which time hearing is back to normal.

Ear canal infection

Infection of the ear canal, also known as otitis externa, can occur when milk or food gets into the ear, or sometimes when the ear isn't dried after bathtime. Babies that crawl may poke dirty fingers into their ears. Your baby may try scratching the ear, and you may see some redness or a little discharge. Generally, there's no fever and your baby remains well. See your doctor, who may prescribe ear drops for the infection. You can use baby acetaminophen or ibuprofen for pain relief, although discomfort is usually mild.

Middle ear infection

Also known as otitis media, infection of the middle ear, behind the eardrum, can be due to viruses or bacteria. It often happens after a cold when the infection spreads up the eustachian tubes that lead from the back of the nose to the ear. In babies and children, the eustachian tubes are short and run horizontally, which means that they get more middle ear infections than adults. Sometimes only one ear is affected, but it's often both. Babies often have no symptoms that suggest the trouble is in the ear, but they may:

■ Feel very sick
■ Be irritable or cry inconsolably
■ Have a high fever
■ Refuse feedings
■ Vomit.

Some babies pull at the affected ear, although many babies also do this when they are tired.

If your baby has any of the symptoms above, see your doctor promptly so the infection can be treated at an early stage. If the infection is untreated, the eardrum can burst, causing a discharge. This relieves the pressure in the middle ear so the baby may feel better as soon as this happens. However, she still needs treatment for the infection.

SYMPTOM	POSSIBLE CAUSE	WHAT TO DO
Fever	◼ Fever is not a very specific symptom since babies can become feverish for all kinds of reasons. It is most commonly a sign of a viral or bacterial infection (see Fever, p.401).	Give plenty of fluids (breast-feedings, if breast-feeding); keep room cool. See doctor if your baby's temperature is 102.2°F (39°C) or more (100.4°F/38°C if under three months).
Runny nose	◼ A runny nose, commonly producing clear mucus that thickens and turns yellow, green, or gray over about a week, is often caused by a cold (see p.408) and sometimes by the flu. ◼ Other causes include allergy (see p.404), the early stages of bronchiolitis (see p.408), or croup (see p.409).	Make sure your baby has plenty of rest and fluids (breast-feedings, if breast-feeding). Ease her breathing by tilting the head end of the crib upward, if it's safe to do so. Ask your doctor about using saline drops.
Cough	◼ A common symptom, it can be due to a cold (se p.408). ◼ Coughing can also be a symptom of chest infection (see p.409); measles (see p.406); allergy (see p.404); bronchiolitis (see p.408); or asthma (see p.408). A deep cough with a barking sound could be croup (see p.409), and bouts of coughing that end with a big breath in may indicate whooping cough.	Give plenty of fluids (breast-feedings, if breast-feeding). See doctor if a cough persists for more than one week or is accompanied by a high fever or wheeze, if your baby is short of breath, makes a crackling breathing sound, refuses feedings, or is listless.
Rash	◼ Once your baby is on solids, a rash around the mouth is often due to irritation from food. If her lips look swollen or she has other symptoms, suspect an allergy (see p.404). ◼ A rash can be a symptom of many common childhood viral infections, such as chickenpox (see p.405) and measles (see p.406). A rash can also occur with meningitis and septicemia (see p.409). Around the diaper area, the most likely cause is diaper rash (see p.405). Little bumps, or tiny blisters, particularly in skin folds, may be heat rash (see p.408). Eczema (see p.407) causes patches of dry skin.	Treatment depends on the cause of the rash. Do the glass test (see opposite) if the rash appears quickly or your baby isn't well. The more ill your baby seems, the more serious her rash is likely to be, so contact the doctor if you are concerned.
Vomiting	◼ Vomiting affects most babies at some stage and is not usually serious. It is most often due to a problem in the digestive tract, but can indicate a serious infection elsewhere in the body (see Vomiting, p.402).	Give plenty of fluids (breast-feedings, if breast-feeding). If vomiting lasts longer than 12–24 hours, take your baby to the doctor. She may prescribe an oral rehydration solution.
Diarrhea	◼ Diarrhea is a common symptom most often due to infection of the digestive tract (see Diarrhea, p.403).	Treat as for vomiting (above). Use a barrier cream when changing her diaper—loose bowel movements can cause her bottom to become irritated.
Loss of appetite	◼ Babies are sometimes reluctant to be fed when teething, but other causes might be gastroenteritis (see p.403), or almost any other acute infection, including middle ear infection (see opposite) and measles (see p.406).	Keep offering fluids (breast-feedings, if breast-feeding) and food, and note the number of wet diapers to make sure she isn't becoming dehydrated. If she refuses several feedings in a row, contact the doctor.

Common conditions

Developmental concerns

Treating milestones as helpful guidelines only prevents unnecessary anxiety, but seek reassurance if you do have persistent concerns.

Babies are all different and even identical twins develop in their own unique way. Even so, there is a pattern of progression, and babies acquire new skills in the same order (see development charts, below). As a parent, you spend most time with your baby and are often the first person to notice if she isn't developing as expected. A slight delay in one area of development isn't always significant, but delay in two or more areas is important. If your baby was born prematurely, remember to allow for that. For example, a baby born six weeks prematurely won't reach the stage of a six-week-old baby until 12 weeks after the birth.

As your baby grows up and does more, the different areas of development become increasingly interlinked. A baby may not wave bye-bye, for instance, unless she can also see, hear, and understand that someone is leaving.

It can be tempting to compare your baby with others. While other people's babies can give you an overall idea of what happens when, you can't expect your baby to do things at exactly the same time as others. If you have other children, don't expect this baby to have the same development timetable as your previous babies. Some traits do run in families. Bottom-shuffling, for instance, can be familial, but most other

achievements vary hugely from one child to the next. Your baby's development will be checked regularly at six or more doctor visits during her first year.

Signs to watch out for
Speak to your pediatrician if your baby displays any of the following signs, or if she regresses in any area. Your baby will be examined and you may be asked to bring her back for review. Babies can vary from day to day, depending on their mood or whether they are hungry or tired, so it is not always easy to give a definite answer on the first consultation. Alternatively, your baby may be referred to a specialist for further assessment.

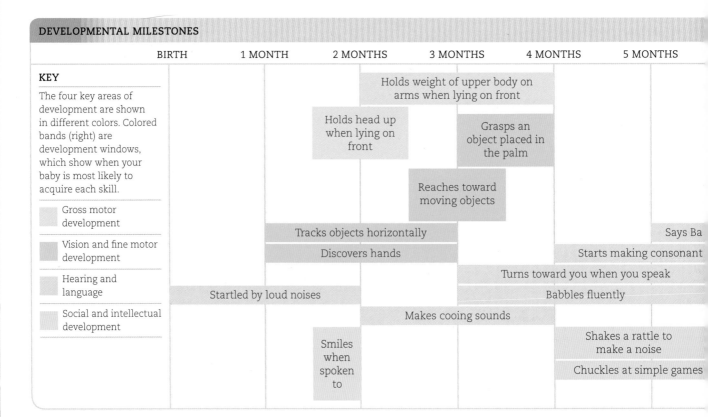

DEVELOPMENTAL MILESTONES

	BIRTH	1 MONTH	2 MONTHS	3 MONTHS	4 MONTHS	5 MONTHS
KEY The four key areas of development are shown in different colors. Colored bands (right) are development windows, which show when your baby is most likely to acquire each skill.				Holds weight of upper body on arms when lying on front		
			Holds head up when lying on front		Grasps an object placed in the palm	
				Reaches toward moving objects		
Gross motor development			Tracks objects horizontally			Says Ba
Vision and fine motor development			Discovers hands		Starts making consonant	
Hearing and language					Turns toward you when you speak	
Social and intellectual development	Startled by loud noises				Babbles fluently	
				Makes cooing sounds		
					Shakes a rattle to make a noise	
			Smiles when spoken to		Chuckles at simple games	

There may be some cause for concern if your baby:

■ Has persistently crossed eyes after six weeks
■ Isn't smiling by 9–10 weeks
■ Tilts her head persistently to one side
■ Doesn't make cooing sounds at about three months
■ Makes no eye contact by three months
■ Doesn't turn her head toward sounds by three months
■ Still has a floppy head by three months (when awake)
■ Doesn't reach for objects by six months
■ Won't turn around when you speak to her at six months
■ Has any crossed eyes at six months
■ Isn't babbling by 10 months or stops babbling after having previously done so (this can be a sign of deafness)
■ Won't sit up by 10 months
■ Doesn't grasp objects at 10 months
■ Doesn't try feeding herself at 12 months
■ Has asymmetry of the limbs, or any movement, at any stage.

YOUR BABY'S VISION

Parents are often concerned about whether their baby can see properly or will need glasses. While conditions such as glaucoma, astigmatism, and near-sightedness can run in families, you don't generally need to be concerned at this stage. However, if you are in doubt or need reassurance, talk to your doctor.

A newborn baby has a very close range of vision, but you should be able to tell whether she can focus on your face at a distance of around 8–10 in (20–25 cm). Also, her pupils should be dark (or red in a flash photograph). Always see the doctor if you notice a white mass in either pupil.

Take note, too, of any abnormal eye movements in your baby, such as crossed eyes, or any wandering or jerking movement, and talk to your pediatrician if you spot these.

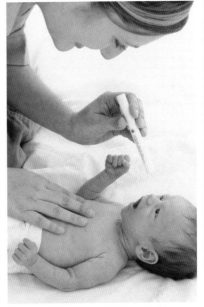

Checking baby's vision Your baby's eyes will be checked at 6–8 weeks, but see your doctor earlier if you think there's a problem.

	6 MONTHS	7 MONTHS	8 MONTHS	9 MONTHS	10 MONTHS	11 MONTHS	12 MONTHS
		Sits unsupported			Walks unaided		
		Crawls or bottom-shuffles					
	Rolls from front to back, and back to front		Pulls up to standing position				
				Cruises around furniture			
					Drops things on purpose		
				Bangs blocks together			
	Can transfer objects from one hand to the other				Can point using index finger		
and Da				Can grasp object between finger and thumb			
sounds					Puts toys in and takes them out of containers		
		Sounds begin to resemble real words					
						Waves bye-bye	
such as peekaboo					Responds to own name		
		Becomes shy with strangers					

Everyday first aid

It's important you know what to do if your baby is injured, and taking a course to learn proper techniques and CPR is advised.

Cuts and scrapes

Babies can become very upset if they get a cut or scrape, so reassure her while you take a look at the injury.

If it's a small scrape or cut, gently clean the area with soap and water using a gauze pad (if you don't have one, you can use any soft, nonfluffy material). If the wound looks dirty, rinse it under running water, pat dry with clean pieces of material, then cover with a clean dressing that is larger than the area of the wound. For a cut lip, apply an ice cube wrapped in a clean piece of burp cloth for about five minutes.

If there is a lot of bleeding, place a clean pad or piece of nonfluffy material over the cut and press down firmly directly on the wound. If possible, raise the injured part above the level of the heart to reduce blood flow. Keep pressing until the bleeding slows down or stops, then apply a dressing large enough to cover the wound.

Take your baby to the ER if:
■ Bleeding isn't under control in 10 minutes
■ The wound is gaping
■ You think there may be a foreign body in the wound.

Bites and stings

If your baby has been bitten or stung by an insect, she is likely to be terrified and in pain, so comfort her. Bites and stings are not usually serious, but in rare cases, a bee or wasp sting can cause a serious allergic reaction, known as anaphylactic shock (see p.404). A bite or sting in or on the mouth can be serious; if this happens, take your baby to the hospital immediately.

If you can see a sting left in the skin, scrape it off with your fingernail. Don't use tweezers since you'll inject more venom into the skin. You can reduce swelling and relieve itching by applying a washcloth or towel soaked in cold water, or an ice cube wrapped in a dry cloth. Hold it on for five minutes while you hug your baby. You can give your baby infant acetaminophen if she's in pain.

Falls, bumps, and bruises

Babies often fall and hurt themselves. Most of the time, all you need to do is comfort your baby and apply a cold compress to the area to relieve swelling and pain (see Bites and stings, left).

Go to the ER if your baby:
■ Has a head injury
■ Cannot move one of her limbs
■ Is bleeding and you can't control it within 10 minutes with direct pressure, or has a gaping wound (see Cuts and scrapes, left)
■ Is or was unconscious
■ You're not sure if it's serious.

Burns

Fire, hot water, steam, sunlight, electricity, and chemicals can all cause burns. The damage depends on the site, size, thickness, and type of burn. The deepest burns are often fairly painless.

Cool the burn under cold running water for at least 10 minutes. Remove (or cut off) clothing around the burn, unless it is stuck to the burn. After cooling, apply a clean dressing or sterile gauze and take your baby to the hospital for assessment. If the area of the burn is small, see your doctor, but do not delay.

Take your baby to an ER right away if:
■ It's a large burn (larger than the palm of your baby's hand)
■ It's on the face/in the mouth, on the hands, or the genitals
■ The burn is chemical or electrical (take the chemical container with you)
■ Your baby seems unwell
■ You're unsure what to do.

Foreign objects

Dirt, dust, or other bits of foreign material can easily get into the eyes, and babies may push small objects, such as beans or buttons, into their ears or nose.

Object in eye Anything in the eye usually causes discomfort and crying. If it's a small speck on the surface of the eye, it can generally be washed out.

Fill a pitcher with warm water. Hold your baby with her head tilted upward and pour the water into her eye, aiming for the inner corner. The eyelids need to be separated so you'll need assistance.

Take your baby to the ER if:
■ An object is embedded in or stuck to the eye. Do not attempt to remove it
■ You've tried to wash out an object on the surface of the eye, but have been unsuccessful
■ The eye remains irritated and sore after the object has been removed.

Object in ear or nose If your baby gets something stuck in her ear or nose, stay calm and reassure her that there's nothing to worry about. Do not try to remove the object even if you can see it because you risk pushing it farther in. Take your baby to the ER, where doctors will be able to remove the object, using

tiny forceps or a suction machine. Sometimes, a baby may not realize there's something stuck in her ears or nose. She may not hear well or one side of her nose may run or have a smelly discharge. If you have any concerns that there could be something in your baby's ear or nose, see your doctor right away.

Choking

This is common in babies. Small objects, such as beans or coins, are often responsible since babies put everything into their mouths. Babies can also choke on food, or on mucus or milk.

Coughing is nature's way of trying to dislodge an obstruction in the airway, so if your baby is choking but still coughing effectively, let her be. If, after two or three minutes, your baby continues to cough, call the doctor.

If your baby cannot breathe, cough, or cry, the choking is severe. She may make strange noises and her face may turn blue. You need to act immediately (see box, below).

Poisoning

If your baby has swallowed something poisonous, call your local Poison Control Center and 911. Tell the medical team what your baby has swallowed, how much, and when, and keep a sample. While waiting for medical help, do not try to make your baby vomit since this can cause further harm. Wash or wipe off any corrosive substances on or around her mouth. If she's eaten a poisonous plant or berries, look in her mouth and remove any remaining pieces.

Deal with choking

If your baby is choking and unable to breathe, take emergency action. Have someone call 911 when you begin first aid. If you're alone, shout for help, then begin.

■ Lay the baby face down on your forearm, her head lower than her body. Support her head with your hand. Using the heel of your other hand, give up to five sharp blows to her upper back.

■ If the obstruction is still present, turn your baby over onto her back and give up to five chest thrusts, pushing down with two fingers in the middle of the breastbone just below the nipples, compressing the chest ⅓ to ½ the depth of the chest.

■ Check her mouth and if you can clearly see a loose object, remove it carefully with your fingertips. Do not sweep the mouth with your finger as this may push the object further down the throat.

■ Continue giving a series of five back blows followed by five chest thrusts and checking the mouth until the object becomes dislodged or the infant becomes unconscious.

■ If your baby loses consciousness, shout for help and have someone else dial 911 while you begin infant CPR. If you are alone, call 911 after performing infant CPR for one minute.

Even if you have successfully dealt with the emergency, any baby who has had chest thrusts must be seen by a doctor to check that her delicate bones haven't been damaged.

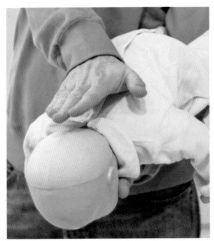

Back blows Make sure the baby's head is lower than her body. Use the heel of your hand to give back blows, making sure the blows land between her shoulder blades.

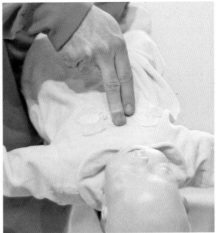

Chest thrusts To avoid injury when giving chest thrusts, your fingers should be on the breastbone, not ribs. Push inward and upward, being firm but not jerky.

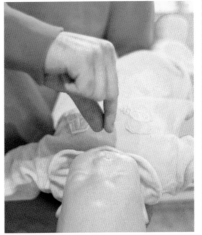

Check mouth Look inside your baby's mouth. If a dislodged object is clearly visible, fish it out carefully with your fingertips, being careful not to push it further in.

Everyday first aid

Resources

Feeding

International Lactation Consultant Association
Find a lactation consultant in your area.
www.ilca.org
(919) 861-5577

La Leche League Canada
Support for breastfeeding moms.
www.lllc.ca
(613) 774-4900

Support groups

Allergy Asthma Information Association
www.aaia.ca
(416) 621-4571 / (800) 611-7011

Autism Society Canada
www.autismsocietycanada.ca
(613) 789-8943 / (866) 476-8440

Canadian Cystic Fibrosis Foundation
www.cysticfibrosis.ca
(416) 485-9149 / (800) 378-2233

Canadian Diabetes Association
www.diabetes.ca
(416) 363-3373 / (800) 226-8464

Canadian Down Syndrome Society
www.cdss.ca
(800) 883-5608

Canadian Foundation for the Study of Sudden Infant Death
www.sidscanada.org
(905) 688-8884 / (800) 363-7437

Canadian Mental Health Association
Information on postpartum depression.
www.cmha.ca/bins/content_page.
   asp?cid=3-86-87-88

Cerebral Palsy Support Foundation of Canada
www.cpsc.ca
(289) 316-0584

Compassionate Friends of Canada
Support for bereaved parents.
tcfcanada.net
(866) 823-0141

Epilepsy Canada
www.epilepsy.ca
(877) 734-0873

Spina Bifida and Hydrocephalus Association of Canada
www.sbhac.ca
(204) 925-3650 / (800) 565-9488

Parent groups

Canadian Association of Family Resource Programs
Provides resources for families and others who care for children.
www.frp.ca
(613) 237-7667 / (866) 637-7226

Canadian Parents
Online parenting community.
www.canadianparents.com

Invest In Kids
A parenting support site to promote healthy child development.
fnih.investinkids.ca
(416) 977-1222 / (877) 583-5437

Multiple Births Canada
Support for those with twins or more.
www.multiplebirthscanada.org
(613) 834-8946 / (866) 228-8824

Parents Matter
Resources for child care and development.
www.parentsmatter.ca
(613) 237-7667 / (866) 637-7226

Parents Without Partners
Support for single parents.
www.parentswithoutpartners.org
(800) 637-7974

Single Parent
Support for single parents.
www.singleparent.ca

Today's Parent
Online parenting community.
www.todaysparent.com

Child care

Au Pair Canada
Resource for au pairs, nannies, and care givers.
www.aupair.ca
(416) 907-0764

Canadian Child Care Federation
cccf-fcsge.ca

Baby and child health and safety

Canadian Red Cross
Health, safety, and first aid information.
www.redcross.ca

Car Seat Information—Transport Canada
www.tc.gc.ca/eng/roadsafety/
   safedrivers-childsafety-car-cartime-
   stage1-221.htm

**Consumer Product Safety—
Health Canada**
List of advisories, warnings,
and recalls.
http://www.hc-sc.gc.ca/cps-spc/index-
    eng.php

Safe Kids Canada
Information and resources about child
safety at home and elsewhere.
www.safekidscanada.ca
(888) 723-3847

St. John Ambulance Canada
Training in first aid and CPR.
www.sja.ca
(613) 236-7461

Rights and benefits

Canada Child Tax Benefit
www.servicecanada.gc.ca/eng/goc/cctb.
    shtml

Child Disability Benefit
www.servicecanada.gc.ca/eng/goc/cdb.
    shtml

**Employment Insurance Family
Supplement**
www.servicecanada.gc.ca/eng/sc/ei/
    family/familysupplement.shtml

**Employment Insurance Maternity
and Parental Benefits**
www.servicecanada.gc.ca/eng/sc/ei/
    benefits/maternityparental.shtml

Quebec Parental Insurance Plan
www.rqap.gouv.qc.ca/index_en.asp

Registered Education Savings Plan
www.servicecanada.gc.ca/eng/goc/resp.
    shtml

Universal Child Care Benefit
www.servicecanada.gc.ca/eng/goc/
    universal_child_care.shtml

General

AboutKidsHealth
Trusted answers from The Hospital
for Sick Children
www.aboutkidshealth.ca

Babycenter Canada
Information on conception, pregnancy,
and birth; free e-newsletters and
forums.
www.babycenter.ca

Canada's Food Guide—Health Canada
Information on healthy eating.
www.hc-sc.gc.ca/fn-an/food-guide-
    aliment/index-eng.php

Caring for Kids
Children's health information from
the Canadian Paediatric Society.
www.caringforkids.cps.ca
(613) 526-9397

College of Family Physicians of Canada
Resources to find a family doctor.
www.cfpc.ca
(905) 629-0900 / (800) 387-6197

**Immunization – Public Health Agency
of Canada**
www.phac-aspc.gc.ca/im/iyc-vve/index-
    eng.php

Motherisk
Information on the safety of medications,
infections, chemicals, personal products
and everyday exposures during
pregnancy and breast-feeding.
www.motherisk.org
(416) 813-6780

Smoker's Helpline
Support for quitting smoking.
smokershelpline.ca
(877) 513-5333

Women's Health Matters
Resources and information on women's
health issues.
www.womenshealthmatters.ca

Index

Index

423

facial expressions 70, 183
and learning 205
making faces 327
"mirror neurons" 126
minerals
in breast milk 275
nutritional requirements 207
in store-bought baby food 271
mint tea 62
"mirror neurons" 126
mirroring, helping baby accept
strong emotions 259
mirrors 127, 208, 236, 372
mites, dust 116
mittens 314, 378
MMR vaccination 103, 406
mobiles 78, 83, 102
mobility 223
bottom shuffling 218, 223,
260, 326
cruising 291, 326, 328, 347
dancing 128, 303, 329, 358
older babies 363
pulling up to standing 263
rolling over 22, 134, 149,
194, 223
toys to encourage 354
see also crawling; walking
moisturizers 129
molars 212, 334
monitors 34, 225
Montgomery's tubercles 26
moods see emotions
Moro reflex 47
Moses baskets 30, 31, 34, 113
mother-and-baby groups see
parent-and-baby groups
mother's helpers 119
motions see bowel movements
mouth
chickenpox in 405
exploring world with 129,
298
hand, foot, and mouth
disease 407
newborn baby checks 43
thrush 405–6
tongue-tie 402
mucus, in stools 236
multiple births see twins
mumps 103, 379, 406
muscles
development of 22, 167, 358
gaining control of 96
legs 137, 218, 358
pectoral 325
pelvic floor exercises 65, 81,
181

six-week checkups 95
tummy time 90, 122, 130,
149
music 303
baby classes 171
background noise 286
benefits of 248
dancing 128, 303, 329
musical ability 21
musical instruments 303
newborn babies and 82, 87
young babies and 102
see also songs
mustard 321

N

nails, trimming 60
nakedness 320
names, recognition of 273, 280
nannies 118, 295
naps
body clock 83
changing routines 280
consistency 320
dropping 188, 292, 370
and early or late bedtimes
240
and early waking 201
instant energy fixes 197
length of 320
older babies 306, 376
one-year-olds 387
routines 31, 91, 151
settling babies 76
and sleeping through the
night 353
young babies 137
nature 215
nature versus nurture 169
naughtiness 196, 276, 288
navel 94
neck muscles 130
neonatal acne 129
neurons (brain cells) 196, 300
newborn babies 40–65
appearance 41
bathing 57
bonding with 52
bottle-feeding 47, 53
breast-feeding 46–7, 49, 50, 53
carrying 71
checkups 43
crying 48, 57, 68–9
diapers 44–5
eyes 57
feeding 44
genitals 41, 47

NICU babies 54–5
outings 61
playing with 75
reflexes 47
sleep 47, 53
sponge bathing 45
weight gain 60
newborn screening test 50
night
body clock 83
comfort feedings 358
fear of dark 337
leaking diapers 177
leaving baby with someone
else 355
nursing sick babies 399
reluctance to go to bed 370
sleeping through the night
352–3
night-lights 34, 337
night waking 105
early waking 201
feeding and 232
separation anxiety 232
young babies 164
nipple cream 34, 46–7
nipple shields 62
89
nipples
bottle-feeding 29, 34
breast-feeding 26, 27
inverted 28
sore 46–7, 58, 59
thrush 59, 405
"no," saying 205, 248, 357,
371, 372
noises
animal noises 175, 273, 312,
360
background noise 286, 350
dropping things 305
learning about 360
startling babies 286, 337
norovirus 403
nose
administering drops 398
colds 408
foreign objects in 414–15
runny nose 411
nudity 320
numbers, counting 173
day-care centers 119, 375, 379
nursery rhymes
action rhymes 174
animals in 340
and speech development
273, 303
tickling games 283

nursing bras 26, 34, 111, 325
nursing sick babies 379, 398–9
nutrition 207
vitamins 237
nutritionists 261
nuts
peanut allergy 62, 241, 261,
404
safety 235, 385

O

oat drinks 247
obesity 200
breast-feeding and 25
demand feeding and 77
object permanence
and dropping things 305
hide-and-seek 245, 335
peekaboo games and 140
and separation anxiety 283
omega oils, in formula 29
oral contraceptives 277
oral rehydration solution 395,
403
orchidopexy 97
orgasm 117
osteoporosis 25, 114, 361
otitis externa 410
otitis media 410
outdoor activities 363, 367, 377
outings
changing routines 280
family outings 127
newborn babies 61
older babies 217
for parents 344
strollers 123
vacations 280, 313, 344
watching animals 340
see also travel
ovarian cancer 25
ovens, safety 327
overstimulated babies 69, 189
overhead press 325
overheating 73
overweight babies 200, 332
breast-feeding and 25
demand feeding and 77
snacks and 267
oxygen, ALTE (Apparent Life-
Threatening Event) 243
oxytocin 26, 52

P

pacifiers 31, 69, 384
paddling pools 381

Acknowledgments

Editor-in-chief's acknowledgments

I would like to thank the authors and entire *Baby Day by Day* team at DK Publishing for their help, guidance, and expert knowledge. I am particularly grateful to Mandy Lebentz and Victoria Heyworth-Dunne for their patient support and enthusiasm throughout the project. Finally I would like to thank my parents and my children for teaching me how to be a parent.

Consultants' acknowledgments

Dr. Carol Cooper would like to thank the team of consultants, who all worked so well together.
Dr. Claire Halsey would like to acknowledge the support of Vicki McIvor of Take3 Management and the love and patient encouragement given by her family, Michael, Rupert, Toby, and Dominic.
Dr. Mary Steen would like to thank the DK team and the other consultants for working so harmoniously as a team.

Publisher's acknowledgments

Editorial assistance Andrea Bagg, Claire Cross, Elizabeth Yeates, Salima Hirani
Design assistance Saskia Janssen, Charlotte Johnson
Production editor Siu Chan
House location agency for photography 1st Option
Assistant to art director for photography Ellie Hoffman, Tom Forge
Prop buying for photography Alison Gardner
Picture librarian Romaine Werblow
Assistance with agency images Susie Peachey
Indexer Hilary Bird
Proofreader Alyson Silverwood
US proofreader Christy Lusiak
DK India Kokila Manchanda (editorial), Neetika Vilash (design), Tina Jindal (proofreader)

Thanks to the models: Sarah and Kaiden Asamoa; Nina and Jamie Bradburn; Unity Brennan, Amelie Grace, and Benjamin Wolski; Selina Chand and Faith Lucy O'Brien; Narae Cho and Alex Park; Nicola and Freya Church; Anna and Eliana Clarke; Archie Clements; Philippa and Noah Dovar; Joe and Dagan Drahota; Jenny and Harry Duggin; Laura and Zoe Forrest; Rachael and Samuel Grady; Kate Heavenor and Nicolas Diaz; Olga and Mia Gelev; Beatriz de Lemos and Isabel Walker; Jordan McRobie, Jenny Parr and Reuben McRobie ; Eden Martin-Osakwe; Poppy Mitchell and Oaklee Wealands; Amelie Victoria Morris; Victoria and Arthur Morton; Oreke Mosheshe and Carter Mbamali; Gabriela and Alba Nardi; Miriam Nelken and Mala Shahi; Laura and Charlie Nickoll; Amie and Rosie Niland; Lauren Overs and Grayson Andrews; Yoan Petkov Petkov; Suzy Richards and Max Snead; Heidi Robinson and Elias Crosby; Jenny Sharp and Joshua Tyler; Matthew, Angela and Jacob Smith; Eve Spaughton and Genevieve Long; Rose and Brooke Thunberg; Anggayasti Trikanti and Carissa Afila; Rachel Weaver and Jacob Marcus; Karen and Milly Westropp; Georgie and Harriet Willock.

Picture credits

The publisher would like to thank the following for their kind permission to reproduce their photographs:

(Key: a-above; b-below/bottom; c-center; f-far; l-left; r-right; t-top)

2 Getty Images: Frank Herholdt (fcla). **18 Corbis:** Tetra Images / Tetra Images (br). **28 Mother & Baby Picture Library:** Paul Mitchell (bc). **38 Getty Images:** Photodisc (fcla). **40 Getty Images:** Frank Herholdt (c). **41 Corbis:** Cameron (cla). **Dorling Kindersley:** Brand X Pictures / PunchStock (br). **42 Corbis:** Larry Williams (cla). **47 Getty Images:** Anthony Bradshaw (c). **55 Alamy Images:** Peter Usbeck (br). **Getty Images:** Louie Psihoyos (tl). **59 Photolibrary:** Philippe Dannic (tc). **60 Getty Images:** Ian Hooton / Spl (br). **Mother & Baby Picture Library:** Ian Hooton (tl). **Photolibrary:** Gyssels (bc). **61 Science Photo Library:** Dr. P. Marazzi (crb). **63 Mother & Baby Picture Library:** Ruth Jenkinson (br). **85 Dorling Kindersley:** Antonia Deutsch (bc, br, fbr). **99 Mother & Baby Picture Library:** Ian Hooton (cla). **103 Mother & Baby Picture Library:** Ian Hooton (cla). **105 Getty Images:** PM Images (br). **107 Mother & Baby Picture Library:** Ian Hooton (cra). **109 Getty Images:** Anthony-Masterson (br). **115 Corbis:** Sean Justice (cra). **Getty Images:** Jupiterimages (br). **123 Getty Images:** Plattform (tl). **135 Getty Images:** Ghislain & Marie David de Lossy (br). **136 Mother & Baby Picture Library:** Angela Spain (tl). **147 Corbis:** Fabrik Studios / Index Stock (cra). **150 Corbis:** Tetra Images (cla). **154 Getty Images:** Joshua Hodge Photography (br). **182 Getty Images:** Fabrice LEROUGE (cla). **183 Corbis:** Norbert Schaefer (cla). **197 Corbis:** eyetrigger Pty Ltd (tl); Ocean (br). **203 Alamy Images:** Peter Griffin (ca). **207 Corbis:** Tim Pannell (tl). **215 Corbis:** Lisa B. (bl). **217 Alamy Images:** thislife pictures (cla). **Mother & Baby Picture Library:** Ian Hooton (br). **241 Getty Images:** Tara Moore (bl). **245 Getty Images:** Jamie Grill (bc). **262 Corbis:** Radius Images (bl). **268 Mother & Baby Picture Library:** Ian Hooton (bl). **276 Corbis:** moodboard (bl). **289 Alamy Images:** Paul Hakimata (cra). **301 Corbis:** Image Source (bl). **316 Getty Images:** Lilly Dong (tl). **322 Alamy Images:** PhotoAlto sas (br). **325 Alamy Images:** MARKA (cla). **331 Getty Images:** Fabrice LEROUGE (cra). **340 Getty Images:** Paul Viant (bl). **344 Getty Images:** Ghislain & Marie David de Lossy (bl). **345 Getty Images:** BJI / Blue Jean Images (br). **349 Corbis:** Jose Luis Pelaez, Inc. / Blend Images (cla). **355 Alamy Images:** moodboard (br). **361 Corbis:** Brigitte Sporrer (cla). **365 Dorling Kindersley:** Ruth Jenkinson Photography (cla). **373 Getty Images:** Betsie Van der Meer (cla). **377 Corbis:** RCWW, Inc. (cla). **381 Getty Images:** David M. Zuber (br). **384 Getty Images:** Betsie Van der Meer (cla). **389 Alamy Images:** Ian nolan (cla). **392 Mother & Baby Picture Library:** Ian Hooton (ca). **393 Alamy Images:** Agencja FREE (cla). **396 Mother & Baby Picture Library:** Ian Hooton (ca). **399 Dorling Kindersley:** dave king (cra). **400 Mother & Baby Picture Library:** Ian Hooton (c). **402 Science Photo Library:** Dr. P. Marazzi (bc). **405 Science Photo Library:** Chris Knapton (tr). **406 Science Photo Library:** Lowell Georgia (tr). **407 Science Photo Library:** Dr. H. C. Robinson (bl). **409 Getty Images:** Ruth Jenkinson / Spl (tl). **410 Meningitis Trust www.meningitis-trust.org:** (cl). **413 Mother & Baby Picture Library:** Ruth Jenkinson (tr)

All other images © Dorling Kindersley
For further information see: www.dkimages.com